Taking Sides: Clashing Views
in Science, Technology,
and Society, 12/e

Thomas A. Easton

http://create.mheducation.com

ISBN-10: 1259398943   ISBN-13: 9781259398940

Contents

Detailed Table of Contents

Peter Bronski et al., of the Rocky Mountain Institute (RMI) argue that the combination of home solar power with storage technologies such as batteries offer to make the electricity grid optional for many consumers, perhaps as early as the 2020s. Utilities have an opportunity to exploit the spread of "distributed electricity generation" to provide a robust, reliable electricity supply. Peter Kind, executive director of Energy Infrastructure Advocates, argues that increased interest in "distributed energy resources" such as home solar power and energy efficiency, among other factors, is threatening to reduce revenue and increase costs for electrical utilities. In order to protect investors and capital availability, electrical utilities must consider new charges for customers who reduce their electricity usage, decreased payments to homeowners using net metering, and even new charges to users of "distributed energy resources" to offset "stranded costs" (such as no longer needed power plants).

John Andrews and Bahman Shabani argue that hydrogen gas can play an important role in a sustainable energy system. The key will be a hierarchy of spatially distributed hydrogen production, storage, and distribution centers that minimizes the need for expensive pipelines. Electricity will power battery-electric vehicles for short-range transportation and serve as the major long-distance energy vector. Ulf Bossel argues that although the technology for widespread use of hydrogen energy is available, generating hydrogen is a very inefficient way to use energy. A hydrogen economy will never make sense.

Unit: Human Health and Welfare

Dennis Dimick argues that new projections of higher population growth through the twenty-first century are reason for concern, largely because of the conflict between population size and resource use. The environmental impact of population also depends on technology, affluence, and waste, but educated women have smaller families and technology (electric lights, for instance) aids education. Controlling population appears to be essential. Tom Bethell argues that population alarmists project their fears onto popular concerns, currently the environment, and every time their scare-mongering turns out to be based on faulty premises. Blaming environmental problems will be no different. Societies are sustained not by population control but by belief in God.

Arjun Walia argues that the scientific consensus on the safety of vaccines may be suspect because "the corporate media is owned by the major vaccine manufacturers." He describes 22 studies that suggest that the connection between childhood vaccines and autism is real or that suggest possible mechanisms for the connection. Jeffrey S. Garber and Paul A. Offit argue that the scientific evidence neither shows a link between vaccines and autism nor supports any of the popular suggested mechanisms. Research should focus on more promising leads.

Jim Thomas, Eric Hoffman, and Jaydee Hanson, representing the Civil Society on the Environmental and Societal Implications of Synthetic Biology, argue that the risks posed by synthetic biology to human health, the environment, and natural ecosystems are so great that Congress should declare an immediate moratorium on releases to the environment and commercial uses of synthetic organisms and require comprehensive environmental and social impact reviews of all federally funded synthetic biology research. Gregory E. Kaebnick of the Hastings Center argues that although synthetic biology is surrounded by genuine ethical and moral concerns—including risks to health and environment—which warrant discussion, the potential benefits are too great to call for a general moratorium.

Kevin Drum argues that we are about to make very rapid progress in artificial intelligence, and by about 2040, robots will be replacing people in a great many jobs. On the way to that "robot paradise," corporate managers and investors will expand their share of national wealth, at the expense of labor's share, even more than they have in recent years. That trend, however, depends on an ample supply of consumers—workers with enough money to buy the products the machines are making. It is thus already time to start rethinking how the nation ensures that its citizens have enough money to be consumers and keep the economy going. Peter Gorle and Andrew Clive argue that robots are not a threat to human employment. Historically, increases in the use of automation almost always increase both productivity and employment. Over the next few years, the use of robotics will generate 700,000–1,000,000 new jobs.

Issue: Can Technology Protect Americans from International Cybercriminals?
Yes: Randy Vanderhoof, from "Testimony before the Committee on Science, Space, and Technology, Subcommittees on Oversight and Research and Technology, hearing on 'Can Technology Protect Americans from International Cybercriminals?'" U.S. House of Representatives (2014).
No: Charles H. Romine, from "Testimony before the Committee on Science, Space, and Technology, Subcommittees on Oversight and Research and Technology, hearing on 'Can Technology Protect Americans from International Cybercriminals?'" U.S. House of Representatives (2014).

Randy Vanderhoof argues that as the United States' payment system shifts from credit cards with magnetic stripes (whose data, stored on merchant computer systems, are a prime target for hackers) to smart cards with embedded microchips (which do not make data available to hackers), the rate of credit card fraud will decline rapidly, as it already has in other countries. Charles H. Romine, Director of the National Institute of Standards and Technology's (NIST) Information Technology Laboratory, argues that technology is not enough to solve the cybercrime problem. The NIST works on smart card systems, but also develops guidelines, standards, and best practices essential to making the technology work. Fighting cybercriminals requires not just technology, but also policy, legal, and economic efforts.

Issue: Does the Public Have a Stake in How Drones Are Used?
Yes: Amie Stepanovich, from testimony at U.S. Senate Judiciary hearing on The Future of Drones in America: Law Enforcement and Privacy Considerations, Judiciary Committee of the U.S. Senate (2013).
No: Department of Homeland Security, Office of Inspector General, from "CBP's Use of Unmanned Aircraft Systems in the Nation's Border Security", United States Department of Homeland Security, Office of Inspector General (2012).

Amie Stepanovich argues that the increased use of unmanned aerial systems (or "drones") to conduct surveillance in the United States must be accompanied by increased privacy protections. The current state of the law is insufficient to address the drone surveillance threat to the interests of the general public, who clearly have a stake (are stakeholders) in the issue. The U.S. Department of Homeland Security, Office of Inspector General, argues that planning is inadequate for the use of resources devoted to serving the purposes of the U.S. Customs and Border Protection (CBP) unmanned aircraft systems program, to provide reconnaissance, surveillance, targeting, and acquisition capabilities to serve the needs of stakeholders. The list of stakeholders does not include the general public, and privacy concerns are not mentioned.

Unit: Ethics

Issue: Is "Animal Rights" Just Another Excuse for Terrorism?
Yes: John J. Miller, from "In the Name of the Animals: America Faces a New Kind of Terrorism", *National Review* (2006).
No: Steven Best, from "Dispatches from a Police State: Animal Rights in the Crosshairs of State Repression", *International Journal of Inclusive Democracy* (2007).

Journalist John Miller argues that animal rights extremists have adopted terrorist tactics in their effort to stop the use of animals in scientific research. Because of the benefits of such research, if the terrorists win, everyone loses. Professor Steven Best argues that the new Animal Enterprise Protection Act is excessively broad and vague, imposes disproportionate penalties, endangers free speech, and detracts from prosecution of real terrorism. The animal liberation movement, on the other hand, is both a necessary effort to emancipate animals from human exploitation, and part of a larger resistance movement opposed to exploitation and hierarchies of any and all kinds.

Issue: Should We Reject the "Transhumanist" Goal of the Genetically Electronically and Mechanically Enhanced Human Being?
Yes: M.J. McNamee and S.D. Edwards, from "Transhumanism, Medical Technology, and Slippery Slopes", *Journal of Medical Ethics* (2006).
No: Maxwell J. Mehlman, from "Biomedical Enhancements: Entering a New Era", *Issues in Science and Technology* (2009).

M. J. McNamee and S. D. Edwards argue that the difficulty of showing that the human body should (rather than can) be enhanced in ways espoused by the transhumanists amounts to an objection to transhumanism. Maxwell J. Mehlman argues that the era of routine biomedical enhancements is coming. Since the technology cannot be banned, it must be regulated and even subsidized to ensure that it does not create an unfair society.

Preface

Those who must deal with scientific and technological issues—scientists, politicians, sociologists, business managers, and anyone who is concerned about energy policy, genetically modified foods, government intrusiveness, expensive space programs, or the morality of medical research, among many other issues—must be able to consider, evaluate, and choose among alternatives. Making choices is an essential aspect of the scientific method. It is also an inescapable feature of every public debate over a scientific or technological issue, for there can be no debate if there are no alternatives.

The ability to evaluate and to select among alternatives—as well as to know when the data do not permit selection—is called critical thinking. It is essential not only in science and technology but in every other aspect of life as well. *Taking Sides: Clashing Views in Science, Technology, and Society* is designed to stimulate and cultivate this ability by holding up for consideration issues that have provoked substantial debate. Each of these issues has at least two sides, usually more. However, each issue is expressed in terms of a single question in order to draw the lines of debate more clearly. The ideas and answers that emerge from the clash of opposing points of view should be more complex than those offered by the students before the reading assignment.

The issues in this book were chosen because they are currently of particular concern to both science and society. They touch on the nature of science and research, the relationship between science and society, the uses of technology, and the potential threats that technological advances can pose to human survival. And they come from a variety of fields, including computer and space science, biology, environmentalism, law enforcement, and public health.

Organization of the book For each issue, I have provided an *Issue Introduction,* which provides some historical background and discusses why the issue is important. I then present two selections, one pro and one con, in which the authors make their cases. Each issue concludes with an *Exploring the Issue* section that provides discussion questions and additional resources, including Internet links.

Which answer to the issue question—yes or no—is the correct answer? Perhaps neither. Perhaps both.

Students should read, think about, and discuss the readings and then come to their own conclusions without letting my or their instructor's opinions (which sometimes show!) dictate theirs. The additional readings mentioned in both the introductions and the exploring the issue sections should prove helpful. It is worth stressing that the issues covered in this book are all *live* issues; that is, the debates they represent are active and ongoing. In fact, they are so active and ongoing that when I teach this course, it often feels like a current events course!

Taking Sides: Clashing Views in Science, Technology, and Society is only one title in the Taking Sides series. If you are interested in seeing other titles, please visit http://create.mheducation.com.

Thomas A. Easton
Thomas College

Editor of This Volume

THOMAS A. EASTON is a professor of science at Thomas College in Waterville, Maine, where he has been teaching environmental science; science, technology, and society; and computer science since 1983. He received a BA in biology from Colby College in 1966 and a PhD in theoretical biology from the University of Chicago in 1971. He writes and speaks frequently on scientific and futuristic issues. His books include *Focus on Human Biology,* 2nd ed., coauthored with Carl E. Rischer (HarperCollins, 1995), *Careers in Science,* 4th ed. (VGM Career Horizons, 2004), *Classic Edition Sources: Environmental Studies* (McGraw-Hill), *Taking Sides: Clashing Views on Controversial Issues in Science, Technology, and Society,* (McGraw-Hill), and *Taking Sides: Clashing Views on Controversial Environmental Issues,* (McGraw-Hill). Dr. Easton is also a well-known writer and critic of science fiction.

Academic Advisory Board Members

Members of the Academic Advisory Board are instrumental in the final selection of articles for each edition of Taking Sides. Their review of articles for content, level, and appropriateness provides critical direction to the editors and staff. We think that you will find their careful consideration well reflected in this volume.

Grace Auyang
University of Cincinnati

Claudius A. Carnegie
Florida International University

Robert Cole
Saint Louis University

Paul DiBara
Curry College

Michael Efthimiades
Vaughn College of Aeronautics

Sarah Greenwald
Appalachian State University

James Hollenbeck
Indiana University Southeast

John A. Kromkowski
The Catholic University of America

Michael Martel
Ohio University

Timothy McGettigan
Colorado State University, Pueblo

Robert Moody
Fort Hays State University

Joseph B. Mosca
Monmouth University

Mike Theiss
University of Wisconsin Marathon

Introduction

In his 2008 inaugural address, President Barack Obama said, "We will build the roads and bridges, the electric grids, and digital lines that feed our commerce and bind us together. We will restore science to its rightful place and wield technology's wonders to raise health care's quality and lower its costs." At the 2010 meeting of the American Association for the Advancement of Science, Eric Lander, cochair of the President's Council of Advisors on Science and Technology, asked, "What is the rightful place of science?" and answered that it belongs "in the president's cabinet and policy-making, in the nation's classrooms; as an engine to propel the American economy; as a critical investment in the federal budget, even in times of austerity; as a tool for diplomacy and international understanding and as an organizing principle for space exploration." (See Eric S. Lander, "Obama Advisor Weighs 'The Rightful Place of Science'," *Science News* (June 5, 2010); the question is also discussed in Daniel Sarewitz, "The Rightful Place of Science," *Issues in Science and Technology* (Summer 2009).) However, John Marburger, science advisor to President George W. Bush, notes in "Science's Uncertain Authority in Policy," *Issues in Science and Technology* (Summer 2010), that policymakers often ignore science in favor of preference, prejudice, and expedience.

The discussion of "the rightful place of science" is important for several reasons. One is simply that previous administrations have often made decisions based less on evidence than on politics and ideology. Today, the conservative or right-wing side of American society is waging what has been called a "war on science," refusing to accept scientific truths that threaten religious beliefs (e.g., evolution), desperate wishes (e.g., vaccine safety and alternative medicine), profit (e.g., global warming), and more; see Shawn Lawrence Otto, *Fool Me Twice: Fighting the Assault on Science in America* (Rodale, 2011); John Grant, *Denying Science: Conspiracy Theories, Media Distortions, and the War Against Reality* (Prometheus, 2011); and Shawn Lawrence Otto, "America's Science Problem," *Scientific American* (November 2012).

The other—closely related—reason for discussing "the rightful place of science" is that a great many of the issues that the United States and the world face today cannot be properly understood without a solid grounding in climatology, ecology, physics, and engineering (among other areas). This is not going to change. In the twenty-first century, we cannot escape science and technology. Their fruits—the clothes we wear, the foods we eat, the tools we use—surround us. They also fill us with both hope and dread for the future, for although new discoveries promise us cures for diseases and other problems, new insights into the wonders of nature, new gadgets, new industries, and new jobs (among other things), the past has taught us that technological developments can have unforeseen and terrible consequences.

Those consequences do *not* belong to science, for science is nothing more (or less) than a systematic approach to gaining knowledge about the world. Technology is the application of knowledge (including scientific knowledge) to accomplish things we otherwise could not. It is not just devices such as hammers and computers and jet aircraft, but also management systems and institutions and even political philosophies. And it is of course such *uses* of knowledge that affect our lives for good and ill.

We cannot say, "for good *or* ill." Technology is neither an unalloyed blessing nor an unmitigated curse. Every new technology offers both new benefits and new problems, and the two sorts of consequences cannot be separated from each other. Automobiles provide rapid, convenient personal transportation, but precisely because of that benefit, they also create suburbs, urban sprawl, crowded highways, and air pollution, and even contribute to global climate change.

Optimists Vs. Pessimists

The inescapable pairing of good and bad consequences helps to account for why so many issues of science and technology stir debate in our society. Optimists focus on the benefits of technology and are confident that we will be able to cope with any problems that arise. Pessimists fear the problems and are sure their costs will outweigh any possible benefits.

Sometimes the costs of new technologies are immediate and tangible. When new devices—steamship boilers or space shuttles—fail or new drugs prove to have unforeseen side effects, people die. Sometimes the costs are less obvious.

The proponents of technology answer that if a machine fails, it needs to be fixed, not banned. If a drug has side effects, it may need to be refined or its permitted recipients may have to be better defined (the banned tranquilizer thalidomide is famous for causing birth defects when taken early in pregnancy; it is apparently quite safe for men and nonpregnant women).

Certainty Vs. Uncertainty

Another root for the debates over science and technology is uncertainty. Science is by its very nature uncertain. Its truths are provisional, open to revision.

Unfortunately, most people are told by politicians, religious leaders, and newspaper columnists that truth is certain. They therefore believe that if someone admits uncertainty, their position is weak and they need not be heeded. This is, of course, an open invitation for demagogues to prey upon fears of disaster or side effects or upon the wish to be told that the omens of greenhouse warming and ozone holes (etc.) are mere figments of the scientific imagination. Businesses may try to emphasize uncertainty to forestall government regulations; see David Michaels, *Doubt Is Their Product: How Industry's Assault on Science Threatens Your Health* (Oxford University Press, 2008).

Is Science Just Another Religion?

Science and technology have come to play a huge role in human culture, largely because they have led to vast improvements in nutrition, health care, comfort, communication, transportation, and humanity's ability to affect the world. However, science has also enhanced understanding of human behavior and of how the universe works, and in this it frequently contradicts what people have long thought they knew. Furthermore, it actively rejects any role of God in scientific explanation.

Many people therefore reject what science tells us. They see science as just another way of explaining how the world and humanity came to be; in this view, science is no truer than religious accounts. Indeed, some say science is just another religion, with less claim on followers' allegiance than other religions that have been divinely sanctioned and hallowed by longer traditions. Certainly, they see little significant difference between the scientist's faith in reason, evidence, and skepticism as the best way to achieve truth about the world and the religious believer's faith in revelation and scripture. This becomes very explicit in connection with the debates between creationists and evolutionists. Even religious people who do not favor creationism may reject science because they see it as denying both the existence of God and the importance of "human values" (meaning behaviors that are affirmed by traditional religion). This leads

to a basic antipathy between science and religion, especially conservative religion, and especially in areas—such as human origins—where science and scripture seem to be talking about the same things but are contradicting each other. This point can be illustrated by mentioning the Italian physicist Galileo Galilei (1564–1642), who in 1616 was attacked by the Roman Catholic Church for teaching Copernican astronomy and thus contradicting the teachings of the Church. Another example arose when evolutionary theorist Charles Darwin first published *On the Origin of Species by Means of Natural Selection* in 1859. Mano Singham notes in "The Science and Religion Wars," *Phi Delta Kappan* (February 2000), that "In the triangle formed by science, mainstream religion, and fringe beliefs, it is the conflict between science and fringe beliefs that is usually the source of the most heated, acrimonious, and public debate." Michael Ruse takes a more measured tone when he asks "Is Evolution a Secular Religion?" *Science* (March 7, 2003); his answer is that "Today's professional evolutionism is no more a secular religion than is industrial chemistry" but there is also a "popular evolutionism" that treads on religious ground and must be carefully distinguished. In recent years, efforts to counter "evolutionism" by mandating the teaching of creationism or "intelligent design" (ID) in public schools have made frequent appearances in the news, but so have the defeats of those efforts. One of the most recent defeats was in Dover, Pennsylvania, where the judge declared that "ID is not science." See Jeffrey Mervis, "Judge Jones Defines Science—And Why Intelligent Design Isn't," *Science* (January 6, 2006), and Sid Perkins, "Evolution in Action," *Science News* (February 25, 2006).

Even if religion does not enter the debate, some people reject new developments in science and technology (and in other areas) because they seem "unnatural." For most people, "natural" seems to mean any device or procedure to which they have become accustomed. Very few realize how "unnatural" are such ordinary things as circumcision and horseshoes and baseball.

Yet new ideas are inevitable. The search for and the application of knowledge is perhaps the human species' single most defining characteristic. Other creatures also use tools, communicate, love, play, and reason. Only humans have embraced change. We are forever creating variations on our religions, languages, politics, and tools. Innovation is as natural to us as building dams is to a beaver.

Efforts to encourage innovation are a perennial topic in discussions of how nations can deal with problems and stimulate their economies (see David H. Guston,

"Innovation Policy: Not Just a Jumbo Shrimp," *Nature* (August 21, 2008)). India has a National Innovation Foundation, and a similar government agency has been suggested for the United States (see Robert Atkinson and Howard Wial, "Creating a National Innovation Foundation," *Issues in Science and Technology* (Fall 2008); see also Robert Atkinson and Howard Wial, *Boosting Productivity, Innovation, and Growth through a National Innovation Foundation* (Washington, DC: Brookings Institution and Information Technology and Innovation Foundation, 2008), available online at www.brookings.edu/~/media/Files /rc/reports/2008/04_federal_role_atkinson_wial/NIF%20Report .pdf or www.itif.org/files/NIF.pdf). The closest we have come so far is the Defense Advanced Research Projects Agency (DARPA; www.darpa.mil/), famous for its initiation of Internet technology, and ARPA-Energy (http://arpa-e.energy .gov/), launched in 2007 with hopes for equally impressive results in the field of energy.

Voodoo Science

Public confusion over science and technology is increased by several factors. One is the failure of public education. In 2002, the Committee on Technological Literacy of the National Academy of Engineering and the National Research Council published a report (*Technically Speaking: Why All Americans Need to Know More About Technology*) that said that although the United States is defined by and dependent on science and technology, "its citizens are not equipped to make well-considered decisions or to think critically about technology. As a society, we are not even fully aware of or conversant with the technologies we use every day."

A second factor is the willingness of some to mislead. Alarmists stress awful possible consequences of new technology without paying attention to actual evidence, they demand certainty when it is impossible, and they reject the new because it is untraditional or even "unthinkable." And then there are the marketers, hypesters, fraudsters, activists, and even legitimate scientists and critics who oversell their claims. Robert L. Park, author of *Voodoo Science: The Road from Foolishness to Fraud* (Oxford University Press, 2002), lists seven warning signs "that a scientific claim lies well outside the bounds of rational scientific discourse" and should be viewed warily:

- The discoverer pitches his claim directly to the media, without permitting peer review.
- The discoverer says that a powerful establishment is trying to suppress his or her work.

- The scientific effect involved is always at the very limit of detection.
- Evidence for a discovery is only anecdotal.
- The discoverer says a belief is credible because it has endured for centuries.
- The discoverer has worked in isolation.
- The discoverer must propose new laws of nature to explain an observation.

The Soul of Science

The standard picture of science—a world of observations and hypotheses, experiments and theories, a world of sterile white coats and laboratories and cold, unfeeling logic—is a myth of our times. It has more to do with the way science is presented by both scientists and the media than with the way scientists actually do their work. In practice, scientists are often less orderly, less logical, and more prone to very human conflicts of personality than most people suspect.

The myth remains because it helps to organize science. It provides labels and a framework for what a scientist does; it may thus be especially valuable to student scientists who are still learning the ropes. In addition, it embodies certain important ideals of scientific thought. It is these ideals that make the scientific approach the most powerful and reliable guide to truth about the world that human beings have yet devised.

The Ideals of Science: Skepticism, Communication, and Reproducibility

The soul of science is a very simple idea: *Check it out.* Scholars used to think that all they had to do to do their duty by the truth was to say "According to . . ." some ancient authority such as Aristotle or the Bible. If someone with a suitably illustrious reputation had once said something was so, it was so. Arguing with authority or holy writ could get you charged with heresy and imprisoned or burned at the stake.

This attitude is the opposite of everything that modern science stands for. As Carl Sagan says in *The Demon-Haunted World: Science as a Candle in the Dark* (Random House, 1995, p. 28), "One of the great commandments of science is, 'Mistrust arguments from authority'." Scientific knowledge is based not on authority but on reality itself. Scientists take nothing on faith. They are *skeptical*. When they want to know something, they do not look it up in the library or take others' word for it. They go into the laboratory, the forest, the desert—wherever they can find the phenomena they wish to know about—and they ask those phenomena directly. They look for answers in the book of nature. And if they think they know the answer already, it is not of books that they ask, "Are we right?" but of nature. This is the point of "scientific experiments"—they are how scientists ask nature whether their ideas check out.

This "check it out" ideal is, however, an ideal. No one can possibly check everything out for himself or herself. Even scientists, in practice, look things up in books. They too rely on authorities. But the authorities they rely on are other scientists who have studied nature and reported what they learned. In principle, everything those authorities report can be checked. Observations in the lab or in the field can be repeated. New theoretical or computer models can be designed. What is in the books can be confirmed.

In fact, a good part of the official "scientific method" is designed to make it possible for any scientist's findings or conclusions to be confirmed. Scientists do not say, "Vitamin D is essential for strong bones. Believe me. I know." They say, "I know that vitamin D is essential for proper bone formation because I raised rats without vitamin D in their diet, and their bones turned out soft and crooked. When I gave them vitamin D, their bones hardened and straightened. Here is the kind of rat I used, the kind of food I fed them, the amount of vitamin D I gave them. Go thou and do likewise, and you will see what I saw."

Communication is therefore an essential part of modern science. That is, in order to function as a scientist, you must not keep secrets. You must tell others not just what you have learned by studying nature, but how you learned it. You must spell out your methods in enough detail to let others repeat your work.

Scientific knowledge is thus *reproducible* knowledge. Strictly speaking, if a person says "I can see it, but you can't," that person is not a scientist. Scientific knowledge exists for everyone. Anyone who takes the time to learn the proper techniques can confirm it. They don't have to believe in it first.

As an exercise, devise a way to convince a red-green colorblind person, who sees no difference between red and green, that such a difference really exists. That is, show that a knowledge of colors is reproducible, and therefore scientific knowledge, rather than something more like belief in ghosts or telepathy.

Here's a hint: Photographic light meters respond to light hitting a sensor. Photographic filters permit light of only a single color to pass through.

The Standard Model of the Scientific Method

As it is usually presented, the scientific method has five major components. They include *observation, generalization* (identifying a pattern), stating a *hypothesis* (a tentative extension of the pattern or explanation for why the pattern exists), and *experimentation* (testing that explanation). The results of the tests are then *communicated* to other members of the scientific community, usually by publishing the findings. How each of these components contributes to the scientific method is discussed briefly below.

Observation

The basic units of science—and the only real facts the scientist knows—are the individual *observations*. Using them, we look for patterns, suggest explanations, and devise tests for our ideas. Our observations can be casual, as when we notice a black van parked in front of the fire hydrant on our block. They may also be more deliberate, as what a police detective notices when he or she sets out to find clues to who has been burglarizing apartments in our neighborhood.

Generalization

After we have made many observations, we try to discern a pattern among them. A statement of such a pattern is a *generalization*. We might form a generalization if we realized that every time there was a burglary on the block, that black van was parked by the hydrant.

Cautious experimenters do not jump to conclusions. When they think they see a pattern, they often make a few more observations just to be sure the pattern holds up. This practice of strengthening or confirming findings by *replicating* them is a very important part of the scientific process. In our example, the police would wait for the van to show up again and for another burglary to happen. Only then might they descend on the alleged villains. Is there loot in the van? Burglary tools?

The Hypothesis

A tentative explanation suggesting why a particular pattern exists is called a *hypothesis*. In our example, the hypothesis that comes to mind is obvious: The burglars drive to work in that black van.

The mark of a good hypothesis is that it is *testable*. The best hypotheses are *predictive*. Can you devise a predictive test for the "burglars use the black van" hypothesis?

Unfortunately, tests can fail even when the hypothesis is perfectly correct. How might that happen with our example?

Many philosophers of science insist on *falsification* as a crucial aspect of the scientific method. That is, when a test of a hypothesis shows the hypothesis to be false, the hypothesis must be rejected and replaced with another.

The Experiment

The *experiment* is the most formal part of the scientific process. The concept, however, is very simple: An experiment is nothing more than a test of a hypothesis. It is what a scientist—or a detective—does to check an idea out.

If the experiment does not falsify the hypothesis, that does not mean the hypothesis is true. It simply means that the scientist has not yet come up with the test that falsifies it. The more times and the more different ways that falsification fails, the more probable it is that the hypothesis is true. Unfortunately, because it is impossible to do all the possible tests of a hypothesis, the scientist can never *prove* it is true.

Consider the hypothesis that all cats are black. If you see a black cat, you don't really know anything at all about all cats. If you see a white cat, though, you certainly know that not all cats are black. You would have to look at every cat on Earth to prove the hypothesis. It takes just one to disprove it.

This is why philosophers of science say that *science is the art of disproving,* not proving. If a hypothesis withstands many attempts to disprove it, then it may be a good explanation of what is going on. If it fails just one test, it is clearly wrong and must be replaced with a new hypothesis.

However, researchers who study what scientists actually do point out that the truth is a little different. Almost all scientists, when they come up with what strikes them as a good explanation of a phenomenon or pattern, do *not* try to disprove their hypothesis. Instead, they design experiments to *confirm* it. If an experiment fails to confirm the hypothesis, the researcher tries another experiment, not another hypothesis.

Police detectives may do the same thing. Think of the one who found no evidence of wrongdoing in the black van but arrested the suspects anyway. Armed with a search warrant, he later searched their apartments. He was saying, in effect, "I *know* they're guilty. I just have to find the evidence to prove it."

The logical weakness in this approach is obvious, but that does not keep researchers (or detectives) from falling in love with their ideas and holding onto them

as long as possible. Sometimes they hold on so long, even without confirmation of their hypothesis, that they wind up looking ridiculous. Sometimes the confirmations add up over the years and whatever attempts are made to disprove the hypothesis fail to do so. The hypothesis may then be elevated to the rank of a *theory, principle,* or *law.* Theories are explanations of how things work (the theory of evolution *by means of* natural selection). Principles and laws tend to be statements of things that happen, such as the law of gravity (masses attract each other, or what goes up comes down) or the gas law (if you increase the pressure on an enclosed gas, the volume will decrease and the temperature will increase).

Communication

Each scientist is obligated to share her or his hypotheses, methods, and findings with the rest of the scientific community. This sharing serves two purposes. First, it supports the basic ideal of skepticism by making it possible for others to say, "Oh, yeah? Let me check that." It tells those others where to see what the scientist saw, what techniques to use, and what tools to use.

Second, it gets the word out so that others can use what has been discovered. This is essential because science is a cooperative endeavor. People who work thousands of miles apart build with and upon each other's discoveries, and some of the most exciting discoveries have involved bringing together information from very different fields, as when geochemistry, paleontology, and astronomy came together to reveal that what killed off the dinosaurs 65 million years ago was apparently the impact of a massive comet or asteroid with the Earth.

Scientific cooperation stretches across time as well. Every generation of scientists both uses and adds to what previous generations have discovered. As Isaac Newton said, "If I have seen further than [other men], it is by standing upon the shoulders of Giants" (Letter to Robert Hooke, February 5, 1675/6).

The communication of science begins with a process called "peer review," which typically has three stages. The first occurs when a scientist seeks funding—from government agencies, foundations, or other sources—to carry out a research program. He or she must prepare a report describing the intended work, laying out background, hypotheses, planned experiments, expected results, and even the broader impacts on other fields. Committees of other scientists then go over the report to see whether the scientist knows his or her area, has the necessary abilities, and is realistic in his or her plans.

Once the scientist has the needed funding, has done the work, and has written a report of the results, that report will go to a scientific journal. Before publishing the report, the journal's editors will show it to other workers in the same or related fields and ask whether the work was done adequately, the conclusions are justified, and the report should be published.

The third stage of peer review happens after publication, when the broader scientific community gets to see and judge the work.

This three-stage quality-control filter can, of course, be short-circuited. Any scientist with independent wealth can avoid the first stage quite easily, but such scientists are much, much rarer today than they were a century or so ago. Those who remain are the object of envy. Surely it is fair to say that they are not frowned upon as are those who avoid the later two stages of the "peer review" mechanism by using vanity presses and press conferences.

On the other hand, it is certainly possible for the standard peer review mechanisms to fail. By their nature, these mechanisms are more likely to approve ideas that do not contradict what the reviewers think they already know. Yet unconventional ideas are not necessarily wrong, as Alfred Wegener proved when he tried to gain acceptance for the idea of continental drift in the early twentieth century. At the time, geologists believed the crust of the Earth—which was solid rock, after all—did not behave like liquid. Yet Wegener was proposing that the continents floated about like icebergs in the sea, bumping into each other, tearing apart (to produce matching profiles like those of South America and Africa), and bumping again. It was not until the 1960s that most geologists accepted his ideas as genuine insights instead of hare-brained delusions.

The Need for Controls

Many years ago, I read a description of a wish machine. It consisted of an ordinary stereo amplifier with two unusual attachments. The wires that would normally be connected to a microphone were connected instead to a pair of copper plates. The wires that would normally be connected to a speaker were connected instead to a whip antenna of the sort we usually see on cars.

To use this device, one put a picture of some desired item between the copper plates. It could be a photo of a person with whom one wanted a date, a lottery ticket, a college, anything. One test case used a photo of a pest-infested cornfield. One then wished fervently for the date, a winning ticket, a college acceptance, or whatever else one craved. In the test case, that meant wishing that all the cornfield pests should drop dead.

Supposedly the wish would be picked up by the copper plates, amplified by the stereo amplifier, and then sent via the whip antenna wherever wish-orders have to go. Whoever or whatever fills those orders would get the message, and then. . . . Well, in the test case, the result was that when the testers checked the cornfield, there was no longer any sign of pests.

What's more, the process worked equally well whether the amplifier was plugged in or not.

I'm willing to bet that you are now feeling very much like a scientist—skeptical. The true, dedicated scientist, however, does not stop with saying, "Oh, yeah? Tell me another one!" Instead, he or she says something like, "Mmm. I wonder. Let's check this out." (Must we, really? After all, we can be quite sure that the wish machine does not work because if it did, it would be on the market. Casinos would then be unable to make a profit for their backers. Deadly diseases would not be deadly. And so on.)

Where must the scientist begin? The standard model of the scientific method says the first step is observation. Here, our observations (as well as our necessary generalization) are simply the description of the wish machine and the claims for its effectiveness. Perhaps we even have an example of the physical device itself.

What is our hypothesis? We have two choices, one consistent with the claims for the device, one denying those claims: The wish machine always works, or the wish machine never works. Both are equally testable, but perhaps one is more easily falsifiable. (Which one?)

How do we test the hypothesis? Set up the wish machine, and perform the experiment of making a wish. If the wish comes true, the device works. If it does not, it doesn't.

Can it really be that simple? In essence, yes. But in fact, no.

Even if you don't believe that wishing can make something happen, sometimes wishes do come true by sheer coincidence. Therefore, if the wish machine is as nonsensical as most people think it is, sometimes it will *seem* to work. We therefore need a way to shield against the misleading effects of coincidence. We need a way to *control* the possibilities of error.

Coincidence is not, of course, the only source of error we need to watch out for. For instance, there is a very human tendency to interpret events in such a way as to agree with our preexisting beliefs, our prejudices. If we believe in wishes, we therefore need a way to guard against our willingness to interpret near misses as not quite misses at all. There is also a human tendency not to look for mistakes when the results agree with our prejudices. That cornfield, for instance, might not have been as badly infested as the testers said it was, or a farmer might have sprayed it with pesticide whether the testers had wished or not, or the field they checked might have been the wrong one.

We would also like to check whether the wish machine does indeed work equally well plugged in or not, and then we must guard against the tendency to wish harder when we know it's plugged in. We would like to know whether the photo between the copper plates makes any difference, and then we must guard against the tendency to wish harder when we know the wish matches the photo.

Coincidence is easy to protect against. All that is necessary is to repeat the experiment enough times to be sure we are not seeing flukes. This is one major purpose of replication.

Our willingness to shade the results in our favor can be defeated by having someone else judge the results of our wishing experiments. Our eagerness to overlook "favorable" errors can be defeated by taking great care to avoid any errors at all; peer reviewers also help by pointing out such problems.

The other sources of error are harder to avoid, but scientists have developed a number of helpful *control* techniques. One is "blinding." In essence, it means setting things up so the scientist does not know what he or she is doing.

In the pharmaceutical industry, this technique is used whenever a new drug must be tested. A group of patients are selected. Half of them—chosen randomly to avoid any unconscious bias that might put sicker, taller, shorter, male, female, homosexual, black, or white patients in one group instead of the other—are given the drug. The others are given a dummy pill, or a sugar pill, also known as a placebo. In all other respects, the two groups are treated exactly the same. Drug (and other) researchers take great pains to be sure groups of experimental subjects are alike in every way but the one way being tested. Here that means the only difference between the groups should be which one gets the drug and which one gets the placebo.

Unfortunately, placebos can have real medical effects, apparently because we *believe* our doctors when they tell us that a pill will cure what ails us. We have faith in them, and our minds do their best to bring our bodies into line. This mind-over-body "placebo effect" seems to be akin to faith healing.

Single Blind.   The researchers therefore do not tell the patients what pill they are getting. The patients are "blinded" to what is going on. Both placebo and drug then gain equal advantage from the placebo effect. If the drug seems to work better or worse than the placebo, then the researchers can be sure of a real difference between the two.

Double Blind. Or can they? Unfortunately, if the researchers know what pill they are handing out, they can give subtle, unconscious cues. Or they may interpret any changes in symptoms in favor of the drug. It is therefore best to keep the researchers in the dark too; since both researchers and patients are now blind to the truth, the experiment is said to be "double blind." Drug trials often use pills that differ only in color or in the number on the bottle, and the code is not broken until all the results are in. This way nobody knows who gets what until the knowledge can no longer make a difference.

Obviously, the double-blind approach can work only when there are human beings on both sides of the experiment, as experimenter and as experimental subject. When the object of the experiment is an inanimate object such as a wish machine, only the single-blind approach is possible.

With suitable precautions against coincidence, self-delusion, wishful thinking, bias, and other sources of error, the wish machine could be convincingly tested. Yet it cannot be perfectly tested, for perhaps it works only sometimes, when the aurora glows green over Copenhagen, in months without an "r," or when certain people use it. It is impossible to rule out all the possibilities, although we can rule out enough to be pretty confident as we call the gadget nonsense.

Very similar precautions are essential in every scientific field, for the same sources of error lie in wait wherever experiments are done, and they serve very much the same function. However, we must stress that no controls and no peer review system, no matter how elaborate, can completely protect a scientist—or science—from error.

Here, as well as in the logical impossibility of proof (experiments only fail to disprove) and science's dependence on the progressive growth of knowledge (its requirement that each scientist make his or her discoveries while standing on the shoulders of the giants who went before, if you will) lies the uncertainty that is the hallmark of science. Yet it is also a hallmark of science that its methods guarantee that uncertainty will be reduced (not eliminated). Frauds and errors will be detected and corrected. Limited understandings of truth will be extended.

Those who bear this in mind will be better equipped to deal with issues of certainty and risk.

Something else to bear in mind is that argument is an inevitable part of science. The combination of communication and skepticism very frequently leads scientists into debates with each other. The scientist's willingness to be skeptical about and hence to challenge received wisdom leads to debates with everyone else. A book like this one is an unrealistic portrayal of science only because it covers such a small fraction of all the arguments available.

Is Science Worth It?

What scientists do as they apply their methods is called *research*. Scientists who perform *basic or fundamental research* seek no specific result. Basic research is motivated essentially by curiosity. It is the study of some intriguing aspect of nature for its own sake. Basic researchers have revealed vast amounts of detail about the chemistry and function of genes, explored the behavior of electrons in semiconductors, revealed the structure of the atom, discovered radioactivity, and opened our minds to the immensity in both time and space of the universe in which we live.

Applied or strategic research is more mission-oriented. Applied scientists turn basic discoveries into devices and processes, such as transistors, computers, antibiotics, vaccines, nuclear weapons and power plants, and communications and weather satellites. There are thousands of such examples, all of which are answers to specific problems or needs, and many of which were quite surprising to the basic researchers who first gained the raw knowledge that led to these developments.

It is easy to see what drives the effort to put science to work. Society has a host of problems that cry out for immediate solutions. Yet there is also a need for research that is not tied to explicit need because such research undeniably supplies a great many of the ideas, facts, and techniques that problem-solving researchers then use in solving society's problems. Basic researchers, of course, use the same ideas, facts, and techniques as they continue their probings into the way nature works.

In 1945—after the scientific and technological successes of World War II—Vannevar Bush argued in *Science, the Endless Frontier* (National Science Foundation, 1990) that science would continue to benefit society best if it were supported with generous funding but not controlled by society. On the record, he was quite right, for the next half-century saw an unprecedented degree of progress in medicine, transportation, computers, communications, weapons, and a great deal more.

There have been and will continue to be problems that emerge from science and its applications in technology. Some people respond like Bill Joy, who argues in "Why the Future Doesn't Need Us," *Wired* (April 2000), that some technologies—notably robotics, genetic engineering, and nanotechnology—are so hazardous that we should refrain

from developing them. On the whole, however, argue those like George Conrades ("Basic Research: Long-Term Problems Facing a Long-Term Investment," *Vital Speeches of the Day* (May 15, 1999)), the value of the opportunities greatly outweighs the hazards of the problems. Others are less sanguine. David H. Guston and Kenneth Keniston ("Updating the Social Contract for Science," *Technology Review* (November/December 1994)) argue that despite the obvious successes of science and technology, public attitudes toward scientific research also depend on the vast expense of the scientific enterprise and the perceived risks. As a result, the public should not be "excluded from decision making about science." That is, decisions should not be left to the experts alone.

Conflict also arises over the function of science in our society. Traditionally, scientists have seen themselves as engaged in the disinterested pursuit of knowledge, solving the puzzles set before them by nature with little concern for whether the solutions to these puzzles might prove helpful to human enterprises such as war, health care, and commerce, among many more. Yet again and again the solutions found by scientists have proved useful. They have founded industries. And scientists love to quote Michael Faraday, who, when asked by politicians what good the new electricity might be, replied: "Someday, sir, you will tax it."

Not surprisingly, society has come to expect science to be useful. When asked to fund research, it feels it has the right to target research on issues of social concern, to demand results of immediate value, to forbid research it deems dangerous or disruptive, and to control access to research results that might be misused by terrorists or others.

Private interests such as corporations often feel that they have similar rights in regard to research they have funded. For instance, tobacco companies have displayed a strong tendency to fund research that shows tobacco to be safe and to cancel funding for studies that come up with other results, which might interfere with profits.

One argument for public funding is that it avoids such conflict-of-interest issues. Yet politicians have their own interests, and their control of the purse strings—just like a corporation's—can give their demands a certain undeniable persuasiveness.

Public Policy

The question of targeting research is only one way in which science and technology intersect the broader realm of public policy. Here the question becomes how society should allocate its resources in general: toward education or prisons; health care or welfare; research or trade; and encouraging new technologies or cleaning up after old ones?

The problem is that money is finite. Faced with competing worthy goals, we must make choices. We must also run the risk that our choices will turn out, in hindsight, to have been wrong.

The Purpose of This Book

Is there any prospect that the debates over the proper function of science, the acceptability of new technologies, or the truth of forecasts of disaster will soon fall quiet? Surely not, for some of the old issues will forever refuse to die (think of evolution versus creationism), and there will always be new issues to debate afresh. Some of the new issues will strut upon the stage of history only briefly, but they will in their existence reflect something significant about the way human beings view science and technology. Some will remain controversial as long as has evolution or the population explosion (which has been debated ever since Thomas Malthus' 1798 "Essay on the Principle of Population"). Some will flourish and fade and return to prominence; early editions of this book included the debate over whether the last stocks of smallpox virus should be destroyed; they were not, and the war on terrorism has brought awareness of the virus and the need for smallpox vaccine back onto the public stage. The loss of the space shuttle *Columbia* reawakened the debate over whether space should be explored by people or machines. Some issues will remain live but change their form, as has the debate over government interception of electronic communications. And there will always be more issues than can be squeezed into a book like this one—think, for instance, of the debate over whether elections should use electronic voting machines (discussed by Steve Ditlea, "Hack the Vote," *Popular Mechanics* (November 2004)).

Since almost all of these science and technology issues can or will affect the conditions of our daily lives, we should know something about them. We can begin by examining the nature of science and a few of the current controversies over issues in science and technology. After all, if one does not know what science, the scientific mode of thought, and their strengths and limitations are, one cannot think critically and constructively about any issue with a scientific or technological component. Nor can one hope to make informed choices among competing scientific, technological, or political and social priorities.

Unit 1

UNIT

The Place of Science and Technology in Society

*T*he partnership between human society and science and technology is an uneasy one. Science and technology offer undoubted benefits, in both the short and long term, but they also challenge received wisdom and political ideology. The issues in this section deal with whether public access to publicly funded research should take precedence over the right of private interests to make money, whether the full results of scientific research should be available to all, and whether commerce or freedom is a better foundation for regulation.

Selected, Edited, and with Issue Framing Material by:
Thomas A. Easton, *Thomas College*

ISSUE

Is the Distinction Between Basic and Applied Research Useful?

YES: Nils Roll-Hansen, from "Why the Distinction Between Basic (Theoretical) and Applied (Practical) Research Is Important to the Politics of Science," Original Work (2010)

NO: Venkatesh Narayanamurti, Tolu Odumosu, and Lee Vinsel, from "RIP: The Basic/Applied Research Dichotomy," *Issues in Science and Technology* (2013)

Learning Outcomes
After reading this issue, you will be able to: • Explain the different roles of basic and applied research.   • Describe the different criteria for success of basic and applied research.   • Explain why government policymakers seem to prefer applied research.   • Describe how basic research reflects liberal democratic values.

ISSUE SUMMARY

YES: Nils Roll-Hansen argues that the difference between basic and applied research is important to studies of the history of science and to science policy. The two differ profoundly in their criteria for success or failure, their effects on social processes, and in their degree of autonomy from political and economic interests. The distinction must not be blurred over in the interest of promoting innovation and economic growth.

NO: Venkatesh Narayanamurti, Tolu Odumosu, and Lee Vinsel argue that the distinction between basic and applied research fails to reflect what actually happens in scientific research. They urge an "invention/discovery" model and hence a more holistic, long-term view of the research process in order to enhance innovation that has public utility and identify ways to intervene with public policy.

One of the major activities of scientists is scientific research. Traditionally, research is divided into two types. *Basic research* (also known as pure or fundamental research) seeks no specific result. It is motivated essentially by curiosity. It is the study of some intriguing aspect of nature for its own sake. It has revealed vast amounts of detail about the chemistry and function of genes, discovered ways to cut and splice genes at will, and learned how to insert into one organism genes from other organisms. It has revealed the structure of the atom and discovered radioactivity. It has opened our minds to the immensity in both time and space of the universe in which we live.

It has yielded photos of the surface of Mars. And a great deal more.

Applied research is more mission oriented. A great many of the scientists who work for government and industry are applied researchers. They seek answers to specific problems. They want cures for diseases, methods for analyzing problems, and ways to control various phenomena. They develop means for realizing the dreams of basic researchers (such as the spacecraft that have yielded photos of other planets). They have taken the knowledge and techniques developed by basic research in genetics, molecular biology, quantum physics, electronics, and other areas and created wondrous technologies (genetic engineering, computers, communications). In the process, they have created new industries with immense potentials for growth and impact on human welfare.

The unexpected fruits or "spinoffs" of basic research have been used to justify steady growth in funding for this side of science ever since Vannevar Bush's 1945 report, *Science, the Endless Frontier* (Washington, DC: National Science Foundation, reprinted 1990). Yet the debate over the value of basic research has been going on for decades. As early as 1953, Warren Weaver ("Fundamental Questions in Science," *Scientific American,* September 1953) was concerned that the successes of applied science meant neglect of basic science. By the 1990s, there was a movement to focus on "national goals" and "science in the national interest" and to emphasize applied research over basic research. The thrust was toward commercial success, international competitiveness, more jobs, and increased prosperity. See Eliot Marshall, "R&D Policy that Emphasizes the 'D,'" *Science* (March 26, 1993).

A similar message has come from the Carnegie Commission on Science, Technology, and Government, which in September 1992 issued a report (*Enabling the Future: Linking Science and Technology to Societal Needs*) calling for a "National Forum on Science and Technology Goals" to help define, debate, focus, and articulate science and technology goals and to monitor the development and implementation of policies to achieve them. For a good discussion of this topic, see Gary Chapman, "The National Forum on Science and Technology Goals," *Communications of the ACM* (January 1994). "A coordinator of the 21st Century Project, a national campaign to reorient U.S. science and technology policy in the post–Cold War era," Chapman strongly favors "new . . . models that incorporate public participation, diversity, equity, and attention to national needs."

Today, the rhetoric involves the need to foster innovation and improve the nation's competitive position *vis-a-vis* other nations. As President Obama said in his January 2011 State of the Union address, "The first step to winning the future is encouraging American innovation." We need new industries, new products, and new processes, and the world's fastest growing economies are encouraging specific industries and development projects with government policy and funding. See Fareed Zakaria, "Innovate Better," *Time* (June 13, 2011). China is already one of the world's economic powerhouses. With its eye on maintaining and improving that status, it is rapidly building a national innovation system; see Tang Yuankai, "Growth Through Innovation," *Beijing Review* (July 19, 2012). At a February 6, 2013, hearing of the United States House Committee on Science, Space, and Technology,

Richard K. Templeton, Chairman, President, and CEO of Texas Instruments, testified that "federal funding of fundamental scientific research is critical to our nation's continued competitiveness, economic growth and workforce development. It will shape our future" and the interaction of industry, universities, and government is a key element of "the U.S. innovation ecosystem." At the same hearing, Charles M. Vest, President of the National Academy of Engineering, said that "if we invest well in basic research and in education, we undoubtedly will be surprised by what new innovations arise."

It is easy to see what drives this rhetoric. Society has a host of problems that cry out for solutions as soon as possible. They involve health care, global warming, energy supply, weather forecasting, and of course keeping the economy booming in order to provide jobs and wealth. The answers lie in the relatively short-term fruits of applied research, though commentators such as Chapman recognize that there is a great deal of interplay between basic and applied research and argue that even basic research (though they may avoid the term in favor of research and development, or R&D) should be directed toward societal needs.

There is also resistance by conservative politicians to basic research that reveals truths that run counter to their beliefs. We thus see attempts to ignore the fruits of evolutionary biology and climate science research, as well as demands that the National Science Foundation fund only political science research that the NSF director "certifies as promoting national security or the economic interests of the United States"; see Jeffrey Mervis, "Bill Would Set New Rules for Choosing NSF Grants," *Science* (May 3, 2013), and Dante D'Orazio, "National Science Foundation Dodges Congressional Politics by Canceling New Political Science Research," *The Verge* (August 3, 2013) (http://www.theverge.com/2013/8/3/4585464/nsf-dodges -congressional-politics-by-canceling-2013-political-science -research-funding). Applied research is politically safer.

Looking back at our initial definitions, we see that research that is directed toward society's problems cannot be basic research. Yet basic research undeniably supplies a great many of the ideas, facts, and techniques which applied researchers then use in their search for answers to society's problems. Basic researchers, of course, use the same ideas, facts, and techniques (as well as the fruits of applied research) as they continue their probing into the way nature works. And basic research also creates applied researchers. When the late Howard E. Simmons (1929–1997), received the American Chemical Society's Priestley Medal, he spoke strongly in favor of basic research, emphasizing its value to long-term progress (see *Chemical*

& *Engineering News*, March 14, 1994). He also encouraged more attention to science education and stressed that from industry's perspective, basic research at the university level plays a crucial role in producing "bright young scientists, broadly trained, but solid in the fundamentals, whose curiosity about the world has been piqued."

In "Endangered Support of Basic Science," a short essay in the May 1994 *Scientific American*, the late Victor F. Weisskopf (1908–2002), an MIT emeritus professor of physics and a Manhattan Project leader, wrote that "Today we cannot afford the kind of lavish funding that basic science enjoyed during the decades following World War II." However, we cannot afford to abandon basic research. "Basic science . . . creates important educational, ethical and political values. It fosters a critical, antidogmatic spirit, a readiness to say, 'I was wrong,' and an idealistic inclination to do work where there is little financial gain. Basic science establishes a bond between humans and nature; it does not recognize industrial, national, racial and ideological barriers. . . . Science cannot flourish unless it is pursued for the sake of pure knowledge and insight."

Unfortunately, because of its lack of specific direction, many government decision makers see basic research as a luxury society cannot afford. The payoff is not immediate, society has other needs that require funding, and the money is limited. Indeed, policymakers argue over whether even applied research should receive government funding, on the grounds that the private sector, guided by markets, should handle this task. In July 2012, *The Economist* ran an online debate on "Research Funding: Should Public Money Finance Applied Research?" (http://www.economist.com/debate/days/view/863). Andrew Miller,

Labour MP and Chair of the House of Commons Science and Technology Select Committee, argued that the private sector would only rarely invest in the long-term, low-return applied research that was crucial to the early development of space technology or future energy potential such as advanced battery technology. There is thus a need for public funding. If he seems to be talking about basic research rather than applied, he also questioned the validity of distinguishing the one from the other. He said, "I do not believe these labels can be used precisely enough to justify funding decisions." His opponent, Terence Kealey, Vice Chancellor of the University of Buckingham, argued against public funding of basic research on the grounds that private firms will choose not to invest in the same research. Indeed, it does seem rational to wait to reap the fruits of the public funding.

In the YES selection, Nils Roll-Hansen argues that the difference between basic and applied research is important to studies of the history of science and to science policy. The two differ profoundly in their criteria for success or failure, their effects on social processes, and in their degree of autonomy from political and economic interests. The distinction must not be blurred over in the interest of promoting innovation and economic growth. In the NO selection, Venkatesh Narayanamurti, Tolu Odumosu, and Lee Vinsel argue that the distinction between basic and applied research fails to reflect what actually happens in scientific research. They urge an "invention/discovery" model and hence a more holistic, long-term view of the research process in order to enhance innovation that has public utility and identify ways to intervene with public policy.

YES

Nils Roll-Hansen

Why the Distinction Between Basic (Theoretical) and Applied (Practical) Research Is Important to the Politics of Science

Introduction

The distinction between "basic" and "applied" research or science was taken for granted half a century ago, in the aftermath of World War II. Basic science was often called "pure science" or simply "science." It had a double social role. On the one hand it was a crucial ingredient in the ideology of liberal democracy, and on the other it was a knowledge base that served practical tasks through applied science. According to this ideal of science, truthfulness is the root value. And scientific research, perceived as search for generally valid knowledge, ought to be as free as possible from the interference of special economic, political, ideological and religious interests. This Weberian ideal type "science" was championed by defenders of classical liberal and enlightenment political ideals, like Karl Popper and Michael Polanyi. It was most famously codified by the sociologist Robert Merton in his "ethos of science." His set of norms for scientific behaviour described an international scientific community committed to produce knowledge, valid and accessible for all, in a critical spirit free from discrimination on grounds of race, sex, religion, ethnic group, etc.

In the 1960s this classical liberal ideal of science came under double pressure, from above and below, so to speak. From above it was eroded by growing political and administrative steering of science in order to serve economic growth. From below political radicalism, inspired by Marxist theory of science and symbolized by the "student revolution," reacted against ideas of "objectivity" and "truth" that served capitalism. Thus government planning and grass roots radicalism alike perceived the academic "ivory tower" as an obstacle to progressive science and technology. Elsewhere I have argued that present politics of science is still reluctant to squarely face this ambiguous ideological legacy. The present paper will focus on the

economic framing that has tended to dominate science studies and science policy since after 1960.

My distinction between basic and applied research reflects the different social functions of science and politics as social institutions. Basic science is dedicated to increasing and managing knowledge of general validity, and research is its dynamic element. The role of politics is to produce agreement, decisions, and collective action. Applied science can roughly be understood as the area of overlap between science and politics. The superior goal is solution of practical economic, social, and political problems, but success depends on properly taking into account the most advanced scientific knowledge and methods.

The purpose of distinctions between basic research, applied research, and technological development is not to separate these activities, but to grasp the differences in order to better coordinate and combine their activities. The concepts are ideal types and not sharply defined and exclusive categories. In spite of overlap and intertwining they carry different expectations and have different societal effects, which the politics of science needs to address. My paper focuses on the difference between basic research on the one hand and applied research and technological development on the other. Where nothing else is stated, the term "applied research" will stand for "applied research and technological development."

1. A Traditional Conception of Applied and Basic Research

During the second half of the 19th century, applied research expanded rapidly. In universities it was growing to a volume that demanded clearer rules of responsibility and public accountability. This led to the establishment of new special institutions for applied research, "practical-scientific" work, in fisheries, agriculture, geological surveying, statistics, etc., in many countries.

The present paper discusses primarily three kinds of difference between applied and basic research:

1. Different criteria for success or failure.
2. Different effects on social processes.
3. Institutional differences, e.g., in degree of autonomy from political and economic interests.

It is the way these differences are combined that gives the distinction between applied and basic research substance and political importance.

In applied research the dominant criterion is solution of specific practical problems. Practical technical success is the superior yardstick of evaluation both in advance, of projects, and retrospectively, of results. Adequate scientific competence is a necessary condition, but the choice of problem as well as the success of the result is decided politically rather than scientifically. Applied research is funded by government agencies, private firms, non-governmental interest organizations, etc., to further their respective goals—improvement in social and medical services, technical efficiency and economic profitability, ideological and political acclaim, etc.

Basic research, on the other hand, is successful when it discovers new phenomena or invents new ideas of general interest. The importance is judged in the first instance by the discipline in question. But interdisciplinary relevance is characteristic of much significant basic research. And the ultimate criterion is contributions to our general world picture. The aim of basic research is theoretical, to improve general understanding. It has no specific aim outside of this. But it is, of course, not by accident that improved understanding of the world increases our ability to act rationally and efficiently, to develop new, efficient, and beneficial technologies. Briefly, the result of successful basic research is what we find in the textbooks.

Applied research is an instrument in the service of its patron, helping to solve practical problems as recognized by politicians, government bureaucrats, commercial entrepreneurs, etc. It helps to interpret and refine the problems of the patron, to make them researchable, and then investigate and develop solutions. The missions of applied research are framed by the problems set by the patron. In this sense it is subordinate to social, economic and political aims external to science.

Basic research is not subject to the same kind of external steering. It has in principle no obligations of loyalty to specific patrons, and its ideal is autonomy from particular political and economic interests. It is responsible only to common human and societal interests—the "common good." This concept of basic science has been understood as a crucial principle of the enlightenment tradition of the West. The autonomy from politics, religion and economic interests builds on a belief that knowledge and understanding is in general a good thing, and that increasing such knowledge and understanding will mostly lead to a better life. However, it is part of the tradition that such beliefs are subjected to critical scrutiny.

In accordance with the enlightenment tradition, a main role of basic scientific research is to improve our understanding of the world. Science is a major source of the concepts and ideas needed for a precise formulation of political and other practical problems. In this sense it is prior to politics. Sometimes basic research has a direct and dramatic effect by discovering new threatening problems and thus immediately setting a new political agenda. The present grave concern over climate change is a striking example of how politics depends on science to assess and respond to a threatening problem.

Thus science does not only provide means (instruments) for solving problems set by politics, it also shapes political values and goals. Applied research is set up to serve the first task while basic research also serves the second. From the point of view of liberal democratic decision-making, there is an important difference between solving recognized problems and introducing new problems. In the first case, science has an *instrumental* role subordinate to politics. In the second case, the role is political *enlightenment*, which is highly dependent on autonomy and independence from political authorities. When science is asked for advice on a threat like climate change, which is still mainly a prediction about future events, the importance of autonomy becomes particularly acute and correspondingly hard to maintain against political pressure.

2. The OECD Classification of Research

In the early 1960s the OECD set up an international comparative system for research statistics. The purpose was to help economic growth and development, and it therefore took a broad view of scientific research, including not only "basic research" but also "applied research" and "experimental development." The OECD classification in this way followed the contemporary trend to expand the concept of scientific research to cover all of "research and development" ("R&D"). Within a few decades this broad concept of "research" had largely replaced the traditional concept of "science" in public discourse.

Nevertheless, the OECD classification of the early 1960s with its distinctions between basic research, applied research and experimental development is still used in international research statistics:

> R&D is a term covering three activities: basic research, applied research and experimental development. . . . Basic research is experimental or theoretical work undertaken primarily to acquire new knowledge of the underlying foundation of phenomena and observable facts, without any particular application or use in view. Applied research is also original investigation undertaken in order to acquire new knowledge. It is, however, directed primarily towards a practical aim or objective. Experimental development is systematic work, drawing on existing knowledge gained from research and/or practical experience that is directed to producing new materials, products or devices, to installing new processes, systems and services, or to improving substantially those already produced or installed.

These OECD categories and definitions have been much criticized for not being sufficiently clear and objective as the basis for a dependable and stable statistics. For instance critics have argued that the distinction between basic and applied appears highly dependent on the subjective attitude of the researcher. And individual projects will often include so much both of basic and applied aspects that they do not comfortably fit either category. This balance may also shift as a project develops. Over time a statistics built on such subjective and flexible categories seems liable to reflect changes in fashions and attitudes rather than register changes in substance of research, critics have argued. But as noted above the OECD classification was based on a traditional conception of science developed from historical experience. This gave substance to the distinction between basic and applied research in terms of intellectual content as well as social effects, institutional differentiation, and criteria for success.

The primary interest of OECD was natural science and its applications in industry, agriculture and medicine. However, the system also included social science and the humanities. These latter fields do not easily fit the British-American concept of "science," though they are well covered by the continental European term "Wissenschaft." The ideal of scientific knowledge as knowledge of universal laws was foreign, especially to the humanities. Their knowledge, often defined as "understanding," was typically embodied in accounts of individual phenomena and events. It was "idiographic" (individually descriptive) and radically different from the "nomothetic" (lawlike) knowledge of natural science. The feeling of being pressed into alien and unsuitable categories has motivated criticism and rejection of the OECD distinction between basic and applied research in the humanities.

By the early 21st century this criticism has less force. As biology has displaced physics as the leading natural science the ideal of scientific knowledge as a knowledge of universal laws has given way to more limited generalizations and explanation in terms of mechanisms. Apt and accurate general terms for description and classification have emerged as an essential basis in natural science much like in the humanities and social science, and the philosophical tension is likely to ease.

In recent decades both scholarly studies and practical politics of science have tended to concentrate on the inclusive category of "research" (R&D) and not take much interest in the differences between basic and applied. There is concern that this will undermine the autonomy of science. Basic research consumes only a small fraction of the total resources for R&D and can easily be overshadowed by applied research and technological development backed by strong external political and economic interests.

There is also concern that preoccupation with the broad category of "research" also makes comparison between countries less meaningful because it obscures critical differences in their needs for research of different kinds. For instance, keeping up an independent and strong military capability demands large investments in development of defence technology. Similarly, a large high-tech industry, producing pharmaceuticals, advanced electronics, etc., goes with high investment in appropriate applied research and technological development. On the other hand, countries mostly exporting semi-fabricated or raw materials have smaller needs for this type of research.

But in spite of scholarly neglect and political-administrative doubts the expression "basic research," and implicitly a distinction between "basic" and "applied," seems to be indispensable in debates over science policy. There is a widespread feeling that "basic research" designates a valuable social activity in need of defence against commercialization and bureaucratic control. In a survey interview with scientists and policy-makers Jan Calvert has shown how ambiguous the term "basic research" is and how the meaning shifts with user and context. However, she thinks this vigorous flora of different meanings and definitions also indicates how "resilient and necessary the term must be."

However imperfect, the OECD statistics over basic research, applied research and experimental development do in a useful way monitor changes over time as well as differences between countries. And as long as participants in science policy debates are aware of the ambiguities, and clearly understand the differences, communication need not suffer.

3. The Economic Approach to Science Policy

After World War II, in the early years of the cold war, intellectual freedom was a main topic in political debates about science. Left wing enthusiasm for a socially useful science on the Soviet model had subsided and scientific freedom became the leading idea. The European scientific tradition was seen as a crucial support for liberal democracy against totalitarian regimes of the left as well as the right. By the early 1960s the focus of science policy had shifted to economic growth and social development. Science was recognized as a fundamental motor in economic growth and supported by public money on a scale unknown before the war. How to distribute resources between different kinds and areas of research now became the main issue. In this economic perspective the justification of applied research and experimental development was easy to see, but basic research became a problem.

The nuclear physicist and science administrator Alvin M. Weinberg considered two possible justifications of basic research: Either as a "Branch of High Culture" or as "An Overhead Charge on Applied Science and Technology." The philosopher and historian of science Stephen Toulmin did not find a simple high culture doctrine reassuring. It was unlikely to impress governments geared to economic growth. He opted instead for basic science as a "tertiary industry." This new branch of "industry" would soak up the work force otherwise doomed to unemployment by the rapid progress of technological efficiency in production of all the goods needed for a comfortable life. Liberating people from trivial production tasks and giving them the opportunity to pursue science for its own sake would be an important contribution to a superior quality of life in the new society that was emerging. Down to earth economists were hesitant to acclaim Toulmin's utopian dream and insisted that basic science had to be considered either as investment or consumption. Resources for basic research could be justified either because of "positive output consequences" or "because it is a pleasurable consumption activity."

In other words: On closer economic scrutiny Toulmin's argument did not get beyond science as "high culture." This implied that public spending on basic research had to be justified politically in competition with other cultural activities like art and literature, or even sport—if it was not simply seen as a necessary overhead on applied research and technological development. It is striking how the science policy debate in the 1960s had narrowed down to an economic perspective. The idea of (basic) science as a pillar of liberal democracy had receded to the background.

Recent analysis and discussion in the "economics of science" still largely follows the 1960s tradition in framing basic research in economic categories. For instance, [Mirowski's and Sent's] *Science Bought and Sold* (2002) is a collection of papers ranging from classic contributions by Charles Sanders Peirce, Richard R. Nelson, Kenneth Arrow, and Michael Polanyi, to recent contributions by historians, philosophers, economists and sociologists of science like Paul Foreman, Philip Kitcher, Michel Callon, Paul David and Steve Fuller.

Kenneth Arrow in a paper on "Economics of Welfare and the Allocation of Resources for Innovation" starts by defining "invention" as roughly synonymous to "the production of knowledge." He cited a paper by Richard Nelson,"The Simple Economics of Basic Science," where the economic and technological perspective on scientific research had been more explicitly presented. Nelson argued that the US should spend more on "basic science" in order to be internationally competitive economically and technologically. The paper, first published in 1959, starts by referring to the Sputnik-shock, still fresh in the public mind. Nelson's epistemology has an instrumentalist flavour which makes good sense in economics but is more problematic for theories of natural science. . . .

Nelson stressed that basic research is not a "homogeneous commodity." But his concerns hardly went beyond an economic perspective. He argued that a free-enterprise economy will under-invest in common welfare commodities like education and public health, which are important economic factors, because such investment is not profitable for private firms. Nelson's worry is that this problem of "external economies" also applies to "basic science." He still uses the term "science" rather than "research." . . .

From the 1960s on the OECD has promoted radical reform of the research system. Traditional basic research has been seen as locked up in the academic "ivory tower," bound in a straight-jacket of old-fashioned scientific disciplines and lacking contact with the practical problems of society. To make science socially useful, governments must intervene more actively by increased funding of applied research, by directing basic research toward national goals, and by supporting interdisciplinary research suitable to illuminate and solve pressing social problems. Science and scholarship, according to OECD policy, have to become much more integrated with public administration, social services, business and industry, was the repeated message to OECD member countries.

By the mid-1990s there was a growing feeling that a radical change had taken place both in the size of the research system and in its organization and social functions. The differences and the distance between basic and applied research seemed to shrink and disappear. The academic ivory tower was finally crumbling, and the OECD economic approach to science policy appeared to have been fruitful. But there was also a notable uneasiness about the effects. *The New Production of Knowledge*, sponsored by the Swedish research policy establishment and published in 1994, distinguishes two different ways of doing scientific research, Mode 1 and Mode 2, corresponding roughly to two different kinds of knowledge, theoretical and practical. Mode 1 stands for the traditional academic and discipline-oriented research and knowledge. Mode 2 is "different in nearly every respect." It "operates within a context of application" and is "transdisciplinary rather than mono- or multidisciplinary." Though Mode 2 has a number of characteristics typical of applied research the inclusive and open character suggests that "research and development" (R&D) is the appropriate statistical category. However, Gibbons et al. do not discuss the OECD statistical classification. They are apparently groping for a new approach which is inspired by humanities and social science and demands radically new categories: "The problem of language is particularly difficult when trying to describe the nature of Mode 2 in areas where natural science is involved."

The thesis of the *The New Production of Knowledge* is that Mode 2 is expanding in economic as well as epistemic importance and threatens to marginalize or swallow up the traditional academic and disciplinary Mode 1 way of doing science. Mode 2 implies political and economic steering, which the old institutions of Mode 1 will have to adapt to. Interpreted as a unification of theoretical and practical science under the governance of politics and economics, Mode 2 comes into conflict with the traditional liberal ideal of scientific autonomy. Basic science as an autonomous institution responsible for true knowledge, cultural enlightenment, education, etc., but not for direct economic social usefulness, becomes more difficult to discern and harder to legitimate. . . .

The Mode 2 picture of science has dominated science policy discourse in recent years, supported by the influential broad trends of social constructivism. Historical and sociological studies of science have concentrated on the social and individual conditions of knowledge production rather than the way in which science achieves progress in dependable (true) knowledge about the objects under study. In this "subjectivist" perspective the legitimacy for external control and governing of the scientific enterprise looms large and the arguments for scientific autonomy become hard to discern.

But there have also been persistent critics arguing that there are important differences between basic and applied research and that it undermines sound science policy if these differences are rejected or neglected. Illka Niiniluoto, for instance, characterizes basic and applied by two fundamentally different goals, epistemic and practical. The primary task of basic research is "cognitive" to help us "*explain* and *understand* reality" and develop a "*world view*." Applied research and technological development on the other hand are also subject to practical technical goals. They are governed by "technological utility" and should be assessed according to this. . . .

4. "Pasteur's Quadrant"

In spite of theories that see basic and applied research as a seamless whole, practical science policy perceives a persistent dilemma in dividing resources between the two. "Basic research" and [the] more or less equivalent wordings "curiosity drive research," "blue skies research," "bottom up research," and "pure science," keep cropping up as expressions of Mode 1 ideals. Science administrators and politicians have given much attention to an attempt to overcome this dilemma by Donald Stokes, [a] political scientist with extensive practical experience in American science policy. In *Pasteur's Quadrant. Basic Science and Technological Innovation* (1997), he argues that the difficulties can be overcome by concentrating on the most outstanding research because here the theoretical and practical come together. The paradigm example is Louis Pasteur. His contributions are truly outstanding both with respect to basic theoretical and applied technological results.

To explain his solution to the perceived dilemma Stokes drew a four box diagram where Pasteur [occupies] the box for research that aims simultaneously for theoretical as well as practical results:

"Quadrant Model of Scientific Research"		
Research is inspired by:		
	Considerations of use?	
	No	Yes
Quest for fundamental understanding — Yes	Pure basic research (Bohr)	Use-inspired basic research (Pasteur)
Quest for fundamental understanding — No		Pure applied research (Edison)

Stokes holds that since World War II it has been widely believed that "the categories of basic and applied research are radically separate" and that their "goals are inevitably in tension." The solution, he argues, lies in taking note of an historical insight: The annals of science are "rich with cases of research that is guided both by understanding and by use, confounding the view of basic and applied science as inherently separate realms." This historical experience points to a research policy that gives priority to the upper left hand corner of his diagram, 'Pasteur's quadrant.' Here belongs the "major work of John Maynard Keynes, the fundamental research of the Manhattan project, and Irving Langmuir's surface physics" as well as Pasteur's biomedical contributions, according to Stokes.

But how well does this solution stand up to the concepts of basic and applied research sketched in this paper? First: The Manhattan project appears misplaced. It was primarily applied research and experimental development, aiming to produce a fission bomb. Second: The troublesome dilemmas are not between the lifelong contributions of prominent scientists. Individual scientists can, of course, participate in basic as well as in applied projects. Some of the best draw inspiration from such rotation. At the ground level, however, the choice is between individual projects with a well specified goal. When the problem or theme is clearly defined and thus made accessible to effective research the individual projects usually emerge with either a theoretical or a practical purpose. The lifelong careers of Pasteur, Keynes, and Langmuir are probably best understood as a series of interacting individual projects. Some were derived of their theoretical interests; some were commissions to help solve practical social or economic problems.

Some "research projects" are large and can more properly be called "research programmes." On a closer look they usually contain many individual projects focused on different problems some of basic scientific character some practical. The pioneering Norwegian acid rain project of the 1970s is a characteristic example. It investigated the effects of acid rain on fresh water fish and on forests and contributed important new understanding of the basic natural processes involved as well [as] answers on the extent and character of damage done.

Other large scale projects have a clearly defined primary purpose that classifies them primarily as applied or basic. But this does not prevent there being parts which qualify as clearly belonging in the other category. The Apollo "project" of the 1960s successfully put a human being on the Moon, but also gave important basic results, like geological knowledge about the Moon. On the other hand, the Large Hadron Collider at CERN . . . is a very large and complicated specialized machine built to investigate basic phenomena in high energy particle physics. Its main purpose is basic research. But in building and operating the machine numerous problems of technological development had to be solved. It is all the applied sub-projects that make this CERN project in basic research so costly.

These two examples, Apollo and the CERN experiment, illustrate the difference in criteria for success. In the first case, research was primarily the necessary instrument for putting a man on the Moon. In the second, new understanding of the nature of the smallest components of matter is the goal. In large projects interesting spin-off in terms of unexpected theoretical discoveries or new technology is likely. But this was not the reason for funding them.

The important and valid point in Stokes' promotion of "Pasteur's quadrant" is that interaction between the most challenging theoretical and practical problems can be highly productive. Theory provides practice with new concepts and theories, and practice presents theory with unexpected facts. Some of the most important achievements, both in basic and applied research, have their origin in settings which include both. This indicates that interaction between basic and applied research is most effectively secured by institutions and individuals that are in some way concerned with both.

Pasteur, for instance, started his career in crystallography investigating the difference of organic from inorganic chemistry. He found asymmetry in crystals of organic compounds to be explained by asymmetry in molecular structure, and speculated that the asymmetry of organic molecules was the secret of life. This "organismic" view inspired his refutation of spontaneous generation in micro-organisms and development of a germ theory. Together these theories remained a continuing hard core in his later researches in applied microbiology, on brewing, diseases of animals and plants, vaccination, etc. This conceptual and theoretical framework was not a result of his involvement in practical technological problems, as has been assumed by economists referring to Stokes' ideas about "Pasteur's quadrant." Rather it was a precondition for his ability to formulate soluble and fruitful questions in applied research.

On this background a general research policy that gives priority to Pasteur's quadrant appears problematic. Increasing scientific specialization makes decision-makers more and more dependent on formal criteria deriving from experts' schematic reports. If individual research projects are rated by adding their score in the basic and applied dimension the result may be to favour projects with an average score in both over those which excel in one. When competition is tough and only a small fraction are funded there is increasing risk that the most innovative projects are squeezed out because they are so clearly either theoretical or practical. It is hardly a good idea to cut support for Edison and Bohr because Pasteur apparently solves the dilemma of choosing between basic and applied research. . . .

5. Subordinating Science to Politics?

One of the "hardest, most neglected problems in contemporary philosophy of science" is "the question of how we balance epistemic values against other kinds of concern." In his *Science, Truth, and Democracy* Kitcher develops the idea of a "well-ordered science" to solve this problem. On one central point there is apparently a direct contradiction to the present paper. Kitcher rejects the distinction between science and technology: Not only does it lack a sound empirical basis; it is directly harmful by blocking important criticism of science and technology. However, his concept of basic research is quite different from mine.

In Kitcher's view the traditional conception of basic research is built on the myth of "pure science." This myth holds that the aim of scientific "inquiry is *merely* to discover truth" (my emphasis). With the cloning of Dolly as his example Kitcher argues convincingly that all science aims not only at any truth but at truths that are socially *significant*, i.e., not isolated and independent of social and moral values. Thus traditional "basic science" does not exist in the real world, and Kitcher draws the general conclusion that "moral and social values" are "intrinsic to the practice of the sciences," i.e., to all kinds of scientific activity.

It is not difficult to agree that all science, including basic research, must in the last instance be judged on its contribution to human well-being. The question is whether this principle leads to the view that there are no politically significant differences between basic and applied research. Perhaps it is the other way around that this distinction is necessary in order to organize a science that will effectively contribute to the desired goal? . . .

[T]he third edition of [Hackett's] *The Handbook of Science and Technology Studies* (2008) appears dismissive of the distinction between basic ("pure") and applied science or research, in line with Kitcher's view. The papers in the section on "Institutions and Economics" suggest that it is "no longer possible to focus on science's institutional autonomy as it was understood in the time of Merton or Polanyi." A weakness in the approach that dominates this *Handbook* is its preoccupation with the period after World War II and the impact of the Cold War on the organization

and funding of American science and technology. Ideas of "pure science," "academic freedom," etc., are narrowly related to this context. Their roots in the political and ideological conflicts of the inter-war period are neglected, and there are repeated references to a "Mertonian" view which is quite different from the ethos of science described by Robert Merton. He did not "treat science as subsisting beyond and outside of politics."

Contrary to the conception of science as separated from politics, Merton was concerned about science as an essential component of modern liberal democracy. His worry was that totalitarian ideologies like German Nazism and Soviet Communism were destroying the institution of science. Merton's ethos of science was formulated well before the advent of the Cold War. . . . When Merton used the term "science" he had in mind basic science as something different from technology. Throughout the *Handbook*, however, the primary interest is in science and technology as a whole, "technoscience" as it is often called. When the term science is used it usually refers to science and technology, not to science in Merton's sense.

Conclusion

This paper aims to delineate and make plausible a distinction between basic research on the one hand and applied research and technological development on the other. It is argued that this distinction, even if poorly understood, lies at the core of present controversies in science policy. Basic research differs from applied by its internal scientific criteria for success, its enlightenment social effects, and the relative autonomy of its institutions.

This distinction has long been central to the politics of scientific research and scientific institutions. It was instrumental in the institutional differentiation of scientific research between universities, technical colleges, industrial laboratories and government institutions of applied research in the late 19th century. It was a main issue in the ideologically charged debates over democracy and freedom in society and science around the Second World War. It was recognized as a fundamental premise in the 1960s seminal debates on criteria of scientific choice. It became marginalized and sometimes explicitly rejected as meaningless and harmful by the new wave of science studies starting around 1970. But there are now signs that a new recognition of the political and cultural importance of this distinction is emerging.

I argue that the distinction makes good philosophical sense when not interpreted in terms of rigid and exclusive metaphysical categories, and that the interaction between science and politics in politically sensitive areas like genetics is more adequately understood with this distinction than without. . . .

The problem with external political and economic steering of scientific research is not that it in general is misguided. On the contrary, strong external steering is good for some kinds of research and bad for others. Typical applied research belongs to the first kind and typical basic research to the second. Applied research is appropriately subject to practical economic and political interests, while basic research needs autonomy in its service of human welfare. I do not claim to have given a convincing argument for this view, but I hope to have shown that there are good reasons to take it more seriously than has been done in science studies during recent decades.

NILS ROLL-HANSEN is a professor emeritus of history and philosophy at the University of Oslo.

**Venkatesh Narayanamurti,
Tolu Odumosu, and Lee Vinsel**

 **NO**

RIP: The Basic/Applied Research Dichotomy

U.S. science policy since World War II has in large measure been driven by Vannevar Bush's famous paper *Science—The Endless Frontier*. Bush's separation of research into "basic" and "applied" domains has been enshrined in much of U.S. science and technology policy over the past seven decades, and this false dichotomy has become a barrier to the development of a coherent national innovation policy. Much of the debate centers on the appropriate federal role in innovation. Bush argued successfully that funding basic research was a necessary role for government, with the implication that applied research should be left to the auspices of markets. However, the original distinction does not reflect what actually happens in research, and its narrow focus on the stated goals of an individual research project prevents us from taking a more productive holistic view of the research enterprise.

By examining the evolution of the famous linear model of innovation, which holds that scientific research precedes technological innovation, and the problematic description of engineering as "applied science," we seek to challenge the existing dichotomies between basic and applied research and between science and engineering. To illustrate our alternative view of the research enterprise, we will follow the path of knowledge development through a series of Nobel Prizes in Physics over several decades.

This mini-history reveals how knowledge grows through a richly interwoven system of scientific and technological research in which there is no clear hierarchy of importance and no straightforward linear trajectory. Accepting this reality has profound implications for the design of research institutions, the allocation of resources, and the national policies that guide research. This in turn can open the door to game-changing discoveries and inventions and put the nation on the path to a more sustainable science and technology ecosystem.

History of an Idea

Although some observers cite Vannevar Bush as the source of the linear model of innovation, the concept actually has deep roots in long-held cultural assumptions that give priority to the work of the head over the work of the hand and thus to the creation of scientific knowledge over technical expertise. If one puts this assumption aside, it opens up a new way of understanding the entire innovation process. We will focus our attention on how it affects our understanding of research.

The question of whether understanding always precedes invention has long been a troubling one. For example, it is widely accepted that many technologies reached relatively advanced stages of development before detailed scientific explanations about how the technologies worked emerged. In one of the most famous examples, James Watt invented his steam engine before the laws of thermodynamics were postulated. In fact, the science of thermodynamics owes a great deal to the steam engine. This and other examples should make it clear that assumptions about what has been called basic and applied research do not accurately describe what actually happens in research.

In 1997, Donald Stokes's book *Pasteur's Quadrant: Basic Science and Technological Innovation* was published posthumously. In this work, Stokes argued that scientific efforts were best carried out in what he termed "Pasteur's Quadrant," where researchers are motivated simultaneously by expanding understanding and increasing our abilities (technological, including medicine) to improve the world. Stokes's primary contribution was in expanding the linear model into a two-dimensional plane that sought to integrate the idea of the unsullied quest for knowledge with the desire to solve a practical problem.

Stokes's model comprises three quadrants, each exemplified by a historical figure in science and technology. The pure basic research quadrant exemplified by Niels Bohr represents the traditional view of scientific research as being inspired primarily by a desire to extend fundamental understanding. The pure applied research quadrant is exemplified in Edison, who represents the classical inventor, driven to solve a practical problem. Louis Pasteur's quadrant is a perfect mix of the two, inventor and scientist in one, expanding knowledge in the pursuit of practical problems. Stokes described this final quadrant as "use-inspired basic research." The fourth quadrant is not fully described in Stokes' framework.

The publication of Stokes's book excited many in the science policy and academic communities, who believed it would free us from the blinders of the linear model. A blurb on the back of the book quotes U.S. Congressman George E. Brown Jr.: "Stokes's analysis will, one hopes, finally lay to rest the unhelpful separation between 'basic' and 'applied' research that has misinformed science policy for decades." However, it has become clear that although Stokes's analysis cleared the ground for future research, it did not go far enough, nor did his work result in sufficient change in how policymakers discuss and structure research. Whereas Stokes notes how "often technology is the inspiration of science rather than the other way around," his revised dynamic model does not recognize the full complexity of innovation, preferring to keep science and technology in separate worlds that mix only in the shared agora of "use-inspired basic research." It is also significant that Stokes's framework preserves the language of the linear model in the continued use of the terms basic and applied as descriptors of research.

We see a need to jettison this conception of research in order to understand the complex interplay among the forces of innovation. We propose a more dynamic model in which radical innovation often arises only through the integration of science and technology.

Invention and Discovery

A critical liability of the basic/applied categorization is that it is based on the motivation of the individual researcher at the time of the work. The efficacy and effectiveness of the research endeavor cannot be fully appreciated in the limited time frame captured by a singular attention to the motivations of the researchers in question. Admittedly, motivations are important. Aiming to find a cure for cancer or advance the frontiers of communications can be a powerful incentive, stimulating groundbreaking research. However, motivations are only one aspect of the research process. To more completely capture the full arc of research, it is important to consider a broader time scale than that implied by just considering the initial research motivations. Expanding the focus

from research motivations to also include questions of how the research is taken up in the world and how it is connected to other science and technology allows us to escape the basic/applied dichotomy. The future-oriented aspects of research are as important as the initial motivation. Considering the implications of research in the long term requires an emphasis on visionary future technologies, taking into account the well-being of society, and not being content with a porous dichotomy between basic and applied research.

We propose using the terms "invention" and "discovery" to describe the twin channels of research practice. For us, invention is the "accumulation and creation of knowledge that results in a new tool, device, or process that accomplishes a specific purpose." Discovery is the "creation of new knowledge and facts about the world." Considering the phases of invention and discovery along with research motivations and institutional settings enables a much more holistic and long-term view of the research process. This allows us to examine the ways in which research generates innovation and leads to further research in a virtuous cycle.

Innovation is a complex, nonlinear process. Still, straightforward and sufficiently realized representations such as Stokes's Pasteur's quadrant are useful as analytical aids. We propose the model of the discovery-invention cycle, which will serve to illustrate the interconnectedness of the processes of invention and discovery, and the need for consideration of research effectiveness over longer time frames than is currently the case. Such a model allows for a more reliable consideration of innovation through time. The model could also aid in discerning possible bottlenecks in the functioning of the cycle of innovation, indicating possible avenues for policy intervention.

A Family of Nobel Prizes

To illustrate this idea, [let us] trace the evolution of the current information and communication age. What can be said about the research that has enabled the recent explosion of information and communication technologies? How does our model enable a deeper understanding of the multiplicity of research directions that have shaped the current information era? To fully answer this question, it is necessary to examine research snapshots over time, paying attention to the development of knowledge and the twin processes of invention and discovery, tracing their interconnections through time. To our mind, the clearest place for selecting snapshots that illustrate the evolution of invention and discovery that enables the information age is the Nobel Prize awards.

We have thus examined the Nobel Prizes in Physics from 1956, 1964, 1985, 1998, 2000, and 2009, which were all related to information technologies. We describe these kinds of clearly intersecting Nobels as a family of prizes in that they are all closely related. Similar families can be found in areas such as nuclear magnetic resonance and imaging.

The birth of the current information age can be traced to the invention of the transistor. This work was recognized with the 1956 Physics Nobel Prize awarded jointly to William Shockley, John Bardeen, and Walter Brattain "for their researches on semiconductors and their discovery of the transistor effect." Building on early work on the effect of electric fields on metal semiconductor junctions, the interdisciplinary Bell Labs team built a working bipolar-contact transistor and clearly demonstrated (discovered) the transistor effect. This work and successive refinements enabled a class of devices that successfully replaced electromechanical switches, allowing for successive generations of smaller, more efficient, and more intricate circuits. Although the Nobel was awarded for the discovery of the transistor effect, the team of Shockley, Bardeen, and Brattain had to invent the bipolar-contact transistor to demonstrate it. Their work was thus of a dual nature, encompassing both discovery and invention. The discovery of the transistor effect catalyzed a whole body of further research into semiconductor physics, increasing knowledge about this extremely important phenomenon. The invention of the bipolar contact transistor led to a new class of devices that effectively replaced vacuum tubes and catalyzed further research into new kinds of semiconductor devices. The 1956 Nobel is therefore exemplary of a particular kind of knowledge-making that affects both later discoveries and later inventions. We call this kind of research radical innovation. The 1956 prize is situated at the intersection of invention and discovery, and it is from this prize that we begin to trace the innovation cycle for the prize family that describes critical moments in the information age.

The second prize in this family is the 1964 Nobel Prize, which was awarded jointly to Charles Townes and the other half to both Nicolay Basov and Aleksandr Prokhorov. Most global communications traffic is carried by transcontinental fiber optic networks, which use light as the signal carrier. Townes's work on the stimulated emission of microwave radiation earned him his half of the Nobel. This experimental work showed that it was possible to build amplifier oscillators with low noise characteristics capable of the spontaneous emission of microwaves with almost perfect amplification. The maser (microwave amplification by the stimulated emission of radiation

effect) was observed in his experiments. Later, Basov and Prokhorov, along with Townes, extended the maser effect to consideration of its application in the visible spectrum, and thus the laser was invented. Laser light allows for the transmission of very high-energy pulses of light at very high frequencies and is crucial for modern high-speed communication systems. This Nobel acknowledges critical work that was also simultaneously discovery (the maser effect) and invention (the maser and the laser), both central to the rise of the information and communication age. Thus, the 1964 Nobel is also situated at the intersection of invention and discovery. The work on lasers built directly on previous work by Einstein, but practical and operational masers and lasers were enabled by advancements in electronic amplifiers made possible by the solid-state electronics revolution, which began with the invention of the transistor.

Although scientists and engineers conducted a great deal of foundational work on the science of information technology in the 1960s, the next wave of Nobel recognition for this research did not come until the 1980s. Advancements in the semiconductor industry led to the development of new kinds of devices such as the metal oxide silicon field effect transistor (MOSFET). The two-dimensional nature of the conducting layer of the MOSFET provided a convenient avenue to study electrical conduction in reduced dimensions. Klaus von Klitzing discovered that under certain conditions, voltage across a current-carrying wire increased in uniform steps. Von Klitzing received the 1985 Nobel Prize for what is known as the quantized Hall effect. This work belongs in the discovery category, although it did have important useful applications.

The 2000 Nobel Prize was awarded jointly to Zhores Alferov and Herbert Kroemer for "developing semiconductor heterostructures" and to Jack Kilby for "his part in the invention of the integrated circuit." Both of these achievements can be classified primarily as inventions, and both built on work done by Shockley et al. This research enabled a new class of semiconductor device that could be used in high-speed circuits and optoelectronics. Alferov and Kroemer showed that creating a double junction with a thin layer of semiconductors would allow for much higher concentrations of holes and electrons, enabling faster switching speeds and allowing for laser operation at practical temperatures. Their invention produced tangible improvements in lasers and light-emitting diodes. It was the work on heterostructures that enabled the modern room-temperature lasers used in fiber optic communication systems. Alferov and Kroemer's work on heterostructures also led to the discovery of a new form of matter, as discussed below.

Jack Kilby's work on integrated circuits at Texas Instruments earned him his half of the Nobel for showing that entire circuits could be realized with semiconductor substrates. Shockley, Bardeen, and Brattain had invented semiconductor-based transistors, but these were discrete components and were used in circuits with components made from other materials. The genius of Kilby's work was in realizing that semiconductors could be arranged in such a way that the entire circuit, not just the transistor, could be realized on a chip. This invention of a process of building entire circuits out of semiconductors allowed for economies of scale, bringing down the cost of circuits. Further research into process technologies allowed escalating progress on the shrinking of these circuits, so that in a few short years, chips containing billions of transistors were possible.

Alferov and Kroemer's work was also valuable to Horst Stormer and his collaborators, who combined it with advancements in crystal growth techniques to produce two-dimensional electron layers with mobility orders of magnitude greater than in silicon MOSFETs. Stormer and Daniel Tsui then began exploring some observed unusual behavior that occurred in two-dimensional electrical conduction. They discovered a new kind of particle that appeared to have only one-third the charge of the previously thought-indivisible electron. Robert Laughlin then showed through calculations that what they had observed was a new form of quantum liquid where interactions between billions of electrons in the quantum liquid led to swirls in the liquid behaving like particles with a fractional electron charge. This phenomenon is clearly a new discovery, but it was enabled by previous inventions and resulted in important practical applications such as the high-frequency transistors used in cell phones. For their work, Laughlin, Stormer, and Tsui were awarded the 1998 Nobel Prize in Physics, an achievement situated firmly in the discovery category.

The 2009 Nobel was awarded to Charles Kao for "groundbreaking achievements concerning the transmission of light in fibers for optical communication" and to Willard Boyle and George Smith for "the invention of the imaging semiconductor circuit—the CCD." Both of these achievements were directly influenced by previous inventions and discoveries in this area. Kao was primarily concerned [with] building a workable waveguide for light for use in communications systems. His inquiries led to astonishing process improvements in glass production, as he predicted that glass fibers of a certain purity would allow long-distance laser light communication. Of course, the work on heterostructures that allowed for room-temperature lasers was critical to assembling the technologies of fiber communication. Kao, however, not only created new processes for measuring the purity of glass but also actively encouraged various manufacturers to improve their processes in this respect. Working directly in industry, Kao's work built on the work by Alferov and Kromer, enabling the physical infrastructure of the information age. Boyle and Smith continued the tradition of Bell Labs inquiry. Adding a brilliant twist to the work that Shockley et al. had done on the transistor, they designed and invented the charge-coupled device (CCD), a semiconductor circuit that enabled digital imagery and video. Kao's work was clearly aimed at discovering the ideal conditions for the propagation of light in fibers of glass, but he also went further in shepherding the invention and development of the new fiber optic devices.

These six Nobel Prizes highlight the multiple kinds of knowledge that play into the innovations that have enabled the current information and communications age. From the discovery of the transistor effect, which relied on the invention of the bipolar junction transistor and led to all the marvelous processors and chips in everything from computers to cars, to the invention of the integrated circuit, which made the power of modern computers possible while shrinking their cost and increasing accessibility. The invention of fiber optics built on previous work on heterostructures and made the physical infrastructure and speed of the global communications networks possible. In fact, the desire to improve the electrical conductivity of heterostructures led to the unexpected discovery of fractional quantization in two-dimensional systems and a new form of quantum fluid. Each of these could probably be classified as "basic" or "applied" research, but that classification obscures the complexity and multiple nature of the research described above and does not help remove the prejudices of many against what is now labeled as "applied research." Thinking in terms of invention and discovery through time helps reconstruct the many pathways that research travels along in the creation of radical innovations.

In our model, the discovery-invention cycle can be traversed in both directions, and research knowledge is seen as an integrated whole that mutates over time (as it traverses the cycle). The bidirectionality of the cycle reflects the reality that inventions are not always the product of discovery but can also be the product of other inventions. Simultaneously, important discoveries can arise from new inventions. Observing the cycle of research over time is essential to understanding how progress occurs.

Seeing with Fresh Eyes

The switch from a basic/applied nomenclature to discovery-invention is not a mere semantic refinement. It enables us to see the entire research enterprise in a new way.

First, it eliminates the tendency to see research proceeding on two fundamentally different and separate tracks. All types of research interact in complex and often surprising ways. To capitalize on these opportunities, we must be willing to see research holistically. Also, by introducing new language, we hope to escape the cognitive trap of thinking about research solely in terms of the researcher's initial motivations. All results must be understood in their larger context.

Second, adopting a long time frame is essential to attaining a full understanding of the path of research. The network of interactions traced in the Nobel Prizes discussed above becomes clear only when one takes into account a 50-year history. This extended view is important to understanding the development of both novel science and novel technologies.

Third, the discovery-invention cycle could be useful in identifying problematic bottlenecks in research. Once we recognize the complex interrelationship of discovery and invention, we are more likely to see that problems can occur in many parts of the cycle and that we need to heed the interactions among a variety of institutions and types of research.

Bringing together the notions of research time horizons and bottlenecks, we argue that successful radical innovation arises from knowledge traveling the innovation cycle. If, as argued above, all parts of the innovation process must be adequately encouraged for the cycle to function effectively, then the notion of traveling also emphasizes that we should have deep and sustained communication between scientists and engineers, between theorists and practitioners. Rather than separating researchers according to their motivation, we must strive to bring all forms of research into deeper congress.

This fresh view of the research enterprise can lead us to rethinking the design of research institutions to align with the principles of long time frames, a premium on futuristic ideas, and the encouragement of interaction among different elements of the research ecosystem. This is especially pertinent in the case of the mission-oriented agencies such as the Department of Energy and the National Institutes of Health.

Implications for Research Policy

The pertinent question is how these insights play out in the messy world of policymaking. First, there is an obvious need to complicate the simple and unhelpful distinction between basic and applied research. The notion of the innovation cycle is a very useful aid in thinking about research holistically. It draws attention to the entirety of research practice and allows one to pose the question of public utility to an entire range of activities.

Second, the nature of the public good, and thus the appropriate role for the federal government, changes. The simple and clear notions of basic and applied were useful in one way: They provided a clear litmus test for limits to federal involvement in the research process. The idea that government funding is necessary to pursue research opportunities that aren't able to attract private funding is a useful one that has contributed to the long-term well-being and productivity of the nation. But through the lens of the discovery-invention cycle, we can see that it would deny federal funding to some types of research that are essential to long-term progress. We suggest that federal support is most appropriate for research that focuses on long-term projects with clear public utility. The difference here is that such research could have its near-term focus on either new knowledge or new technology.

The public good must be understood over the long term, and the best way to ensure that the research enterprise contributes as much as possible to meeting our national goals is to make funding decisions about discovery and invention research in a long-term holistic context.

Venkatesh Narayanamurti is the Benjamin Peirce Professor of technology and public policy and professor of physics at Harvard University and the director of the Science, Technology, and Public Policy Program at the Harvard Kennedy School.

Tolu Odumosu is a postdoctoral research fellow in the Science, Technology, and Public Policy Program at the Harvard Kennedy School and at Harvard's School of Engineering and Applied Sciences.

Lee Vinsel is a postdoctoral research fellow in the Science, Technology, and Society Program at the Harvard Kennedy School and at Harvard's School of Engineering and Applied Sciences.

EXPLORING THE ISSUE

Is the Distinction Between Basic and Applied Research Useful?

Critical Thinking and Reflection

1. Many scientific research projects have both basic and applied elements. Is it always possible to separate these elements?
2. In the invention/discovery model, invention corresponds at least roughly to applied research and discovery to basic. Is there a reason why invention comes first in the name of the model?
3. Should scientific research aim primarily at benefiting national security and the economy or at discovering truths about nature?
4. Is it possible to choose basic research that has "clear public utility" for funding?
5. In what ways does basic research influence politics and policymaking? In what ways does applied research influence politics and policymaking?

Is There Common Ground?

There is little disagreement that scientific research has both basic and applied (or discovery and invention) elements. Policymakers argue over which deserves government funding (and why), as well as over the nature of the eventual benefits.

1. Construct an argument that the increased understanding of the world that comes from basic research is more important than the economic benefits of applied research.
2. Construct an argument that the economic benefits of applied research are more important than the increased understanding of the world that comes from basic research.
3. Can one actually separate increased understanding from economic benefits?

Create Central

www.mhhe.com/createcentral

Additional Resources

Vannevar Bush, *Science, the Endless Frontier: A Report to the President* (Washington, DC: U.S. GovernmentPrinting Office, 1945).

Royal Society of Great Britain, *The Scientific Century: Securing Our Future Prosperity* (London: Royal Society, 2010).

Nils Roll-Hansen, "Why the Distinction Between Basic (Theoretical) and Applied (Practical) Research Is Important in the Politics of Science," *Centre for Philosophy of Natural and Social Science. Technical report No. 04/09* (London School of Economics, 2009).

Internet References . . .

Basic versus Applied Research

http://psych.csufresno.edu/psy144/Content/Design/Types/appliedvsbasic.html

Federation of American Scientists

https://www.fas.org/

Research and Development: Essential Foundation for U.S. Competitiveness in a Global Economy

http://www.nsf.gov/statistics/nsb0803/start.htm

Selected, Edited, and with Issue Framing Material by:
Thomas A. Easton, *Thomas College*

ISSUE

Should the Public Have to Pay to See the Results of Federally Funded Research?

YES: Ralph Oman, from "The Fair Copyright in Research Works Act," testimony regarding H.R 6845, before the Subcommittee on Courts, the Internet, and Intellectual Property of the Committee on the Judiciary (September 11, 2008)

NO: Stuart M. Shieber, from "Testimony Before the U.S. House of Representatives Committee on Science, Space and Technology, Subcommittee on Investigations and Oversight, Hearing on Examining Public Access and Scholarly Publication Interests" (March 29, 2012)

Learning Outcomes

After studying this issue, students will be able to:

- Explain how peer review helps to assure the quality of scientific publications.
- Explain why peer review and open access can coexist.
- Explain why university and college libraries favor open access publishing.
- Explain the role of profit in academic publishing.

ISSUE SUMMARY

YES: Attorney and past register of copyrights Ralph Oman contends that "If the NIH [National Institutes of Health] succeeds in putting all of the NIH-related peer-reviewed articles on its online database for free within one year of publication, the private publishers will be hard-pressed to survive." Allowing private publishers to continue to profit by publishing the results of publically funded research is the best way to ensure public benefit.

NO: Stuart M. Shieber argues that the concerns of traditional journal publishers that open access publishing will endanger their survival are not justified. The data show that publisher profitability has increased despite the recent economic downturn. Providing open access to the publicly funded research literature amplifies the diffusion of knowledge and benefits researchers, taxpayers, and everyone who gains from new medicines, new technologies, new jobs, and new solutions to long-standing problems of every kind.

According to Peter Suber's "Open Access Overview" (www.earlham.edu/~peters/fos/overview.htm), "open access" refers to the broad-based movement to put peer-reviewed research articles online, free of charge, and without most copyright and licensing restrictions. According to his "Timeline of the Open Access Movement" (www.earlham.edu/~peters/fos/timeline.htm), the movement has roots in the 1960s, well before the Internet came to exist as we know it today. Project Gutenberg (www.gutenberg.org/wiki/Main_Page), which makes public-domain novels and other books freely available, was launched in 1971. For many years, the open access movement was no threat to the standard modes of scientific publishing, but by 2004 it was clear that scientific (and other) journals were becoming so expensive that university and college libraries were being forced to cut back on the number of journals they could subscribe to; on April 17, 2012, Harvard's Faculty Advisory Council sent a memo to faculty saying "Major Periodical Subscriptions Cannot Be Sustained" (http://isites.harvard.edu/icb/icb.do?keyword=k77982&tabgroupid=icb.tabgroup143448).

In response to a report from the House Appropriations Committee urging the National Institutes of Health to require NIH-funded research reports to be deposited in NIH's Internet archive, PubMed Central, NIH director Elias Zerhouni convened meetings with representatives of academic publishers, and others. Publishers expressed concern that making reports freely available would threaten their continued existence. See Jocelyn Kaiser, "House Weighs Proposal to Block Mandatory 'Open Access'," *Science* (September 19, 2008).

Pressure was rising to do something about the problem, and open access looked like a possible solution, as exemplified by the Public Library of Science (PLoS) (see Theodora Bloom, et al., "PLoS Biology at 5: The Future Is Open Access," *PLoS Biology* (October 2008). Leah Hoffman, "Open for Business," *Communications of the ACM* (April 2012), notes that "Open access is growing fast in both recognition and popularity, making it a force to be reckoned with in the future of academic publishing."

According to Walt Crawford, "Open Access: It's Never Simple," *Online* (July/August 2008), one major objection to the traditional mode of scholarly publication—meaning that university and college libraries pay to subscribe to a journal—is that subscriptions have become remarkably expensive. Springer-Verlag's journal prices for 2010 can be seen at www.springer.com/librarians/price+lists? SGWID=0-40585-0-0-0; sixteen of those journals are priced at over $10,000 a year. The prices of Elsevier's titles are listed at www.elsevier.com/wps/find/journalpricing.cws_home/ subscrippricelistlibr/description; *Life Sciences* cost a library $7,399 for 2012 compared to $4,031 a year in 2000 and $2,325 in 1995. Subscription prices for print journals have grown about 10 percent per year, with electronic access and mixed access being priced even higher. Aggregated (multijournal) electronic-access packages appeared in 2001 to help stabilize prices; see Frances L. Chen, Paul Wrynn, and Judith L. Rieke, "Electronic Journal Access: How Does It Affect the Print Subscription Price?" *Bulletin of the Medical Library Association* (October 2001). Michael P. Taylor, "Opinion: Academic Publishing Is Broken: The Current System by Which Academics Publish Their Scientific Discoveries Is a Massive Waste of Money," *The Scientist* (March 19, 2012), reinforces these points.

Today aggregated packages (such as Ebsco) are commonplace, with many academic libraries using them to replace paper subscriptions. But even these can be expensive. It is no surprise that libraries are among the strongest backers of the open access movement in the United States and elsewhere (for a Canadian view, see Heather Morrison and Andrew Waller, "Open Access and Evolving Scholarly Communication," *C&RL News*, September 2008). Some researchers are addressing the concern that open access journals are somehow inferior to subscription journals in terms of quality control by studying their "impact factor" (how often papers are cited); K. A. Clauson, et al., "Open-Access Publishing for Pharmacy-Focused Journals," *American Journal of Health-System Pharmacists* (August 15, 2008), find that impact factors are actually greater for journals with some form of open access. Yet as open access journals proliferate, it is clear that some are of much less quality than others; see Martin Enserink, "As Open Access Explodes, How to Tell the Good from the Bad and the Ugly?" *Science* (November 23, 2012).

The pressure for open access does not come only from government agencies such as NIH. Some see open access as a movement to democratize what has until recently been an elite resource; see Ron Miller, "Open Access Battles to

Democratize Academic Publishing," *EContent* (April 2009). Leslie Chan, Subbiah Arunachalam, and Barbara Kirsop, "Open Access: A Giant Leap Towards Bridging Health Inequities," *Bulletin of the World Health Organization* (August 2009), argue that only through open access publishing can the latest research results reach those who need them. Harvard University's arts and sciences faculty "has directly challenged the authority of academic journals to control access to research results" by voting to put faculty work in a free online repository, following similar moves by the Howard Hughes Medical Institute and the Wellcome Trust in London. A comment by Patricia Schroeder of the Association of American Publishers that "Publishers may not be as quite as excited to take articles from Harvard" seems more than a little wishful, considering Harvard's reputation. See Andrew Lawler, "Harvard Faculty Votes to Make Open Access Its Default Mode," *Science* (February 22, 2008). In December 2009, Robin Peek, "OAW [Open Access Week] 2009 Exceeds Expectations," *Information Today*, noted that 100 universities had already announced plans to require researchers to deposit research information in open access repositories. The Obama administration has opened discussions over whether to broaden open access beyond the NIH program; see Jocelyn Kaiser, "White House Mulls Plan to Broaden Access to Published Papers," *Science* (January 15, 2010). In July 2010, the Information Policy, Census, and National Archives Subcommittee of the House Committee on Oversight and Government Reform held a hearing to discuss the open access debate, touching on two bills, one that would extend the NIH policy to eleven other research agencies and shorten the 12-month delay before depositing papers in an open archive to just 6 months, and one that would revise copyright law to forbid the practice entirely. Testimony recapitulated many of the points mentioned here; see Jocelyn Kaiser, "House Hearing Explores Debate over Free Access to Journal Articles," *ScienceInsider* (July 30, 2010).

Are print journals actually threatened by the open access movement? Many commentators remark that journals offer much more than just research reports. However, they may not prove able to sustain high subscription prices. They will be obliged to adapt, as many are already doing, according to Jennifer Howard, "Scholarly Presses Discuss How They're Adapting to a Brave New E-World," *Chronicle of Higher Education* (July 11, 2008). One such adaptation is publishing books that can be freely downloaded in hope that actual book sales will follow; see John Murphy, "New Entry Tries New Publishing Model," *Research Information* (December 2008). Charles Oppenheim, "Electronic Scholarly Publishing and Open Access," *Journal of Information Science* (vol. 34, no. 4, 2008), expects pressure for open access publishing to continue, and not just in the United States. In 2012 the United Kingdom announced a requirement to require open access publishing of publicly funded research. Still, no one really expects open access publishing to completely displace the traditional mode; see Jocelyn Kaiser, "Free Journals Grow Amid Ongoing Debate," *Science* (August 20, 2010).

In 2007, legislation mandated that federally funded research reports be given to PubMed Central. The resulting Public Access Policy is described in Robin Peek, "Coming to Grips with the NIH Policy," *Information Today* (September 2008); see also Robin Peek, "The Battle over PubMed Central Continues," *Information Today* (November 2008). The debate continued into 2012, but when journal publisher Elsevier pulled its support from the latest bill, it appeared dead, at least for now; see Jennifer Howard, "Legislation to Bar Public-Access Requirement on Federal Research Is Dead," *The Chronicle of Higher Education* (February 27, 2012). On February 22, 2013, the White House's Office of Science and Technology Policy issued a "policy memorandum" directing all Federal agencies with more than $100 million in R&D spending to develop plans to make publically accessible within one year of publication the results of all their research; see Jocelyn Kaiser, "U.S. Agencies Directed to Make Research Papers Available," *Science* (March 1, 2013).

A hearing on an earlier bill was held on September 11, 2008. Publisher representatives such as Martin Frank, executive director of the American Physiological Society, supported the bill, arguing that "By protecting copyright for research works, [it] will continue to provide incen-tives for private-sector investment in the peer review process which helps to ensure the quality and integrity of scientific research." In the YES selection, attorney and past register of copyrights Ralph Oman contends in his testimony that "If the NIH [National Institutes of Health] succeeds in putting all of the NIH-related peer-reviewed articles on its online database for free within one year of publication, the private publishers will be hard-pressed to survive." Allowing private publishers to continue to profit by publishing the results of publically funded research is the best way to ensure public benefit. In the NO selection, from a 2012 hearing of the House Committee on Science, Space and Technology, Subcommittee on Investigations and Oversight, on Examining Public Access and Scholarly Publication, Stuart M. Shieber argues that the concerns of traditional journal publishers that open access publishing will endanger their survival are not justified. The data show that publisher profitability has increased despite the recent economic downturn. Providing open access to the publicly funded research literature amplifies the diffusion of knowledge and benefits researchers, taxpayers, and everyone who gains from new medicines, new technologies, new jobs, and new solutions to long-standing problems of every kind.

YES ↵

Ralph Oman

The Fair Copyright in Research Works Act

Mr. Chairman and members of the Subcommittee. It is a great honor to appear again before this distinguished panel. It has been a few years since my last appearance.

Thank you for the opportunity to testify on this matter of importance to copyright generally, and to the public, to the research community, to the authors of scientific, technical, and medical articles, and to the publishers of STM journals. I would like to focus on the larger policy issues that undergird the American copyright system and discuss the proposal of the National Institutes of Health that requires recipients of NIH research grants to effectively renounce copyright in their peer-reviewed article manuscripts just 12 months after publication. I will also briefly mention the bill introduced by Chairman Conyers that seeks to moderate the impact of the NIH proposal in a way that will encourage the broadest possible dissemination of high quality, peer-reviewed articles without running roughshod over the rights of authors and copyright owners.

This hearing is important on another level. The language in the appropriations bill that has given rise to this controversy was never vetted by the Judiciary Committee—the committee with intellectual property expertise. With your scrutiny today, the Subcommittee puts this narrow dispute in the larger context of the constitutional mandate—to promote the progress of science for the public interest. Other than celebrating the Judiciary Committee's involvement, I will not comment on the wisdom of legislating on appropriations bills. Into that Serbonian Bog I will not wade.

Instead, I simply applaud your decision, Mr. Chairman, to give a full airing of these issues before your expert Subcommittee. They bear directly on the copyright policies of our government and the incentives to authorship and publication under U.S. copyright law. For reasons I will discuss, the NIH proposal seems short-sighted, counterproductive, damaging to U.S. creativity, which this subcommittee fosters and safeguards, and contrary to the NIH's own interests in encouraging broad public dissemination of peer-reviewed learned articles. The Appropriations Committee, to its credit, sensed that the NIH proposal ventured into sensitive territory and added a very important proviso. That proviso directed the NIH to "implement the public access policy in a manner consistent with copyright law." In my opinion, the NIH has fallen short of that dictate in several respects, and, with this committee's expert

guidance, they should refine their proposal in ways that are true to both the letter and spirit of the copyright law, and the essential policies behind it.

In this debate, three key questions must be answered. First, what policy will result in the broadest dissemination of high quality, peer-reviewed scholarly articles? Second, is it fair for the U.S. government to appropriate the value-added contributions of the private STM publishers? And, third, is the NIH correct in its assumption that the STM publishers will continue to publish their journals even if they lose 50 percent of their paid subscriptions?

Many of my colleagues in academia recognize that the STM publishers perform many vital functions in bringing these articles into the public forum. For one thing, they make substantial investments in the peer-review process. While they do not as a general rule pay the reviewers, the publishers hire in-house teams to support outside specialists. These teams arrange and coordinate effective distribution, stay close to the academic experts in the discipline personally and professionally, follow the literature, and engage in on-going communications with the authors about the reviewers' comments and the incorporation of those comments into the manuscript.

In addition to the peer-review process, the publishers make judgments about which of the manuscripts to publish, depending on their quality and the level of interest in the research itself. They also edit the manuscripts and make them presentable for publication.

My basic concern about the NIH proposal is that it will, sooner rather than later, destroy the commercial market for these scientific, technical, and medical journals. If this dark prophesy comes to pass, who, I wonder, will handle all of these expensive and sensitive administrative details? Some of my academic colleagues are confident that this change in the mechanics of scientific publishing will have little or no impact on the private sector, and that it will remain as robust as ever, even if the NIH freely publishes all of the NIH peer-reviewed article manuscripts shortly after private publication. Some claim that they have "evidence" that STM publishing will continue to flourish. I have not seen that evidence. To me, it suggests an element of wishful thinking. In my experience, Congress is normally reluctant to hang major legislative change in copyright policy on the thin reed of wishful thinking. With the prospect of free copies available in the near term, who in the face of experience and reality can reasonably expect that subscribers to STM journals, faced

Oman, Ralph. The U.S. House of Representatives, September 11, 2008.

with their own budgetary constraints and needs, will not look with real favor on alternative free sources? I can't. It is belied by common sense. Certainly, many university and industry librarians will cancel their subscriptions to these learned journals, with some estimates of a cancellation rate approaching 50 percent. With plummeting sales, how could the STM publishers stay in business? This is a critical point, and one that this committee has a special sensitivity to. It really goes to the heart of the matter, in terms of public policy.

It is a basic premise of copyright that the law is designed to benefit the public, not reward authors or publishers. But, as James Madison wrote in the Federalist Papers, "the public good fully coincides" with the rights of authors and copyright owners. With that admonition, we consider the NIH proposal. It seems clear that Congress would not want the NIH free access policy to cause many or all of the private STM publishers to fade away. Of course, if fair market competition, or a change in the culture of academic publishing, or costly overhead were eventually to drive the private publishers out of business, so be it. It is one thing that they should suffer demise because of changes in the marketplace, and it is another to be brought down by an ill-considered governmental fiat. The NIH does not intend to perform any of the vetting, selection, and editing functions now performed by the learned societies, by the professional organizations, and by the STM publishers, and I doubt if Congress wants to increase their budget so they can take on these additional responsibilities. So the question occurs: who is going to do it? I do not see replacements for the publishers raising their hands to volunteer. For this reason alone, I question the wisdom of the NIH provision. And there are larger issues as well. Experience teaches that as a general rule Congress prefers to keep the hairy snout of the federal government out of the peer-review and manuscript selection process. We live in an open society, and, with a weather eye on the First Amendment, we try to keep the government at arms length from these delicate publication decisions, so as not to skew the process.

That being said, the NIH provision brings back vivid memories of the debate we had in 1980 with the Small Business and University Patent Procedure Act. In that debate, Senator Russell Long, Chairman of the Senate Finance Committee, following the script written by Admiral Rickover, the father of the nuclear submarine, argued in favor of existing government policy—that patents developed with government research money belong to the taxpayers who subsidize the research. Senator Bayh and Senator Dole reasoned that the taxpayers would get a far greater return on their investment if we instead facilitated private sector ownership and commercialization of the inventions, putting these inventions to work for the people. We are about to celebrate the 30th anniversary of Bayh/Dole, and no one is arguing for its repeal.

The same policy arguments apply in the NIH case. If the NIH succeeds in putting all of the NIH-related peer-reviewed articles on its online database for free within one year of publication, the private publishers will be hard-pressed to survive. To me, it seems far more likely that the U.S. taxpayer will achieve the desired objective—the broadest possible dissemination of the peer-reviewed article manuscripts—under the current system. With the private STM publishers running the peer-review process, selecting the articles, and aggressively marketing their journals to libraries and other research institutions, both foreign and domestic, the current system lets the publishers bring their professional judgment and expertise into the process and ensures high quality scholarship. Paid subscriptions keep the current system perking along, without intrusive government involvement, and without an infusion of funds from the government fisc. If the NIH provision is fully implemented, it will almost certainly end this self-policing and self-financing system and get the federal government deeply into the STM publishing business.

Finally, Mr. Chairman, I would like to mention a few related issues. First, I wonder if any of the manuscript articles that the NIH will publish contain preexisting materials that the NIH researcher did not create and therefore does not own. Here, I am thinking of charts, diagrams, photographs, and illustrations. Will the NIH commandeer the rights of those creators as well, or will it require the NIH researcher to clear all of those ancillary rights as part of the "contract." Today, of course, the publishers often help the author clear these rights, including electronic distribution rights. Will the NIH undertake this task if the publishers drop out of the picture?

Second, I wonder if the NIH proposal really serves our international interests. Our trade negotiators are constantly fighting for strong intellectual property protection, which is under siege in many countries around the world. I assume that some of the authors (or at least co-authors) are foreign nationals, and would fall under the protection of the Berne Convention. And I assume some of the impacted publisher/copyright owners are foreign as well. As I will note in a moment, the NIH policy will seriously threaten the protection of American authored and published works in foreign countries. This government edict from the NIH, not promulgated "in a manner consistent with copyright law," has a crippling effect on the value of the copyright in these works. Some of my academic colleagues argue that the Berne Convention has no relevance to the NIH policy. They see it as a simple contract matter, and they note that the researchers get very valuable consideration for their assignment of copyright to the NIH under the contract. Granted, the researchers do receive a generous stipend, averaging $400,000, but that fact also makes the whole arrangement suspect. To a serious researcher, an NIH grant is a matter of life and death professionally. To claim that the assignment of the reproduction right is "voluntary"—the product of a free market negotiation—strikes me as disingenuous.

In fact, the government involvement puts the NIH "contract" in a suspect category in the Berne and TRIPs context. It is not a private contract between commercial interests. Let me draw a hypothetical. The U.S. motion picture industry is now permitted to exhibit theatrically only 10 or so films per year in China. Suppose the government of China were to offer the American film producers a deal: "If you sign a contract waiving your reproduction right, we will allow you to exhibit 100 films a year." The producers would crunch the numbers and calculate the bottom line, even while complaining bitterly that the deal is outrageous and clearly a violation of the spirit of copyright and the Berne Convention. Nonetheless, they might conclude that on balance they would make more money with the proffered deal than they now make with limited access to the huge Chinese market. So, in the end, they might sign on the dotted line. Could the United States take that "contract" to the WTO and press a claim under TRIPs that China is not complying with its treaty obligations? I think so. The ensuing mass piracy of American films in China would be a direct result of this unwaivering government action that diminishes copyright, disguised as a "contract." In any case, the NIH free access policy is an unfortunate international precedent for a country like the United States, whose great strength is intellectual property.

The NIH should reconsider the long term consequences of its proposal. The dedicated researchers who benefit from the NIH grants take great professional pride in being published in prestigious learned journals, all of which constitute a valuable and reliable resource for future research. The NIH itself recognizes that "publication in peer-reviewed journals is a major factor in determining the professional standing of scientists; institutions use publication in peer-reviewed journals in making hiring, promotion, and tenure decisions."

Despite some grumbling about high subscription prices, very few researchers, academics, or librarians are suggesting that the journals have outlived their usefulness. The STM publishers should be given the right to compete fairly in a changing marketplace, in which they will innovate and have the opportunity to flourish on their own merits, as long as their copyrights are protected. Congress should require the NIH to demonstrate convincingly that their free access policy will not jeopardize the existence of the STM publishers and the indispensable role they play in vetting and selecting peer-reviewed articles. Absent that proof, the NIH should rethink their current policy of involuntary assignment. Current law gives the NIH some discretion in implementing their open access policy in a manner consistent with copyright. If the NIH do not amend their policy, Congress should direct them to do so. The Chairman's bill will allow the publishers to continue publishing. It will preserve the STM journals as valuable professional tools for scientific research, thereby promoting the progress of science. By restoring the status quo ante, the Chairman's bill will give the evolving free market a chance to come to grips with the new online technologies without undercutting the incentives that publishers have relied on for two hundred years. I would urge its enactment.

RALPH OMAN is Pravel Professorial Lecturer in Intellectual Property Law and fellow of the Creative and Innovative Economy Center, The George Washington University Law School. He is a counsel for the intellectual property practice group of the firm Dechert, LLP, and has served as register of copyrights of the United States and as chief counsel of the Senate Subcommittee on Patents, Copyrights, and Trademarks.

Stuart M. Shieber

Testimony Before the U.S. House of Representatives Committee on Science, Space and Technology, Subcommittee on Investigations and Oversight, Hearing on Examining Public Access and Scholarly Publication Interests

The Potential for Open Access

The mission of the university is to create, preserve, and disseminate knowledge to the benefit of all. In Harvard's Faculty of Arts and Sciences (FAS), where I hold my faculty post, we codify this in the FAS Grey Book, which states that research policy "should encourage the notion that ideas or creative works produced at the University should be used for the greatest possible public benefit. This would normally mean the widest possible dissemination and use of such ideas or materials."

At one time, the widest possible dissemination was achieved by distributing the scholarly articles describing the fruits of research in the form of printed issues of peer-reviewed journals, sent to the research libraries of the world for reading by their patrons, and paid for by subscription fees. These fees covered the various services provided to the authors of the articles—management of the peer review process, copy-editing, typesetting, and other production processes—as well as the printing, binding, and shipping of the physical objects.

Thanks to the forward thinking of federal science funding agencies, including NSF, DARPA, NASA, and DOE, we now have available computing and networking technologies that hold the promise of transforming the mechanisms for disseminating and using knowledge in ways not imaginable even a few decades ago. The internet allows nearly instantaneous distribution of content for essentially zero marginal cost to a large and rapidly increasing proportion of humanity. Ideally, this would ramify in a universality of access to research results, thereby truly achieving the widest possible dissemination.

The benefits of such so-called *open access* are manifold. The signatories of the 2002 Budapest Open Access Initiative state that

> The public good [open access] make[s] possible is the world-wide electronic distribution of the peer-reviewed journal literature and completely free and unrestricted access to it by all scientists,

scholars, teachers, students, and other curious minds. Removing access barriers to this literature will accelerate research, enrich education, share the learning of the rich with the poor and the poor with the rich, make this literature as useful as it can be, and lay the foundation for uniting humanity in a common intellectual conversation and quest for knowledge.

From a more pragmatic point of view, a large body of research has shown that public research has a large positive impact on economic growth, and that access to the scholarly literature is central to that impact. Martin and Tang's recent review of the literature concludes that "there have been numerous attempts to measure the economic impact of publicly funded research and development (R&D), all of which show a large positive contribution to economic growth." It is therefore not surprising that Houghton's modeling of the effect of broader public access to federally funded research shows that the benefits to the US economy come to the billions of dollars and are eight times the costs.

Opening access to the literature makes it available not only to human readers, but to computer processing as well. There are some million and a half scholarly articles published each year. No human can read them all or even the tiny fraction in a particular subfield, but computers can, and computer analysis of the text, known as *text mining,* has the potential not only to extract high-quality structured data from article databases but even to generate new research hypotheses. My own field of research, computational linguistics, includes text mining. I have collaborated with colleagues in the East Asian Languages and Civilization department on text mining of tens of thousands of classical Chinese biographies and with colleagues in the History department on computational analysis of pre-modern Latin texts. Performing similar analyses on the current research literature, however, is encumbered by proscriptions of copyright and contract because the dominant publishing mechanisms are not open.

Shieber, Stuart M. From statement before U.S. House of Representatives, March 29, 2012.

In Harvard's response to the Office of Science and Technology Policy's request for information on public access, Provost Alan Garber highlighted the economic potential for the kinds of reuse enabled by open access.

Public access not only facilitates innovation in research-driven industries such as medicine and manufacturing. It stimulates the growth of a new industry adding value to the newly accessible research itself. This new industry includes search, current awareness, impact measurement, data integration, citation linking, text and data mining, translation, indexing, organizing, recommending, and summarizing. These new services not only create new jobs and pay taxes, but they make the underlying research itself more useful. Research funding agencies needn't take on the job of provide all these services themselves. As long as they ensure that the funded research is digital, online, free of charge, and free for reuse, they can rely on an after-market of motivated developers and entrepreneurs to bring it to users in the forms in which it will be most useful. Indeed, scholarly publishers are themselves in a good position to provide many of these value-added services, which could provide an additional revenue source for the industry.

Finally, free and open access to the scholarly literature is an intrinsic good. It is in the interest of the researchers generating the research and those who might build upon it, the public who take interest in the research, the press who help interpret the results, and the government who funds these efforts. All things being equal, open access to the research literature ought to be the standard.

Systemic Problems in the Journal Publishing System

Unfortunately, over the last several years, it has become increasingly clear to many that this goal of the "widest possible dissemination" was in jeopardy because of systemic problems in the current mechanisms of scholarly communication, which are not able to take full advantage of the new technologies to maximize the access to research and therefore its potential for social good.

By way of background, I should review the standard process for disseminating research results. Scholars and researchers—often with government funding—perform research and write up their results in the form of articles, which are submitted to journals that are under the editorial control of the editor-in-chief and editorial boards made up of other scholars. These editors find appropriate reviewers, also scholars, to read and provide detailed reviews of the articles, which authors use to improve the quality of the articles. Reviewers also provide advice to the editors on whether the articles are appropriate for publication in the journal, the final decisions being made by the editors.

Participants in these aspects of the publishing process are overwhelmingly volunteers, scholars who provide their time freely as a necessary part of their engagement in the research enterprise. The management of this process, handling the logistics, is typically performed by the journal's publisher, who receives the copyright in the article from the author for its services. The publisher also handles any further production process such as copy-editing and typesetting of accepted articles and their distribution to subscribers through print issue or more commonly these days through online access. This access is provided to researchers by their institutional libraries, which pay for annual subscriptions to the journals.

Libraries have observed with alarm a long-term dramatic rise in subscription costs of journals. The Association of Research Libraries, whose members represent the leading research libraries of the United States and Canada, have tracked serials expenditures for over three decades. From 1986 through 2010 (the most recent year with available data), expenditures in ARL libraries have increased by a factor of almost 5. Even discounting for inflation, the increase is almost 2.5 times. These increases correspond to an annualized rate of almost 7% per year, during a period in which inflation has averaged less than 3%.

Another diagnostic of the market dysfunction in the journal publishing system is the huge disparity in subscription costs between different journals. Bergstrom and Bergstrom showed that even within a single field of research, commercial journals are *on average* five times more expensive per page than non-profit journals. When compared by cost per citation, which controls better for journal quality, the disparity becomes even greater, a factor of 10 times. Odylzko notes that "The great disparity in costs among journals is a sign of an industry that has not had to worry about efficiency." Finally, the extraordinary profit margins, increasing even over the last few years while research libraries' budgets were under tremendous pressure, provide yet another signal of the absence of a functioning competitive market.

The Harvard library system is the largest academic library in the world, and the fifth largest library of any sort. In attempting to provide access to research results to our faculty and students, the university subscribes to tens of thousands of serials at a cost of about 9 million dollars per year. Nonetheless, we too have been buffeted by the tremendous growth in journal costs over the last decades, with Harvard's serials expenditures growing by a factor of 3 between 1986 and 2004. Such geometric increases in expenditures could not be sustained indefinitely. Over the years since 2004 our journal expenditure increases have been curtailed through an aggressive effort at deduplication, elimination of print subscriptions, and a painful series of journal cancellations. As a researcher, I know that Harvard does not subscribe to all of the journals that I would like access to for my own research, and if Harvard, with its scale, cannot provide optimal subscription access, other universities without our resources are in an even more restricted position.

Correspondingly, the articles that we ourselves generate as authors are not able to be accessed as broadly as we would like. We write articles not for direct financial gain—we are not paid for the articles and receive no royalties—but rather so that others can read them and make use of the discoveries they describe. To the extent that access is limited, those goals are thwarted.

The economic causes of these observed phenomena are quite understandable. Journal access is a monopolistic good. Libraries can buy access to a journal's articles only from the publisher of that journal, by virtue of the monopoly character of copyright. In addition, the high prices of journals are hidden from the "consumers" of the journals, the researchers reading the articles, because an intermediary, the library, pays the subscriptions on their behalf. The market therefore embeds a moral hazard. Under such conditions, market failure is not surprising; one would expect inelasticity of demand, hyperinflation, and inefficiency in the market, and that is what we observe. Prices inflate, leading to some libraries canceling journals, leading to further price increases to recoup revenue—a spiral that ends in higher and higher prices paid by fewer and fewer libraries. The market is structured to provide institutions a Hobson's choice between unsustainable expenditures or reduced access.

The unfortunate side effect of this market dysfunction has been that as fewer libraries can afford the journals, access to the research results they contain is diminished. In 2005, then Provost of Harvard Steven Hyman appointed an ad hoc committee, which I chaired, to examine these issues and make recommendations as to what measures Harvard might pursue to mitigate this problem of access to our writings. Since then, we have been pursuing a variety of approaches to maximize access to the writings of Harvard researchers.

Addressing Insufficient Access Through an Open Access Policy

One of these approaches involves the self-imposition by faculty of an open-access policy according to which faculty grant a license to the university to distribute our scholarly articles and commit to providing copies of our manuscript articles for such distribution. By virtue of this kind of policy, the problem of access limitation is mitigated by providing a supplemental venue for access to the articles. Four years ago, in February of 2008, the members of the Faculty of Arts and Sciences at Harvard became the first school to enact such a policy, by unanimous vote as it turned out.

In order to guarantee the freedom of faculty authors to choose the rights situation for their articles, the license is waivable at the sole discretion of the author, so faculty retain control over whether the university is granted this license. But the policy has the effect that by default, the university holds a license to our articles, which can therefore be distributed from a repository that we have set up for that purpose. Since the FAS vote, six other schools at Harvard—Harvard Law School, Harvard Kennedy School of Government,

Harvard Graduate School of Education, Harvard Business School, Harvard Divinity School, and Harvard Graduate School of Design—have passed this same kind of policy, and similar policies have been voted by faculty bodies at many other universities as well, including Massachusetts Institute of Technology, Stanford, Princeton, Columbia, and Duke. Notably, the policies have seen broad faculty support, with faculty imposing these policies on themselves typically by unanimous or near unanimous votes.

Because of these policies in the seven Harvard schools, Harvard's article repository, called DASH (for Digital Access to Scholarship at Harvard), now provides access to over 7,000 articles representing 4,000 Harvard-affiliated authors. Articles in DASH have been downloaded almost three-quarters of a million times. The number of waivers of the license has been very small; we estimate the waiver rate at about 5%. Because of the policy, as faculty authors we are retaining rights to openly distribute the vast majority of the articles that we write.

The process of consultation in preparation for the faculty vote was a long one. I started speaking with faculty committees, departments, and individuals about two years before the actual vote. During that time and since, I have not met a single faculty member or researcher who objected to the principle underlying the open-access policies at Harvard, to obtain the widest possible dissemination for our scholarly results, and have been struck by the broad support for the kind of open dissemination of articles that the policy and the repository allow.

This approach to the access limitation problem, the provision of supplemental access venues, is also seen in the extraordinarily successful public access policy of the National Institutes of Health (NIH), which Congress mandated effective April, 2008. By virtue of that policy, researchers funded by NIH provide copies of their articles for distribution from NIH's PubMed Central (PMC) repository. Today, PMC provides free online access to 2.4 million articles downloaded a million times per day by half a million users. NIH's own analysis has shown that a quarter of the users are researchers. The hundreds of thousands of articles they are accessing per day demonstrates the large latent demand for articles not being satisfied by the journals' subscription base. Companies account for another 17%, showing that the policy benefits small businesses and corporations, who need access to scientific advances to spur innovation. Finally, the general public accounts for 40% of the users, some quarter of a million people per day, demonstrating that these articles are of tremendous interest to the taxpayers who fund the research in the first place and who deserve access to the results that they have underwritten.

The Standard Objection to Open Access Policies

The standard objection to these open-access policies is that supplemental access to scholarly articles, such as that provided by institutional repositories like Harvard's DASH or subject-based repositories like NIH's PubMed Central, could supplant subscription access to such an extent that subscriptions would come under substantial price pressure. Sufficient price pressure, in this scenario, could harm the publishing industry, the viability of journals, and the peer review and journal production processes.

There is no question that the services provided by journals are valuable to the research enterprise, so such concerns must be taken seriously. By now, however, these arguments have been aired and addressed in great detail. I recommend the report "The Future of Taxpayer-Funded Research: Who Will Control Access to the Results?" by my co-panelist Elliott Maxwell, which provides detailed support for the report's conclusion that "There is no persuasive evidence that increased access threatens the sustainability of traditional subscription-supported journals, or their ability to fund rigorous peer review." The reasons are manifold, including the fact that supplemental access covers only a fraction of the articles in any given journal, is often delayed relative to publication, and typically provides a manuscript version of the article rather than the version of record. Consistent with this reasoning, the empirical evidence shows no such discernible effect. After four years of the NIH policy, for instance, subscription prices have continued to increase, as have publisher margins. The NIH states that "while the U.S. economy has suffered a downturn during the time period 2007 to 2011, scientific publishing has grown: The number of journals dedicated to publishing biological sciences/agriculture articles and medicine/health articles increased 15% and 19%, respectively. The average subscription prices of biology journals and health sciences journals increased 26% and 23%, respectively. Publishers forecast increases to the rate of growth of the medical journal market, from 4.5% in 2011 to 6.3% in 2014."

Open Access Journal Publishing as an Alternative to Subscription Journal Publishing

Nonetheless, it does not violate the laws of economics that increased supplemental access (even if delayed) to a sufficiently high proportion of articles (even if to a deprecated version) could put price pressure on subscription journals, perhaps even so much so that journals would not be able to recoup their costs. In this hypothetical case, would that be the end of journals? No, because even if publishers (again, merely by hypothesis and counterfactually) add no value for the readers (beyond what the readers are already getting in the [again hypothetical] universal open access), the author and the author's institution gain much value: vetting, copyediting, typesetting, and most importantly, imprimatur of the journal. This is value that authors and their institutions should be, would be, and are willing to pay for. The upshot is that journals will merely switch to a different business model, in which the journal charges a one-time *publication fee* to cover the costs of publishing the article.

I state this as though this publication-fee revenue model is itself hypothetical, but it is not. Open-access journals already exist in the thousands. They operate in exactly the same way as traditional subscription journals—providing management of peer review, production services, and distribution—with the sole exception that they do not charge for online access, so that access is free and open to anyone. The publication-fee revenue model for open-access journals is a proven mechanism. The prestigious non-profit open-access publisher Public Library of Science is generating surplus revenue and is on track to publish some 3% of the world biomedical literature through its journal *PLoS ONE* alone. The BioMed Central division of the commercial publisher Springer is generating profits for its parent company using the same revenue model. Indeed, the growth of open-access journals over the past few years has been meteoric. There are now over 7,000 open-access journals, many using the publication-fee model, and many of the largest, most established commercial journal publishers—Elsevier, Springer, Wiley-Blackwell, SAGE—now operate open-access journals using the publication-fee revenue model. Were supplemental access to cause sufficient price pressure to put the subscription model in danger, the result would merely be further uptake of this already burgeoning alternative revenue model.

In this scenario, the cost of journal publishing would be borne not by the libraries on behalf of their readers, but by funding agencies and research institutions on behalf of their authors. Already, funding agencies such as Wellcome Trust and Howard Hughes Medical Institute underwrite open access author charges, and in fact mandate open access. Federal granting agencies such as NSF and NIH allow grant funds to be used for open-access publication fees as well (though grantees must prebudget for these unpredictable charges). Not all fields have the sort of grant funding opportunities that could underwrite these fees. For those fields, the researcher's employing institution, as de facto funder of the research, should underwrite charges for publication in open-access journals. Here again, Harvard has taken an early stand as one of the initial signatories—along with Cornell, Dartmouth, MIT, and University of California, Berkeley—of the Compact for Open-Access Publishing Equity, which commits these universities and the dozen or so additional signatories to establishing mechanisms for underwriting reasonable open-access publication fees. The Compact acknowledges the fact that the services that journal publishers provide are important, cost money, and deserve to be funded, and commits the universities to doing so, albeit with a revenue model that avoids the market dysfunction of the subscription journal system.

Advantages of the Open Access Publishing System

The primary advantage of the open-access journal publishing system is the open access that it provides. Since revenue does not depend on limiting access to those willing to pay, journals have no incentive to limit access, and in fact have incentive to provide as broad access as possible to increase the value of their brand. In fact, open-access journals can provide access not only in the traditional sense, allowing anyone to access the articles for the purpose of reading them, but can provide the articles unencumbered by any use restrictions, thereby allowing the articles to be used, re-used, analyzed, and data-mined in ways we are not even able to predict.

A perhaps less obvious advantage of the publication-fee revenue model for open-access journals is that the factors leading to the subscription market failure do not inhere in the publication-fee model. Bergstrom and Bergstrom explain why:

> Journal articles differ [from conventional goods such as cars] in that they are not substitutes for each other in the same way as cars are. Rather, they are complements. Scientists are not satisfied with seeing only the top articles in their field. They want access to articles of the second and third rank as well. Thus for a library, a second copy of a top academic journal is not a good substitute for a journal of the second rank. Because of this lack of substitutability, commercial publishers of established second-rank journals have substantial monopoly power and are able to sell their product at prices that are much higher than their average costs and several times higher than the price of higher quality, non-profit journals.
>
> By contrast, the market for authors' inputs appears to be much more competitive. If journals supported themselves by author fees, it is not likely that one Open Access journal could charge author fees several times higher than those charged by another of similar quality. An author, deciding where to publish, is likely to consider different journals of similar quality as close substitutes. Unlike a reader, who would much prefer access to two journals rather than to two copies of one, an author with two papers has no strong reason to prefer publishing once in each journal rather than twice in the cheaper one.
>
> If the entire market were to switch from Reader Pays to Author Pays, competing journals would be closer substitutes in the view of authors than they are in the view of subscribers. As publishers shift from selling complements to selling substitutes, the greater competition would be likely to force commercial publishers to reduce their profit margins dramatically.

Again, the empirical evidence supports this view. Even the most expensive open-access publication fees, such as those of the prestigious Public Library of Science journals, are less than $3,000 per article, with a more typical value in the $1,000–1,500 range. By contrast, the average revenue per article for subscription journal articles is about $5,000. Thus, the open-access model better leverages free market principles: Despite providing unencumbered access to the literature, it costs no more overall per article, and may end up costing much less, than the current system. The savings to universities and funding agencies could be substantial.

Conclusion

I began my comments by quoting the mission of academics such as myself to provide the widest possible dissemination—open access—to the ideas and knowledge resulting from our research. Government, too, has an underlying goal of promoting the dissemination of knowledge, expressed in Thomas Jefferson's view that "by far the most important bill in our whole code is that for the diffusion of knowledge among the people." The federal agencies and science policies that this committee oversees have led to knowledge breakthroughs of the most fundamental sort—in our understanding of the physical universe, in our ability to comprehend fundamental biological processes, and, in my own field, in the revolutionary abilities to transform and transmit information.

Open access policies build on these information technology breakthroughs to maximize the return on the taxpayers' enormous investment in that research, and magnify the usefulness of that research. They bring economic benefits that far exceed the costs. The NIH has shown one successful model, which could be replicated at other funding agencies, as envisioned in the recently re-introduced bipartisan Federal Research Public Access Act (FRPAA).

Providing open access to the publicly-funded research literature—amplifying the "diffusion of knowledge"—will benefit researchers, taxpayers, and every person who gains from new medicines, new technologies, new jobs, and new solutions to longstanding problems of every kind.

STUART M. SHIEBER is the James O. Welch, Jr., and Virginia B. Welch Professor of computer science at Harvard University. As a faculty member, he led the development and enactment of Harvard's open access policies. He also serves as the faculty director of Harvard's Office for Scholarly Communication.

EXPLORING THE ISSUE

Should the Public Have to Pay to See the Results of Federally Funded Research?

Critical Thinking and Reflection

1. How does peer review help to ensure the quality of scientific publications?
2. Are "open access" and "peer review" mutually contradictory concepts?
3. Why can university libraries not subscribe to all available high-quality academic journals?
4. Should academic publishing be profit oriented?

Is There Common Ground?

At the core of the debate lie two points: the right of academic publishers to make a profit and the right of the public to have access to the fruits of scientific research. High journal prices favor the former while impeding the latter. In one form, open access publishing says the academic publishers can make a profit for a limited time before articles get put into open access archives. On the other hand, no one really expects open access publishing to completely displace the traditional mode; see Jocelyn Kaiser, "Free Journals Grow Amid Ongoing Debate," *Science* (August 20, 2010).

1. Is this form of open access publishing a viable compromise?
2. Some areas of science have long circulated preprints of articles to give other scientists and even the public a first look at reports. Journals later publish edited, peer-reviewed versions of the reports. Is this a viable compromise?
3. What services do journal publishers provide to researchers? Do these services justify high journal prices?

4. If we reject the idea that academic publishing should be profit oriented, how can the publishers remain in business? Should academic publishing be run by the government?

Create Central

www.mhhe.com/createcentral

Additional Resources

Theodora Bloom, et al., "PLoS Biology at 5: The Future Is Open Access," *PLoS Biology* (October 2008).

Jennifer Howard, "Legislation to Bar Public-Access Requirement on Federal Research Is Dead," *The Chronicle of Higher Education* (February 27, 2012).

Jocelyn Kaiser, "Free Journals Grow Amid Ongoing Debate," *Science* (August 20, 2010).

Michael P. Taylor, "Opinion: Academic Publishing Is Broken: The Current System by Which Academics Publish Their Scientific Discoveries Is a Massive Waste of Money," *The Scientist* (March 19, 2012).

Internet References . . .

Directory of Open Access Journals

The Directory of Open Access Journals lists over 8,000 free, full-text, quality-controlled scientific and scholarly journals, many of which can be searched at the article level.

www.doaj.org/

BioMed Central Open Access Charter

BioMed Central calls itself the "open access publisher." It defines open access publishing as making materials "universally and freely accessible via the Internet, in an easily readable format . . . immediately upon publication" and commits itself to maintaining an open access policy.

www.biomedcentral.com

Selected, Edited, and with Issue Framing Material by:
Thomas A. Easton, *Thomas College*

ISSUE

Can Science Be Trusted Without Government Regulation?

YES: David R. Franz, from "The Dual Use Dilemma: Crying Out for Leadership," *Saint Louis University Journal of Health Law & Policy* (2013)

NO: Robert Gatter, from "Regulating Dual Use Research to Promote Public Trust: A Reply to Dr. Franz," *Saint Louis University Journal of Health Law & Policy* (2013)

Learning Outcomes

After reading this issue, you will be able to:

- Explain what "dual-use" research is.
- Explain why a government agency would ask researchers and journal editors to leave details out of a scientific paper.
- Describe the role of responsible laboratory leadership in preventing breaches of biosecurity.
- Discuss the role of government regulation in preventing breaches of biosecurity.

ISSUE SUMMARY

YES: David R. Franz argues that "when rules for the few become too disruptive to the work of the many, communities of trust can break down." Exceptional research leaders create a culture of responsibility in which safety rulebooks can be thin and their laboratories will be safer, more secure, and more productive. Government regulation leads to thicker rulebooks and more wasted effort without increasing safety and security.

NO: Robert Gatter argues that the research enterprise must be trustworthy to the public at large. Because scientists share a bias in favor of discovery rather than public safety, they cannot be trusted to regulate themselves. Government regulation is essential.

"**D**ual Use Research of Concern," or DURC, is now a widespread concern. According to the National Science Advisory Board for Biosecurity (NSABB), it means "research that, based on current understanding, can be reasonably anticipated to provide knowledge, products, or technologies that could be directly misapplied by others to pose a threat to public health and safety, agricultural crops and other plants, animals, the environment or materiel." A major question being debated among scientists, bureaucrats, and legislators, among others, is how to enjoy the benefits of DURC without having to face the risks.

The topic came to prominence with research on the H5N1 bird flu. H5N1 is deadly to domestic poultry. Occasionally it infects people, and the death rate among those who are taken to hospitals is about 60 percent (no one knows how many cases are not taken to hospitals; the actual death rate may be much less). Fortunately, the virus does not spread easily from human to human. In an effort to understand why, research teams led by Ron Fouchier of Erasmus MC in Rotterdam, the Netherlands, and Yoshihiro Kawaoka of the University of Wisconsin, Madison, modified the virus so that it could move more easily through the air between ferrets (which respond to flu similarly to humans), and potentially from human to human. In the fall of 2011, the two teams submitted papers to *Nature* and *Science* explaining how they had modified the virus. The journals accepted the papers but delayed publication while the United States' National Science Advisory Board for Biosecurity (NSABB) deliberated over whether key details should be removed or "redacted" from the papers (and made available only to researchers with a clear need to know) in order to prevent terrorists from learning how to create a flu pandemic (widespread epidemic). Critics called the modified virus an "Armageddon virus," and the media—*CNN*, the *New York Times*, *Time*, and many other magazines and blogs—gave the story major attention. There was even a call on Facebook to suppress the research. The potentials for bioterrorism and accidental releases from labs were major concerns; see Laurie Garrett, "The Bioterrorist Next Door," *Foreign Policy* (December 15, 2011), Fred Guterl, "Waiting to Explode," *Scientific American* (June 2012), and Tina Hesman Saey, "Designer Flu," *Science News* (June 2, 2012).

Those who oppose redaction argue that the details may be crucial to identifying a dangerous pandemic in its early stages and mounting an appropriate response; see Jon Cohen, "Does Forewarned = Forearmed with Lab-Made Avian Influenza Strains?" *Science* (February 17, 2012). In December 2011 the NSABB recommended redaction, and soon thereafter the researchers announced a 60-day moratorium on further research (the moratorium has since then been extended); see Josh Fischman, "Science and Security Clash on Bird-Flu Papers," *Chronicle of Higher Education* (January 6, 2012), and Alice Park, "Scientists Agree to Halt Work on Dangerous Bird Flu Strain," *Time* (January 20, 2012).

Some scientists cautioned that the modified flu virus may not actually be a serious threat and urged the NSABB to reconsider its decision. In February 2012, the World Health Organization (WHO) convened a group of flu researchers, public health officials, and journal editors from eleven countries to discuss the issue. The group recommended that the papers be published with all their details. On March 29, 2012, the U.S. government issued a "Policy for Oversight of Life Sciences Dual Use Research of Concern" (http://oba.od.nih.gov/oba/biosecurity /pdf/united_states_government_policy_for_oversight_of_durc _final_version_032812.pdf). Very shortly afterwards, the NSABB re-reviewed the H5N1 papers and recommended publication in full. See Jon Cohen and David Malakoff, "On Second Thought, Flu Papers Get Go-Ahead," *Science* (April 6, 2012). The *Nature* paper, Masaki Imai, et al., "Experimental Adaptation of an Influenza H5 HA Confers Respiratory Droplet Transmission to a Reassortant H5

HA/H1N1 Virus in Ferrets" (http://www.nature.com/nature /journal/vaop/ncurrent/full/nature10831.html), appeared online May 2, 2012, and on paper June 21, 2012. The *Science* paper, Sander Herfst, et al., "Airborne Transmission of Influenza A/H5N1 Virus Between Ferrets" (http://www .sciencemag.org/content/336/6088/1534.full), was published on June 22, 2012, along with several essays reviewing the situation and an attempt to assess the likelihood that the virus could actually jump to humans and cause problems. Critics remain concerned that, as Thomas Ingleby of the Center for Biosecurity of the University of Pittsburgh Medical Center said, "We are playing with fire"; see Libby Lewis, "Science Journal Could Give Recipe for Deadly Avian Flu Virus," *CNN* (May 12, 2012) (http://www.cnn.com/2012/05/12/us/journal-avian-flu/index .html). By late 2012, a National Institutes of Health (NIH) plan that would call for stringent reviews of whether similar research should receive government funding, or even be classified, was being discussed by the NSABB; see David Malakoff, "Proposed H5N1 Research Reviews Raise Concerns," *Science* (December 7, 2012), and David Malakoff and Martin Enserink, "New U.S. Rules Increase Oversight of H5N1 Studies, Other Risky Science," *Science* (March 1, 2013).

The debate over whether publication of the details of the bird-flu papers should be redacted or not has been intense. Concern that they may lead to new and more onerous controls on research and publication seem to have been justified; see David Malakoff, "U.S. Agencies to Start Screening Biomedical Proposals for Dual Use," *Science* (April 6, 2012). Despite new controls, however, researchers are eager to resume research in this area; see David Malakoff, "H5N1 Researchers Ready as Moratorium Nears End," *Science* (January 4, 2013).

The basic question of control over scientific and technical knowledge is not new. In 2001, the destruction of New York's World Trade Towers and the unrelated mailing of anthrax spores to several public figures created a climate of fear and mistrust that led to heightened concern about security. Part of that fear and mistrust was aimed at science and technology, for the al Qaeda terrorists had used computers and the Internet for communicating with each other and the person responsible for the anthrax scare (currently thought to be anthrax researcher Bruce Ivins; see David Willman, *The Mirage Man: Bruce Ivins, the Anthrax Attacks, and America's Rush to War* [Bantam, 2011]) obviously knew too much about anthrax.

"Even before . . . 2001, White House directives and agencies used the label SBU [sensitive but unclassified] to safeguard from public disclosure information that does not meet the standards for classification"; see Genevieve J. Knezo, "'Sensitive but Unclassified' and Other Federal Security Controls on Scientific and Technical Information: History and Current Controversy" (Congressional Research Service Report for Congress, April 2, 2003). See also John D. Kraemer and Lawrence O. Gostin, "The Limits of Government Regulation of Science," *Science* (March 2, 2012). In March 2002, the Bush Administration declared that some information—notably the results of scientific research, especially in the life sciences—might not be classified in the ways long familiar to researchers in nuclear physics (for instance), but it could still be considered "sensitive" and thus worthy of restrictions on publication and dissemination. The Defense Department announced—and promptly dropped—plans to restrict the use and spread of unclassified DoD-funded research. However, a National Academy of Sciences report on agricultural bioterrorism that contained no classified information was censored on the insistence of the Department of Agriculture "to keep potentially dangerous information away from enemies of the United States." National security experts warned "that the current system of openness in science could lead to dire consequences." See Richard Monastersky, "Publish and Perish?" *Chronicle of Higher Education* (October 11, 2002). However, many have objected to inventing and attempting to restrict the new "sensitive but unclassified" category of information. Steven Teitelbaum, president of the Federation of American Societies for Experimental Biology, said, "information should be either classified or not classified." Charles M. Vest, in "Response and Responsibility: Balancing Security and Openness in Research and Education," *Report of the President for the Academic Year 2001–2002* (Cambridge, MA: Massachusetts Institute of Technology, 2002), argued that openness in science must preempt fears of the consequences of scientific knowledge falling into the wrong hands.

In July 2002, researchers announced that they had successfully assembled a polio virus from biochemicals and the virus's gene map. Members of Congress called for more care in releasing such information, and the American Society for Microbiology (ASM) began to debate voluntary restrictions on publication. By August 2002, the ASM had policy guidelines dictating that journal submissions that contain "information . . . that could be put to inappropriate use" be carefully reviewed and even rejected; see David Malakoff, "Researchers See Progress in Finding the Right Balance," *Science* (October 18, 2002). Soon thereafter, the federal government took its own steps in the same direction with the formation of the NSABB; see Jennifer

Couzin, "U.S. Agencies Unveil Plan for Biosecurity Peer Review," *Science* (March 12, 2004).

In October 2005, scientists reassembled the deadly 1918 flu from synthesized subunits (see Phillip A. Sharp, "1918 Flu and Responsible Science" [Editorial], *Science,* October 7, 2005). In 2006, there were calls for authors, journal editors, and reviewers to do risk-benefit analysis before publishing "dual-use" work (see Yudhijit Bhattacharjee, "U.S. Panel Calls for Extra Review of Dual-Use Research," *Science,* July 21, 2006, and Robert F. Service, "Synthetic Biologists Debate Policing Themselves," *Science,* May 26, 2006). The relevance of the debate outside biology became clear when researchers omitted important details from a study of how a dirty-bomb attack could affect Los Angeles harbor (see Yudhijit Bhattacharjee, "Should Academics Self-Censor Their Findings on Terrorism?" *Science,* May 19, 2006).

A paper by Lawrence M. Wein and Yifan Liu, "Analyzing a Bioterror Attack on the Food Supply: The Case of Botulinum Toxin in Milk," on how terrorists might attack the U.S. milk supply and on how to safeguard it, was scheduled for the May 30, 2005, issue of the *Proceedings of the National Academy of Sciences.* However, Stewart Simonson, Assistant Secretary of the Department of Health and Human Services, asked the NAS not to publish the paper on the grounds that it provides "a road map for terrorists and publication is not in the interests of the United States." The journal put the paper on hold while it studied the issue; it appeared online (http://www.pnas.org /cgi/content/abstract/0408526102v1) on June 28, 2005, and in print in the July 12, 2005, issue of *PNAS.* The Department of Health and Human Services continues to believe publication is a mistake, for the "consequences could be dire." It should come as no surprise that Frida Kuhlau, Anna T. Hoglund, Kathinka Evers, and Stefan Eriksson, "A Precautionary Principle for Dual Use Research in the Life Sciences," *Bioethics* (January 2011), note that the precautionary principle—more familiar in environmental and public health contexts—may reasonably be applied to dual-use biological research.

When in March/April 2006, *Technology Review* published Mark Williams' "The Knowledge," which stressed the ominous implications of current knowledge and the ready availability of materials and equipment (DNA synthesizers can be bought on eBay!), it also published a rebuttal. Allison M. Macfarlane, "Assessing the Threat," *Technology Review* (March/April 2006), noted that turning biological agents of destruction into useful weapons is much harder than it seems and the real hazards are impossible to estimate without more research. For now, she thinks, it makes more sense to focus on more imminent threats, such as those involving nuclear weapons.

Are there other possible answers besides restricting—voluntarily or otherwise—publication of potentially hazardous work? In an editorial, "Dual-Use Research of Concern: Publish *and* Perish?" *Indian Journal of Medical Research* (January 2011), K. Satyanarayana finds that "the real challenges would continue to be governance and enforcement as scientists are clearly averse to any external intervention." John D. Steinbruner and Elisa D. Harris, "Controlling Dangerous Pathogens," *Issues in Science and Technology* (Spring 2003), call for a global body that could oversee and regulate potentially dangerous disease research. Robert H. Sprinkle proposes "The Biosecurity Trust," *Bioscience* (March 2003). Ruth R. Faden and Ruth A. Karron, "The Obligation to Prevent the Next Dual-Use Controversy," *Science* (February 11, 2012), argue that the need for some such oversight mechanism is urgent. No such organization yet exists, although the new screening rules are a step in that direction.

On February 22, 2013, the *Saint Louis University Journal of Health Law & Policy* and the Center for Health Law Studies at that school held a symposium on "Regulating Dual-Use Research in Life Sciences." At the same time, the U.S. government released proposed rules for regulating DURC, which led to lively discussions during the symposium. Two participants in those discussions were David R. Franz and Robert Gatter. In the YES selection, Dr. Franz argues that "when rules for the few become too disruptive to the work of the many, communities of trust can break down." Exceptional research leaders create a culture of responsibility in which safety rulebooks can be thin and their laboratories will be safer, more secure, and more productive. Government regulation leads to thicker rulebooks and more wasted effort without increasing safety and security. In the NO selection, Dr. Gatter argues that the research enterprise must be trustworthy to the public at large. Because scientists share a bias in favor of discovery rather than public safety, they cannot be trusted to regulate themselves. Government regulation is essential.

YES

David R. Franz

The Dual Use Dilemma: Crying Out for Leadership

I. Introduction

Between October 2011 and March 2012, a controversy regarding the publication of results of H5N1 influenza virus research by two scientists led to additional oversight of a relatively broad segment of the infectious disease research enterprise in the U.S. The episode has been described as an example of the "dual use dilemma," legitimate and open research that could be exploited for harm by others. Why is *leadership* important in the context of the dual use dilemma? Is not dual use about technology and knowledge being misused for harm? Can we not just control the knowledge and technologies? How is the dual use dilemma related to the *insider threat* in research and clinical laboratories? What is our interest in these low likelihood events in twenty-first century America? The recent concern regarding Dual Use Research (DUR) is focused on the traditional agents of biological warfare and the influenza viruses. Yet, these *Select Agents* are but a small part of the spectrum of biological threats and risks we humans, our animals, and plants face today. Therefore, Dual Use Research of Concern (DURC) cannot be understood in isolation. What follows is a short history of the misuse—and use—of biology in what will always be a dangerous world. We cannot reduce risk to zero, but we can increase safety, security, and productivity in our laboratories without layering another set of regulations over the enterprise each time an individual scientist does something thoughtless or even malevolent.

II. DURC Background

A. A Short History of Laboratory Biosafety—1940s Onward

The U.S. conducted offensive biological warfare research, development, and field-testing from mid-1942 until late 1969, when President Nixon traveled to Fort Detrick,

Maryland, to announce that the U.S. would end its biological weapons program two National Security memoranda, the first dated November 25, 1969, and the second February 20, 1970, the U.S. Government renounced development, production, and stockpiling of biological weapons. Further, the U.S. declared its intent to maintain only quantities of agents necessary for the development of vaccines, drugs, and diagnostics. While I am convinced the weapons testing during the more than 25 years of the offensive program demonstrated *nuclear equivalence* of biological weapons, the real legacy of this program is the development and implementation of the foundational principles of modern laboratory biological *safety*.

During the 1960s, Dr. Arnold G. Wedum, M.D., Ph.D, Director of Industrial Health and Safety at Fort Detrick, was the principal proponent and leader of a system of containment facilities, equipment, and procedures developed to greatly enhance the safety of the employees of the offensive program and the rural community in which the core laboratories were operated. Many of Dr. Wedum's principles of biological safety served as the basis for the U.S. Centers for Disease Control and Prevention's (CDC) publication called *Biosafety in Microbiological and Biomedical Laboratories* (BMBL). The BMBL is now updated regularly and has become the biosafety *bible* in laboratories around the globe. Thus, in what we might today call a reverse dual use model, some very important good has ultimately come from a program that was designed to do harm.

By the end of the twentieth century, the principles of biosafety—facilities, equipment, and procedures—were codified, enhanced, respected, and followed by the scientists in the relatively few high containment labs in the U.S. The original U.S. high-containment labs were commissioned from 1971 to 1972 at Fort Detrick within the U.S. Army Medical Research Institute of Infectious Diseases (USAMRIID), and in Atlanta at the CDC just a few years later.

Franz, David R., "The Dual Use Dilemma: Crying Out for Leadership," 7 St. Louis U. J. Health L. & Pol'y 5 (2013) Reprinted with permission of the Saint Louis University Journal of Health Law & Policy © 2013. St. Louis University School of Law, St. Louis, Missouri.

I served as Deputy Commander (1993–1995) and Commander (1995–1998) of USAMRIID. My command briefings during the mid-90s often listed three top priorities—"biosafety, biosafety, and biosafety." We had good people in harm's way during peacetime and in war in Biosafety Level-4 (BSL-4) labs where one needle stick, one bone fragment through a surgical glove, or even the bite of an infected laboratory animal could mean almost certain death to a scientist or technician. While the institute was located on a fenced and guarded military installation with twenty-four hour unarmed guards, as well as redundant locking systems with personal identification number codes for laboratory suite entry, my focus was on the safety of the employees and the community, as well as the productivity of our laboratory. I learned in those six years that the same leadership approach that makes people safe, makes an organization productive, and gives a community a sense of well being, is based on nurturing a culture of responsibility and trust.

B. Laboratory Biosecurity—Mid-90s and Beyond

In 1995, Mr. Larry Wayne Harris mailed a letter requesting an isolate of *Yersinia pestis (Y. pestis)*, the plague bacillus, from the American Type Culture Collection (ATCC) in Manassas, Virginia. It was eventually discovered that the letterhead he used—"Small Animal Microbiology Laboratory, 266 Cleveland Avenue, Lancaster, Ohio" and the "Ohio Environmental Protection Agency approval number 890"—were fraudulent. While the ATCC ultimately shipped the vials of *Y. pestis*, Mr. Harris became impatient and called to follow up on his order. In doing so, he alerted authorities and the Federal Bureau of Investigation (FBI) became involved. While other incidents—Aum Shinrikyo sarin attack in Tokyo on March 20, 1995 and the B'nai B'rith incident in Washington D.C. involving a petri dish of *B. cereus* in 1997—contributed to our increased concern about both the illicit acquisition and malevolent use of biological agents, it was the Harris incident that most greatly influenced our thinking regarding laboratory biological *security* in the U.S.

The Select Agent Rule became law and was implemented in 1997. This new rule made the transfer between laboratories illegal for designated bacteria, viruses, or toxins without CDC approval. Intially, the rule only affected agent transfers, which meant that many academic and clinical labs with select agent pathogens could maintain them without breaking the law. Only after an inspection by the CDC (or, for some pathogens, the U.S. Department of Agriculture) could a laboratory be certified to transfer pathogens on the list, and then once certified, transfer only to a similarly certified laboratory. The era of laboratory biosecurity had begun. As a result of his actions, Harris, the individual most directly responsible for the Select Agent Rule, was required to complete 200 hours of community service. Legitimate research with the listed agents would forever be more costly and probably less productive in government, academic, and industrial labs where the new rules were promulgated.

C. DURC—2003 and Beyond

The World Trade Center attacks on September 11, 2001 (9/11), and the first case of inhalational anthrax concerning the anthrax letters discovered on October 4, 2001 (1 0/4), changed everything. The U.S. biosecurity budget went from $137 million in 1997, to $14.5 billion spent on biodefense from 2001 to 2004. Soon many more laboratories sought and received Select Agent certification.

Today, it is almost impossible to put one's mind back into the state of infectious disease research before 2002, when thousands of new scientists began working with this short list of threat agents. After 9/11, 10/4, and the increased funding for new high-containment labs and Select Agent research, the next layer of DURC regulation in the life sciences was beginning to unfold. It would take another legitimate, even respected scientist, this time not trying to do harm, but possibly for personal or professional gain, to drive the U.S. Government to further regulate the traditional select agents and influenza viruses.

About ten years before the 2012 controversy regarding the publication of information on the intentional development of a recombinant H5N1 influenza virus transmissible between mammals, there was the reasonable observation by the U.S. biological sciences community that it should "think about policing itself" before the government intervened with undue regulation. The now well-known Fink Report by the National Academies of Science, *Biotechnology Research in an Age of Terrorism: The Dual-Use Dilemma*, was a direct result. At that time, factors that triggered the perceived need for the study and subsequent report included: (1) a surprise result of Australian attempts to design a rodent sterilization virus, (2) the second *de novo* synthesis of poliovirus from a "web recipe," and (3) a new understanding of the implications of the Smallpox Inhibitor of Complement Enzymes "SPICE gene" in orthopox viruses.

The nation was now working in a backdrop of 9/ll and l0/4, so misuse of biology was on our minds. Although the term "dual use" had been used in other settings, it was the Fink Report that really codified the term in this context. The Fink Report also suggested that a national-level committee be formed and composed of equal numbers of biology and security experts to help the government cope with the dual use dilemma. The eventual response from the U.S. Government was the formation of the National Science Advisory Board for Biosecurity (NSABB) in 2004. Initially, the NSABB described DUR as "research yielding new technologies or information with the potential for both benevolent and malevolent applications. . . ." Later, after realizing that a significant percentage of the technology and knowledge in the life sciences enterprise could be used for good or harm, the NSABB chose the term DURC to define a subset of dual use knowledge and technologies. The NSABB described DURC as "research that, based on current understanding, can be reasonably anticipated to provide knowledge, products, or technologies that could be directly misapplied by others to pose a threat to public health and safety, agricultural crops and other plants, animals, the environment or materiel." . . .

III. Regulatory Approaches: Value and Cost

. . . Actions to protect us have taken place in the name of public safety and security. The Antiterrorism and Effective Death Penalty Act of 1996, the Select Agent Rule, Army Regulation 50- 1, and the new DURC policies are all domestic U.S. Government actions. These regulations are wide nets cast, rather than leadership-based approaches, to deal with troubled or frustrated personnel more broadly. Due to the nature of the dual use dilemma (technical surprise or ethical lapse) and insider threat (individual or small group sociopathic behavior), these wide cast, but superficial regulatory nets are, at best, very blunt instruments. Very few studies have looked at the productivity of the enterprise before and after 2001, but the subject deserves our attention. At least anecdotally, compliance with these regulatory approaches has forced laboratories to hire additional contractors to manage the programs, which has diverted funds from legitimate research, subsequently slowing progress. Even with these regulations in place, the U.S. Government cannot assure increased security.

Possibly the greatest value in the international laws and resolutions is in their role as norms, tools of education, and awareness. Further, dialogues around international laws and resolutions have led to some increased understanding by bringing experts from many nations together to discuss them, as well as the visible boundary lines which they paint on the life sciences court. In other cases, the international laws have been barriers to communication and understanding. Regulations may do harm when they overburden the life sciences community or build walls internationally, instead of simply painting the boundary lines. Internationally, there have been more focused actions for nations who crossed the line: the Trilateral Agreements (because of Former Soviet Union behavior) and UNSCR 687 (in response to Iraqi behavior). Domestically, . . . individual acts . . . have increased oversight, and broad regulatory management has become the norm within the life sciences community.

IV. Why So Little Emphasis on Leadership?

A. Leadership Models

During the past 20 years, the role of leaders, particularly in U.S. Government laboratories where insider threats seem to be of greater concern than DURC, have changed dramatically. In this regard, the period before 9/11 can be clearly differentiated from the period after. In the past, laboratory leaders grew up within their organizations, took personal responsibility for their organizations, and molded laboratory cultures in a way that resulted in productivity and safety. Security was viewed differently before 9/11, but was appropriate for that day and time. Patriotism and teamwork were underlying principles, and the mission and focus on scientific ethics was the norm.

Leaders who knew their organizations well also knew their people well enough to practice preventive intervention in the rare case of outlier behavior. The troubled scientist would seek out the leader for help if trust was there or the leader would observe and intervene in time if the leader was enlightened and appropriately engaged. Outlier employees were counseled and helped or weeded from the organization. A self-centered, arrogant, or insensitive manager would miss the warning signs, and thus, be unable to avert disaster. Such poor leaders did not last in those days. Today, there is much less thought given to these issues. Rather, much more time is spent trying to assure compliance with regulations. The challenge of heavy-handed regulation is also facing academic researchers in this country today.

B. Really Hard, but Rare Problems with No Perfect Solution

We are dealing with two very hard problems in a very complex, even messy, world today. The spectrum of natural disease kills millions of people globally each year. Our government has focused enormous energy and treasure on hopefully rare, but potentially high-impact intentional events. Much of this is related to the *terror* factor and the vast unknowns. Most Americans do not notice the deaths of 50,000 humans from seasonal influenza complications, 30,000 from auto accidents, or even the 10,000 deaths associated with gun homicides annually, unless they involve one of our loved ones. Yet, the unknowns frighten us. As we face fiscal constraints nationally, the challenge is to balance our preparations and resolve regarding those vast unknowns.

Dr. Lederberg told us "there is no technical solution." He proposed ethical or moral solutions, but acknowledged that such personal controls would not appeal to an individual set on doing harm. Just as epidemiologists tell us that protecting a percentage of a population with a vaccine will indirectly protect unvaccinated individuals within a population, so too, establishing a corporate culture of responsibility will help reduce the likelihood that an individual within that culture will go astray.

Secretary of the Navy, Richard Danzig, Ph.D., has told us that "we are driving in the dark" with regard to understanding the risk in national security. We cannot know what lies ahead. We have spent time and hundreds of millions of dollars trying to predict what is coming and for what to prepare. The insider threat is a very hard case while the DURC challenge is also difficult, but more easily dealt with. Interestingly, both respond to a very similar set of behavioral tools. We are much more likely to divert, dissuade, deter, or just discover individuals prone to either course in a healthy corporate culture than in an unhealthy one. So we get two-for-one—DURC and the insider threat—protection in a healthy life sciences laboratory culture.

C. Rethinking DURC: Did the Science Community Do the Right Thing?

It's not surprising that we have focused our energies on the technologies, the science, and the microbiological agents rather than on the behavior of the scientists. At the national level, our elected officials seek to do something to make the public feel safer, so they regulate what they cannot directly control. For DUR, it started with the beloved Fink Report, so we must bear part of the responsibility. When we called it DUR and listed the seven examples of research that might be misused, we forced ourselves to look at the technologies, the knowledge, and the science. If we had instead called for "Responsible Life Science Research," the term now preferred by many of our

international colleagues, we would have had to focus on human behavior. I believe more effective outcomes would have resulted if we had focused more on individual and corporate responsibility than on regulation to control technologies and knowledge. No matter if the individual scientist is armed with an oligonucleotide synthesizer or the organization with a freezer full of Select Agents, they are less likely to do harm with them in a healthy laboratory culture than in an unhealthy one.

D. Leadership and DURC or Actually "Responsible Life Sciences Research"

Leadership is related only indirectly to DUR, but it is very much related to responsibility, which is the real problem. Leaders, by definition, demonstrate personal responsibility and they, by definition, develop cultures of responsibility in the organizations that they lead. Responsible organizations contribute, again with enormous influence by their leaders, to networks of responsibility. Responsible leaders, groups of responsible individuals, and networks of responsible groups provide *herd immunity* that protects the whole. It's simple, but it requires smart, caring, humble, and strong leaders throughout the organization. . . .

Humility is not the first word that comes to mind when the average person thinks about leadership; it is probably power, authority, or even arrogance. But humility is absolutely essential to great leadership and what is sometimes perceived as arrogance is often simply confidence. Humility facilitates another characteristic of a great leader—appreciating employees who are smarter than you. Bo Peabody, in his book, *Lucky or Smart? Secrets to an Entrepreneurial Life,* tells would-be entrepreneurs to create an environment where smart people gather and then be smart enough to stay out of the way. He goes on to say that managers are A-students and entrepreneurs are B-students. Likewise, it is not unusual to find that the best leaders are very comfortable when surrounded by people who are smarter than they.

In industry and even in academia today, the great leaders rise to the top on merit. As the moral underpinnings of the electorate weaken, elected officials in a democracy can become more interested in their own position of authority than the good of their electorate or even their nation. When they do, their inclination is to try to *control* when the issues are too complex for them to resolve quickly and easily. As in the case with DURC and the insider threat, they often choose to regulate and in doing so, upset the balance between appropriate regulation and freedom. An over-regulated individual, organization, or nation will not attain its full potential.

V. Conclusion

A. Our Place in the World

Exceptional leaders and thinkers drafted the intellectual and legal foundation of the U.S. We were made a free and powerful nation by great leaders. Leaders in our most productive laboratories demonstrate personal responsibility and inculcate corporate responsibility. With the global proliferation of biological technologies and knowledge, we now face well-qualified and serious competition in the life sciences. Patrick Lencioni, in his book, *Healthy Organizations,* states "because of this global competition, it will become ever more difficult to have a competitive advantage based on knowledge and technologies," but a healthy organization can compete on this new, more level playing field. DURC issues and insider threat are rare, but potentially harmful outcomes of the life sciences enterprise. Both are outlier risks that are more likely to occur in an unhealthy or poorly led organization.

Personal and corporate responsibility provide herd immunity, which can protect, rehabilitate, or ferret out the outliers in an organization. Communities of trust characterize the kind of corporate responsibility typically orchestrated by enlightened leadership. Every organization needs regulation; we must know the boundaries of the playing field and the rules of the game. The greater the potential for injury in the game, the thicker the rulebook. The safety rulebook in a high-containment infectious disease laboratory is *thick* and applies to everyone. The DURC and the insider threat rulebooks are there for the outliers, but they impact all of us. When rules for the few become too disruptive to the work of the many, communities of trust can break down. Laboratories with exceptional leaders armed with well thought-out and *thin* DURC and insider threat rulebooks will always be safer, more secure, and far more productive than laboratories where the many are overregulated because of the few. It takes courage to do the right thing—to mentor, grow leaders, and then give them the responsibility, authority, and the freedom to succeed. Will we find leaders with the wisdom and the moral courage to rebalance our approach to DURC and the insider threat?

DAVID R. FRANZ is former Commander of the U.S. Army Medical Research Institute of Infectious Diseases (AMRIID) and a founding member of the National Science Advisory Board for Biosecurity. His current focus is responsible life sciences research and the role of international engagement as a component of global biosecurity policy.

Robert Gatter    **NO**

Regulating Dual Use Research to Promote Public Trust: A Reply to Dr. Franz

. . . **D**r. David Franz makes a persuasive argument that protecting the public against risks posed by dual use research of concern (DURC) requires strong leadership among scientists who manage the laboratories in which such research takes place. Among other things, he calls on scientists, regulators, and others interested in DURC oversight to devote as much attention to developing stronger laboratory leadership as has been spent on creating rules and regulations.

Importantly, Dr. Franz is skeptical of the government's regulating scientists and research institutions, including the newly proposed federal rules concerning DURC. He writes that regulations cannot make us safe in the face of dual use risks and that, instead, they create compliance tasks that distract scientists and divert resources from research.

More fundamentally, Dr. Franz depicts life science research as "over-regulated" and argues that such regulation is antithetical to maintaining laboratories as "communities of trust" in which safe and productive research can take place. Indeed, this is the closing message of his article. After acknowledging that regulations are necessary to establish "the boundaries of the playing field and the rules of the game," he observes that, in the context of DURC, "[t]he safety rulebook in a high-containment infectious disease laboratory is *thick*. . . ." Moreover, he explains that many of the rules respond to the conduct of very few bad actors, and yet those rules apply to every scientist and lab worker. From this, Dr. Franz warns that, "[w]hen rules for the few become too disruptive to the work of the many, communities of trust can break down." Meanwhile, "[l]aboratories with exceptional leaders armed with well thought-out, and *thin* . . . rulebooks," he says, "will always be safer, more secure, and far more productive than labs where the many are overregulated. . . ."

Dr. Franz's observations bring into play a complicated relationship between regulation and trust, which has significant implications for how the law should be used to steer conduct with respect to DURC in life science research. Both trust and regulation are necessary components to the research enterprise. I defer to Dr. Franz's view that trust among laboratory workers and scientists is vital to safety and productivity. Equally vital, however, is *public* trust in researchers and research institutions. Put another way, it is not enough for scientists to trust each other and the leadership of their research institutions; the research enterprise generally must also be trustworthy to the public at large.

Controversy over the publication of two studies in which scientists manipulated the genes of a certain strain of highly pathogenic avian influenza (H5N1) to create new pathogens that are easily transmissible among ferrets (a model for human influenza transmission) draws into question the trustworthiness of researchers and research institutions. This research involved significant risks to public safety by creating new and potentially virulent pathogens that could be accidentally released or misused, and demonstrated methods for creating other potentially dangerous pathogens, which could be misused in war or bioterrorism. Yet, it does not appear that those risks were acknowledged or discussed by the scientists or research institutions involved until just before the studies were to be published, and then only when outsiders raised questions.

Under these circumstances, regulators, legislators, news media, and voters are more than justified to question whether research oversight is sufficient to assure public safety. The public may fairly interpret the story of the ferret flu studies as an example of how a single-minded drive toward discovery can blind scientists to the full measure of the risks their work imposes on the public.

The ferret studies were designed to create new influenza strains that were not only highly pathogenic, but also easily transmissible between mammals. It was no surprise, then, that each of the studies resulted in new strains of

H5N1 that were transmitted between ferrets. Given the risks inherent in the objectives and design of these experiments, why were the public safety risks not discussed and compared to the benefits of the research until the eleventh hour prior to publication, well after the studies were completed? Why did the lead researchers not present a risk-benefit analysis as part of their research proposals? Why did their research institutions not require such a risk-benefit analysis as a condition for allowing the studies to be conducted on their premises? Why did the National Institutes of Health (NIH) approve government funding for each of the studies without first conducting a risk-benefit analysis and without first questioning whether the value of two studies was worth doubling the safety risks to the public?

The thesis of this essay is that a discovery imperative lies at the core of science, that this drive to discover causes scientists to undervalue research risks, and that public trust in life sciences research requires a regulatory check on that bias. Despite Dr. Franz's observation that research regulation diminishes trust within laboratories, I argue that the right kind of regulation will create a foundation for public trust in researchers and their institutions. Moreover, I claim that the newly proposed DURC regulations are the right kind of regulation.

A. The Ferret Studies, Their Approval, and Their Publication

In 2012, two different research teams completed similar experiments proving that H5N1 is susceptible to genetic modifications that will make it easily transmissible among humans. As an avian influenza, H5N1 most commonly infects a variety of domestic and wild birds. Yet, it is capable of leaping the species barrier to infect humans. To date, more than 600 human infections have been recorded worldwide with a mortality rate of close to 60%. Despite these infections, there has not been an outbreak of H5N1 among humans because the strains of H5N1 involved in these infections were not easily transmitted from human-to-human through, for example, sneezing. This led some scientists to question whether H5N1 poses much of a pandemic threat. These scientists hypothesized that the genetic alterations necessary to permit an avian H5N1 to both infect a human and to become easily transmissible among humans are so numerous as to be highly unlikely to ever occur in nature. To address this hypothesis, the two research teams designed experiments to identify what, if any, genetic modifications to H5N1 would make it easily transmissible among humans.

Both of the studies were funded in part by the National Institute of Allergy and Infectious Diseases (NIAID), which is the division of NIH responsible for influenza research. Yet, the funding review at NIH and NIAID was purely scientific and was unlikely to have included any assessment of the dual use risks posed by either project. Federal regulations provide that NIH assess "the scientific merit and significance of the project, the competency of the proposed staff . . . the feasibility of the project, the likelihood of its producing meaningful results, the proposed project period, and the adequacy of the applicant's resources available for the project. . . ." Likewise, grant application guidelines under the NIAID state that reviewers should judge an application solely on "its ability to make a strong impact on its field," which "is a function of . . . the importance of the topic," defined as "the significance and innovation of the research problem—its ability to move the frontier of knowledge forward."

One of the two studies—the one designed by Yoshihiro Kawaoka, Ph.D.—was conducted at the University of Wisconsin-Madison, and involved recombinant DNA (rDNA) methods. The research team clipped a gene from a H5N1 cell and "stitched" it together with genes from a human H1N1 virus cell. Research, like Dr. Kawaoka's that uses rDNA techniques, is subject to NIH Guidelines which instruct the research institution not to permit any such research unless it has first been reviewed and approved by an Institutional Biosafety Committee (IBC). An IBC consists of at least five members, including two community members, who collectively have "experience and expertise in recombinant [DNA] technology and the capability to assess the safety of recombinant [DNA] research and to identify any potential risk to public health or the environment." The University of Wisconsin-Madison's IBC that reviewed and approved Dr. Kawaoka's study had 17 members, 15 of whom were employed by the University as faculty or staff.

An IBC's review determines the level of biosafety laboratory standards that should be applied to proposed research pursuant to NIH's rDNA Guidelines (Guidelines). These Guidelines specify for IBCs the level of biosafety standards to be employed based on the biological material on which the research is being conducted. When the research involves H5N1 and when it could result in creating a more virulent and less treatable form of influenza, then more stringent biosafety standards might apply than provided for in the Guidelines. In this case, an IBC is instructed to refer the matter as a "major action" to NIH and its Recombinant DNA Advisory Committee (RAC). The University of Wisconsin-Madison's IBC reviewed Dr. Kawaoka's study proposal, but the IBC did not refer the proposal to NIH and RAC for federal review, even though the research team proposed creating a new strain of H5N1 that was virulent and much more transmissible among humans than what otherwise occurred in nature. Instead, the University of Wisconsin's IBC approved the study locally and, with that approval, the research began.

In both of the studies, researchers created a new pathogen through genetic manipulation of a naturally occurring H5N1 virus. They then infected laboratory ferrets with the new pathogen. Ferrets are considered to be a good model for human influenza infection because, like humans, ferrets can spread seasonal influenza. The researchers next observed that the genetically modified H5N1 was transmitted to uninfected ferrets. It was through this observation that the researchers concluded it was possible for an avian H5N1 strain that infected a mammal to undergo genetic changes so as to also become easily transmissible among those mammals.

The researchers also discovered that very few genetic changes may be necessary to convert an H5N1 strain capable of leaping the species barrier to infect a human into a strain that is also capable of airborne transmission between humans. Each of the two research teams found only four or five genetic changes between the H5N1 strain with which they started and the modified H5N1 that was easily transmitted between the ferrets. This led the researchers to their final conclusions that avian H5N1 is not incapable of making the genetic changes necessary to become easily transmissible among humans, and that those genetic changes may be so few as to justify the view that an H5N1 pandemic is a real public health threat.

Each of the research teams drafted their experiments, results, and conclusions and submitted their articles for publication. One of the articles was accepted for publication in *Science* and the other in *Nature*. Just before publication, however, the journals' editors became concerned that publication of these studies posed a bioterror risk. The editors sought input from NIH and its National Science Advisory Board for Biosecurity (NSABB) as to whether the publication of the studies created an unacceptable biosecurity risk. The concern was that the publications could provide a blueprint for creating a lethal and transmissible pathogen that could be misused for terrorism. NSABB reviewed the studies and recommended that both journals publish only redacted versions to eliminate the description of how the research teams created the new pathogens they studied.

NSABB's recommendation started a firestorm of controversy. At issue was the value of these research findings to influenza scientists and public health officials who sought to prepare for an influenza pandemic, as compared to the risk that the research posed to national security.

Once it became clear that the new pathogens had not been lethal among the ferrets in either experiment, and that the methods of the experiments were available as a result of earlier published papers and presentations at scientific conferences, NSABB reversed itself. It recommended that both journals publish each of the articles without redaction. The articles were published later in 2012.

B. The Discovery Imperative and Bias in Science

To the scientist, "discovery is *everything*." That is how Harvard biologist Edward O. Wilson, Ph.D., describes it. Scientists, he says, "know the first rule of the professional game book: Make an important discovery, and you are a successful scientist. . . . You go into the textbooks." It goes deeper than success and fame, however. Discovery drives the scientist at an emotional level. It is "thrilling," Dr. Wilson says. "There is no feeling more pleasant, no drug more addictive, than setting foot on virgin soil." Meanwhile, if, as a scientist, you "[f]ail to discover . . . you are little or nothing in the culture of science, no matter how much you learn and write about science."

If Dr. Wilson is to be believed, then discovery is an imperative in the professional ethos of science. As such, it demands of researchers a single-minded zeal to add to the body of scientific knowledge. To punctuate his point, Dr. Wilson borrows a quote: "The scientific method is doing your damnedest, no holds barred."

Such "investigative zeal" leads, in turn, to a professional bias toward conducting research and blinding scientists to the risks that an experiment can pose to the public. It is a close kin to what others refer to as a "White Hat Bias" in science; a "bias leading to distortion of information," which, in the case of DURC, is a protocol's risks and benefits "in the service of what may be perceived to be righteous ends." Because it arises from the *profession's* imperative to discover, this bias affects not only the scientist who designs and conducts an experiment, but also every other scientist who might have a role in reviewing the experiment for funding or for institutional approval. In short, this bias of the profession travels from one degree to another with each and every scientist no matter the role he or she plays, if any, with respect to a particular experiment.

In particular, the discovery imperative creates a bias among scientists to overvalue the benefits of an experiment and to undervalue its risks, even among scientists whose roles are limited to participating in the institutional review of an experiment proposed by a colleague. The bias is so pervasive that one experienced chair of an Institutional Review Board (IRB) wrote about it. He observed that researchers on IRBs "share a constantly reinforced bias for experimentation per se," which, he said, "normally follow[ed] the socialization of scientists." This professional bias, the author opined, created a real "potential for inappropriate overvaluation of benefits over risks. . . ." Other commentators have found additional anecdotal evidence of such a bias. For example, Professor Richard Saver describes instances in which investigators conducting human subjects research and the IRBs that approved the research have been criticized for allowing the researchers' "investigative zeal" to result in subjects being exposed to potentially unjustifiable research risks, even in the absence of financial conflicts of interest.

All of the above suggests that the ever-present bias associated with the discovery imperative could have been at work during the design, funding, and institutional approval of the ferret studies. It certainly would explain why there were several lost opportunities prior to the onset of the research to account for the dual use risks of each study and to assure that they were more than offset by research benefits. For example, the discovery imperative can explain why the lead scientists on each of the studies designed their research protocols without expressly completing a dual use risk-benefit analysis. Likewise, it also can explain why the IBC that reviewed and approved Dr. Kawaoka's study failed to account for the full measure of the biosafety risks of the experiment.

The discovery imperative and its associated biases also explain, at least in part, why a public policy that relies completely on scientists to identify and manage dual use risks is unsustainable. There must be some external check on that bias before we can expect the public to trust researchers and research institutions to manage DURC effectively. This provides one way that regulation generally, and the proposed federal rules for oversight of DURC in particular, play a vital role.

C. Bounded Self-Regulation as a Means for Promoting Public Trust in Scientists

As I have written elsewhere, regulating for trust is tricky. The law is a powerful vehicle for expressing and enforcing important social norms. It can signal to researchers and research institutions that they are obligated to protect the public from dual use risks that are not clearly justified by the benefits of that research which give rise to those risks. By creating a means to hold science accountable when its practitioners breach that obligation, the law can also provide a basis for the public to trust that science has a strong incentive to live up to its obligation.

For this to work, however, the law must tread somewhat lightly. If, in the hope of gaining greater compliance, the law takes primary control of DURC oversight, the entire effort to promote public trust in the research enterprise could backfire. By taking primary control of DURC oversight, the law would signal that scientists and research institutions cannot be trusted to sufficiently protect public safety. Why else would it be necessary to regulate them so completely?

In the end, promoting public trust in researchers and research institutions to manage dual use risks requires the law to hit a regulatory sweet spot—enough regulation to provide a foundation for the public to believe that scientists have a strong incentive to abide by the norm of protecting public safety, but not so much regulation as to signal that scientists are not sufficiently trustworthy to be given substantial authority to oversee DURC. A model for hitting that sweet spot is bounded self-regulation. Under this model, regulators set boundary procedures and standards by which a target of regulation must abide or suffer some form of legally mandated penalty. Within these boundaries, however, those who are subject to the regulations are permitted to exercise their own judgment about how to apply the boundary standards, and regulators defer to those judgments.

This regulatory technique is particularly useful where the goal of regulation is to signal the trustworthiness of the targets of regulation so as to increase public trust. Accordingly, it has a unique application in health law where trust is viewed as exceptionally important.

The value of promoting trust in the context of scientific research is clear. Society needs the expertise of scientists to advance our collective knowledge about our world, which, of course, requires experimentation. Society might want to assess the risks and benefits of scientists' experiments on a case-by-case basis. Even then, however, it requires the expertise of scientists to identify those risks and benefits; to assess the probability that the risks and benefits actually materialize; and to place those risks, benefits, and probabilities into context for lay people. In short, there is no way to escape our reliance on scientists to conduct experiments, as well as to help us determine whether the risks of research are worth the benefits. Given the reality of our reliance on the expertise of scientists, society needs a basis for trusting not only in the technical expertise of scientists, but also in their fidelity to our collective interests, which, at times, may mean halting the pursuit of discovery in the name of public safety.

Given the importance of public trust in scientific research, it is not surprising to find the regulatory model of bounded self-regulation already in use. Medical researchers and their institutions have been deputized by federal law to review proposed research involving human research subjects to assure that the benefits of research outweigh the risks, and that human subjects participate on an informed and voluntary basis. Likewise, federal policy deputizes scientists and their institutions to review proposed research involving rDNA techniques to assure that the research will comply with applicable biosafety standards under federal guidelines. In each instance, procedures and standards are set by federal law and the task of administering those standards is delegated to researchers at the research institutions in which proposed research will take place if approved. Research institutions that fail to abide by the boundary procedures and standards are subject to losing their eligibility for federal research funds, which is a powerful incentive for compliance. In this way, these laws fall within the realm of bounded self-regulation because the law signals, through its delegation of authority, that researchers and research institutions are trustworthy, while also providing boundaries for the exercise of discretion and a substantial penalty for violating those boundaries.

Using this model of bounded self-regulation does not guarantee success. Despite employing this model, the regulations both for protecting human subjects and for overseeing rDNA research are rife with flaws. Where the government regulates as a tool to promote public trust, the model of bounded self-regulation gives the government an opportunity to succeed where a command and control model does not.

D. New Federal Policies for DURC Oversight

In response to the ferret studies, the federal government developed two new policies for the oversight of DURC. The first policy was released on March 29, 2012 (2012 Policy), and it requested that all federal agencies conducting or funding life sciences research review their projects to determine if any involve DURC and to report their findings to the Assistant to the President for Homeland Security and Counterterrorism. Additionally, if an agency finds that it is funding or conducting any DURC, the 2012 Policy provides that the agency should work with the researcher and research institution to develop a plan to mitigate the dual use risks. If those risks cannot be mitigated adequately, then agencies may take more extreme measures, such as classifying the research or terminating its federal funding.

The second policy is a policy in name only. From an administrative law perspective, it is proposed rule-making for which notice was provided and comments requested on February 22, 2013 (2013 Proposed Rules). The 2013 Proposed Rules describe the DURC oversight responsibilities of researchers, research institutions, and federal agencies. Researchers would be obligated to assess whether their proposed research meets the definition of DURC and, if so, to work with the research institution's review board to develop a dual use risk mitigation plan. If finalized, the 2013 Proposed Rules would require research institutions that receive federal funding to establish a board to review research proposals for the purpose of determining if they involve DURC and, if so, develop and enforce dual use risk mitigation plans for the research. The board may be internal or external to the research institution, and it may be a unique committee or an existing committee (such as an IBC) whose charge is expanded to include DURC oversight. The 2013 Proposed Rules do not require a particular make-up of the committee's membership, so long as it has "sufficient breadth of expertise to assess the dual use potential of the range of relevant life sciences research conducted at a given research facility" and has knowledge of dual use issues, federal law, and available risk mitigation alternatives. Additionally, a research institution must notify the agency funding the research, if and when, the institution's review board identifies the funded research as DURC, and it must provide that agency with a copy of the dual use risk mitigation plan developed by the institution. As for funding agencies, the 2013 Proposed Rules incorporate the powers and responsibilities described in the 2012 Policy. Any institution subject to the 2013 Proposed Rules would risk losing its eligibility for federal research funding if it failed to comply.

The 2012 Policy and the 2013 Proposed Rules are positive steps to promoting public trust in scientists and research institutions conducting DURC, because they employ the bounded self-regulation model. Together they set boundary standards and procedures that will add to the accountability of researchers and research institutions with respect to the dual use risks that their research imposes on the public. First, they require researchers and research institutions to be deliberate in assessing whether their proposed research meets the definition of DURC and, if so, to identify the precise dual use risks at issue and then develop a plan of mitigation. This diminishes the likelihood that proposed research will proceed on the assumption that the research does not pose any dual use risks or that dual use risks are simply a price of pursuing discovery. Second, they provide for the funding agency to make a fresh assessment of dual use risks and mitigation plans for DURC that they fund. Moreover, they empower the funding agency to classify research or even refuse to fund research that the agency perceives to have dual use risks that cannot be sufficiently mitigated. In this way, the agency's review is a potentially powerful check on the ability of the researcher and research institution to identify and manage dual use risks effectively. It forces scientists and their institutions either to stand in the shoes of the funding agency when managing DURC, or risk that the funding agency will step in to manage or withhold funding for the research.

At the same time, the 2012 Policy and the 2013 Proposed Rules rely on researchers and research institutions to take the lead in the oversight of DURC. They defer to the researcher and his or her institution to identify DURC and to develop plans for mitigation. Federal regulators override the institutional plan to manage DURC only where they find it significantly lacking. This leaves plenty of opportunity and an incentive for science to develop its own norms for protecting the public in the case of DURC.

This is not to say that the 2012 Policy and the 2013 Proposed Rules are perfect. They are not. In particular, the 2013 Proposed Rules should instruct scientists and their institutions to not only assess and mitigate dual use risks, but to articulate why those risks, once mitigated, are justified by the likely benefits of the research. The rules should also identify whether research benefits must merely, clearly, or substantially outweigh dual use risks, and they should require that the institutional review process apply that standard. Finally, the 2013 Proposed Rules should do more than demand life sciences expertise on the institutional committees that review DURC. Those committees should be required to have a sufficient number of institutionally unaffiliated members to act as an additional check on the bias created by the discovery imperative.

In the end, Dr. Franz and I agree that life scientists and their research institutions should not be over-regulated because doing so undermines trust. Yet, fear of over-regulation should not result in closing the door on all regulation. Instead, the answer is finding the right regulatory technique that allows scientists to regulate themselves within legal boundaries that help assure the public that the profession of science has a strong incentive to protect society while pursuing the next discovery.

Robert Gatter is a Distinguished Scholar at the University of Pittsburgh Medical Center's Center for Biosecurity and a professor of public health and medicine at the University of Pittsburgh. During the 1960s, he headed the international effort to eliminate smallpox.

EXPLORING THE ISSUE

Can Science Be Trusted Without Government Regulation?

Critical Thinking and Reflection

1. What is "discovery bias"? Is there anything similar in other fields (such as "treatment bias" in medicine or "driving bias" in errand-running)?
2. Is there anything similar to "discovery bias" in other fields (such as "treatment bias" in medicine or "driving bias" in errand-running)?
3. Do such biases limit our ability to see alternatives?
4. Does publishing the full methods and results of the Fouchier and Kawaoka H5N1 studies seem likely to increase our ability to protect public health from a future H5N1 pandemic?

Is There Common Ground?

David R. Franz sees a role for regulation in setting the boundaries of the field of play and defining the rules of the game. Robert Gatter thinks that much more is necessary if life scientists are to warrant the public's trust, but he does say at the end of his paper, "life scientists and their research institutions should not be over-regulated because doing so undermines trust." They thus agree that over-regulation can be a problem. They differ in how much regulation is over-regulation.

1. Is more-regulated research more trustworthy than less-regulated research?
2. Does "discovery bias" blind a researcher to the ethical and moral dimensions of research?
3. If exceptional laboratory leadership makes regulation less necessary, is it reasonable to try to rely on such leadership?

Additional Resources

Jon Cohen, "Does Forewarned = Forearmed with Lab-Made Avian Influenza Strains?" *Science* (February 17, 2012).

Fred Guterl, "Waiting to Explode," *Scientific American* (June 2012).

Sander Herfst, et al., "Airborne Transmission of Influenza A/H5N1 Virus Between Ferrets," *Science* (June 22, 2012) (http://www.sciencemag.org /content/336/6088/1534.full).

Masaki Imai, et al., "Experimental Adaptation of an Influenza H5 HA Confers Respiratory Droplet Transmission to a Reassortant H5 HA/H1N1 Virus in Ferrets," *Nature* (June 21, 2012) (http:// www.nature.com/nature/journal/vaop/ncurrent/full /nature10831.html).

Carl Zimmer, "Could Information about a Lab-Made Virus Really Help Evildoers Create a Biological Weapon?" *Slate* (December 22, 2011) (http://www .slate.com/articles/technology/future_tense/2011/12 /h5n1_the_lab_made_virus_the_u_s_fears_could_be _made_into_a_biological_weapon_.html).

Internet References . . .

National Science Advisory Board for Biosecurity (NSABB)

http://oba.od.nih.gov/biosecurity/about_nsabb.html

Office of Declassification: History of Classification and Declassification

http://fas.org/irp/doddir/doe/history.htm

United States Senate Committee on Homeland Security & Government Affairs Hearing on "Biological Security: The Risk of Dual-Use Research"

http://www.hsgac.senate.gov/hearings/biological-security-the-risk-of-dual-use-research

Unit 2

UNIT

Energy and the Environment

*A*s the damage that human beings do to their environment in the course of obtaining food, water, wood, ore, energy, and other resources has become clear, many people have grown concerned. Some of that concern is for the environment—the landscapes and living things with which humanity shares its world. Some of that concern is more for human welfare; it focuses on the ways in which environmental damage threatens human health, prosperity, or even survival.

Among the major environmental issues are those related to energy. By releasing vast amounts of carbon dioxide, fossil fuels threaten to change the world's climate. Potential solutions include warding off excess solar heating, greatly expanding the use of hydroelectric power, and replacing fossil fuels with hydrogen.

Selected, Edited, and with Issue Framing Material by:
Thomas A. Easton, *Thomas College*

ISSUE

Is Anthropogenic Global Warming Real and Dangerous?

YES: Intergovernmental Panel on Climate Change, from "Climate Change 2014: Synthesis Report," IPCC (2014)

NO: Steve Goreham, from *The Mad, Mad, Mad World of Climatism,* New Lenox Books (2013)

Learning Outcomes

After reading this issue, you will be able to:

- Describe the evidence that the global climate is warming.
- Explain why climate scientists consider the evidence for human-caused climate change "unequivocal."
- Describe how climate change puts human society and ecosystems at risk.
- Describe what is meant by "climatism."

ISSUE SUMMARY

YES: The Intergovernmental Panel on Climate Change argues that warming of the world's climate system is unequivocal, and many of the observed changes are unprecedented over decades to millennia. The atmosphere and ocean have warmed, the amounts of snow and ice have diminished, sea level has risen, and the concentrations of greenhouse gases have increased, driven largely by population growth and economic development. Warming can be expected to continue for centuries with profound effects on the environment and on human well-being. Yet there is much we can do to limit future risks.

NO: Steve Goreham argues that the scientific data do not support the IPCC's projections of catastrophe, vast amounts of money are being wasted, and "the theory of man-made global warming" will soon be seen to be completely false. After all, carbon dioxide is not a pollutant—it is an essential plant nutrient!

The idea that the heat-trapping ability of infrared-absorbing gases in the atmosphere is similar to that of the glass panes in a greenhouse (hence the "greenhouse effect") was first proposed by the French mathematical physicist Jean-Baptiste-Joseph Fourier in 1827. In 1896, the Swedish chemist Svante Arrhenius, who later won the 1903 Nobel Prize in chemistry, predicted that if atmospheric carbon dioxide (CO_2) levels doubled due to the burning of fossil fuels, the resulting increase in the average temperature at the Earth's surface would amount to four to six degrees Celsius (seven to ten degrees Fahrenheit).

The Arrhenius prediction about global warming was all but forgotten for more than half a century until direct observations and historical data demonstrated that by 1960, atmospheric CO_2 levels had risen to 315 ppm from the preindustrial level of 280 ppm. Careful measurements since then have shown that the CO_2 level is now above 400 ppm, and rising (http://www.esrl.noaa.gov/gmd/ccgg/trends/). The Arrhenius prediction that the average temperature on Earth will rise more than four degrees Celsius may well come true before the end of the twenty-first century if present fossil fuel use and forest destruction trends continue. Most atmospheric scientists agree that such a warming will be accompanied by changes in the world's weather patterns and a significant increase in sea levels. The data on which these conclusions are based, as well as the conclusions themselves, have been vigorously debated for years.

In 1988, due to concern about the potentially serious disruptive effects that would result from significant, short-term changes in world climate, the United Nations Environment Programme joined with the World Meteorological Organization to establish the Intergovernmental Panel on Climate Change (IPCC) to assess the available scientific, technical, and socioeconomic information regarding greenhouse gas-induced climate change. Thousands of meteorologists and other atmospheric and climate scientists have participated in periodic reviews of the data. The Fifth Assessment Report of the IPCC appeared in 2013–2014. It is very clear that global climate change is real, it is caused by human activities, and its impacts on ecosystems and human well-being (especially in developing nations) will be serious. It also outlined the steps that must be taken to prevent, ease, or cope with these impacts. Other reports (see Nicholas Stern, *Stern Review: The Economics of Climate Change*, Executive Summary, October 30, 2006 [http://www.hm-treasury.gov.uk/independent_reviews/stern _review_economics_climate_change/sternreview_index .cfm]) make it clear that although taking steps now to limit future impacts of global warming would be very expensive, "the benefits of strong, early action considerably outweigh the costs . . . . Ignoring climate change will eventually damage economic growth . . . . Tackling climate change is the pro-growth strategy for the longer term, and it can be done in a way that does not cap the aspirations for growth of rich or poor countries. The earlier effective action is taken, the less costly it will be."

Exactly what will global warming do to the world and its people? Richard B. Primack, *Walden Warming* (University of Chicago Press, 2014), has compared wildflower blooming times, as recorded in Henry David Thoreau's mid-1800s notebooks and found that warming has already shifted those times as much as six weeks earlier in the year. This does not sound very catastrophic, but our future is much more than a matter of wildflower blooming times. Projections have grown steadily worse; see Eli Kintisch, "Projections of Climate Change Go from Bad to Worse, Scientists Report," *Science* (March 20, 2009). Effects include rising sea level, more extreme weather events, reduced global harvests, reduced nutrient levels of crops (Mary Macvean, "Rising Carbon Dioxide Levels Affect Nutrients in Crops, Study Says," *Los Angeles Times*, May 7, 2014; http://www .latimes.com/science/sciencenow/la-sci-sn-carbon-dioxide -crops-20140507-story.html), and threats to the economies and security of nations (Michael T. Klare, "Global Warming

Battlefields: How Climate Change Threatens Security," *Current History*, November 2007; and Scott G. Bergerson, "Arctic Meltdown: The Economic and Security Implications of Global Warming," *Foreign Affairs*, March/April 2008). As rainfall patterns change and the seas rise, millions of people will flee their homelands; see Alex de Sherbinin, Koko Warner, and Charles Erhart, "Casualties of Climate Change," *Scientific American* (January 2011). The potential for conflict is emphasized in the IPCC's Fifth Assessment Report.

It seems clear that something must be done, but what? How urgently? And with what aim? Should we be trying to reduce or prevent human suffering? Or to avoid political conflicts? Or to protect the global economy—meaning standards of living, jobs, and businesses? The humanitarian and economic approaches are obviously connected, for protecting jobs certainly has much to do with easing or preventing suffering. However, these approaches can also conflict. In October 2009, the Government Accountability Office (GAO) released "Climate Change Adaptation: Strategic Federal Planning Could Help Government Officials Make More Informed Decisions" (GAO-10-113; http://www. gao.gov/products/GAO-10-113), which noted the need for multiagency coordination and strategic (long-term) planning, both of which are often resisted by bureaucrats and politicians. Robert Engelman, *Population, Climate Change, and Women's Lives* (Worldwatch Institute, 2010), notes that addressing population size and growth would help but "Despite its key contribution to climate change, population plays little role in current discussions on how to address this serious challenge."

U.S. President Barack Obama indicated that his administration would take global warming more seriously than did his predecessors. In June 2009, the U.S. House of Representatives passed an Energy and Climate bill that promised to cap carbon emissions and stimulate use of renewable energy. The Senate version of the bill failed to pass; see Daniel Stone, "Who Killed the Climate and Energy Bill?" *Newsweek* (September 15, 2010). The Obama administration also said it was committed to negotiating seriously at the Copenhagen Climate Change Conference in December 2009. Unfortunately, the Copenhagen meeting ended with little accomplished except agreements to limit global temperature increases to two degrees Celsius by 2100, but only through voluntary cuts in carbon emissions; to have developed nations report their cuts; to have developed nations fund mitigation and adaptation in developing nations; and to continue talking about the problem (see Elizabeth Finkel, "Senate Looms as Bigger Hurdle after Copenhagen," *Science*, January 1, 2010). There were few signs that the world is ready to take the extensive actions deemed necessary by many; see, e.g., Janet L.

Sawin and William R. Moomaw, "Renewing the Future and Protecting the Climate," *World Watch* (July/August 2010). However, when the U.N. Framework Convention on Climate Change met in Lima, Peru, in December 2014, it was able to report agreement among 190 nations, both developed and developing, that they would develop actions plans immediately; see David Talbot, "Lima Climate Accord Might Boost Renewables," *Technology Review* (December 16, 2014) (http://www.technologyreview.com/news/533581/lima-climate-accord-might-boost-renewables/).

According to David Rotman, "Climate Change: The Moral Choices," *Technology Review* (April 11, 2013) (http://www.technologyreview.com/review/513526/climate-change-the-moral-choices/), ethicists are only now addressing the question of what ethical behavior means in the global warming context. Is it right to value present benefits (such as cheap, convenient energy) more than benefits to future generations (such as freedom from the consequences of global warming)?

In May 2010, the National Research Council released three books, *Advancing the Science of Climate Change* (http://www.nap.edu/catalog.php?record_id=12782), *Limiting the Magnitude of Future Climate Change* (http://www.nap.edu/catalog.php?record_id=12785), and *Adapting to the Impacts of Climate Change* (http://www.nap.edu/catalog.php?record_id=12783). Together, they stress the reality of the problem, the need for immediate action to keep the problem from getting worse, and the need for advance planning and preparation to deal with the impacts. Computer simulations suggest that since 1980, climate changes have reduced maize and wheat harvests by 3.8–5.5 percent; see D. B. Lobell, W. Schlenker, and J. Costa-Roberts, "Climate Trends and Global Crop Production Since 1980," *Science* (published online May 5, 2011). At a meeting of the International Emissions Trading Association, Christiana Figueres, executive secretary of the United Nations framework convention on climate change, said that the situation is urgent and the world must immediately agree to change its goal from limiting global warming to 2.0°C to limiting it to 1.5°C, or "we are in big trouble"; see Fiona Harvey, "UN Chief Challenges World to Agree to Tougher Target for Climate Change," *The Guardian* (June 1, 2011). In May 2014, the U.S. Global Change Research Program released the National Climate Assessment (http://nca2014.globalchange.gov/), which stresses that global warming is real, serious (with effects varying by region), and primarily due to human activities, chiefly the burning of fossil fuels. In the same month, NASA released "A new study [currently in press with *Geophysical Research Letters*] by researchers at NASA and the University of California, Irvine, [that] finds a rapidly melting section of the West Antarctic Ice Sheet appears to be in an irreversible state of decline, with nothing to stop the glaciers in this area from melting into the sea . . . . These glaciers . . . contain enough ice to raise global sea level by 4 feet (1.2 meters) and are melting faster than most scientists had expected . . . . [T]hese findings will require an upward revision to current predictions of sea level rise" (http://www.nasa.gov/press/2014/may/nasa-uci-study-indicates-loss-of-west-antarctic-glaciers-appears-unstoppable/). In 2014, the Climate Science Panel of the American Association for the Advancement of Science (AAAS) released "What We Know: The Reality, Risks and Response to Climate Change," and stressed in no uncertain terms that global warming and climate change are real, that they are caused by human activities, and that we face serious consequences if we do nothing.

However, there remains resistance to the idea that global climate change is real, is caused by human activities, or poses any threat to the environment or human well-being. Most of the remaining critics of the reality of global warming are either employed by or funded by industries and nations that have a financial stake in resisting proposals for significant reductions in the release of greenhouse gases. Some fossil-fuel-industry funding is funneled through conservative organizations such as the Heartland Institute (http://heartland.org/), which in 2013 made news by spreading disinformation about scientific acceptance of global warming; see Phil Plait, "The Heartland Institute and the American Meteorological Society," *Slate* (December 10, 2013) (http://www.slate.com/blogs/bad_astronomy/2013/12/10/heartland_institute_sowing_global_warming_doubt.html?wpisrc=burger_bar). Earlier in 2013, it mailed copies of Steve Goreham's *The Mad, Mad, Mad World of Climatism* to college professors all over the country.

In the YES selection, the Intergovernmental Panel on Climate Change argues that warming of the world's climate system is unequivocal, and many of the observed changes are unprecedented over decades to millennia. The atmosphere and ocean have warmed, the amounts of snow and ice have diminished, sea level has risen, and the concentrations of greenhouse gases have increased, driven largely by population growth and economic development. Warming can be expected to continue for centuries with profound effects on the environment and on human well-being. Yet there is much we can do to limit future risks. The NO selection is taken from Steve Goreham's *The Mad, Mad, Mad World of Climatism*, which argues that the scientific data do not support projections of catastrophe, vast amounts of money are being wasted, and "the theory of man-made global warming" will soon be seen to be completely false. After all, carbon dioxide is not a pollutant—it is an essential plant nutrient!

YES

Intergovernmental Panel on Climate Change

Climate Change 2014: Synthesis Report

Summary for Policymakers

SPM Introduction

This Synthesis Report is based on the reports of the three Working Groups of the Intergovernmental Panel on Climate Change (IPCC), including relevant Special Reports. It provides an integrated view of climate change as the final part of the IPCC's Fifth Assessment Report (AR5).

This summary follows the structure of the longer report, which addresses the following topics: Observed changes and their causes; Future climate change, risks and impacts; Future pathways for adaptation, mitigation and sustainable development; Adaptation and mitigation.

In the Synthesis Report, the certainty in key assessment findings is communicated as in the Working Group Reports and Special Reports. It is based on the author teams' evaluations of underlying scientific understanding and is expressed as a qualitative level of confidence (from *very low* to *very high*) and, when possible, probabilistically with a quantified likelihood (from *exceptionally unlikely* to *Virtually certain*) Where appropriate, findings are also formulated as statements of fact without using uncertainty qualifiers . . . .

SPM 1. Observed Changes and their Causes

> **Human influence on the climate system is clear, and recent anthropogenic emissions of greenhouse gases are the highest in history. Recent climate changes have had widespread impacts on human and natural systems.**

SPM 1.1 Observed changes in the climate system

> **Warming of the climate system is unequivocal, and since the 1950s, many of the observed changes are unprecedented over decades to millennia. The atmosphere and ocean have warmed, the amounts of snow and ice have diminished, and sea level has risen.**

Each of the last three decades has been successively warmer at the Earth's surface than any preceding decade since 1850. The period from 1983 to 2012 was *likely* the warmest 30-year period of the last 1400 years in the Northern Hemisphere, where such assessment is possible (*medium confidence*). The globally averaged combined land and ocean surface temperature data as calculated by a linear trend, show a warming of 0.85 [0.65 to 1.06] °C[2] over the period 1880 to 2012, when multiple independently produced datasets exist.

In addition to robust multi-decadal warming, the globally averaged surface temperature exhibits substantial decadal and interannual variability. Due to this natural variability, trends based on short records are very sensitive to the beginning and end dates and do not in general reflect long-term climate trends. As one example, the rate of warming over the past 15 years (1998–2012; 0.05 [–0.05 to 0.15] °C per decade), which begins with a strong El Niño, is smaller than the rate calculated since 1951 (1951–2012; 0.12 [0.08 to 0.14] °C per decade).

Ocean warming dominates the increase in energy stored in the climate system, accounting for more than 90% of the energy accumulated between 1971 and 2010 (*high confidence*), with only about 1% stored in the atmosphere. On a global scale, the ocean warming is largest near the surface, and the upper 75 m warmed by 0.11 [0.09 to 0.13] °C per decade over the period 1971 to 2010. It is *virtually certain* that the upper ocean (0–700 m) warmed from 1971 to 2010, and it *likely* warmed between the 1870s and 1971.

Averaged over the mid-latitude land areas of the Northern Hemisphere, precipitation has increased since 1901 (*medium confidence* before and *high confidence* after 1951). For other latitudes, area-averaged longterm positive or negative trends have *low confidence*. Observations of changes in ocean surface salinity also provide indirect evidence for changes in the global water cycle over the ocean (*medium confidence*). It is *very likely* that

Climate Change 2014: Synthesis Report. Contribution of Working Groups I, II, and III to the Fifth Assessment Report of the Intergovernmental Panel on Climate Change, pp. 1–2, 4–8, 10, 12–18. Core Writing Team, Pachauri, R.K. and Meyer, L. (eds.) IPCC, Geneva, Switzerland. Reprinted by permission. All rights reserved.

regions of high salinity, where evaporation dominates, have become more saline, while regions of low salinity, where precipitation dominates, have become fresher since the 1950s.

Since the beginning of the industrial era, oceanic uptake of CO_2 has resulted in acidification of the ocean; the pH of ocean surface water has decreased by 0.1 (*high confidence*), corresponding to a 26% increase in acidity, measured as hydrogen ion concentration.

Over the period 1992 to 2011, the Greenland and Antarctic ice sheets have been losing mass (*high confidence*), *likely* at a larger rate over 2002 to 2011. Glaciers have continued to shrink almost worldwide (*high confidence*). Northern Hemisphere spring snow cover has continued to decrease in extent (*high confidence*). There is *high confidence* that permafrost temperatures have increased in most regions since the early 1980s in response to increased surface temperature and changing snow cover.

The annual mean Arctic sea-ice extent decreased over the period 1979 to 2012, with a rate that was *very likely* in the range 3.5 to 4.1% per decade. Arctic sea-ice extent has decreased in every season and in every successive decade since 1979, with the most rapid decrease in decadal mean extent in summer (*high confidence*). It is *very likely* that the annual mean Antarctic sea-ice extent increased in the range of 1.2 to 1.8% per decade between 1979 and 2012. However, there is *high confidence* that there are strong regional differences in Antarctica, with extent increasing in some regions and decreasing in others.

Over the period 1901 to 2010, global mean sea level rose by 0.19 [0.17 to 0.21] m. The rate of sea-level rise since the mid-19th century has been larger than the mean rate during the previous two millennia (*high confidence*).

SPM 1.2   Causes of climate change

> Anthropogenic greenhouse gas emissions have increased since the pre-industrial era, driven largely by economic and population growth, and are now higher than ever. This has led to atmospheric concentrations of carbon dioxide, methane and nitrous oxide that are unprecedented in at least the last 800,000 years. Their effects, together with those of other anthropogenic drivers, have been detected throughout the climate system and are *extremely likely* to have been the dominant cause of the observed warming since the mid-20th century.

Anthropogenic greenhouse gas (GHG) emissions since the pre-industrial era have driven large increases in the atmospheric concentrations of CO_2, CH_4 and N_2O.

Between 1750 and 2011, cumulative anthropogenic CO_2 emissions to the atmosphere were 2040 ± 310 GtCO2. About 40% of these emissions have remained in the atmosphere (880 ± 35 GtCO2); the rest was removed from the atmosphere and stored on land (in plants and soils) and in the ocean. The ocean has absorbed about 30% of the emitted anthropogenic CO_2, causing ocean acidification. About half of the anthropogenic CO_2 emissions between 1750 and 2011 have occurred in the last 40 years (*high confidence*).

Total anthropogenic greenhouse gas emissions have continued to increase over 1970 to 2010 with larger absolute increases between 2000 and 2010, despite a growing number of climate change mitigation policies. Anthropogenic greenhouse gas emissions in 2010 have reached 49 ± 4.5 GtCO2 eq/yr. Emissions of CO_2 from fossil fuel combustion and industrial processes contributed about 78% of the total greenhouse gas emissions increase from 1970 to 2010, with a similar percentage contribution for the increase during the period 2000 to 2010 (*high confidence*). Globally, economic and population growth continued to be the most important drivers of increases jn CO_2 emissions from fossil fuel combustion. The contribution of population growth between 2000 and 2010 remained roughly identical to the previous three decades, while the contribution of economic growth has risen sharply. Increased use of coal has reversed the long-standing trend of gradual decarbonization (i.e., reducing the carbon intensity of energy) of the world's energy supply (*high confidence*).

The evidence for human influence on the climate system has grown since the Fourth Assessment Report (AR4). It is *extremely likely* that more than half of the observed increase in global average surface temperature from 1951 to 2010 was caused by the anthropogenic increase in greenhouse gas concentrations and other anthropogenic forcings together. The best estimate of the human-induced contribution to warming is similar to the observed warming over this period. Anthropogenic forcings have *likely* made a substantial contribution to surface temperature increases since the mid-20th century over every continental region except Antarctica. Anthropogenic influences have *likely* affected the global water cycle since 1960 and contributed to the retreat of glaciers since the 1960s and to the increased surface melting of the Greenland ice sheet since 1993. Anthropogenic influences have *very likely* contributed to Arctic sea-ice loss since 1979 and have *very likely* made a substantial contribution to increases in global upper ocean heat content (0–700 m) and to global mean sea-level rise observed since the 1970s.

SPM 1.3   Impacts of climate change

> **In recent decades, changes in climate have caused impacts on natural and human systems on all continents and across the oceans. Impacts are due to observed climate change, irrespective of its cause, indicating the sensitivity of natural and human systems to changing climate.**

Evidence of observed climate-change impacts is strongest and most comprehensive for natural systems. In many regions, changing precipitation or melting snow and ice are altering hydrological systems, affecting water resources in terms of quantity and quality (*medium confidence*). Many terrestrial, freshwater, and marine species have shifted their geographic ranges, seasonal activities, migration patterns, abundances, and species interactions in response to ongoing climate change (*high confidence*). Some impacts on human systems have also been attributed to climate change, with a major or minor contribution of climate change distinguishable from other influences. Assessment of many studies covering a wide range of regions and crops shows that negative impacts of climate change on crop yields have been more common than positive impacts (*high confidence*). Some impacts of ocean acidification on marine organisms have been attributed to human influence (*medium confidence*).

SPM 1.4   Extreme events

> **Changes in many extreme weather and climate events have been observed since about 1950. Some of these changes have been linked to human influences, including a decrease in cold temperature extremes, an increase in warm temperature extremes, an increase in extreme high sea levels and an increase in the number of heavy precipitation events in a number of regions.**

It is *very likely* that the number of cold days and nights has decreased and the number of warm days and nights has increased on the global scale. It is *likely* that the frequency of heat waves has increased in large parts of Europe, Asia and Australia. It is *very likely* that human influence has contributed to the observed global scale changes in the frequency and intensity of daily temperature extremes since the mid-20th century. It is *likely* that human influence has more than doubled the probability of occurrence of heat waves in some locations. There is *medium confidence* that the observed warming has increased

heat-related human mortality and decreased cold-related human mortality in some regions.

There are *likely* more land regions where the number of heavy precipitation events has increased than where it has decreased. Recent detection of increasing trends in extreme precipitation and discharge in some catchments imply greater risks of flooding at regional scale (*medium confidence*). It is *likely* that extreme sea levels (for example, as experienced in storm surges) have increased since 1970, being mainly a result of rising mean sea level.

Impacts from recent climate-related extremes, such as heat waves, droughts, floods, cyclones, and wildfires, reveal significant vulnerability and exposure of some ecosystems and many human systems to current climate variability (*very high confidence*).

SPM 2.   Future Climate Changes, Risks and Impacts

> **Continued emission of greenhouse gases will cause further warming and long-lasting changes in all components of the climate system, increasing the likelihood of severe, pervasive and irreversible impacts for people and ecosystems. Limiting climate change would require substantial and sustained reductions in greenhouse gas emissions which, together with adaptation, can limit climate change risks.**

SPM2.1   Key drivers of future climate

> **Cumulative emissions of CO_2 largely determine global mean surface warming by the late 21st century and beyond. Projections of greenhouse gas emissions vary over a wide range, depending on both socioeconomic development and climate policy.**

Anthropogenic greenhouse gas emissions are mainly driven by population size, economic activity, lifestyle, energy use, land-use patterns, technology and climate policy. The "Representative Concentration Pathways" (RCPs) which are used for making projections based on these factors describe four different 21st century pathways of greenhouse gas emissions and atmospheric concentrations, air pollutant emissions and land-use. The RCPs include a stringent mitigation scenario (RCP2.6), two intermediate scenarios (RCP4.5 and RCP6.0), and one scenario with very high greenhouse gas emissions (RCP8.5). Scenarios without additional efforts to constrain emissions ("baseline scenarios") lead to pathways ranging between RCP6.0 and RCP8.5. RCP2.6 is representative of a scenario that aims to keep global warming *likely* below 2°C above preindustrial temperatures. The RCPs are consistent with the wide range of scenarios in the literature as assessed by WGIII.

Multiple lines of evidence indicate a strong, consistent, almost linear relationship between cumulative CO_2 emissions and projected global temperature change to the year 2100 in both the RCPs and the wider set of mitigation scenarios analysed in WGIII. Any given level of warming is associated with a range of cumulative CO_2 emissions, and therefore, e.g., higher emissions in earlier decades imply lower emissions later.

Multi-model results show that limiting total human-induced warming to less than 2°C relative to the period 1861–I880 with a probability of >66% would require cumulative CO_2 emissions from all anthropogenic sources since 1870 to remain below about 2900 GtCO2 (with a range of 2550–3150 GtCO2 depending on non-C02 drivers). About 1900 GtC02 had already been emitted by 2011 . . . .

SPM 2.2   Projected changes in the climate system
The projected changes in Section SPM 2.2 are for 2081–2100 relative to 1986–2005, unless otherwise indicated.

> **Surface temperature is projected to rise over the 21st century under all assessed emission scenarios. It is *very likely* that heat waves will occur more often and last longer, and that extreme precipitation events will become more intense and frequent in many regions. The ocean will continue to warm and acidify, and global mean sea level to rise.**

Future climate will depend on committed warming caused by past anthropogenic emissions, as well as future anthropogenic emissions and natural climate variability. The global mean surface temperature change for the period 2016–2035 relative to 1986–2005 is similar for the four RCPs and will *likely* be in the range 0.3°C–0.7°C (*medium confidence*). This assumes that there will be no major volcanic eruptions or changes in some natural sources (e.g., CH_4 and N_2O), or unexpected changes in total solar irradiance. By mid-2l st century, the magnitude of the projected climate change is substantially affected by the choice of emissions scenario.

Relative to 1850–1900, global surface temperature change for the end of the 21st century (2081–2100) is projected to *likely* exceed I.5°C for RCP4.5, RCP6.0 and RCP8.5 (*high confidence*). Warming is *likely* to exceed 2°C for RCP6.0 and RCP8.5 (*high confidence*), *more likely than not* to exceed 2°C for RCP4.5 (*medium confidence*), but *unlikely* to exceed 2°C for RCP2.6 (*medium conjidence*).

The increase of global mean surface temperature by the end of the 21st century (2081–2100) relative to 1986–005 is *likely* to be 0.3°C-1.7°C under RCP2.6, 1.1°C–2.6°C under RCP4.5, I.4°C–3.1°C under RCP6.0, and 2.6°C–4.8°C under RCP8.5. The Arctic region will continue to warm more rapidly than the global mean.

It is *virtually certain* that there will be more frequent hot and fewer cold temperature extremes over most land areas on daily and seasonal timescales, as global mean surface temperature increases. It is *very likely* that heat waves will occur with a higher frequency and longer duration. Occasional cold winter extremes will continue to occur.

Changes in precipitation will not be uniform. The high-latitudes and the equatorial Pacific are *likely* to experience an increase in annual mean precipitation under the RCP8.5 scenario. In many mid-latitude and subtropical dry regions, mean precipitation will *likely* decrease, while in many mid-latitude wet regions, mean precipitation will *likely* increase under the RCP8.5 scenario. Extreme precipitation events over most of the mid-latitude land masses and over wet tropical regions will *very likely* become more intense and more frequent.

The global ocean will continue to warm during the 21st century, with the strongest warming projected for the surface in tropical and Northern Hemisphere subtropical regions.

Earth System Models project a global increase in ocean acidification for all RCP scenarios by the end of the 21st century, with a slow recovery after mid-century under RCP2.6. The decrease in surface ocean pH is in the range of 0.06 to 0.07 (15–17% increase in acidity) for RCP2.6, 0.14 to 0.15 (38–41%) for RCP4.5, 0.20 to 0.21 (58–62%) for RCP6.0, and 0.30 to 0.32 (100–109%) for RCP8.5.

Year-round reductions in Arctic sea ice are projected for all RCP scenarios. A nearly ice-free Arctic Ocean in the summer sea-ice minimum in September before mid-century is *likely* for RCP8.5. (*medium confidence*).

It is *virtually certain* that near-surface permafrost extent at high northern latitudes will be reduced as global mean surface temperature increases, with the area of permafrost near the surface (upper 3.5 m) projected to decrease by 37% (RCP2.6) to 81% (RCP8.5) for the multi-model average (*medium confidence*).

The global glacier volume, excluding glaciers on the periphery of Antarctica (and excluding the Greenland and Antarctic ice sheets), is projected to decrease by 15 to 55% for RCP2.6, and by 35 to 85% for RCP8.5 (*medium confidence*).

There has been significant improvement in understanding and projection of sea-level change since the AR4. Global mean sea-level rise will continue during the 21st century, *very likely* at a faster rate than observed from 1971 to 2010. For the period 2081–2100 relative to 1986–2005, the rise will *likely* be in the ranges of 0.26 to 0.55 m for RCP2.6, and of 0.45 to 0.82 m for RCP8.5 (*medium confidence*). Sea-level rise will not be uniform across regions. By the end of the 21st century, it is *very likely* that sea level will rise in more than about 95% of the ocean area. About 70% of the coastlines worldwide are projected to experience a sea-level change within ± 20% of the global mean.

SPM 2.3 Future risks and impacts caused by a changing climate

> **Climate change will amplify existing risks and create new risks for natural and human systems. Risks are unevenly distributed and are generally greater for disadvantaged people and communities in countries at all levels of development.**

Risk of climate-related impacts results from the interaction of climate-related hazards (including hazardous events and trends) with the vulnerability and exposure of human and natural systems, including their ability to adapt. Rising rates and magnitudes of warming and other changes in the climate system, accompanied by ocean acidification, increase the risk of severe, pervasive, and in some cases irreversible detrimental impacts. Some risks are particularly relevant for individual regions, while others are global. The overall risks of future climate change impacts can be reduced by limiting the rate and magnitude of climate change, including ocean acidification. The precise levels of climate change sufficient to trigger abrupt and irreversible change remain uncertain, but the risk associated with crossing such thresholds increases with rising temperature (*medium confidence*). For risk assessment, it is important to evaluate the widest possible range of impacts, including low-probability outcomes with large consequences.

A large fraction of species faces increased extinction risk due to climate change during and beyond the 21st century, especially as climate change interacts with other stressors (*high confidence*). Most plant species cannot naturally shift their geographical ranges sufficiently fast to keep up with current and high projected rates of climate change in most landscapes; most small mammals and freshwater molluscs will not be able to keep up at the rates projected under RCP4.5 and above in flat landscapes in this century (*high confidence*). Future risk is indicated to be high by the observation that natural global climate change at rates lower than current anthropogenic climate change

caused significant ecosystem shifts and species extinctions during the past millions of years. Marine organisms will face progressively lower oxygen levels and high rates and magnitudes of ocean acidification (*high confidence*), with associated risks exacerbated by rising ocean temperature extremes (*medium confidence*). Coral reefs and polar ecosystems are highly vulnerable. Coastal systems and low-lying areas are at risk from sea-level rise, which will continue for centuries even if the global mean temperature is stabilized (*high confidence*).

Climate change is projected to undermine food security. Due to projected climate change by the mid-21st century and beyond, global marine species redistribution and marine biodiversity reduction in sensitive regions will challenge the sustained provision of fisheries productivity and other ecosystem services (*high confidence*). For wheat, rice, and maize in tropical and temperate regions, climate change without adaptation is projected to negatively impact production for local temperature increases of 2°C or more above late-20th century levels, although individual locations may benefit (*medium confidence*). Global temperature increases of ~4°C or more above late-20th century levels, combined with increasing food demand, would pose large risks to food security globally (*high confidence*). Climate change is projected to reduce renewable surface water and groundwater resources in most dry subtropical regions (*robust evidence, high agreement*), intensifying competition for water among sectors (*limited evidence, medium agreement*).

Until mid-century, projected climate change will impact human health mainly by exacerbating health problems that already exist (*very high confidence*). Throughout the 21st century, climate change is expected to lead to increases in ill-health in many regions and especially in developing countries with low income, as compared to a baseline without climate change (*high confidence*). By 2100 for RCP8.5, the combination of high temperature and humidity in some areas for parts of the year is expected to compromise common human activities, including growing food and working outdoors (*high confidence*).

In urban areas, climate change is projected to increase risks for people, assets, economies and ecosystems, including risks from heat stress, storms and extreme precipitation, inland and coastal flooding, landslides, air pollution, drought, water scarcity, sea-level rise, and storm surges (*very high confidence*). These risks are amplified for those lacking essential infrastructure and services or living in exposed areas.

Rural areas are expected to experience major impacts on water availability and supply, food security, infrastructure, and agricultural incomes, including shifts in the production areas of food and non-food crops around the world (*high confidence*).

Aggregate economic losses accelerate with increasing temperature (*limited evidence, high agreement*) but global economic impacts from climate change are currently difficult to estimate. From a poverty perspective, climate change impacts are projected to slow down economic growth, make poverty reduction more difficult, further erode food security, and prolong existing and create new poverty traps, the latter particularly in urban areas and emerging hotspots of hunger (*medium confidence*). International dimensions such as trade and relations among states are also important for understanding the risks of climate change at regional scales.

Climate change is projected to increase displacement of people (*medium evidence, high agreement*). Populations that lack the resources for planned migration experience higher exposure to extreme weather events, particularly in developing countries with low income. Climate change can indirectly increase risks of violent conflicts by amplifying well-documented drivers of these conflicts such as poverty and economic shocks (*medium confidence*).

SPM 2.4 Climate change beyond 2100, irreversibility and abrupt changes

> Many aspects of climate change and associated impacts will continue for centuries, even if anthropogenic emissions of greenhouse gases are stopped. The risks of abrupt or irreversible changes increase as the magnitude of the warming increases.

Warming will continue beyond 2100 under all RCP scenarios except RCP2.6. Surface temperatures will remain approximately constant at elevated levels for many centuries after a complete cessation of net anthropogenic CO_2 emissions. A large fraction of anthropogenic climate change resulting from CO_2 emissions is irreversible on a multi-century to millennial time scale, except in the case of a large net removal of CO_2 from the atmosphere over a sustained period.

[S]tabilization of global average surface temperature does not imply stabilization for all aspects of the climate system. Shifting biomes, soil carbon, ice sheets, ocean temperatures and associated sea-level rise all have their own intrinsic long timescales which will result in changes lasting hundreds to thousands of years after global surface temperature is stabilized.

There is *high confidence* that ocean acidification will increase for centuries if CO_2 emissions continue, and will strongly affect marine ecosystems.

It is *virtually certain* that global mean sea-level rise will continue for many centuries beyond 2100, with the amount of rise dependent on future emissions. The threshold for the loss of the Greenland ice sheet over a millennium or more, and an associated sea-level rise of up to 7 m, is greater than about 1°C (*low confidence*) but less than about 4°C (*medium confidence*) of global warming with respect to pre-industrial temperatures. Abrupt and irreversible ice loss from the Antarctic ice sheet is possible, but current evidence and understanding is insufficient to make a quantitative assessment.

Magnitudes and rates of climate change associated with medium- to high-emission scenarios pose an increased risk of abrupt and irreversible regional-scale change in the composition, structure, and function of marine, terrestrial and freshwater ecosystems, including wetlands (*medium confidence*). A reduction in permaforst extent is *virtually certain* with continued rise in global temperatures.

SPM 3. Future Pathways for Adaptation, Mitigation and Sustainable Development

> Adaptation and mitigation are complementary strategies for reducing and managing the risks of climate change. Substantial emissions reductions over the next few decades can reduce climate risks in the 21st century and beyond, increase prospects for effective adaptation, reduce the costs and challenges of mitigation in the longer term, and contribute to climate-resilient pathways for sustainable development.

SPM 3.1 Foundations of decision-making about climate change

> Effective decision making to limit climate change and its effects can be informed by a wide range of analytical approaches for evaluating expected risks and benefits, recognizing the importance of governance, ethical dimensions, equity, value judgments, economic assessments and diverse perceptions and responses to risk and uncertainty.

Sustainable development and equity provide a basis for assessing climate policies. Limiting the effects of climate change is necessary to achieve sustainable development and equity, including poverty eradication. Countries' past and future contributions to the accumulation of GHGs in the atmosphere are different, and countries also face varying challenges and circumstances and have different capacities to address mitigation and adaptation. Mitigation and adaptation raise issues of equity, justice, and fairness. Many of those most vulnerable to climate change have contributed and contribute little to GHG emissions. Delaying mitigation shifts burdens from the present to the future, and insufficient adaptation responses to emerging impacts are already eroding the basis for sustainable development. Comprehensive strategies in response to climate change that are consistent with sustainable development take into account the co-benefits, adverse side-effects and risks that may arise from both adaptation and mitigation options.

The design of climate policy is influenced by how individuals and organizations perceive risks and uncertainties and take them into account. Methods of valuation from economic, social and ethical analysis are available to assist decision making. These methods can take account of a wide range of possible impacts, including low-probability outcomes with large consequences. But they cannot identify a single best balance between mitigation, adaptation and residual climate impacts.

Climate change has the characteristics of a collective action problem at the global scale, because most greenhouse gases accumulate over time and mix globally, and emissions by any agent (e.g., individual, community, company, country) affect other agents. Effective mitigation will not be achieved if individual agents advance their own interests independently. Cooperative responses, including international cooperation, are therefore required to effectively mitigate GHG emissions and address other climate change issues. The effectiveness of adaptation can be enhanced through complementary actions across levels, including international cooperation. The evidence suggests that outcomes seen as equitable can lead to more effective cooperation.

SPM 3.2 Climate change risks reduced by mitigation and adaptation

> Without additional mitigation efforts beyond those in place today, and even with adaptation, warming by the end of the 21st century will lead to high to very high risk of severe, widespread, and irreversible impacts globally (*high confidence*). Mitigation involves some level of co-benefits and of risks due to adverse side-effects, but these risks do not involve the same possibility of severe, widespread, and irreversible impacts as risks from climate change, increasing the benefits from near-term mitigation efforts.

Mitigation and adaptation are complementary approaches for reducing risks of climate change impacts over different time scales (*high confidence*). Migitation, in the near-term and through the century, can substantially reduce climate change impacts in the latter decades of the 21st century and beyond. Benefits from adaptation can already be realized in addressing current risks, and can be realized in the future for addressing emerging risks.

Five "Reasons For Concern" (RFCs) aggregate climate change risks and illustrate the implications of warming and of adaptation limits for people, economies, and ecosystems across sectors and regions. The Five RFCs are associated with : (1) Unique and threatened systems, (2) Extreme weather events, (3) Distribution of impacts, (4) Global aggregate impacts, and (5) Large-scale singular events. In this report, the RFCs provide information relevant to Article 2 of UNFCCC.

Without additional mitigation efforts beyond those in place today, and even with adaptation, warming by the end of the 21st century will lead to high to very high risk of severe, widespread, and irreversible impacts globally (*high confidence*). In most scenarios without additional mitigation efforts (those with 2100 atmospheric concentrations > 1000ppm CO_2-eq), warming is *more likely than not* to exceed 4°C above pre-industrial levels by 2100. The risks associated with temperatures at or above 4°C include substantial species extinction, global and regional food insecurity, consequential constraints on common human activities, and limited potential for adaptation in some cases (*high confidence*). Some risks of climate change, such as risks to unique and threatened systems and risks associated with extreme weather events, are moderate to high at temperatures 1°C to 2°C above pre-industrial levels.

Substantial cuts in greenhouse gas emissions over the next few decades can substantially reduce risks of climate change by limiting warming in the second half of the 21st century and beyond. Cumulative emissions of CO_2 largely determine global mean surface warming by the late 21st century and beyond. Limiting risks across RFCs would imply a limit for cumulative emissions of CO_2. Such a limit would require that global net emissions of CO_2 eventually decrease to zero and would constrain annual emissions over the next few decades (*high confidence*). But some risks from climate damages are unavoidable, even with mitigation and adaptation.

Mitigation involves some level of co-benefits and risks, but these risks do not involve the same possibility of severe, widespread, and irreversible impacts as risks from climate change. Inertia in the economic and climate system and the possibility of irreversible impacts from climate change increase the benefits from near-term mitigation efforts (*high confidence*). Delays in additional mitigation or constraints on technological options increase the longer-term mitigation costs to hold climate change risks at a given level.

THE INTERGOVERNMENTAL PANEL ON CLIMATE CHANGE (IPCC) is the leading international body for the assessment of climate change. It was established by the United Nations Environment Programme (UNEP) and the World Meteorological Organization (WMO) in 1988 to provide the world with a clear scientific view on the current state of knowledge in climate change and its potential environmental and socio-economic impacts.

Steve Goreham    **NO**

The Mad, Mad, Mad World of Climatism: Mankind and Climate Change Mania

Introduction

I'll bet I know your thoughts about the climate. For years you've heard about how Earth is warming up. How people are the cause of global warming. How the polar bears are threatened with extinction. How we each must change our lifestyle for the good of the planet.

Television specials show calving glaciers and raging torrents from an ice melt in Greenland and voice concern over greenhouse gas emissions. Scientists report from Antarctica about pending disasters. A news story says that the flood in Pakistan is due to global warming. And wasn't Hurricane Katrina caused by climate change?

If you listen to the news, your national leaders promote new policies to fight climate change. Your nation must embrace renewable energy and reduce greenhouse gas emissions. There is talk about new taxes and regulations that will require sacrifices, but these are necessary to solve the climate crisis.

Of course, as a good citizen, you try to follow the lead. You've purchased some of the new compact fluorescent lights. They're a little expensive and it takes a while for them to get bright. They contain mercury—so you don't want to break one. Is it true that you can't buy any of the old incandescent bulbs anymore?

You're told that electric cars are the hot new technology. But they seem a little small and are said to have only a 40-mile range. Will they be available as a minivan or a pickup truck? If you buy one, where can you charge it?

You might have a new Vice President of Sustainability at your company. Purchases of expensive green energy and estimating the carbon dioxide output from processes are new policies. It's politically incorrect to question these policies, so you remain silent.

Your high school student comes home with concerns about climate change. It seems she has just seen Al Gore's movie in class. She asks if your family is doing enough to help save the planet.

A group of wind turbines was recently constructed in the next county. They look majestic, towering above fields and grazing livestock. But when you drive past them, many seem to be standing idle.

Yes, the world is certainly a greener place in response to all these changes. Yet, something deep down in your gut says that all this alarm about global warming just doesn't ring true. Maybe you've heard the demands for change, but they don't make sense in your daily life. Maybe you remember the 1970s, when scientists were concerned about global cooling and a pending ice age. But friends tell you now that your memory is faulty—there was no fear of an ice age back then.

You've been told that our air is being filled with "dangerous carbon pollution." But, you don't see any evidence of this. You recall the smog in our cities and foul-smelling polluted air when you were a child. Somehow it seems like the quality of air has improved during the last 30 years, despite the alarms from the news media.

Maybe you've just been through a tough winter, with mountainous drifts of snow and cold temperatures. Didn't the seasonal forecast call for a warm, dry winter? And what about Climategate—something about a scandal over temperature data at a university in Britain?

Well, your intuition about global warming is right. There is no direct scientific evidence that man-made greenhouse gases are causing catastrophic global warming. Instead, the world has been captured by the ideology of Climatism—the belief that man-made greenhouse gases are destroying Earth's climate. Most of the leaders in government, at universities, in scientific organizations, and in business say they believe in Climatism.

The astonishing thing is that *CO_2 is green!* Rather than being a pollutant, carbon dioxide makes plants grow! In a world turned upside down, every community and every company measures their "carbon footprint" and tries to reduce emissions of a harmless, invisible gas that is essential for photosynthesis and the growth of plants.

Don't misunderstand me. There are real pollutants that we need to control. For more than 25 years, I've had the joy of kayaking many of the great white water rivers of North America. From Texas to Idaho to Quebec, rivers have been a love of my life. I've paddled creeks on the Cumberland Plateau in Tennessee, Al Gore's home turf. Rivers are highlights of this amazing and beautiful world. We all want our water to be pure and our air to be clean. We're all environmentalists. But we must use sound science to determine man-made impacts on our climate. Sensible economics should drive our energy policy, not unfounded fears about global warming.

This book will take a common-sense look at global warming mania. We'll provide a down-to-earth discussion of the science, which increasingly shows that natural cycles of Earth are the dominant cause of climate change—not man-made greenhouse gas emissions. We'll discuss how climate science has been corrupted and look at the money and special interests that continue to drive the dogma of Climatism forward. We'll discuss renewable energy, which is proposed as a primary solution to stop climate change.

The arguments of this book are not just opinions, but are based on the work of hundreds of scientists across the world who challenge the theory of man-made global warming. Graphs and scientific data from peer-reviewed papers are used to show that man-made influences are actually only a very small part of Earth's climate. The evidence is available for all to see.

Chapters 1–2 discuss how our leaders have been captured by the false ideology of Climatism and the remedies proposed to change the life of every person on Earth. Climate science is discussed in Chapters 3–5. I encourage you to read the down-to-earth science in these chapters, but of course feel free to skip these if you're just interested in how the world has been smitten by climate madness. Chapters 6–7 discuss alarming claims about Earth's icecaps and weather, and show that these claims are not supported by scientific data. Chapter 8 exposes some of the biggest whoppers of global warming mania. Chapters 9–10 discuss bad science and the powerful role that money plays in this whole affair. Chapter 11 discusses the continuing shortcomings of renewable energy, despite many decades of media hype and promotion by governments. Don't miss Chapter 12, "You Can't Make This Stuff Up!"

Climate change is a serious topic. Government policies are proposed or already in place that will affect the light bulbs you buy, the construction of your house, the car or appliance you purchase, the price of your energy, your workplace, what your children are taught in school, and almost every aspect of your life. This book will help you sort fact from fiction in the global warming debate. It will remove the fear and paranoia that you and your family may be feeling from daily bombardment of climate change nonsense from work, school, and community.

Along the way, we'll have some fun. We'll discuss the wackiness of mankind turned on its head by global warming alarmism. This whole charade has moved from the serious to the absurd. Beware the sidebars, since a few of these are spoofs. But the rest are true headlines or quotes from our mad, mad, mad world of Climatism. Enjoy and, as the great Paul Harvey used to say, learn "the rest of the story" about climate change.

Climatism—Headed for a Crash

"It ain't what you don't know that gets you into trouble. It's what you know for sure that just ain't so."

—Mark Twain

For more than 20 years, the Intergovernmental Panel on Climate Change (IPCC) and the supporting scientific community, led by climate computer modelers, have successfully promoted the theory of man-made global warming. Almost every nation has accepted prophesies of disaster, responding with bizarre programs of every kind. Researchers at universities and government laboratories have cried "Alarm! Alarm!," gathering billions in funding to "solve" the climate crisis. Vast sums have been spent on dilute, intermittent, and expensive renewable energy projects—money that could be used instead to solve the real pressing problems of mankind. Businesses both large and small promote sustainability and sell green products, trusting that they are helping the environment. But as we discussed in Chapters 4 and 5, climate change is due to natural processes, probably driven by the sun, and man-made emissions play only a very small part. So the world is living in climate madness, certain of a pending climate catastrophe that isn't going to happen.

Climatism is headed for a fall. Recent trends in scientific data indicate the IPCC projections of catastrophe appear more and more far-fetched. Political leaders, once marching down the road of Climatism, are no longer certain of the right path. The renewable energy revolution is now threatened by the hard realities of economics and a new abundance of hydrocarbon energy. And citizens are questioning the scary scenario of man-made global warming. The coming disaster will not be about Earth's climate, but will instead be the destruction of the theory of man-made global warming.

Trends Show That the Models Are Wrong

We've now had 20 years to assess IPCC projections, and the projections are found wanting. Based on climate model simulations, the IPCC 1990 First Assessment Report told the world to expect a temperature rise of 0.3°C per decade, leading to 2025 temperatures that would be 1°C higher than 1990 temperatures. But satellite data shows that global temperatures have been flat to declining over at least the last ten years. Temperatures remain about 0.2°C above 1990 levels, but the rise has been substantially lower than the IPCC "low estimate" projection.

In a 2005 paper, Dr. James Hansen, head of NASA's Goddard Institute, warned of an "energy imbalance" due to rising atmospheric CO_2 that was causing Earth's oceans to absorb energy. He stated that this was confirmed by "precise measurements over the last 10 years." But measurements of ocean heat content before 2005 were based on sporadic data taken by passing ships, which was anything but precise.

Since 2000, 24 nations and the European Union have cooperated to deploy the Argo network. Argo is a global array of 3,500 buoys that measure temperature and salinity of the upper 2,000 meters of the ocean. With better ocean coverage and consistent measurements, Argo shows a surprising result. For the last eight years, there has been *no change* in ocean heat content, despite climate model predictions of a steady heat content rise. Dr. Kevin Trenberth of the National Center for Atmospheric Research was baffled by the "missing heat," stating in a 2009 paper:

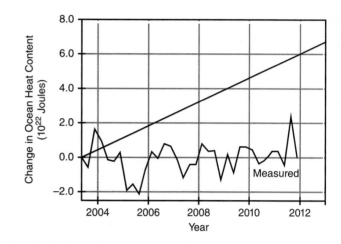

Model Projections and Actual Ocean Heat Content. Model projections diverging from Argo buoy measurements. (Hansen, 2005; National Oceanic Data Center; Evans, 2012)

. . . Was it because a lot of the heat went into melting Arctic sea ice or parts of Greenland and Antarctica, and other glaciers? Was it because the heat was buried in the ocean and sequestered, perhaps well below the surface? . . . Perhaps all of these things are going on?

In addition to the actual measurements of surface temperatures and ocean heat, natural climate cycles appear to be moving against the theory of man-made warming. Within the last ten years, two of the Earth's major climate cycles, the Pacific Decadal Oscillation and the Atlantic Multidecadal Oscillation, appear to have moved into a cool phase. Many solar physicists now predict a period of low solar activity in the current and coming Sunspot Cycles 24 and 25. All of these trends point to a coming period of cooler global temperatures, rather than the feared warming.

Science Does Not Support Climate Alarm

After 20 years, it's clear that climate catastrophe is not occurring. The modest 0.5°C warming from 1975 to 2000 was not abnormal compared to the Medieval Warm Period and other eras, and there has been no global warming for the last ten years. There is no evidence of increasing water vapor in Earth's atmosphere, and the model-predicted hot spot over the tropics has not appeared.

Water vapor is Earth's most abundant greenhouse gas. Contributions of carbon dioxide to Earth's atmosphere are overwhelmingly due to releases from the oceans, biosphere, and volcanoes. Man-made emissions produce only about one percent of Earth's greenhouse effect. Carbon

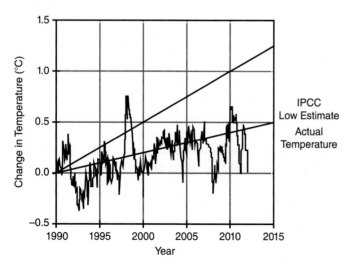

IPCC Projections and Actual Global Temperature. High, best, and low IPCC projections for global temperature from the IPCC First Assessment Report in 1990, compared to actual global temperature from satellite data. (IPCC First Assessment Report, 1990; UAH Satellite Data; Evans, 2012)

dioxide is plant food and the best substance humanity could release into the biosphere.

The Antarctic Icecap, which contains 90 percent of Earth's ice, continues to slowly expand. Ocean levels are rising at seven to eight inches per century, not the 20 feet per century predicted by Dr. Hansen and Mr. Gore. Hurricanes and tornados are neither more frequent nor more powerful on a global scale than those of the past. Polar bear populations are at a 50-year high, and stories of the bear's demise are greatly exaggerated. The fear of ocean acidification is based solely on computer model projections, without empirical evidence that changes in ocean pH are historically abnormal.

Climate science jumped to a wrong conclusion more than 20 years ago, and Climatism is now driven by money. The Climategate emails revealed that lead authors of the IPCC reports were strongly biased to develop data to support the false theory of man-made global warming. Despite the mounting evidence, NOAA, NASA, National Academy of Sciences, the Royal Society, and all major scientific organizations of the world continue to support the theory of man-made global warming. Many will be dining on a generous helping of crow when the world returns to climate reality.

The Failure of Global Negotiations

The year 2009 was set to be a year of triumph for Climatism. In 2007, the IPCC's Fourth Assessment Report declared that mankind was very likely the cause of global temperature increase. That same year, Al Gore and the IPCC shared the Nobel Peace Prize. In 2008, Barack Obama was elected President of the United States, heralding a rebirth of a more environmentally conscious nation. After securing the majority of primary delegates in June 2008, candidate Obama declared:

> . . . this was the moment when the rise of the oceans began to slow and our planet began to heal . . .

Following the President's lead, the US House of Representatives passed the Waxman-Markey cap-and-trade bill in June 2009 and sent it to the US Senate.

The Copenhagen Conference in December 2009, part of the United Nations Framework Convention on Climate Change (UNFCCC), was to be the major next step to control global emissions. Climate activists called for a successor treaty to replace and expand the Kyoto Protocol and establish binding emissions limits on all countries. In January 2009, the European Community (EC) proposed

a 30-percent emissions cut by year 2020 for developed nations and a 15- to 30-percent reduction in emissions from "business as usual" levels by large developing nations. More than 15,000 conference attendees, including President Obama and more than 100 other heads of state, traveled to Copenhagen. Despite differences between the developed and developing nations, conference delegates were cautiously optimistic.

But then the momentum collapsed. Throughout 2008 and 2009, opposition to the theory of man-made global warming gained headway with world opinion. The Heartland Institute sponsored the first of eight International Conferences on Climate Change in 2008 and 2009, providing skeptical scientists with a forum for realist climate views. In 2009, the Nongovernmental International Panel on Climate Change issued *Climate Change Reconsidered,* an 880-page volume that was the most extensive critique of the IPCC at the time. The report cited thousands of peer-reviewed articles and concluded that "natural causes are very likely to be the dominant cause" of global warming. Citizens began to recognize that man-made warming alarm was a political movement.

Then in late November 2009, just one week prior to the Copenhagen summit, the release of the Climategate emails shook the science of man-made warming. On their home turf of Copenhagen, European delegates had intended to use the conference to lead the world to a more aggressive climate treaty. But they were shocked when their proposals were ignored by developing nations. On the last day, Brazil, China, India, South Africa, and the United States crafted a weak, voluntary agreement named the Copenhagen Accord, which was then adopted. Delegates left the conference without either a binding agreement on emissions limits or a successor treaty to the Kyoto Protocol.

The combination of the failure at Copenhagen and the release of the Climategate emails shook many in the world community. German Chancellor Angela Merkel and other European leaders returned from the conference disillusioned and discouraged about the prospects for a global treaty. Copenhagen shattered the illusion that the world would join a Europe-led climate crusade.

In 2010, more bad news arrived from the United States. First, the Waxman-Markey cap-and-trade bill died in the Senate without even being called to a vote. Then in fall of 2010, mid-term elections saw Republicans capture a majority in the House of Representatives and gain seats in the Senate. Many first-term Republican representatives openly challenged the theory of man-made warming.

The 2010 Cancun and 2011 Durban climate conferences did little to restore the stalled momentum of the global warming movement. At Cancun, Mexico, representatives reaffirmed their commitment to limit the global temperature rise to 2°C and their pledge to establish a $100-billion climate fund for developing nations. Not that there was any new evidence that mankind could control global temperatures. The Durban, South Africa, conference called on members to negotiate a new agreement on binding emissions that would include all nations, to go into effect by 2020. The conference also proposed an extension of the Kyoto Protocol for another five years.

But key delegates to Durban were not pleased. Representatives from China and India made it clear that they were unhappy with emissions restrictions, stating that the industrial nations were responsible for emissions that caused the global warming problem. Shortly after the end of the Durban conference, Canada announced that it would not participate in an extension of the Kyoto Protocol. Japan and Russia subsequently also declined to participate, and the United States repeated that it would remain outside of the treaty.

After 20 years of climate negotiations and millions of hours of delegate time, the misguided nations of the world have achieved little. The Kyoto treaty ends in 2012, and a wide policy position gap continues to exist between the developed and developing nations. By 2010, global greenhouse gas emissions were *up 45 percent* from 1990 levels. Despite massive efforts to convert to renewables and to enact cap-and-trade and other foolish climate laws, *the growth rate in global emissions from 1990 to 2010 was the same as the growth rate from 1970 to 1990.* It's no wonder most Climatists are in despair.

Renewable Remedies Are Bankrupt

It's increasingly clear that the remedies of Climatism have failed. As we discussed in Chapter 11, wind and solar cannot replace conventional power plants if continuity of electrical supply is to be maintained. As we discussed in Chapter 11, the use of wind turbines forces backup plants to cycle inefficiently, releasing more harmful pollutants and CO_2 emissions than conventional power plants without wind. Similarly, when land usage is taken into account, vehicles using biofuel produce more pollutants and CO_2 emissions than gasoline or diesel-powered vehicles. "Sustainable" renewable sources use dozens of times more land than hydrocarbon or nuclear alternatives, and the production of biofuels requires much more water than gasoline or diesel fuel.

Rather than being at a point of peak oil and gas, we may be at a point of peak renewables, at least as a percentage of global energy usage. The great hope of Climatism

was that the cost of hydrocarbons would continue to rise, making renewables competitive. But the hydraulic fracturing revolution has driven the cost of natural gas down 70 percent in the US over the last decade. Electricity from natural gas plants is cheaper, generates lower emissions than combined wind-gas systems, and has a much smaller land footprint than wind systems. It appears that fracking will provide mankind with a supply of low-cost gas for at least 200 years. Why subsidize another wind turbine?

Faced with massive commitments for renewable subsidies, Germany, Greece, the Netherlands, Spain, the United Kingdom, and the United States have all recently cut subsidies for renewables. How many subsidies will remain when people realize that humans are not destroying Earth's climate? When the subsidies disappear, will fields and hills remain scarred by rusting turbines, with wind howling past unturning blades? Who will clean up the acres of solar cell panels, broken and weed-infested?

Europe and Decarbonization Folly

Europe is living in a fantasy world. The EC continues to push for a zero-carbon future, calling for an 80-percent emissions reduction by the year 2050. Although 2010 CO_2 emissions from 27 European nations were down 7 percent since 1990, much of this is due to a shift from production to imports. For example, official UK government numbers showed a 22-percent decline in CO_2 emissions from UK industry from 1990 to 2009. But total CO_2 missions associated with UK consumption *rose* 12 percent over the same period, because more goods were imported from abroad. When imports are considered, European nations aren't cutting anything.

Energy economics will preclude deep emissions cuts short of economic destruction. Solar systems don't deliver enough energy to make a difference. Wind systems, when considered with required hydrocarbon backup, don't reduce emissions. Nuclear, the only viable decarbonization choice, has been rejected by Austria, Belgium, Denmark, Germany, Italy, and Spain.

Transportation poses a special problem for decarbonization. European emissions from the transportation sector increased 36 percent from 1990 to 2007. As we discussed in Chapter 11, studies now show that ethanol and biodiesel fuels *do not* reduce emissions when used in place of gasoline, diesel, and aviation fuels. The EC has no alternative but to stop the use of cars, trucks, and planes, if transportation emissions are to be cut.

Nevertheless, Europe continues to march down the road of climate madness. Even a patio heater ban has been proposed to halt climate change. When will European citizens wake up to reality?

Sustainability: A House Built on Sand

According to the United Nations, "sustainable development" is development that meets "the needs of the present without compromising the needs of the future." Sustainability is now widely accepted by governments, businesses, universities, and most major organizations.

Economics taught us that resource scarcity was resolved by market pricing through supply and demand and substitution of goods. But sustainability tells us this isn't good enough. Instead, intellectual elites must direct the activities of mankind to preserve the planet for future generations.

At the core of sustainable development is a belief in man-made global warming. The United Nations and other proponents of sustainability call for reduced consumption, reduced production, and reduced energy usage. Wind, solar, and biofuels are defined as "sustainable," despite their ineffectiveness and land-hogging qualities when compared to traditional fuels. But since nature, not man, controls the climate, the philosophy of sustainable development is built on falsehood.

One Trillion Dollars Down a Green Drain

Every day, 25,000 people die from hunger-related issues in developing nations. More than 1 billion people are trying to survive on less than $1.25 per day. Two and one-half billion people do not have adequate sanitation, 1.4 billion do not have electricity, and almost 1 billion do not have access to clean drinking water. Every year, 2 million die from AIDS. Almost 2 million die from

tuberculosis. Malaria, pneumonia, and diarrheal diseases kill millions more.

The tragedy of Climatism is a misuse of resources on a vast scale. The world spent $243 billion in 2010 on renewable energy, trying to "decarbonize" energy systems. *More than $1 trillion was spent over the last ten years,* and governments and industries are on pace to waste another $1 trillion in the next four years on foolish climate programs. Each year, twice as much is spent in a futile attempt to stop global warming as is spent for total international aid. Imagine the benefits to the world's poor if decarbonization expenditures could be redirected to solve the problems of hunger, disease, and poverty.

Billions Will Figure It Out

Today, billions of people believe in the theory of man-made global warming. But year after year, temperatures do not follow model predictions, sea levels do not rise abnormally, the polar bears thrive, and predicted disasters do not occur. The world's citizens will figure it out. Changes in public opinion already show that citizens are beginning to learn the real story. The crash of Climatism will be thunderous.

Let's hasten the fall of Climatism and the awakening of mankind to climate reality. Climate change is natural and cars are innocent. Let's reallocate the vast funds spent in foolish efforts to fight global warming, to instead solve the real pressing problems of mankind.

STEVE GOREHAM is a speaker, author, and researcher on environmental issues and the executive director of the Climate Science Coalition of America.

EXPLORING THE ISSUE

Is Anthropogenic Global Warming Real and Dangerous?

Critical Thinking and Reflection

1. Does one's stance on global warming depend on one's source of funding?
2. Why do some people deny the weight of scientific evidence on matters of social importance (not just global warming)?
3. The IPCC's Fifth Assessment Report uses more recent data than the data Steve Goreham criticizes. Does this affect the believability of the two sides?

Is There Common Ground?

Both sides in this issue agree that human activities are increasing the carbon dioxide content of Earth's atmosphere. They differ in whether this is a problem.

1. If carbon dioxide is indeed a good thing (as a plant nutrient), is it possible to have too much of a good thing?
2. What is a "pollutant"?
3. Are there other pollutants (besides carbon dioxide) that can be seen as good things in certain circumstances?

Additional Resources

National Research Council, *Advancing the Science of Climate Change* (http://www.nap.edu/catalog.php?record _id=12782) (May 2010).

National Research Council, *Limiting the Magnitude of Future Climate Change* (http://www.nap.edu/catalog .php?record_id=12785) (May 2010).

National Research Council, *Adapting to the Impacts of Climate Change* (http://www.nap.edu/catalog.php?record _id=12783), (May 2010).

Nicholas Stern, *Stern Review: The Economics of Climate Change*, Executive Summary, October 30, 2006 (http://www.hm-treasury.gov.uk/independent_reviews /stern_review_economics_climate_change/stern review_index.cfm).

Internet References . . .

350.org

http://www.350.org/

The National Renewable Energy Laboratory

http:// www.nrel.gov/

Intergovernmental Panel on Climate Change

http://ipcc.ch/

Climate Change

http://www.unep.org/themes/climatechange/

Selected, Edited, and with Issue Framing Material by:
Thomas A. Easton, *Thomas College*

ISSUE

Is Home Solar the Wave of the Future?

YES: Peter Bronski et al., from "The Economics of Grid Defection," Rocky Mountain Institute (2014)

NO: Peter Kind, from "Disruptive Challenges: Financial Implications and Strategic Responses to a Changing Retail Electric Business," Edison Electric Institute (2013)

Learning Outcomes
After reading this issue, you will be able to: • Explain the benefits of home solar power.   • Explain why electric utilities see home solar as a threat.   • Explain why home solar power users still need the electric utility's infrastructure (or grid).   • Discuss ways utilities can raise the money to maintain the infrastructure (or grid).

ISSUE SUMMARY

YES: Peter Bronski et al., of the Rocky Mountain Institute (RMI) argue that the combination of home solar power with storage technologies such as batteries offer to make the electricity grid optional for many consumers, perhaps as early as the 2020s. Utilities have an opportunity to exploit the spread of "distributed electricity generation" to provide a robust, reliable electricity supply.

NO: Peter Kind, executive director of Energy Infrastructure Advocates, argues that increased interest in "distributed energy resources" such as home solar power and energy efficiency, among other factors, is threatening to reduce revenue and increase costs for electrical utilities. In order to protect investors and capital availability, electrical utilities must consider new charges for customers who reduce their electricity usage, decreased payments to homeowners using net metering, and even new charges to users of "distributed energy resources" to offset "stranded costs" (such as no longer needed power plants).

We have known how to generate electricity from the sun for many years. One technique that has actually been put to use by electric utilities uses mirrors to concentrate sunlight on a boiler, generate steam, and spin the turbines of electrical generators. The largest and most recent example is the Ivanpah solar farm in California's Mojave Desert; it was designed to produce over a million megawatt-hours of electricity per year, but weather and start-up issues have affected its performance (see Pete Danko, "At Ivanpah Solar Power Plant, Energy Production Falling Well Short of Expectations," *Breaking Energy*, October 29,

2014; http://breakingenergy.com/2014/10/29/at-ivanpah -solar-power-plant-energy-production-falling-well-short -of-expectations/).

A more direct use of sunlight to generate electricity relies on solar cells. They can be deployed anywhere a flat surface faces the sun—on rooves, on free-standing frameworks, and even on roads (the first example is a portion of a bike path in the Netherlands—see http://www .npr.org/blogs/thetwo-way/2014/11/10/363023227 /solar-bike-path-opens-this-week-in-the-netherlands. Of course, no solar power system can generate electricity when the sun isn't shining, as at night or in cloudy weather.

An effective solar power system therefore needs backup electricity sources or storage mechanisms such as batteries. It could also be an interconnected system spread out across multiple time zones. One solution is the "smart grid" that has been under discussion for the last few years. Russell Kay, "The Smart Grid," *Computerworld* (May 11, 2009), describes it as a more advanced and efficient version of the current grid (the network of power plants, power lines, substations, and computerized control stations that controls the distribution of electricity even when disrupted by storms, power plant failures, and other problems), with digital controls to coordinate a host of small and intermittent electricity sources, such as home solar and wind power. See also Mike Martin, "The Great Green Grid," *E Magazine* (July–August 2010).

As the price of solar cells has come down, their popularity has been increasing, aided by federal corporate investment credits and federal and state tax breaks, and even local subsidies, for homeowners. It now seems entirely possible that the technology could become very widely used. James M. Higgins, "Your Solar-Powered Future: It's Closer than You Thought," *The Futurist* (May–June 2009), tells us that "Ten years from now, power generation will be much more widely distributed. Homes and businesses alike will install solar-energy conversion systems for most—if not all—of their electrical needs." Ken Zweibel, James Mason, and Vasilis Fthenakis, "A Solar Grand Plan," *Scientific American* (January 2008), believe that with appropriate investment, solar can replace most or all conventional electricity generation; Mark Z. Jacobson and Mark A. Delucchi, "A Path to Sustainable Energy by 2030," *Scientific American* (November 2009), think it will take longer. But the process is already under way. At present, businesses such as SolarCity (http://www.solarcity.com/), Sungevity (http://www.sungevity.com/), Sunrun (http://www.sunrun.com/), and Vivint (http://www.vivintsolar.com/) offer consumers the chance to let the company install solar cells on home rooftops, use some of the electricity generated, and sell the rest to utilities. People can also buy solar systems outright, with or without battery backup.

In November 2014, Deutsche Bank released a report on Vivint which predicted that the cost of rooftop solar electricity, already equal to or less than the cost of coal and oil-fueled electricity in ten states of the United States, would match or beat those costs in all 50 states by 2016. And the technology is expected to get even cheaper. See Lucas Mearian, "Rooftop Solar Electricity on Pace to Beat Coal, Oil," *Computerworld* (November 18, 2014) (http://www.computerworld.com/article/2848875/rooftop-solar-electricity-on-pace-to-beat-coal-oil.html).

It is not surprising that consumers find rooftop solar appealing. It's already cheaper than utility electricity in some places, some states have implemented "net metering" (meaning that a homeowner who generates more electricity than needed can sell it to the local power company, and the power company has to buy it), in operation it does not emit greenhouse gases and thus contribute to global warming, and it offers independence from external systems. It also offers advantages to utilities, for if rooftop solar spreads, there will be less need to build huge new power plants. If homeowners opt to combine rooftop solar with battery storage systems, the need for poles and wires declines as well. However, that need does not seem likely to go away entirely; solar power depends on a steady supply of sunshine, and battery systems have finite capacity. Given a long spell of cloudy weather, people would still need the power company.

But, according to David Biello, "Solar Wars," *Scientific American* (November 2014), the trend is already worrying electrical utilities. As more and more states mandate that utilities buy surplus electricity from home providers and as home providers proliferate, the utilities see a day coming when their profits will be seriously affected. Worse yet, regulators require them to maintain the electrical grid—poles, wires, transformers, and power plants—that currently supplies everyone with a dependable supply of electricity and to recoup the costs by charging their customers. If they lose customers, they must either charge the remaining customers more or find a way to bill noncustomers. In Florida, local government seems prepared to help by preventing people from disconnecting from the grid (http://www.nbc-2.com/story/24790572/cape-woman-living-of-the-grid-challenged-by-city#.VGjCsMltgpE). In Hawaii, utilities restrict or block rooftop solar. In other states, they are pushing hard to do the same.

Is home solar power really a threat to utilities? If you take the stance that utilities have a right to keep making money and attracting investors the same way they have for the last century, perhaps it is. But if you think that home solar power offers ways to retool their business model, perhaps not. In the YES selection, Peter Bronski et al. of the Rocky Mountain Institute argue that the combination of home solar power with storage technologies such as batteries offers to make the electricity grid optional for many consumers, perhaps as early as the 2020s. Utilities have opportunities to exploit the spread of "distributed electricity generation" to provide a robust, reliable electricity supply. The authors are working on a second report about the implications of these "disruptive opportunities" for utility business models. In the NO selection, Peter Kind, executive director of Energy Infrastructure Advocates, argues that increased interest in "distributed energy resources" such as home solar power and energy efficiency, among other factors, is threatening to reduce revenue and increase costs for electrical utilities. In order to protect investors and capital availability, electrical utilities must consider new charges for customers who reduce their electricity usage, decreased payments to homeowners using net metering, and even new charges to users of "distributed energy resources" to offset "stranded costs" (such as no longer needed power plants).

YES

Peter Bronski et al.

The Economics of Grid Defection

Introduction

Utilities in the United States today face a variety of challenges to their traditional business models. An aging grid makes substantial investment in maintaining and modernizing system infrastructure a looming need. Meanwhile, myriad factors are making kWh sales decay a real concern, threatening the traditional mechanism by which regulated utilities recover costs and earn allowed market returns associated with infrastructure investment, as well as threatening the business model for all other types of utilities. These factors include:

- The falling costs and growing adoption of distributed generation (DG) and the prevalence of net-metering policies for integrating that DG
- Flat or even declining electricity demand, driven in part by increasing energy efficiency efforts as well as expanding demand-side strategies to manage electricity consumption

In addition, the electricity sector faces increasing social and regulatory pressures to reduce the carbon intensity and other environmental and health impacts of power generation.

Together, these forces undermine the "old" model of central power generation, transmission, and distribution. In particular, the combination of increasing costs and declining revenues creates upward price pressure. Yet higher retail electricity prices further prompt customers to invest in efficiency and distributed generation, creating a self-reinforcing cycle sometimes known as the utility death spiral.

The idea of a utility death spiral, while not new, is increasingly relevant in its potential reality. Once upon a time, the utility death spiral was considered a potential outcome of efficiency. The growth of grid-connected distributed generation later added to death spiral concern. And while some customers have more choice than others, the trend of increasing options for electricity supply is likely here to stay. Now, there's also a fundamentally different growing threat and emerging opportunity wrapped up into one: combined distributed generation and energy storage. Other challenges, such as DG alone and energy efficiency, still maintain customers' grid dependence. Combined DG and storage, and in particular, solar-plus-battery systems, give a customer the option to go from grid connected to grid defected—customers could secede from the macro grid entirely.

Utilities have recently acknowledged this day could come. The Edison Electric Institute's January 2013 report, *Disruptive Challenges,* noted:

> Due to the variable nature of renewables, there is a perception that customers will always need to remain on the grid. While we would expect customers to remain on the grid until a fully viable and economic distributed non-variable resource is available, one can imagine a day when battery storage technology or micro turbines could allow customers to be electric grid independent.

Two mutually reinforcing accelerants—declining costs for distributed energy technologies and increasing adoption of those technologies—are rapidly transforming the electricity market in ways that suggest grid parity (i.e., economic and technical service equality with the electrical grid) for solar-plus-battery systems is coming sooner than many had anticipated.

Declining Costs for Distributed Energy Technologies

Trends for Solar PV

The distributed U.S. solar industry has experienced robust growth in recent years, delivering an average annual installed capacity increase of 62% from 2010 to 2012. Lower hardware costs (largely thanks to the collapse in PV module prices) and the rapid expansion of third-party financing for residential and commercial customers have fueled this growth.

We expect solar PV's levelized cost of energy (LCOE) to continue to decline through 2020 and beyond, despite both the likely end of the residential renewable energy tax credit and the reduction (from 30% to 10%) of the business energy investment tax credit in 2016. Further drops in upfront costs per installed Watt and additional improvements in solar PV finance (i.e., reduced cost of capital) will help drive the continued declines in solar PV's LCOE.

Trends for Battery Technology

Electric vehicle (EV) market growth has driven the lithium-ion (Li-ion) battery industry's recent expansion. Though it lags behind the growth of the solar PV market, it has still been significant in recent years. Coupled with greater opportunities for on-grid energy storage, including those enabled by regulations such as the Federal Energy Regulatory Commission's (FERC) Order 755 and California's AB 2514, battery demand is surging. Opportunities in both the vehicle and grid markets will continue to drive the energy storage industry for the foreseeable future, yielding lower costs for batteries for mobile and stationary applications.

Support Technologies Unlock More Value

The evolution of support systems—including improved energy systems controls—is progressing apace. Synergistically, these controls have improved the value proposition of solar PV and batteries, thus creating further demand. In addition, smart inverters have seen price reductions and continue to offer new capabilities, unlocking new opportunities for their application and the increased integration of distributed energy resources.

Given the fast-moving technology landscape, we took a conservative view that represents steady progress and is aligned with published projections. However, with high innovation rates in solar, storage, and support technologies, it is conceivable that we underestimate progress in our base case.

Forces Driving Adoption of Off-Grid Systems

Based on our research and interviews with subject matter experts, we identified at least five forces driving the increased adoption of off-grid hybrid distributed generation and storage systems:

- Interest in reliability and resilience
- Demand for cleaner energy
- Pursuit of better economics

- Utility and grid frustration
- Regulatory changes

Interest in Reliability and Resilience

From severe weather events such as Superstorm Sandy, to direct physical attacks on grid infrastructure in Arkansas and Silicon Valley, to reports on the potential for major system damage from geomagnetic storms, the fragility of the U.S. electric grid is now a nearly constant media topic. As a byproduct of the U.S.'s early advance into the electrical age, our systems are among the oldest on the planet and experience triple the frequency disruptions and ten times the duration of system outages compared to some OECD peer nations such as Germany and Denmark. In fact, in little over a decade, the U.S. has witnessed some of the most severe power outages in its history.

An increasingly popular solution to these reliability challenges is islandable microgrids, which produce and consume power locally in small, self-balancing networks capable of separating from and rejoining the larger grid on demand. They have a point of common coupling to the grid, and include both generation and loads that can be managed in a coordinated manner. Navigant Research forecasts the microgrid market to reach as high as $40 billion in the U.S. by 2020.

A more extreme example of this trend, yet similarly connected to reliability and resilience interests, is permanently off-grid buildings. Prior to 2000 off-grid solar installations made up over 50% of solar PV projects. While currently a minute portion of total solar PV sales, such off-grid solar has actually continued its growth in absolute sales. Though the majority of solar PV was off grid prior to 2000 primarily because it was used in remote locations where grid connection was a more difficult and expensive proposition, we're likely in the midst of a new era of off-grid solar PV (with batteries) within grid-accessible locations. The conversation has shifted from being off grid out of necessity to being off grid out of choice.

Demand for Cleaner Energy

Demand for cleaner energy with a lower carbon intensity and softer environmental footprint is on the rise.

On the commercial side, major corporations such as Walmart, Costco, IKEA, and Apple are increasingly "going solar." According to the World Wildlife Fund's *Power Forward* report, nearly 60% of Fortune 100 and Global 100 companies have renewable energy targets, greenhouse gas emissions goals, or both. These commitments are driving increased investment in renewable energy, including distributed solar PV. As of mid-2013, cumulative U.S. commercial solar installations totaled 3,380 MW, a 40% increase over the previous year.

On the residential side, a 2012 survey of nearly 200 solar homeowners found that even if solar's economics weren't favorable, 1 in 4 would *still* have chosen to install a solar PV system because of their passion for the environment. An earlier survey of more than 640 solar installs—primarily residential—found that reducing one's carbon footprint ranked nearly equal with reducing one's energy bill among the top reasons customers chose to go solar. Small residential applications for completely off-grid homes have existed within the United States for many years. These homes and businesses were usually owned by the environmentally-driven consumer, as these buildings had to be energy sippers, because of the then-high cost of renewable energy technologies such as solar, wind, and storage.

Pursuit of Better Economics

Most remote locations without substantial energy infrastructure—like many islands—have been largely dependent on diesel fuel and diesel gensets to meet their electrical needs. In places such as Hawaii, Puerto Rico, Alaskan villages, and the U.S. Virgin Islands, expensive imported petroleum (e.g., diesel, fuel oil) provides 68%–99% of electricity generation, resulting in retail electricity prices of $0.36–$0.50 per kWh or more.

Thus on islands and anywhere with high retail electricity prices, there is a strong economic case for reducing the use of diesel fuel as a primary fuel source for electrical power, especially considering that the retail price of diesel in the U.S. has increased 233%-real in the past 15 years.

Yet in 2013, liquid fuels were used for nearly 5% of global electricity production, accounting for 948 billion kilowatt-hours of generation, 387 GW of installed capacity, and nearly 5 million barrels/day of fuel consumption. Further, projections from a new Navigant Research report suggest that annual installations of standby diesel generators will reach 82 GW per year by 2018, signifying a growing opportunity for solar-plus-battery systems.

Utility and Grid Frustration

While in the past the grid barely warranted a second thought for most people, sentiment is changing. This change will only get worse as interconnection delays and red tape, arguments over net metering, and potentially rising prices continue to affect consumers. This reputational erosion poses additional challenges to utilities, above and beyond the increasingly competitive economics of off-grid solutions.

For example, in Hawaii, where utility interconnection limitations are making it impossible for many customers to take on grid-connected solar, off-grid development is increasing. Similar desires from individuals for some semblance of energy independence—particularly the right to garner external financing for systems on their private property—led to an unlikely political alliance between conservatives and liberals in Georgia in 2012, as well as current, similarly across-the-aisle political activities in Arizona.

Regulatory Changes

Rapid scaling of solar PV, and now grid-connected solar-plus-battery systems, are requiring federal, utility, state, and local regulators to explore new regulatory frameworks. Distributed generation and storage don't fit neatly into the traditional utility model of generation, distribution, and load or existing pricing structures that recover utilities' fixed costs through energy sales.

In California, where battery storage targets and incentives have made solar-plus-battery systems more attractive, utilities including Southern California Edison, PG&E, and Sempra Energy have made it challenging for system owners with storage to net meter their power. The utilities expressed concern that customers could store grid electricity on their batteries and then sell it back to the grid at higher prices. This upset current customers who have had battery storage for some time and were surprised by the utilities' decisions. The matter impacts both California Public Utility Commission regulation as well as the state's Renewable Portfolio Standard.

Perceived negative outcomes from regulation can drive customers, who desire solar PV and batteries for other factors, to pursue off-grid solutions.

In addition, incentives to promote storage could accelerate battery price declines, thereby increasing uptake of off-grid solutions. Several pro-storage regulations have recently been enacted. While they were primarily created with grid connectivity in mind, the overall development of the storage market and accompanying controls and other integration systems likely will lead to more robust and affordable off-grid storage applications. . . .

Conclusion

Rising retail electricity prices (driven in part by rising utility costs), increasing energy efficiency, falling costs for distributed energy technologies such as solar-plus-battery systems, and increasing adoption of distributed energy options are fundamentally shifting the landscape of the electricity system. Our analysis shows that solar-plus-battery systems will reach grid parity—for growing numbers of customers in certain geographies, especially those with high retail electricity prices—well within the 30-year period by which utilities capitalize major power assets. Millions of customers, commercial earlier than residential, representing billions of dollars in utility revenues will find themselves in a position to cost effectively defect from the grid if they so choose.

The so-called utility death spiral is proving not just a hypothetical threat, but a real, near, and present one. The coming grid parity of solar-plus-battery systems in the foreseeable future, among other factors, signals the eventual demise of traditional utility business models. Furthermore, early adopters and kWh sales decay will make utilities feel the pinch even before the rapidly approaching day of grid parity is here, while more aggressive technology improvements and investments in demand-side improvements beyond our base case would accelerate grid parity. Though utilities could and should see this as a threat, especially if they cling to increasingly challenged legacy business models, they can also see solar-plus-battery systems as an opportunity to add value to the grid and their business. When solar-plus-battery systems are integrated into a network, new opportunities open up that generate even greater value for customers and the network (e.g., potentially better customer-side economics, additional sizing options, ability of distributed systems to share excess generation or storage). The United States' electric grid is in the midst of transformation, but that shift need not be an either/or between central and distributed generation. Both forms of generation, connected by an evolving grid, have a role to play.

Having conducted an analysis of when and where grid parity will happen in this report, the important next question is how utilities, regulators, technology providers, and customers might work together to reshape the market—either within existing regulatory frameworks or under an evolved regulatory landscape—to tap into and maximize new sources of value offered by these disruptive opportunities to build the best electricity system of the future that delivers value and affordability to customers and society. The implications of these disruptive opportunities on business model design are the subject of ongoing work by the authors and their institutions, covered in a forthcoming report to follow soon.

PETER BRONSKI is the editorial director at the Rocky Mountain Institute, a nonprofit "think-and-do" tank that promotes the cost-effective shift from fossil fuels to efficiency and renewables.

JON CREYTS is a managing director at the Rocky Mountain Institute, a nonprofit "think-and-do" tank that promotes the cost-effective shift from fossil fuels to efficiency and renewables.

LEIA GUCCIONE is a manager with the Rocky Mountain Institute's electricity and industrial practices, where she specializes in microgrids, campus energy systems, industrial ecosystems, distributed generation and storage, and renewable energy procurement strategies.

MAITE MADRAZO is currently a research assistant in the Institute for Sustainable Enterprise, University of Michigan.

JAMES MANDEL is a principal at the Rocky Mountain Institute, working in industrial and electricity practices.

BODHI RADER is an associate with RMI's electricity practice, where he specializes in microgrids, distributed renewable generation, energy storage, vehicle-to-grid technology, and smart grids.

DAN SEIF is a former principal with RMI's electricity and industrial practices, and is focusing on industrial efficiency and solar PV thrusts.

PETER LILIENTHAL is the original developer of the HOMER® software at the National Renewable Energy Laboratory and founded HOMER Energy in 2009 to enhance and commercialize the software.

JOHN GLASSMIRE is a globally-minded engineer at HOMER Energy who has worked across a wide-range of infrastructure projects. He has interests in sustainable design, renewable energy, project management, and international development.

JEFFREY ABROMOWITZ worked with HOMER Energy, which provides software and consulting services for distributed power systems.

MARK CROWDIS is president of Reznick Think Energy, which he founded in 2000.

JOHN RICHARDSON is an investment banking analyst with Reznick Capital Markets Securities.

EVAN SCHMITT is currently a financial analyst at Infigen Energy.

HELEN TOCCO is a civil engineer with CohnReznick Think Energy.

Peter Kind  **NO**

Disruptive Challenges: Financial Implications and Strategic Responses to a Changing Retail Electric Business

Executive Summary

Recent technological and economic changes are expected to challenge and transform the electric utility industry. These changes (or "disruptive challenges") arise due to a convergence of factors, including: falling costs of distributed generation and other distributed energy resources (DER); an enhanced focus on development of new DER technologies; increasing customer, regulatory, and political interest in demand-side management technologies (DSM); government programs to incentivize selected technologies; the declining price of natural gas; slowing economic growth trends; and rising electricity prices in certain areas of the country. Taken together, these factors are potential "game changers" to the U.S. electric utility industry, and are likely to dramatically impact customers, employees, investors, and the availability of capital to fund future investment. The timing of such transformative changes is unclear, but with the potential for technological innovation (e.g., solar photovoltaic or PV) becoming economically viable due to this confluence of forces, the industry and its stakeholders must proactively assess the impacts and alternatives available to address disruptive challenges in a timely manner.

This paper considers the financial risks and investor implications related to disruptive challenges, the potential strategic responses to these challenges, and the likely investor expectations to utility plans going forward. There are valuable lessons to be learned from other industries, as well as prior utility sector paradigm shifts, that can assist us in exploring risks and potential strategic responses.

The financial risks created by disruptive challenges include declining utility revenues, increasing costs, and lower profitability potential, particularly over the long-term. As DER and DSM programs continue to capture "market share," for example, utility revenues will be reduced.

Adding the higher costs to integrate DER, increasing subsidies for DSM and direct metering of DER will result in the potential for a squeeze on profitability and, thus, credit metrics. While the regulatory process is expected to allow for recovery of lost revenues in future rate cases, tariff structures in most states call for non-DER customers to pay for (or absorb) lost revenues. As DER penetration increases, this is a cost-recovery structure that will lead to political pressure to undo these cross subsidies and may result in utility stranded cost exposure.

While the various disruptive challenges facing the electric utility industry may have different implications, they all create adverse impacts on revenues, as well as on investor returns, and require individual solutions as part of a comprehensive program to address these disruptive trends. Left unaddressed, these financial pressures could have a major impact on realized equity returns, required investor returns, and credit quality. As a result, the future cost and availability of capital for the electric utility industry would be adversely impacted. This would lead to increasing customer rate pressures.

The regulatory paradigm that has supported recovery of utility investment has been in place since the electric utility industry reached a mature state in the first half of the 20th century. Until there is a significant, clear, and present threat to this recovery paradigm, it is likely that the financial markets will not focus on these disruptive challenges, despite the fact that electric utility capital investment is recovered over a period of 30 or more years (i.e., which exposes the industry to stranded cost risks). However, with the current level of lost load nationwide from DER being less than 1 percent, investors are not taking notice of this phenomenon, despite the fact that the pace of change is increasing and will likely increase further as costs of disruptive technologies benefit further from scale efficiencies.

Investors, particularly equity investors, have developed confidence throughout time in a durable industry financial recovery model and, thus, tend to focus on earnings growth potential over a 12- to 24-month period.

So, despite the risks that a rapidly growing level of DER penetration and other disruptive challenges may impose, they are not currently being discussed by the investment community and factored into the valuation calculus reflected in the capital markets. In fact, electric utility valuations and access to capital today are as strong as we have seen in decades, reflecting the relative safety of utilities in this uncertain economic environment.

In the late 1970s, deregulation started to take hold in two industries that share similar characteristics with the electric utility industry—the airline industry and the telecommunications industry (or "the telephone utility business"). Both industries were price- and franchise-regulated, with large barriers to entry due to regulation and the capital-intensive nature of these businesses. Airline industry changes were driven by regulatory actions (a move to competition), and the telecommunications industry experienced technology changes that encouraged regulators to allow competition. Both industries have experienced significant shifts in the landscape of industry players as a result.

In the airline sector, each of the major U.S. carriers that were in existence prior to deregulation in 1978 faced bankruptcy. The telecommunication businesses of 1978, meanwhile, are not recognizable today, nor are the names of many of the players and the service they once provided ("the plain old telephone service"). Both industries experienced poor financial market results by many of the former incumbent players for their investors (equity and fixed-income) and have sought mergers of necessity to achieve scale economies to respond to competitive dynamics.

The combination of new technologies, increasing costs, and changing customer-usage trends allow us to consider alternative scenarios for how the future of the electric sector may develop. Without fundamental changes to regulatory rules and recovery paradigms, one can speculate as to the adverse impact of disruptive challenges on electric utilities, investors, and access to capital, as well as the resulting impact on customers from a price and service perspective. We have the benefit of lessons learned from other industries to shift the story and move the industry in a direction that will allow for customers, investors, and the U.S. economy to benefit and prosper.

Revising utility tariff structures, particularly in states with potential for high DER adoption, to mitigate (or eliminate) cross subsidies and provide proper customer price signals will support economic implementation of DER while limiting stress on non-DER participants and utility finances. This is a near-term, must-consider action by all policy setting industry stakeholders.

The electric utility sector will benefit from proactive assessment and planning to address disruptive challenges. Thirty year investments need to be made on the basis that they will be recoverable in the future in a timely manner. To the extent that increased risk is incurred, capital deployment and recovery mechanisms need to be adapted accordingly. The paper addresses possible strategic responses to competitive threats in order to protect investors and capital availability. While the paper does not propose new business models for the industry to pursue to address disruptive challenges in order to protect investors and retain access to capital, it does highlight several of the expectations and objectives of investors, which may lead to business model transformation alternatives.

Background

As a result of a confluence of factors (i.e., technological innovation, public policy support for sustainability and efficiency, declining trends in electricity demand growth, rising price pressures to maintain and upgrade the U.S. distribution grid, and enhancement of the generation fleet), the threat of disruptive forces (i.e., new products/markets that replace existing products/markets) impacting the utility industry is increasing and is adding to the effects of other types of disruptive forces like declining sales and end-use efficiency. While we cannot lay out an exact roadmap or timeline for the impact of potential disruptive forces, given the current shift in competitive dynamics, the utility industry and its stakeholders must be prepared to address these challenges in a way that will benefit customers, long-term economic growth, and investors. Recent business history has provided many examples of companies and whole industries that either failed or were slow to respond to disruptive forces and suffered as a result.

Today, a variety of disruptive technologies are emerging that may compete with utility-provided services. Such technologies include solar photovoltaics (PV), battery storage, fuel cells, geothermal energy systems, wind, micro turbines, and electric vehicle (EV) enhanced storage. As the cost curve for these technologies improves, they could directly threaten the centralized utility model. To promote the growth of these technologies in the near-term, policymakers have sought to encourage disruptive competing energy sources through various subsidy programs, such as tax incentives, renewable portfolio standards, and net metering where the pricing structure of utility services allows customers to engage in the use of new technologies, while shifting costs/lost revenues to remaining non-participating customers.

In addition, energy efficiency and DSM programs also promote reduced utility revenues while causing the utility to incur implementation costs. While decoupling recovery mechanisms, for example, may support recovery of lost revenues and costs, under/over recovery charges are typically imposed based on energy usage and, therefore, adversely impact non-participants of these programs. While the financial community is generally quite supportive of decoupling to capture lost revenues, investors have not delved into the long-term business and financial impact of cross subsidization on future customer rates inherent in most decoupling models and the effective recovery thereof. In other words, will non-DER participants continue to subsidize participants or will there be political pressure to not allow cost pass thru over time?

The threat to the centralized utility service model is likely to come from new technologies or customer behavioral changes that reduce load. Any recovery paradigms that force cost of service to be spread over fewer units of sales (i.e., kilowatt-hours or kWh) enhance the ongoing competitive threat of disruptive alternatives. While the cost—recovery challenges of lost load can be partially addressed by revising tariff structures (such as a fixed charge or demand charge service component), there is often significant opposition to these recovery structures in order to encourage the utilization of new technologies and to promote customer behavior change.

But, even if cross-subsidies are removed from rate structures, customers are not precluded from leaving the system entirely if a more cost-competitive alternative is available (e.g., a scenario where efficient energy storage combined with distributed generation could create the ultimate risk to grid viability). While tariff restructuring can be used to mitigate lost revenues, the longer-term threat of fully exiting from the grid (or customers solely using the electric grid for backup purposes) raises the potential for irreparable damages to revenues and growth prospects. This suggests that an old-line industry with 30-year cost recovery of investment is vulnerable to cost-recovery threats from disruptive forces.

Generators in organized, competitive markets are more directly exposed to threats from new technologies and enhanced efficiency programs, both of which reduce electricity use and demand. Reduced energy use and demand translate into lower prices for wholesale power and reduced profitability. With reduced profitability

comes less cash flow to invest and to support the needs of generation customers. While every market-driven business is subject to competitive forces, public policy programs that provide for subsidized growth of competing technologies and/or participant economic incentives do not provide a level playing field upon which generators can compete fairly against new entrants. As an example subsidized demand response programs or state contracted generation additions create threats to the generation owner (who competes based upon free market supply and demand forces).

According to the Solar Electric Power Association (SEPA), there were 200,000 distributed solar customers (aggregating 2,400 megawatts or MW) in the United States as of 2011. Thus, the largest near-term threat to the utility model represents less than 1 percent of the U.S. retail electricity market. Therefore, the current level of activity can be "covered over" without noticeable impact on utilities or their customers. However, at the present time, 70 percent of the distributed activity is concentrated within 10 utilities, which obviously speaks to the increased risk allocated to a small set of companies. As previously stated, due to a confluence of recent factors, the threat to the utility model from disruptive forces is now increasingly viable. One prominent example is in the area of distributed solar PV, where the threats to the centralized utility business model have accelerated due to:

- The decline in the price of PV panels from $3.80/watt in 2008 to $0.86/watt in mid-2012. While some will question the sustainability of cost-curve trends experienced, it is expected that PV panel costs will not increase (or not increase meaningfully) even as the current supply glut is resolved. As a result, the all-in cost of PV solar installation approximates $5/watt with expectations of the cost declining further as scale is realized;

- An increase in utility rates such that the competitive price opportunity for PV solar is now "in the market" for approximately 16 percent of the U.S. retail electricity market where rates are at or above $0.15/kWh. In addition, projections by PV industry participants suggest that the "in the money" market size will double the share of contestable revenue by 2017 (to 33 percent, or $170 billion of annual utility revenue);

- Tax incentives that promote specific renewable resources, including the 30-percent Investment Tax Credit (ITC) that is effective through 2016 and five-year accelerated depreciation recovery of net asset costs;

- Public policies to encourage renewable resource development through Renewable Portfolio Standards (RPS), which are in place in 29 states and the District of Columbia and which call for renewable generation goals within a state's energy mix;
- Public policies to encourage net metering, which are in effect in 43 states and the District of Columbia (3 additional states have utilities with voluntary net metering programs) and which typically allow customers to sell excess energy generated back to the utility at a price greater than the avoided variable cost;
- Time-of-use rates, structured for higher electric rates during daylight hours, that create incentives for installing distributed solar PV, thereby taking advantage of solar benefit (vs. time-of-use peak rates) and net metering subsidies; and
- The evolution of capital markets' access to businesses that leverage the dynamics outlined above to support a for-profit business model. Examples include tax equity financing, project finance lending, residential PV leasing models (i.e., "no money down" for customers), and public equity markets for pure play renewable resource providers and owners. As an illustration, U.S. tax equity investment is running at $7.5 billion annualized for 2012. Add other sources of capital, including traditional equity, and this suggests the potential to fund a large and growing industry.

Bloomberg New Energy Finance (BNEF) projects that distributed solar capacity will grow rapidly as a result of the competitive dynamics highlighted. BNEF projects 22-percent compound annual growth in PV installations through 2020, resulting in 30 gigawatts (GW) of capacity overall (and approximately 4.5 GW coming from distributed PV). This would account for 10 percent of capacity in key markets coming from distributed resources and even a larger share of year-round energy generated.

Assuming a decline in load, and possibly customers served, of 10 percent due to DER with full subsidization of DER participants, the average impact on base electricity prices for non-DER participants will be a 20 percent or more increase in rates, and the ongoing rate of growth in electricity prices will double for non-DER participants (before accounting for the impact of the increased cost of serving distributed resources). The fundamental drivers previously highlighted could suggest even further erosion of utility market share if public policy is not addressed to normalize this competitive threat.

While the immediate threat from solar PV is location dependent, if the cost curve of PV continues to bend

and electricity rates continue to increase, it will open up the opportunity for PV to viably expand into more regions of the country. According to ThinkEquity, a boutique investment bank, as the installed cost of PV declines from $5/watt to $3.5/watt (a 30-percent decline), the targeted addressable market increases by 500 percent, including 18 states and 20 million homes, and customer demand for PV increases by 14 times. If PV system costs decline even further, the market opportunity grows exponentially. In addition, other DER technologies being developed may also pose additional viable alternatives to the centralized utility model.

Due to the variable nature of renewable DER, there is a perception that customers will always need to remain on the grid. While we would expect customers to remain on the grid until a fully viable and economic distributed non-variable resource is available, one can imagine a day when battery storage technology or micro turbines could allow customers to be electric grid independent. To put this into perspective, who would have believed 10 years ago that traditional wire line telephone customers could economically "cut the cord?"

The cost of providing interconnection and back-up supply for variable resources will add to the utility cost burden. If not properly addressed in the tariff structure, the provision of these services will create additional lost revenues and will further challenge non-DER participants in terms of being allocated costs incurred to serve others.

Another outcome of the trend of rising electricity prices is the potential growth in the market for energy efficiency solutions. Combining electricity price trends, customer sustainability objectives, and ratemaking incentives via cross-subsidies, it is estimated that spending on energy efficiency programs will increase by as much as 300 percent from 2010 to 2025, within a projected range of $6 to $16 billion per year. This level of spending on energy efficiency services will have a meaningful impact on utility load and, thus, will create significant additional lost revenue exposure.

The financial implications of these threats are fairly evident. Start with the increased cost of supporting a network capable of managing and integrating distributed generation sources. Next, under most rate structures, add the decline in revenues attributed to revenues lost from sales foregone. These forces lead to increased revenues required from remaining customers (unless fixed costs are recovered through a service charge tariff structure) and sought through rate increases. The result of higher electricity prices and competitive threats will encourage a higher rate of DER additions, or will promote greater use of efficiency or demand-side solutions.

Increased uncertainty and risk will not be welcomed by investors, who will seek a higher return on investment and force defensive-minded investors to reduce exposure to the sector. These competitive and financial risks would likely erode credit quality. The decline in credit quality will lead to a higher cost of capital, putting further pressure on customer rates. Ultimately, capital availability will be reduced, and this will affect future investment plans. The cycle of decline has been previously witnessed in technology-disrupted sectors (such as telecommunications) and other deregulated industries (airlines).

Disruptive Threats—Strategic Considerations

A disruptive innovation is defined as "an innovation that helps create a new market and value network, and eventually goes on to disrupt an existing market and value network (over a few years or decades), displacing an earlier technology. The term is used in business and technology literature to describe innovations that improve a product or service in ways that the market does not expect, typically first by designing for a different set of consumers in the new market and later by lowering prices in the existing market."

Disruptive forces, if not actively addressed, threaten the viability of old-line exposed industries. Examples of once-dominant, blue chip companies/entities being threatened or succumbing to new entrants due to innovation include Kodak and the U.S. Postal Service (USPS). For years, Kodak owned the film and related supplies market. The company watched as the photo business was transformed by digital technology and finally filed for bankruptcy in 2012.

Meanwhile, the USPS is a monopoly, government-run agency with a mission of delivering mail and providing an essential service to keep the economy moving. The USPS has been threatened for decades by private package delivery services (e.g., UPS and FedEx) that compete to offer more efficient and flexible service. Today, the primary threat to USPS' viability is the delivery of information by email, including commercial correspondence such as bills and bill payments, bank and brokerage statements, etc. Many experts believe that the USPS must dramatically restructure its operations and costs to have a chance to protect its viability as an independent agency.

Participants in all industries must prepare for and develop plans to address disruptive threats, including plans to replace their own technology with more innovative, more valuable customer services offered at competitive prices. The traditional wire line telephone players, including AT&T and Verizon, for example, became leaders in U.S. wireless telephone services, which over time could make the old line telephone product extinct. But these innovative, former old-line telephone providers had the vision to get in front of the trend to wireless and lead the development of non-regulated infrastructure networks and consumer marketing skills. As a result, they now hold large domestic market shares. In fact, they have now further leveraged technology innovation to create new products that expand their customer offerings.

The electric utility sector has not previously experienced a viable disruptive threat to its service offering due to customer reliance and the solid economic value of its product. However, a combination of technological innovation, public/regulatory policy, and changes in consumer objectives and preferences has resulted in distributed generation and other DER being on a path to becoming a viable alternative to the electric utility model. While investors are eager to support innovation and economic progress, they do not support the use of subsidies to attack the financial viability of their invested capital. Utility investors may not be opposed to DER technologies, but, in order for utilities to maintain their access to capital, it is essential that the financial implications of DER technologies be addressed so that non-DER participants and investors are not left to pay for revenues lost (and costs unrecovered) from DER participants. . . .

Strategic Implications of Distribution 2020 Disruptive Forces

The threats posed to the electric utility industry from disruptive forces, particularly distributed resources, have serious long-term implications for the traditional electric utility business model and investor opportunities. While the potential for significant immediate business impact is currently low (due to low DER participation to date), the industry and its stakeholders must begin to seriously address these challenges in order to mitigate the potential impact of disruptive forces, given the prospects for significant DER participation in the future.

One example of a significant potential adverse impact to utility investors stems from net metering. Utilities have witnessed the implementation of net metering rules in all but a handful of states. Lost revenues from DER are being recovered from non-DER customers in order to encourage distributed generation implementation. This type of lost revenue recovery drives up the prices of those non-participating customers and creates the environment for ongoing loss of additional customers as the system cost is transferred to a smaller and smaller base of remaining customers.

Utility investors are not being compensated for the risks associated with customer losses resulting from increasing DER. It is difficult to identify a rate case in which the cost-of-capital implications of net metering were considered. At the point when utility investors become focused on these new risks and start to witness significant customer and earnings erosion trends, they will respond to these challenges. But, by then, it may be too late to repair the utility business model.

DER is not the only disruptive risk the industry faces. Energy efficiency and DSM programs that promote lower electricity sales pressure earnings required to support capital investment. Without a tariff structure that properly allocates fixed vs. variable costs, any structure for lost revenues would come at a cost to non-participating customers, who will then be more motivated to find alternatives to reduce their consumption. While it is not the objective of this paper to outline new business model alternatives to address disruptive challenges, there are a number of actions that utilities and stakeholders should consider on a timely basis to align the interests of all stakeholders, while avoiding additional subsidies for non-participating customers.

These actions include:

Immediate Actions:

- Institute a monthly customer service charge to all tariffs in all states in order to recover fixed costs and eliminate the cross-subsidy biases that are created by distributed resources and net metering, energy efficiency, and demand-side resources;
- Develop a tariff structure to reflect the cost of service and value provided to DER customers, being off-peak service, back-up interruptible service, and the pathway to sell DER resources to the utility or other energy supply providers; and
- Analyze revision of net metering programs in all states so that self-generated DER sales to utilities are treated as supply-side purchases at a market-derived price. From a load provider's perspective, this would support the adoption of distributed resources on economically driven bases, as opposed to being incentivized by cross subsidies.

Longer-term Actions:

- Assess appropriateness of depreciation recovery lives based on the economic useful life of the investment, factoring the potential for disruptive loss of customers;
- Consider a stranded cost charge in all states to be paid by DER and fully departing customers to recognize the portion of investment deemed stranded as customers depart;
- Consider a customer advance in aid of construction in all states to recover upfront the cost of adding new customers and, thus, mitigate future stranded cost risk;
- Apply more stringent capital expenditure evaluation tools to factor-in potential investment that may be subject to stranded cost risk, including the potential to recover such investment through a customer hook-up charge or over a shorter depreciable life;
- Identify new business models and services that can be provided by electric utilities in all states to customers in order to recover lost margin while providing a valuable customer service—this was a key factor in the survival of the incumbent telephone players post deregulation; and
- Factor the threat of disruptive forces in the requested cost of capital being sought.

Investors have no desire to sit by and watch as disruptive forces slice away at the value and financial prospects of their investment. While the utility sector provides an important public good for customers, utilities and financial managers of investments have a fiduciary responsibility to protect the value of invested capital. Prompt action to mitigate lost revenue, while protecting customers from cross-subsidization better aligns the interests of customers and investors.

As growth in earnings and value is a major component of equity investment returns, what will investors expect to see as a strategic response from the industry to disruptive forces? The way to realize growth in earnings is to develop profit streams to counterbalance the impact of disruptive forces. Examples of new profit sources would include ownership of distributed resources with the receipt of an ongoing service fee or rate basing the investment and financial incentives for utilities to encourage demand side/energy efficiency benefits for customers. From an investor perspective, this may be easier said than done because the history of the electric utility industry in achieving non-regulated profits/value creation streams has not been a pleasant experience. So, investors will want to see very clear cut programs to capture value that are consistent with the core strengths of utilities: ability to execute construction projects, to provide dependable service with high reliability, and to access relatively low-cost capital.

Summary

While the threat of disruptive forces on the utility industry has been limited to date, economic fundamentals and public policies in place are likely to encourage significant future disruption to the utility business model. Technology innovation and rate structures that encourage cross subsidization of DER and/or behavioral modification by customers must be addressed quickly to mitigate further damage to the utility franchise and to better align interests of all stakeholders.

Utility investors seek a return on investment that depends on the increase in the value of their investment through growth in earnings and dividends. When customers have the opportunity to reduce their use of a product or find another provider of such service, utility earnings growth is threatened. As this threat to growth becomes more evident, investors will become less attracted to investments in the utility sector. This will be manifested via a higher cost of capital and less capital available to be allocated to the sector. Investors today appear confident in the utility regulatory model since the threat of disruptive forces has been modest to date. However, the competitive economics of distributed energy resources, such as PV solar, have improved significantly based on technology innovation and government incentives and subsidies, including tax and tariff-shifting incentives. But with policies in place that encourage cross subsidization of proactive customers, those not able or willing to respond to change will not be able to bear the responsibility left behind by proactive DER participating customers. It should not be left to the utility investor to bear the cost of these subsidies and the threat to their investment value.

This paper encourages an immediate focus on revising state and federal policies that do not align the interests of customers and investors, particularly revising utility tariff structures in order to eliminate cross subsidies (by non-DER participants) and utility investor cost-recovery uncertainties. In addition, utilities and stakeholders must develop policies and strategies to reduce the risk of ongoing customer disruption, including assessing business models where utilities can add value to customers and investors by providing new services.

While the pace of disruption cannot be predicted, the mere fact that we are seeing the beginning of customer disruption and that there is a large universe of companies pursuing this opportunity highlight the importance of proactive and timely planning to address these challenges early on so that uneconomic disruption does not proceed further. Ultimately, all stakeholders must embrace change in technology and business models in order to maintain a viable utility industry. . . .

Peter Kind is the executive director of Energy Infrastructure Advocates.

EXPLORING THE ISSUE

Is Home Solar the Wave of the Future?

Critical Thinking and Reflection

1. What do people mean when they call a technology "disruptive"?
2. What other industries might feel threatened by the growth in home solar power?
3. In what ways do early adopters of home solar power hasten the utility "death spiral"?

Is There Common Ground?

Both of our selections agree that the growing use of home solar power is likely to mean changes in the way that homeowners gain their electricity supply. To the Rocky Mountain Institute's team, these changes are desirable, for they promise lower prices, less dependence on fossil fuels, less contribution to global warming, and opportunities for utilities to retool their business models. To the electric utilities, these changes are not desirable, for they threaten loss of revenue, loss of investor confidence, and pressure to change traditional ways of doing business.

1. Both the Rocky Mountain Institute's team and Peter Kind agree that there is a need to identify new business models and services. What else can an electric utility do besides sell electricity?

2. Why do electric utilities need income even if they aren't selling electricity?
3. How can electric utilities take advantage of the trend toward home solar power?

Additional Resources

David Biello, "Solar Wars," *Scientific American* (November 2014).

Michael Boxwell, *Solar Electricity Handbook, 2014 Edition: A Simple Practical Guide to Solar Energy— Designing and Installing Photovoltaic Solar Electric Systems* (Greenstream, 2013).

John Schaeffer, *Real Goods Solar Living Sourcebook: Your Complete Guide to Living beyond the Grid with Renewable Energy Technologies and Sustainable Living* (New Society, 2014).

Internet References . . .

Rocky Mountain Institute

http://www.rmi.org/

The Edison Electric Institute

http://www.eei.org/Pages/default.aspx

Vivint Solar

http://www.vivintsolar.com/

Selected, Edited, and with Issue Framing Material by:
Thomas A. Easton, *Thomas College*

ISSUE

Does a Hydrogen Economy Make Sense?

YES: John Andrews and Bahman Shabani, from "Reenvisioning the Role of Hydrogen in a Sustainable Energy Economy," *International Journal of Hydrogen Energy* (January 2012)

NO: Ulf Bossel, from "Does a Hydrogen Economy Make Sense?" *Proceedings of the IEEE* (October 2006)

Learning Outcomes

After studying this issue, students will be able to:

- Explain why hydrogen is a potential replacement for fossil fuels.
- Describe the difficulties of converting to a sustainable hydrogen economy.
- Explain why hydrogen is a less efficient form of energy than fossil fuels or electricity.

ISSUE SUMMARY

YES: John Andrews and Bahman Shabani argue that hydrogen gas can play an important role in a sustainable energy system. The key will be a hierarchy of spatially distributed hydrogen production, storage, and distribution centers that minimizes the need for expensive pipelines. Electricity will power battery-electric vehicles for short-range transportation and serve as the major long-distance energy vector.

NO: Ulf Bossel argues that although the technology for widespread use of hydrogen energy is available, generating hydrogen is a very inefficient way to use energy. A hydrogen economy will never make sense.

The 1973 "oil crisis" heightened awareness that the world—even if it was not yet running out of oil—was extraordinarily dependent on that fossil fuel (and therefore on supplier nations) for transportation, home heating, and electricity generation. Recent price increases have repeated the lesson. Since the supply of oil and other fossil fuels is clearly finite, some people worry that there will come a time when demand cannot be satisfied, and our dependence will leave us helpless. We are also acutely aware of the many unfortunate side-effects of fossil fuels, including air pollution, strip mines, oil spills, global warming, and more.

The 1970s saw the modern environmental movement gain momentum. The first Earth Day was in 1970. Numerous governmental steps were taken to deal with air pollution, water pollution, and other environmental problems. In response to the oil crisis, a great deal of public money went into developing alternative energy supplies. The emphasis was on "renewable" energy, meaning conservation, wind, solar, and fuels such as hydrogen gas (which when burned with pure oxygen produces only water vapor as exhaust). However, when the crisis passed and oil supplies were once more ample (albeit more expensive), most

public funding for alternative-energy research and demonstration projects vanished. What work continued was at the hands of a few enthusiasts and those corporations that saw future opportunities. In 2001, the Worldwatch Institute published Seth Dunn's *Hydrogen Futures: Toward a Sustainable Energy System*. In 2002, MIT Press published Peter Hoffman's *Tomorrow's Energy: Hydrogen, Fuel Cells, and the Prospects for a Cleaner Planet*.

What drives the continuing interest in hydrogen and other alternative or renewable energy systems is the continuing problems associated with fossil fuels, concern about dependence and potential political instability, rising oil and gasoline prices, and the growing realization that the availability of petroleum will peak in the near future. Will that interest come to anything? There are, after all, a number of other ways to meet the need. Coal can be converted into oil and gasoline (though the air pollution and global warming problems remain). Cars can be made more efficient (and mileage efficiency is much greater than it was in the seventies despite the popularity of SUVs). Hybrid gas-electric cars are available.

Hydrogen as a fuel offers definite benefits. As Joan M. Ogden notes in "Hydrogen: The Fuel of the Future?" *Physics Today* (April 2002), the technology is available and compared to the alternatives it "offers the greatest potential environmental and energy-supply benefits." To put hydrogen to use, however, will require massive investments in facilities for generating, storing, and transporting the gas, as well as manufacturing hydrogen-burning engines and fuel cells. Currently, large amounts of hydrogen can easily be generated by "reforming" natural gas or other hydrocarbons. Hydrolysis—splitting hydrogen from water molecules with electricity—is also possible, and in the future this may use electricity from renewable sources such as wind or from nuclear power. The basic technologies are available right now. See Thammy Evans, Peter Light, and Ty Cashman, "Hydrogen—A Little PR," *Whole Earth* (Winter 2001). Daniel Sperling notes, in "Updating Automotive Research," *Issues in Science and Technology* (Spring 2002), that "Fuel cells and hydrogen show huge promise. They may indeed prove to be the Holy Grail, eventually taking vehicles out of the environmental equation," but making that happen will require research, government assistance in building a hydrogen distribution system, and incentives for both industry and car buyers. See also Piotr Tomczyk, "Fundamental Aspects of the Hydrogen Economy," *World Futures* (July 2009). M. Z. Jacobson, W. G. Colella, and D. M. Golden, "Cleaning the Air and Improving Health with Hydrogen Fuel-Cell Vehicles," *Science* (June 24, 2005), conclude that if all on road vehicles are replaced with fuel-cell vehicles using hydrogen generated by wind power, air pollution and human health impacts will both be reduced and overall costs will be less than for gasoline. Joan Ogden, "High Hopes for Hydrogen," *Scientific American* (September 2006), agrees that the potential is great but stresses that the transition to a hydrogen future will take decades. Michael K. Heiman and Barry D. Solomon, "The Hydrogen Economy and Its Alternatives," *Environment* (October 2007), argue that hydrogen may serve as a bridge to the future in some ways, but it is not likely to play much role in the transportation sector.

I. P. Jain, "Hydrogen the Fuel for 21st Century," *International Journal of Hydrogen Energy* (September 2009), believes that "the day is not far when hydrogen will take over oil." Jeremy Rifkin, "Hydrogen: Empowering the People," *Nation* (December 23, 2002), says local production of hydrogen could mean a much more decentralized energy system. He may be right, as John A. Turner makes clear in "Sustainable Hydrogen Production," *Science* (August 13, 2004), but Henry Payne and Diane Katz, "Gas and Gasbags . . . or, the Open Road and Its Enemies," *National Review* (March 25, 2002), contend that a major obstacle to hydrogen is market mechanisms that will keep fossil fuels in use for years to come, local hydrogen production is unlikely, and adequate supplies will require that society invest heavily in nuclear power. There are also technical obstacles, according to M. Balat and E. Kirtay, "Major Technical Barriers to a 'Hydrogen Economy'," *Energy*

Sources, Part A: Recovery, Utilization & Environmental Effects (June 2010). Jim Motavalli, "Hijacking Hydrogen," *E—The Environmental Magazine* (January–February 2003), worries that the fossil fuel and nuclear industries will dominate the hydrogen future. The former wishes to use "reforming" to generate hydrogen from coal (which means a continuing contribution to global warming), and the latter sees hydrolysis as creating demand for nuclear power. In Iceland, Freyr Sverrisson, "Missing in Action: Iceland's Hydrogen Economy," *World Watch* (November/December 2006), notes that the demand of industry for electricity has shifted plans to develop hydrogen to the development of hydroelectric dams instead.

The difficulty of developing a hydrogen economy is underlined by Robert F. Service in "The Hydrogen Backlash," *Science* (August 13, 2004) (the lead article in a special section titled "Toward a Hydrogen Economy"). According to Paul Ekins and Nick Hughes, "The Prospects for a Hydrogen Economy (1): Hydrogen Futures," *Technology Analysis & Strategic Management* (October 2009), one major difficulty is the sheer scale of the task of replacing one mature energy industry (fossil fuels) with another. Jeff Tollefson, "Fuel of the Future?" *Nature* (April 29, 2010), sees signs of increasing interest in hydrogen-fueled vehicles but notes that whether electric or hydrogen-fueled vehicles will rule future roads is far from settled. See also Laurie Wiegler, "The Future of Hydrogen Cars," *Technology Review* (September 21, 2011) (www.technologyreview.com/energy/38647/). Nadya Anscombe, "Hydrogen: Hype or Hope?" *Engineering & Technology* (May 8–28, 2010), notes that we will not have a hydrogen economy until we first have a renewable energy economy. In Germany, the marriage of hydrogen and renewables seems well begun. The country aims to produce 80 percent of its electricity from renewable sources such as wind and solar by 2050, and the Siemens corporation is developing large-scale hydrogen production and storage systems to handle electricity supply when the sun isn't shining and the wind isn't blowing; see Kevin Bullis, "Hydrogen Storage Could Be Key to Germany's Energy Plans," *Technology Review* (March 29, 2012) (www.technologyreview.com/energy/40001/).

In the YES selection, John Andrews and Bahman Shabani argue that hydrogen gas can play an important role in a sustainable energy system. The key will be a hierarchy of spatially distributed hydrogen production, storage, and distribution centers that minimizes the need for expensive pipelines. Electricity will power battery-electric vehicles for short-range transportation and serve as the major long-distance energy vector. In the NO selection, Ulf Bossel argues that although the technology for widespread use of hydrogen energy is available, generating hydrogen is a very inefficient way to use energy. A hydrogen economy will never make sense.

YES

John Andrews and Bahman Shabani

Reenvisioning the Role of Hydrogen in a Sustainable Energy Economy

Introduction

Where does hydrogen fit into a sustainable energy economy? To the forebears of the hydrogen economy, the answer to this core question was clear. The electrochemist, John Bockris, describes the genesis of this concept of a hydrogen economy in his pioneering book *Energy: The Solar Hydrogen Alternative* first published in 1975 as follows:

> The phrase 'A Hydrogen Economy' arose for the first time in a discussion between Bockris and Triner of the General-Motors Technical Center, 3 February 1970. They had been discussing (along with others in a Group) the various fuels which could replace polluting gasoline in transportation and had come to the conclusion that hydrogen would be the eventual fuel for all types of transports. The discussion went to other applications of hydrogen in providing energy to households and industry, and it was suggested that we might live finally in what could be called 'A Hydrogen Society'. The phrase 'A Hydrogen Economy' was then used later in the same conversation.

The original vision for such a Hydrogen Economy (HE) was conceived at a time when concerns about running out of oil, natural gas, and ultimately coal in the face of exponential growth in global primary energy use, and the associated rising pollution levels, were first being raised. The seminal meeting described above took place just before the release of the Club of Rome's controversial *Limits to Growth* report, and three years before the first major oil crisis occurred leading to a major hike in the price of crude oil and risks about the security of future supplies from the Middle East. Presciently, Bockris in his 1975 book does refer to the fact that increasing coal consumption could lead to increasing carbon dioxide in the atmosphere

and global warming. But it is a cursory mention, since the threat of looming climate change was then only dimly recognized, and in no way a driving force behind the transition to a HE as it is today.

In essence, Bockris' HE vision centered on the production of hydrogen by electrolysis of fresh and sea water by electricity generated by large-scale solar power stations located in hot remote parts of the world—most notably the desert regions of North Africa, Saudi Arabia, and Australia—and/or by nuclear fission reactors. The hydrogen produced would then be transmitted to distant population centers by long pipelines for consumption in all sectors of the economy.

Now that we confront the three-pronged threat of irreversible climate change, a deficit between oil demand and supply, and rising levels of pollution generally, the original HE concept needs re-envisioning. In transport applications, there have been significant developments in battery technology, with lithium ion and lithium polymer batteries becoming available with much higher gravimetric and volumetric energy densities than traditional lead acid batteries. Hence there is a major effort worldwide to commercialize electric vehicles, particularly cars and light commercial vehicles, as an alternative to conventional gasoline and diesel vehicles. If electric vehicles are to be a true zero-emission mode of transport, however, the electricity for battery charging must come from renewable energy (RE) sources of electricity (or the more problematic nuclear, or fossil fuel power stations with carbon capture and storage). Yet the very same is the case for the electricity to produce hydrogen by electrolysis, the most likely early production technology, for use in hydrogen fuel cell vehicles. Why then traverse the apparently more circuitous and energy lossy route of converting electricity to hydrogen, transporting and storing it, and then reconverting it back to electricity on board a vehicle in a fuel cell,

Abbreviation: A, Aircraft; AC, Alternating Current; AHC, Autonomous Hydrogen Center; B, Bus; BEV, Battery Electric Vehicle; C, Cycle; CCS, Carbon Capture and Storage; CHC, Coastal Hydrogen Center; DC, Direct Current; DoE, Department of Energy; EERE, Energy Efficiency and Renewable Energy; EO, Electric Overhead; EU, European Union; HE, Hydrogen Economy; HFC, Hydrogen Fuel Cell; HFCV, Hydrogen Fuel Cell Vehicle; HHV, High Heating Value; HISE, Hydrogen in a Sustainable Energy (strategy); IHC, Inland Hydrogen Center; IPCC, Intergovernmental Panel on Climate Change; JetLH, Liquid Hydrogen Jet Fuel; kWh$_e$, Kilowatt Hours (electrical); LHV, Low Heating Value; LPG, Liquid Petroleum Gas; NHA, National Hydrogen Association; OHC, Off-shore Hydrogen Center; PV, Photovoltaic; R, Rail; R&D, Research and Development; RE, Renewable Energy; S, Ship; T, Tram; UPT, Urban Public Transport; W, Walking; WWS, Wind, Water, and Sunlight.

Andrews, John and Shabani, Bahman. From *International Journal of Hydrogen Energy,* January 2012, excerpts pp. 1184–1187, 1192–1196, 1198–1199, 1200–1201. Copyright © 2012 by the International Association for Hydrogen Energy. Reprinted by permission of International Association for Hydrogen Energy—IAHE.

rather than simply charging batteries in vehicles using grid electricity generated from renewables? With batteries, it is electricity in and electricity out directly from the one electrochemical device.

Another alternative that has emerged to hydrogen as a transport fuel is biofuel, including principally ethanol, various bio-oils and biodiesel. All such biofuels are produced from organic materials—starch, sugar or cellulosic plants, or algae—that have absorbed carbon dioxide from the atmosphere by photosynthesis during their growth phase so that on combustion the same quantity of carbon dioxide is emitted once again. Provided then the energy used to produce and distribute these biofuels is also obtained from renewable resources, they are a zero-emission option like hydrogen produced from renewables. Biofuels for transport can be used as blends with existing fuels without any modification to today's internal combustion engines, the remainder of vehicle technology, and fuel distribution, storage and delivery infrastructure, and as 100% alternatives with relatively minor changes to existing engines and fuel distribution infrastructure. To many, biofuels are thus seen as a much more readily implementable substitute for petroleum fuels than taking on the apparently herculean challenge of switching to hydrogen, which indeed would require a completely new fuel distribution, storage and dispensing infrastructure, as well as a radical change in vehicle motive power systems and associated vehicle design.

In the original HE, hydrogen further played the critical role of providing the energy storage that would allow continuous base-load electricity supply in a system relying substantially on intermittent and variable RE sources such as solar, wind and ocean power. In recent years this role for hydrogen too has come under strong challenge from a number of alternatives, including batteries, supercapacitors, thermal storage, and multiple RE inputs geographically distributed over a large-scale grid.

Over the past decade, there have been many notable and useful works that have sought to develop and modify the original vision of a hydrogen economy to reflect more recent environmental, resource, and political-economic contexts, and technological developments. In the area of more specific and quantitative scenario-based studies, the International Energy Agency researched the consequences of introducing hydrogen globally, finding that hydrogen and fuel cells could reduce carbon dioxide emissions by a further 5% (1.4 Gt/year) by 2050 compared to just deploying efficiency measures (such as petrol-electric hybrid vehicles) and alternative fuels like ethanol.

One of the most thorough studies of the potential role of hydrogen in a sustainable energy economy conducted to date has been the HyWays European hydrogen roadmap supported by the European Union (EU) and ten of its member countries. In the high policy support, fast learning, hydrogen-emphasis scenario evaluated by Hyways, the penetration of hydrogen fuel cell vehicles in passenger transport rises rapidly from 3% in 2020, to 25% in 2030, and tends towards saturation at just under 75% in 2050. The corresponding hydrogen production mix in 2030 is 31% from nuclear fission power, 27% from RE sources, 26% from steam reforming of natural gas, and 14% from coal via integrated gasification combined cycle plants and carbon capture and storage. In this scenario, transport greenhouse gas emissions in 2050 for the ten countries modelled were projected to be more than 60% lower than 2000 levels.

Drawing on the HyWays study and the earlier European Commission-supported World Energy Technology Outlook hydrogen study, Doll and Wietschel concluded that the use of hydrogen in a sustainable transport future could significantly reduce carbon dioxide emissions of the transport sector, taking into account tailpipe and upstream emissions, and importantly reduce local air pollutants by up to 80%. Possible negative impacts identified were accident risks, increased nuclear waste, and increased biomass demand (for hydrogen production alongside other sources).

The prospects for a transition to a hydrogen economy based on RE sources in Spain were discussed by Brey *et al.*, considering a short-term target of 10% of transport energy demand being met by hydrogen. This study concluded that most of the Spanish regions could be self-sufficient for supplying their energy demand via renewable sources and hydrogen, except for Madrid which would require transfer of hydrogen from nearby regions. The main barriers to a transition to hydrogen were identified as the lack of development of technologies for hydrogen production, storage, transport, and distribution, and high costs compared with the current system. Balat analyzed the potential importance of hydrogen produced from coal and natural gas (with carbon sequestration), nuclear power, and large-scale renewables as a future solution to environmental and transportation problems. Hydrogen from steam reforming of natural gas was identified as the most economical production method among the current commercial processes, yielding a unit cost of between 1.25 US$/kg for large systems to about 3.50 US$/kg for small systems with a natural gas price of 6 US$/GJ, compared to 8 US$/kg for hydrogen from electrolytic processes. The role of hydrogen in road transport in a sustainable energy system in Korea has been examined by Kim and Moon, in Austria by Ajanovic, and in all sectors of the United Arab Emirates' economy by Kazim. Carton and Olabi propose the use of hydrogen produced by electrolysers using surplus wind power to allow wind farms in Ireland to provide much more consistent electricity supply to the main grid, particularly as the problems of variability and intermittency are exacerbated as the country heads towards a target of 40% electricity from renewables by 2020. Focusing on the European Union, Bleischwitz and Bader concluded that the [then] EU policy framework neither hindered nor enhanced hydrogen development, and that the large-scale market development of hydrogen and fuel cells would require a new policy approach with technology-specific and regionally-based support.

The global potential for the production of hydrogen from multiple biomass feedstocks via a two-stage bioprocess in a cost-effective and environmentally friendly manner was reviewed by Urbaniec *et al.,* based on the preliminary results of the Hyvolution Integrated Research Project supported by the 6th Framework Programme of the European Union.

The greenhouse gas reduction benefits and costs of a large-scale transition to hydrogen in the USA were investigated by Dougherty *et al.* The hydrogen production options considered were on-site and centralised steam reforming of natural gas and electrolysis using RE, and centralised coal and biomass reforming with and without sequestration of carbon dioxide. Dougherty *et al.* concluded that a coordinated shift towards hydrogen, focussed on displacing gasoline and diesel (non-military) in cars, light trucks, heavy-duty vehicles, marine vessels, and trains, and avoiding serious economic disruption, would likely entail a several decades transition and higher costs in the short-term, but is technically feasible.

The National Hydrogen Association released a report on energy-economic modeling of a hydrogen-emphasis scenario in transport in the USA. This report found that a scenario in which hydrogen fuel cell vehicles dominated the marketplace in the USA, in conjunction with hybrids, plug-in hybrids and biofuels, could cut greenhouse gas pollution by 80% below 1990 levels by 2100; allow America to become essentially independent of petroleum fuels by the latter year; eliminate nearly all controllable urban air pollution by 2100; and reduce societal costs of transport by up to $US 600 billion per year by 2100. Hydrogen is made initially from natural gas, transitioning to hydrogen from biomass, from coal with carbon capture and storage (CCS), from natural gas with CCS, and eventually from electrolysis of water using renewable and nuclear electricity. On the other hand, McKay rejects hydrogen in his sustainable energy strategies for the UK on the grounds that converting energy to and from hydrogen can only be done inefficiently, and it has "a whole bunch of practical defects", opting instead to use primarily Battery Electric Vehicles (BEVs) with charging from low or zero-emission electricity, and their collective battery banks for energy storage on grids as the renewables input increases.

The critical issue of whether there is enough RE available to provide all the primary energy required by a global sustainable energy economy relying substantially on hydrogen for storage and as a transport energy carrier has been addressed by Kleijn and van der Voet and Jacobson and Delucchi. Both these studies answer this question in the affirmative, but with some important conditions.

It is our view that the original HE concept now needs radical re-envisioning. As in many of the strategic sustainable energy studies referred to above, and drawing on Andrews' preliminary sketch of a sustainable hydrogen economy, we argue in the present paper that, rather than seeing hydrogen as the exclusive fuel for the future, the specific roles to which it is uniquely suited in each major sector within an overall sustainable energy strategy need to be identified. With this approach we expect that hydrogen would still play a substantive and crucial role, but a role in concert rather than competition with that of electricity and technologies such as BEVs and a variety of shorter-term energy storage options for grid power.

We therefore propose six principles that could guide the role played by hydrogen in a truly sustainable energy economy based on taking energy efficiency to its economic limit and ideally using only RE sources. We elaborate on and discuss the implications of these principles in turn, in sketching a sustainable energy economy with a strong emphasis on hydrogen. The focus is thus on the potential role of hydrogen, rather than other equally-important aspects of a global sustainable energy strategy. Our intention is to keep this vision as general as possible at this stage so that it is potentially applicable to most countries and regions around the world. Inevitably, many important issues cannot be dealt with in detail in the present work, including, for example, a comparison of the relative merits of biofuels and hydrogen in various forms of land, sea and air transport.

However, our recommendation is that these principles for hydrogen deployment in the strategic context of global sustainable energy may in the future be applied in detailed and quantitative energy-economic modeling of the global economy and the economies of individual geo-political regions and nations. Evidently it will only be after the findings of such studies are assessed that any claims of the economic, environmental and social merits of the approach we propose can be verified.

Principles

The six principles we propose to guide the role played by hydrogen in sustainable energy strategies, both globally and at national levels, are the following:

1. A hierarchy of sustainable hydrogen production, storage and distribution centers relying on local RE sources producing hydrogen as required
2. Complementary use of hydrogen and electricity as energy vectors to minimize the extent of new hydrogen pipeline distribution networks
3. Production of hydrogen from a range of RE sources and feedstocks, without dependence on nuclear fission power or carbon capture and storage, but with the application of energy efficiency measures to the economic limit across all sectors of the economy
4. Recognition of the complementary roles of hydrogen and battery storage across a range of transport vehicles and transport services
5. Use of hydrogen for longer-duration energy storage on centralized grids relying extensively on RE inputs

6. Employment of bulk hydrogen storage as the strategic energy reserve to guarantee national and global energy security in a world relying increasingly on RE.

As a snapshot, the key differences between the original HE concept and the re-envisioned role for 'Hydrogen In a Sustainable Energy' (HISE) strategy presented here are the following:

HISE is set firmly in the context of a zero greenhouse gas emission economy in terms of both the production of hydrogen from renewables and consumption, rather than just as a response to depleting reserves of fossil fuel. While HE involved centralized production of hydrogen from mainly solar and wind energy occupying vast areas of generally remote land, as well as nuclear fission reactors, and hence very long distance transmission of hydrogen via pipelines to centers of consumption, HISE involves decentralized distributed production of hydrogen from a wide variety of renewables and feedstocks. In HISE, hydrogen and electricity play complementary roles as energy vectors, and hydrogen and batteries complementary roles as energy stores, in the transport sector and industrial, commercial and residential sectors—no longer is hydrogen the sole and exclusive energy carrier and store in every sector of the economy.

While HE accepted primary energy inputs from nuclear fission power, as well as in some variants from natural gas and coal too, in its ideal manifestation HISE focuses exclusively on renewables, coupled with an equally strong emphasis on energy efficiency and demand management, in an overall sustainable energy strategy akin to that espoused over many years by Amory Lovins and his coworkers. However, in a more pragmatic vein, we also briefly canvas the roles hydrogen could play in the event of a substantial shift to nuclear power, and proven economical use of carbon capture and storage to allow continued use of natural gas and coal. The six principles underlying the HISE strategy and their implications will now be elaborated in turn.

A Hierarchy of Sustainable Hydrogen Centers With

Overview of the Hierarchy

Given the spatial dispersion of RE sources, and the desirability of producing hydrogen near to where it is consumed, a hierarchy of distributed sustainable hydrogen production, storage and distribution centers would be established. These centers would draw upon a range of RE sources to produce hydrogen from a number of different feedstocks for a variety of end-use applications. While the precise structure of the hierarchy would depend on the local conditions in a particular country or region, the following principal types of center would be expected: off-shore, coastal, inland, and autonomous local. . . .

Complementary Use of Hydrogen and Electricity as Energy Vectors to Minimise the Hydrogen Pipeline Distribution Network

The complementary role of electricity and hydrogen as energy vectors is evident. Wherever practical, the long-distance transmission and distribution of the RE supply is via electricity, probably in the future increasingly by high-voltage DC transmission or even superconducting electricity transmission lines, which have much lower losses than current high-voltage AC transmission networks. The transmission of hydrogen by pipeline is restricted so far as possible from hydrogen production plants (mainly electrolyzers) near to solar, wind and wave energy sources, to the nearby cities and towns.

Clearly the construction of a new hydrogen distribution network involving compressed hydrogen gas piped from location to location, together with the required plant for pressurization, safety regulation and storage, would be an expensive piece of infrastructure investment per kilometre of pipeline. Hence an important guiding principle in the design of a sustainable hydrogen system is to seek to minimize the extent of the required hydrogen distribution network. The hierarchical network of sustainable hydrogen production, storage and distribution centers has been designed in accordance with this principle.

The central design feature to minimize the extent of the hydrogen pipeline network is to create a geographically distributed network of hydrogen production centers, so that so far as possible hydrogen is produced regionally or even locally for refueling vehicles, or energy storage for use in combined electricity and heating systems, in that same region or locality. As Dougherty *et al.* and McDowell and Eames point out, decentralized production is one way to overcome many of the infrastructural barriers to a hydrogen transition. Along the same lines, Rifkin and Sorenson proposed decentralized or on-site hydrogen production actually in residential or commercial buildings, for refueling vehicles, and via fuel cells electricity and heat as well.

Ideally, the only need for a hydrogen pipeline distribution system would be in major cities to transport hydrogen from bulk storage facilities (associated with off-shore, coastal or major inland hydrogen centers nearby) to:

- a network of medium-sized hydrogen storages from which hydrogen could be transferred on demand (most likely by road tankers initially) to a network of refueling stations for road transport vehicles—cars, commercial vehicles and trucks
- facilities for producing liquefied hydrogen for use by aircraft (probably only one or two such facilities for each major city)
- hydrogen storages at major ports for refueling ships

- hydrogen storages at major railway terminals for refueling long-distance freight and passenger trains
- fuel cell power stations for supplying electricity to the grid at periods of low RE input, or during national emergencies that resulted in disruptions to normal supplies. . . .

Production of Hydrogen from Renewable Energy Sources and Feedstocks, Without Nuclear Fission Power or Carbon Capture and Storage

The ultimate and ideal sustainable energy economy would rely solely on the earth's RE income, from solar, wind, wave, tidal, hydro, biomass and geothermal sources, and use energy to meet end-use needs in the most energy-efficient manner possible. Furthermore, hydrogen would be produced from a diverse range of RE sources ensuring zero-emissions in production, and hence no contribution to aggregate global greenhouse gas emissions from the overall system given that the consumption of hydrogen in fuel cells, internal combustion engines or simply by external combustion to deliver end-use services simply leads to water vapour. During the transition to a truly sustainable economy, some hydrogen is also likely to be produced by steam reforming of natural gas, the lowest emission fossil-fuel source and process.

The fundamental question thus arises as to whether there are sufficient RE sources available, and economically deployable, to meet global demands for the services energy can provide, taking into account forecast population growth and rises in material standards of living, particularly in developing countries. The potential resource constraints in a HE based on RE sources were investigated by Kleijn and van der Voet. They estimated that the primary energy requirements of a global economy in 2050 that were 2.5 times those in 2005 could be met entirely from potentially collectable solar radiation (80% of the total supply), wind power (15%) and other renewables (5%). However, it was pointed out that the infrastructure to harvest that amount of RE would require massive investments, and that extensive transmission networks may be necessary since optimal energy harvesting locations are often far from the centres of consumption. A highly decentralised sustainable energy economy along the lines suggested in the present work was not considered.

Jacobson and Delucchi have recently completed one of the most thorough studies to date into the potential of Wind, Water and Sunlight (WWS) energy sources to provide the primary energy required by a global sustainable energy economy in 2030. Referring to US Energy Information Administration (2008) projections, Jacobson

and Delucchi base their scenarios on the current average world rate of energy consumption for all end-uses rising from 12.5 TW (10^{12} W) in 2008 to 16.9 TW in 2030 on the basis of the current range of primary fuels employed, primarily fossil fuels, nuclear and a small contribution from renewables. However, they estimate that a shift to renewable WWS sources to replace all fossil fuel and wood combustion by 2030, together with a shift to electricity and hydrogen as energy carriers, and strong energy efficiency measures in all sectors, could reduce the global demand to be met in that year to just 11.5 TW, that is, 8% less than in 2008. Jacobson and Delucchi show how this demand could be met entirely from WWS sources including wind, wave, hydro, geothermal, photovoltaic and solar thermal power technologies. The estimated total new land area—excluding land already used for renewables such as hydroelectric plants, and the space occupied by offshore wind, wave and tidal power devices—would be only 1% of the total global land area, and hence in principle potentially feasible. These authors conclude that barriers to a 100% conversion to WWS power worldwide are primarily social and political, not technological or even economic. . . .

Complementary Roles for Hydrogen and Battery Storage in Transport

To reduce transport-related greenhouse gas emissions, and effect a transition away from petroleum fuels, a number of more sustainable demand-side, primary energy resource, and technology options are being considered around the world, including:

- urban restructuring and land-use planning to reduce average trip and freight movement distances,
- modal shifts to urban public transport, high-speed intercity rail, and rail freight,
- use of hybrid petrol/gas electric vehicles
- deployment of internal combustion engine vehicles running on biofuels such as ethanol, methanol, or bio-oils produced from biomass crops
- [Battery electric vehicles (BEVs)] charged from the main electricity grid, assuming an increasing proportion of electricity supply derives from zero-emission sources
- development of hydrogen fuel cell vehicles (HFCVs) with hydrogen produced from renewables.

Clearly reducing the passenger and freight task per capita, and mode shifts that lower energy intensity are desirable and deserve full support in their own right. To the extent that they are successful, the remaining transport task to be met by the alternative fuel supply options is facilitated.

Petrol/gas hybrid vehicles are likely to be an important short to medium term option, because of their improved emission performance compared to standard petrol and diesel vehicles and compatibility with existing infrastructure. Yet they are not zero emission technologies as long as petroleum fuels are used as the primary energy input. Inevitably in the medium to longer term they will need to be replaced by BEVs or HFCVs. . . .

Both BEVs and HFCVs offer a completely zero-emission transport solution, provided the electricity to charge batteries, and electricity (or other energy source) to make the hydrogen, is also zero emission, that is, renewable, nuclear or fossil fuel with carbon capture and storage. . . .

As alternative routes for zero-emission hydrogen production, taking some of the pressure off the renewable sources of electricity. Such relief would not be available in an exclusive BEV scenario. . . .

Hydrogen storage currently has, and will probably extend in the future, a substantial advantage over batteries in gravimetric and volumetric energy densities when used in vehicles with a range similar to that of today's petrol and diesel vehicles. Other things being equal, this advantage should mean that hydrogen fuel cell vehicles will have a much greater range (two to three times) that of a comparable battery electric vehicle for a given volume and mass of the storage system.

However, the figures arrived at here are merely indicative of the general case, so that it remains essential to compare hydrogen and battery storages of particular kinds employed in specific comparable vehicles to be sure about their relative merits in each case. Moreover, technological development is continually leading to improved energy densities in both battery (especially lithium ion) and hydrogen storage systems. Consequently, any changes in relative energy densities through technological advances will need to be watched closely. Indeed a necessary condition for use of hydrogen for transport in a sustainable energy strategy is that hydrogen storage maintains a substantial advantage over battery storage in terms of gravimetric and volumetric energy densities.

The optimal energy storage system for vehicles requiring a range equivalent to today's petrol and diesel vehicles is actually likely to employ a combined hydrogen and battery system. The hydrogen system would provide the bulk energy storage, while a relatively small energy capacity battery would allow regenerative braking, meet peak power demands, and generally buffer the fuel cell against load changes to extend its lifetime. This complementary use of hydrogen and battery storage is precisely the arrangement employed by Honda in its FCX Clarity hydrogen car that is now available commercially in limited numbers.

The complementarity of hydrogen and battery storage may well be extended to the question of which type of vehicle is best across a range of transport applications. [This is] a 'horses for courses' approach to meeting the gamut of end-use transport services by a combination of hydrogen fuel cell, battery electric, hydrogen-fuelled jet engines, and electric vehicles supplied by overhead electricity, drawing

entirely upon RE sources, and after implementing a number of mode shifts to preserve service levels while reducing total transport energy demand.

A mode shift to walking, cycling and urban public transport is highly desirable for urban short trips. The remaining demand for short trips (less than 100 km typically) could conveniently be met using plug-in battery-electric cars, small station wagons and commercial vehicles (that is, BEVs), to take full advantage of the relatively high round-trip energy efficiency of batteries when the period between charging is not long.

For medium to longer distance urban, regional, and intercity trips over land (>100 km), a mode shift to electric rail (supplied by overhead or power rail) would reduce the overall demand for transportable fuel. Hydrogen fuel cell cars, buses, and trains (where new overhead construction is too expensive or impractical) would meet the remaining demand for journeys of more than 100 km, with ranges of more than 450 km between refueling. HFC vehicles would usually employ a small energy capacity battery to allow regenerative braking and meet short-term maximum power demands.

BEVs are also highly suited for urban goods delivery over short distances (<100 km). For medium and long-distance road freight, hydrogen fuel cell trucks, without any battery storage, are likely to be preferable since the vehicles operate for long periods at relatively constant speeds, rapid acceleration is not so critical, and regenerative braking would not offer significant savings. The more stop-start the usage, the more the balance would tip to including a small energy capacity battery into the system as well.

Coastal and international shipping where the range required is large are also likely to employ hydrogen storage and electric drive supplied by fuel cells. A mode shift to very fast electric rail for land-based intercity travel where possible would be beneficial. For trips that still have to be undertaken by air, jet and turboprop aircraft will almost certainly have to rely on liquid hydrogen to get mass and energy densities down to at least the same order of magnitude as current aviation fuel (kerosene and aviation diesel).

Use of Hydrogen for Longer-Duration Energy Storage on Centralised Grids Relying Extensively on Renewable Energy Inputs

Just as batteries have emerged as a major competitor to hydrogen energy storage and fuel cells in the area of transport, so a number of alternatives to hydrogen are currently being mooted to allow electricity grids to maintain continuous and reliable supply as the primary energy inputs to electricity generation from inherently intermittent and variable renewables increase in order to meet greenhouse gas reduction targets. Among these means are, most notably:

- batteries,
- supercapacitors,
- thermal storage, particularly for night-time supply with solar-thermal power systems,
- geothermal power stations, which can supply power on a near continuous basis,
- a large-scale grid covering a vast geographical area with distributed RE inputs of many kinds—such as solar PV, solar thermal, wind power, and biomass power generation—so that the complementarity over time of these variable inputs can reduce the variations in aggregate supply and reduce the requirement for any other form of energy storage such as hydrogen, and
- pumped hydroelectric schemes.

The first three options—batteries, supercapacitors and thermal storage—essentially provide just short-term storage: in the order of seconds for supercapacitors, a few days to a week in the case of batteries, and from day to night for thermal storage. Such storage will undoubtedly be highly valuable on many grids, especially given the diurnal cycle of solar radiation, and hence will probably find many applications of this kind. However, in locations where there are variations in renewable input over longer cycles, in particular from season to season, a longer-term form of storage such as hydrogen will probably still be necessary for security of supply and be advantageous economically. . . .

A large-scale grid drawing on inputs from a range of different renewables that are geographically dispersed would have a reduced need for storage to meet demand continuously and reliably throughout the year. Hence it clearly makes sense to encourage this diverse range of distributed renewable inputs. However, a number of factors militate against this strategy eliminating the need altogether for a substantial capacity of some guaranteed form of energy storage such as hydrogen:

- Renewables such as solar, wind, waves and tidal stream all follow seasonal patterns of variation, so these variations will not be eliminated by taking inputs from varying locations at a given time (at least in the same hemisphere).
- Inputs from distributed renewables will vary from location to location over the whole grid, but transmission losses are likely to be very high if the entire grid has to be supplied at certain times from just a few sources located in one region.
- The installation of very high voltage DC transmission lines in place of the AC lines currently used has been suggested as one way to minimize such losses, but such an upgrading of the entire grid infrastructure would be very expensive.
- Considerable excess generating capacity would need to be installed in each area if at times the output from this area had to meet a major proportion

of the total demand from the entire grid when there is a deficiency of aggregate input from the generating capacity from other areas.
- Reliance on a joint probability distribution for the supply of power from a diverse range of types and locations of RE generators, each subject to its own probability distribution over an annual period, should indeed give a greater continuity and reliability of supply than that obtainable from a small number of very large renewable power stations. However, there will remain a finite probability of low supply that is insufficient to meet the demand. This situation cannot be tolerated in modern grid systems that are usually bound by legally enforceable supply reliability and continuity contracts, not to mention consumer demands. Hence there will remain a need for a secure and totally reliable source of supply that can be relied upon with total confidence when necessary. Hydrogen storage and fuel cells can meet this requirement for a guaranteed back up supply, both to meet any deficit from renewables, and to be called upon in times of national emergency.

Pumped hydroelectric schemes in which surplus power is used to pump water to the high reservoir of a hydroelectric facility, and then allowed to run back to the lower reservoir through the turbines at times of supply shortage, offer a reasonably high roundtrip energy efficiency (above 70%). However, the global availability of additional environmentally-acceptable sites for such schemes, which require very large reservoir capacities, is generally now very limited. Even at 100% energy conversion efficiency and 100 m head the volumetric energy density of pumped hydroelectric storages is only 0.273 Wh_e/litre, compared to up to 0.47 kWh_e/L achieved with metal hydrides and fuel cells, that is, well over a thousand times lower.

For all these reasons, hydrogen energy storage is likely to have some role to play, especially for longer-term storage in most grids that rely heavily on RE inputs, often (as in transport) in concert with other forms of storage. However, the extent of this role will vary from one grid to another, and can only be investigated with any confidence through full system modeling of each grid on an annual basis, and taking into account climate variations over the longer term.

Bulk Hydrogen Storage for Energy Security When Relying on Renewable Energy

As national economies, and thus in turn the international economy, shift to relying increasingly on RE sources for both electrical power generation and transport to achieve stringent global greenhouse gas emission reduction targets over the coming decades, entirely novel challenges arise to ensure national and international energy security compared to those we face today in the fossil-fuel era. Coal, oil and natural gas resources are located in specific geographical regions and must be transported around the globe to consuming countries, most of which do not have sufficient indigenous supplies to meet their own needs. Hence energy security considerations today focus largely on guaranteeing a continuous and sufficient supply of fossil fuels to the main consuming nations, particularly the USA, the European Union, China, India and Japan, from the main fossil fuel supply nations such as the OPEC nations in the Middle East, Russia, Mexico, and Australia. By contrast, in the sustainable energy economy being sketched here, a large proportion of the primary energy input would be in the form of distributed RE sources. Each country, and indeed wherever possible each region therein, will therefore draw its energy to a large extent from local and indigenous energy sources, with much less dependence on energy imports from other countries. Since most renewables are inherently intermittent and variable both on short (hourly, daily, weekly) time scales, medium or seasonal time scales, and to some extent also on longer time scales (years and decades, especially if there is significant climate change), the challenge of energy security shifts to ensuring energy supply in the face of this inevitable variability. The reliance on a diverse range of renewables (solar, wind, biomass, waves) that are themselves geographically distributed will mitigate the effects of the variable inputs from particular sources at any time. Certain renewables such as biomass and geothermal can provide more continuous supply. Yet there will remain a need for a strategic energy reserve that is available with effective certainty to meet demand in periods of low availability of aggregate primary energy from the renewables, and in the event of any major breakdowns in supply or distribution technology, or catastrophic events such as volcanic eruptions, cyclones, bushfires, floods, droughts, or during wars or terrorist attacks.

In the sustainable energy vision proposed here, a number of bulk hydrogen storages as integral parts of offshore, coastal and inland hydrogen centers would serve as strategic energy reserves both within nations, and preferably internationally too, organized via the United Nations. This hydrogen reserve would be able to maintain supply to both the transport and electricity supply sectors in the event of unforeseen interruptions or deficiencies from the primary renewable supply sources. Hydrogen can store energy near permanently, so that bulk hydrogen storage would play a role akin to that of fossil fuels today, with one critical difference: the hydrogen storage can be regularly replenished with more hydrogen produced using the earth's RE income, while fossil fuels once used are irreversibly depleted.

Conclusions and Recommendations

In this paper we have sought to re-envision the role of hydrogen in a sustainable energy strategy broadly applicable at national and international levels, taking into account the need to confront the three-pronged challenge of irreversible climate change, uncertain oil supply, and rising pollution levels of diverse kinds, and the strong

challenges to hydrogen storage that have arisen from a range of competing technologies.

We suggest that the time for proposing an exclusively HE has passed, since the sustainable energy strategy proposed here, ideally based only on RE inputs but taking energy efficiency to its economic limits, would also make extensive use of electricity, batteries and probably other storage technologies and zero-emission fuels too. But hydrogen would still have a critical and substantial role to play: in the transport sector, in road and rail vehicles requiring a range comparable to today's petrol and diesel vehicles, in coastal and international shipping, and in air transport; and in the electricity sector to provide longer-term seasonal storage on electricity grids relying exclusively on variable RE inputs.

A core difference between this vision and earlier concepts of a HE is that a hierarchy of spatially-distributed sustainable hydrogen production, storage and distribution centers relying on a range of local RE sources and feedstocks would be created. Hydrogen would be produced, stored and consumed locally so far as practical, rather than being produced at a few large-scale facilities and then transmitted via long-distance pipelines centralized to distant cities. The required hydrogen pipeline distribution system would be limited to separate distribution networks for the main metropolitan areas and regions, by complementary use of hydrogen and electricity as energy vectors. Bulk hydrogen storage would, however, provide the strategic energy reserve to guarantee national and global energy security in a world relying increasingly on RE.

This vision of a sustainable HE has intentionally been outlined in a generic form so that it is applicable to many different countries and regions. The vision remains merely a thumbnail sketch at this stage, without detailed quantification of its associated primary energy supply, storage, distribution and consumption profiles, and without a detailed comparison on triple bottom line—that is, economic, environmental (including principally greenhouse gas emissions), and social—criteria with alternative energy scenarios.

What is needed now as a next step is to apply this vision to specific countries (or groupings of nations) by conducting detailed energy-economic-environmental modeling to quantify its key characteristics in particular contexts. A quantitative scenario for a transition to a hydrogen-based sustainable energy strategy over time will need to be developed in these contexts, and an evaluation conducted into its overall economic, environmental and social benefits compared with alternative scenarios.

A number of features included tentatively in the vision presented here require in particular further investigation:

- The most suitable methods for producing hydrogen from biomass resources of various kinds including cellulosic and algal sources, and a triple bottom line comparison of these methods with direct production of biofuels for use in internal combustion engines, or aircraft jet engines.

- The magnitude of the hydrogen storage capacity needed to provide the required level of supply security on national electricity grids of various structures, and with different levels and types of variable and distributed RE input, along with the use of other types of short-duration energy storage such as supercapacitors and batteries.
- The technical feasibility, and triple bottom line evaluation, of storing hydrogen in very large quantities in subsea or subterranean depleted natural gas or oil reservoirs, or other on and off-shore geological formations, whether in their natural or artificially altered forms.
- The most appropriate methods for bulk storage of hydrogen at Coastal and Inland Hydrogen Centers prior to regional/local distribution, including high-pressure (350 or 700 bar) gas, in metal or chemical hydrides, in slurries (such as alane slurry), or in carbon-based materials. Given the enormous quantities of hydrogen and hence hydrogen storage material that will be needed in a fully-fledged HISE strategy, ultimately carbon-based storage materials would clearly be preferable from the perspective of material availability (and hence price) on a global basis.
- The development of hydrogen storage and fuel cell systems suitable for large transport vehicles, in particular, long-distance road trucks (semi-trailers and B-doubles), long-distance buses, intercapital freight and passenger trains, tractors and other heavy mobile machinery, and international and coastal ships.

- The development of liquid hydrogen fuelled jet aircraft, and associated on-board storage, and airport refueling systems. In addition, R&D to develop the most cost-efficient methods of liquefying hydrogen using just RE sources is necessary, and/or to find an alternative high-density form of hydrogen storage suitable for aircraft.

While the concept of a HE may now need re-envisioning, the role of hydrogen in a sustainable energy economy deserves full and urgent consideration in terms of policy studies, and research, development, demonstration and commercialization of the enabling technologies.

JOHN ANDREWS is an associate professor in the School of Aerospace, Mechanical and Manufacturing Engineering, RMIT University, Melbourne, Australia. He directs the school's Master of Engineering (Sustainable Energy) and RMIT-NORTH Link Greenhouse Emission Reduction programs and leads the renewable-energy hydrogen R&D group. His book *Living Better with Less* (Penguin, 1981) was one of the first works to propose sustainable development for Australia.

BAHMAN SHABANI is a lecturer in the Master of Engineering Sustainable Energy program at the School of Aerospace, Mechanical and Manufacturing Engineering, RMIT University, Melbourne, Australia.

Ulf Bossel

 **NO**

Does a Hydrogen Economy Make Sense?

Introduction

The technology needed to establish a hydrogen economy is available or can be developed. Two comprehensive 2004 studies by the U.S. National Research Council and the American Physical Society summarize technical options and identify needs for further improvements. They are concerned with the cost of hydrogen obtained from various sources, but fail to address the key question of the overall energy balance of a hydrogen economy. Energy is needed to synthesize hydrogen and to deliver it to the user, and energy is lost when the gas is converted back to electricity by fuel cells. How much energy is needed to liberate hydrogen from water by electrolysis or high-temperature thermodynamics or by chemistry? Where does the energy come from and in which form is it harvested? Do we have enough clean water for electrolysis and steam reforming? How and where do we safely deposit the enormous amounts of carbon dioxide if hydrogen is derived from coal?

This paper extends a previous analysis of the parasitic energy needs of a hydrogen economy. It argues that the energy problem cannot be solved in a sustainable way by introducing hydrogen as an energy carrier. Instead, energy from renewable sources and high energy efficiency between source and service will become the key points of a sustainable solution. The establishment of an efficient "electron economy" appears to be more appropriate than the creation of a much less efficient "hydrogen economy."

The Challenge

The following examples illustrate the nature of the challenge involved in creating a hydrogen economy.

It takes about 1 kg of hydrogen to replace 1 U.S. gal of gasoline. About 200 MJ (55 kWh) of dc electricity are needed to liberate 1 kg of hydrogen from 9 kg of water by electrolysis. Steam reforming of methane (natural gas) requires only 4.5 kg of water for each kilogram of hydrogen, but 5.5 kg of CO_2 emerge from the process. One kilogram of hydrogen can also be obtained from 3 kg of coal and 9 kg of water, but 11 kg of CO_2 are released and need to be sequestered. Even with most efficient fuel cell systems, at most 50% of the hydrogen energy can be converted back to electricity.

The full dimensions of the challenge become apparent when these numbers are translated to a specific case. The following case study may serve to illustrate the point. About 50 jumbo jets leave Frankfurt Airport every day, each loaded with 130 tons of kerosene. If replaced on a 1 : 1 energy base by 50 tons of liquid hydrogen, the daily needs would be 2500 tons or 36 000 m^3 of the cryogenic liquid, enough to fill 18 Olympic-size swimming pools. Every day 22 500 tons of water would have to be electrolyzed. The continuous output of eight 1-GW power plants would be required for electrolysis, liquefaction, and transport of hydrogen. If all 550 planes leaving the airport were converted to hydrogen, the entire water consumption of Frankfurt (650 000 inhabitants) and the output of 25 full-size power plants would be needed to meet the hydrogen demand of air planes leaving just one airport in Germany.

For hydrogen derived from fossil hydrocarbons, the availability of water and the safe sequestration of CO_2 may pose serious problems, not because of inadequate technology, but with respect to logistics, infrastructure, costs, safety, and energy consumption. To fuel the 50 jumbo jets with hydrogen, about 7500 tons of coal and 11 250 tons of water are needed daily and 27 500 tons of carbon dioxide must be liquefied for transport, shipped to a suitable disposal site (perhaps in the deep waters of the mid-Atlantic) and safely deposited. The significant energy needs for hydrogen liquefaction and transport are the same for any source of hydrogen. Fueling the 50 jumbo jets at Frankfurt airport is only an insignificant part of a hydrogen economy. Has the magnitude of the task been recognized?

Questions of this nature need to be addressed before resources are invested in a hydrogen infrastructure. The mission should not be the development of technology and the introduction of new energy carriers, but the establishment of a sustainable energy future. There are other options to be considered before we make major commitments to a hydrogen future.

Sustainable Energy Future

In this paper, fossil and nuclear energy are defined as unsustainable because the resources are finite and the waste cannot be absorbed by nature. If one accepts this definition, renewable energy harvested in a sustainable way becomes the key to a sustainable energy future.

With the exception of biomass, all renewable energy is of a physical nature: heat (solar, geothermal), solar radiation (photovoltaic) and mechanical energy (wind, hydro, waves, etc.). Heat obtained from solar collectors, geothermal sources, and waste incineration may also be converted to electricity. Thus, in one vision of a sustainable future, electricity from renewable sources will become the dominant primary energy carrier replacing chemical carriers of today's economy.

Physical energy provided by nature is best distributed as physical energy without intermediate chemical carriers, because, excepting food, people need physical energy for transport, space conditioning, fabrication processes, cooking, lighting, and communication. Hydrogen would make sense only if its production, distribution, and use are superior to the distribution of electricity by wires.

For centuries hydrogen has fascinated people. Hydrogen can be derived from water and other chemical compounds. The conversion of hydrogen to heat or power is often simplified by the popular equation "hydrogen plus air yields electricity and drinking water." Also, hydrogen, the most common chemical element on the planet, is hailed as an everlasting energy source. But nature does not provide hydrogen in its elemental form. High-grade energy (electricity or heat) is needed to liberate hydrogen from its chemical source.

Economy means trade. A hydrogen economy involves all economic stages between hydrogen production and hydrogen use, i.e., between renewable electricity received to electrolyzers and useful electricity drawn from fuel cells. Between the two ends of the economic chain hydrogen has to be packaged by compression or liquefaction to become a commodity. In the transportation, hydrogen has to be produced, packaged, transported, stored, transferred to cars, then stored and transported again before it is finally admitted to fuel cells.

All these processes require energy. Compared to natural gas (methane) or liquid fuels much more energy is required for the marketing of hydrogen. This is directly related to the physical properties of hydrogen (density 0.09 kg/m^3, boiling point 20.3 K). Compared to methane, the volumetric energy density of hydrogen is less than one third. Even in the liquid state, the density of hydrogen (70 kg/m^3) is not much above the density of heavy duty styrofoam. Gasoline and even wood pellets carry 3.5 or 1.2 times more energy per volume than liquefied hydrogen. One cubic meter of the cold liquid holds 70 kg, the same volume of gasoline 128 kg of hydrogen. The best way to store hydrogen is in chemical combination with carbon. . . .

Energy Needs of a Hydrogen Economy

The energy needed to produce, compress, liquefy, transport, transfer, and store hydrogen and the energy lost for its conversion back to electricity with fuel cells can never be recovered. The heat of formation or [higher heat in value (HHV)] has been used throughout to base the analysis on true energy contents in agreement with the law of energy conservation.

In contrast, the lower heating value (LHV), a man-created accounting convention, is appropriate only when energetic processes are compared for identical fuels. In many "well-to-wheel" studies, hydrogen solutions are embellished by 10% as a result of an LHV accounting. When hydrogen is made by whatever process at least the heat of formation HHV of the synthetic energy carrier has to be invested in form of electricity, heat, or HHV energy content of precursor materials. For a correct accounting the output of a fuel cell should also be related to the HHV, not the LHV energy content of the hydrogen gas. Also, LHV accounting may turn conventional energy equipment into perpetual motion machines with efficiencies exceeding 100%. The use of the higher heating value HHV is appropriate for all serious energy analyses.

Although cost of energy is an important issue, this study is only concerned with energy balances. Energy is needed for solving the energy problem and energy waste has to be minimized. However, a quick visit to the market is helpful. . . . Every GJ of hydrogen energy will cost around $5.60 when produced from natural gas, $10.30 from coal, and $20.10 from electrolysis of water. Before taxes, gasoline costs about $3.00 per GJ.

Production of Hydrogen by Electrolysis

Making hydrogen from water by electrolysis is an energy-intensive process. However, in a sustainable energy future, this is the direct route from renewable electricity to a chemical energy carrier. The standard potential for the water formation is 1.48 V, corresponding to the heat of formation or the higher heating value HHV of hydrogen. . . .

The electrolysis is frequently performed under pressure. In that case, part of the electrical energy input is used for an isothermal compression. Pressure is not obtained for free, but by this meaningful procedure compression losses and equipment costs are reduced. Pressure electrolysis offers energetic and commercial advantages over atmospheric electrolyzers.

Electrolysis may be the only practical link between renewable energy and hydrogen. Although solar or nuclear heat can also be used for high-temperature cyclic processes, it is unlikely that a recognizable fraction of the global energy demand can be served with hydrogen from solar concentrators or high-temperature reactors. Local wind farms may deliver energy at lower costs than distant solar or nuclear installations.

Hydrogen from Biomass

Hydrogen from biomass is another option with uncertain future. Biomass has to be converted to biomethane by aerobic fermentation or gasification before hydrogen can be made. However, biomethane of natural gas quality (above 96% CH$_4$) is already a perfect fuel for transport and stationary applications. Why reform it to hydrogen? In many European countries, biomethane from sewage digesters is already sold at fueling stations to a growing number of satisfied drivers.

In a sustainable future, hydrogen could also be obtained by reforming of alcohols or wood. This is not likely to happen, because the listed biofuels are much better energy carriers than hydrogen. The inherent value of these substances is the natural bond of hydrogen and carbon atoms. By chemical rearrangement (e.g., Fischer Tropsch) it is possible to synthesize liquid hydrocarbons for long distance transport by air, ship, rail, or road. Hydrogen production from biomass shall not be considered in this context.

Using autothermal processes the conversion can be very efficient. The process heat obtained by burning some of the biomass is transferred to the hydrogen stream. Industrial natural gas reformers generate hydrogen with energetic HHV efficiencies of 90%. Today, this is the most economical method to obtain hydrogen. As stated earlier, hydrogen production from fossil hydrocarbons is not here considered sustainable.

Packaging of Hydrogen by Compression

Compressing gas requires energy. . . . Compared to methane, about nine times more energy per kg is required to compress hydrogen, and 15 times more (ratio of molecular masses) than for air. The energy consumption for compression of hydrogen is substantial and has to be considered.

Multistage compressors with intercoolers operate somewhere between the isothermal and adiabatic limits. Compared with methane, hydrogen passes the compression heat faster to the cooler walls thus bringing the process closer to isothermal. Data provided by a leading manufacturer of hydrogen compressors show that the energy required for a five-stage compression of 1000 kg of hydrogen per hour from ambient pressure to 20 MPa is about 7.2% of its HHV. . . .

For multistage compression to a final pressure of 20 MPa, about 8% of the HHV energy content of hydrogen is required. This analysis does not include any losses in the electrical power supply system. At least 1.08 units of energy must be invested in compression to obtain 1 unit of hydrogen HHV at 20 MPa. The number becomes 1.12 for compression to 80 MPa for hydrogen transfer to the proposed 70 MPa standard vehicle tanks of automobiles. If mechanical and electrical losses are also considered, the total electricity needs for compression may reach 20% of the HHV hydrogen energy leaving the process.

Packaging of Hydrogen by Liquefaction

Even more energy is needed to compact hydrogen by liquefaction. Theoretically, only about 14.2 $MJ/kgLH_2$ have to be removed to cool hydrogen gas from 298 K (25 °C) to 20.3 K and to condense the gas at 20.3 K and atmospheric pressure. However, at such low temperatures, no heat sinks exist for cooling and condensing hydrogen. Generally, a three-stage propane refrigeration system is used for cooling hydrogen gas from ambient temperature to about 170 K, followed by multistage nitrogen expansion to obtain 77 K, and a multistage helium compression–expansion to complete the liquefaction of hydrogen at 20.3 K and atmospheric pressure. The energy consumed by these three stages is much higher than the exergetic limit mentioned above. Therefore, published data of representative hydrogen liquefaction plants are used for reference.

The medium size liquefaction plant of Linde Gas AG at Ingolstadt in Germany produces 182 kg/h of LH_2 at a specific energy consumption of about 54 $MJ/kgLH_2$. Advanced larger plants in the United States require 36 $MJ/kgLH_2$ to liquefy hydrogen. In a Japanese feasibility study of a hydrogen liquefaction plant of 300 metric tons LH_2 per day or 12 500 $kgLH_2/h$, the best case power consumption is given at 105.2 MW. This corresponds to 30.3 $MJ/kgLH_2$ for a plant about six times larger than any existing facility. The use of helium–neon mixture for the low-temperature cycle has been suggested to reduce the energy consumption to, perhaps, 25.2 $MJ/kgLH_2(= 7 kWh/kgLH_2)$ for a plant producing 7200 $kgLH_2$ per hour, or 173 metric tons LH_2 per day. However, experimental results are not yet available.

The real-world requirements are much higher. Twenty-five hundred metric tons of liquid hydrogen would be required daily to fuel 50 jumbo jets departing from Frankfurt Airport. For this, 22 500 m^3 of clean water must be split by electrolysis. Hydrogen production and liquefaction consumes the continuous output of eight 1-GW power plants. The numbers may be multiplied by five if Frankfurt airport were totally converted to hydrogen.

Large liquefaction plants are more efficient than small facilities. . . . More electrical energy is consumed for the liquefaction of hydrogen in small plants than in large facilities.

For very small liquefaction plants (> 5 $kgLH_2/h$), the energy needed to liquefy hydrogen may exceed the HHV energy. Even 10 000 $kgLH_2/h$ plants (perhaps four times larger than any existing liquefaction facility) would consume about 25% of the HHV energy of the liquefied hydrogen. For the available technology, 40% would be a reasonable number. [In] other words, 1.4 units of energy would have to be supplied to the liquefier as hydrogen and electricity to obtain 1 HHV unit of liquid hydrogen. However, no liquefaction plants of comparable performance have yet been built.

Moreover, liquid hydrogen storage systems lose some hydrogen gas by boiloff. This is due to unavoidable heat leakage, and must be permitted for safety reasons. The loss rate is dependent on the size of the store, but would be significant for those used in vehicles, and may amount to 3%–4% a day. Boiloff hydrogen has to be vented from parked vehicles. For example, when a car is left at an airport for two weeks, 50% of the original hydrogen may be lost by evaporation.

Physical Metal Hydrides

Hydrogen may be stored physically, e.g., by adsorption in spongy matrices of special alloys of metal hydrides. The hydrogen forms a very close physical, but not a perfect chemical bond with alloys like $LaNi_5$ or $ZrCr_2$.

The energy balance shall be described in general terms. Again, energy is needed to produce and compress hydrogen. Some of this energy is lost. Also, heat is released and normally lost when metal hydride storage containers are filled with hydrogen. Conversely, heat must be added to liberate the stored hydrogen from the hydrides. The energy needed to store hydrogen in physical metal hydrides and to liberate it later is significantly more than the energy needed to compress the gas to 3 MPa, the typical filling pressure of hydride storage containers.

However, metal hydrides store only around 55–60 kg of hydrogen per m^3 of storage volume. For comparison, liquid hydrogen has a volumetric density of 70 kg/m^3. Moreover, metal hydride cartridges are heavy. A small metal hydride container holding less than 2 g of hydrogen has a weight of 230 g. Hence, around 50 kg of hydrides are required to store 1 kg of hydrogen, the equivalent of about 4 L or 1 U.S. gal of gasoline. Hydride storage of hydrogen is not practical for automotive application, unless the volumetric and gravimetric energy density of the storage medium can be raised. Today, the specific energy density of metal hydride storage devices is comparable to that of advanced Li–Ion batteries.

Chemical Metal Hydrides

Hydrogen may also be stored chemically in alkali metal hydrides. Alkali metal hydrides have high energy densities with gravimetric energy content comparable to firewood. The weight of alkali hydride materials poses no problems. One kg of CaH_2 or LiH reacting with water yields 13.6 or 36.1 MJ of HHV hydrogen energy, respectively. However, the energy needed to produce the alkali metal hydrides would discourage their commercial use on a larger scale.

There are many options in the alkali group like LiH, NaH, KH, and CaH_2. Complex binary hydride compounds like $LiBH_4$, $NaBH_4$, KBH_4, $LiAlH_4$, or $NaAlH_4$ have also been proposed for hydrogen storage. None of these compounds can be found in nature. All have to be synthesized from pure metals and hydrogen. . . .

For hydrogen storage in hydrides, at least 1.6 times more high-grade energy has to be invested to produce 1 HHV energy unit of hydrogen, resulting in a stage efficiency of less than 60%.

Road Delivery of Hydrogen

Although pipeline transport is preferred for gases, hydrogen transport by trucks will play a role in a hydrogen economy. Because of the low density of the gaseous energy carrier, transport of pressurized or liquid hydrogen is extremely inefficient. Forty-ton trucks can carry only 350 kg of hydrogen at 200 bar in the gaseous, or 3500 kg in the liquid state. The bulk weight is steel for pressure tanks and cryogenic vessels. It takes about 22 hydrogen tube trailers to deliver the same amount of energy as a single gasoline tanker.

The energy analysis is based on information obtained from some of the leading providers of industrial gases in Germany and Switzerland. . . . [The] following assumptions are made. Hydrogen gas (at 20 MPa = 200 bar), liquid hydrogen, methanol, ethanol, propane, and octane (representing gasoline) are trucked from the refinery or hydrogen plant to the consumer. Trucks with a gross weight of 40 metric tons are fitted with suitable containers. Fuel consumption is 40 kg of diesel fuel per 100 km and metric ton. The engine efficiency does not depend on the vehicle weight.

The 40-metric-ton tanker trucks are designed to carry a maximum of fuel. For liquids like gasoline, ethanol, and methanol, the payload is about 26 metric tons. One hundred percent of the liquid fuels are delivered to the customer. In contrast, only 80% of the compressed gases are transferred by blow-down. The remaining 20% of the gas load is returned to the gas plant. Such pressure cascades are standard practice today. As a consequence, the payload of pressurized gas carriers is 80% of the load. However, in anticipation of technical developments, this analysis assumes that in future, trucks will be able to carry 4000 kg methane or 500 kg of hydrogen, of which 80% (3200 kg or 400 kg, respectively) are delivered to the consumer.

The transport of liquid hydrogen is limited by volume, not by weight. A large trailer-truck may have a useful box volume of 2.4-m width, 2.5-m height, and 10-m length, i.e., 60 m^3. As the density of 70 kg/m^3, only 4200 kg of liquid hydrogen could possibly be loaded. But space is needed for the cryogenic container, thermal insulation, safety equipment, etc. In fact, a large truck has room for about 2100 kg of the cryogenic liquid. However, trucking liquid hydrogen is more energy efficient than delivering the pressurized gas.

. . . The energy needed to transport any of the liquid hydrocarbon fuels is reasonably small. For a one-way delivery distance of 100 km, the diesel fuel consumption remains below 0.5% of the HHV energy content of the delivered liquid fuels. However, for delivering pressurized hydrogen, the parasitic energy consumption is significant. About 7% of the delivered energy is consumed for delivery, about 13 times more than for gasoline. For liquid hydrogen the ratio is about 3.5.

Pipeline Delivery of Hydrogen

Hydrogen pipelines exist to transport the chemical commodity "hydrogen" from sources to production sites. The energy required to deliver the gas is part of the production process and energy costs are absorbed in the final price of the product. People do not mind paying for hydrogen in aspirin, plastic materials, or steel. However, energy is the currency in pipeline transport of hydrogen. Parasitic energy losses reduce the amount of energy available for useful purposes. Hydrogen transport by pipelines has to compete with electricity transport by wires.

The assessment of the energy required to pump hydrogen through pipelines is derived from natural gas pipeline operating experience. It is assumed that the same amount of energy is delivered through identical pipelines. In reality, existing pipelines must be modified for hydrogen, because of diffusion losses (mainly in sealing areas), brittleness of materials and seals, compressor lubrication, and other technical issues. Also, as the volumetric HHV energy content of hydrogen is about 3.5 times less than that of natural gas, pipes of larger diameters are needed to accommodate similar energy flow rates. Natural gas is diluted by adding hydrogen, not upgraded. . . .

Typically, a compressor is installed every 150 km for natural gas transport through pipelines at 10 m/s. The compressor motors are fueled from the gas taken from the stream, each compressor consuming about 0.3% of the local energy flow. Applying this model to the transport of hydrogen through the same pipeline, each compressor would require 3.85 more energy or 1.16% of the local energy flow. The remaining mass flow is decreasing with pipeline length. This crude model needs to be refined by pipeline experts. It does not consider the higher energy needs for hydrogen compression discussed above.

For a pipeline length of 3000 km (e.g., for gas from Russian fields to Germany), the mass fraction consumed for transporting natural gas is about 20%, while transporting hydrogen gas over the same distance would require about 35% of the original mass flow. This result was obtained for pipes of equal diameter. . . .

For a transport distance of 3000 km, at least 1.5 kg of hydrogen must be fed into the line for the delivery of 1 kg to the customer. Moving hydrogen over long distances by pipeline is not a good option. However, hydrogen pipelines have been suggested for the transport of solar energy from northern Africa or the Middle East to central Europe.

On-Site Generation of Hydrogen

One option for providing hydrogen at filling stations and dispersed depots is on-site generation of the gas by electrolysis. Again, the energy needed to generate and compress hydrogen by this scheme is compared to the HHV energy content of the hydrogen transferred to cars. Natural gas reforming is not a sustainable solution and thus not considered for the reasons stated earlier.

Consider a filling station now pumping 60 000 L of fuel (gasoline or diesel) into 1000 cars, trucks, or buses per day. This number is typical for service areas along European freeways. In most parts of the United States, many smaller filling stations are located roadside at freeway exits. On a 1 : 1 energy base, 60 000 L of fuel corresponds to about 17 000 kg of hydrogen. However, hydrogen vehicles are assumed to have a 1.5 times higher tank-to-wheel efficiency than IC engine cars. The frequently cited number of 2.5 cannot be justified any

longer in light of the high efficiency of diesel or hybrid vehicles. In fact, the well-to-wheel studies of 2002 are based on lower heating values, optimistic assumptions of fuel cells, and disregard of the efficiency potentials of diesel engines and hybrid systems. Furthermore, more recent well-to-wheel studies appropriately based on the higher heating values do not identify hydrogen-fuel-cell cars as the best transportation option. In fact, the efficiency of all-electric cars is three times better than for hydrogen-fuel-cell vehicles.

Under the favorable assumption of a 1.5 advantage of hydrogen versus gasoline, 60 000 liters of fuel will be replaced by 12 000 kg of hydrogen per day. The electrolyzer efficiency may be 75%. Also, losses occur in the ac-dc power conversion. Making 12 000 kg of hydrogen per day by electrolysis requires 25 MW of continuous power and 108 000 liters of water must be pumped and demineralized. Compression power is needed for storing the hydrogen to 10 MPa and for transfer at 40 MPa to vehicle tanks at 35 MPa. In all, to generate and store 12 000 kg of hydrogen per day, the filling station must be supplied with continuous electric power of about 28 MW. There are many sites in arid regions where neither the electricity nor the water is available for hydrogen production.

For 12 000 kg of hydrogen per day (this corresponds to 1000 conventional vehicles per day), about 1.65 units of energy must be invested to obtain 1 unit of hydrogen HHV, giving a stage efficiency of 60%.

Assuming continuous operation, a 1-GW electric power plant must be available for every 20–30 hydrogen filling stations on European freeways. Today, about one fifth of the total energy consumption is electricity. The national electric power generating capacity must be significantly increased to power the transition from fossil fuels to hydrogen. It may be difficult to derive the needed electrical energy from "renewable sources" as suggested by hydrogen promoters. One would certainly use off-peak power from wind and solar sources for hydrogen production. However, electrolyzers, pumps, and storage tanks must be sized for peak demand during rush hours and vacation traffic. Not only must the electric peak power demand be considered, but also the storage of substantial amounts of hydrogen to meet the daily and seasonal demands at filling stations. . . .

Energy Efficiency of a Hydrogen Economy

When the original report was published in 2003, the parasitic energy needs of a hydrogen economy had not even been considered by promoters of a hydrogen economy. The intent of the original study was to create an awareness of the fundamental energetic weaknesses of using hydrogen as an energy vector. Since then equations and results for producing, packaging, distributing, storing, and transferring hydrogen have been checked by others and found correct.

For selected hydrogen strategies, the accumulated parasitic energy needs of all important stages can be determined by multiplication or addition of the losses of the stages involved. Four cases may serve to illustrate the point

a. Hydrogen is produced by electrolysis, compressed to 20 MPa and distributed by road to filling stations, stored at 10 MPa, then compressed to 40 MPa for rapid transfer to vehicles at 35 MPa. Energy input to hydrogen energy delivered: 1.59

b. Hydrogen is produced by electrolysis, liquefied, and distributed by road to filling stations, then transferred to vehicles.
Energy input to hydrogen energy delivered: 2.02

c. Hydrogen is produced by electrolysis on-site at filling stations or consumers, stored at 10 MPa, and subsequently compressed to 40 MPa for rapid transfer to vehicles at 35 MPa.
Energy input to hydrogen energy delivered: 1.59

d. Hydrogen is produced by electrolysis and used to make alkali metal hydrides. Hydrogen is then released by reaction of the hydride with water.
Energy input to hydrogen energy delivered: 1.90

The analysis reveals that between 1.6 and 2.0 electrical energy units must be harvested from renewable sources for every energy unit of hydrogen gas sold to the user. The high energy losses may be tolerated for some niche markets, but it is unlikely that hydrogen will ever become an important energy carrier in a sustainable energy economy built on renewable sources and efficiency.

Moreover, the delivered hydrogen must be converted to motion for all transport applications. IC engines convert hydrogen within 45% efficiency directly into mechanical motion, while equally efficient fuel cells systems produce dc electricity for traction motors. Further losses may occur in transmissions, etc. All in all, hardly 50% of the hydrogen energy contained in a vehicle tank is converted to motion of a car. The overall efficiency between electricity from renewable sources and wheel motion is only 20 to 25%. In comparison, over 60% of the original electricity can be used for transportation, if the energy is not converted to hydrogen, but directly used in electric vehicles. The energy advantages of battery-electric cars over hydrogen-fuel-cell-electric vehicles are obvious. However, further work is needed in the area of electricity storage, converters, drive systems, and electricity transfer.

Hydrogen Economy or Electron Economy

The foregoing analysis of the parasitic energy losses within a hydrogen economy shows that a hydrogen economy is an extremely inefficient proposition for the distribution of electricity from renewable sources to useful electricity from fuel cells. Only about 25% of the power generated from wind, water, or sun is converted to practical use. If the original electricity had been directly supplied by wires, as much as 90% could have been put to service. This has two serious consequences to be considered in future energy strategies.

a. About four renewable power plants have to be erected to deliver the output of one plant to stationary or mobile consumers via hydrogen and fuel cells. Three of these plants generate energy to cover the parasitic losses of the hydrogen economy while only one of them is producing useful energy. Can we base our energy future on such wasteful schemes?

b. As energy losses will be charged to the customer, electricity from hydrogen fuel cells will be at least four times more expensive than electricity from the grid. Who wants to use fuel cells? Who wants to drive a hydrogen-fuel-cell car?

Fundamental laws of physics expose the weakness of a hydrogen economy. Hydrogen, the artificial energy carrier, can never compete with its own energy source, electricity, in a sustainable future.

The discussion about a hydrogen economy is adding irritation to the energy debate. We need to focus our attention on sustainable energy solutions. It seems that the establishment of an efficient electron economy should become the common goal. There are many topics to be addressed, like electricity storage and automatic electricity transfer to vehicles, yet electric cars equipped with Li–Ion-batteries already have a driving range of 250 km. In 2010, Mitsubishi will commercialize an electric car with 260 hp on four wheels and a driving range of 500 km (300 mi). It seems that by focusing attention on hydrogen we are missing the chance to meet the challenges of a sustainable energy future.

The title question "Does a hydrogen economy make sense?" must be answered with a definite "Never." However, niche applications for the use of hydrogen energy are abundant and should be addressed.

ULF BOSSEL is on the Board of Advisors of the European Fuel Cell Forum in Lucerne, Switzerland.

EXPLORING THE ISSUE

Does a Hydrogen Economy Make Sense?

Critical Thinking and Reflection

1. Discuss why we need one or more replacements for fossil fuel energy (natural gas, oil, and coal).
2. What requirements must a replacement for fossil fuel energy satisfy?
3. Why can't the various energy-conversion efficiency factors discussed by Ulf Bossel be improved?

Is There Common Ground?

Does a hydrogen economy make sense? Both sides agree that we need to develop a replacement for the fossil fuel economy we are accustomed to and that there are serious difficulties in implementing a hydrogen-based replacement (among which is the need to distribute fuel). Both also agree that there is a place for electricity-powered vehicles.

1. What technological changes would make electricity-powered vehicles more satisfactory to all concerned?
2. What changes in the structure of society might make hydrogen a more affordable option?

Additional Resources

M. Balat and E. Kirtay, "Major Technical Barriers to a 'Hydrogen Economy'," *Energy Sources, Part A: Recovery, Utilization & Environmental Effects* (June 2010).

Joan M. Ogden, "Hydrogen: The Fuel of the Future?" *Physics Today* (April 2002).

Piotr Tomczyk, "Fundamental Aspects of the Hydrogen Economy," *World Futures* (July 2009).

Laurie Wiegler, "The Future of Hydrogen Cars," *Technology Review* (September 21, 2011) (www.technologyreview.com/energy/38647/).

Create Central

www.mhhe.com/createcentral

Internet References . . .

International Association for Hydrogen Energy

The International Association for Hydrogen Energy works toward the time when hydrogen energy will be the principal means by which the world achieves its long-sought goal of abundant clean energy for mankind.

www.iahe.org/

Some other groups and sites with a similar mission are:

Renewable Energy World

www.renewableenergyworld.com/rea/tech/hydrogen

Hydrogen Energy Center

www.h2eco.org/

U.S. Department of Energy Hydrogen and Fuel Cells Program

www.hydrogen.energy.gov/

Unit 3

UNIT

Human Health and Welfare

*M*any people are concerned about new technological and scientific discoveries because they fear their potential impacts on human health and welfare. In the past, fears have been expressed concerning nuclear bombs and power plants, irradiated food, the internal combustion engine, medications such as thalidomide and diethylstilbestrol, vaccines, pesticides and other chemicals, and more. Because human birth rates have declined, at least in developed nations, the hazards of excess population have fallen out of the headlines, but a few people do still struggle to remind us that a smaller population makes many problems less worrisome. On the public-health front, people worry about whether new "synthetic biology" organisms pose a threat and about whether research into infectious animal diseases such as hoof-and-mouth disease should be kept far away from livestock operations. It is worth stressing that risks may be real (as they are with toxic chemicals), but there may be a trade-off for genuine health benefits.

Selected, Edited, and with Issue Framing Material by:
Thomas A. Easton, *Thomas College*

ISSUE

Do We Have a Population Problem?

YES: **Dennis Dimick**, from "As World's Population Booms, Will Its Resources Be Enough for Us?" *National Geographic* (2014)

NO: **Tom Bethell**, from "Population, Economy, and God," *The American Spectator* (2009)

Learning Outcomes

After reading this issue, you will be able to:

- Explain why unrestrained population growth is not sustainable.
- Explain why past predictions of population disaster have not come true.
- Explain the potential benefits of stabilizing or reducing population.
- Explain the potential drawbacks of stabilizing or reducing population.

ISSUE SUMMARY

YES: **Dennis Dimick** argues that new projections of higher population growth through the twenty-first century are reason for concern, largely because of the conflict between population size and resource use. The environmental impact of population also depends on technology, affluence, and waste, but educated women have smaller families and technology (electric lights, for instance) aids education. Controlling population appears to be essential.

NO: **Tom Bethell** argues that population alarmists project their fears onto popular concerns, currently the environment, and every time their scare-mongering turns out to be based on faulty premises. Blaming environmental problems will be no different. Societies are sustained not by population control but by belief in God.

I n 1798 the British economist Thomas Malthus published his *Essay on the Principle of Population*. In it, he pointed with alarm at the way the human population grew geometrically (a hockey-stick-shaped curve of increase) and at how agricultural productivity grew only arithmetically (a straight-line increase). It was obvious, he said, that the population must inevitably outstrip its food supply and experience famine. Contrary to the conventional wisdom of the time, population growth was not necessarily a good thing. Indeed, it led inexorably to catastrophe. For many years, Malthus was something of a laughing stock. The doom he forecast kept receding into the future as new lands were opened to agriculture, new agricultural

technologies appeared, new ways of preserving food limited the waste of spoilage, and the birth rate dropped in the industrialized nations (the "demographic transition"). The food supply kept ahead of population growth and seemed likely—to most observers—to continue to do so. Malthus's ideas were dismissed as irrelevant fantasies.

Yet overall population kept growing. In Malthus's time, there were about 1 billion human beings on Earth. By 1950—when Warren S. Thompson worried that civilization would be endangered by the rapid growth of Asian and Latin American populations during the next five decades (see "Population," *Scientific American*, February 1950)— there were a little over 2.5 billion. In 1999 the tally passed 6 billion. It passed 7 billion in 2011. By 2025 it will be over 8 billion. Until fairly recently, most experts thought that population would peak at about 9 billion around 2050 and then begin to level off and even decline. Some projected a 2100 world population of about 10 billion; see Jocelyn Keiser, "10 Billion Plus: Why World Population Projections Were Too Low," *Science Insider* (May 4, 2011) (http://scim.ag/_worldpop). However, in 2014 the United Nations released estimates indicating that population would not level off before 2100. Indeed, it could reach 12 billion, or even a bit more, largely due to continuing high growth rates in Africa; see Patrick Gerland, et al., "World Population Stabilization Unlikely This Century," *Science* (October 10, 2014).

While global agricultural production has also increased, it has not kept up with rising demand, and— because of the loss of topsoil to erosion, the exhaustion of aquifers for irrigation water, and the high price of energy for making fertilizer (among other things)—the prospect of improvement seems exceedingly slim to many observers. Two centuries never saw Malthus's forecasts of doom come to pass. Population continued to grow, and environmentalists pointed with alarm at a great many problems that resulted from human use of the world's resources (air and water pollution, erosion, loss of soil fertility and groundwater, loss of species, and a great deal more). "Cornucopian" economists such as the late Julian Simon insisted that the more people there are on Earth, the more people there are to solve problems and that humans can find ways around all possible resource shortages. See Simon's essay, "Life on Earth Is Getting Better, Not Worse," *The Futurist* (August 1983). See also David Malakoff, "Are More People Necessarily a Problem?" *Science* (July 29, 2011) (a special issue on population).

Was Malthus wrong? Both environmental scientists and many economists now say that if population continues to grow, problems are inevitable. But some experts still project that population will level off and then decline. Fred Pearce, *The Coming Population Crash: and Our Planet's Surprising Future* (Beacon, 2010), is optimistic about the effects on human well-being of the coming decline in population. Do we still need to work on controlling population? Historian Matthew Connolly, *Fatal Misconception: The Struggle to Control World Population* (Belknap Press, 2010), argues that the twentieth-century movement to control population was an oppressive movement that failed to deliver on its promises. Now that population growth is slowing, the age of population control is over. Yet there remains the issue of "carrying capacity," defined very simply as the size of the population that the environment can support, or "carry," indefinitely, through both good years and bad. It is not the size of the population that

can prosper in good times alone, for such a large population must suffer catastrophically when droughts, floods, or blights arrive or the climate warms or cools. It is a long-term concept, where "long-term" means not decades or generations, nor even centuries, but millennia or more. See Mark Nathan Cohen, "Carrying Capacity," *Free Inquiry* (August/September 2004); T. C. R. White, "The Role of Food, Weather, and Climate in Limiting the Abundance of Animals," *Biological Reviews* (August 2008); and David Pimentel, et al., "Will Limited Land, Water, and Energy Control Human Population Numbers in the Future?" *Human Ecology* (August 2010).

What is Earth's carrying capacity for human beings? It is surely impossible to set a precise figure on the number of human beings the world can support for the long run. As Joel E. Cohen discusses in *How Many People Can the Earth Support?* (W. W. Norton, 1996), estimates of Earth's carrying capacity range from under a billion to over a trillion. The precise number depends on our choices of diet, standard of living, level of technology, willingness to share with others at home and abroad, and desire for an intact physical, chemical, and biological environment (including wildlife and natural environments), as well as on whether or not our morality permits restraint in reproduction and our political or religious ideology permits educating and empowering women. The key, Cohen stresses, is human choice, and the choices are ones we must make within the next 50 years. Phoebe Hall, "Carrying Capacity," *E—The Environmental Magazine* (March/April 2003), notes that even countries with large land areas and small populations, such as Australia and Canada, can be overpopulated in terms of resource availability. The critical resource appears to be food supply; see Russell Hopfenberg, "Human Carrying Capacity Is Determined by Food Availability," *Population & Environment* (November 2003).

Andrew R. B. Ferguson, in "Perceiving the Population Bomb," *World Watch* (July/August 2001), sets the maximum sustainable human population at about 2 billion. Sandra Postel, in the Worldwatch Institute's *State of the World 1994* (W.W. Norton, 1994), says, "As a result of our population size, consumption patterns, and technology choices, we have surpassed the planet's carrying capacity. This is plainly evident by the extent to which we are damaging and depleting natural capital" (including land and water). The point is reiterated by Robert Kunzig, "By 2045 Global Population Is Projected to Reach Nine Billion. Can the Planet Take the Strain?" *National Geographic* (January 2011) (*National Geographic* ran numerous articles on population-related issues during 2011). Thomas L. Friedman, "The Earth Is Full," *New York Times* (June 7, 2011), thinks a crisis is imminent but we will learn and move on; see also Paul

Gilding, *The Great Disruption: Why the Climate Crisis Will Bring On the End of Shopping and the Birth of a New World* (Bloomsbury Press, 2011).

Or is the crisis less urgent? Many people, relying on pre-2014 estimates of future population, think population growth is now declining and world population will actually begin to decline during this century. See Jeff Wise, "About that Overpopulation Problem," *Slate* (January 9, 2013) (http://www.slate.com /articles/technology/future_tense/2013/01/world _population_may_actually_start_declining_not _exploding.html. If they are right, there is clearly hope. But most estimates of carrying capacity put it at well below the current world population size, and it will take a long time for global population to fall far enough to reach such levels. Perhaps we are moving in the right direction, but it remains an open question whether our numbers will decline far enough soon enough (i.e., before environmental problems become critical). On the other hand, Jeroen Van den Bergh and Piet Rietveld, "Reconsidering the Limits to World Population: Meta-Analysis and Meta-Prediction," *Bioscience* (March 2004), set their best estimate of human global carrying capacity at 7.7 billion, which is distinctly reassuring. J. T. Trevors, "Total Abuse of the Earth: Human Overpopulation and Climate Change," *Water, Air, and Soil Pollution* (January 2010, Suppl. 1), is less optimistic, noting that we are in unsustainable territory and "The party [of endless growth and consumption] is over. . . . Humans cannot bribe nor buy nature."

How high a level will population actually reach? Fertility levels are definitely declining in many developed nations; see Alan Booth and Ann C. Crouter (eds.), *The New population problem: Why Families in Developed Countries Are Shrinking and What It Means* (Lawrence Erlbaum Associates, 2005). The visibility of this fertility decline is among the reasons mentioned by Martha Campbell, "Why the Silence on Population?" *Population and Environment* (May 2007). Yet Doug Moss, "What Birth Dearth?" *E— The Environmental Magazine* (November–December 2006), reminds us that there is still a large surplus of births— and therefore a growing population—in the less developed world. If we think globally, there is no shortage of people. However, many countries are so concerned about changing age distributions that they are trying to encourage larger—not smaller—families. See Robert Engelman, "Unnatural Increase? A Short History of Population Trends and Influences," *World Watch* (September/October 2008—a special issue on population issues), "Population and Sustainability," *Scientific American Earth 3.0* (Summer 2009), and his book *More: Population, Nature, and What Women Want* (Island Press, 2008). On the other hand,

David E. Bloom, "7 Billion and Counting," *Science* (July 29, 2011), notes that "Despite alarmist predictions, historical increases in population have not been economically catastrophic. Moreover, changes in population age structure [providing for more workers] have opened the door to increased prosperity." Jonathan A. Foley, "Can We Feed the World & Sustain the Planet?" *Scientific American* (November 2011), thinks that with revisions to the world's agricultural systems, a growing population's demand for food can be met, at least through 2050.

Some people worry that a decline in population will not be good for human welfare. Michael Meyer, "Birth Dearth," *Newsweek* (September 27, 2004), argues that a shrinking population will mean that the economic growth that has meant constantly increasing standards of living must come to an end, government programs (from war to benefits for the poor and elderly) will no longer be affordable, a shrinking number of young people will have to support a growing elderly population, and despite some environmental benefits, quality of life will suffer. China is already feeling some of these effects; see Wang Feng, "China's Population Destiny: The Looming Crisis," *Current History* (September 2010), and Mara Hvistendahl, "Has China Outgrown the One-Child Policy?" *Science* (September 17, 2010). Julia Whitty, "The Last Taboo," *Mother Jones* (May–June 2010), argues that even though the topic of overpopulation has become unpopular, it is clear that we are already using the Earth's resources faster than they can be replenished and the only answer is to slow and eventually reverse population growth. Scott Victor Valentine, "Disarming the Population Bomb," *International Journal of Sustainable Development and World Ecology* (April 2010), calls for "a renewed international focus on managed population reduction as a key enabler of sustainable development." As things stand, the current size and continued growth of population threaten the United Nations' Millennium Development Goals (including alleviating global poverty, improving health, and protecting the environment; see http://www.un.org /millenniumgoals/); see Willard Cates, Jr., et al., "Family Planning and the Millennium Development Goals," *Science* (September 24, 2010). Paul R. Ehrlich and Anne H. Ehrlich, "Solving the Human Predicament," *International Journal of Environmental Studies* (August 2012), stress the contribution of population to environmental problems and see hope in a wide variety of grassroots movements.

In the YES selection, Dennis Dimick argues that new projections of higher population growth through the twenty-first century are reason for concern, largely because of the conflict between population size and resource use. The environmental impact of population also depends on technology, affluence, and waste, but educated women have smaller families and technology (electric lights, for instance) aids education. Controlling population appears to be essential. In the NO selection, Tom Bethell argues that population alarmists project their fears onto popular concerns, currently the environment, and every time their scaremongering turns out to be based on faulty premises. Blaming environmental problems will be no different. Societies are sustained not by population control but by belief in God.

YES

Dennis Dimick

As World's Population Booms, Will Its Resources Be Enough for Us?

This week, two conflicting projections of the world's future population were released. . . . [A] new United Nations and University of Washington study in the journal *Science* says it's highly likely we'll see 9.6 billion Earthlings by 2050, and up to 11 billion or more by 2100. These researchers used a new "probabilistic" statistical method that establishes a specific range of uncertainty around their results. Another study in the journal *Global Environmental Change* projects that the global population will peak at 9.4 billion later this century and fall below 9 billion by 2100, based on a survey of population experts. Who is right? We'll know in a hundred years.

Population debates like this are why, in 2011, *National Geographic* published a series called "7 Billion" on world population, its trends, implications, and future. After years of examining global environmental issues such as climate change, energy, food supply, and freshwater, we thought the time was ripe for a deep discussion of people and how we are connected to all these other issues—issues that are getting increased attention today, amid the new population projections.

After all, how many of us there are, how many children we have, how long we live, and where and how we live affect virtually every aspect of the planet upon which we rely to survive: the land, oceans, fisheries, forests, wildlife, grasslands, rivers and lakes, groundwater, air quality, atmosphere, weather, and climate.

World population passed 7 billion on October 31, 2011, according to the United Nations. Just who the 7 billionth person was and where he or she was born remain a mystery; there is no actual cadre of census takers who go house to house in every country, counting people. Instead, population estimates are made by most national governments and international organizations such as the UN. These estimates are based on assumptions about existing population size and expectations of fertility, mortality, and migration in a geographic area.

We've been on a big growth spurt during the past century or so. In 1900, demographers had the world's population at 1.6 billion, in 1950 it was about 2.5 billion, by 2000 it was more than 6 billion. Now, there are about 7.2 billion of us.

In recent years we've been adding about a billion people every 12 or 13 years or so. Precisely how many of us are here right now is also a matter of debate, depending on whom you consult: The United Nations offers a range of current population figures and trends, the U.S. Census Bureau has its own estimate, and the Population Reference Bureau also tracks us.

The new UN study out this week projects that the world's population growth may not stop any time soon. That is a reversal from estimates done five years ago, when demographers—people who study population trends—were projecting that by 2045, world population likely would reach about 9 billion and begin to level off soon after.

But now, the UN researchers who published these new projections in the journal *Science* say that a flattening of population growth is not going to happen soon without rapid fertility declines—or a reduction in the number of children per mother—in most parts of sub-Saharan Africa that are still experiencing rapid population growth. As Rob Kunzig wrote for *National Geographic*, the new study estimates that "there's an 80 percent chance . . . that the actual number of people in 2100 will be somewhere between 9.6 and 12.3 billion."

A History of Debates Over Population

In a famous 1798 essay, the Reverend Thomas Malthus proposed that human population would grow more rapidly than our ability to grow food, and that eventually we would starve.

He asserted that the population would grow geometrically—1, 2, 4, 8, 16, 32—and that food production would increase only arithmetically—1, 2, 3, 4, 5, 6. So food production would not keep up with our expanding appetites. You might imagine Malthus' scenario on geometric population growth as being like compound interest: A couple have two children and those children each produce two children. Those four children produce two children each to make eight, and those eight children each have their own two kids, leaving 16 kids in that generation. But worldwide, the current median fertility rate is about 2.5, (or five children between two couples), so, like compound interest, the population numbers can rise even faster.

Even though more than 800 million people worldwide don't have enough to eat now, the mass starvation Mathus envisioned hasn't happened. This is primarily because advances in agriculture—including improved plant breeding and the use of chemical fertilizers—have kept global harvests increasing fast enough to mostly keep up with demand. Still, researchers such as Jeffrey Sachs and Paul Ehrlich continue to worry that Malthus eventually might be right.

Ehrlich, a Stanford University population biologist, wrote a 1968 bestseller called *The Population Bomb*, which warned of mass starvation in the 1970s and 1980s because of overpopulation. Even though he drastically missed that forecast, he continues to argue that humanity is heading for calamity. Ehrlich says the key issue now is not just the number of people on Earth, but a dramatic rise in our recent consumption of natural resources, which Elizabeth Kolbert explored in 2011 in an article called "The Anthropocene—The Age of Man."

As part of this human-dominated era, the past half century also has been referred to as a period of "Great Acceleration" by Will Steffen at The International Geosphere-Biosphere Program. Besides a near tripling of human population since the end of World War II, our presence has been marked by a dramatic increase in human activity—the damming of rivers, soaring water use, expansion of cropland, increased use of irrigation and fertilizers, a loss of forests, and more motor vehicles. There also has been a sharp rise in the use of coal, oil, and gas, and a rapid increase in the atmosphere of methane and carbon dioxide, greenhouse gases that result from changes in land use and the burning of such fuels.

Measuring Our Rising Impact

As a result of this massive expansion of our presence on Earth, scientists Ehrlich, John Holdren, and Barry Commoner in the early 1970s devised a formula to measure our rising impact, called IPAT, in which (I)mpact equals (P)opulation multiplied by (A)ffluence multiplied by (T)echnology.

The IPAT formula, they said, can help us realize that our cumulative impact on the planet is not just in population numbers, but also in the increasing amount of natural resources each person uses. . . . [T]rise in our cumulative impact since 1950—rising population combined with our expanding demand for resources—has been profound.

IPAT is a useful reminder that population, consumption, and technology all help shape our environmental impact, but it shouldn't be taken too literally. University of California ecologist John Harte has said that IPAT ". . . conveys the notion that population is a linear multiplier. . . . In reality, population plays a much more dynamic and complex role in shaping environmental quality."

One of our biggest impacts is agriculture. Whether we can grow enough food sustainably for an expanding world population also presents an urgent challenge, and this becomes only more so in light of these new population projections. Where will food for an additional 2 to 3 billion people come from when we are already barely keeping up with 7 billion? Such questions underpin a 2014 *National Geographic* series on the future of food.

As climate change damages crop yields and extreme weather disrupts harvests, growing enough food for our expanding population has become what The 2014 World Food Prize Symposium calls "the greatest challenge in human history."

Population's Structure: Fertility, Mortality, and Migration

Population is not just about numbers of people. Demographers typically focus on three dimensions—fertility, mortality, and migration—when examining population trends. Fertility examines how many children a woman bears in her lifetime, mortality looks at how long we live, and migration focuses on where we live and move. Each of these population qualities influences the nature of our presence and impact across the planet.

The newly reported higher world population projections result from continuing high fertility in sub-Saharan Africa. The median number of children per woman in the region remains at 4.6, well above both the global mean of 2.5 and the replacement level of 2.1. Since 1970, a global decline in fertility—from about 5 children per woman to about 2.5—has occurred across most of the world: Fewer babies have been born, family size has shrunk, and population growth has slowed. In the United States, fertility is now slightly below replacement level.

Reducing fertility is essential if future population growth is to be reined in. Cynthia Gorney wrote about the dramatic story of declining Brazilian fertility as part of *National Geographic's* 7 Billion series. Average family size dropped from 6.3 children to 1.9 children per woman over two generations in Brazil, the result of improving education for girls, more career opportunities, and the increased availability of contraception.

Mortality—or birth rates versus death rates—and migration (where we live and move) also affect the structure of population. Living longer can cause a region's population to increase even if birth rates remain constant. Youthful nations in the Middle East and Africa, where there are more young people than old, struggle to provide sufficient land, food, water, housing, education, and employment for young people. Besides the search for a life with more opportunity elsewhere, migration also is driven by the need to escape political disruption or declining environmental conditions such as chronic drought and food shortages.

A paradox of lower fertility and reduced population growth rates is that as education and affluence improves, consumption of natural resources increases per person. In other words, . . . as we get richer, each of us consumes more natural resources and energy, typically carbon-based fuels such as coal, oil, and gas. This can be seen in consumption patterns that include higher protein foods such as meat and dairy, more consumer goods, bigger houses, more vehicles, and more air travel.

When it comes to natural resources, studies indicate we are living beyond our means. An ongoing Global Footprint Network study says we now use the equivalent of 1.5 planets to provide the resources we use, and to absorb our waste. A study by the Stockholm Resilience Institute has identified a set of "nine planetary boundaries" for conditions in which we could live and thrive for generations, but it shows that we already have exceeded the institute's boundaries for biodiversity loss, nitrogen pollution, and climate change.

Those of us reading this article are among an elite crowd of Earthlings. We have reliable electricity, access to Internet-connected computers and phones, and time available to contemplate these issues.

About one-fifth of those on Earth still don't have access to reliable electricity. So as we debate population, things we take for granted—reliable lighting and cooking facilities, for example—remain beyond the reach of about 1.3 billion or more people. Lifting people from the darkness of energy poverty could help improve lives.

Improved education, especially for girls, is cited as a key driver of declining family size. Having light at night can become a gateway to better education for millions of young people and the realization that opportunities and choices besides bearing many children can await.

So when we debate population, it's important to also discuss the impact—the how we live—of the population equation. While new projections of even higher world population in the decades ahead are cause for concern, we should be equally concerned about—and be willing to address—the increasing effects of resource consumption and its waste.

Dennis Dimick is *National Geographic's* executive editor for the Environment.

Tom Bethell

 **NO**

Population, Economy, and God

World population, once "exploding," is still increasing, and "momentum" ensures that it will do so for decades to come. But fertility rates have tumbled. In Europe every country has fallen below replacement level. Some governments, especially France's, are beginning to use financial incentives to restore fertility rates but the effort, if generous enough to work—by paying women to have a third child—could bankrupt the welfare state.

In rich countries, a total fertility rate of 2.1 babies per woman is needed if population is to remain stable. But in the European Union as a whole the rate is down to 1.5. Germany is at 1.4, and Italy, Spain, and Greece are at 1.3. The fertility rate in France is now 2.0, or close to replacement. But the uneasy question is whether this is due to subsidies or to the growing Muslim population.

All over the world, with a few anomalies, there is a strong inverse correlation between GDP per capita and babies per family. It's a paradox, because wealthier people can obviously afford lots of children. But very predictably they have fewer. Hong Kong (1.02), Singapore, and Taiwan are three of the richest countries in the world, and three of the four lowest in total fertility. The countries with the highest fertility rates are Mali (7.4), Niger, and Uganda. Guess how low they are on the wealth chart.

Here's a news item. Carl Djerassi, one of the inventors of the birth control pill, recently deplored the sharp decline of total fertility in Austria (1.4), the country of his birth. A Catholic news story seized on that and reported that one of the pill's inventors had said the pill had caused a "demographic catastrophe." Austria's leading Catholic, Cardinal Schönborn, said the Vatican had predicted 40 years ago that the pill would promote a dramatic fall in birth rates.

Djerassi, 85, an emeritus professor of chemistry at Stanford, did warn of a catastrophe and he said that Austria should admit more immigrants. But he denied that people have smaller families "because of the availability of birth control." They do so "for personal, economic, cultural, and other reasons," of which "changes in the status of women" was the most important. Japan has an even worse demographic problem, he said, "yet the pill was only legalized there in 1999 and is still not used widely." (Japan's fertility rate is 1.22.) (In fact, if the pill and abortion really were illegal more children surely would be born, if only because unintentional pregnancies would come to term.)

Austrian families who had decided against children wanted "to enjoy their schnitzels while leaving the rest of the world to get on with it," Djerassi also said. That may have rankled because the country had just put his face on a postage stamp.

So what is causing these dramatic declines? It's under way in many countries outside Europe too. In Mexico, fertility has moved down close to replacement level—having been as high as six babies per woman in the 1970s.

Obviously economic growth has been the dominant factor but there are other considerations.

Young couples hardly read Paul Ehrlich before deciding whether to have children, but scaremongering authors have played a key role in creating our anti-natalist mood. Books warning of a (then) newfangled emergency, the "population explosion," began appearing soon after World War II. Consider *Road to Survival* (1948), by William Vogt, or *People! Challenge to Survival*, by the same author. An anti-people fanatic before his time, Vogt was hypnotized by the Malthusian doctrine that population growth would overtake the food supply. That would lead to a war of all against all. Paul Ehrlich projected that the 1980s would see massive die-offs from starvation. (Obesity turned out to be the greater health threat.)

In that earlier period, the population controllers didn't feel they had to mince words. Vogt wrote in 1960 that "tens of thousands of children born every year in the United States should, solely for their own sakes, never have seen the light of day. . . . There are hundreds of thousands of others, technically legitimate since their parents have engaged in some sort of marriage ritual, but whose birth is as much of a crime against them as it is against the bastards."

At a time when the world population still had not reached 3 billion—today it is 6.7 billion—Vogt thought "drastic measures are inescapable." He warned of "mounting population pressures in the Soviet Union," where, by the century's end, "there may be 300 million Russians." It was time for them "to begin control of one of the most powerful causes of war—overpopulation."

Note: the population of Russia by 2000 was 145 million; today it is 141 million. (Fertility rate: 1.4.)

Population alarmists have long enjoyed the freedom to project their fears onto whatever cause is uppermost in the progressive mind. Then it was war. Today it is the environment, which, we are told, human beings are ruining. This will be shown to have been as false as the earlier warnings, but not before our environmental scares have done much harm to a fragile economy (at the rate things are going with Obama). All previous scares were based on faulty premises, and the latest one, based on "science," will be no different.

I believe that two interacting factors shape population growth or decline: economic prosperity and belief in God. As to the first, there is no doubt that rising material prosperity discourages additional children. Fewer infants die; large families are no longer needed to support older parents. The welfare state—which only rich countries can afford—has greatly compounded this effect. When people believe that the government will take care of them, pay their pensions and treat their maladies, children do seem less essential.

A rise in prosperity also encourages people to think that they can dispense with God. Religion diminishes when wealth increases—that's my theory. But with a twist that I shall come to. Wealth generates independence, including independence from God, or (if you will) Providence. God is gradually forgotten, then assumed not to exist. This will tend to drive childbearing down even further. Hedonism will become predominant. Remember, Jesus warned that it's the rich, not the poor, who are at spiritual hazard.

The legalization of abortion reflected the decline of religious faith in America, but it must also have led others to conclude that God was no longer to be feared. That's why I don't quite believe Djerassi when he tries to disassociate the pill from fertility. The ready availability of the pill told society at large that sex without consequences was perfectly acceptable. Then, by degrees, that self-indulgent view became an anti-natalist worldview.

It became so ingrained that many people now think it obvious. Sex became a "free" pastime as long as it was restricted to consenting adults. Furthermore, anyone who questioned that premise risked denunciation as a bigot.

The U.S. has been seen as the great stumbling block to any theory linking prosperity, lack of faith, and low fertility. Prosperity here has been high, and overall fertility is at replacement. But I am wary of this version of American exceptionalism. How much lower would U.S. fertility fall without the influx of Latino immigrants and their many offspring? Nicholas Eberstadt, a demographer at AEI, tells me that Mexican immigrants now actually have a higher fertility rate in the U.S. than they do in Mexico. (Maybe because they come to American hospitals for free medical care?)

I wonder also if religious vitality here is what it's cracked up to be. Surely it has weakened considerably. A recent survey by Trinity College in Hartford, funded by the Lilly Endowment, showed that the percentage of Americans identifying themselves as Christian dropped to 76 percent from 86 percent in 1990; those with "no" religion, 8.2 percent of the population in 1990, are now 15 percent.

As a social force, the U.S. Catholic bishops have withered away to a shocking extent. Hollywood once respected and feared their opinion. Today, the most highly placed of these bishops are unwilling to publicly rebuke proabortion politicians who call themselves Catholic, even when they give scandal by receiving Communion in public. How the mitered have fallen. They daren't challenge the rich and powerful.

But there is another factor. Calling yourself a Christian when the pollster phones imposes no cost and selfreported piety may well be inflated. We have to distinguish between mere self-labelers and actual churchgoers. And beyond that there are groups with intense religious belief who retain the morale to ignore the surrounding materialism and keep on having children.

The ultra-Orthodox in Israel are the best example. Other Jewish congregations may go to synagogue, but they have children at perhaps one-third the ultra-Orthodox rate. At about seven or eight children per family, theirs is one of the highest fertility rates in the world. And they don't permit birth control—Carl Djerassi, please note. In the U.S. Orthodox Jews again far outbreed their more secular sisters.

The Mormons are also distinctive. Utah, about twothirds Mormon, has the highest fertility rate (2.63 in 2006) among the 50 states; Vermont has the lowest (1.69). In the recent Trinity Survey, Northern New England is now "the least religious section of the country." Vermont is the least religious state; 34 percent of residents say they have "no religion." So minimal faith and low fertility are demonstrably linked. Mormon fertility is declining, to be sure, and I recognize that I am flirting with a circular argument: deciding which groups are the most fervent by looking at their birth rates.

Then there's the Muslim concern. It's hard to avoid concluding that the lost Christian zeal has been appropriated by Islam. In the U.S., Muslims have doubled since 1990 (from a low base, to 0.6% of the population). The rise of Islam suggests that the meager European fertility rates would be even lower if Muslims had not contributed disproportionately to European childbearing.

It's hard to pin down the numbers, though. Fertility in France has risen, but Nick Eberstadt tells me that the French government won't reveal how many of these babies are born to Muslim parents. "They treat it as a state secret," he said. In other countries such as Switzerland, where lots of guest workers are employed, the fertility rate would be much lower than it already is (1.44) were it not for the numerous offspring of those guest workers.

When a population is not replacing itself, the welfare state creates its own hazard. Lots of new workers are needed to support the retirees. Germany's low fertility will require an annual immigration of 200,000 just to maintain the current population. Where will they come from? Many arrive from Turkey, where the fertility rate has also declined (to about 2.0). But not as far as it has declined among native Germans. So the concern is that in the welfare states of Europe, believing Muslims are slowly replacing the low-morale, low-fertility, materialistic non-believers who once formed a Christian majority.

I could summarize the argument with this overstatement: The intelligentsia stopped believing in God in the 19th century. In the 20th it tried to build a new society, man without God. It failed. Then came a new twist. Man stopped believing in himself. He saw himself as a mere polluter—a blot on the landscape. Theologians tell us that creatures cannot exist without the support of God. A corollary may be that societies cannot long endure without being sustained by a *belief* in God.

TOM BETHELL is a senior editor of *The American Spectator*.

EXPLORING THE ISSUE

Do We Have a Population Problem?

Critical Thinking and Reflection

1. Is it possible to have too many people on Earth?
2. What is wrong with the statement that there is no population problem because all of Earth's human population could fit inside the state of Texas?
3. What does population have to do with sustainability?
4. What is more important for long-term survival of the human species—population control or belief in God?

Is There Common Ground?

The essayists for this issue agree that human population continues to grow and that long-term human survival (or sustainability) matters. They disagree on the best way to achieve long-term human survival.

1. Does quality of life seem likely to suffer more with a declining population or a growing population?
2. What are the key features of "quality of life"? (One good place to start your research is www.foe.co.uk/community/tools/isew/)
3. How might we determine what the Earth's carrying capacity for human beings really is?
4. What is the influence (if any) of religious faith on carrying capacity?

Additional Resources

Matthew Connolly, *Fatal Misconception: The Struggle to Control World Population* (Belknap Press, 2010).

Jonathan A. Foley, "Can We Feed the World & Sustain the Planet?" *Scientific American* (November 2011).

David Malakoff, "Are More People Necessarily a Problem?" *Science* (July 29, 2011).

Fred Pearce, *The Coming Population Crash: And Our Planet's Surprising Future* (Beacon, 2010).

Julia Whitty, "The Last Taboo," *Mother Jones* (May–June 2010).

Internet References . . .

Facing the Future: People and the Planet

www.facingthefuture.org/

United States & World Population Clocks

www.census.gov/main/www/popclock.html

Population Reference Bureau

www.prb.org/

Selected, Edited, and with Issue Framing Material by:
Thomas A. Easton, *Thomas College*

ISSUE

Can Vaccines Cause Autism?

YES: Arjun Walia, from "Scientific Evidence Suggests the Vaccine-Autism Link Can No Longer Be Ignored," *Collective Evolution* (2013)

NO: Jeffrey S. Gerber and Paul A. Offit, from "Vaccines and Autism: A Tale of Shifting Hypotheses," *Clinical Infectious Diseases* (2009)

Learning Outcomes

After reading this issue, you will be able to:

- Explain why many people have thought childhood vaccines can cause autism.
- Explain how scientific evidence fails to support the idea that vaccines can cause autism.
- Explain why many people continue to believe that childhood vaccines can cause autism.
- Discuss where research into the causes of autism should focus.

ISSUE SUMMARY

YES: Arjun Walia argues that the scientific consensus on the safety of vaccines may be suspect because "the corporate media is owned by the major vaccine manufacturers." He describes 22 studies that suggest that the connection between childhood vaccines and autism is real or that suggest possible mechanisms for the connection.

NO: Jeffrey S. Garber and Paul A. Offit argue that the scientific evidence neither shows a link between vaccines and autism nor supports any of the popular suggested mechanisms. Research should focus on more promising leads.

Not so long ago, childhood infectious diseases claimed an astonishing number of young lives:

- Between 1940 and 1948, whooping cough (pertussis) killed 64 of every 100,000 children less than one year old. By 1974, extensive use of vaccines had reduced that toll to less than 1 per 100,000 (James D. Cherry, "Historical Perspective on Pertussis and Use of Vaccines to Prevent It: 100 Years of Pertussis (the Cough of 100 Days)," *Microbe*, March 2007)
- Before the measles vaccine came into wide use in the 1960s, "nearly all children got measles by the time they were 15 years of age. Each year in the United States about 450–500 people died because of measles, 48,000 were hospitalized, 7,000 had seizures, and about 1,000 suffered permanent

brain damage or deafness. Today there are only about 60 cases a year reported in the United States, and most of these originate outside the country" (http://www.cdc.gov/measles/about/overview.html).
- Before the polio vaccine became available, the United States saw about 50,000 polio cases per year, with thousands of victims, mostly children, needing braces, crutches, wheelchairs, or iron lungs. Today polio is rare in the United States.
- Before the mumps vaccine became available, about 200,000 cases of mumps and 20–30 deaths occurred each year in the United States. Mumps outbreaks still occur but are much smaller; in 2009–2010 an outbreak consisted of 1,521 cases.
- In 1921, the United States saw 206,000 cases of diphtheria, with 15,520 deaths. The diphtheria vaccine came into use in the 1920s, and since then the incidence of this disease has declined

tremendously. There were no cases at all in the 2004–2008 period.

- Hib (Haemophilus influenzae type b) meningitis kills up to 1 in 20 of infected children and leaves 1 in 5 with brain damage or deafness. "Before the Hib vaccine was available, Hib caused serious infections in 20,000 children and killed about 1,000 children each year. Since the vaccine's introduction in 1987, the incidence of severe Hib disease has declined by 99 percent in the United States" (http://www.vaccinateyourbaby.org/why/history /hib.cfm).

It is perhaps unfortunate that the Bad Old Days those numbers describe were so long ago. Whole generations have grown up with no memory of what vaccines have saved us from. Today a baby gets stuck with a needle and cries, and a parent feels that this is horrible, that the baby is being hurt for no good reason. At the same time, vaccines have always had side-effects (including occasionally causing the disease they are intended to ward off), and when one of these side-effects shows up, there is again a sense that children are being endangered without good reason. As a result, some parents today choose not to vaccinate their children. When enough parents make that choice, the old diseases can and do crop up again, and children die.

In addition, there is a fear that childhood vaccines can cause autism, which is rooted in a 1998 study by Andrew Wakefield, a British gastroenterologist. The study proved to have major ethical and procedural lapses and was retracted; Wakefield himself lost his position and his medical license. However he considers himself a victim of the medical establishment and insists that his results were sound and he will be vindicated; see Andrew J. Wakefield, *Callous Disregard: Autism and Vaccines—The Truth Behind a Tragedy* (Skyhorse, 2011). An enormous number of parents of autistic children have come to view him as a hero, for only he has an answer to why their children suffer and to how that suffering might have been prevented—by refusing vaccinations. This view has been promoted by uncritical media and celebrities such as Jenny McCarthy (who wrote the foreword to Wakefield's book; see also Michael Specter, "Jenny McCarthy's Dangerous Views," *The New Yorker*, July 16, 2013, http://www.newyorker.com/tech /elements/jenny-mccarthys-dangerous-views). One claim is that the government has admitted that vaccines cause autism because the federal Vaccine Court (National Vaccine Injury Compensation Program [NVICP; http://www.hrsa .gov/vaccinecompensation/index.html]) has awarded damages to autism cases. It is worth stressing that the

Vaccine Court awards damages for "table injuries." A "table injury" is an injury listed as known to follow vaccines at least occasionally; if medical records show a child has such an injury soon after vaccination, the correlation is enough to justify awarding damages. Autism is not a table injury, but possibly related conditions such as encephalopathy are. Many parents now use the purported connection between childhood vaccines and autism to justify refusing to have their children vaccinated.

As evidence against the vaccines-autism link has accumulated, the idea that parents have the right to choose whether to have their children vaccinated has gained momentum; the "essential handbook for the vaccination choice movement" is Louise Kuo Habakus, Mary Holland, and Kim Mack Rosenberg, eds., *Vaccine Epidemic: How Corporate Greed, Biased Science, and Coercive Government Threaten Our Human Rights, Our Health, and Our Children* (Skyhorse, 2011, 2012). The opposing view is that vaccinations protect public health by preventing not just infection by deadly diseases but also the spread of these diseases through a population, and indeed in numerous cases the declining popularity of vaccinations has resulted in outbreaks of disease and the deaths of both children and adults. One strong supporter of the view that vaccines do not cause autism is Alison Singer, who left Autism Speaks, an organization that promotes the need for more research into the vaccines-autism link, to found the Autism Science Foundation, which promotes the need for more research into the causes of autism; see Meredith Wadman, "A Voice for Science," *Nature* (November 3, 2011).

Seth Mnookin, *The Panic Virus: The True Story Behind the Vaccine-Autism Controversy* (Simon and Schuster, 2011), reviews the history of vaccines and earlier anti-vaccine movements, the Wakefield story, and the exploitation of families with autistic children by quacks who use the supposed vaccine connection to encourage distrust of the medical establishment and peddle expensive, useless, and even damaging treatments.

Those who believe there is a connection between childhood vaccines and autism are only rarely convinced by evidence that there is no connection. It does not help that no one has a good idea of how the connection might work. Is it the mercury-based preservative, thimerosal, in the vaccines? When thimerosal was removed from vaccines the upward trend of autism diagnoses did not change. Is it the sheer number of vaccinations children undergo? Is it the age at which vaccines are administered? Do vaccines damage the intestinal lining and allow nerve-damaging proteins to enter the blood? There are a number of studies that suggest possible mechanisms, but none can say anything stronger than "maybe." It has even been suggested (controversially) that an imbalance of bacterial types in the mix that inhabits the intestine may be involved; see http://theconversation.com/can -a-gut-bacteria-imbalance-really-cause-autism-9128. In the YES selection, Arjun Walia describes 22 studies that suggest the connection between childhood vaccines is real or that suggest possible mechanisms for the connection. He notes that the scientific consensus may be suspect because "the corporate media is owned by the major vaccine manufacturers." In the NO selection, Jeffrey S. Garber and Paul A. Offit argue that the scientific evidence neither shows a link between vaccines and autism nor supports any of the popular suggested mechanisms. Research should focus on more promising leads.

YES ⤶   **Arjun Walia**

Scientific Evidence Suggests the Vaccine-Autism Link Can No Longer Be Ignored

Concerns regarding vaccinations continue to increase exponentially in light of all of the information and documentation that has surfaced over the past few years. As a result, corporate media has responded to alternative media, stating that the increase of persons who are choosing to opt out of vaccines and the recommended vaccine schedule is a result of 'fear mongering.' This may not be too surprising as the corporate media is owned by the major vaccine manufacturers, and the major vaccine manufacturers are owned by corporate media. Given this fact, it's easy to fathom the possibility that these institutions are desperately trying to protect the reputation of their product.

For example, if we take a look at GlaxoSmithKline and Pfizer, they are owned by the same financial institutions and groups that own Time Warner (CNN, HBO etc.) and General Electric (NBC, Comcast, Universal Pictures etc.). This is seen throughout all of the major vaccine manufacturers and all of the 6 corporations that control our mainstream media. Keep in mind that these are the major funders of all 'medical research' that's used to administer drugs and vaccinations. Despite these connections, medical research and documentation exists to show that vaccines might indeed be a cause for concern.

Vaccines and Autism, Both Sides of the Coin

Here we will simply present information from both sides of the coin because many are not even aware that two sides exist. We've presented multiple studies, citing multiple research papers and published research conducted by doctors and universities from all across the world. . . . We'd also like to present medical research that indicates the many dangers associated with vaccines, and have done this on multiple occasions. We do this because the safety of vaccinations is commonly pushed by the mainstream

media, without ever mentioning or citing the abundant medical research that should also be taken into consideration when discussing vaccinations. **Please keep in mind that there is evidence on both sides.** At the same time, some of the evidence on the side that negates a positive outlook on vaccination has been labelled fraudulent, but then again many haven't.

The vaccine-autism debate has been going on for years. It has been a tale of shifting beliefs as child vaccination rates remain high. On February 1998, Andrew Wakefield, a British gastroenterologist and his colleagues published a paper that supposedly linked Autism to Vaccines. More specifically, he claimed that the MMR vaccine was responsible for intestinal inflammation that led to translocation of usually non-permeable peptides to the bloodstream and, subsequently, to the brain, where they affected development. His work was unpublished, and he lost his medical license despite the fact multiple studies seem to support Andrew Wakefield's work (here (http://vran.org/wp-content/documents/VRAN-Abnormal%20 Measles-Mumps-Rubella-Antibodies-CNS-Autoimmunity -Children-Autism-Singh-Lin-Newell-Nelson.pdf) is one example, and here (http://www.mdpi.com/1099-4300/14/11/2227) is another.) He has been labelled a fraud by the mainstream medical world, some experts claim that his research and methods are weak and based on very little evidence. **Dr. Wakefield's research will NOT be used in this article.**

At the same time I must mention that multiple studies from around the world have concluded that there is no link between autism and the MMR vaccine. It can become quite a confusing subject given that we have multiple medical studies contradicting each other. Was Dr. Wakefield exposing something that the medical industry did not want you to know? It is known that vaccine manufacturers suppress harmful data regarding their product, as mentioned and illustrated earlier in the article. Regardless of the MMR vaccine and autism debate, there are still a number of studies that link vaccines to a possible autism connection. Please keep in mind that multiple courts worldwide have ruled in favour of vaccines causing autism, brain damage and other complications, that include the MMR vaccine.

Here (http://www.collective-evolution.com/2012/09/07 /rob-schneider-speaks-out-against-vaccines) is a great video narrated by Rob Schneider outlining the vaccine-autism link. Below that you will find a list of 22 medical studies that show possible connections to vaccines and autism. Please keep in mind that we've only presented 22 studies here, there are many more published papers that document the link. Hopefully this inspires you to further your research on the subject. Also keep in mind that autism is only one of the multiple shown consequences of vaccine administration, as they have been linked to a number of other ailments.

1. A study published in the journal *Annals of Epidemiology* (http://www.ncbi.nlm.nih.gov/pubmed /21058170) has shown that giving the Hepatitis B vaccine to newborn baby boys could triple the risk of developing an autism spectrum disorder compared to boys who were not vaccinated as neonates. The research was conducted at Stony Brook University Medical Centre, NY.

2. A study published in the *Journal of Inorganic Biochemistry* (http://omsj.org/reports/tomljenovic%20 2011.pdf) by researchers at the Neural Dynamics Group, Department of Ophthalmology and Visual Sciences at the University of British Columbia determined that aluminum, a highly neurotoxic metal and the most commonly used vaccine adjuvant may be a significant contributing factor to the rising prevalence of ASD in the Western World. They showed that the correlation between ASD prevalence and the aluminum adjuvant exposure appears to be the highest at 3–4 months of age. The studies also show that children from countries with the highest ASD appear to have a much higher exposure to aluminum from vaccines. The study points out that several prominent milestones of brain development coincide with major vaccination periods for infants. These include the onset of synaptogenesis (birth), maximal growth velocity of the hippocampus and the onset of amygdala maturation. Furthermore, major developmental transition in many bio-behavioural symptoms such as sleep, temperature regulation, respiration and brain wave patterns, all of which are regulated by the neuroendocrine network. Many of these aspects of brain function are known to be impaired in autism, such as sleeping and brain wave patterns.

According to the FDA, vaccines represent a special category of drugs as they are generally given to healthy individuals. Further according to the FDA, "this places significant emphasis on their vaccine safety." While the FDA does set an upper limit for aluminum in vaccines at no more than 850/mg/dose, it is important to note that this amount was selected empirically from data showing that aluminum in such amounts enhanced the antigenicity of the vaccine, rather than from existing safety. Given that the scientific evidence appears to indicate that vaccine safety is not as firmly established as often believed, it would seem ill advised to exclude paediatric vaccinations as a possible cause of adverse long-term neurodevelopment outcomes, including those associated with autism.

3. A study published in the *Journal of Toxicology and Environmental Health, Part A: Current Issues* (http:// www.ncbi.nlm.nih.gov/pubmed/21623535) by the Department of Economics and Finance at the University of New York shows how researchers suspect one or more environmental triggers are needed to develop autism, regardless of whether individuals have a genetic predisposition or not. They determined that one of those triggers might be the "battery of vaccinations that young children receive." Researchers found a positive and statistically significant relationship between autism and vaccinations. They determined that the higher the proportion of children receiving recommended vaccinations, the higher the prevalence of autism. A [1%] increase in vaccination was associated with an additional 680 children having autism. The results suggest that vaccines may be linked to autism and encourages more in depth study before continually administering these vaccines.

4. A study published in the *Journal of Toxicology* (http://www.hindawi.com/journals/jt/2013/801517/) by the Department of Neurosurgery at The Methodist Neurological Institute in Houston has shown that ASD is a disorder caused by a problem in brain development. They looked at B-cells and their sensitivity levels to thimerosal, a commonly used additive in many vaccines. They determined that ASD patients have a heightened sensitivity to thimerosal which would restrict cell proliferation that is typically found after vaccination. The research shows that individuals who have this hypersensitivity to thimerosal could make them highly susceptible to toxins like thimerosal, and that individuals with a mild mitochondrial defect may be affected by

thimerosal. The fact that ASD patients' B cells exhibit hypersensitivity to thimerosal tells us something.

5. A study published in the *Journal of Biomedical Sciences* (http://www.ncbi.nlm.nih.gov/pubmed/12145534) determined that the autoimmunity to the central nervous system may play a causal role in autism. Researchers discovered that because many autistic children harbour elevated levels of measles antibodies, they should conduct a serological study of measles-mumps-rubella (MMR) and myelin basic protein (MBP) autoantibodies. They used serum samples of 125 autistic children and 92 controlled children. Their analysis showed a significant increase in the level of MMR antibodies in autistic children. The study concludes that the autistic children had an inappropriate or abnormal antibody response to MMR. The study determined that autism could be a result from an atypical measles infection that produces neurological symptoms in some children. The source of this virus could be a variant of MV, or it could be the MMR vaccine.

6. Study published in the *Annals of Clinical Psychiatry* (http://www.collective-evolution.com/2013/09/12/22-medical-studies-that-show-vaccines-can-cause-autism/Study%20published%20in%20the%20Annals%20of%20Clinical%20Psychiatry) suggests that autism is likely triggered by a virus, and that measles virus (MV and/or MMR vaccine) might be a very good candidate. It supports the hypothesis that a virus-dincued autoimmune response may play a causal role in autism.

7. A study published in the *American Journal of Clinical Nutrition* (http://ajcn.nutrition.org/content/80/6/1611.full) determined that an increased vulnerability to oxidative stress and decreased capacity for methylation may contribute to the development and clinical manifestation of autism. It's well known that viral infections cause increased oxidative stress. Research suggests (http://www.ncbi.nlm.nih.gov/pubmed/11895129) that metals, including those found in many vaccines are directly involved in increasing oxidative stress.

8. A study published by the Department of Pharmaceutical Sciences [http://www.ncbi.nlm.nih.gov/pubmed/14745455] at Northeastern University, Boston determined that a novel growth factor signalling pathway that regulates methionine synthase (MS) activity and thereby modulates methylation reactions. The potent inhibition of this pathway by ethanol, lead, mercury, aluminum and thimerosal suggests that it may be an important target of neurodevelopmental toxins. . . .

9. A study published in the *Journal of Child Neurology* (http://jcn.sagepub.com/content/22/11/1308.abstract) examined the question of what is leading to the apparent increase in autism. They expressed that if there is any link between autism and mercury, it is crucial that the first reports of the question are not falsely stating that no link occurs. Researchers determined that a significant relation does exist between the blood levels of mercury and the diagnosis of an autism spectrum disorder.

10. A study published in the *Journal of Child Neurology* (http://jcn.sagepub.com/content/21/2/170.abstract) noted that autistic spectrum disorders can be associated with mitochondrial dysfunction. Researchers determined that children who have mitochondrial-related dysfunctional cellular energy metabolism might be more prone to undergo autistic regression between 18 and 30 months of age if they also have infections or immunizations at the same time.

11. A study conducted by Massachusetts General Hospital (http://www.ncbi.nlm.nih.gov/pubmed/16151044) at the Centre for Morphometric Analysis by the Department of Paediatric Neurology illustrates how autistic brains have a growth spurt shortly after birth and then slow in growth a few short years later. Researchers have determined that neuroinflammation appears to be present in autistic brain tissue from childhood through adulthood. The study excerpt reads:

> Oxidative stress, brain inflammation and microgliosis have been much documented in association with toxic exposures including various heavy metals. The awareness that the brain as well as medical conditions of children with autism may be conditioned by chronic biomedical abnormalities such as inflammation opens the possibility that meaningful biomedical interventions may be possible well past the window of maximal neuroplasticity in early childhood because the basis for assuming that all deficits can be attributed to fixed early developmental alterations in net

12. A study conducted by the Department of Paediatrics at the University of Arkansas (http://www.ncbi.nlm.nih.gov/pubmed/15527868) determined that thimerosal-induced cytotoxicity was associated with the depletion of intracellular glutathione (GSH) in both cell lines. The study

outlines how many vaccines have been neurotoxic, especially to the developing brain. Depletion of GSH is commonly associated with autism. Although thimerosal has been removed from most children's vaccines, it is still present in flu vaccines given to pregnant women, the elderly and to children in developing countries.

13. A study published in the *Public Library of Science (PLOS)* (http://www.plosone.org/article/info%3Adoi%2F10.1371%2Fjournal.pone.0068444) determined that elevation in peripheral oxidative stress is consistent with, and may contribute to more severe functional impairments in the ASD group. We know that oxidative stress is triggered by heavy metals, like the ones contained in multiple vaccines.

14. A study conducted by the University of Texas Health Science Centre (http://www.ncbi.nlm.nih.gov/pubmed/16338635) by the Department of Family and Community Medicine determined that for each 1,000 Ib of environmentally released mercury, there was a 43% increase in the rate of special education services and a 61% increase in the rate of autism. Researchers emphasized that further research was needed regarding the association between environmentally released mercury and developmental disorders such as autism.

15. A study published in the *International Journal of Toxicology* (http://www.ncbi.nlm.nih.gov/pubmed/12933322) determined that in light of the biological plausibility of mercury's role in neurodevelopment disorders, the present study provides further insight into one possible mechanism by which early mercury exposures could increase the risk of autism.

16. A study published in the *Journal of Toxicology and Environmental Health* (http://www.ncbi.nlm.nih.gov/pubmed/17454560) determined that mercury exposure can induce immune, sensory, neurological, motor and behavioural dysfunctions similar to traits defining or associated with ASDs. Based upon differential diagnoses, 8 of 9 patients examined were exposed to significant mercury from thimerosal-containing vaccine preparations during their fetal/infant developmental periods. These previously normal developing children suffered mercury encephalopathies that manifested with clinical symptoms consistent with regressive ASDs. Evidence for mercury intoxication should be considered in the differential diagnosis as contributing to some regressive ASDs.

17. A study published by the US National Library of Medicine (http://civileats.com/wp-content/uploads/2009/01/palmer2008.pdf) conducted by the University of Texas Health Science Centre suspected that persistent low-dose exposures to various environmental toxicants including mercury, that occur during critical windows of neural development among genetically susceptible children, may increase the risk for developmental disorders such as autism.

18. A study conducted by the Department of Obstetrics and Gynaecology (http://www.ane.pl/pdf/7020.pdf) at University of Pittsburgh's School of Medicine showed that macaques are commonly used in pre-clinical vaccine safety testing. Collective evolution does not support animals testing, we feel there is a large amount of evidence and research that already indicated the links to vaccines in which some animals have been used to illustrate. The objective of this study was to compare early infant cognition and behaviour with amygdala size and opioid binding in rhesus macaques receiving the recommended childhood vaccines. The animal model, which examines for the first time, behavioural, functional and neuromorphometric consequences of the childhood vaccine regimen, mimics certain neurological abnormalities of autism. These findings raise important safety issues while providing a potential model for examining aspects of causation and disease pathogenesis in acquired disorders of behaviour and development.

19. A study conducted by The George Washington University School of Public Health (http://www.ncbi.nlm.nih.gov/pubmed/18482737) from the Department of Epidemiology and Biostatistics determined that significantly increased rate ratios were observed for autism and autism spectrum disorders as a result of exposure to mercury from thimerosal-containing vaccines.

20. A study published in the journal *Cell Biology and Toxicology* (http://www.ncbi.nlm.nih.gov/pubmed/19357975) by Kinki University in Osaka, Japan determined that in combination with the brain pathology observed in patients diagnosed with autism, the present study helps to support the possible biological plausability for how low-dose exposure to mercury from thimerosal-containing vaccines may be associated with autism.

21. A study published by the *Journal Lab Medicine* (http://labmed.ascpjournals.org/content/33/9/708.full.pdf) determined that vaccinations may be one of the triggers for autism. Researchers discovered that substantial data demonstrates immune abnormality in many autistic children consistent with impaired resistance to infection, activation of inflammatory responses and autoimmunity.

Impaired resistance may predispose to vaccine injury in autism.

22. A study published in the journal *Neurochemical Research* (http://www.ncbi.nlm.nih.gov/pmc/articles/PMC3264864/?tool=pubmed) determined that since excessive accumulation of extracellular glutamate is linked with excitotoxicity, data implies that neonatal exposure to thimerosal-containing vaccines might induce excitotoxic brain injuries, leading to neurodevelopmental disorders.

ARJUN WALIA writes for *Collective Evolution*, a website and magazine that is "about creating change and talking about how we can get there."

Jeffrey S. Gerber and Paul A. Offit

 **NO**

Vaccines and Autism: A Tale of Shifting Hypotheses

A worldwide increase in the rate of autism diagnoses—likely driven by broadened diagnostic criteria and increased awareness—has fueled concerns that an environmental exposure like vaccines might cause autism. Theories for this putative association have centered on the measles-mumps-rubella (MMR) vaccine, thimerosal, and the large number of vaccines currently administered. However, both epidemiological and biological studies fail to support these claims.

MMR

On 28 February 1998, Andrew Wakefield, a British gastroenterologist, and colleagues published a paper in *The Lancet* that described 8 children whose first symptoms of autism appeared within 1 month after receiving an MMR vaccine. All 8 of these children had gastrointestinal symptoms and signs and lymphoid nodular hyperplasia revealed on endoscopy. From these observations, Wakefield postulated that MMR vaccine caused intestinal inflammation that led to translocation of usually nonpermeable peptides to the bloodstream and, subsequently, to the brain, where they affected development.

Several issues undermine the interpretation by Wakefield et al. of this case series. First, the self-referred cohort did not include control subjects, which precluded the authors from determining whether the occurrence of autism following receipt of MMR vaccine was causal or coincidental. Because ~50,000 British children per month received MMR vaccine between ages 1 and 2 years—at a time when autism typically presents—coincidental associations were inevitable. Indeed, given the prevalence of autism in England in 1998 of 1 in 2000 children, ~25 children per month would receive a diagnosis of the disorder soon after receiving MMR vaccine by chance alone. Second, endoscopic or neuropsychological assessments were not blind, and data were not collected systematically or completely. Third, gastrointestinal symptoms did not predate autism

in several children, which is inconsistent with the notion that intestinal inflammation facilitated bloodstream invasion of encephalopathic peptides. Fourth, measles, mumps, or rubella vaccine viruses have not been found to cause chronic intestinal inflammation or loss of intestinal barrier function. Indeed, a recent study by Hornig et al. found that the measles vaccine virus genome was not detected more commonly in children with or without autism. Fifth, putative encephalopathic peptides traveling from the intestine to the brain have never been identified. In contrast, the genes that have been associated with autism spectrum disorder to date have been found to code for endogenous proteins that influence neuronal synapse function, neuronal cell adhesion, neuronal activity regulation, or endosomal trafficking.

Although no data supporting an association between MMR vaccine and autism existed and a plausible biological mechanism was lacking, several epidemiologic studies were performed to address parental fears created by the publication by Wakefield et al. Fortunately, several features of large-scale vaccination programs allowed for excellent descriptive and observational studies—specifically, large numbers of subjects, which generated substantial statistical power; high-quality vaccination records, which provided reliable historical data; multinational use of similar vaccine constituents and schedules; electronic medical records, which facilitated accurate analysis of outcome data; and the relatively recent introduction of MMR vaccine in some countries, which allowed for before and after comparisons.

Ecological studies. Researchers in several countries performed ecological studies that addressed the question of whether MMR vaccine causes autism. Such analyses employ large databases that compare vaccination rates with autism diagnoses at the population level.

1. In the United Kingdom, researchers evaluated 498 autistic children born from 1979 through 1992 who were identified by computerized

U.S. Dept of Health and Human Services , 2009.

health records from 8 health districts. Although a trend toward increasing autism diagnoses by year of birth was confirmed, no change in the rates of autism diagnoses after the 1987 introduction of MMR vaccine was observed. Further, MMR vaccination rates of autistic children were similar to those of the entire study population. Also, investigators did not observe a clustering of autism diagnoses relative to the time that children received MMR vaccine, nor did they observe a difference in age at autism diagnosis between those vaccinated and not vaccinated or between those vaccinated before or after 18 months of age. These authors also found no differences in autism rates among vaccinated and unvaccinated children when they extended their analysis to include a longer time after MMR exposure or a second dose of MMR.

2. Also in the United Kingdom, researchers performed a time-trend analysis using the General Practice Research Database—a high-quality, extensively validated electronic medical record with virtually complete vaccination data. More than 3 million person-years of observation during 1988–1999 confirmed an increase in autism diagnoses despite stable MMR vaccination rates.

3. In California, researchers compared year-specific MMR vaccination rates of kindergarten students with the yearly autism case load of the California Department of Developmental Services during 1980–1994. As was observed in the United Kingdom, the increase in the number of autism diagnoses did not correlate with MMR vaccination rates.

4. In Canada, researchers estimated the prevalence of pervasive developmental disorder with respect to MMR vaccination in 27,749 children from 55 schools in Quebec. Autism rates increased coincident with a decrease in MMR vaccination rates. The results were unchanged when both exposure and outcome definitions varied, including a strict diagnosis of autism.

Additional population-based studies considered the relationship between MMR vaccine and the "new variant" form of autism proposed by Wakefield et al.—specifically, developmental regression with gastrointestinal symptoms. Although it is difficult to analyze such a phenomenon when it is unclear that one exists (which complicates the formulation of a case definition), conclusions may be gleaned from the data with respect to developmental regression alone (i.e., autism irrespective of coincident bowel problems).

1. In England, researchers performed a cross-sectional study of 262 autistic children and demonstrated no difference in age of first parental concerns or rate of developmental regression by exposure to MMR vaccine. No association between developmental regression and gastrointestinal symptoms was observed.

2. In London, an analysis of 473 autistic children used the 1987 introduction of MMR to compare vaccinated and unvaccinated cohorts. The incidence of developmental regression did not differ between cohorts, and the authors observed no difference in the prevalence of gastrointestinal symptoms between vaccinated and unvaccinated autistic children.

Two conclusions are evident from these data. First, the explicit consideration of developmental regression among autistic children does not alter the consistent independence of MMR vaccine and autism. Second, these data argue against the existence of a new variant form of autism.

Retrospective, observational studies. Four retrospective, observational studies addressed the relationship between MMR vaccine and autism.

1. In the United Kingdom, 71 MMR-vaccinated autistic children were compared with 284 MMR-vaccinated matched control children through use of the Doctor's Independent Network, a general practice database. The authors observed no differences between case and control children in practitioner consultation rates—a surrogate for parental concerns about their child's development—within 6 months after MMR vaccination, which suggests that the diagnosis of autism was not temporally related to MMR vaccination.

2. In Finland, using national registers, researchers linked hospitalization records to vaccination records in 535,544 children vaccinated during 1982–1986. Of 309 children hospitalized for autistic disorders, no clustering occurred relative to the time of MMR vaccination.

3. In Denmark, again using a national registry, researchers determined vaccination status and autism diagnosis in 537,303 children born during 1991–1998. The authors observed no differences in the relative risk of autism between those who did and those who did not receive MMR vaccine. Among autistic children, no relationship between date of vaccination and development of autism was observed.

4. In metropolitan Atlanta, using a developmental surveillance program, researchers compared

624 autistic children with 1824 matched control children. Vaccination records were obtained from state immunization forms. The authors observed no differences in age at vaccination between autistic and nonautistic children, which suggests that early age of MMR vaccine exposure was not a risk factor for autism.

Prospective observational studies. Capitalizing on a long-term vaccination project maintained by the National Board of Health, investigators in Finland performed 2 prospective cohort studies. Researchers prospectively recorded adverse events associated with MMR-vaccinated children during 1982–1996 and identified 31 with gastrointestinal symptoms; none of the children developed autism. A further analysis of this cohort revealed no vaccine-associated cases of autism among 1.8 million children. Although this cohort was analyzed using a passive surveillance system, the complete absence of an association between gastrointestinal disease and autism after MMR vaccination was compelling.

Thimerosal

Thimerosal—50% ethylmercury by weight—is an antibacterial compound that has been used effectively in multidose vaccine preparations for >50 years (thimerosal is not contained in live-virus vaccines, such as MMR). In 1997, the US Food and Drug Administration Modernization Act mandated identification and quantification of mercury in all food and drugs; 2 years later, the US Food and Drug Administration found that children might be receiving as much as 187.5 μg of mercury within the first 6 months of life. Despite the absence of data suggesting harm from quantities of ethylmercury contained in vaccines, in 1999, the American Academy of Pediatrics and the Public Health Service recommended the immediate removal of mercury from all vaccines given to young infants. Widespread and predictable misinterpretation of this conservative, precautionary directive, coupled with a public already concerned by a proposed but unsubstantiated link between vaccination and autism, understandably provoked concern among parents, which led to the birth of several antimercury advocacy groups. However, because the signs and symptoms of autism are clearly distinct from those of mercury poisoning, concerns about mercury as a cause of autism were—similar to those with MMR vaccine—biologically implausible; children with mercury poisoning show characteristic motor, speech, sensory, psychiatric, visual, and head

circumference changes that are either fundamentally different from those of or absent in children with autism. Consistent with this, a study performed by scientists at the Centers for Disease Control and Prevention years later showed that mercury in vaccines did not cause even subtle signs or symptoms of mercury poisoning.

Despite the biological implausibility of the contention that thimerosal in vaccines caused autism, 7 studies—again descriptive or observational—were performed. Four other studies have been reviewed in detail elsewhere but are not discussed here because their methodology is incomplete and unclear and, thus, cause difficulty in drawing meaningful conclusions.

Ecological studies. Three ecological studies performed in 3 different countries compared the incidence of autism with thimerosal exposure from vaccines. In each case, the nationwide removal of thimerosal—which occurred in 1992 in Europe and in 2001 in the United States—allowed robust comparisons of vaccination with thimerosal-containing and thimerosal-free products, as follows:

1. In Sweden and Denmark, researchers found a relatively stable incidence of autism when thimerosal-containing vaccines were in use (1980–1990), including years when children were exposed to as much as 200 μg of ethylmercury (concentrations similar to peak US exposures). However, in 1990, a steady increase in the incidence of autism began in both countries and continued through the end of the study period in 2000, despite the removal of thimerosal from vaccines in 1992.

2. In Denmark, researchers performed a study comparing the incidence of autism in children who had received 200 μg (1961–1970), 125 μg (1970–1992), or 0 μg of thimerosal (1992–2000) and again demonstrated no relationship between thimerosal exposure and autism.

3. In Quebec, researchers grouped 27,749 children from 55 schools by date of birth and estimated thimerosal exposure on the basis of the corresponding Ministry of Health vaccine schedules. School records were obtained to determine age-specific rates of pervasive developmental disorder. Thimerosal exposure and pervasive developmental disorder diagnosis were found to be independent variables. Similar to previous analyses, the highest rates of pervasive developmental disorder were found in cohorts exposed to thimerosal-free vaccines. The results were unchanged when both exposure and outcome definitions varied.

Cohort studies. Four cohort studies that examined thimerosal exposure and autism have been performed, as follows:

1. In Denmark, researchers examined >1200 children with autism that were identified during 1990–1996, which comprised ~3 million person-years. They found that the risk of autism did not differ between children vaccinated with thimerosal-containing vaccines and those vaccinated with thimerosal-free vaccines or between children who received greater or lower quantities of thimerosal. They also found that the rates of autism increased after the removal of thimerosal from all vaccines.
2. In the United States, using the Vaccine Safety Data Link, researchers at the Centers for Disease Control and Prevention examined 140,887 US children born during 1991–1999, including >200 children with autism. The researchers found no relationship between receipt of thimerosal-containing vaccines and autism.
3. In England, researchers prospectively followed 12,810 children for whom they had complete vaccination records who were born during 1991–1992, and they found no relationship between early thimerosal exposure and deleterious neurological or psychological outcomes.
4. In the United Kingdom, researchers evaluated the vaccination records of 100,572 children born during 1988–1997, using the General Practice Research Database, 104 of whom were affected with autism. No relationship between thimerosal exposure and autism diagnosis was observed.

Too Many Vaccines

When studies of MMR vaccine and thimerosal-containing vaccines failed to show an association with autism, alternative theories emerged. The most prominent theory suggests that the simultaneous administration of multiple vaccines overwhelms or weakens the immune system and creates an interaction with the nervous system that triggers autism in a susceptible host. This theory was recently popularized in the wake of a concession by the Vaccine Injury Compensation Program with regard to the case of a 9-year-old girl with a mitochondrial enzyme deficiency whose encephalopathy, which included features of autism spectrum disorder, was judged to have worsened following the receipt of multiple vaccines at age 19 months. Despite reassurances by the Centers for Disease Control and Prevention that the Vaccine Injury Compensation Program's action should not be interpreted as scientific

evidence that vaccines cause autism, many in the lay press and the public have not been reassured.

The notion that children might be receiving too many vaccines too soon and that these vaccines either overwhelm an immature immune system or generate a pathologic, autism-inducing autoimmune response is flawed for several reasons:

1. Vaccines do not overwhelm the immune system. Although the infant immune system is relatively naive, it is immediately capable of generating a vast array of protective responses; even conservative estimates predict the capacity to respond to thousands of vaccines simultaneously. Consistent with this theoretical exercise, combinations of vaccines induce immune responses comparable to those given individually. Also, although the number of recommended childhood vaccines has increased during the past 30 years, with advances in protein chemistry and recombinant DNA technology, the immunologic load has actually decreased. The 14 vaccines given today contain <200 bacterial and viral proteins or polysaccharides, compared with >3000 of these immunological components in the 7 vaccines administered in 1980. Further, vaccines represent a minute fraction of what a child's immune system routinely navigates; the average child is infected with 4–6 viruses per year. The immune response elicited from the vast antigen exposure of unattenuated viral replication supersedes that of even multiple, simultaneous vaccines.
2. Multiple vaccinations do not weaken the immune system. Vaccinated and unvaccinated children do not differ in their susceptibility to infections not prevented by vaccines. In other words, vaccination does not suppress the immune system in a clinically relevant manner. However, infections with some vaccine-preventable diseases predispose children to severe, invasive infections with other pathogens. Therefore, the available data suggest that vaccines do not weaken the immune system.
3. Autism is not an immune-mediated disease. Unlike autoimmune diseases such as multiple sclerosis, there is no evidence of immune activation or inflammatory lesions in the CNS of people with autism. In fact, current data suggest that genetic variation in neuronal circuitry that affects synaptic development might in part account for autistic behavior. Thus, speculation that an exaggerated or inappropriate immune response to vaccination precipitates autism is at

variance with current scientific data that address the pathogenesis of autism.

4. No studies have compared the incidence of autism in vaccinated, unvaccinated, or alternatively vaccinated children (i.e., schedules that spread out vaccines, avoid combination vaccines, or include only select vaccines). These studies would be difficult to perform because of the likely differences among these 3 groups in health care seeking behavior and the ethics of experimentally studying children who have not received vaccines.

Conclusions

Twenty epidemiologic studies have shown that neither thimerosal nor MMR vaccine causes autism. These studies have been performed in several countries by many different investigators who have employed a multitude of epidemiologic and statistical methods. The large size of the studied populations has afforded a level of statistical power sufficient to detect even rare associations. These studies, in concert with the biological implausibility that vaccines overwhelm a child's immune system, have effectively dismissed the notion that vaccines cause autism. Further studies on the cause or causes of autism should focus on more-promising leads.

Jeffrey S. Gerber is a physician with the Division of Infectious Diseases at the Children's Hospital of Philadelphia. Among his interests are the adverse effects of antimicrobial use in children.

Paul A. Offit is the chief of the Division of Infectious Diseases and the director of the Vaccine Education Center at the Children's Hospital of Philadelphia. He is also the Maurice R. Hilleman Professor of Vaccinology and a Professor of Pediatrics at the University of Pennsylvania School of Medicine. Among his many awards are the J. Edmund Bradley Prize for Excellence in Pediatrics from the University of Maryland Medical School, the Young Investigator Award in Vaccine Development from the Infectious Disease Society of America, and a Research Career Development Award from the National Institutes of Health.

EXPLORING THE ISSUE

Can Vaccines Cause Autism?

Critical Thinking and Reflection

1. Vaccines work by stimulating the body's immune system to attack bacteria and viruses that are composed of proteins and other chemicals not native to the body. How then can they stimulate immune systems into attacking things that belong to the body? (Hint: think of "mistaken identity.")
2. With so much evidence that vaccines do not cause autism, why do people continue to believe they do?
3. Vaccines have side effects. Sometimes those side effects kill. Are vaccines worth the risk?
4. Many of the diseases we vaccinate against, such as whooping cough, are caused by bacteria. Why don't we just use antibiotics?

Is There Common Ground?

No one argues that we should not do everything we can to keep our children healthy. Vaccines have side effects, but if we stop using them, we risk returning to the days when childhood diseases killed children in large numbers. Antibiotics don't work against viruses such as those that cause measles and mumps, and they have side-effects too. One of the most notable, thanks to natural selection, is antibiotic-resistant bacteria.

1. Must we just accept the risks?
2. How many children must die or develop autism as a result of disease-prevention efforts before we give up trying to prevent disease?
3. If we look to history for guidance in answering that last question, how far back should we look?

Additional Resources

Louise Kuo Habakus, Mary Holland, and Kim Mack Rosenberg, eds., *Vaccine Epidemic: How Corporate Greed, Biased Science, and Coercive Government Threaten Our Human Rights, Our Health, and Our Children* (Skyhorse, 2011, 2012).

Seth Mnookin, *The Panic Virus: The True Story Behind the Vaccine-Autism Controversy* (Simon and Schuster, 2011).

Andrew J. Wakefield, *Callous Disregard: Autism and Vaccines—The Truth Behind a Tragedy* (Skyhorse, 2011).

Internet References . . .

Autism Speaks

http://www.autismspeaks.org/

The Autism Science Foundation

http://www.autismsciencefoundation.org/

Vaccinate Your Baby

http://www.vaccinateyourbaby.org/

Selected, Edited, and with Issue Framing Material by:
Thomas A. Easton, *Thomas College*

ISSUE

Should Society Impose a Moratorium on the Use and Release of "Synthetic Biology" Organisms?

YES: Jim Thomas, Eric Hoffman, and Jaydee Hanson, from "Offering Testimony from Civil Society on the Environmental and Societal Implications of Synthetic Biology" (May 27, 2010)

NO: Gregory E. Kaebnick, from "Written Testimony of Gregory E. Kaebnick to the House Committee on Energy and Commerce" (May 27, 2010)

Learning Outcomes

After studying this issue, students will be able to:

- Explain what "dual-use" technologies are and why they warrant special regulation.
- Discuss the impact of the ability to make "synthetic cells" on traditional views of life.
- Discuss the difficulty of preventing all the potential risks of a new technology.
- Make a reasonable forecast of future developments of synthetic biology technology.

ISSUE SUMMARY

YES: Jim Thomas, Eric Hoffman, and Jaydee Hanson, representing the Civil Society on the Environmental and Societal Implications of Synthetic Biology, argue that the risks posed by synthetic biology to human health, the environment, and natural ecosystems are so great that Congress should declare an immediate moratorium on releases to the environment and commercial uses of synthetic organisms and require comprehensive environmental and social impact reviews of all federally funded synthetic biology research.

NO: Gregory E. Kaebnick of the Hastings Center argues that although synthetic biology is surrounded by genuine ethical and moral concerns—including risks to health and environment—which warrant discussion, the potential benefits are too great to call for a general moratorium.

In the past century, biologists have learned an enormous amount about how the cell—the basic functional unit of all living things—works. By the early 1970s, they were beginning to move genes from one organism to another and dream of designing plants and animals (including human beings) with novel combinations of features. By 2002, with Defense Department funding, Jeronimo Cello, Aniko Paul, and Eckard Wimmer were able to construct a live poliovirus from raw laboratory chemicals. This feat was a long way from constructing a bacterium or animal from raw chemicals, but it was enough to set alarm bells of many kinds ringing. Some people thought this work challenged the divine monopoly on creation. Others feared that if one could construct one virus from scratch, one could construct others, such as the smallpox virus, or even tailor entirely new viruses with which natural immune systems and medical facilities could not cope. Some even thought that the paper was irresponsible and should not have been published because it pointed the way toward new kinds of terrorism. See Michael J. Selgelid and Lorna Weir, "Reflections on the Synthetic Production of Poliovirus," *Bulletin of the Atomic Scientists* (May/June 2010).

In 2010, the next step was taken. Craig Venter's research group announced that they had successfully synthesized a bacterial chromosome (the set of genes that specifies the function and form of the bacterium) and implanted it in a bacterium of a different species whose chromosome had been removed. The result was the conversion of the recipient bacterium into the synthesized chromosome's species. See Daniel G. Gibson, et al., "Creation of a Bacterial Cell Controlled by a Chemically Synthesized Genome," *Science* (July 2, 2010). The report received a great deal of media attention, much of it saying that Venter's group had created a living cell, even though only the chromosome had been synthesized. The chromosome's biochemically complex container—a cell minus its chromosome—had *not* been synthesized.

The goal of this work is not the creation of life, but rather the ability to exert unprecedented control over what cells do. In testimony before the House Committee on Energy and Commerce Hearing on Developments in Synthetic Genomics and Implications for Health and Energy (May 27, 2010), Venter said "The ability to routinely write the 'software of life' will usher in a new era in science, and with it, new products and applications such as advanced biofuels, clean water technology, food products, and new vaccines and medicines. The field is already having an impact in some of these areas and will continue to do so as long as this powerful new area of science is used wisely." See also Pamela Weintraub, "J. Craig Venter on Biology's Next Leap: Digitally Designed Life-Forms that Could Produce Novel Drugs, Renewable Fuels, and Plentiful Food for Tomorrow's World," *Discover* (January/February 2010); and Michael A. Peters and Priya Venkatesan, "Bioeconomy and Third Industrial Revolution in the Age of Synthetic Life," *Contemporary Readings in Law and Social Justice* (vol. 2, no. 2, 2010). However, the ETC Group, which anticipated a synthetic organism in 2007, condemns the lack of rules governing synthetic biology, calls it "a quintessential Pandora's box moment," and calls for a global moratorium on further work; see "Synthia Is Alive . . . and Breeding: Panacea or Pandora's Box?" ETC Group News Release (May 20, 2010) (www.etcgroup.org/en/node/5142). A number of artists have also joined the debate; see Sara Reardon, "Visions of Synthetic Biology," *Science* (September 2, 2011). Some biologists have already established do-it-yourself "community labs," looking ahead to the day when synthetic biology is something anyone can do; see Sam Kean, "A Lab of Their Own," *Science* (September 2, 2011). And the FBI's Weapons of Mass Destruction Directorate's Biological Countermeasures Unit encourages "a kind of neighborhood watch" among the do-it-yourselfers; see Delthia Ricks, "Bio Hackers," *Discover* (October 2011).

Researchers had been working on synthetic biology for a number of years, and well before Craig Venter's group announced their accomplishment, prospects and consequences were already being discussed. Michael Specter, "A Life of Its Own," *New Yorker* (September 28, 2009), describes progress to date and notes "the ultimate goal is to create a synthetic organism made solely from chemical parts and blueprints of DNA." If this sounds rather like manipulating living things the way children manipulate Legos, Drew Endy of MIT and colleagues created in 2005 the BioBricks Foundation to make that metaphor explicit. See also Rob Carlson, *Biology Is Technology: The Promise, Peril, and Business of Engineering Life* (Harvard University Press, 2010). David Deamer, "First Life and Next Life," *Technology Review* (May/June 2009), notes that the next step is to create entire cells, not just a single bacterial chromosome. Charles Petit, "Life from Scratch," *Science News* (July 3, 2010), describes

the even more ambitious work of Harvard's Jack Szostak, who is trying to understand how life began by constructing a pre-cell just sophisticated enough to take in components, grow, divide, and start evolving. Szostak expects to succeed within a few years. Such efforts, say Steven A. Benner, Zunyi Yang, and Fei Chen, "Synthetic Biology, Tinkering Biology, and Artificial Biology: What Are We Learning?" *Comptes Rendus Chimie* (April 2011), will drive a better understanding of biology in ways that mere analysis cannot. Some researchers are more focused on modifying existing cells with genetic engineering; see Alexandra Witze, "Factory of Life," *Science News* (January 12, 2013).

We are a long way from designing or modifying cells at will, but that is not to say that we will not get there; see Allen A. Cheng and Timothy K. Lu, "Synthetic Biology: An Emerging Engineering Discipline," *Annual Review of Biomedical Engineering* (August 2012). Immediately after the Venter group's announcement of their accomplishment, Vatican representatives declared that synthetic biology was "a potential time bomb, a dangerous double-edged sword for which it is impossible to imagine the consequences" and "Pretending to be God and parroting his power of creation is an enormous risk that can plunge men into barbarity"; see "Vatican Greets First Synthetic Cell with Caution," *America* (June 7–14, 2010). Chuck Colson, "Synthetic Life: The Danger of God-Like Pretensions," *Christian Post* (June 16, 2010), says "God-like control [of risks] isn't only hubris, it's pure fantasy. The only real way to avoid the unthinkable is not to try and play God in the first place. But that would require the kind of humility that Venter and company reject out-of-hand." Nancy Gibbs, "Creation Myths," *Time* (June 28, 2010), says "The path of progress cuts through the four-way intersection of the moral, medical, religious and political—and whichever way you turn, you are likely to run over someone's deeply held beliefs. Venter's bombshell revived the oldest of ethical debates, over whether scientists were playing God or proving he does not exist because someone reenacted Genesis in suburban Maryland." The "playing God" objection seems likely to grow louder as synthetic biology matures, but it is also likely to fade just as it has done after previous advances such as in vitro fertilization and surrogate mothering. Henk van den Belt, "Playing God in Frankenstein's Footsteps: Synthetic Biology and the Meaning of Life," *NanoEthics* (December 2009), notes that "While syntheses of artificial life forms cause some vague uneasiness that life may lose its special meaning, most concerns turn out to be narrowly anthropocentric. As long as synthetic biology creates only new microbial life and does not directly affect human life, it will in all likelihood be considered acceptable." On the other hand, we may owe our creations the same moral regard we owe to natural species; see Robin Attfield, "Biocentrism, Religion and Synthetic Biology," *Worldviews: Global Religions, Culture & Ecology* (vol. 17, no. 1, 2013).

What will be more significant will be discussions such as Gautam Mukunda, Kenneth A. Oye, and Scott C.

Mohr, "What Rough Beast? Synthetic Biology, Uncertainty, and the Future of Biosecurity," *Politics and the Life Sciences* (September 2009). Mukunda, et al., see synthetic biology as seeking "to create modular biological parts that can be assembled into useful devices, allowing the modification of biological systems with greater reliability, at lower cost, with greater speed, and by a larger pool of people than has been the case with traditional genetic engineering." It is thus a "dual-use" technology, meaning that it has both benign and malign applications. This has clear implications for national security, both offensive and defensive, but they find those implications least alarming in the short term. In the long term, the defensive implications are most important. Because the offensive implications are there, regulation and surveillance of research and development will be necessary in order to forestall terrorists and criminals. Jonathan B. Tucker, "Could Terrorists Exploit Synthetic Biology?" *New Atlantis: A Journal of Technology & Society* (Spring 2011), sees potential problems. Mildred K. Cho and David A. Relman, "Synthetic 'Life,' Ethics, National Security, and Public Discourse," *Science* (July 2, 2010), caution that some concerns about biosecurity and ethics are real but some are imagined; being realistic and avoiding exaggeration are essential if the science is not to become a victim of public mistrust. Meera Lee Sethi and Adam Briggle, "Making Stories Visible: The Task for Bioethics Commissions," *Issues in Science and Technology* (Winter 2011), caution that the stories we tell ourselves about technology (such as "synthetic biology is like computers") may hide issues that warrant deep and careful thought. Paul B. Thompson, "Synthetic Biology Needs a Synthetic Bioethics," *Ethics, Policy, & Environment* (2012), argues that proper consideration of the ethics of synthetic biology will require integrating biomedical and environmental ethics. Walter E. Block, on the other hand, objects that "Synthetic Biology Does Not Need a Synthetic Bioethics: Give Me That Old Time (Libertarian) Ethics," *Ethics, Policy & Environment* (2012). The Biotechnology Industry Organization's Brent Erickson, Rina Singh, and Paul Winters, "Synthetic Biology: Regulating Industry Uses of New Biotechnologies," *Science* (September 2, 2011), think it crucial that regulation not impede innovation and development of new products. See also Tania Bubela, Gregory Haden, and Edna Einsiedel, "Synthetic Biology Confronts Publics and Policy Makers: Challenges for Communication, Regulation, and Commercialization," *Trends in Biotechnology* (May 2012).

In the YES selection, Jim Thomas, Eric Hoffman, and Jaydee Hanson, representing the Civil Society on the Environmental and Societal Implications of Synthetic Biology, argue that the risks posed by synthetic biology to human health, the environment, and natural ecosystems are so great that Congress should declare an immediate moratorium on releases to the environment and commercial uses of synthetic organisms and require comprehensive environmental and social impact reviews of all federally funded synthetic biology research. In the NO selection, Gregory E. Kaebnick of the Hastings Center argues that although synthetic biology is surrounded by genuine ethical and moral concerns—including risks to health and environment—which warrant discussion, the potential benefits are too great to call for a general moratorium.

YES

Jim Thomas, Eric Hoffman, and Jaydee Hanson

Offering Testimony from Civil Society on the Environmental and Societal Implications of Synthetic Biology

. . . Last week, the J. Craig Venter Institute announced the creation of the first living organism with a synthetic genome claiming that this technology would be used in applications as diverse as next generation biofuels, vaccine production and the clean up of oil spills. We agree that this is a significant technical feat however; we believe it should be received as a wake-up call to governments around the world that this technology must now be accountably regulated. While attention this week has been on the activities of a team from Synthetic Genomics Inc, the broader field of synthetic biology has in fact quickly and quietly grown into a multi-billion dollar industry with over seventy DNA foundries and dozens of "pure play" synthetic biology companies entering the marketplace supported by large investments from Fortune 500 energy, forestry, chemical and agribusiness companies. That industry already has at least one product in the marketplace (Du Pont's 'Sorona' bioplastic), and another recently cleared for market entry in 2011 (Amyris Biotechnology's 'No Compromise' biofuel) as well as several dozen near to market applications. We believe the committee should consider the implications of this new industry as a whole in its deliberations not just the technical breakthrough reported last week. Without proper safeguards in place, we risk introducing synthetically constructed living organisms into the environment, intentionally or inadvertently through accident and worker error, that have the potential to destroy ecosystems and threaten human health. We will see the widespread commercial application of techniques with grave dual-use implications. We further risk licensing their use in industrial applications that will unsustainably increase the pressure of human activities on both land and marine ecologies through the increased take of biomass, food resources, water and fertilizer or displacement of wild lands to grow feedstocks for bio-based fuel and chemical production.

We call on Congress to:

1. Implement a moratorium on the release of synthetic organisms into the environment and also their use in commercial settings. This moratorium should remain in place until there is an adequate scientific basis on which to justify such activities, and until due consideration of the associated risks for the environment, biodiversity, and human health, and all associated socio-economic repercussions, are fully and transparently considered.
2. As an immediate step, all federally funded synthetic biology research should be subject to a comprehensive environmental and societal impact review carried out with input from civil society, also considering indirect impacts on biodiversity of moving synthetic organisms into commercial use for fuel, chemicals and medicines. This should include the projects that received $305 million from the Department of Energy in 2009 alone.
3. All synthetic biology projects should also be reviewed by the Recombinant DNA Advisory Committee.

On Synthetic Biology for Biofuels—Time for a Reality Check

Much of the purported promise of the emerging Synthetic Biology industry resides in the notion of transforming biomass into next generation biofuels or bio-based chemicals where synthetic organisms work as bio-factories transforming sugars to high value products. On examination much of this promise is unrealistic and unsustainable and if allowed to proceed could hamper ongoing efforts to conserve biological diversity, ensure food security and prevent dangerous climate change. The sobering reality is that a switch to a bio-based industrial economy could exert much more pressure on land, water, soil, fertilizer, forest resources and conservation areas. It may also do little to address greenhouse gas emissions, potentially worsening climate change.

By way of an example, the team associated with Synthetic Genomics Inc who have recently announced the creation of a synthetic cell have specifically claimed that they would use the same technology to develop an algal species that efficiently converts atmospheric carbon dioxide into hydrocarbon fuel, supposedly addressing both the climate crisis and peak oil concerns in one fell swoop. Yet, contrary to the impression put forth by these researchers in the press, algae, synthetic or otherwise, requires much more than just carbon dioxide to grow—it also requires water,

Thomas et al., Jim. U.S. House of Representatives Committee on Energy and Commerce, May 27, 2010.

nutrients for fertilizer and also sunlight (which therefore means one needs land or open ocean—this can't be done in a vat without also consuming vast quantities of sugar).

In order for Synthetic Genomics or their partners to scale up algal biofuel production to make a dent in the fuel supply, the process would likely exert a massive drain on both water and on fertilizers. Both fresh water and fertilizer (especially phosphate-based fertilizers) are in short supply, both are already prioritized for agricultural food production and both require a large amount of energy either to produce (in the case of fertilizers) or to pump to arid sunlight-rich regions (in the case of water). In a recent life-cycle assessment of algal biofuels published in the journal *Environmental Science and Technology* researchers concluded that algae production consumes more water and energy than other biofuel sources like corn, canola, and switch grass, and also has higher greenhouse gas emissions. "Given what we know about algae production pilot projects over the past 10 to 15 years, we've found that algae's environmental footprint is larger than other terrestrial crops," said Andres Clarens, an assistant professor in U.Virginia's Civil and Environmental Department and lead author on the paper. Moreover scaling-up this technology in the least energy-intensive manner will likely need large open ponds sited in deserts, displacing desert ecosystems. Indeed the federally appointed Invasive Species Advisory Committee has recently warned that non-native algal species employed for such biofuel production could prove ecologically harmful and is currently preparing a fuller report on the matter.

Meanwhile it is not clear that the yield from algal biofuels would go far to meeting our energy needs. MIT inventor Saul Griffiths has recently calculated that even if an algae strain can be made 4 times as efficient as an energy source than it is today it would still be necessary to fill one Olympic-size swimming pool of algae every second for the next twenty five years to offset only half a terawatt of our current energy consumption (which is expected to rise to 16 TW in that time period). That amounts to massive land use change. Emissions from land use change are recognized as one of the biggest contributors to anthropogenic climate change.

Moving Forward—Time for New Regulation

The rapid adoption of synthetic biology is moving the biotechnology industry into the driving seat of industrial production across many previously disparate sectors with downstream consequences for monopoly policy.

Meanwhile its application in commercial settings uses a set of new and extreme techniques whose proper oversight and limits has not yet been debated. It also enables many more diverse living organisms to be produced using genetic science at a speed and volume that will challenge and ultimately overwhelm the capacity of existing biosafety regulations. For example, Craig Venter has claimed in press and in his patent applications that when combined with robotic techniques the technology for producing a synthetic cell can be perfected to make millions of new species per day. Neither the US government nor any other country has the capacity to assess such an outpouring of new synthetic species in a timely or detailed manner. The Energy and Commerce Committee urgently needs to suggest provisions for regulating these new organisms and chemicals derived from them under the Toxic Substances Control Act, Climate Change legislation and other legislation under its purview before allowing their release into the environment. It also needs to identify how it intends to ensure that the use of such organisms whether in biorefineries, open ponds or marine settings does not impinge on agriculture, forestry, desert and marine protection, the preservation of conservation lands, rural jobs or livelihoods.

To conclude, Congress must receive this announcement of a significant new lifeform as a warning bell, signifying that the time has come for governments to fully regulate all synthetic biology experiments and products. It is imperative that in the pursuit of scientific experimentation and wealth creation, we do not sacrifice human health, the environment, and natural ecosystems. These technologies could have powerful and unpredictable consequences. These are life forms never seen on the planet before now. Before they are unleashed into the environment and commercial use, we need to understand the consequences, evaluate alternatives properly, and be able to prevent the problems that may arise from them.

JIM THOMAS is a program manager at ETC Group (Action Group on Erosion, Technology and Concentration) (www.etcgroup.org/en/issues/synthetic_biology).

ERIC HOFFMAN is a genetic technology policy campaigner with Friends of the Earth (www.foe.org).

JAYDEE HANSON is a policy director at the International Center for Technology Assessment (www.icta.org).

Gregory E. Kaebnick    **NO**

Written Testimony of Gregory E. Kaebnick to the House Committee on Energy and Commerce

...The ethical issues raised by synthetic biology are familiar themes in an ongoing conversation this nation has been having about biotechnologies for several decades. . . .

The concerns fall into two general categories. One has to do with whether the creation of synthetic organisms is a good or a bad thing in and of itself, aside from the consequences. These are thought of as intrinsic concerns. Many people had similar intrinsic concerns about reproductive cloning, for example; they just felt it was wrong to do, regardless of benefits. Another has to do with potential consequences—that is, with risks and benefits. The distinction between these categories can be difficult to maintain in practice, but it provides a useful organizational structure.

1. Intrinsic Concerns

I will start with the more philosophical, maybe more baffling, kind of concern—the intrinsic concerns. They are an appropriate place to start because the work just published by researchers at Synthetic Genomics, Inc., has been billed as advancing our understanding of these issues in addition to making a scientific advance.

This announcement is not the first time we have had a debate about whether biotechnology challenges deeply held views about the status of life and the power that biotechnology and medicine give us over it. There was a similar debate about gene transfer research in the 1970s and 1980s, about cloning and stem cell research in the 1990s, and—particularly in the last decade but also earlier—about various tools for enhancing human beings. They have been addressed by the President's Commission for the Study of Ethical Problems in Medicine and Biomedical and Behavioral Research in 1983, by President Clinton's National Bioethics Advisory Council, and by President Bush's President's Council on Bioethics. These concerns are related to even older concerns in medicine about decisions to withhold or withdraw medical treatment at the end of life.

The fact that we have had this debate before speaks to its importance. I believe the intrinsic concerns deserve respect, and with some kinds of biotechnology I think

they are very important, but for synthetic biology, I do not think they provide a basis for decisions about governance.

A. Religious or Metaphysical Concerns

The classic concern about synthetic biology is that it puts human beings in a role properly held by God—that scientists who do it are "playing God," as people say. Some may also believe that life is sacred, and that scientists are violating its sacredness. Prince Charles had this in mind in a famous polemic some years ago when he lamented that biotechnology was leading to "the industrialisation of Life."

To object to synthetic biology along these lines is to see a serious moral mistake in it. This kind of objection may be grounded in deeply held beliefs about God's goals in creating the world and the proper role of human beings within God's plan. But these views would belong to particular faiths—not everybody would share them. Moreover, there is a range of opinions even within religious traditions about what human beings may and may not do. Some people celebrate human creativity and science. They may see science as a gift from God that God intends human beings to develop and use.

The announcement that Synthetic Genomics, Inc., has created a synthetic cell appears to some to disprove the view that life is sacred, but I do not agree. Arguably, what has been created is a synthetic genome, not a completely synthetic cell. Even if scientists manage to create a fully synthetic cell, however, people who believe that life is sacred, that it is something more than interacting chemicals, could continue to defend that belief. A similar question arises about the existence of souls in cloned people: If people have souls, then surely they would have souls even if they were created in the laboratory by means of cloning techniques. By the same reasoning, if microbial life is more than a combination of chemicals, then even microbial life created in the laboratory would be more than just chemicals. In general, beliefs about the sacredness of life are not undermined by science. Moreover, even the creation of a truly synthetic cell would still start with existing materials. It would not be the kind of creating with which God is credited, which is creating something from nothing—creation ex nihilo.

Kaebnick, Gregory E. From statement before U.S. House of Representatives Committee on Energy and Commerce, May 27, 2010.

B. Concerns that Synthetic Biology Will Undermine Morally Significant Concepts

A related but different kind of concern is that synthetic biology will simply undermine our shared understanding of important moral concepts. For example, perhaps it will lead us to think that life does not have the specialness we have often found in it, or that we humans are more powerful than we have thought in the past. This kind of concern can be expressed without talking about God's plan.

Synthetic biology need not change our understanding of the value of life, however. The fact that living things are created naturally, rather than by people, would be only one reason for seeing them as valuable, and we could continue to see them as valuable when they are created by people. Further, in its current form, synthetic biology is almost exclusively about engineering single-celled organisms, which may be less troubling to people than engineering more complex organisms. If the work is contained within the laboratory and the factory, then it might not end up broadly changing humans' views of the value of life.

Also, of course, the fact that the work challenges our ideas may not really be a moral problem. It would not be the first time that science has challenged our views of life or our place in the cosmos, and we have weathered these challenges in the past.

C. Concerns about the Human Relationship to Nature

Another way of saying that there's something intrinsically troubling about synthetic biology, again without necessarily talking about the possibility that people are treading on God's turf, is to see it as a kind of environmentalist concern. Many environmentalists want to do more than make the environment good for humans; they also want to save nature from humans—they want to save endangered species, wildernesses, "wild rivers," old-growth forests, and mountains, canyons, and caves, for example. We should approach the natural world, many feel, with a kind of reverence or gratitude, and some worry that synthetic biology—perhaps along with many other kinds of biotechnology—does not square with this value.

Of course, human beings have been altering nature throughout human history. They have been altering ecosystems, affecting the survival of species, affecting the evolution of species, and even creating new species. Most agricultural crop species, for example, are dramatically different from their ancestral forebears. The issue, then, is where to draw the line. Even people who want to preserve nature accept that there is a balance to be struck between saving trees and harvesting them for wood. There might also be a balance when it comes to biotechnology. The misgiving is that synthetic biology goes too far—it takes human control over nature to the ultimate level, where we are not merely altering existing life forms but creating new forms.

Another environmentalist perspective, however, is that synthetic biology could be developed so that it is beneficial to the environment. Synthetic Genomics, Inc. recently contracted with Exxon Mobil to engineer algae that produce gasoline in ways that not only eliminate some of the usual environmental costs of producing and transporting fuel but simultaneously absorb large amounts of carbon dioxide, thereby offsetting some of the environmental costs of burning fuel (no matter how it is produced). If that could be achieved, many who feel deeply that we should tread more lightly on the natural world might well find synthetic biology attractive. In order to achieve this benefit, however, we must be confident that synthetic organisms will not escape into the environment and cause harms there.

Concerns Involving Consequences

The second category of moral concerns is about consequences—that is, risks and benefits. The promise of synthetic biology includes, for example, better ways of producing medicine, environmentally friendlier ways of producing fuel and other substances, and remediation of past environmental damage. These are not morally trivial considerations. There are also, however, morally serious risks. These, too, fall into three categories.

Concerns about Social Justice

Synthetic biology is sometimes heralded as the start of a new industrial age. Not only will it lead to new products, but it will lead to new modes of production and distribution; instead of pumping oil out of the ground and shipping it around the world, we might be able to produce it from algae in places closer to where it will be used. Inevitably, then, it would have all sorts of large-scale economic and social consequences, some of which could be harmful and unjust. Some commentators hold, for example, that if synthetic biology generates effective ways of producing biofuels from feedstocks such as sugar cane, then farmland in poor countries would be converted from food production to sugar cane production. Another set of concerns arises over the intellectual property rights in synthetic biology. If synthetic biology is the beginning of a new industrial age, and a handful of companies received patents giving them broad control over it, the results could be unjust.

Surely we ought to avoid these consequences. It is my belief that we can do so without avoiding the technology. Also, traditional industrial methods themselves seem to be leading to disastrous long-term social consequences; if so, synthetic biology might provide a way toward better social outcomes.

Concerns about Biosafety

Another concern is about biosafety—about mechanisms for containing and controlling synthetic organisms, both during research and development and in industrial applications. The concern is that organisms will escape, turn out to have properties, at least in their new environment, different from what was intended and predicted, or maybe mutate to acquire them, and then pose a threat to public health, agriculture, or the environment. Alternatively, some of their genes might be transferred to other, wild microbes, producing wild microbes with new properties.

Controlling this risk means controlling the organisms—trying to prevent industrial or laboratory accidents, and then trying to make sure that, when organisms do escape, they are not dangerous. Many synthetic biologists argue that an organism that devotes most of its energy to producing jet fuel or medicine, that is greatly simplified (so that it lacks the genetic complexity and therefore the adaptability of a wild form), and that is designed to work in a controlled, contained environment, will simply be too weak to survive in the wild. For added assurance, perhaps engineering them with failsafe mechanisms will *ensure* that they are incapable of surviving in the wild.

Concerns about Deliberate Misuse

I once heard a well-respected microbiologist say that he was very enthusiastic about synthetic biology, and that the only thing that worries him is the possibility of catastrophe. The kind of thing that worries him is certainly possible. The 1918 flu virus has been recreated in the laboratory. In 2002, a scientist in New York stitched together stretches of nucleotides to produce a string of DNA that was equivalent to RNA polio virus and eventually produced the RNA virus using the DNA string. More recently, the SARS virus was also created in the laboratory. Eventually, it will almost certainly be possible to recreate bacterial pathogens like smallpox. We might also be able to enhance these pathogens. Some work in Australia on mousepox suggests ways of making smallpox more potent, for example. In theory, entirely new pathogens could be created. Pathogens that target crops or livestock are also possible.

Controlling this risk means controlling the people and companies who have access to DNA synthesis or the tools they could use to synthesize DNA themselves. There are some reasons to think that the worst will never actually happen. To be wielded effectively, destructive synthetic organisms would also have to be weaponized; for example, methods must be found to disperse pathogens in forms that will lead to epidemic infection in the target population while sparing one's own population. Arguably, terrorists have better forms of attacking their enemies than with bioweapons, which are still comparatively hard to make and are very hard to control. However, our policy should amount to more than hoping for the best.

Governance

In assessing these risks and establishing oversight over synthetic biology, we do not start from square one. There is an existing framework of laws and regulations, put into action by various agencies and oversight bodies, that will apply to R&D and to different applications. The

NIH is extending its guidelines for research on genetic engineering to ensure that they are applicable to research on synthetic biology. These Guidelines are enforced by the NIH's Recombinant DNA Advisory Committee and a network of Institutional Biosafety Committees at research institutions receiving federal funding. Many applications would fall under the purview of various federal laws and the agencies that enforce them. For example, a plan to release synthetic organisms into the sea to produce nutrients that would help rebuild ocean food chains would have to pass muster with the EPA. The USDA and FDA also have regulatory authority over applications. The FBI and the NIH's National Science Advisory Board for Biosecurity are formulating policy to regulate the sale of synthetic DNA sequences that might pose a threat to biosecurity.

At the same time, the current regulatory framework may need to be augmented. First, there are questions about whether the existing laws leave gaps. Research conducted by entirely privately funded laboratory might not [be] covered by the NIH's Guidelines, for example. Field testing of a synthetic organism—that is, release into the environment as part of basic research—might not be covered by the existing regulations of the EPA or the USDA. Questions about the adequacy of existing regulations are even more pointed when it comes to concerns about biosecurity, particularly if or when powerful benchtop synthesizers are available in every lab.

The other big question is whether the regulatory bodies' ability to do risk assessment of synthetic biology is adequate. Synthetic biology differs from older forms of genetic engineering in that a synthetic organism could combine DNA sequences found originally in many different organisms, or might even contain entirely novel genetic code. The eventual behavior of these organisms in new environments, should they accidentally end up in one, may therefore be hard to predict.

The synthetic biologists' goal of simplicity is crucial. One of the themes of traditional biology is that living things are usually more complex than they first appear. We should not assume at the outset that synthetic organisms will shed the unpredictability inherent to life. Life tends to find a way. As a starting assumption, we should expect that artificial life will try to find a way as well.

Another difficulty in assessing concerns about both biosafety and deliberate misuse is that, if the field evolves so that important and even innovative work could be done in small, private labs, even in homes, then it could be very difficult to monitor and regulate. The threats of biosafety and deliberate misuse would have to be taken yet more seriously.

Concluding Comments

I take seriously concerns that synthetic biology is bad in and of itself, and I believe that they warrant a thorough public airing, but I do not believe that they provide a good basis for restraining the technology, at least if we can be confident that the organisms will not lead to environmental damage. Better yet would be to get out in front of the technology and ensure that it benefits the environment. Possibly, some potential applications of synthetic biology are more troubling than others and should be treated differently.

Ultimately, I think the field should be assessed on its possible outcomes. At the moment, we do not understand the possible outcomes well enough. We need, I believe:

- more study of the emergence, plausibility, and impact of potential risks;
- a strategy for studying the risks that is multidisciplinary, rather than one conducted entirely within the field;
- a strategy that is grounded in good science rather than sheer speculation, yet flexible enough to look for the unexpected; and

- an analysis of whether our current regulatory framework is adequate to deal with these risks and how the framework should be augmented.

Different kinds of applications pose different risks and may call for different responses. Microbes intended for release into the environment, for example, would pose a different set of concerns than microbes designed to be kept in specialized, contained settings. Overall, however, while the risks of synthetic biology are too significant to leave the field alone, its potential benefits are too great to call for a general moratorium.

GREGORY E. KAEBNICK is a research scholar at The Hastings Center and editor of the *Hastings Center Report*.

EXPLORING THE ISSUE

Should Society Impose a Moratorium on the Use and Release of "Synthetic Biology" Organisms?

Critical Thinking and Reflection

1. What are "dual-use" technologies?
2. Does creating a synthetic cell disprove the idea that life is sacred?
3. How long do you think it will be before synthetic biology can be done at home? Is the prospect frightening?
4. Can all risks be prevented?

Is There Common Ground?

As with many technologies, some people see mostly risks and would, if they could, stop the development of the technology. Others see mostly benefits and think that those benefits are worth putting up with the risks. A more nuanced approach is to determine which risks and benefits seem most likely and then to carefully weigh them against each other. This approach is known as risk–benefit or cost–benefit analysis, and it is used in medicine, engineering, business, and other areas.

1. What seem to be the most likely or worrisome risks associated with synthetic biology technology?
2. What seem to be the most likely benefits associated with synthetic biology technology?
3. Do you think the benefits are worth the risks?

Create Central

www.mhhe.com/createcentral

Additional Resources

Michael A. Peters and Priya Venkatesan, "Bioeconomy and Third Industrial Revolution in the Age of Synthetic Life," *Contemporary Readings in Law and Social Justice* (vol. 2, no. 2, 2010).

Michael J. Selgelid and Lorna Weir, "Reflections on the Synthetic Production of Poliovirus," *Bulletin of the Atomic Scientists* (May/June 2010).

Jonathan B. Tucker, "Could Terrorists Exploit Synthetic Biology?" *New Atlantis: A Journal of Technology & Society* (Spring 2011).

Pamela Weintraub, "J. Craig Venter on Biology's Next Leap: Digitally Designed Life-Forms that Could Produce Novel Drugs, Renewable Fuels, and Plentiful Food for Tomorrow's World," *Discover* (January/February 2010).

Internet Reference . . .

The J. Craig Venter Institute

The J. Craig Venter Institute, formed in October 2006, is a world leader in genomics research, including the effort to create synthetic cells.

www.jcvi.org

Selected, Edited, and with Issue Framing Material by:
Thomas A. Easton, *Thomas College*

ISSUE

Can Infectious Animal Diseases Be Studied Safely in Kansas?

YES: Bruce Knight, from "Statement on the National Bio- and Agro-Defense Facility," before the Subcommittee on Oversight and Investigation, House Energy and Commerce Committee (May 22, 2008)

NO: Ray L. Wulf, from "Written Testimony," submitted for the Record to the Subcommittee on Oversight and Investigation, House Energy and Commerce Committee (May 22, 2008)

Learning Outcomes

After studying this issue, students will be able to:

- Explain the need for reliable isolation or containment measures when doing research on infectious animal and human diseases.
- Compare the advantages of geographic and technological isolation or containment measures.
- Discuss the economic impact of an outbreak of foot-and-mouth disease.

ISSUE SUMMARY

YES: Bruce Knight argues that although the U.S. Department of Agriculture's research facility at Plum Island, New York, has served well since it was built over half a century ago, modern technology is capable of ensuring safety at a mainland facility, which would also be cheaper to operate, more easily accessible, and more responsive to potential disease threats.

NO: Ray L. Wulf argues that an island location is much more effective at containing infectious diseases such as foot-and-mouth disease. A mainland research facility would permit unhampered spread of such diseases throughout the continental United States, with devastating consequences for the agricultural economy. Modern technology is not adequate to ensure safety, and federal, state, and local authorities are not prepared to deal with an outbreak.

Plum Island, located off the coast of Long Island in New York State, became a center of research into deadly animal diseases in 1954. At that time, responding to outbreaks of foot-and-mouth disease (FMD) in Mexico and Canada, the U.S. Army gave the island to the U.S. Department of Agriculture (USDA) to establish a research center for studying FMD. The island location was chosen because it was isolated from the mainland and the prevailing winds blow out to sea. FMD can be spread by the wind, and it is highly contagious. The island location was regarded as the safest possible place to work with diseases such as FMD.

Today, the Plum Island Animal Disease Center is responsible for protecting the U.S. livestock industry against catastrophic economic losses caused by foreign animal disease agents accidentally or deliberately introduced into the United States. It does this by performing research into disease detection and diagnosis, vaccines, drugs, and risk assessment. It also trains animal health professionals. It is proud of its safety record; its Web site claims that "Not once in our nearly 50 years of operation has an animal pathogen escaped from the island."

The island was transferred from the USDA to the Department of Homeland Security (DHS) in 2003. The DHS soon began to rethink the facility as the National Bio- and Agro-Defense Facility, upgraded to provide more space for the study of diseases that can infect both animals and humans. Such research would require Biosafety Level 4 laboratories, the highest security level. Plum Island at the time had only Biosafety Level 3 laboratories, and area residents had resisted proposals to upgrade the laboratories to Level 4. DHS also thought it would be advantageous to move the research facility to the mainland and soon narrowed the list of candidate sites to six (including Plum Island). The final choice was Manhattan, Kansas, near to a major university and research community but also very close to large populations of livestock. Critics have objected that the choice of Kansas was unduly influenced by aggressive lobbying by the state's senators and governor; see Yudhijit Bhattacharjee, "How Kansas Nabbed the New Bio- and Agro-Defense Lab," *Science* (December 12, 2008). As of late 2010, the Kansas choice stands, and Plum Island is to be sold.

At the hearing of the Subcommittee on Oversight and Investigation, House Energy and Commerce Committee, for which the testimony presented in the NO selection was prepared, the U.S. Government Accounting Office (GAO) testified that the DHS had not suitably evaluated the risks of moving the Plum Island Animal Disease Center to the mainland. On December 12, 2008, DHS released a final Environmental Impact Statement (EIS), and on January 16, 2009, it announced its choice of Manhattan, Kansas, as the new location, basing the choice on the information and analysis in the final EIS (http://www.dhs .gov) and other factors.

The GAO then undertook to analyze the EIS, noting that DHS was restricted by law from moving the Plum Island facility to the mainland until it had completed a risk assessment on whether FMD research can be done there as safely as on the island. The GAO specifically assessed the evidence DHS said supported its decision. Unfortunately, said the GAO, "DHS's analyses did not effectively characterize and differentiate the risks associated with the release of FMD virus at the six sites. . . . The economic analyses did not incorporate market response to an FMD outbreak—which would be related to the number of livestock in the site's vicinity. They also did not consider the effect of establishing a containment zone to control the effects of a national export ban on the domestic livestock industry—which could have been used to differentiate across National Bio and Agro-Defense Facility sites. The analyses were constrained by limited scope and detail. They did not incorporate worst-case outbreak scenarios. . . . Given the significant limitations in DHS's analyses that we found, the conclusion that FMD work can be done as safely on the mainland as on Plum Island is not supported." See the GAO report at http://www.gao .gov/products/GAO-09-747. In November 2010, the National Research Council issued a safety report, which concluded that there is a 70 percent chance of pathogen release from the proposed Manhattan, Kansas BioLab-4 over a

50-year period; see "National Research Council Questions Safety of Proposed Biocontainment Lab in Kansas," http:// www.thefreelibrary.com/National+research+council+questions +safety+of+proposed+biocontainment...-a0243277969. New York officials are objecting to the move on the grounds of expense and jobs, among other things.

According to Carol D. Leonnig, "Infectious Diseases Study Site Questioned: Tornado Alley May Not Be Safe, GAO Says," *Washington Post* (July 27, 2009), DHS officials are claiming that the GAO exceeded its authority in reviewing the DHS risk assessment. They are also pushing to delay further hearings of the Subcommittee on Oversight and Investigation, House Energy and Commerce Committee. No such hearings had been held by the end of 2010.

It is worth noting that risk assessment is a complex activity. One recent textbook, Paolo F. Ricci's *Environmental and Health Risk Assessment and Management: Principles and Practices* (Springer Netherlands, 2009), stresses the need for "sound causal arguments," which is where the GAO says the DHS falls short. However, the president of Kansas State University in Manhattan, Kansas, remains delighted that his campus was chosen by DHS to house Plum Island's replacement, according to a press release, "President Kirk Schulz Keeping K-State at the Forefront of National Animal Health."

In the YES selection taken from testimony before the Subcommittee on Oversight and Investigation, House Energy and Commerce Committee, Bruce Knight, then the USDA's Under Secretary for Marketing and Regulatory Programs, argues that although the USDA's research facility at Plum Island, New York, has served well since it was built over half a century ago, modern technology is capable of ensuring safety at a mainland facility, which would also be cheaper to operate, more easily accessible, and more responsive to potential disease threats. In the NO selection, farmer and rancher Ray L. Wulf argues that an island location is much more effective at containing infectious diseases such as FMD. A mainland research facility would permit unhampered spread of such diseases throughout the continental United States, with devastating consequences for the agricultural economy. Modern technology is not adequate to ensure safety, and federal, state, and local authorities are not prepared to deal with an outbreak.

YES ⤶

Bruce Knight

Statement on the National Bio- and Agro-Defense Facility

. . . Agriculture is a vital component of our nation's economy. Of particular importance to homeland security is the significant increase in agricultural trade. This year, we expect agriculture exports to reach approximately $101 billion, making it the highest export sales year ever in our history—and significant to our balance of trade. Agriculture imports are rising as well—increasing from nearly $58 billion in 2005 to an estimated $76.5 billion this year.

We face many challenges in protecting this important infrastructure. As goods move back and forth across the border, we must remain vigilant to safeguard U.S. agriculture from unwelcome pest and disease threats. Our sector is particularly concerned about security because food production is not constrained by political boundaries, and as we all know, diseases and pathogens do not respect state or national borders. The interconnected nature of the global food system is our strength and allows us to feed the world, but it is also a disadvantage in the event of attack or natural disease outbreak. Additionally, one of the agricultural sector's greatest contributions to the quality of life is the fact that products flow quickly through interstate commerce—one of our greatest assets is also one of our greatest concerns because intentionally or unintentionally contaminated products could quickly spread a pest, disease, or other agent.

USDA works diligently to protect U.S. agriculture from the potential introduction of human and animal disease agents, whether unintentionally or through agroterrorism. Many of these pathogens such as the Nipah and Hendra viruses are zoonotic, that is, they cause both human and animal disease, and can pass from animals to humans. If a significant zoonotic or animal disease were to penetrate our borders, it could devastate the agricultural industry, cause numerous casualties, and harm the economy.

We've seen just how disastrous the effects of a foreign animal disease outbreak can be in the 2001 foot-and-mouth disease (FMD) outbreak in the United Kingdom. In that case, over 6 million pigs, sheep, and cattle were destroyed, with the epidemic costing the U.K. economy an estimated $13 billion. This example highlights the need for the best tools and diagnostics to safeguard the U.S. livestock industry from significant foreign animal disease threats such as FMD. At the same time, the 2007 suspected release of live FMD virus from the Pirbright campus in England amplifies the balance needed in undertaking such work. This is why USDA and the Department of Homeland Security (DHS) will use the most modern biosafety practices and procedures, and stringent and rigorous safety measures within NBAF.

Because of the continued emergence of new animal diseases, the leaping of dangerous animal diseases across species, and the possibility of a bioterrorist release, it is even more essential that USDA have a sufficient understanding of these diseases and be well prepared to protect the U.S. livestock industry from their damage. To achieve this, USDA works through its Agricultural Research Service (ARS) and Animal and Plant Health Inspection Service (APHIS) to meet its responsibilities in animal health. ARS is the primary intramural science research agency of USDA, operating a network of over 100 research laboratories across the nation that work on all aspects of agricultural science. APHIS is responsible for safeguarding U.S. agricultural health from foreign pests and diseases of plants and animals.

In order to be able to rapidly identify, respond to, and control outbreaks of foreign animal and zoonotic disease, USDA needs secure, state-of-the-art biocontainment laboratories with adequate space for advanced research, diagnostics, and training. Recognizing this need, the President directed USDA and DHS, via Homeland Security Presidential Directive 9: "Defense of the United States Agriculture and Food," to develop a plan to provide for such facilities. As I will explain further, USDA is working closely with our partners in DHS to fulfill this important need.

Plum Island Animal Disease Center

In 1954, USDA began work at the Plum Island Animal Disease Center (PIADC) in research and diagnostics on foreign animal diseases that, either by accidental or deliberate introduction to the United States, pose significant health and/or economic risks to the U.S. livestock industry. The Plum Island Animal Disease Center has served U.S. agriculture well. It's no accident that this country has the healthiest and most abundant livestock populations in the world. Producers and all of us at USDA work hard every day to keep this up.

An integral part of maintaining animal health is preventing the entry of exotic pest and disease threats. The Plum Island Animal Disease Center, through its diagnostic, research, and reagent production and distribution activities, has stood as American agriculture's bulwark

Knight, Bruce. From statement before U.S. House of Representatives, May 22, 2008.

against potentially devastating foreign animal diseases. Each working day since the facility opened over 50 years ago, the dedicated and highly skilled Plum Island Animal Disease Center staff has equipped veterinarians, scientists, professors, and other animal health professionals here and around the world with the tools they need to fight exotic disease incursions that threaten livestock. In addition to FMD and classical swine fever, other livestock diseases that our scientists have studied at the Plum Island Animal Disease Center include African swine fever, rinderpest, Rift Valley fever, West Nile fever, vesicular stomatitis, and Capri pox (sheep pox and lumpy skin disease).

As you know, in June 2003, operational responsibility for the Plum Island Animal Disease Center transferred from USDA to DHS under the Homeland Security Act of 2002. Since the transfer, we've developed a strong, collaborative partnership with DHS and put in place an interagency agreement to clarify roles and responsibilities. A Board of Directors and Senior Leadership Group were created to facilitate decision-making regarding facility operations and policies, while also allowing the three agencies to focus on accomplishing their specific missions and goals. I believe our relationship with DHS is a very positive one that allows both Departments to achieve our similar goals while making the most of each other's specialized expertise.

After the Plum Island Animal Disease Center transfer, USDA remained responsible for conducting basic and applied research and diagnostic activities at the Plum Island Animal Disease Center to protect U.S. agriculture from foreign animal disease agents. DHS, in turn, assumed responsibility for coordinating the overall national effort to protect key U.S. resources and infrastructure, including agriculture. Science programs at the Plum Island Animal Disease Center now include the APHIS Foreign Animal Disease Diagnostic Laboratory (FADDL), ARS' Foreign Animal Disease Research Unit, and DHS' Targeted Advanced Development Unit. . . .

APHIS scientists perform diagnostic testing of samples collected from U.S. livestock that are showing clinical signs consistent with an exotic disease, as well as testing animal products and live animals being imported into the United States to ensure that unwanted diseases are not accidentally introduced through importation. APHIS scientists at the Plum Island Animal Disease Center have the capability to diagnose more than 30 exotic animal diseases, and perform thousands of diagnostic tests each year. They also prepare diagnostic reagents and distribute them to laboratories throughout the world, and test the safety and efficacy of vaccines for selected foreign animal diseases. Other APHIS activities include improving techniques for the diagnosis or control of foreign animal diseases and validating tests for foreign animal diseases that are deployed to the National Animal Health Laboratory Network (NAHLN). Through the use of these tests in surveillance, the NAHLN provides for early detection and the surge capability needed in the case of an outbreak.

In addition, FADDL staff, in conjunction with APHIS' Professional Development Staff, train veterinarians, scientists, professors, and veterinary students on recognition of clinical signs and pathological changes caused by foreign animal diseases. This training provides the backbone of APHIS' animal disease surveillance and safeguarding programs. These foreign animal disease diagnosticians trained by FADDL are located throughout the country, and can be on-site to conduct an investigation and collect samples within 16 hours of receiving a report of a suspect foreign animal disease. Based on their assessment of the situation and prioritization of the threat, APHIS can then take appropriate steps if necessary to protect the U.S. livestock industry.

Through its involvement in the Plum Island Animal Disease Center, ARS develops new strategies to prevent and control foreign or emerging animal disease epidemics through a better understanding of the nature of infectious organisms, pathogenesis in susceptible animals, host immune responses, and the development of novel vaccines and diagnostic tests. The ARS Foreign Animal Disease Research Unit focuses on developing vaccines that can be produced safely in the United States and used safely on U.S. farms, diagnostic techniques to differentiate between a vaccinated and an infected animal, and methods for identifying carrier animals. Currently, ARS' work at the Plum Island Animal Disease Center includes active research programs working with FMD, Classical Swine Fever, and vesicular stomatitis viruses.

ARS scientists have recently carried out extensive work on FMD, including early development of a FMD vaccine that is safe to produce on the mainland; discovery of an antiviral treatment that prevents FMD replication and spread within 24 hours; and determination of many key aspects of FMD virus structure, function, and replication at the molecular level, leading to highly specific diagnostic tests.

Meeting the Needs of American Agriculture

The Plum Island Animal Disease Center has played a critical role in developing the tools and expertise needed to protect the country from the deliberate or unintentional introduction of significant foreign animal diseases. However, much has changed since the Plum Island Animal Disease Center was first built, and we are even more cognizant of the threat from foreign animal diseases due to the increasingly interconnected world we live in. This need is echoed by our American livestock industries that could be devastated by the introduction of a significant foreign animal disease. Groups such as the United States Animal Health Association and National Institute for Animal Agriculture have appealed for accelerated research to protect their industries. Also, the National Cattlemen's Beef Association, Animal Agriculture Coalition, and National Milk Producers Federation have written to Congress, to show their support for NBAF.

To continue providing U.S. agriculture with the latest research and technological services, as well as world-class approaches to agricultural health safeguarding and foreign-animal disease diagnostics, USDA needs additional space and upgraded biosecurity measures to work on those animal-borne diseases that pose the greatest risk to U.S. livestock industries, and those that can also be transmitted to humans. The Plum Island Animal Disease Center is aging and nearing the end of its lifecycle, and the state of current facilities has created a backlog of needed space for important experiments, diagnostic development, and training efforts.

In particular, USDA is in need of enhanced research and diagnostic capabilities for animal diseases, particularly zoonotic diseases of large animals that require agriculture BSL-3 and BSL-4 capabilities. However, since we cannot currently carry out BSL-4 activities at the Plum Island Animal Disease Center, the nation is left lacking a large animal facility to address high-consequence animal diseases that can be transmitted to humans, such as Nipah and Hendra, as well as Rift Valley Fever (which requires vaccinated personnel; however vaccine is in short supply).

Specifically, USDA would utilize the BSL-4 space to develop diagnostic assays for Rift Valley Fever and Nipah and Hendra viruses, using specimens collected from animals in the BSL-4 lab. In addition, in the event of an emerging pathogen, it would often be necessary to inoculate animals in a BSL-4 suite in order to determine the clinical course of the disease, determine appropriate diagnostic specimens, isolate the agent, and develop diagnostic tools.

In order to protect U.S. agriculture and human health, it is critical that USDA have the capability of diagnosing and working with the disease agents I have mentioned, as well as any new highly infectious pathogen that may emerge. In response, our agencies have begun planning for the next generation facility which we call the NBAF, to replace the current structures at the Plum Island Animal Disease Center. NBAF will integrate research, development, and testing in foreign animal diseases and zoonotic diseases, which will support the complimentary missions of USDA and DHS. NBAF will address USDA needs that are currently not being met by the facilities at the Plum Island Animal Disease Center, including inadequate lab space for processing diagnostic samples, limitations in diagnostic capability for BSL-4 agents, and lack of space to expand to include the development, feasibility testing, and validation of new and emerging technologies for detection of exotic and emerging diseases. In addition, it will provide room to grow as we further enhance our abilities to respond to increasing threats to the U.S. livestock industry.

The NBAF will also have a synergistic effect, to the benefit of each of our agencies, by utilizing the expertise of the academic and scientific community in the area. In addition, we expect that by sharing a well-equipped core facility, we will see a more cost effective utilization of

funding. This will also continue to provide a number of opportunities for enhanced interaction among the three agencies. For example, research done by ARS and DHS may identify possible new diagnostic tools that APHIS can use; APHIS' repository of foreign animal disease agents obtained from outbreaks around the world will provide a resource for ARS and DHS research and bioforensics; and APHIS' diagnostic investigations and surveillance will help identify emerging or re-emerging diseases in the field, in turn helping set research priorities for ARS and DHS.

Site Selection

At the time Plum Island was built, biosecurity was much different than it is today. Agriculture biosecurity was defined by biological isolation, so that if there was a problem at the laboratory, there was physical separation from susceptible livestock populations and any breaches were localized. Today, with much more advanced technologies, the ability to manage effective biosecurity and biosafety practices is not dictated by location or physical barriers.

We recognize that there is concern about building the NBAF on the mainland. Since the determination was made over 60 years ago to build the Plum Island Animal Disease Center on an island, assessments have shown that technological advances would allow for safe research and diagnostics of foreign animal diseases to take place on the U.S. mainland. A 2002 study completed by the Science Applications International Corporation (SAIC) and commissioned by USDA found that the FMD virus and other exotic foreign animal diseases of concern to the Department could be fully and safely contained within a BSL-3 laboratory, as was being done in other countries at the time including Canada, Germany, and Brazil. A second SAIC study also concluded that there was a valid USDA need for a BSL-4 facility, and that a BSL-4 facility for large animal work could be safely located on the mainland.

In planning for the NBAF, we recognize the absolutely essential need for state-of-the-art biosafety practices and procedures, including stringent and rigorous safety measures within the laboratories themselves, to prevent disease organisms from escaping into the environment. Situations such as the recent suspected release of live FMD virus from the Pirbright campus in England only serve to highlight this importance. We can use that example as a learning opportunity and make sure that the design and maintenance of the NBAF facility enables us to carry out the essential activities needed to protect the nation from foreign animal diseases while ensuring the highest level of biosafety.

This is why the NBAF will utilize the redundancies built into modern research laboratory designs and the latest biosecurity and containment systems, coupled with continued training and monitoring of employees, to effectively minimize any risks. Personnel controls for the NBAF will include background checks, biometric testing for lab entry, and no solitary access to BSL-4 microorganisms. The NBAF will also feature biological safety cabinets in the wet labs designed to meet the needs of BSL-3 labs, while in BSL-4 labs, these biological safety cabinets will include additional security measures or be used in combination with full-body, air-supplied personal protective suits.

In terms of facility design, the BSL-4 lab at the NBAF will employ a box-in-box principle with a pressure-controlled buffer. All water and air leaving the lab will be purified—that is, no research microorganism will enter the sewage system or outside air. All critical functions will have redundant systems. The design of the BSL-4 laboratories and animal space will comply with the appropriate recommendations and requirements of the Centers for Disease Control and Prevention, National Institutes of Health, Department of Defense, and National Research Council.

I would also like to note some potential advantages to locating the NBAF on the mainland. For example, the lower cost of living, as compared to that in the communities surrounding the Plum Island Animal Disease Center, would likely make recruiting personnel easier for our agencies. This would also eliminate the costs of moving people on and off an island every day, as we currently do. A mainland facility would be more accessible if air traffic is shut down due to weather conditions or an emergency situation, and would not be subject to the occasional wind closures that we experience at the Plum Island Animal Disease Center due to rough waters. And, as I mentioned earlier, locating the facility near an established research community would facilitate innovative collaboration.

A key advantage to locating NBAF on the mainland would be the ability to quickly respond to a potential foreign animal disease threat. Placing the NBAF on the mainland could eliminate the need for additional transport of samples to the island via boat or aircraft, as is currently done at Plum Island. Having a more accessible location, where diagnostic capabilities could be utilized within the first 24 hours of an emergency, is essential. For example, in June 2007, APHIS conducted an investigation into swine showing signs consistent with a significant foreign animal disease. In such a situation, every hour counts when it comes to being able to quickly rule out major diseases. Incidents such as this can have a significant impact on the economy, stop movement and trade in multiple species of livestock, and spread fear throughout the industry.

Although DHS is ultimately responsible for the selection of a NBAF site, USDA has been closely involved throughout this process. APHIS and ARS have provided detailed program requirements to DHS, and have representatives on the site selection committee and site inspection team. We support the criteria used to select the sites: proximity to research capabilities linked to the NBAF mission requirements, site proximity to a skilled workforce, as well as acquisition/construction/operations, and com-

munity acceptance, and look forward to the next steps in the process.

DHS is currently preparing an environmental impact statement (EIS) looking at the six sites, which include Plum Island and five mainland locations. The EIS, on which USDA and DHS are working, will consider the risk and potential consequences of an accidental release of a foreign animal disease, and will be integral to moving forward with a sound NBAF site selection.

It is important that we move forward in a timely manner with planning and construction of NBAF so that we can develop the diagnostics and tools needed to protect U.S. agriculture from the threats of dangerous foreign animal diseases. Just as the science behind bioterrorism has advanced in recent years, and new and changing diseases continue to emerge, so too must we arm ourselves with more sophisticated ways of preventing harm to the U.S. livestock industry. If we don't, then bioterrorists will continue to find innovative ways to attack our livestock, new diseases will continue to emerge, and U.S. agriculture will be left vulnerable to these dangers. This is why USDA is committed to working with DHS to move forward with plans for NBAF, after a thorough analysis of the options and development of plans to ensure the utmost biosafety and biosecurity.

Authority to Conduct FMD Research on the Mainland

Lastly, I would like to briefly mention recent legislative activity related to live FMD virus. Current statute (21 U.S.C. 113a.) restricts research involving live FMD virus and other animal diseases that present a significant risk to domestic U.S. livestock to laboratories on coastal islands separated from the mainland United States by deep water. Research involving live FMD virus is carried out at the Plum Island Animal Disease Center under this statute, which dates back to the 1950s. The statute was amended by the 1990 Farm Bill to authorize the Secretary of Agriculture, when necessary, to allow the movement of live FMD virus, under permit, to research facilities on the U.S. mainland.

USDA recognizes DHS' interest in the Secretary being directed, via statute, to issue a permit for live FMD virus at the NBAF. This direction will provide clarity in this important area as DHS moves forward in selecting a site for the NBAF and then in contracting for the construction of the facility. For these reasons, the Administration included in our Farm Bill Proposal an authorization for USDA to conduct research and diagnostics for highly infectious disease agents, such as FMD and rinderpest, on the U.S. mainland. Consistent with the Administration's proposal, section 7524 of the Food, Conservation, and Energy Act of 2008 directs the Secretary to issue a permit for live FMD virus at NBAF, while preserving the Secretary's discretion and ensuring that all biosafety and select agent requirements are being met at the facility.

Conclusion

. . . We believe the planned NBAF is necessary to replace the aging Plum Island Animal Disease Center and provide additional capacity for much needed animal disease research, diagnostics, training, and countermeasures development. The NBAF will play a crucial role in protecting against the future introduction of foreign animal and zoonotic diseases, and ensuring the continued health and vitality of our agricultural industries. We are committed to continuing our work in partnership with DHS in planning the NBAF and making the facility a reality.

BRUCE KNIGHT spent several years as the under secretary for Marketing and Regulatory Programs at the U.S. Department of Agriculture. He is now a consultant focusing on conservation and environmental issues related to agriculture.

Ray L. Wulf

 **NO**

Written Testimony

. . . **O**n behalf of American Farmers & Ranchers [I] thank you for the opportunity to testify on the Department of Homeland Security's recent proposal to close the Plum Island Animal Disease Center and move its biological research laboratory, including, but not limited to, research on foot-and-mouth disease, to a new location on the mainland United States. This is an issue that is of particular interest and concern to our organization and companies.

At the committee's request I will address the following questions:

- Does your organization support moving foot-and-mouth disease from Plum Island to a research facility on the mainland United States?
- What would be the estimated cost to your membership of an outbreak of foot-and-mouth disease in the United States?
- Does your organization believe modern technology is adequate to prevent the accidental release of foot-and-mouth disease—or other contagious diseases affecting livestock—from a research facility located on the mainland United States?
- If an outbreak of foot-and-mouth disease were to occur on the mainland United States, does your organization believe that Federal, State, and local authorities are prepared to identify, isolate, and halt the spread of such an outbreak before it caused significant damage?

Does your organization support moving foot-and-mouth disease from Plum Island to a research facility on the mainland United States?

NO, AFR is *opposed* to the movement of the Plum Island Animal Disease Center to a research facility on the mainland U.S. The Plum Island Animal Disease Center is the only place in the country where certain highly infectious foreign animal diseases are studied, such as foot-and-mouth disease. Foot-and-mouth disease is a highly contagious virus that affects cloven-hoofed animals such as cattle, sheep, pigs, goats and deer.

Foot-and-mouth disease can be carried by the wind, on clothing, footwear, skin, through nasal passages, and on equipment. The current location or one with similar natural barriers should continue to be the site for research and diagnostic activities that protect our nation's food supply. There are simply too many possibilities for error,

either by negligence, or accident, that could pose extreme economic impacts on U.S. agriculture producers and consumers.

Specifically foot-and-mouth disease creates a serious threat to the U.S. livestock industry, the overall agriculture economy, as well as the U.S. economy. A GAO report released December of 2005 stated that nationally recognized animal disease experts were interviewed and agreed that foot-and-mouth disease constitutes the greatest threat to American livestock. Furthermore GAO provided a letter on December 17, 2007 stating that some of the pathogens maintained at Plum Island, such as foot-and-mouth disease, are highly contagious to livestock and could cause catastrophic economic losses in the agricultural sector if it was released outside of the facility.

Infrastructure

The results of a possible outbreak on the mainland are magnified and accelerated by the efficiencies of the U.S. infrastructure and the transportation industry. The U.S. infrastructure for moving livestock is second to none, allowing livestock to move rapidly across the U.S. [In] five days cattle were trucked from the Oklahoma City National Livestock Market to 39 states. In addition, other animals that carry foot-and-mouth disease, such as swine, sheep, and goats are also rapidly distributed. Within a matter of days livestock can be transported hundreds to thousands of miles away and intermingled with other livestock. Amplifying the situation is the fact that foot-and-mouth disease is expelled over four to five days after an animal has been infected and may occur several days before the onset of clinical signs. In a matter of a couple of weeks the entire country could be infected.

What would be the estimated cost to your membership of an outbreak of foot-and-mouth disease in the United States?

The economic impacts to AFR members would no doubt be severe and devastating and reach far beyond the livestock industry. Quarantines affecting large areas would be established stopping all incoming and outgoing commerce in the quarantined area. Depending on the time of year, a quarantine could halt grain harvest, a major economic impact to many areas. Trucks and equipment would not be allowed in or out for harvesting, milk trucks would not be allowed in or out and, in addition, travel to and from

Wulf, Ray L. From statement before U.S. House of Representatives, May 22, 2008.

school, for business or leisure would be halted. The impact would not only be felt by the producer, but also the local community, region, nation and could cause irreparable damage to the financial community. In addition the U.S. could expect severe economic consequences in the global market.

Many studies have attempted to assess the economic implications of an outbreak of foot-and-mouth disease in the U.S. Results can vary, but at the same time all point out the significant economic losses as a result of a foot-and-mouth outbreak. Direct economic losses would result from lost production, the cost of destroying disease-ridden livestock, indemnification and the cost of disease containment measures, such as drugs, diagnostics, vaccines, and veterinary services. Indirect costs and multiplier effects from dislocations in agriculture sectors would include the feed and inputs industry, transportation, retail and the loss of export markets.

A foot-and-mouth outbreak would not only be a problem for agriculture. In Britain the outbreak of foot-and-mouth disease resulted in postponing a general election for a month, the cancellation of many sporting events and leisure activities, the cancellation of large events likely to be attended by those from infected areas.

Research at Oklahoma State University

Dr. Clem Ward of Oklahoma State University outlines how estimating the effects is difficult to gauge:

- First, the effects would depend upon how isolated or widespread the incidence was and how quickly it was contained.
- Second, the effects would depend upon the type of livestock operations that were infected and how frequently or recently animals have moved from the sites.
- Third, impacts would depend on how the media handles the news reporting of the outbreak.
- And fourth, markets would likely react immediately to the news, and how long it would take them to rebound to a more normal level would depend on the first three factors mentioned.

Dr. Ward also looked at two studies that estimate the economic impacts of a foot-and-mouth outbreak based on a given set of wide ranging scenarios.

1. A 1979 study with impacts adjusted to 2000; estimated economic impacts from $2.4 billion to $27.6 billion.
2. A 1999 study estimated the impacts for California alone at $8.5 billion to $13.5 billion.

Kansas Research

An article in *ScienceDaily* (Nov. 29, 2007), "Foot-and-mouth Disease Could Cost Kansas Nearly A Billion Dollars," referenced research by Dustin L. Pendell, John

Leatherman, Ted C. Schroeder, and Gregory S. Alward— THE ECONOMIC IMPACTS OF A FOOT-AND-MOUTH DISEASE OUTBREAK: A REGIONAL ANALYSIS. The team of researchers analyzed a 14-county region in southwest Kansas that has a high concentration of large cattle feeding operations, as well as other livestock enterprises and beef processing plants. They considered three scenarios:

- one where the disease was introduced at a single cow-calf operation;
- one where a medium-sized feedlot, 10,000 to 20,000 head of cattle, was initially infected;
- one where five large feedlots, each with more than 40,000 head of cattle, were simultaneously exposed.

Schroeder said the first two scenarios were used to predict what could happen if the disease were introduced accidentally, while the larger scenario shows what could happen were there an intentional release.

Generally, researchers found that the greater the number of animals infected in an operation, the longer an outbreak would last and the more it would likely spread—all directly correlating to the level of economic ruin.

- Under the small cow-calf scenario, researchers predicted that 126,000 head of livestock would have to be destroyed and that a foot-and-mouth disease outbreak would last 29 days.
- In the medium-sized operation, those numbers went up to 407,000 animals and 39 days.
- In the scenario where five large feedlots were exposed at the same time, researchers predicted that 1.7 million head of livestock would have to be destroyed and that an outbreak would last nearly three months.

From smallest to largest operation, that translated into regional economic losses of $23 million, $140 million and $685 million, respectively. For the state of Kansas as a whole, those numbers climb to $36 million, $199 million and $945 million.

"Kansas produces about 1.5 million calves, markets 5.5 million head of fed cattle, and slaughters 7.5 million head of cattle annually. The large commercial cattle feedlot and beef packing industries together bring more than 100,000 head of cattle per week on average into the state for feeding or processing," Schroeder said. "Such large volumes of livestock movement provide avenues for contagious animal disease to spread."

Leatherman estimated the statewide impacts of foot-and-mouth for this study and said the effects of an outbreak would go way beyond producers. "This study tells us what the overall stake of the region and state has in preventing such an occurrence," he said. "It isn't just farmers, ranchers, feed lots and packers who would suffer—it's all of us, in some measure."

Other Research

Another report titled "Potential Revenue Impact of an Outbreak of Foot-and-Mouth Disease in the United Sates" by Paarlbwerg, Lee, and Seitzinger was published in the *Journal of American Veterinary Medical Association* in April of 2002. The report stated an outbreak similar to that which occurred in the U.K. during 2001, would cause an estimated U.S. farm income losses of $14 billion. Losses in gross revenue for each sector were estimated to be the following: live swine, −34%; pork, −24%; live cattle −17%; beef, −20%; milk, −16%; live lambs and sheep, −14%; lamb and sheep meat, −10%; forage, −15%; and soybean meal, −7%.

Other Agriculture Markets Impacted

Livestock markets are not the only markets impacted by an outbreak. Feed grains and protein meal feeds would also be impacted. A CRS Report titled "Agroterrorism: Options in Congress," December 19, 2001 states—According to industry officials, every other bushel of U.S. grain goes to animal feed. In addition, information from the U.S. Meat Export Federation states that:

- One milk cow will eat 3 tons of hay and 1,460 lbs of distiller's grain over the course of a year
- It takes 150 lbs of soybean meal to feed a pig to its finished weight
- Every pound of U.S. pork exported utilizes 1.5 pounds of U.S. soybeans
- More than 54 million bushels of soybeans were exported through U.S. red meat in 2006
- More than 300 million bushels of corn were exported through U.S. red meat in 2006
- While direct corn exports have increased by 25% since 1990, indirect exports of corn through the value added process of exporting red meat has increased by 196%

Trade Impact

Ninety-four to ninety-six percent of the world's consumers live outside the U.S. making trade a critical part of U.S. Agriculture. Examples from the pork industry are as follows:

- Source: USDA
  - U.S. has 27% share of the world pork exports
- Source: U.S. Meat Export Federation
  - 2007 Pork Exports add $22.00 per hog
  - The net benefit of U.S. pork exports to the pork industry in 2007 equates to $22 added dollars per market hog
  - Japan, Mexico, Canada and Korea account for 75% of all U.S. pork exports—10% of total production
  - One in every four pounds of pork traded in the world originates from the U.S.
  - The U.S. exports the equivalent of 49,500 market hogs daily

Foot-and-mouth disease is a *"Trade Disease."* To avoid foot-and-mouth disease it is common practice among foot-and-mouth disease-free countries to allow imports only from other foot-and-mouth disease-free countries. This action by countries that are foot-and-mouth disease free is consistent with the provisions of the World Trade Organization's "Agreement on Application of Sanitary and Phytosanitary Measures," which allows countries to adopt and enforce measures necessary to protect human, animal, or plant health. The World Organization of Animal Health (OIE), an independent international organization founded in 1924, monitors and disseminates information about animal diseases throughout the world, and provides a list of countries declared free of foot-and-mouth disease.

Global competition is fierce and in the event a foot-and-mouth outbreak occurred in the U.S., life as we know would no longer exist. Operating as a foot-and-mouth positive country would exclude the U.S. from premium meat markets.

While a foot-and-mouth disease vaccine is available it is used only in emergencies, to create a "disease-free" buffer zone around an infected area. Because vaccinated animals will test positive, they cannot be shipped internationally and protocols require the animals to be destroyed as soon as the disease is eradicated.

Consumer Issues

Foot-and-mouth is not readily transmissible to humans. Only a few cases of human infections, none requiring hospitalization, occurring as a result of direct contact with infected animals have been documented. Even though foot-and-mouth disease does not pose a health risk to humans, consumer fear would occur. Because the average consumer has a lack of knowledge about the disease, more than likely there would be a drop in meat consumption.

. . .

Does your organization believe modern technology is adequate to prevent the accidental release of foot-and-mouth disease—or other contagious diseases affecting livestock—from a research facility located on the mainland United States?

NO, AFR does not believe that there are adequate technologies and safety precautions that can assure U.S. producers and consumers that there would not be an accidental or intentional release of foot-and mouth disease or for that fact any other contagious disease affecting livestock from a research facility located on the mainland U.S. Regardless of how much technology has improved, it does not safeguard from human error, harmful intentions or lack of preparedness.

Plum Island's research and diagnostic activities work to accomplish an important mission to protect U.S. animal industries and exports from deliberate or accidental introductions of foreign animal diseases. Although steps have been taken to implement better security measures at

Plum Island, an outbreak is not out of the question. The U.S. should take note of the most recent U.K. outbreak in August of 2007. Investigations determined that the U.K. outbreak was caused by a strain of virus used for vaccine research at laboratories associated with the institute for Animal Health at Pirbright.

If an outbreak of foot-and-mouth disease were to occur on the mainland United States, does your organization believe that Federal, State, and local authorities are prepared to identify, isolate, and halt the spread of such an outbreak before it caused significant damage?

NO, Although Federal, State and local authorities continue to try to prepare themselves for a foreign animal disease outbreak, AFR believes there are entirely too many unknown variables that would hinder a successful containment of the disease. A U.S. Government simulated outbreak in 2002 called "Crimson Sky" ended with fictional riots in the streets after the simulation's National Guardsmen were ordered to kill tens of millions of farm animals, so many that troops ran out of bullets. In the exercise, the government said it would have been forced to dig a ditch in Kansas 25 miles long to bury carcasses. In the simulation, protests broke out in some cities amid food shortages.

In addition, AFR has concerns about the transportation of infectious disease samples that may need to come into or out of the facility and travel through populated areas. Furthermore AFR has concerns about the number of employees that would be traveling in and out of the facility. The Department of Homeland Security states that a new proposed National Bio and Agro-Defense Facility would generally include between 250 and 350 employees.

Traceability Is Critical

AFR believes that a critical part of being able to control the spread of foot-and-mouth or any animal disease is a national animal identification system. The capacity to trace livestock and product movements is critical for the early control of an outbreak. USDA has been pursuing implementation of an effective animal identification system since the BSE discovery in a U.S. cow in 2003. The U.S. has yet to establish a workable I.D. program. Until

traceability is mandatory and in place moving the Plum Island Animal Disease Center to the mainland should *not* be considered and even then it should be reviewed carefully and any consideration should be focused on a remote area with little or no livestock or wild game habitation.

Conclusion

In conclusion, AFR strongly supports full funding for the research performed at Plum Island, including research on foot-and-mouth disease. In addition AFR fully supports funding to update research facilities to the highest standards.

However, AFR believes the U.S. should not risk bringing highly contagious animal disease research to the mainland with so many variables that could wreak havoc on the U.S. livestock industry, communities, the U.S. and global economy.

AFR believes further activities are needed to prepare for an animal disease outbreak. Activities should include:

- An analysis of communication between all stakeholders
- A full economic study that includes control and compensation including businesses reliant on livestock and global trade impacts
- How to adequately establish a quarantine area around an outbreak
- How movement restrictions will be handled
- Procedures in regard to slaughtering all infected herds and other herds that have been in contact with them
- Disposing of animals—Environmental impacts—burial contamination of ground water by leakages from a disposal pit
- Disinfecting properties
- Compensating stock owners for the livestock slaughtered
- Carrying out clinical inspection a surveillance to ensure the disease has not spread

RAY L. WULF is an Oklahoma farmer and rancher. Until 2009, he was the president and CEO of American Farmers and Ranchers Mutual Insurance Company in Oklahoma City.

EXPLORING THE ISSUE

Can Infectious Animal Diseases Be Studied Safely in Kansas?

Critical Thinking and Reflection

1. Why was Plum Island initially favored for working with highly infectious animal diseases?
2. Why does the Department of Homeland Security think Plum Island is no longer an appropriate location?
3. Why is foot-and-mouth disease considered a "trade disease?"
4. How would an outbreak of foot-and-mouth disease affect the U.S. economy?

Is There Common Ground?

All involved in this debate agree that infectious diseases—whether of animals or of humans—should not be permitted to escape from research facilities. One significant difference is in the degree of trust people are willing to put in technological means of preventing such escape.

1. Google on "biodefense labs" and summarize the news stories and reports you find.
2. Do people seem willing to trust isolation or containment measures to work? Why not?
3. What could be done to make isolation or containment measures more reliable, or at least more worthy of public trust?

Create Central

www.mhhe.com/createcentral

Additional Resources

David Malakoff, "Kansas Veterinary Biosecurity Lab Trampled in Spending Plan," *Science* (February 24, 2012).

National Research Council, *Evaluation of the Updated Site-Specific Risk Assessment for the National Bio- and Agro-Defense Facility in Manhattan, Kansas* (National Academies Press, 2012) (www.nap.edu/catalog.php?record_id=13418).

Internet Reference . . .

Plum Island Animal Disease Center

Since 1954, the Plum Island Animal Disease Center has been protecting America's livestock from foreign animal diseases (diseases not present in the United States) such as foot-and-mouth disease.

**www.ars.usda.gov/main/site_main.htm?
modecode=19-40-00-00**

Selected, Edited, and with Issue Framing Material by:
Thomas A. Easton, *Thomas College*

ISSUE

Are Genetically Modified Foods Safe to Eat?

YES: **Henry I. Miller and Gregory Conko,** from "Scary Food," *Policy Review* (June/July 2006)

NO: **Vandana Shiva,** from *Introduction to the GMO Emperor Has No Clothes: A Global Citizens Report on the State of GMOs—False Promises, Failed Technologies* (Navdanya International, 2011) (www.navdanya.org/publications)

Learning Outcomes

After studying this issue, students will be able to:

- Describe the potential benefits of applying genetic engineering to food crops.
- Describe the potential adverse effects of genetically modified foods.
- Explain why and on what basis new technologies should be regulated.

ISSUE SUMMARY

YES: Henry I. Miller and Gregory Conko of the Hoover Institution argue that genetically modified (GM) crops are safer for the consumer and better for the environment than non-GM crops.

NO: Vandana Shiva argues that we need to create a GMO-free world to protect biodiversity, human health, and the freedom to choose GMO-free seed and food.

In the early 1970s, scientists first discovered that it was technically possible to move genes—biological material that determines a living organism's physical makeup—from one organism to another and thus (in principle) to give bacteria, plants, and animals new features and to correct genetic defects of the sort that cause many diseases, such as cystic fibrosis. Most researchers in molecular genetics were excited by the potentialities that suddenly seemed within their grasp. However, a few researchers—as well as many people outside the field—were disturbed by the idea; they thought that genetic mix-and-match games might spawn new diseases, weeds, and pests. Some people even argued that genetic engineering should be banned at the outset, before unforeseeable horrors were unleashed.

Researchers in support of genetic experimentation responded by declaring a moratorium on their own work until suitable safeguards could be devised. Once those safeguards were in place in the form of government regulations, work resumed. James D. Watson and John Tooze document the early years of this research in *The DNA Story: A Documentary History of Gene Cloning* (W. H. Freeman, 1981). For a shorter, more recent review of the story, see Bernard D. Davis, "Genetic Engineering: The Making of Monsters?" *The Public Interest* (Winter 1993).

By 1989 the technology had developed tremendously: Researchers could obtain patents for mice with artificially added genes ("transgenic" mice); firefly genes had been added to tobacco plants to make them glow (faintly) in the dark; and growth hormone produced by genetically engineered bacteria was being used to grow low-fat pork and increase milk production by cows. Critics argued that genetic engineering was unnatural and violated the rights of both plants and animals to their "species integrity"; that expensive, high-tech, tinkered animals gave the competitive advantage to big agricultural corporations and drove small farmers out of business; and that putting human genes into animals, plants, or bacteria was downright offensive. See Betsy Hanson and Dorothy Nelkin, "Public Responses to Genetic Engineering," *Society* (November/December 1989). Most of the initial attention aimed at genetic engineering focused first on its use to modify bacteria and other organisms to generate drugs needed to fight human disease and second on its potential to modify human genes and attack hereditary diseases at their roots. See Eric B. Kmiec, "Gene Therapy," *American Scientist* (May–June 1999).

Pharmaceutical and agricultural applications of genetic engineering have been very successful, the latter largely because, as Robert Shapiro, CEO of Monsanto Corporation, said in 1998, it "represents a potentially sustainable solution to the issue of feeding people." In "Biotech's

Plans to Sustain Agriculture," *Scientific American* (October 2009) interviewed several industry representatives, who see biotechnology—including genetic engineering—as essential to meeting future demand in a sustainable way.

Between 1996 and 2012, the area planted with genetically engineered crops jumped from 1.7 million hectares to 170 million hectares, according to the International Service for the Acquisition of Agri-Biotech Applications, "ISAAA Brief 44-2012: Executive Summary: Global Status of Commercialized Biotech/GM Crops: 2012" (www.isaaa .org/resources/publications/briefs/44/executivesummary/default .asp). Many people are not reassured by such data. They see potential problems in nutrition, toxicity, allergies, and ecology. Brian Halweil, "The Emperor's New Crops," *World Watch* (July/August 1999), notes that although genetically engineered crops may have potential benefits, they may also have disastrous effects on natural ecosystems and— because high-tech agriculture is controlled by major corporations such as Monsanto—on less-developed societies. He argues that "ecological" agriculture (using, e.g., organic fertilizers and natural enemies instead of pesticides) offers much more hope for the future. Similar arguments are made by those who demonstrate against genetically modified (GM) foods—sometimes by destroying research labs and test plots of trees, strawberries, and corn—and lobby for stringent labeling requirements or for outright bans on planting and importing these crops. See Claire Hope Cummings, "Risking Corn, Risking Culture," *World Watch* (November/December 2002). Protestors argue against GM technology in terms of the precautionary principle; see "GMOs and Precaution in EU countries," *Outlook on Science Policy* (September 2005). Georgina Gustin, "Seeds of Change?" *Columbia Journalism Review* (January/February 2010), reviews press coverage of GM crops and notes that despite the numerous objections by environmental groups there are no data that indicate problems. She adds that there is a need for more research on safety.

Many researchers see great hope in GM foods. In July 2000, the Royal Society of London, the U.S. National Academy of Sciences, the Indian Academy of Sciences, the Mexican Academy of Sciences, and the Third World Academy of Sciences issued a joint report titled "Transgenic Plants and World Agriculture" (www.nap.edu/catalog. php?record_id=9889). This report stresses that during the twenty-first century, both the population and the need for food are going to increase dramatically, especially in developing nations. According to the report, "Foods can be produced through the use of GM technology that are more nutritious, stable in storage, and in principle, health promoting . . . . New public sector efforts are required for creating transgenic crops that benefit poor farmers in developing nations and improve their access to food . . . . Concerted, organized efforts must be undertaken to investigate the potential environmental effects, both positive and negative, of GM technologies [compared to those] from conventional agricultural technologies . . . . Public Health regulatory systems need to be put in place in every country to identify and monitor any poten-

tial adverse human health effects." The United States' National Research Council reports that the economic and environmental benefits of GM crops are clear; see Erik Stokstad, "Biotech Crops Good for Farmers and Environment, Academy Finds," *Science* (April 16, 2010), and Committee on the Impact of Biotechnology on Farm-Level Economics and Sustainability, *The Impact of Genetically Engineered Crops on Farm Sustainability in the United States* (National Academies Press, 2010) (www.nap.edu/catalog .php?record_id=12804).

The worries surrounding GM foods and the scientific evidence to support them are summarized by Kathryn Brown, in "Seeds of Concern," and Karen Hopkin, in "The Risks on the Table," both in *Scientific American* (April 2001). Jeffrey M. Smith, *Seeds of Deception: Exposing Industry and Government Lies about the Safety of the Genetically Engineered Foods You're Eating* (Chelsea Green, 2003), argues that the dangers of GM foods have been deliberately concealed. Henry I. Miller and Gregory Conko, in *The Frankenfood Myth: How Protest and Politics Threaten the Biotech Revolution* (Praeger, 2004), address at length the fallacy that GM foods are especially risky. Rod Addy and Elaine Watson, "Forget 'Frankenfood,' GM Crops Can Feed the World, Says FDF," *Food Manufacture* (December 2007), note that "EU trade commissioner Peter Mandelson said that the inability of European politicians to engage in a rational debate about GM was a source of constant frustration. They were also creating barriers to trade by banning GM crops that had repeatedly been pronounced safe by the European Food Safety Authority (EFSA)." Early in 2010, the EFSA reinforced this point; see "EFSA Rejects Study Claiming Toxicity of GMOs," *European Environment & Packaging Law Weekly* (February 24, 2010). According to Gemma Masip, et al., "Paradoxical EU Agricultural Policies on Genetically Engineered Crops," *Trends in Plant Science* (in press, available online April 25, 2013), EU attitudes toward GM crops obstruct policy goals; GM crops are essential to EU agricultural competitiveness. Nevertheless, many people argue that GM foods should be labeled so that people can choose to avoid them. See Robin Mather, "The Threats from Genetically Modified Foods," *Mother Earth News* (April–May 2012), and Amy Harmon and Andrew Pollack, "Battle Brewing over Labeling of Genetically Modified Food," *New York Times* (May 24, 2012). Jane Black, "As Nature Made Them," *Prevention* (April 2012), adds a call for more independent (not sponsored by seed companies) research into GMO safety.

Is the issue safety? Human welfare? Or economics? In the YES selection, Henry I. Miller and Gregory Conko of the Hoover Institution argue that GM crops are safer for the consumer and better for the environment than non-GM crops. People have failed to embrace them because news coverage has been dominated by the outlandish claims and speculations of antitechnology activists. In the NO selection, activist Vandana Shiva argues that we need to create a GMO-free world to protect biodiversity, human health, and the freedom to choose GMO-free seed and food.

YES ↵

**Henry I. Miller and
Gregory Conko**

Scary Food

Like a scene from some Hollywood thriller, a team of U.S. Marshals stormed a warehouse in Irvington, New Jersey, last summer to intercept a shipment of evildoers from Pakistan. The reason you probably haven't heard about the raid is that the objective was not to seize Al Qaeda operatives or white slavers, but $80,000 worth of basmati rice contaminated with weevils, beetles, and insect larvae, making it unfit for human consumption. In regulation-speak, the food was "adulterated," because "it consists in whole or in part of any filthy, putrid, or decomposed substance, or if it is otherwise unfit for food."

Americans take food safety very seriously. Still, many consumers tend to ignore Mother Nature's contaminants while they worry unduly about high technology, such as the advanced technologies that farmers, plant breeders, and food processors use to make our food supply the most affordable, nutritious, varied, and safe in history.

For example, recombinant DNA technology—also known as food biotechnology, gene-splicing, or genetic modification (GM)—is often singled out by critics as posing a risk that new allergens, toxins, or other nasty substances will be introduced into the food supply. And, because of the mainstream media's "if it bleeds, it leads" approach, news coverage of food biotech is dominated by the outlandish claims and speculations of anti-technology activists. This has caused some food companies—including fastfood giant McDonald's and baby-food manufacturers Gerber and Heinz—to forgo superior (and even cost-saving) gene-spliced ingredients in favor of ones the public will find less threatening.

Scientists agree, however, that gene-spliced crops and foods are not only better for the natural environment than conventionally produced food crops, but also safer for consumers. Several varieties now on the market have been modified to resist insect predation and plant diseases, which makes the harvested crop much cleaner and safer. Ironically (and also surprisingly in these litigious times), in their eagerness to avoid biotechnology, some major food companies may knowingly be making their products less safe and wholesome for consumers. This places them in richly deserved legal jeopardy.

Don't Trust Mother Nature

Every year, scores of packaged food products are recalled from the American market due to the presence of all-natural contaminants like insect parts, toxic molds, bacteria, and viruses. Because farming takes place out-of-doors and in dirt, such contamination is a fact of life. Fortunately, modern technology has enabled farmers and food processors to minimize the threat from these contaminants.

The historical record of mass food poisoning in Europe offers a cautionary tale. From the ninth to the nineteenth centuries, Europe suffered a succession of epidemics caused by the contamination of rye with ergot, a poisonous fungus. Ergot contains the potent toxin ergotamine, the consumption of which induces hallucinations, bizarre behavior, and violent muscle twitching. These symptoms gave rise at various times to the belief that victims were possessed by evil spirits. Witch-hunting and persecution were commonplace—and the New World was not immune. One leading explanation for the notorious 1691–92 Salem witch trials also relates to ergot contamination. Three young girls suffered violent convulsions, incomprehensible speech, trance-like states, odd skin sensations, and delirious visions in which they supposedly saw the mark of the devil on certain women in the village. The girls lived in a swampy meadow area around Salem; rye was a major staple of their diet; and records indicate that the rye harvest at the time was complicated by rainy and humid conditions, exactly the situation in which ergot would thrive.

Worried villagers feared the girls were under a spell cast by demons, and the girls eventually named three women as witches. The subsequent panic led to the execution of as many as 20 innocent people. Until a University of California graduate student discovered this link, a reasonable explanation had defied historians. But the girls' symptoms are typical of ergot poisoning, and when the supply of infected grain ran out, the delusions and persecution likewise disappeared.

In the twenty-first century, modern technology, aggressive regulations, and a vigorous legal liability system in industrialized countries such as the United States are able to mitigate much of this sort of contamination. Occasionally, though, Americans will succumb to tainted food picked from the woods or a backyard garden. However, elsewhere in the world, particularly in less-developed countries, people are poisoned every day by fungal toxins that contaminate grain. The result is birth defects, cancer, organ failure, and premature death.

About a decade ago, Hispanic women in the Rio Grande Valley of Texas were found to be giving birth to an unusually large number of babies with crippling and lethal neural tube defects (NTDS) such as spina bifida, hydrocephalus, and anencephaly—at a rate approximately six times higher than the national average for non-Hispanic women. The cause remained a mystery until recent research revealed a link between NTDS and consumption of large amounts of unprocessed corn like that found in tortillas and other staples of the Latino diet.

The connection is obscure but fascinating. The culprit is fumonisin, a deadly mycotoxin, or fungal toxin, produced by the mold *Fusarium* and sometimes found in unprocessed corn. When insects attack corn, they open wounds in the plant that provide a perfect breeding ground for *Fusarium*. Once molds get a foothold, poor storage conditions also promote their postharvest growth on grain.

Fumonisin and some other mycotoxins are highly toxic, causing fatal diseases in livestock that eat infected corn and esophageal cancer in humans. Fumonisin also interferes with the cellular uptake of folic acid, a vitamin that is known to reduce the risk of NTDS in developing fetuses. Because fumonisin prevents the folic acid from being absorbed by cells, the toxin can, in effect, induce functional folic acid deficiency—and thereby cause NTDS—even when the diet contains what otherwise would be sufficient amounts of folic acid.

The epidemiological evidence was compelling. At the time that the babies of Hispanic women in the Rio Grande Valley experienced the high rate of neural tube defects, the fumonisin level in corn in that locale was two to three times higher than normal, and the affected women reported much higher dietary consumption of homemade tortillas than in women who were unaffected.

Acutely aware of the danger of mycotoxins, regulatory agencies such as the U.S. Food and Drug Administration and Britain's Food Safety Agency have established recommended maximum fumonisin levels in food and feed products made from corn. Although highly processed cornstarch and corn oil are unlikely to be contaminated with fumonisin, unprocessed corn or lightly processed corn (e.g., cornmeal) can have fumonisin levels that exceed recommended levels.

In 2003, the Food Safety Agency tested six organic cornmeal products and twenty conventional cornmeal products for fumonisin contamination. All six organic cornmeals had elevated levels—from nine to 40 times greater than the recommended levels for human health—and they were voluntarily withdrawn from grocery stores.

A Technical Fix

The conventional way to combat mycotoxins is simply to test unprocessed and processed grains and throw out those found to be contaminated—an approach that is both wasteful and dubious. But modern technology—specifically in the form of gene-splicing—is already attacking the fungal problem at its source. An excellent example is "Bt corn," crafted by splicing into commercial corn varieties a gene from the bacterium *Bacillus thuringiensis*. The

"Bt" gene expresses a protein that is toxic to corn-boring insects but is perfectly harmless to birds, fish, and mammals, including humans.

As the Bt corn fends off insect pests, it also reduces the levels of the mold *Fusarium*, thereby reducing the levels of fumonisin. Thus, switching to the gene-spliced, insect-resistant corn for food processing lowers the levels of fumonisin—as well as the concentration of insect parts—likely to be found in the final product. Researchers at Iowa State University and the U.S. Department of Agriculture found that Bt corn reduces the level of fumonisin by as much as 80 percent compared to conventional corn.

Thus, on the basis of both theory and empirical knowledge, there should be potent incentives—legal, commercial, and ethical—to use such gene-spliced grains more widely. One would expect public and private sector advocates of public health to demand that such improved varieties be cultivated and used for food—not unlike requirements for drinking water to be chlorinated and fluoridated. Food producers who wish to offer the safest and best products to their customers—to say nothing of being offered the opportunity to advertise "New and Improved!"—should be competing to get gene-spliced products into the marketplace.

Alas, none of this has come to pass. Activists have mounted intractable opposition to food biotechnology in spite of demonstrated, significant benefits, including reduced use of chemical pesticides, less runoff of chemicals into waterways, greater use of farming practices that prevent soil erosion, higher profits for farmers, and less fungal contamination. Inexplicably, government oversight has also been an obstacle, by subjecting the testing and commercialization of gene-spliced crops to unscientific and draconian regulations that have vastly increased testing and development costs and limited the use and diffusion of food biotechnology.

The result is jeopardy for everyone involved in food production and consumption: Consumers are subjected to avoidable and often undetected health risks, and food producers have placed themselves in legal jeopardy. The first point is obvious, the latter less so, but as described first by Drew Kershen, professor of law at the University of Oklahoma, it makes a fascinating story: Agricultural processors and food companies may face at least two kinds of civil liability for their refusal to purchase and use fungus-resistant, gene-spliced plant varieties, as well as other superior products.

Food for Thought

In 1999 the Gerber foods company succumbed to activist pressure, announcing that its baby food products would no longer contain any gene-spliced ingredients. Indeed, Gerber went farther and promised it would attempt to shift to organic ingredients that are grown without synthetic pesticides or fertilizers. Because corn starch and corn sweeteners are often used in a range of foods, this could mean changing Gerber's entire product line.

But in its attempt to head off a potential public relations problem concerning the use of gene-spliced ingredients, Gerber has actually increased the health risk for its baby consumers—and, thereby, its legal liability. As noted above, not only is gene-spliced corn likely to have lower levels of fumonisin than conventional corn; organic corn is likely to have the highest levels, because it suffers greater insect predation due to less effective pest controls.

If a mother some day discovers that her "Gerber baby" has developed liver or esophageal cancer, she might have a legal case against Gerber. On the child's behalf, a plaintiff's lawyer can allege liability based on mycotoxin contamination in the baby food as the causal agent of the cancer. The contamination would be considered a *manufacturing defect* under product liability law because the baby food did not meet its intended product specifications or level of safety. According to Kershen, Gerber could be found liable "even though all possible care was exercised in the preparation and marketing of the product," simply because the contamination occurred.

The plaintiff's lawyer could also allege a *design defect* in the baby food, because Gerber knew of the existence of a less risky design—namely, the use of gene-spliced varieties that are less prone to *Fusarium* and fumonisin contamination—but deliberately chose not to use it. Instead, Gerber chose to use non-gene-spliced, organic food ingredients, knowing that the foreseeable risks of harm posed by them could have been reduced or avoided by adopting a reasonable alternative design—that is, by using gene-spliced Bt corn, which is known to have a lower risk of mycotoxin contamination.

Gerber might answer this design defect claim by contending that it was only responding to consumer demand, but that alone would not be persuasive. Product liability law subjects defenses in design defect cases to a risk-utility balancing in which consumer expectations are only one of several factors used to determine whether the product design (e.g., the use of only non-gene-spliced ingredients) is reasonably safe. A jury might conclude that whatever consumer demand there may be for non-biotech ingredients does not outweigh Gerber's failure to use a technology that is known to lower the health risks to consumers.

Even if Gerber was able to defend itself from the design defect claim, the company might still be liable because it failed to provide adequate instructions or warnings about the potential risks of non-gene-spliced ingredients. For example, Gerber could label its non-gene-spliced baby food with a statement such as: "This product does not contain gene-spliced ingredients. Consequently, this product has a very slight additional risk of mycotoxin contamination. Mycotoxins can cause serious diseases such as liver and esophageal cancer and birth defects."

Whatever the risk of toxic or carcinogenic fumonisin levels in non-biotech corn may be (probably low in industrialized countries, where food producers generally are cautious about such contamination), a more likely scenario is potential liability for an allergic reaction.

Six percent to 8 percent of children and 1 to 2 percent of adults are allergic to one or another food ingredient, and an estimated 150 Americans die each year from exposure to food allergens. Allergies to peanuts, soybeans, and wheat proteins, for example, are quite common and can be severe. Although only about 1 percent of the population is allergic to peanuts, some individuals are so highly sensitive that exposure causes anaphylactic shock, killing dozens of people every year in North America.

Protecting those with true food allergies is a daunting task. Farmers, food shippers and processors, wholesalers and retailers, and even restaurants must maintain meticulous records and labels and ensure against cross-contamination. Still, in a country where about a billion meals are eaten every day, missteps are inevitable. Dozens of processed food items must be recalled every year due to accidental contamination or inaccurate labeling.

Fortunately, biotechnology researchers are well along in the development of peanuts, soybeans, wheat, and other crops in which the genes coding for allergenic proteins have been silenced or removed. According to University of California, Berkeley, biochemist Bob Buchanan, hypoallergenic varieties of wheat could be ready for commercialization within the decade, and nuts soon thereafter. Once these products are commercially available, agricultural processors and food companies that refuse to use these safer food sources will open themselves to products-liability, design-defect lawsuits.

Property Damage and Personal Injury

Potato farming is a growth industry, primarily due to the vast consumption of french fries at fast-food restaurants. However, growing potatoes is not easy, because they are preyed upon by a wide range of voracious and difficult-to-control pests, such as the Colorado potato beetle, virus-spreading aphids, nematodes, potato blight, and others.

To combat these pests and diseases, potato growers use an assortment of fungicides (to control blight), insecticides (to kill aphids and the Colorado potato beetle), and fumigants (to control soil nematodes). Although some of these chemicals are quite hazardous to farm workers, forgoing them could jeopardize the sustainability and profitability of the entire potato industry. Standard application of synthetic pesticides enhances yields more than 50 percent over organic potato production, which prohibits most synthetic inputs.

Consider a specific example. Many growers use methamidophos, a toxic organophosphate nerve poison, for aphid control. Although methamidophos is an EPA-approved pesticide, the agency is currently reevaluating the use of organophosphates and could ultimately prohibit or greatly restrict the use of this entire class of pesticides. As an alternative to these chemicals, the Monsanto Company developed a potato that contains a gene from the bacterium *Bacillus thuringiensis* (Bt) to control the

Colorado potato beetle and another gene to control the potato leaf roll virus spread by the aphids. Monsanto's NewLeaf potato is resistant to these two scourges of potato plants, which allowed growers who adopted it to reduce their use of chemical controls and increase yields.

Farmers who planted NewLeaf became convinced that it was the most environmentally sound and economically efficient way to grow potatoes. But after five years of excellent results it encountered an unexpected snag. Under pressure from anti-biotechnology organizations, McDonald's, Burger King, and other restaurant chains informed their potato suppliers that they would no longer accept gene-spliced potato varieties for their french fries. As a result, potato processors such as J.R. Simplot inserted a nonbiotech-potato clause into their farmer-processor contracts and informed farmers that they would no longer buy gene-spliced potatoes. In spite of its substantial environmental, occupational safety, and economic benefits, NewLeaf became a sort of contractual poison pill and is no longer grown commercially. Talk about market distortions.

Now, let us assume that a farmer who is required by contractual arrangement to plant nonbiotech potatoes sprays his potato crop with methamidophos (the organophosphate nerve poison) and that the pesticide drifts into a nearby stream and onto nearby farm laborers. Thousands of fish die in the stream, and the laborers report to hospital emergency rooms complaining of neurological symptoms.

This hypothetical scenario is, in fact, not at all far-fetched. Fish-kills attributed to pesticide runoff from potato fields are commonplace. In the potato-growing region of Prince Edward Island, Canada, for example, a dozen such incidents occurred in one 13-month period alone, between July 1999 and August 2000. According to the UN's Food and Agriculture Organization, "normal" use of the pesticides parathion and methamidophos is responsible for some 7,500 pesticide poisoning cases in China each year.

In our hypothetical scenario, the state environmental agency might bring an administrative action for civil damages to recover the cost of the fish-kill, and a plaintiff's lawyer could file a class-action suit on behalf of the farm laborers for personal injury damages.

Who's legally responsible? Several possible circumstances could enable the farmer's defense lawyer to shift culpability for the alleged damages to the contracting food processor and to the fast-food restaurants that are the ultimate purchasers of the potatoes. These circumstances include the farmer's having planted Bt potatoes in the recent past; his contractual obligation to the potato processor and its fast-food retail buyers to provide only nonbiotech varieties; and his demonstrated preference for planting gene-spliced, Bt potatoes, were it not for the contractual proscription. If these conditions could be proved, the lawyer defending the farmer could name the contracting processor and the fast-food restaurants as cross-defendants, claiming either contribution in tort law or indemnification in contract law for any damages legally imposed upon the farmer client.

The farmer's defense could be that those companies bear the ultimate responsibility for the damages because they compelled the farmer to engage in higher-risk production practices than he would otherwise have chosen. The companies chose to impose cultivation of a non-gene-spliced variety upon the farmer although they knew that in order to avoid severe losses in yield, he would need to use organophosphate pesticides. Thus, the defense could argue that the farmer should have a legal right to pass any damages (arising from contractually imposed production practices) back to the processor and the fast-food chains.

Why Biotech?

Companies that insist upon farmers' using production techniques that involve foreseeable harms to the environment and humans may be—we would argue, *should* be—legally accountable for that decision. If agricultural processors and food companies manage to avoid legal liability for their insistence on nonbiotech crops, they will be "guilty" at least of externalizing their environmental costs onto the farmers, the environment, and society at large.

Food biotechnology provides an effective—and cost-effective—way to prevent many of these injurious scenarios, but instead of being widely encouraged, it is being resisted by self-styled environmental activists and even government officials.

It should not fall to the courts to resolve and reconcile what are essentially scientific and moral issues. However, other components of society—industry, government, and "consumer advocacy" groups—have failed abjectly to fully exploit a superior, life-enhancing, and life-saving technology. Even the biotechnology trade associations have been unhelpful. All are guilty, in varying measures, of sacrificing the public interest to self-interest and of helping to perpetuate a gross public misconception—that food biotechnology is unproven, untested, and unregulated.

If consumers genuinely want a safer, more nutritious, and more varied food supply at a reasonable cost, they need to know where the real threats lie. They must also become better informed, demand public policy that makes sense, and deny fringe anti-technology activists permission to speak for consumers.

Henry I. Miller is a research fellow at Stanford University's Hoover Institution. His research focuses on public policy toward science and technology, especially biotechnology. He is the coauthor, with Gregory Conko, of *The Frankenfood Myth: How Protest and Politics Threaten the Biotech Revolution* (Praeger, 2004).

Gregory Conko is a senior fellow at the Competitive Enterprise Institute. He is the coauthor, with Henry I. Miller, of *The Frankenfood Myth: How Protest and Politics Threaten the Biotech Revolution* (Praeger, 2004).

Vandana Shiva

 **NO**

Introduction to the GMO Emperor Has No Clothes: A Global Citizens Report on the State of GMOs—False Promises, Failed Technologies

We have been repeatedly told that genetically engineered (GE) crops will save the world by increasing yields and producing more food. They will save the world by controlling pests and weeds. They will save the world by reducing chemical use in agriculture. They will save the world with GE drought tolerant seeds and other seed traits that will provide resilience in times of climate change.

However, the GE emperor (Monsanto) has no clothes. All of these claims have been established as false over years of experience all across the world. The Global Citizens Report "The Emperor Has No Clothes" brings together evidence from the ground of Monsanto's and the industry's false promises and failed technology.

Failure to Yield

Contrary to the claim of feeding the world, genetic engineering has not increased the yield of a single crop. Navdanya's research in India has shown that contrary to Monsanto's claim of Bt cotton yield of 1500 kg per acre, the reality is that the yield is an average of 400–500 kg per acre. Although Monsanto's Indian advertising campaign reports a 50 percent increase in yields for its Bollgard cotton, a survey conducted by the Research Foundation for Science, Technology and Ecology found that the yields in all trial plots were lower than what the company promised.

Bollgard's failure to deliver higher yields has been reported all over the world. The Mississippi Seed Arbitration Council ruled that in 1997, Monsanto's Roundup Ready cotton failed to perform as advertised, recommending payments of nearly $2 million to three cotton farmers who suffered severe crop losses.

Failure to Yield, a report by the Union of Concerned Scientists in the U.S., has established that genetic engineering has not contributed to yield increases in any crop. According to this report, increases in crop yields in the U.S. are due to yield characteristics of conventional crops, not genetic engineering.

Australian research shows that conventional crops outperform GE crops.

Yield Comparison of GE Canola Trials in Australia

	2001	
Conventional	1144	
Round UP	1055	(Two application of Round Up)
Ready GE	977	(One application of Round Up)

New South Wales	2001
In Vigor (GE)	109
Hyola (Conventional)	120

Despite Monsanto adding the Roundup Ready gene to "elite varieties," the best Australian trials of Roundup Ready Canola yielded only 1.055 t/ha, at least 16 percent below the national average of 1.23 t/ha (www.non-gm-farmers.com/documents/ GM Canola report-full.pdf).

As Marc Lappe and Britt Bailey report in their book *Against the Grain* 1998, herbicide-resistant soybeans yielded 36 to 38 bushels per acre, while hand tilled soybeans yielded 38.2 bushels per acre. According to the authors, this raises the possibility that the gene inserted into these engineered plants may selectively disadvantage their growth when herbicides are not applied. "If true, data such as these cast doubt on Monsanto's principal point that their genetic engineering is both botanically and environmentally neutral," the authors write.

While increased food productivity is the argument used to promote genetic engineering, when the issue of potential economic impacts on farmers is brought up, the biotechnology industry itself argues that genetic engineering does not lead to increased productivity. Robert Shapiro, CEO of Monsanto, referring to Posilac (Monsanto's bovine growth hormone) in *Business Ethics*, said on the one hand that "There is need for agricultural productivity, including dairy productivity, to double if we want to feed all the people who will be joining us, so I think this is unequivocally a good product." On the other hand, when asked about the product's economic impact on farmers, he said that it would "play a relatively small role in the process of increasing dairy productivity."

In twenty years of commercialization of GE crops, only two traits have been developed on a significant scale: herbicide tolerance and insect resistance.

Failed Technology: GE Crops Do Not Control Pests and Weeds, They Create Super Pests and Super Weeds

Herbicide tolerant (Roundup Ready) crops were supposed to control weeds and Bt crops were intended to control pests. Instead of controlling weeds and pests, GE crops have led to the emergence of super weeds and super pests. In the U.S., Round Up Ready crops have produced weeds resistant to Round Up. Approximately 15 million acres are now overtaken by Roundup resistant "superweeds," and, in an attempt to stop the spread of these weeds, Monsanto has started offering farmers a "rebate" of up to $6 per acre for purchasing and using other, more lethal herbicides. These rebates offset approximately 25 to 35 percent of cost of purchasing the other herbicides.

In India, Bt cotton sold under the trade name "Bollgard" was supposed to control the Bollworm pest. Today, the Bollworm has become resistant to Bt cotton and now Monsanto is selling Bollgard II with two additional toxic genes in it. New pests have emerged and farmers are using more pesticides.

Bt Crops: A Recipe for Super Pests

Bt is a naturally occurring organism, *Bacillus thuringiensis*, which produces a toxin. Corporations are now adding genes for Bt toxins to a wide array of crops to enable the plants to produce their own insecticide.

Monsanto sells its Bt potato as "Nature Mark" in Canada and describes it as a plant using "sunshine, air and soil nutrients to make a biodegradable protein that affects just one specific insect pest, and only those individual insects that actually take a bite of the plants."

The camouflaged description of a transgenic crop hides many of the ecological impacts of genetically engineered crops. The illusion of sustainability is manufactured through the following distortions.

1. The Bt Plant does not merely use "sunshine, air, and soil nutrients." Bt crops are transgenic and have a gene from a bacterium called bacillus thuringiensis (bt) which produces the Bttoxin. In addition it has antibiotic resistance marker genes and genes from viruses as promoters.
2. The so called "biodegradable protein" is actually a toxin which the gene continuously produces in the plant. This protein has been found in the blood of pregnant women and their fetuses.
3. Insect pests like the cotton bollworm which destroy cotton can actually evolve resistance because of continuous release of the toxin and hence become "super pests."
4. The Bt crop does not affect "just one specific pest." Beneficial insects like bees and ladybirds

can be seriously affected. A Cornell study showed that the Bt toxin affected the Monarch butterfly. Navdanya's studies have shown that soil microorganisms are negatively affected.

The primary justification for the genetic engineering of Bt into crops is that this will reduce the use of insecticides. Bt cotton is among the "miracles" being pushed by corporations like Monsanto as a solution to the pesticide crisis. One of the Monsanto brochures had a picture of a few worms and stated, "You will see these in your cotton and that's O.K. Don't spray." However, in Texas, Monsanto faced a lawsuit filed by 25 farmers over Bt cotton planted on 18,000 acres which suffered cotton bollworm damage and on which farmers had to use pesticides in spite of corporate propaganda that genetic engineering meant an end to the pesticide era. In 1996, two million acres in the US were planted with Monsanto's transgenic Bollgard cotton.

However, cotton bollworms were found to have infested thousands of acres planted with the new breed of cotton in Texas. Not only did the genetically engineered cotton not survive cotton bollworm attack, there are also fears that the strategy will create super bugs by inducing Bt resistance in pests. The question is not whether superpests will be created, but when they will become dominant. The fact that the Environmental Protection Agency (EPA) of the US requires refugia of non-engineered crops to be planted near the engineered crops reflects the reality of the creation of resistant strains of insects.

The widespread use of Bt containing crops could accelerate the development of insect pest resistance to Bt which is used for organic pest control. Already eight species of insects have developed resistance to Bt toxins, either in the field or laboratory, including the diamond back moth, Indian meal moth, tobacco budworm, Colorado potato beetle, and two species of mosquitoes.

The genetically engineered Bt crops continuously express the Bt toxin throughout its growing season. Long term exposure to Bt toxins promotes development of resistance in insect populations, this kind of exposure could lead to selection for resistance in all stages of the insect pest on all parts of the plant for the entire season.

Due to this risk of pest resistance, the EPA offers only conditional and temporary registration of varieties producing Bt. The EPA requires four percent "refugia" with Bt cotton, meaning four percent of planted cotton is conventional and does not express the Bt toxin. It therefore acts as a refuge for insects to survive and breed, and hence keeps the overall level of resistance in the population low. Even at a 4 percent refugia level, insect resistance will evolve in as little as three to four years.

Herbicide Resistant Crops: A Recipe for Superweeds

Herbicide resistant crops such as Roundup Ready cotton can create the risk of herbicide resistant "superweeds" by transferring the herbicide resistance to weeds. Monsanto has confirmed that a notorious Australian weed, rye grass, has developed tolerance to its herbicide Roundup, thus rendering genetic engineering of herbicide resistant crops a useless strategy.

In 1994, research scientists in Denmark reported strong evidence that an oilseed rape plant genetically engineered to be herbicide tolerant transmitted its transgene to a weedy natural relative, *Brassica campestris ssp. Campestris*. This transfer can become established in the plant in just two generations.

In Denmark, *B. campestris* is a common weed in cultivated oilseed rape fields, where selective elimination by herbicides is now impossible. The wild relative of this weed is spread over large parts of the world. One way to assess the risk of releasing transgenic oilseed rape is to measure the rate of natural hybridization with *B. campestris*, because certain transgenes could make its wild relative a more aggressive weed, and even harder to control.

Although crosses with *B. campestris* have been used in the breeding of oilseed rape, natural interspecific crosses with oilseed rape was generally thought to be rare. Artificial crosses by hand pollination carried out in a risk assessment project in the U.K. were reported unsuccessful. However, a few studies have reported spontaneous hybridization between oilseed rape and the parental species *B. campestris* in field experiments. As early as 1962, hybridization rates of zero percent to 88 percent were measured for oilseed rape and wild *B. campestris*. The results of the Danish team showed that high levels of hybridization can occur in the field. Their field tests revealed that between nine percent and 93 percent of hybrid seeds were produced under different conditions.

The scientists also warn that as the gene for herbicide resistance is likely to be transferred to the weed, this herbicide strategy will be useless after a few years. Like many other weeds, *B. campestris* is characterized by seed dormancy and longevity of the seeds. Therefore, *B. campestris* with transgenes from oilseed rape may be preserved for many years in spite of efforts to exterminate it. They conclude that weedy *B. campestris* with this herbicide tolerant transgene may present economic risks to farmers and the biotechnology industry. Finally, natural ecosystems may also be affected.

Other concerned scientists add that the potential spread of the transgene will indeed be wide because oilseed rape is insect-pollinated and bees are known to fly far distances. The existence of the wild relative of *B. campestris* in large parts of the world poses serious hazards once the transgenic oilseed rape is marketed commercially. In response to the Danish findings, the governments of Denmark and Norway have acted against the commercial planting of the engineered plant, but the U.K. Government has approved its marketing.

Wild beets have become a major problem in European sugar beet production since the 1970s. These weedy populations arise from seeds originating from the accidental pollinations of cultivated beets by adventitious beets in the seed production area. The existence of gene exchange via seed and pollen between weed beets and cultivated beets shows genetically engineered sugar beets to be herbicide resistant, with the possibility of becoming "superweeds." In this case, the efficacy of herbicide resistant crops is totally undermined.

Current surveys indicate that almost 20 percent of U.S. producers have found glyphosate resistant (Roundup Resistant) weeds on their farms.

Referring to Round Up Resistant weeds, Andrew Wargo III, the President of the Arkansas Association of Conservation Districts said, "It is the single largest threat to production agriculture that we have ever seen."

There are now ten resistant species in at least 22 states infesting millions of acres, predominantly soybeans, cotton, and corn. Roundup Resistant weeds include pig weed, rag weed, and horse weed.

Today, Roundup Ready crops account for 90 percent of soybeans and 70 percent of corn and cotton grown in the U.S.

Mike Owen, a Weed Scientist at Iowa State University has cautioned: "What we're talking about here is Darwinian evolution in fast-forward."

As a result of this weed resistance, farmers are being forced to use more herbicides to combat weeds. As Bill Freese of the Center for Food Safety in Washington, D.C., says "The biotech industry is taking us into a more pesticide dependent agriculture, and we need to be going in the opposite direction."

The problem of "superweeds" is so severe that U.S. Congress organized a hearing on it titled "Are Superweeds on Outgrowth of USDA Biotech Policy".

As Roy Troush, an Indiana farmer, stated in his testimony: "In 2005 we first began to encounter problems with glyphosate-resistance in both our soybean and corn crops. Despite well documented proof that glyphosate tolerant weeds were becoming a significant problem, the Monsanto scientist insisted that resistance existed and instructed me to increase my application rates. The increase in application proved ineffectual. In 2008, we were forced to include the use of 2,4-D and an AIS residual in our program. Like most farmers, we are very sensitive to environmental issues, and we were very reluctant to return to using tillage and more toxic herbicides for weed control. However, no other solutions were then or now readily available to eradicate the weed problems caused by development of glyphosate resistance."

When introduced to regions such as China, Taiwan, Japan, Korea and former USSR where wild relatives of soy are found, Monsanto's Roundup Ready Soya bean could transfer the herbicide resistant genes to wild relatives leading to new weed problems.

The native biodiversity richness of the Third World thus increases the environmental risks of introduced genetically modified species.

The genetic engineering miracle is quite clearly faltering in farmers' fields. Yet the information on the hazards and risks does not accompany the sales promotion of genetically engineered crops in India. Nor does the false promise of the biotech miracle inform farmers that the genetic engineering era of farming also requires "high-tech slavery" for farmers.

False Promises

1. Reduced Use of Chemicals

Despite claims that genetically modified organisms (GMOs) will lower the levels of chemicals (pesticides and herbicides) used, this has not been the case. This is of great concern both because of the negative impacts of these chemicals on ecosystems and humans, and because there is the danger that increased chemical use will cause pests and weeds to develop resistance, requiring even more chemicals in order to manage them. . . .

2. Climate Resilience

Monsanto has been claiming that through genetic engineering it can breed crops for drought tolerance and other climate-resilient traits. This is a false promise. As the U.S. Department of Agriculture (USDA) has said in its draft environmental assessment of the new drought-resistant GE corn, "Equally comparable varieties produced through conventional breeding techniques are readily available in irrigated corn production reviews."

Helen Wallace of GeneWatch UK cautions: "The GE industry must now stop its cynical attempts to manipulate the public into believing that GE crops are needed to feed the world."

Other biotech industries also falsely claim that they are inventing climate resilient traits. As Ram Kaundiya, CEO of Advanta, India and Chairman of Biotech Led Enterprises—Agriculture Group—writes, "Very exciting input traits are in the pipeline. For example, a water use efficiency trait will reduce the water requirements of the crops considerably and can help vast numbers of farmers who cultivate rainfed crops in the country in more than 100 million ha. Similarly, the nitrogen use efficiency trait which will reduce the use of nitrogenous fertilizer on the crops by an estimated 30 percent. Another trait that is waiting in the wings is a salt tolerance trait which can help farmers grow crops in saline soils of more than 20 million ha in India." There are 1600 patents on climate resilient crops.

But all these traits have already been evolved the traditional way by Indian farmers. Navdanya's seed collections have drought tolerant varieties like Nalibakuri, Kalakaya, Atia, Inkiri etc., flood tolerant varieties like Nalidhulia, Ravana, Seulapuni, Dhosarakhuda etc., and salt tolerant varieties like Bhundi, Kalambank, Lunabakada, Sankarchin etc.

Pulses and beans are nitrogen fixing crops. None of these traits are "invented" by genetic engineering. They are pirated from nature and farmers.

3. Health Safety

While the GE Emperor has no clothes—i.e., GE crops cannot feed the world, it has the potential for harming the world and enslaving the world. Among the false claims made by Monsanto and the Biotechnology industry is that GE foods are safe. However, there are enough independent studies to show that GE foods can cause health damage.

For example, Dr. Arpad Pusztai's research has shown that rats fed with GE potatoes had enlarged pancreases, their brains had shrunk, and their immunity had been damaged. Dr. Eric Seralini's research demonstrated that organ damage can occur.

The Committee of Independent Research and Information on Genetic Engineering (CRIIGEN) and universities at Caen and Rouen were able to get raw data of Monsanto's 2002 feeding trials on rats at the European Council order and made it public in 2005. The researchers found that rats fed with three approved corn varieties of GE corn—Mon 863, insecticide products, Mon 810, and Roundup Ready herbicide—suffered organ damage. The data "clearly underlines adverse impacts on kidneys and liver, the dietary, detoxifying organs as well as different levels of damages to the heart, adrenal glands, spleen and haematopoietic systems," according to Dr. Gilles Eric Seralini, a molecular biologist at the University of Caen.

The Biotechnology Industry attacked Dr. Pusztai and Dr. Seralini and every scientist who has done independent research on GMOs. GMOs cannot co-exist with the independence and freedom of science.

A Canadian study showed that traces of the Bt toxin from Monsanto Bt corn were found in the blood of 93 percent of women and 80 percent of their umbilical cord and fetal blood.

Monsanto's false argument for safety was that the Bt toxin in Bt crops poses no danger to human health because the protein breaks down in the human gut. However, the study shows that the Bt toxin survives in the blood of pregnant women and is also detected in fetal blood.

Evidence of liver and kidney toxicity appeared when rats were fed an approved GE maize variety (Mon 863) Similar effects were observed when Monsanto fed its GT-73 Roundup Ready canola variety to rats. The rats showed a 12 percent to 16 percent increase in liver weight. . . .

4. The Myth of Substantial Equivalence

The safety debate has been repeatedly suppressed by bad science. One of the unscientific strategies used to extinguish the safety discussion is to tautologically define a novel organism or novel food created through genetic engineering as "substantially equivalent" to conventional organisms and foods. However, 9 genetically engineered crop or food is different because it has genes from unrelated organisms—it cannot, therefore, be treated as equivalent to a non-genetically engineered crop or food. In fact, the biotechnology industry itself gives up the claim of "substantial equivalence" when it claims patents on GMOs on grounds of novelty.

While governments and government agencies promoting genetic engineering refer to "sound science" as the basis for their decisions, they are manipulating scientific data and research to promote the interests of the biotechnology industry while putting citizen health and the environment at risk. The report by EPA scientists entitled "Genetic Gene: The premature commercial release of genetically engineered bacteria" and the report by Andrew Christiansen "Recombinant Bovine Growth Hormone: Alarming Tests, Unfounded Approval: The Story Behind the Rush to Bring rBGH to the market" show in detail how regulatory agencies have been manipulated on issues of safety.

Scientific agencies have been split and polarized into two communities—a corporate science community and a public science community. The corporate science community participates in distorting and manipulating science. Among the distortions of corporate science is the assumption of "substantial equivalence" which is falsified both by the research done by the public science community as well as by the intellectual property rights claims of the biotechnology industry itself.

When industry wants to avoid risk assessment and issues of liability, the argument used is that the genetically engineered organism is "substantially equivalent" to the non-engineered parent. However, when industry wants property rights, the same GMO becomes "novel" or substantially inequivalent to the parent organism.

When a safety and intellectual property rights discourse of the genetic engineering industry is put side by side what emerges is an unscientific, incoherent undemocratic structure for total control through which absolute rights are claimed and all responsibility is denied and disclaimed. . . .

Another strategy used to suppress good science by bad science is in the design of trials, and the extrapolation of data from artificially constructed contexts to real ecosystems.

The final strategy used is of direct arm twisting, used by the U.S. administration repeatedly to kill the Biosafety protocol in the Convention of Biological Diversity (CBD), even though the US is not a party to the Convention. In spite of it, the countries of the world adopted the Cartagena Protocol on Biosafety in 2000. It was also the strategy used against labeling of genetically engineered foods. However, the world agreed to GMO labelling in the Codex Alimentarius.

While constantly referring to science the US government is in fact promoting bad science, and with it, promoting ecological and human health risks. Instead of generating scientific understanding of the impacts of transferring genes, it is promoting deliberate ignorance.

'Don't Look, Don't See' "The Strategy of Deliberate Ignorance"

The false assumption of "substantial equivalence" of GMOs and non-engineered organisms establishes a strategy of deliberate ignorance. Ignorance of the risks is then treated as proof of safety. "Don't look—don't see" leads to total lack of information about the ecological impacts of genetic engineering.

It is often claimed that there have been no adverse consequences from more than 500 field releases in the U.S. However, the term "releases" is completely misleading. Those tests were largely not scientific tests of realistic ecological concerns, yet "this sort of non-data on non-releases has been cited in policy circles as though 500 true releases have now informed scientists that there are no legitimate scientific concerns."

Recently, for the first time, the data from the U.S. Department of Agriculture field trials were evaluated to see whether they support the safety claims. The Union of Concerned Scientists (UCS) that conducted the evaluation found that the data collected by the USDA on small-scale tests have little value for commercial risk assessment. Many reports fail to even mention—much less measure—environmental risks. Of those reports that allude to environmental risk, most have only visually scanned field plots looking for stray plants or isolated test crops from relatives. The UCS concluded that the observations that "nothing happened" in those hundreds of tests do not say much. In many cases, adverse impacts are subtle and would never be registered by scanning a field. In other cases, failure to observe evidence of the risk is due to the contained conditions of the tests. Many test crops are routinely isolated from wild relatives, a situation that guarantees no outcrossing. The UCS cautioned that ". . . care should be taken in citing the field test record as strong evidence for the safety of genetically engineered crops" (Jane Rissler & Margaret Mellon, *The Ecological Risks of Engineered Crops*, The MIT Press, 1996).

The myth of safety of genetic engineering is manufactured through deliberate ignorance. Deliberate ignorance of the impacts is not proof of safety; it is a guarantee for disaster.

The scientific corruption by the biotech industry and the sacrifice of knowledge sovereignty began in 1992 with the concoction of the false principle of substantial equivalence. The false assumption of "susbtantial equivalence" was introduced by President George H.W. Bush in US policy immediately after the Earth Summit in Rio de Janeiro to blunt the call for biosafety regulation. It was later formalized and introduced in 1993 by OECD (UN Organization for Economic Cooperation and Development), and subsequently endorsed by FAO (UN Food and Agriculture Organization) and WHO (World Health Organization). The OECD document states:

> "For foods and food components from organisms developed by the application of modern biotechnology, the most practical approach to the determination is to consider whether they are substantially equivalent to analogous food products if such exist. The concept of substantial equivalence embodies the idea that existing organisms used as foods, or as a source of food, an be used as the basis for comparison when assessing the safety of human consumption of food or food component that has been modified or is new."

Apart from being vague, this definition is unsound. Foods with Bt toxin genes are not the same as foods without. Herbicide-resistant crops are different from existing varieties because they have new genes for resistance to herbicide. An article by Marc Lappe and others in the Journal of Medicinal Food (1999) has established that Monsanto's Round Up Ready soya beans change the levels of phytoestrogens by 12 to 14 percent. To treat these differences as insignificant when it is a question of safety, and as significant when it is a question of patentability, is totally unscientific. . . .

5. Genetic Contamination Is Inevitable, Co-existence Is Not Possible

In addition to causing harm to public health and ecosystems, GE seeds and crops provide a pathway for corporations to "own" seeds through patents and intellectual property rights (IPRs). Patents provide royalties for the patent holder and corporate monopolies. This translates into super profits for Monsanto. For the farmers this means debt. For example, more than 250,000 Indian farmers have been pushed to suicide in the last decade and a half. Most of the suicides are in the cotton belt where Monsanto has established a seed monopoly through Bt cotton.

At a conference in Washington, D.C. on the Future of Farming, U.S. Secretary of Agriculture, Tom Vilsack, referring to organic farming and GMOs said, "I have two sons, I love them both and I want them to coexist." Filmmaker Debra Grazia responded from the floor "but one of your sons is a bully."

GMOs contaminate non-GE crops. Contamination is inevitable, since cross-pollination is inevitable, within the same species or with close relatives.

The most dramatic case of contamination and genetic pollution is the case of Percy Schmeiser, a Canadian Canola seed grower, whose crop was contaminated by Monsanto's Round-Up Ready Canola. Instead of paying Percy for the damage of contamination in accordance with the "Polluter Pays" principle, Monsanto sued Percy for "Intellectual Property theft."

The contamination of canola in Canada is so severe that 90 percent of certified non-GE Canola seed samples contain GE material.

As Arnold Taylor, Chair of the Organic Agriculture Protection Fund said:

> "There is no organic canola in Canada any more, virtually none, because the seed stock is basically contaminated . . . we've lost that crop."

In the Agriculture Canada study, scientists in Saskatoon found that nearly half of the 70 certified seed samples tested were contaminated with the Roundup Ready gene. Thirty-seven percent had the Liberty Link gene and 59 percent had both.

Another study in the US found that virtually all samples of non-GE corn, soy beans, and canola seed were contaminated by GE varieties. . . .

6. Patents on Seeds and Seed Monopolies

GMOs are intimately linked to seed patents. In fact, patenting of seeds is the real reason why industry is promoting GMOs.

Monopolies over seeds are being established through patents, mergers and cross licensing arrangement.

Monsanto now controls the world's biggest seed company, Scminis, which has bought up [many others]. . . .

Monsanto has cross-licensing arrangements with BASF, Bayer, Dupont, Sygenta and Dow. They have agreements to share patented genetically engineered seed traits with each other. The giant seed corporations are not competing with each other. They are competing with peasants and farmers over the control of the seed supply.

The combination of patents, genetic contamination and the spread of monocultures means that society is rapidly losing its seed freedom and food freedom. Farmers are losing their freedom to have seed and grow organic food free of the threat of contamination by GE crops. Citizens are losing their freedom to know what they are eating, and the choice of whether or not to eat GE free food.

An example of seed monopolies is cotton in India. In a decade, Monsanto gained control of 95 percent of the cotton seed market, and seed prices jumped 8,000 percent. India's Anti-Trust Court, the Monopoly and Restrictive Trade Practices Commission, was forced to rule against Monsanto. High costs of seed and chemicals have pushed 250,000 farmers to suicide with most suicides concentrated in the cotton belt. Monsanto does not just control the seed through patents. It also spreads its control through contamination. After spreading genetic contamination, Monsanto sues farmers as "intellectual property thieves" as it did in the case of Percy Schmeiser. That is why a case has been brought against Monsanto by a coalition of more than 80 groups to stop Monsanto from suing farmers after polluting their crops. (www.pubpat.org/assets/files/seed/OSGATA-v-Monsanto-Complaint.pdf)

Denial of Labeling as the Denial to Consumers of Their Democratic "Right to Know" and "Right to Choose"

In June 1997, the US Trade Representative Charlene Barshefshy warned the European Union Agriculture Commission Franz Fischler not to go through with proposals to require the labeling of genetically modified organisms (GMOs) or their segregation from regular products. The Trade Representative told the Senate Agriculture Committee that the U.S. cannot tolerate a step which would cause a major disruption in US exports to the E.U.

The E.U. Commissioner was under pressure from European Consumers to label GMO foods as their democratic right to inform ation and choice. However, consumer rights were defined by the U.S. trade representative as "arbitrary, politicized and scientifically unjustified" rules. The insistence of consumers to pursue "non-science based restrictions" would lead to a "trade war of major dimensions."

In a letter to the U.S. Secretary on June 12th, 1997, US agribusiness corporations stated the segregation of crops for labeling is both scientifically unjustified and commercially unfeasible.

According to U.S. industry, labeling of foods violates the WTO agreement on free trade. The Sanitary and Phyto-Sanitary measures in WTO are thus viewed by industry as protecting their interests. But the right to information is about democracy and democratic rights cannot be sanctioned by arbitrary technocratic and corporate decision making about what is "sound science" and what is not.

The denial of labelling is one dimension of totalitarian structures associated with the introduction of genetical engineering in food and agriculture. Navdanya filed a case in India demanding labeling of GM foods but the direct intervention by the U.S. embassy prevented the labeling law from being introduced by the Indian Health Ministry.

On July 5, 2011 Codex Alimentarius, the international food safety body, recognized the right of countries to label GMO foods. This ended twenty years of an international struggle. As the Consumer International states: "The new Codex agreement means that any country wishing to adopt GM food labeling will no longer face the threat of a legal challenge from the World Trade Organization (WTO). This is because national measures based on Codex guidance or standards cannot be challenged as a barrier to trade."

We now need to build on this right-to–know principle and ensure GMO labeling in all countries.

GMOs Are an Issue of Food Democracy

This is why GE crops are an issue for democracy. Food democracy is everyone's right and responsibility. We have food democracy when we can exercise our choice to have GMO free seed and food. This choice is being undermined as seed is genetically engineered and patented, as food systems are increasingly controlled by giant corporations, as chemical pollution and genetic pollution spread uncontrolled, making our food unsafe. Each of us must defend our food freedom and urge our governments to protect the rights of their citizens and stop supporting corporate takeover of our seeds and foods. Each of us is vital in creating food democracy. We invite you to join us to defend the most fundamental freedom: our food freedom.

VANDANA SHIVA is an Indian physicist, environmentalist, and campaigner for sustainability and social justice. She is director/founder of The Research Foundation for Science, Technology and Ecology (RFSTE) and director/founder of Navdanya. She has received many awards, including the Right Livelihood Award and most recently the Sydney Peace Prize. Her most recent book is *Staying Alive: Women, Ecology, and Development* (South End Press, 2010).

EXPLORING THE ISSUE

Are Genetically Modified Foods Safe to Eat?

Critical Thinking and Reflection

1. What does it mean to say that a particular technology is "unnatural"?
2. What is the greatest threat to human health posed by genetically modified (GM) foods?
3. Should tests of GM foods performed by industry scientists be trusted?
4. Should regulation of a new technology be based on demonstrated risks? On potential risks? On the nature of the press coverage?

Is There Common Ground?

The participants in the debate over GM foods agree that it is important to ensure a healthy, safe, and abundant food supply. They differ on whether genetic engineering helps to achieve this aim.

1. It can be instructive to consider other threats to a healthy, safe, and abundant food supply. Among these threats are plant diseases known as rusts and blights. Read Rachel Ehrenberg, "Rust Never Sleeps," *Science News* (September 25, 2010), and discuss the global effects of a massive rust outbreak.
2. List as many other threats to a healthy, safe, and abundant food supply as you can.
3. How many of these threats might be addressed using genetic engineering? Using other technologies?

Additional Resources

Robin Mather, "The Threats from Genetically Modified Foods," *Mother Earth News* (April–May 2012).

Henry I. Miller and Gregory Conko, *The Frankenfood Myth: How Protest and Politics Threaten the Biotech Revolution* (Praeger, 2004).

National Research Council and Committee on the Impact of Biotechnology on Farm-Level Economics and Sustainability, *The Impact of Genetically Engineered Crops on Farm Sustainability in the United States* (National Academies Press, 2010) (www.nap.edu/catalog.php?record_id=12804).

Jeffrey M. Smith, *Seeds of Deception: Exposing Industry and Government Lies about the Safety of the Genetically Engineered Foods You're Eating* (Chelsea Green, 2003).

Create Central

www.mhhe.com/createcentral

Internet References . . .

World Health Organization

The World Health Organization of the United Nations provides links to recent reports and meetings about the safety of GM foods on its Biotechnology page.

www.who.int/foodsafety/biotech/en/

National Institute of Environmental Health Sciences

The National Institute of Environmental Health Sciences studies the health risks of numerous environmental factors, many of which are associated with the use of technology.

www.niehs.nih.gov

Unit 4

UNIT

SPACE

*M*any interesting controversies arise in connection with technologies that are so new that they may sound more like science fiction than fact. Some examples are technologies that allow the exploration of space, the detection (and perhaps prevention) of space-based threats, and the search for extraterrestrial intelligence. We have capabilities undreamed of in earlier ages, and they raise genuine, important questions about what it is to be a human being, the limits on human freedom in a technological age, the degree to which humans are helpless victims of fate, and the place of humanity in the broader universe. They also raise questions of how we should respond: Should we accept the new devices and abilities offered by scientists and engineers? Or should we reject them? Should we use them to make human life safer and more secure? Or should we remain, as in past ages, at the mercy of the heavens?

Selected, Edited, and with Issue Framing Material by:
Thomas A. Easton, *Thomas College*

ISSUE

Can We Stop an Asteroid or Comet Impact?

YES: Michael F. A'Hearn, from "Testimony Before the House Committee on Science, Space, and Technology— Threats from Space: A Review of Private and International Efforts to Track and Mitigate Asteroids and Meteors, Part II," U.S. House of Representatives (2013)

NO: Clark R. Chapman, from "What Will Happen When the Next Asteroid Strikes?" *Astronomy Magazine* (2011)

Learning Outcomes

After reading this issue, you will be able to:

- Explain why asteroid and comet impacts are considered a risk to society.
- Explain what options are available to prevent asteroid and comet impacts or mitigate their effects.
- Explain the importance of advance planning to deal with potential disasters such as asteroid and comet impacts.

ISSUE SUMMARY

YES: Michael F. A'Hearn argues that even impacts by small (less than 140 meters in diameter) near-Earth-objects (NEOs) can be damaging and that present detection programs focus only on larger NEOs and will take many years to complete their inventory. The probability that even a small NEO will strike Earth in the near future is small, but the potential damage is so great that investing in identifying and tracking NEOs, and researching ways of preventing impact, is worthwhile.

NO: Clark R. Chapman argues that though the consequences of an asteroid or comet impact would be catastrophic, efforts to prevent the impact would be futile. It is far more appropriate to incorporate such impact disasters into more conventional disaster planning.

Thomas Jefferson once said that he would rather think scientists were crazy than believe that rocks could fall from the sky. Since then, we have recognized that rocks do indeed fall from the sky. Most are quite small and do no more than make pretty streaks across the sky as they burn up in the atmosphere; they are known as meteors. Some—known as meteorites—are large enough to reach the ground and even to do damage. Every once in a while, the news reports one that crashed through a car or house roof, as indeed one did in January 2007 in New Jersey. Very rarely, a meteorite is big enough to make a crater in the Earth's surface, much like the ones that mark the face of the Moon. An example is Meteor Crater in Arizona, almost

a mile across, created some 50,000 years ago by a meteorite 150 feet in diameter. (The Meteor Crater website, http://www.meteorcrater.com/, includes an animation of the impact.) A more impressive impact is the one that occurred 65 million years ago, when a comet or asteroid 10 kilometers (6 miles) in diameter struck near what is now Chicxulub, Mexico: The results included the extinction of the dinosaurs (as well as a great many other species). Chicxulub-scale events are very rare; a hundred million years may pass between them. Meteor Crater-scale events may occur every thousand years, releasing as much energy as a 100-megaton nuclear bomb and destroying an area the size of a city. And it has been calculated that a human being is more likely to die as the result of such an event than in an airplane crash (crashes are much more common but they don't kill as many people as a large impact would).

It is not just Hollywood sci-fi, *Deep Impact* and *Armageddon*. Some people think we really should be worried. We should be doing our best to identify meteoroids (as they are called before they become meteors or meteorites) in space, plot their trajectories, tell when they are coming our way, and even develop ways of deflecting them before they cause enormous losses of life and property. In 1984, Thomas Gehrels, a University of Arizona astronomer, initiated the Spacewatch project, which aimed to identify space rocks that cross Earth's orbit. In the early 1990s, NASA workshops considered the hazards of these rocks. NASA now funds the international Spaceguard Survey, which finds about 25 new near-Earth asteroids every month and has identified more than 600 asteroids over 1 kilometer (2/3 of a mile) in diameter; none seem likely to strike Earth in the next century. On the other hand, in February 2013 an asteroid the size of a skyscraper missed Earth by about 17,000 miles and a 10-ton meteor exploded over Chelyabinsk, Russia (the shock wave broke windows and caused numerous injuries; see Richard Stone, "Siberian Meteor Spurs Dash for Data, Calls for Safeguards," *Science*, March 8, 2013). There are many other large rocks in space, and eventual large impacts on Earth are very likely. According to NASA, there are some 4,700 asteroids more than 100 meters (330 feet) across, of which only 20–30 percent have actually been discovered so far. Greg Easterbrook, "The Sky Is Falling," *Atlantic* (June 2008), argues that human society faces so much risk from asteroid and comet impacts that Congress should place a much higher priority on detecting potential impactors and devising ways to stop them.

In the debate over the risks of near-Earth object (NEO) impacts on Earth, there are a few certainties: They have happened before, they will happen again, and they come in various sizes. As Mike Reynolds says, in "Earth Under Fire," *Astronomy* (August 2006), the question is not whether impacts will happen in the future. "It's just a matter of when and how big the object will be." Many past craters mark the Earth, even though many more have been erased by plate tectonics and erosion. Ivan Semeniuk, "Asteroid Impact," *Mercury* (November/December 2002), says, "If there is one question that best sums up the current state of thinking about the impact hazard, it is this: At what size do we need to act? In the shooting gallery that is our solar system, everyone agrees we are the target of both cannonballs and BBs. The hard part is deciding where to draw the line that separates them. For practical reasons, that line is now set at 1 kilometer. Not only are objects of this diameter a global threat (no matter where they hit, we're all affected to some degree), they are

also the easiest to spot." However, as Richard A. Kerr notes, "The Small Ones Can Kill You, Too," *Science* (September 19, 2003). Edward T. Lu, "Stop the Killer Rocks," *Scientific American* (December 2011), argues that "All civilizations that inhabit planetary systems must eventually deal with the asteroid threat, or they will go the way of the dinosaurs." Action is essential.

What if a "killer rock" does present a threat? In September 2002, NASA held a "Workshop on Scientific Requirements for Mitigation of Hazardous Comets and Asteroids," which concluded "that the prime impediment to further advances in this field is the lack of any assigned responsibility to any national or international organization to prepare for a disruptive collision and the absence of any authority to act in preparation for some future collision mitigation attempt" and urged that "NASA be assigned the responsibility to advance this field" and "a new and adequately funded program be instituted at NASA to create, through space missions and allied research, the specialized knowledge base needed to respond to a future threat of a collision from an asteroid or comet nucleus." The results of the workshop appeared as *Mitigation of Hazardous Impacts Due to Asteroids and Comets* (Cambridge University Press, 2004).

The Organization for Economic Cooperation and Development (OECD) Global Science Forum held a "Workshop on Near Earth Objects: Risks, Policies and Actions" in January 2003. It too concluded that more work is needed. In May 2005, the House Science Committee approved a bill to establish and fund a NASA program to detect and assess near-Earth asteroids and comets down to 100 meters in diameter. As Michael A'Hearn notes in his congressional testimony (see below) that became a Congressional mandate to find 90 percent of NEOs greater than 140 meters in diameter. See also David H. Levy, "Asteroid Alerts: A Risky Business," *Sky & Telescope* (April 2006). NASA's March 2007 "Near-Earth Object Survey and Deflection: Analysis of Alternatives, Report to Congress" argues that although progress is being made, much more would be possible if Congress increased funding.

Given political will and funding, what could be done if a threat were identified? Richard Stone, "Target Earth," *National Geographic* (August 2008), says that "Two facts are clear: Whether in 10 years or 500, a day of reckoning is inevitable. More heartening, for the first time ever we have the means to prevent a natural disaster of epic proportions." There have been numerous proposals, from launching nuclear missiles to pulverize approaching space rocks to sending astronauts (or robots) to install rocket engines and deflect the rocks onto safe paths (perhaps into the sun to forestall future hazards).

A December 2008 study by the U.S. Air Force found that we are woefully unprepared for a NEO impact; see David Shiga, "Asteroid Attack: Putting Earth's Defences to the Test," *New Scientist* (September 23, 2009). Not much has changed since Bill Cooke, "Killer Impact," *Astronomy* (December 2004), warned that for the foreseeable future, our only real hope will be evacuation of the target zone. All proposed methods of warding off disaster require a stronger space program than any nation now has. Lacking such a program, knowing that a major rock is on the way would surely be of little comfort. However, given sufficient notice—on the order of decades—a space program might be mobilized to deal with the threat. Led by ex-astronauts Ed Lu and Rusty Schweickart, the B612 Foundation (http://b612foundation.org/) hopes to address this problem with a privately funded survey satellite called Sentinel; see Robert Irion, "The Save-the -World Foundation," *Science* (August 23, 2013).

At the moment, Europe appears to be taking the lead in the effort to ward off disaster from the skies. In January 2012, the German space agency's (DLR) Institute of Planetary Research in Berlin held the kickoff meeting for Project NEOShield, an international effort to study how to prevent asteroid and comet impacts. See http://www.neoshield .net/en/index.htm.

In the YES selection, Michael F. A'Hearn argues that though the probability that a near-Earth-object (NEO) will strike Earth in the near future is small, the potential damage is so great that investing in identifying and tracking NEOs, and researching ways of preventing impact, is worthwhile. Since much time is likely to be needed to develop technology that can safely and reliably divert a threatening object, it is now time to discuss how to go about it. In the NO selection, planetary scientist Clark R. Chapman argues that though the consequences of an asteroid or comet impact would be catastrophic, efforts to prevent the impact would be futile. It is far more appropriate to incorporate such impact disasters into more conventional disaster planning.

YES ↩

Michael F. A'Hearn

Testimony Before the House Committee on Science, Space, and Technology—Threats from Space: A Review of Private and International Efforts to Track and Mitigate Asteroids and Meteors, Part II

Mr. Chairman and members of the Committee, thank you for the opportunity to appear today to discuss the potential threats of near-Earth objects (NEOs) in the context of the [National Research Council (NRC)] report on this topic that was issued in 2010. I was the chairman of the mitigation sub-panel for the NRC report, but today I am not representing the NRC, nor NASA, nor the University of Maryland.

The NRC Study: As mandated by Congress in the Consolidated Appropriations Act, 2008, NASA commissioned the NRC to study Surveys for Near-Earth Objects and Hazard Mitigation Strategies. The Steering Committee was chaired by Dr. Irwin Shapiro of Harvard University and the two sub-panels, one for Surveys and Characterization and one for Mitigation Strategies, were chaired by Dr. Faith Vilas, then Director of the MMT Observatory in Arizona, and by myself, respectively. The committee had a wide variety of expertise, ranging over the entire scope of the impact hazard problem. Several public hearings were held, with testimony from numerous experts, some of whom were advocates of specific projects while others were experts in impact prediction and risk communication, and yet others were policy experts.

The committee concluded that the money being expended at that time on NEO surveys was inadequate to meet the congressional mandate of finding 90% of potential impactors larger than 140 m on any reasonable time scale. The committee did not make a specific recommendation on the forward path, but described forward paths for surveys and discovery as a function of how much money Congress wished to appropriate to "buy insurance" against an impact. The amount of money to be appropriated would directly affect the timeline. The committee also recom-mended initiating a search for potential impactors in the 50–140-m range. The committee noted that there are basically four approaches to mitigation—evacuation for the smallest impactors, slow push-pull techniques, such as the gravity tractor, for moderately sized impactors with long warning times, and then kinetic impactors and standoff nuclear explosions for successively larger impactors and/or shorter warning times. A research program to better understand these mitigation approaches was recommended. Actual mitigation experiments in space were suggested, provided sufficient funding was provided, and overall programs were described for three different levels of funding.

The committee's report, Defending Planet Earth—Near-Earth-Object Surveys and Hazard Mitigation Strategies, was released in 2010. The remainder of this testimony concerns the details of some of these recommendations, both as recommended by the NRC and including my personal perspectives on the issues.

Impactors <140 meters: At the time of the NRC report, results newly published at that time indicated that previous modeling of impacts, by scaling from nuclear explosions of known yield, were incorrect due to the rapid downward motion of an external impactor compared to a nuclear explosion, for which the source can be considered to be at a fixed altitude. These results, which are still neither refuted nor explicitly confirmed, show that substantial damage can be inflicted by objects that are even smaller than 50 meters in diameter. To be specific, the new calculations suggested that the Tunguska event, which in 1908 flattened every tree over roughly 2000 square km in Siberia, was due to a body in the range of 30–50 meters diameter. Based on our knowledge of the size distribution of NEOs that corresponds to an event that should occur roughly every century or two. For comparison, the best estimate of the Chelyabinsk meteor in February, which caused one building collapse and lots of broken windows with many people injured, is that it had a diameter of 15–20 meters, much smaller than any of the previous estimates of a hazardous size. The size of the Chelyabinsk meteor is better known than most since the trajectory has yielded a reliable velocity and the recovered samples can be used to infer the density of the body. Such an event should occur every several decades. Thus it is clear that objects much smaller than 140 meters are frequent and are capable of significant damage on Earth, although most of these impacts in the past went unnoticed because they occurred over the ocean or over very sparsely inhabited land areas. Detailed modeling of the effects of small impactors, say from Chelyabinsk-size to 140-m diameter, is a gap that should be filled, although most of the computer codes to tackle this problem accurately are under restricted access.

It is widely understood that small objects are much more abundant than large ones in nearly all the populations of the solar system, and specifically among the NEOs. Very roughly, a 14-m NEO is 1000 times more likely than a 140-m NEO. Thus the "next" significant impactor will most likely be closer in size to Chelyabinsk than to 140 meters. It therefore is important to plan for such an event, even if the hazard to life is small.

A key issue for the small impactors is that they are normally so faint prior to impact that we do not know how to detect them very far in advance. Many of them can only be discovered days to weeks before impact. Fortunately, this limitation coincides with the fact that the region of destruction by such an impactor is sufficiently small that evacuation (aka "duck and cover") is a realistic mitigation to minimize loss of life (but not property damage). . . .

Programs at Various Funding Levels: The NRC report noted that any program dealing with NEO hazards as policy, as opposed to programs dealing with NEOs as scientific targets, should be considered as a form of insurance. The hazard is different from other terrestrial hazards, however, in that the insurance can be used to prevent damage rather than paying for restoration after damage. The question should be thought of, therefore, as a question of how much insurance the nation should [buy]. The committee then described three different scenarios, depending on how much insurance was being bought, with rather arbitrary levels being chosen for the scenarios.

At a level of $10 million per year, the then operating survey programs could continue, as could a modest research program into issues related to the NEO hazard. This level would not meet the congressionally mandated George E. Brown survey to detect 90% of potential impactors larger than 140 meters in diameter.

I note that current spending in NASA's NEO program has increased to roughly $20 million per year, allowing some new initiatives such as the ATLAS program, operations of the PanSTARRS system (currently only one telescope but soon to be two telescopes), and research grants into mitigation related topics. Spending for the Large Synoptic Survey Telescope [(LSST)] is not included in these totals – that telescope, if operated in NEO survey mode only, could meet the 140-meter goal relatively quickly.

At a level of $50 million per year, operation of a telescope such as LSST could be funded for NEO-optimized searches, although this assumes construction funding for astronomical research, e.g., from NSF. Alternatively, an in-flight mitigation mission might be feasible if conducted as a minor part of an international partnership.

At a level of $250 million per year for a decade, the advanced surveys to 140 meters could be completed, either from the ground or from space, and a unilateral mitigation experimental mission would be feasible.

None of the NRC's recommended funding levels addressed the question of impactors smaller than 140 meters. With current technology, late detection appears to be the only feasible approach. Limits for the Sentinel system are not readily available to me, nor are the actual limits of the ATLAS system so I cannot comment on their relative contributions. The NEO program office at JPL has funded an independent study to assess the capability of the ATLAS system.

One also needs to remember that, once the George E. Brown survey to 140 meters is complete (90%), the remaining unidentified impactors include both the smaller impactors and the long-period comets. Although the long-period comets very rarely impact Earth, cumulatively they are likely to lead to as many or more deaths as the much more frequent small events. They have been ignored up to this point because they have been such a small fraction of the total threat, but that situation will change dramatically. One has to decide whether to deal with the small, frequent events or with the rare, large events, or both, analogous to deciding whether to deal with frequent auto accidents or infrequent large airliner or ship accidents or both.

International Cooperation and Collaboration: International collaboration is very important in the entire effort to deal with the impact hazard, from discovery, through impact prediction, to mitigation. Unfortunately, despite considerable discussion at the individual scientist level and considerable discussion at the governmental level up to the United Nations, the U. S. is the only nation with a funded, active and effective survey/discovery program. Canada has just launched (February 2013) and Germany will soon launch a small satellite designed to discover sub-populations of NEOs, but the U.S. is still the predominant nation in funding an active program for tracking NEOs, both through the JPL NEO Program Office and through funding the entire operation of the Minor Planet Center that is nominally sponsored by the International Astronomical Union.

It should be pointed out that the only terrestrial impactor ever predicted in advance was 2008 TC_3, an impactor much smaller (roughly 4 meters) than the Chelyabinsk meteor. This was discovered less than one day before impact, by R. Kowalski at the Catalina survey, based in Arizona. The impact was predicted only because the Catalina survey included a (NASA-funded) telescope in Australia in addition to the telescopes in Arizona, which allowed very rapid follow up data, and it was the combination of data from both telescopes that allowed the rapid prediction of the impact, including a prediction of the time and location of impact, both of which were extremely accurate. Thus an internationally distributed, and closely interactive, network of telescopes is critical for predicting small impactors. Fortunately, 2008 TC_3 was so small that it caused no damage on the Sahara Desert in northern Sudan where it entered Earth's atmosphere, although small pieces were subsequently recovered days later.

The area in which international collaboration is even more important is mitigation, due largely to the fact that incorrectly changing the orbit of a potential impactor could merely move the impact site from one country to another, with obvious international implications. Even the Chelyabinsk meteor was claimed by a fringe politician in Russia to be an American weapons test, but fortunately the Russian Academy of Sciences was in the forefront of public announcements, clearly declaring that this was a natural meteor. Unfortunately, there has been even less international discussion on this topic than on the survey/discovery/prediction topic, although there have been discussions within the UN's Action Team 14 of COPUOS [(UN Committee on the Peaceful Uses of Outer Space)]. This is an area in which international collaboration, not just discussion, must be established before action is needed.

Contributions of Basic Research to Detection, Characterization, and Mitigation: There is considerable overlap between basic scientific research on comets and asteroids, *i.e.*, on the bodies that include NEOs, and policy-based work on the issues of hazard prediction and mitigation. However, the focus is very different between the two areas and consequently there are significant activities that are not included in one focus or the other. It is for this reason that NEO hazard activities require a separately identified source of funding, associated with national policy, that is not taken out of the scientific programs.

The research activities related to surveys and discovering bodies are aimed at finding statistically significant samples to enable interpretation, and these were the precursors of the specific hazard surveys, which are aimed at discovering as close to all of the objects as is practical (widely being taken to be 90% of the estimated total population). The research surveys, coupled with the work of dynamical researchers studying the orbits of the bodies, are what led to the recognition of the scale of the hazard and many of the individuals involved in those surveys are also involved in the hazard-driven surveys.

Research activities are also directly related to mitigation, but clearly distinct from actual mitigation planning. One of the key issues in mitigation, and for that matter even in predicting the scale of the damage from an impact, is to understand the physical properties of the impactors. Research programs using remote sensing have shown unambiguously that there is a wide variety of physical characteristics among the NEOs, ranging from likely coherent bodies that are the source of iron meteorites through really porous cometary nuclei that are likely to have been the source of the dinosaur-killer K-T impact 65 million years ago. Remote sensing can study a large number of objects and they are sensitive primarily to surface properties of the objects, to their size, and in some cases to a crude measure of their shape and their density.

Important, detailed characteristics of the NEOs can only be learned from *in situ* studies and PI [(Principle Investigation)]-led, competitively selected missions, under NASA's Discovery and New Frontiers programs, provide the key mechanism to carry out these studies. Such missions can only be used to study a very few targets for budgetary reasons. A team led by Mike Belton and myself proposed the Deep Impact mission to the Discovery Program many years ago purely as a scientific mission, with only two sentences in the proposal about the possible peripheral benefits for NEO hazard mitigation. What the mission did for hazard mitigation was to demonstrate active targeting to impact on a small body, the nucleus of comet 9P/Tempel 1 (a technique needed for our science but also a technique needed for mitigation) and it also demonstrated the very porous nature of cometary nuclei (probably 10% of NEOs are inactive cometary nuclei). The observations of the ejecta were used both to determine the bulk density (much empty space inside!) and to estimate the momentum transfer efficiency of the impact as relatively low (roughly 2), a critical parameter for altering an NEO's orbit with a kinetic impactor. The mission also showed the challenges of attitude control in the last minute of approach to a cometary nucleus. These results have been presented to various groups directly concerned about mitigation, such as the Defense Threat Reduction Agency. The results of the subsequent flyby of comet Hartley 2 as part of the EPOXI mission showed the diversity among cometary nuclei and the heterogeneity from place to place on a single nucleus, both of which must be taken into account in mitigation.

The OSIRIS-REx mission, scheduled for launch in 2016, is a very different mission to a different type of NEO, the asteroid 1999 RQ_{36}. This mission will return a sample of the asteroid to Earth for detailed analysis, but while at the asteroid it will also produce, for example, a detailed map of the gravity. In addition to the material properties learned from the returned sample, gravitational mapping can be used to understand the internal structure of the asteroid, critical information for understanding how to mitigate by changing the orbit, whether by kinetic impact, or nuclear explosion, or even with a gravity tractor, which depends less on the physical structure but does depend on the bulk density and the shape.

These competitively chosen "research" missions are not sufficient to completely address mitigation, but they provide most of the necessary information on the range of physical properties one might encounter. Unfortunately, the NASA budget for planetary exploration has been such that NASA's Discovery program (competitively selected, PIled missions with a cost cap of $425M in the latest round), have been devastated compared to even a decade ago. The NRC's recent decadal survey of planetary science recommended that NASA's priorities should be first to maintain a cadre of good researchers, and then to maintain a regular cadence, averaging a new start every two years, for the smallest missions (the Discovery Program), then the New Frontiers program (similar to the Discovery Program but for missions twice as expensive), and finally flagship missions (center directed missions that have lately cost more than $2 billion). Although not every mission in Discovery and New Frontiers is relevant to hazard mitigation (the most recent selection in the Discovery program is a mission to Mars), restoring Discovery to the originally intended cadence of research missions would significantly help with the mitigation effort by ensuring the existence of other missions to comets and asteroids to provide information necessary for mitigation.

Ultimately, however, specific mitigation missions must be considered as discussed above under program levels. They should be funded over and above the research program and they could be either separately funded add-ons to scientific missions or stand-alone missions, or international collaborations, with the international collaboration a high priority. Note that once the range of physical properties is understood, it is still very difficult to determine the physical properties of an actually threatening NEO without sending a mission to it, a possibility with very early discoveries but not with late discoveries.

What Should Be Done in the Event of an Identified NEO Threat? After an NEO threat is identified, the initial steps are well defined. NASA is the lead agency for identifying threats and they have a reporting path through the U.S. government that covers all relevant federal agencies and the POTUS [(President of the United States)]. Reporting to other countries is also urgent and should be done through the U.N. in order to reach all governments. In addition, there should be direct communication with countries and international agencies that have relevant capabilities for mitigation. Immediately following the alert, it is crucial to share all available data publicly. This is routine for the positional observations of the NEO and for the resultant orbital computations through the Minor Planet Center and through JPL's NEO Program Office. Beyond this, however, it is crucial to share all available information on the physical characteristics of the NEO from whatever source and on the details of the impact prediction. In the case of 2008 TC_3, which presented no hazard, this information was communicated through the channels normally used worldwide by astronomers and information was made readily available to news media.

The next steps depend critically on the nature of the threat—how big the impact will be, how far in the future it will occur, and where it will occur. An all-out effort to determine the characteristics of the particular impactor is crucial—remote sensing being needed in any case and, if time permits, a mission to characterize the NEO should be initiated in order to optimize the mitigation. Short warning times, however, may preclude an advance characterization mission and in that case the range of expected properties must be used to design a fail-safe mitigation. Action paths are, to my limited knowledge, not yet in place domestically. For a small impactor, a plausible route is through FEMA. For a larger impactor, however, either the military or NASA might be the one to take charge. For truly large impactors, the lead country and agency should be coordinated among those countries that have the capability to execute any mitigation. This decision/action tree should be fleshed out and made publicly available long before any specific threat is identified.

Michael F. A'Hearn is Professor Emeritus in the Astronomy Department, University of Maryland. His research for many years has emphasized the study of comets and asteroids.

Clark R. Chapman

 **NO**

What Will Happen When the Next Asteroid Strikes?

On October 6, 2008, I was on my way to the Johns Hopkins Applied Physics Laboratory when I turned on the news in the car and could hardly believe my ears: An asteroid discovered late the previous night was predicted to strike Earth in just a few hours—at 2:46 UT on October 7, to be precise. Ground zero would be in Sudan's Nubian Desert, just south of the Egyptian border.

For 2 decades, astronomers had reported minute chances that an asteroid might strike in the distant future, and also about "close calls" as near-Earth asteroids (NEAs) sailed by our planet at distances comparable to that of the Moon. This, however, was the first confident prediction in history of an impending asteroid impact—and it would happen less than 20 hours after discovery.

Fortunately, the incoming rock wasn't dangerous, measuring just 10 to 13 feet (3 to 4 meters) across. But a larger asteroid would cause significant destruction; would we have enough warning?

Collecting Space Rocks

A congressional hearing in 1998 mandated that scientists discover and catalog 90 percent of NEAs larger than 0.6 mile (1 kilometer) wide within 10 years, thus finding them years or decades before one might strike. Immediately after the mandate, astronomers formed the Spaceguard Survey to do just that. (It is a bit behind schedule, having found about 83 percent of them by late 2010.) The hope is we find an NEA on a likely collision course with enough time to do something about it: for example, design and launch a spacecraft mission to tug on the object or run into it. This would nudge it onto a slightly different path, missing Earth.

The Catalina Sky Survey (CSS) telescopes on Mount Bigelow, north of Tucson, Arizona, are part of the Spaceguard Survey, and it was CSS's Richard Kowalski who first noted the moving spot of light October 6, 2008, which scientists later dubbed 2008 TC3. He immediately

reported it to the Minor Planet Center in Cambridge, Massachusetts, which made a preliminary calculation of the asteroid's orbit. This time, there would be no decades of warning—just hours. Luckily, physicists had calculated that objects like 2008 TC3 would explode brilliantly, but harmlessly, high in the atmosphere. Thus, asteroids smaller than about 100 feet (30m) were nothing to fear, they said.

2008 TC3 exploded high in the atmosphere, but not exactly harmlessly. Thousands of stone fragments struck the desert beneath its flight path (an area perhaps 20 miles [32 km] long and a few miles across). About 600 pieces have been recovered so far. Ground zero was empty except for a small train station, which scientists named the meteorites after (Almahata Sitta means "Station 6" in Arabic).

A Range of Consequences

2008 TC3 was a small rock, so what about larger ones? When will the "Big One" hit? (And what defines the "Big One"?) Asteroids tend to travel at similar speeds—about 100 times faster than a jet airliner—so it is primarily their masses that determine their destructive potential when they strike Earth.

The monster object that struck 65 million years ago—eradicating most species of life, including dinosaurs, and paving the way for the emergence of mammals—was a "Big One." It was probably about 6 to 9 miles (10 to 15 km) wide. Its explosive force of a hundred million megatons of TNT disrupted the planet's ecosphere and caused the mass extinction. (Scientists call this collision the K-T boundary event because it represents the sharp change in fossils at the boundary between the Cretaceous [K] and Tertiary [T] periods.) Such an event could happen again this century, but the odds are exceedingly small; the Spaceguard Survey tells us that no NEA even close to that size will hit. Huge objects impact every hundred million years or so.

Chapman, Clark R. From *Astronomy Magazine*, May 2011, pp. 30–35. Copyright © 2011 by Kalmbach Publishing Co. Reprinted by permission.

A large comet, however, could come from the outer solar system and reach Earth in a couple of years, and we could do nothing about it but fearfully await the demise of our species. But the chances of that happening are almost infinitesimally tiny—maybe one in 10 million during this century.

With modest tweaks to CSS observing protocols, or using modest-sized telescopes dedicated to searching for objects on their final plunge to Earth's surface, we could plausibly have advance warning—of tens of hours to weeks—for perhaps half of infalling asteroids larger than a few feet. The other half, coming from the Sun's direction, would still strike without warning.

Notifications of days to weeks provide no chance for a deflection mission. Even attempting to destroy the object as it approaches would risk converting a precisely known ground-zero location into an unpredictable, scattered-shotgun outcome. However, such warnings, just as those for hurricanes, could enable people to evacuate ground zero, potentially saving many lives. In the case of 2008 TC_3, the warning process didn't work perfectly; luckily, there was almost no one in the desert to warn.

The 2008 TC3 event was mostly good luck: It was the first successful prediction of an asteroid strike (and on such short notice), and the meteorites were recovered (which would have been much less likely if it fell in a swamp or jungle). Largely informal Internet communications enabled many astronomers—professionals and amateurs alike—to observe 2008 TC_3 before it entered Earth's shadow and struck. So, for the first time, we have rocks in our laboratories that we can compare directly with telescopic observations of their progenitor asteroid in space. But 20 hours is extremely short notice. The October 2008 collision showed that we still don't have enough protocols for warning and evacuation in place.

History Shows Collisions

The largest well-documented asteroid impact occurred in 1908. Near the Podkamennaya Tunguska River in Siberia, a multi-megaton atmospheric explosion caused much destruction. Scientists think a roughly 130-foot-wide (40m) asteroid exploded with an energy 30 million times less powerful than the K-T boundary impact. Luckily, the mosquito-infested taiga forest was only sparsely inhabited—the explosion knocked down and burned trees for many miles around. Had the Tunguska blast been over a densely populated region, the natural disaster would have rivaled the worst earthquakes of recent decades. There is a fair chance, maybe one in three or four, that another Tunguska-like impact will happen this century,

but it would likely occur over an ocean or a barren desert because a larger percentage of Earth's area is either one of these environments rather than a city.

Asteroids and comets are much more plentiful, but also less damaging, the smaller they are. Although a few K-T-boundary-sized NEAs exist, interplanetary space is voluminous. The chance that such a large cosmic body and Earth would arrive in the same place in our lifetime at the same time is tiny. 2008 TC_3-like impacts are much more likely (we think they occur roughly annually, but we can't see them all). There are hundreds of such NEAs for every Tunguska-sized object, and hundreds of millions for every K-T boundary impactor. And still smaller-sized objects are visible as meteor flashes on any clear, dark night due to countless tiny pebbles and an occasional larger rock burning up harmlessly in the night sky.

Target Earth

A cosmic body vastly more massive and energetic than Tunguska but 100 times less energetic than the K-T boundary event could have serious consequences. It might kill a billion people, destroy the infrastructure of our civilization, and return us to a dark age—but probably not render the human species extinct. Humanity has never experienced a cataclysm more devastating than the Black Plague of the 14th century, so it is difficult to predict the outcome of an impact by such a 1.2- to 1.9-mile-diameter (2 or 3 km) object. Fortunately, the damage would pale before the ecological collapse at the K-T boundary.

Such an impact will happen, although it's much more likely to be millions of years from now rather than during this century. These events have happened in the past, but probably not since human beings first evolved. With objects this size, it won't matter whether the incoming rock strikes the ocean or a desert—the environmental consequences will be enormous worldwide.

Let's play out the scenario. It would start with someone discovering a comet (the Spaceguard Survey has a complete census of large NEAs showing that no asteroid larger than 1.2 miles [2 km] will hit in this century). After a few nights of additional measurements, scientists would calculate a tentative orbit and soon after realize that Earth might be in its path. They would redouble their efforts to observe the comet. Let's say astronomers find that the comet is 1.5 miles (2.4 km) across—rather small as comets go but twice the size of Comet 103P/Hartley, recently visited by NASA's EPOXI mission. They could then calculate the exact date of impact. (Even when the chance of collision is tiny, scientists can determine what date the object would hit, as well as the location of a narrow path across Earth where it would hit.) After weeks and months, the likelihood of an Earth impact would grow.

There might be talk of trying to deflect the comet with a spacecraft—unfortunately for us, that mission would be futile. We couldn't launch enough mass to crash into it. (Engineers have in mind a sphere of metal or rock several tons in mass.) A "gravity tractor" probably wouldn't work either—it moves small bodies large distances, or larger objects small distances. Just conceivably, a large nuclear blast might be energetic enough to boil off the surface on one side of the comet, forcing it to move slightly in reaction. But we couldn't build and launch such a mission in time to intersect the comet years in advance, which is the time needed for nuclear-blast deflection to work. And most comets move unpredictably because of their own outgassing, so it might just as likely nudge the comet toward Earth as away. If we break apart the comet nucleus, smaller pieces with unknown trajectories could pummel our planet.

The Aftermath

I'll leave it to science fiction to describe how individuals, nations, emergency planners, religions, and economic interests worldwide might respond to the ever-more-confident predictions of a cometary calamity as the months pass. But we can estimate what would happen, physically, when the comet struck.

First, we can calculate the immediate damage in the region where the object hits. Planetary scientist Jay Melosh of Purdue University in West Lafayette, Indiana, and his colleagues have a starting place for the calculation: They created a website application called "Impact: Earth" (www.purdue.edu/impactearth) where you can plug in values to simulate collision aftereffects. In our scenario, we have a comet 1.5 miles (2.4 km) in diameter, with a density of 1,000 kilograms per cubic meter (the density of ice). It strikes at 20 miles/second (32 km/s) into a rural area of sedimentary rock.

At 50 miles (80 km) from ground zero, the fireball of the exploding comet—which would appear 60 times bigger than the Sun—would immediately burn us and every flammable thing around us. Surrounding buildings would suffer major damage from the resulting earthquake—nearly as big as the Chilean one of February 2010—that would reach our charred remains about 16 seconds after impact. Some 4 minutes after impact, an enormous airblast with winds approaching 1,200 mph (1,900 km/h) would sweep away anything left standing.

If we were 300 miles (480 km) away from ground zero, we would likely survive, at least initially. Because we know of the impending impact, we could hide in a well-constructed building to avoid burns from the fireball, protect ourselves from falling rocks, and endure the earthquake and airblast. Either the earthquake about 1.6 minutes after impact or the hurricane-force airblast arriving 24.4 minutes after the impact might badly damage ordinary wood-frame houses.

Our best option would be to evacuate far away from ground zero long before the comet approached Earth. But we still wouldn't be safe. What calculations such as "Impact: Earth" don't describe are the global environmental and infrastructure damage, which could disrupt civilization worldwide for months and years to come. For example, as the comet penetrates the atmosphere, chemical reactions would likely destroy Earth's protective ozone layer. Some scientists think there could be an enormous electromagnetic pulse (EMP) that might disable electrical grids around the world and render communications and electronic equipment (including Earth's orbiting satellites) nonfunctional. Unfortunately, we don't know much about the effect; scientists haven't seriously researched impact-induced EMPs.

In addition, Earth would undergo significant climate changes as Sun-blocking dust is launched into the atmosphere after impact. As dust circles the globe during the ensuing weeks, perhaps crossing the equator into the opposite hemisphere, temperatures would cool dramatically, threatening an agricultural growing season and hence the world's food supply.

With more than a year of warning, the international community could mitigate the worst effects before impact: prepare for unprecedented food shortages, the required medical effort, and the possible collapse of the world's economic infrastructure. Maybe humanity could weather the storm without letting fears of the terrible prognosis exacerbate tensions, which would magnify the unfolding tragedy. With foreknowledge, civilization might survive, depending on whether we can stay resilient as we face such a natural disaster.

Closer to Impact

Fortunately, the chance of a 1.5-mile-wide comet striking within the next few centuries is tiny. Instead of worrying about the highly improbable, let's focus on how we will face more 2008 TC_3-sized objects, and even bigger ones like a Tunguska. Civil defense and emergency managers are not yet sufficiently informed about asteroids, nor are communications channels established and tested to reliably warn people near ground zero in time to evacuate.

We must incorporate our future handling of these infrequent events into the "all hazards" methods that nations and localities use when facing the much more frequent floods, tornadoes, and avalanches. The National Research Council, the President's Office of Science and Technology, and NASA's Planetary Defense Task Force pub-lished reports about the NEA impact hazard in 2010. Our country, along with the United Nations, is taking the first steps toward becoming more robustly prepared. . . .

Clark R. Chapman is a planetary scientist in the Department of Space Studies at the Southwest Research Institute in Boulder, Colorado.

EXPLORING THE ISSUE

Can We Stop An Asteroid or Comet Impact?

Critical Thinking and Reflection

1. Suppose that astronomers announce that an asteroid big enough to destroy the United States will strike Ohio in 10 years. What could we do about it?
2. Make that 25 years. What could we do about it?
3. Given the inevitability of an eventual asteroid impact, how important is it that we plan ahead? How much should we spend per year on preparations for warding off the impact or recovering afterward?

Is There Common Ground?

No one thinks that if an asteroid or comet struck the Earth, the consequences would be trivial. But because such impacts are rare events, many people are inclined to think they don't need to worry *now*, there is nothing that could be done to stop them, and besides, there are a great many other problems—from malaria to global hunger to climate change—that deserve funding more immediately. As the selections for this issue point out, however, it doesn't take huge amounts of funding to maintain a watch on the skies, inventory potential threats, and plan ahead. Our essayists even agree that for small NEO impacts, evacuation and disaster relief programs (e.g., FEMA) are most appropriate. They differ on what can usefully be done about larger impacts.

There are other potential disasters for which a precautionary approach is appropriate. Look up the following terms (begin with the listed URLs) and discuss how people are preparing for future problems.

1. Volcanoes   (http://www.scientificamerican.com/article.cfm?id=volcano-monitoring-jindal)
2. Supervolcanoes   (http://volcanoes.usgs.gov/volcanoes/yellowstone/yellowstone_sub_page_49.html)
3. Tsunamis   (http://www.ess.washington.edu/tsunami/general/warning/warning.html)
4. Earthquakes (http://earthquake.usgs.gov/)

Additional Resources

Committee to Review Near-Earth-Object Surveys and Hazard Mitigation Strategies Space Studies Board, *Defending Planet Earth: Near-Earth Object Surveys and Hazard Mitigation Strategies* (National Academies Press, 2010).

Greg Easterbrook, "The Sky Is Falling," *Atlantic* (June 2008).

Edward T. Lu, "Stop the Killer Rocks," *Scientific American* (December 2011).

National Research Council, *Defending Planet Earth: Near-Earth Object Surveys and Hazard Mitigation Strategies* (National Academies Press, 2010; http://www.nap.edu/catalog.php?record_id=12842).

Richard Stone, "Target Earth," *National Geographic* (August 2008).

Internet References . . .

National Aeronautics and Space Administration

http://www.nasa.gov

Near Earth Object Program

http://neo.jpl.nasa.gov/index.html

NEOShield: Preparing to Protect the Planet

http://www.neoshield.net/en/index.htm

Meteor Explodes above Urals

http://www.youtube.com/watch?v=yWTanCmQAxk&noredirect=1

The Near Earth Object Dynamic Site (NEODyS)

http://newton.dm.unipi.it/neodys/

Selected, Edited, and with Issue Framing Material by:
Thomas A. Easton, *Thomas College*

ISSUE

Will the Search for Extraterrestrial Life Ever Succeed?

YES: Seth Shostak, from "Using Radio in the Search for Extraterrestrial Intelligence," U.S. House of Representatives (2014)

NO: Peter Schenkel, from "SETI Requires a Skeptical Reappraisal," *Skeptical Inquirer* (2006)

Learning Outcomes

After studying this issue, students will be able to:

- Explain why it ever seemed reasonable to use radio telescopes to search for extraterrestrial intelligence.
- Explain why some people think, despite the lack of success to date, that it remains worthwhile to search for extraterrestrial intelligence.
- Explain why some people think SETI is not a worthwhile endeavor.
- Discuss the likely consequences of successful SETI.

ISSUE SUMMARY

YES: Radio astronomer and Search for Extraterrestrial Intelligence (SETI) researcher Seth Shostak defends SETI and argues that if the assumptions behind the search are well grounded, "it is not hyperbole to suggest that scientists could very well discover extraterrestrial intelligence within two decades."

NO: Peter Schenkel argues that SETI's lack of success to date, coupled with the apparent uniqueness of Earth's history and suitability for life, suggests that intelligent life is probably rare in our galaxy and that the enthusiastic optimism of SETI proponents should be reined in.

In the 1960s and early 1970s, the business of listening to the radio whispers of the stars and hoping to pick up signals emanating from some alien civilization was still new. Few scientists held visions equal to those of Frank Drake, one of the pioneers of the SETI field. Drake and scientists like him use radio telescopes—large, dish-like radio receiver-antenna combinations—to scan radio frequencies (channels) for signal patterns that would indicate that the signal was transmitted by an intelligent being. In his early days, Drake worked with relatively small and weak telescopes out of listening posts that he had established in Green Bank, West Virginia, and Arecibo, Puerto Rico. See Carl Sagan and Frank Drake, "The Search for Extraterrestrial Intelligence," *Scientific American*

(May 1975), and Frank Drake and Dava Sobel, *Is Anyone Out There? The Scientific Search for Extraterrestrial Intelligence* (Delacorte Press, 1992).

There have been more than 50 searches for extraterrestrial (ET) radio signals since 1960. The earliest ones were very limited. Later searches have been more ambitious, using multiple telescopes and powerful computers to scan millions of radio frequencies per second. New technologies and techniques continue to make the search more efficient. See Monte Ross, "The New Search for E.T.," *IEEE Spectrum* (November 2006).

At the outset, many people thought—and many still think—that SETI has about as much scientific relevance as searches for the Loch Ness Monster, Bigfoot, and the Abominable Snowman. However, to SETI fans it seems inevitable that with so many stars in the sky, there must be other worlds with life upon them, and some of that life must be intelligent and have a suitable technology and the desire to search for alien life too.

Writing about SETI in the September–October 1991 issue of *The Humanist*, physicist Shawn Carlson compares visiting the National Shrine of the Immaculate Conception in Washington, D.C., to looking up at the stars and "wondering if, in all [the] vastness [of the starry sky], there is anybody out there looking in our direction . . . [A]re there planets like ours peopled with creatures like us staring into their skies and wondering about the possibilities of life on other worlds, perhaps even trying to contact it?" That is, SETI arouses in its devotees an almost religious sense of mystery and awe, a craving for contact with the *other*. Success would open up a universe of possibilities, add immensely to human knowledge, and perhaps even provide solutions to problems that our interstellar neighbors have already defeated.

SETI also arouses strong objections, partly because it challenges human uniqueness. Many scientists have objected that life-bearing worlds such as Earth must be exceedingly rare because the conditions that make them suitable for life as we know it—composition and temperature—are so narrowly defined. Others have objected that there is no reason whatsoever to expect that evolution would produce intelligence more than once or that, if it did, the species would be similar enough to humans to allow communication. Still others say that even if intelligent life is common, technology may not be so common, or technology may occupy such a brief period in the life of an intelligent species that there is virtually no chance that it would coincide with Earth scientists' current search. Whatever their reasons are, SETI detractors agree that listening for ET signals is futile. Ben Zuckerman, "Why SETI Will Fail," *Mercury* (September/October 2002), argues that the simple fact that we have not been visited by ETs indicates that there are probably very few ET civilizations, and SETI is therefore futile.

Are we in fact alone or first? Are the conditions that lead to life and intelligence rare? Are there aliens living in disguise among us? Or are we quarantined? Reservationed? Zooed? Or maybe there is nobody there at all—not even us! (Sure, that could be it—if we are just simulations in some cosmic computer.) In *Where Is Everybody? Fifty Solutions to the Fermi Paradox and the Problem of Extraterrestrial Life* (Copernicus Books, 2002), Stephen Webb describes Fermi and his paradox (if they're out there, why haven't we been visited?) in great detail and offers a variety of answers that have been suggested—most seriously, some a bit tongue-in-cheek—for why the search has not succeeded.

His own opinion is on the pessimistic side. The SETI community, however, remains convinced that their effort is worthwhile.

Astronomers have found a great many stars with planets, but so far they have not seen signs of life. Steve Nadis, "How Many Civilizations Lurk in the Cosmos?" *Astronomy* (April 2010), discusses how the latest data have improved estimates of how many ET civilizations might exist in the galaxy. Nadis quotes Frank Drake as saying that early estimates may have been much too low. There may be 10,000 such civilizations, and detecting even one may require that we examine 20 million stars. There is, however, an even larger obstacle to success. Paul Davies, *The Eerie Silence* (Houghton Mifflin Harcourt, 2010), notes that our efforts at detection are severely limited by the communications technologies we are familiar with, and ET civilizations may use those technologies for only a brief period in their history, moving on to others that we have not yet thought of and have no way to detect. We need new thinking, meaning that we must look for signals in neutrinos from space, embedded in the genes of viruses, and much more. See also Elizabeth Quill, "Can You Hear Me Now?" *Science News* (April 24, 2010). Unfortunately, our efforts at detection are also limited by funding difficulties here at home; M. Mitchell Waldrop, "SETI Is Dead, Long Live SETI," *Nature* (July 28, 2011), discusses the closure of the Allen Telescope Array at the Hat Creek Radio Observatory in California, ending a "big science" approach to SETI (however, private funding has kept the Array open for now; see Nicole Gugliucci, "SETI's Allen Telescope Array Is Back on Track!" *Discovery*, August 27, 2011; http://news.discovery.com/space/setistars-successful-funding-jodie-foster-110817.htm). Smaller projects, however, do continue. There is also more emphasis today on detecting life—not the presumably rarer *intelligent* life—on other worlds, using techniques ranging from Mars rovers seeking sedimentary rocks that bear the chemical signatures of life to spectroscopic analyses of the atmospheres of planets circling distant stars, looking for oxygen, methane, or even industrial pollutants; see Michael D. Lemonick, "The Hunt for Life Beyond Earth," *National Geographic* (July 2014); Bruce Dorminey, "A New Way to Search for Life in Space," *Astronomy* (June 2014); Timothy D. Brandt and David S. Spiegel, "Prospects for Detecting Oxygen, Water, and Chlorophyll on an Exo-Earth," *Proceedings of the National Academy of Sciences of the United States of America* (September 16, 2014); and Henry W. Lin, Gonzalo Gonzalez Abad, and Abraham Loeb, "Detecting Industrial Pollution in the Atmospheres of Earth-Like Exoplanets," http://arxiv.org/abs/1406.3025 (July 21, 2014).

What if SETI succeeds? Frank Drake noted in *Is Anyone Out There? The Scientific Search for Extraterrestrial Intelligence*) that positive results would have to be reported to everyone, at once, in order to prevent attempts to suppress or monopolize the discovery. Albert A. Harrison, "Confirmation of ETA: Initial Organizational Response," *Acta Astronautica* (August 2003), focuses on the need for a response to success, but he is skeptical that an effective response is possible; he says, "Foresight and advance preparation are among the steps that organizations may take to prepare for contact, but conservative values, skepticism towards SETI, and competing organizational priorities make serious preparation unlikely." Should our response include sending an answer back to the source of whatever radio signals we detect? H. Paul Schuch, "The Search for Extraterrestrial Intelligence," *Futurist* (May/June 2003), suggests that there may be dangers in such a move. These dangers are addressed by Ivan Almar and H. Paul Schuch in "The San Marino Scale: A New Analytical Tool for Assessing Transmission Risk," *Acta Astronautica* (January 2007); see also Ivan Almar, "SETI and Astrobiology: The Rio Scale and the London Scale," *Acta Astronautica* (November 2011), and Douglas A. Vakoch, "Responsibility, Capability, and Active SETI: Policy, Law, Ethics, and Communication with Extraterrestrial Intelligence," *Acta Astronautica* (February 2011). A few nonscientists have also begun to consider the implications of successful contact. See, for instance, Thomas Hoffman, "Exomissiology: The Launching of Exotheology," *Dialog: A Journal of Theology* (Winter 2004). David Brin, "The Dangers of First Contact," *Skeptic* (vol. 15, no. 3, 2010), argues that because the idea of free and open exchange of information is a historical anomaly here on Earth, any attempts to reply to a signal should not include our most valuable assets—our art, music, science, and other information. Instead, we should seek equal exchange, *quid pro quo*. He does not agree that those scientists are necessarily right who say that ETs must be highly advanced ethically and thus likely to treat us benignly. At the same time, he argues that we should not count on ET messages to solve our problems; it is better that we rely on ourselves.

Have the results of SETI to date been totally blank? Researchers have found nothing that justified any claim of success, but there have been a few "tantalizing signals." T, Joseph W. Lazio and Robert Naeye discuss them in "Hello? Are You Still There?" *Mercury* (May/June 2003).

In the YES selection, Seth Shostak defends SETI and argues that if the assumptions behind the search are reasonable, "it is not hyperbole to suggest that scientists could very well discover extraterrestrial intelligence within two decades." In the NO selection, Peter Schenkel, a retired political scientist, argues that SETI's lack of success to date, coupled with the apparent uniqueness of Earth's history and suitability for life, suggests that intelligent life is probably rare in our galaxy. It is time, he says, "to dampen excessive ET euphoria and to adopt a . . . stand, compatible with facts."

YES ↩

Seth Shostak

Using Radio in the Search for Extraterrestrial Intelligence

The question of whether we share the universe with other intelligent beings is of long standing. Written speculation on this subject stretches back to the classical Greeks, and it hardly seems unreasonable to suppose that even the earliest *Homo sapiens* gazed at the night sky and wondered if beings as clever as themselves dwelled in those vast and dark spaces.

What is different today is that we have both sufficient scientific knowledge and adequate communications technology to permit us to address this question in a meaningful way.

Finding extraterrestrial intelligence would calibrate humanity's place in the cosmos. It would also complete the so-called Copernican revolution. Beginning about 470 years ago, observation and scientific reasoning led to an accurate understanding of our place in the physical universe. The goal of SETI—the Search for Extraterrestrial Intelligence—is to learn our place in the intellectual universe. Are our cognitive abilities singular, or are they simply one instance among many?

Just as large sailing ships and the compass inaugurated the great age of terrestrial exploration at the end of the 15th century, so too does our modern technology—coupled to a far deeper understanding of the structure of the universe than we had even two decades ago—give us the possibility to discover sentient life elsewhere. SETI is exploration, and the consequences of exploration are often profoundly enlightening and ultimately of unanticipated utility. We know that our species is special, but is it unique? That is the question that SETI hopes to answer.

Why We Think that Life Exists Elsewhere

There is, as of now, no compelling evidence for biology beyond Earth. While the widely reported claims of fossilized microbes in a Martian meteorite generated great excitement in 1996, the opinion of most members of the astrobiology community today is that the claims are unconvincing.

Nonetheless these same astrobiologists, if asked if they think it likely that extraterrestrial life is both commonplace and discoverable, would nod their heads affirmatively.

They would do so largely because of what we've learned in the past two decades concerning the prevalence of life-friendly cosmic habitats. Until 1995, we knew of no planets around other stars, habitable or otherwise. And yes, there was speculation that such worlds might be common, but that sunny thought was *only* speculation.

In the last two decades, astronomers have uncovered one so-called exoplanet after another. The current tally is approximately two thousand, and many more are in the offing thanks to continued analysis of data from NASA's enormously successful Kepler space telescope.

Estimates are that at least 70 percent of all stars are accompanied by planets, and since the latter can occur in systems rather than as individuals (think of our own solar system), the number of planets in the Milky Way galaxy is of order one trillion. It bears mentioning that the Milky Way is only one of 150 billion galaxies visible to our telescopes—and each of these will have its own complement of planets. This is plentitude beyond easy comprehension.

The Kepler mission's principal science objective has been to determine what fraction of this planetary harvest consists of worlds that could support life. The usual metric for whether a planet is habitable or not is to ascertain whether liquid water could exist on its surface. Most worlds will either be too cold, too hot, or of a type (like Jupiter) that may have no solid surface and be swaddled in noxious gases. Recent analyses of Kepler data suggest that as many as one star in five will have a habitable, Earth-size planet in orbit around it. This number could be too large by perhaps a factor of two or three, but even so it implies that the Milky Way is home to 10 to 80 billion cousins of Earth.

There is, in other words, more than adequate cosmic real estate for extraterrestrial life, including intelligent life.

A further datum established by recent research is that the chemical building blocks of life—the various carbon compounds (such as amino acids) that make up all terrestrial organisms—are naturally formed and in great abundance throughout the cosmos. The requisites for biology are everywhere, and while that doesn't guarantee that life will be spawned on all the worlds whose physical conditions are similar to our own, it does encourage the thought that it occurs frequently.

If even only one in a thousand "earths" develop life, our home galaxy is still host to tens of millions of worlds encrusted by flora and fauna.

However, SETI is a class of experiments designed to find not just life, but technologically sophisticated life—beings whose level of intellect and development is at least equal to our own. So it is germane to ask, even assuming that there are many worlds with life, what fraction will eventually evolve a species with the cognitive talents of *Homo sapiens*? This is a question that's both controversial and difficult to answer.

As some evolutionary biologists (including most famously Ernst Mayr and Stephen Jay Gould) have pointed out, the road from early multicellular life forms (e.g., trilobites) to us is an uncertain one with many forks. For example, if the asteroid that wiped out the dinosaurs (and two-thirds of all other land-dwelling species) 65 million years ago had arrived in our neighborhood 15 minutes later, it could have missed the Earth. The stage might never have been cleared for the mammals to assert themselves and eventually produce us. This simple argument suggests that, while life could be commonplace, intelligence might be rare.

On the other hand, recent research has shown that many different species of animals have become considerably more clever in the last 50 million years. These include of course simians—but also dolphins, toothed whales, octopuses, and some birds. One plausible interpretation of these findings is that intelligence has so much survival value that—given a complex biota and enough time—it will eventually arise on any world.

We don't know what the truth is regarding the emergence of cognition. But finding another example of an intelligent species would tell us that *Homo sapiens* is not singular. The possibility of elucidating this evolutionary question is one of the most enticing motives for doing SETI experiments.

Finding Extraterrestrial Intelligence

Although encounters with intelligent aliens are a frequent staple of movies and television, the idea of establishing the existence of these putative beings by traveling to their home planets is one that will remain fiction for the foreseeable future. The planets that orbit the Sun may include other worlds with life (Mars, various moons of the planets Jupiter and Saturn). But they are surely devoid of any life that would be our cerebral equals. Intelligent beings—assuming they exist—are on planets (or possibly large moons) orbiting other stars. Those are presently unreachable: Even our best rockets would take 100 thousand years to traverse the distance to the nearest other stellar systems. The idea that extraterrestrials have come here (the so-called UFO phenomenon), while given credence by approximately one-third of the populace, is not considered well established by the majority of scientists.

However, the methods used by SETI to discover the existence of intelligence elsewhere don't require that either we or they pay a visit. All we need do is find a signal, come to us at the speed of light. The first modern SETI experiment was conducted in 1960, when astronomer Frank Drake used an 85-foot diameter antenna at the newly constructed National Radio Astronomy Observatory in West Virginia in an attempt to "eavesdrop" on signals either deliberately or accidentally transmitted by beings light-years away. Drake used a very simple receiver, and examined two nearby star systems.

By contrast, later SETI experiments have made use of far more sensitive equipment, and have greatly expanded the scope of the search. Project Phoenix—a survey by the SETI Institute of 1,000 star systems—used antennas that ranged from 140—1,000 feet in diameter with receivers that could look for weak signals in ten million radio channels simultaneously. Today's efforts by the Institute use a small grouping of 42 antennas known as the Allen Telescope Array, situated in the Cascade Mountains of northern California. The advantage of this instrument is that it can be used for a very high percentage of time for SETI experiments, unlike previous campaigns that relied on antennas that were shared with radio astronomers doing conventional research projects. This latter circumstance greatly constrained the number of possible searches.

The other large radio SETI group in the U.S. is at the University of California, Berkeley. Their long-running Project SERENDIP uses the very large (1,000-foot diameter) antenna at Arecibo, Puerto Rico in a commensal mode. By piggybacking on this antenna, the Berkeley group gets virtually continuous use of the antenna, but the price is that they have no control of where it is aimed. However, over the course of several years, this random scrutiny covers roughly one-third of the sky. The receiver can simultaneously monitor more than 100 million channels, and some of the Berkeley data are made available for processing by individuals on their home computers using the popular screen saver, SETI@home. Approximately ten million people have downloaded the screen saver.

At the moment, the only other full-time radio SETI experiment is being conducted by a small group at the Medicina Observatory of the University of Bologna, in Italy.

Radio SETI searches preceded efforts to look for brief laser light pulses, known as optical SETI, largely because the development of practical radio occurred more than a half-century before the invention of the laser. Nonetheless, radio remains a favored technique for establishing the existence of intelligence beyond Earth. The amount of energy required to send a bit of information from one star system to another using radio is less than other schemes, and therefore it seems plausible that, no matter what other communication technologies intelligent species might develop, radio will always have a function. As a simple analogy: the wheel is an ancient technology for us, yet we use it every day and undoubtedly always will.

Radio SETI experiments have not yet detected a signal that is unambiguously extraterrestrial. Some people, both in and out of the science community, have ascribed undue significance to this fact, claiming that it indicates that no one is out there. While this may be comforting to those who would prefer to think that our species is the only one with the wit to comprehend the cosmos, it is a thoroughly unwarranted conclusion. Despite a many-decades long history of effort, our scrutiny of star systems still remains tentative. The number of star systems carefully examined over a wide range of the radio dial is no more than a few thousand. In the Milky Way, there are hundreds of billions of star systems. Consequently, our reconnaissance is akin to exploring Africa for megafauna, but one that has so far been limited to a square city block of territory.

While no one knows how prevalent signal generating civilizations might be, the more conservative estimates suggest that—to find a transmission that would prove others are out there—requires surveillance of a million star systems or more. This could be done in the near future, given the relentlessly increasing power of digital electronics. It is not hyperbolic to suggest that scientists could very well discover extraterrestrial intelligence within two decades' time or less, given resources to conduct the search.

However, funding for SETI is perennially problematic. The most ambitious SETI program, the one planned by NASA in the 1980s and 1990s, had scarcely begun observations when Congress canceled funding in the Fall of 1993. Since then, SETI efforts in this country have either been privately funded, or been an incidental part of university research. As a telling metric of the limitations of this approach, note that the total number of scientists and engineers doing full-time SETI in this country is approximately one dozen, or comparable to the tally of employees at a car wash.

Progress and Evolution of Radio SETI

A rough and ready estimate suggests that today's radio SETI experiments are about 100 trillion times more effective—as judged by speed, sensitivity, and range of radio frequencies investigated—than Frank Drake's pioneering 1960 search. The rapid development of both analog and digital electronics has spinoffs that are accelerating the capabilities of SETI.

As example, in 1980 typical SETI efforts sported receivers able to monitor 10 thousand channels simultaneously. Today's experiments sport 10—100 million channels, causing a thousand-fold increase in search speed.

Speed is essential to success. As mentioned above, conservative estimates of the prevalence of broadcasting societies hint that—in order to find a signal from another species—our SETI experiments will need to "listen" in the direction of at least 1 million stellar systems. Cheaper digital technology, which can be read as greater compute power, immediately leads to receivers with more channels—which means that it takes less time to check out all the interesting frequencies for a given SETI target.

In the case of antenna arrays, cheaper computing can also speed observations by increasing the number of star systems looked at simultaneously. As example, the Allen Telescope Array currently has the ability to examine three such systems at once. But this could be increased to hundreds or even thousands with more computing power—bringing with it a concomitant augmentation of speed.

Current and Future Resources

As noted above, the level of radio SETI effort today is small, employing roughly a dozen full- time scientists and engineers. At the height of the NASA SETI program (1992), the annual budget for this activity was $10 million, or one-thousandth of the space agency's budget. This supported equipment development and observations for a two-pronged strategy—a low-sensitivity survey of the entire sky, and a high-sensitivity targeted search of the nearest thousand star systems. The number of scientists involved was five times greater than today.

The financial support for all radio SETI efforts in the United States now is approximately 20 percent of the earlier NASA program, and comes from either private donations or from research activities at the University of California. This is, frankly, a level inadequate for keeping this science alive. The cost of developing and maintaining the requisite equipment and software, as well as paying for the scientists and engineers who do the experiments, is—at minimum—$5 million annually. Without this level of funding, the U.S. SETI efforts are likely to be overtaken by Asian and European initiatives (such as the Square Kilometer Array) in the next decade. SETI is exploration. There's no way to guarantee that if only sufficient effort is made, success will inevitably follow. Like all exploration, we don't know what we'll find, and it's possible that we'll not find anything. But if we don't search, the chances are good that the discovery of intelligence elsewhere in the cosmos will be made by others. That discovery will rank among the most profound in the history of humankind. The first evidence that we share the universe with other intelligence will be viewed by our descendants as an inflection point in history, and a transformative event.

The Public's Interest

The idea of extraterrestrials resonates with the public in a way that little of the arcane research of modern science does. While much was made of the discovery of the Higgs boson in 2012, people who weren't schooled in advanced physics had a difficult time understanding just why this was important, and what justified the multi-billion dollar price tag of the collider used in its discovery.

The idea of life in space on the other hand is science that everyone grasps. Countless creatures from the skies infest both movies and television. In addition, the techniques of SETI—while complex in detail—are simple in principle. Carl Sagan's novel and movie, "Contact," enjoyed considerable popularity, and familiarized millions with the technique of using radio to search for extraterrestrials. Documentaries on SETI and the search for life in general can be found on cable television every week. Compare that with the frequency of programming on, say, organic chemistry.

In other words, SETI is an endeavor that everyone "gets." And that includes school kids. This makes the subject an ideal hook for interesting young people in science. They come for the aliens, but along the way they learn astronomy, biology, and planetary science. Even if SETI fails to find a signal for decades, it does great good by enticing youth to develop skills in science.

It's even possible that we are hard-wired to be interested in extraterrestrial life, in the same way that we are programmed to be interested in the behavior of predators. The latter has obvious survival value (and might explain why so many young people are intrigued by dinosaurs!) Our interest in "aliens" could simply derive from the survival value of learning about our peers. Extraterrestrials are the unknown tribe over the hill—potential competitors or mates, but in any case someone we would like to know more about.

There's no doubt that SETI occasionally provokes derision. It's easy to make fun of an effort whose goal is to find "space aliens." But this is to conflate science fiction with science. As our telescopes continue to peel back the film that has darkened our view of the cosmos since *Homo sapiens* first walked the savannahs, we are learning that the Earth is only one of 100,000 billion planets, spinning quietly in the vast tracts of space. It would be a cramped mind indeed that didn't wonder who might be out there.

Seth Shostak is senior astronomer at the SETI Institute. He frequently presents the Institute's work in the media, through lectures, and via the Institute's weekly radio show, *Are We Alone?*

Peter Schenkel  **NO**

SETI Requires a Skeptical Reappraisal

The possible existence of extraterrestrial intelligence (ETI) has always stirred the imagination of man. Greek philosophers speculated about it. Giordano Bruno was burnt on the stake in Rome in 1600, mainly [for] positing the likelihood of other inhabited worlds in the universe. Kant and Laplace were also convinced of the multiplicity of worlds similar to ours. In the latter part of the nineteenth century Flammarion charmed vast circles with his books on the plurality of habitable worlds. But all these ideas were mainly philosophical considerations or pure speculations. It was only in the second half of the twentieth century that the Search for Extraterrestrial Intelligence (SETI) became a scientifically underpinned endeavor. Since the late 1950s distinguished scientists have conducted research, attempting to receive intelligent signals or messages from space via radio-telescopes. Hundreds of amateur astronomers, members of the SETI-League in dozens of countries, are scanning the sky, trying to detect evidence of intelligent life elsewhere in our galaxy. SETI pioneers, such as Frank Drake and Carl Sagan, held the stance that the Milky Way is teeming with a large number of advanced civilizations. However, the many search projects to date have not succeeded, and this daring prediction remains unverified. New scientific insights suggest the need for a more cautious approach and a revision of the overly optimistic considerations.

The standard argument for the existence of a multiplicity of intelligent life runs like this: There are about 200 to 300 billion stars in our galaxy and probably hundreds of millions, maybe even billions of planets in our galaxy. Many of these planets are likely to be located in the so-called "habitable zone" in relation [to] their star, enjoying Earth-favorable conditions for the evolution of life. The physical laws, known to us, apply also to the cosmos, and far-away stellar formations are composed of the same elements as our solar system. Therefore, it is assumed, many should possess water and a stable atmosphere, considered to be basic requisites for the development of life. Such planets must have experienced geological and biological processes similar to those on Earth, leading to the development of primitive life organisms. Then, in the course of time, following a similar course of Darwin's theory of natural selection, these evolved into more complex forms, some eventually developing cognitive capacities and—as in our case—higher intelligence.

In other words, it is maintained, our solar system, Earth, and its evolution are not exceptional cases, but something very common in our Milky Way galaxy. Consequently it must be populated by a huge number of extraterrestrial civilizations, many of them older and more advanced than ours.

Considering the enormous number of stars and planets, these seem like fair and legitimate assumptions. It indeed appears unlikely that intelligence should have evolved only on our planet. If many of these civilizations are scientifically and technologically superior to us, contact with them would give mankind a boost in many ways.

These optimistic views are based mainly on the famous Drake formula. . . . It considers the formation of stars in the galaxy, the fraction of stars with planetary systems, the number of planets ecologically suited for life, the fraction of these planets on which life and intelligent life evolves, and those reaching a communicative stage and the length of time of technical civilizations. On the basis of this formula it was estimated that a million advanced civilizations probably exist in the galaxy. The nearest one should be at a distance of about 200 to 300 light-years from Earth. German astronomer Sebastian von Hoerner estimated a number between ten thousand and ten million such civilizations.

But because of many new insights and results of research in a number of scientific fields, ranging from paleontology, geology, biology to astronomy, I believe this formula is incomplete and must be revised. The early optimistic estimates are no longer tenable. A more realistic and sober view is required.

I by no means intend to discredit SETI; the search for extraterrestrial intelligent life is a legitimate scientific endeavor. But it seems prudent to demystify this interesting

Schenkel, Peter. From *Skeptical Inquirer,* vol. 30, no. 3, May/June 2006. Copyright © 2006. Committee for Skeptical Inquiry. Reprinted by permission. All rights reserved.

subject, and to reformulate its claims on a new level, free of the romantic flair that adorns it.

Years ago, I readily admit, I myself was quite taken in by the allegations that intelligence is a very common phenomenon in the galaxy. In books, articles, and on radio and television I advocated the idea that our world, beset by problems, could learn a lot from a civilization more advanced than ours. But, in the meantime, I became convinced that a more skeptical attitude would do reality better justice. There are probably only a few such civilizations in the galaxy, if any at all. The following considerations buttress this rather pessimistic appraisal.

First of all, since project OZMA I in 1959 by Frank Drake, about a hundred radio-magnetic and other searches were conducted in the U.S. and in other countries, and a considerable part of our sky was scanned thoroughly and repeatedly, but it remained disappointingly silent. In forty-six years not a single artificial intelligent signal or message from outer space was received. Some specialists try to downplay this negative result, arguing that so far only a small part of the entire spectrum has been covered, and that more time and more sophisticated equipment is required for arriving at a definite conclusion. Technological and economic criteria may thwart the possibility of extraterrestrial civilizations beaming signals into space over long stretches of time, without knowing where to direct their signals. Or, they may use communication methods unknown to us. Another explanation is that advanced ETI may lack interest in contacting other intelligences, especially those less developed. The argument of the Russian rocket expert Konstantin Tsiolkovski is often quoted: "Absence of evidence is not evidence of absence."

But neither of these arguments, which attempt to explain why we have not received a single intelligent signal from space, is convincing. True, future search projects may strike pay dirt and register the reception of a signal of verified artificial origin. But as long as no such evidence is forthcoming, the possibility of achieving success must be considered remote. If a hundred searches were unsuccessful, it is fair to deduce that estimates of a million or many thousands ETI are unsustainable propositions. As long as no breakthrough occurs, the probability of contact with ETI is near to zero. The argument that advanced extraterrestrials may not be interested in contact with other intelligences is also—as I will show—highly implausible.

Second, as recent research results demonstrate, many more factors and conditions than those considered by the Drake formula need to be taken into account. The geologist Peter D. Ward and the astronomer Donald Brownlee present in their book *Rare Earth* a series of such aspects, which turn the optimistic estimates of ETI upside down.

According to their reasoning, the old assumption that our solar system and Earth are quite common phenomena in the galaxy needs profound revision. On the contrary, the new insights suggest, we are much more special than thought. The evolution of life forms and eventually of intelligent life on Earth was due to a large number of very special conditions and developments, many of a coincidental nature. I'll mention only some that seem particularly important: The age, size, and composition of our sun, the location of Earth and inclination of its axis to it, the existence of water, a stable oxygen-rich atmosphere and temperature over long periods of time—factors considered essential for the evolution of life—and the development of a carbon-based chemistry. Furthermore an active interior and the existence of plate tectonics form the majestic mountain ridges like the Alps, the Himalayas and the Andes, creating different ecological conditions, propitious for the proliferation of a great variety of species. Also the existence of the Moon, Jupiter, and Saturn (as shields for the bombardment of comets and meteorites during the early stages of Earth). Also the repeated climatic changes, long ice ages, and especially the numerous and quite fortuitous catastrophes, causing the extinction of many species, like the one 65 million years ago, which led to the disappearance of dinosaurs but opened the way for more diversified and complex life forms.

Though first primitive life forms on Earth, the prokaryotic bacteria, evolved relatively rapidly, only about 500 million years after the cooling off of Earth's crust and the end of the dense bombardment of meteorites and comets, they were the only life forms during the first two billion years of Earth's 4.6-billion-year history. Mammals—including apes and man—developed much later, only after the extinction of the dinosaurs 65 million years ago. The first human-like being, the Proconsul, emerged in the Miocene Period, just about 18 million years ago. The Australopithecus, our antecessor, dates only 5 to 6 million years. In other words, it took almost 4 billion years, or more than 96 percent of the age of Earth, for intelligence to evolve—an awfully long time, even on the cosmic clock.

In this regard we should note also the caveat of the distinguished biologist Ernst Mayr, who underscored the enormous complexity of human DNA and RNA and their functions for the production of proteins, the basic building blocks of life. He estimated that the likelihood that similar biological developments may have occurred elsewhere in the universe was nil.

The upshot of these considerations is the following: Because of the very special geological, biological, and other conditions which propitiated the evolution of life and intelligence on Earth, similar developments in our galaxy are probably very rare. Primitive life forms, Ward and Brownlee conclude, may exist on planets of other stellar systems, but intelligent life, as ours, is probably very rare, if it exists at all.

Third is the so-called "Fermi Paradox," another powerful reason suggesting a skeptical evaluation of the multiplicity of intelligence in the galaxy. Italian physicist Enrico Fermi posed the annoying question, "If so many highly developed ETIs are out there, as SETI specialists claim, why haven't they contacted us?" I already expressed great doubt about some of the explanations given [for] this paradox. Here I need to focus on two more. The first refers to the supposed lack of interest of advanced aliens to establish contact with other intelligent beings. This argument seems to me particularly untrustworthy. I refer to a Norwegian book, which explains why the Vikings undertook dangerous voyages to far-away coasts in precarious vessels. "One reason," it says, "is fame, another curiosity, and a third, gain!" If the Vikings, driven by the desire to discover the unknown, reached America a thousand years ago with a primitive technology, if we—furthermore—a still scientifically and technically young civilization, search for primitive life on other planets of the solar system and their moons, it is incredible that higher developed extraterrestrial intelligences would not be spurred by likewise interests and yearnings. One of the fundamental traits of intelligence is its unquenchable intellectual curiosity and urge to penetrate the unknown. Elder civilizations, our peers in every respect, must be imbued by the same daring and scrutinizing spirit, because if they are not, they could not have achieved their advanced standards.

A second argument often posited is that distances between stars are too great for interstellar travel. But this explanation also stands on shaky ground. Even our scientifically and technically adolescent civilization is exploring space and sending probes—the Voyager crafts—which someday may reach other stellar systems. We are still far from achieving velocities, near the velocity of light, necessary for interstellar travel. But some scientists predict that in 200 or 300 years, maybe even earlier, we are likely to master low "c" velocities, and once we reach them, our civilization will send manned exploratory expeditions to the nearest stars. Automatic unmanned craft may be the initial attempts. But I am convinced that nothing will impede the desire of man to see other worlds with his own eyes, to touch their soil and to perform research that unmanned probes would not be able to perform. Evidently, civilizations tens of thousands or millions of years in our advance will have reached near c velocities, and they will be able to explore a considerable part of the galaxy. Advanced ETI

civilizations would engage in such explorations not only out of scientific curiosity, but in their own interest, for instance for spreading out and finding new habitats for their growing population, or because of the need to abandon their planet due to hazards from their star, and also because with the help of other civilizations it may confront dangers, lurking in the universe, more successfully than alone. The Fermi Paradox should therefore put us on guard, and foster a sound skepticism. Lack of interest in meeting a civilization such as ours is the least plausible reason why we have not heard from ETI.

A little mental experiment illustrates this point. Carl Sagan held once that intelligent aliens would visit Earth at least once every thousand years. But such visits have not taken place. Even extending this period to a million years, we fare no better. Let us assume an extraterrestrial craft landed on Earth any time during the era of the dinosaurs, lasting about 140 million years. It is only logical to assume the aliens would have returned at reasonable intervals to study our world and these fascinating animals, but also to find out if any one of them evolved the capability of reasoning, higher math, and building a civilization. There would have been reason for much surmise. According to paleontologists, Drake stresses, the dinosaur sauronithoides was endowed with such a potential. It was a dinosaur resembling a bird of our size and weight and possessing a mass of brain well above average, and, Drake speculates, if it had survived for an additional ten or twenty million years, it might have evolved into the first intelligent being on Earth. But it didn't happen, because the dinosaurs went extinct due to a cosmic catastrophe. When *Homo australopithecus*, then *Homo faber* and *habilis*, and lastly *Homo sapiens* evolved, shouldn't that have provoked on the part of visiting extraterrestrials a high level of interest? But no such visits are recorded. Only a few mythological, undocumented and highly suspect accounts of alleged visiting aliens exist. It is fair to assume, if advanced aliens had visited Earth during the past 200 million or, at least, during the past 16 million years, they would have left some durable, indestructible and recognizable mark, probably on the moon. But nothing has been detected. The most likely explanation? No such visits took place! There are no advanced extraterrestrial civilizations anywhere in our vicinity. If they existed, they already would have responded to our world's television signals, reaching some 60 light-years into space—another reason invalidating the claim that our galaxy is teeming with intelligence.

Another argument supporting the skeptical point of view sustained here is the fact that none of the detected planets around other stars comes close to having conditions apt for creating and sustaining life. Since Michel

Mayor's Swiss group discovered the first planet outside our solar system around the star 51 Pegasi ten years ago, about 130 other planets have been identified within a distance of 200 light-years. Research results show that most are of gaseous composition, some many times the size of Jupiter, some very close to their stars, very hot and with extremely rapid orbital cycles. So far, not one presents conditions favorable for the development of even the most primitive forms of life, not to speak of more complex species. Again it may be argued that only a very tiny fraction of planets were surveyed and future research might strike upon a suitable candidate. This may well be, and I would certainly welcome it. But so far the evidence fails to nourish optimistic expectations. The conditions in our universe are not as favorable for the evolution of life as optimists like to think.

Even if water or fossils of microorganisms should be found underneath the surface of Mars, the importance of such a finding for the theory of a multiplicity of inhabited worlds would be insignificant. Some astronomers think that Titan, the famous moon of Saturn, may have an ocean, possibly of methane. Primitive life forms may exist in it, but this remains to be seen. Even if it does, the evolutionary path from such primitive forms to complex life as human beings is—as we have seen—a long one, studded with a unique sequence of chance and catastrophes.

I am not claiming that we are probably the only intelligent species in our galaxy. Nor do I suggest that SETI activities are a waste of time and money. Though, so far, they have failed to obtain evidence for the existence of ETI, they enrich man's knowledge about the cosmos in many ways. They helped develop sophisticated search techniques, and they contribute decisively to the perception of man's cosmic destiny. Carl Sagan and Frank Drake, the two most distinguished pioneers of SETI, did ground breaking work. That their efforts and those of other dedicated SETI experts on behalf of this great cause are tinged with a dash of too optimistic expectation is understandable and profoundly human.

However, in the interest of science and sound skepticism, I believe it is time to take the new findings and insights into account, to dampen excessive SETI euphoria and to adopt a more pragmatic and down-to-earth stand, compatible with facts. We should quietly admit that the early estimates—that there may be a million, a hundred thousand, or ten thousand advanced extraterrestrial civilizations in our galaxy—may no longer be tenable. There might not be a hundred, not even ten such civilizations. The optimistic estimates were fraught with too many imponderables and speculative appraisals. What is required is to make contact with a single extraterrestrial intelligence, obtaining irrefutable, thoroughly verified evidence, either via electromagnetic or optical waves or via physical contact, that we are not the only intelligent species in the cosmos. Maybe an alien spacecraft, attracted by our signals, will decide to visit us some day, as I surmised in my novel *Contact: Are We Ready for It?* I would be the first one to react to such a contact event with great delight and satisfaction. The knowledge that we are not alone in the vast realm of the cosmos, and that it will be possible to establish a fruitful dialogue with other, possibly more advanced intelligent beings would mark the biggest event in human history. It would open the door to fantastic perspectives.

But SETI activities so far do not justify this hope. They recommend a more realistic and sober view. Considering the negative search results, the creation of excessive expectations is only grist to the mill of the naysayers—for instance, members of Congress who question the scientific standing of SETI, imputing to it wishful thinking, and denying it financial support. This absolutely negative approach to SETI is certainly wrong, because contrary to the UFO hoax, SETI (as UCLA space scientist Mark Moldwin stressed in a recent issue of this magazine) is based on solid scientific premises and considerations. But exaggerated estimates fail to conform to realities, as they are seen today, tending to backfire and create disappointment and a turning away from this fascinating scientific endeavor. The dream of mankind to find brethren in space may yet be fulfilled. If it is not, man should not feel sorry for his uniqueness. Rather that circumstance should boost the gratitude for his existence and his sense of responsibility for making the most of it.

PETER SCHENKEL is a retired political scientist interested in the question of what contact with advanced aliens would mean to humanity.

EXPLORING THE ISSUE

Will the Search for Extraterrestrial Life Ever Succeed?

Critical Thinking and Reflection

1. Why do SETI fans think searching for extraterrestrial signals is worth the effort?
2. Why do SETI critics think the effort is wasted?
3. If SETI researchers ever detect extraterrestrial signals, should they reply? If so, what should they say?
4. Why aren't real-life extraterrestrials likely to be much like the ones on TV and in the movies?

Is There Common Ground?

In the debate over this issue, there seems to be little common ground. One side thinks it worth continuing SETI. The other side says, "Forget it." But there are related areas of research, such as the search by astronomers for planets circling other stars, which to many have the ultimate goal of finding life-bearing worlds.

1. What are "exoplanets" and why do astronomers search for them? (http://planetquest.jpl.nasa.gov/; www.superwasp.org/exoplanets.htm)
2. One recent exoplanet discovery was briefly dubbed the "Goldilocks planet." Look up the term and discuss why both the astronomers and the media were excited.
3. To many people, the "Fermi Paradox" is no paradox at all. It posits that we have not been visited by aliens, but what about UFOs, the Roswell incident, alien abductions, and so on?

Why don't SETI researchers take such things seriously?

Additional Resources

Ronald D. Ekers, *SETI 2020: A Roadmap for the Search for Extraterrestrial Intelligence* (SETI Press, SETI Institute, 2002).

Michael D. Lemonick, "The Hunt for Life Beyond Earth," *National Geographic* (July 2014).

Alan Penny, "SETI: Peering into the Future," *Astronomy & Geophysics* (February 2011).

H. Paul Shuch, *Searching for Extraterrestrial Intelligence: SETI Past, Present, and Future* (Springer, 2011).

Douglas A. Vakoch, "Responsibility, Capability, and Active SETI: Policy, Law, Ethics, and Communication with Extraterrestrial Intelligence," *Acta Astronautica* (February 2011).

Internet References . . .

SETI at Home

http://setiathome.ssl.berkeley.edu/

SETI Institute

http://www.seti.org

The Allen Telescope Array

http://www.seti.org/ata

The Exoplanet Data Explorer

http://exoplanets.org/

Selected, Edited, and with Issue Framing Material by:
Thomas A. Easton, *Thomas College*

ISSUE

Should the United States Continue Its Human Spaceflight Program?

YES: Committee on Human Spaceflight, from "Pathways to Exploration: Rationales and Approaches for a U.S. Program of Human Space Exploration," National Academies Press (2014)

NO: Amitai Etzioni, from "Final Frontier vs. Fruitful Frontier: The Case for Increasing Ocean Exploration," *Issues in Science and Technology* (2014)

Learning Outcomes

After reading this issue, you will be able to:

- Explain the potential benefits of space exploration.
- Explain the potential benefits of ocean exploration.
- Argue both in favor of and against sending human beings on space missions.
- Explain how political and budgetary factors make it difficult to justify manned space exploration.

ISSUE SUMMARY

YES: The National Research Council's Committee on Human Spaceflight argues that the combination of the pragmatic benefits of and the human aspirations associated with human spaceflight are great enough to justify continuing the United States' human spaceflight program.

NO: Professor Amitai Etzioni argues that the Earth's oceans offer more potential discoveries, more resources for human use, and more contributions to national security and disaster preparedness than outer space. The exploration of space should be replaced by the exploration of the oceans, and the necessary budgetary resources should be taken from NASA.

The dream of conquering space has a long history. The Russian Konstantin Tsiolkovsky (1857–1935) and the American Robert H. Goddard (1882–1945), the pioneers of rocketry, dreamed of exploring other worlds, although neither lived long enough to see the first artificial satellite, the Soviet *Sputnik*, go up in 1957. That success sparked a race between America and the Soviet Union to be the first to achieve each step in the progression of space exploration. The next steps were to put dogs (the Soviet Laika was the first), monkeys, chimps, and finally human beings into orbit. Communications, weather, and spy satellites were designed and launched. And on July 20, 1969, the U.S. Apollo Program landed the first men on the moon.

There were a few more *Apollo* landings, but not many. The United States had achieved its main political goal of beating the Soviets to the moon and, in the minds of the government, demonstrating the United States' superiority. Thereafter, the United States was content to send automated spacecraft (computer-operated robots) off to observe Venus, Mars, and the rings of Saturn; to land on Mars and study its soil; and even to carry recordings of Earth's sights and sounds past the distant edge of the solar system, perhaps to be retrieved in the distant future by intelligent life from some other world. (Those recordings are attached to the *Voyager* spacecraft, launched in 1977; published as a combination of CD, CD-ROM, and book, *Murmurs of Earth: The Voyager Interstellar Record*

[Ballantine, 1978; available from Amazon]). Humans have not left near-Earth orbit for two decades, even though space technology has continued to develop. The results of this development include communications satellites, space shuttles, space stations, and independent robotic explorers such as the *Mariners* and *Vikings,* the Mars rovers *Spirit, Opportunity,* and *Curiosity,* and the polar lander *Phoenix,* which finally found water on Mars in July 2008.

Why has human space exploration gone no further to date? One reason is that robots are now extremely capable. Although some robot spacecraft have failed partially or completely, there have been many grand successes that have added enormously to humanity's knowledge of Earth and other planets. Another is money: Lifting robotic explorers into space is expensive, but lifting people into space—along with all the food, water, air, and other supplies necessary to keep them alive for the duration of a mission—is much more expensive. And there are many people in government and elsewhere who cry that there are many better ways to spend the money on Earth.

Still another reason for the reduction in human space travel seems to be the fear that astronauts will die in space. This point was emphasized by the explosion on takeoff of the space shuttle *Challenger* in January 1986, which killed seven astronauts and froze the entire shuttle program for over two and a half years. The point was reinforced by the breakup of *Columbia* on entry February 1, 2003. After the latter event, the public reaction included many calls for an end to such risky, expensive enterprises. See Jerry Grey, "Columbia—Aftermath of a Tragedy," *Aerospace America* (March 2003); John Byron, "Is Manned Space Flight Worth It?" *Proceedings* (of the U. S. Naval Institute) (March 2003) (and Richard H. Truly's response in the May issue); and "Manned or Unmanned into Space?" *USA Today* (February 26, 2003), among many others. Robert Zubrin, "How Much Is an Astronaut's Life Worth?" *Reason* (February 2012), argues that risk is an inescapable part of manned spaceflight and the refusal to accept risk has hamstrung the space program. "Human spaceflight vehicles . . . are daring ships of exploration that need to sail in harm's way if they are to accomplish a mission critical to the human future. The mission needs to come first."

In 2004 when President George W. Bush announced his plan to send humans to the Moon and Mars, beginning as soon as 2015, the reaction was immediate. James A. Van Allen asked "Is Human Spaceflight Obsolete?" in *Issues in Science and Technology* (Summer 2004). Andrew Lawler asked "How Much Space for Science?" in *Science* (January 30, 2004). Physicist and Nobel laureate

Steven Weinberg, "The Wrong Stuff," *New York Review of Books* (April 8, 2004), argued that nothing needs doing in space that cannot be done without human presence. Until we find something that does need humans on the scene, there is no particular reason to send humans—at great expense—into space.

John Derbyshire, "Space Is for Science," *National Review* (June 5, 2006), argues that the expense and hazards of putting humans in space do not justify the benefits when much cheaper automated spacecraft (robots) can make all necessary observations. Paul D. Spudis, "Who Should Explore Space? Astronaut Explorers Can Perform Science in Space that Robots Cannot," *Scientific American* (Special Edition, January 2008), argues that there is no substitute for human astronauts in installing and maintaining equipment and in conducting field exploration because humans provide skills that are unlikely to be automated in the foreseeable future. Francis Slakey, "Who Should Explore Space? Unmanned Spacecraft Are Exploring the Solar System More Cheaply and Effectively than Astronauts Are," *Scientific American* (Special Edition, January 2008), argues that NASA sends humans into space chiefly for public relations purposes. Unmanned probes are much cheaper and more effective than astronauts, and many scientific organizations have recommended that *space* science should instead be done through robotic and telescopic missions. See also Louis D. Friedman and G. Scott Hubbard, "Examining the Vision," *American Scientist* (July/August 2008).

The question of whether robots can do the job is particularly relevant because of the success of the Mars rovers, *Spirit, Opportunity,* and *Curiosity.* If robots continue to be successful, it seems likely that efforts to promote manned space travel will meet resistance. Funding for space exploration remains low largely because problems on Earth (environmental and other) seem to need money more urgently than space exploration projects do. The prospects for manned space expeditions to the moon, Mars, or other worlds seem very dim, although Paul D. Spudis, "Harvest the Moon," *Astronomy* (June 2003), argues that there are four good reasons for putting people at least on the Moon: "The first motivation to revisit the Moon is that its rocks hold the early history of our own planet and the solar system. Next, its unique environment and properties make it an ideal vantage point for observing the universe. The Moon is also a natural space station where we can learn how to live off-planet. And finally, it gives us an extraterrestrial filling station, with resources to use both locally and in near-Earth space." See also Paul D. Spudis, "The New Moon,"

Scientific American (December 2003). Nader Elhefnawy, "Beyond *Columbia*: Is There a Future for Humanity in Space?" *The Humanist* (September/October 2003), says that we cannot ignore the wealth of resources in space. Alex Ellery, "Humans versus Robots for Space Exploration and Development," *Space Policy* (May 2003), argues that "though robotics and artificial intelligence are becoming more sophisticated, they will not be able to deal with 'thinking-on-one's-feet' tasks that require generalisations from past experience. . . . there will be a critical role for humans in space for the foreseeable future." Carl Gethmann, "Manned Space Travel as a Cultural Mission," *Poiesis & Praxis* (December 2006), argues that costs should not be used to reject manned space travel as a pointless option. The dream and the effort are part of our culture, and we should pursue them as far as we can afford to. Arthur Woods, "The Space Option," *Leonardo* (vol. 41, no. 4, 2008), argues that space resources are the most realistic way to ensure future human survival and success.

Jeff Foust, "The Future of Human Spaceflight," *Technology Review* (January/February 2010), summarizes the report of the Augustine Commission (*Seeking a Human Spaceflight Program Worthy of a Great Nation*, October 2009, http://www.nasa.gov/pdf/396093main_HSF_Cmte_FinalReport .pdf) and argues that the ultimate goal of manned space exploration is to "chart a path for human expansion into the solar system." To support that goal will require extending the life of the International Space Station (ISS), providing more funding for mission development, and encouraging the private sector to take over transportation to and from the ISS. At present, human spaceflight is not sustainable. Early in 2010, President Barack Obama announced plans to cancel existing plans for a new launch system that would replace the present Space Shuttle, shift support missions for the International Space Station to commercial spaceflight companies, and to start work on a new system that would be able to support missions to asteroids and even Mars; see Andrew Lawler, "Obama Backs New Launcher and Bigger NASA Budget," *Science* (January 1, 2010). In May 2012, the first commercial flight—the unmanned SpaceX Dragon—successfully reached the International Space Station; see "SpaceX Dragon Triumph: Only the Beginning," *CNN online* (May 25, 2012) (http://lightyears.blogs.cnn.com/2012/05/25 /spacex-orbital-mission-just-the-beginning/).

In the YES selection, the National Research Council's Committee on Human Spaceflight argues that the combination of the pragmatic benefits of and the human aspirations associated with human spaceflight are great enough to justify continuing the United States' human spaceflight program. In the NO selection, Professor Amitai Etzioni argues that the Earth's oceans offer more potential discoveries, more resources for human use, and more contributions to national security and disaster preparedness than outer space. The exploration of space should be replaced by the exploration of the oceans, and the necessary budgetary resources should be taken from NASA.

YES

Committee on Human Spaceflight

Pathways to Exploration: Rationales and Approaches for a U.S. Program of Human Space Exploration

Summary

The United States has publicly funded its human space-flight program continuously for more than a halfcentury. Today, the United States is the major partner in a massive orbital facility, the International Space Station (ISS), that is a model for how U.S. leadership can engage nations through soft power and that is becoming the focal point for the first tentative steps in commercial cargo and crewed orbital spaceflights. Yet, a national consensus on the long-term future of human spaceflight beyond our commitment to the ISS remains elusive.

The task for the Committee on Human Spaceflight originated in the National Aeronautics and Space Administration [NASA] Authorization Act of 2010, which required that the National Academies perform a human-spaceflight study that would review "the goals, core capabilities, and direction of human space flight." The explicit examination of rationales, along with the identification of enduring questions, set the task apart from numerous similar studies performed over the preceding several decades, as did the requirement that the committee bring broad public and stakeholder input into its considerations. The complex mix of historical achievement and uncertain future made the task faced by the committee extraordinarily challenging and multidimensional. Nevertheless, the committee has come to agree on a set of major conclusions and recommendations, which are summarized here.

Enduring Questions

Enduring questions are questions that serve as motivators of aspiration, scientific endeavors, debate, and critical thinking in the realm of human spaceflight. The questions endure in that any answers available today are at best provisional and will change as more exploration is done. Enduring questions provide motivations that are immune to external forces and policy shifts. They are intended not only to stand the test of time but also to continue to drive work forward in the face of technological, societal, and economic constraints. Enduring questions are clear and intrinsically connect to broadly shared human experience. . . . The committee asserts that the enduring questions motivating human spaceflight are these:

- How far from Earth can humans go?
- What can humans discover and achieve when we get there?

Rationales for Human Spaceflight and the Public Interest

All the arguments that the committee heard in support of human spaceflight have been used in various forms and combinations to justify the program for many years. In the committee's view, these rationales can be divided into two sets. Pragmatic rationales involve economic benefits, contributions to national security, contributions to national stature and international relations, inspiration for students and citizens to further their science and engineering education, and contributions to science. Aspirational rationales involve the eventual survival of the human species (through off-Earth settlement) and shared human destiny and the aspiration to explore. In reviewing the rationales, the committee concluded as follows:

- *Economic matters.* There is no widely accepted, robust quantitative methodology to support comparative assessments of the returns on investment in federal R&D programs in different economic sectors and fields of research. Nevertheless, it is clear that the NASA human spaceflight program, like other government R&D programs, has stimulated economic activity and has advanced development of new products and technologies that have had or may in the future generate significant economic impacts. It is impossible, however, to develop a reliable comparison of the returns on spaceflight versus other government R&D investment.

- *Security*. Space-based assets and programs are an important element of national security, but the direct contribution of human spaceflight in this realm has been and is likely to remain limited. An active U.S. human spaceflight program gives the United States a stronger voice in an international code of conduct for space, enhances U.S. soft power, and supports collaborations with other nations; thus, it contributes to our national interests, including security.

- *National stature and international relations*. Being a leader in human space exploration enhances international stature and national pride. Because the work is complex and expensive, it can benefit from international cooperative efforts. Such cooperation has important geopolitical benefits.

- *Education and inspiration*. The United States needs scientists and engineers and a public that has a strong understanding of science. The challenge and excitement of space missions can serve as an inspiration for students and citizens to engage with science and engineering although it is difficult to measure this. The path to becoming a scientist or engineer requires much more than the initial inspiration. Many who work in space fields, however, report the importance of such inspiration, although it is difficult to separate the contributions of human and robotic spaceflight.

- *Scientific discovery*. The relative benefits of robotic versus human efforts in space science are constantly shifting as a result of changes in technology, cost, and risk. The current capabilities of robotic planetary explorers, such as Curiosity and Cassini, are such that although they can go farther, go sooner, and be much less expensive than human missions to the same locations, they cannot match the flexibility of humans to function in complex environments, to improvise, and to respond quickly to new discoveries. Such constraints may change some day.

- *Human survival*. It is not possible to say whether human off-Earth settlements could eventually be developed that would outlive human presence on Earth and lengthen the survival of our species. That question can be answered only by pushing the human frontier in space.

- *Shared destiny and aspiration to explore*. The urge to explore and to reach challenging goals is a common human characteristic. Space is today a major physical frontier for such exploration and aspiration. Some say that it is human destiny to continue to explore space. While not all share this view, for those who do it is an important reason to engage in human spaceflight.

. . . The pragmatic rationales have never seemed adequate by themselves, perhaps because the benefits that they argue for are not unique to human spaceflight. Those that are—the aspirational rationales related to the human destiny to explore and the survival of the human species—are also the rationales most tied to the enduring questions. Whereas the committee concluded from its review and assessment that no single rationale alone seems to justify the costs and risks of pursuing human spaceflight, the aspirational rationales, when supplemented by the practical benefits associated with the pragmatic rationales, do, in the committee's judgment, argue for a continuation of our nation's human spaceflight program, provided that the pathways and decision rules recommended by the committee are adopted (see below).

The level of public interest in space exploration is modest relative to interest in other public-policy issues such as economic issues, education, and medical or scientific discoveries. Public opinion about space has been generally favorable over the past 50 years, but much of the public is inattentive to space exploration, and spending on space exploration does not have high priority for most of the public.

Horizon Goal

The technical analysis completed for this study shows clearly that for the foreseeable future the only feasible destinations for human exploration are the Moon, asteroids, Mars, and the moons of Mars. Among that small set of plausible goals for human space exploration,[1] the most distant and difficult is a landing by human beings on the surface of Mars; it would require overcoming unprecedented technical risk, fiscal risk, and programmatic challenges. Thus, the "horizon goal" for human space exploration is Mars. All long-range space programs, by all potential partners, for human space exploration converge on that goal.

Policy Challenges

A program of human space exploration beyond low Earth orbit (LEO) that satisfies the pathway principles defined below is not sustainable with a budget that increases only enough to keep pace with inflation. . . . The current program to develop launch vehicles and spacecraft for flight beyond LEO cannot provide the flight frequency required to maintain competence and safety, does not possess the "stepping-stone" architecture that allows the public to see the connection between the horizon goal and near-term accomplishments, and may discourage potential international partners.

Because policy goals do not lead to sustainable programs unless they also reflect or change programmatic, technical, and budgetary realities, the committee notes that those who are formulating policy goals will need to keep the following factors in mind:

- Any defensible calculation of tangible, quantifiable benefits—spinoff technologies, attraction of talent to scientific careers, scientific knowledge, and so on—is unlikely ever to demonstrate a positive economic return on the massive investments required by human spaceflight.
- The arguments that triggered the Apollo investments—national defense and prestige—seem to have especially limited public salience in today's post-Cold War America.
- Although the public is mostly positive about NASA and its spaceflight programs, increased spending on spaceflight has low priority for most Americans. However, although most Americans do not follow the issue closely, those who pay more attention are more supportive of space exploration.

International Collaboration

International collaboration has become an integral part of the space policy of essentially all nations that participate in space activities around the world. Most countries now rarely initiate and carry out substantial space projects without some foreign participation. The reasons for collaboration are multiple, but countries, including the United States, cooperate principally when they benefit from it.

It is evident that near-term U.S. goals for human exploration are not aligned with those of our traditional international partners. Although most major spacefaring nations and agencies are looking toward the Moon, specifically the lunar surface, U.S. plans are focused on redirection of an asteroid into a retrograde lunar orbit where astronauts would conduct operations with it. It is also evident that given the rapid development of China's capabilities in space, it is in the best interests of the United States to be open to its inclusion in future international partnerships. In particular, current federal law that prevents

NASA from participating in bilateral activities with the Chinese serves only to hinder U.S. ability to bring China into its sphere of international partnerships and substantially reduces the potential international capability that might be pooled to reach Mars. Also, given the scale of the endeavor of a mission to Mars, contributions by international partners would have to be of unprecedented magnitude to defray a significant portion of the cost. . . .

Recommendations for a Pathways Approach

NASA and its international and commercial partners have developed an infrastructure in LEO that is approaching maturity—that is, assembly of the ISS is essentially complete. The nation must now decide whether to embark on human space exploration beyond LEO in a sustained and sustainable fashion. Having considered past and current space policy, explored the international setting, articulated the enduring questions and rationales, and identified public and stakeholder opinions, the committee drew on all this information to ask a fundamental question: What type of human spaceflight program would be responsive to these factors? The committee argues that it is a program in which humans operate beyond LEO on a regular basis—a sustainable human exploration program beyond LEO.

A sustainable program of human deep-space exploration requires an ultimate horizon goal that provides a long-term focus that is less likely to be disrupted by major technological failures and accidents along the way or by the vagaries of the political process and the economic scene. There is a consensus in national space policy, international coordination groups, and the public imagination for Mars as a major goal for human space exploration. NASA can sustain a human space-exploration program that pursues the horizon goal of a surface landing on Mars with meaningful milestones and simultaneously reassert U.S. leadership in space while allowing ample opportunity for substantial international collaboration—but only if the program has elements that are built in a logical sequence and if it can fund a frequency of flights sufficiently high to ensure the maintenance of proficiency among ground personnel, mission controllers, and flight crews. In the pursuit of that goal, NASA needs to engage in the type of mission planning and related technology development that address mission requirements and integration and develop high-priority capabilities, such as entry, descent, and landing for Mars; radiation safety;

and advanced in-space propulsion and power. Progress in human exploration beyond LEO will be measured in decades with costs measured in hundreds of billions of dollars and significant risk to human life.

In addition, the committee has concluded that the best way to ensure a stable, sustainable human-spaceflight program that pursues the rationales and enduring questions that the committee has identified is to develop a program through the rigorous application of a set of pathway principles. The committee's highest-priority recommendation is as follows:

NASA should adopt the following pathway principles:

I. Commit to designing, maintaining, and pursuing the execution of an exploration pathway beyond low Earth orbit toward a clear horizon goal that addresses the "enduring questions" for human spaceflight.

II. Engage international space agencies early in the design and development of the pathway on the basis of their ability and willingness to contribute.

III. Define steps on the pathway that foster sustainability and maintain progress on achieving the pathway's long-term goal of reaching the horizon destination.

IV. Seek continuously to engage new partners that can solve technical or programmatic impediments to progress.

V. Create a risk-mitigation plan to sustain the selected pathway when unforeseen technical or budgetary problems arise. Such a plan should include points at which decisions are made to move to a less ambitious pathway (referred to as an "off-ramp") or to stand down the program.

VI. Establish exploration pathway characteristics that maximize the overall scientific, cultural, economic, political, and inspirational benefits without sacrificing progress toward the long-term goal, namely,

a. The horizon and intermediate destinations have profound scientific, cultural, economic, inspirational, or geopolitical benefits that justify public investment.

b. The sequence of missions and destinations permits stakeholders, including taxpayers, to see progress and to develop confidence in NASA's ability to execute the pathway.

c. The pathway is characterized by logical feed-forward of technical capabilities.

d. The pathway minimizes the use of dead-end mission elements that do not contribute to later destinations on the pathway.

e. The pathway is affordable without incurring unacceptable development risk.

f. The pathway supports, in the context of available budget, an operational tempo that ensures retention of critical technical capability, proficiency of operators, and effective use of infrastructure.

The pathway principles will need to be supported by a set of operational decision rules as NASA, the administration, and Congress face inevitable programmatic challenges along a selected pathway. The decision rules that the committee has developed provide operational guidance that can be applied when major technical, cost, and schedule issues arise as NASA progresses along a pathway. Because many decisions will have to be made before any program of record is approved and initiated, the decision rules have been designed to provide the framework for a sustainable program through the lifetime of the selected pathway. They are designed to allow a program to stay within the constraints that are accepted and developed when the pathway principles are applied. The committee recommends that,

Whereas the overall pathway scope and cost are defined by application of the pathway principles, once a program is on a pathway, technical, cost, or schedule problems that arise should be addressed by the administration, NASA, and Congress by applying the following decision rules:

A. If the appropriated funding level and 5-year budget projection do not permit execution of a pathway within the established schedule, do not start down that pathway.

B. If a budget profile does not permit the chosen pathway, even if NASA is well along on it, take an "off-ramp."

C. If the U.S. human spaceflight program receives an unexpected increase in budget for human spaceflight, NASA, the administration, and Congress should not redefine the pathway in such a way that continued budget increases are required for the pathway's sustainable execution; rather, the increase in funds should be applied to rapid retirement of important technology risks or to an increase in operational tempo in pursuit of the pathway's previously defined technical and exploration goals.

D. Given that limitations on funding will require difficult choices in the development of major new technologies and capabilities, give high priority to choices that solve important technological shortcomings, that reduce overall program cost, that allow an acceleration of the schedule, or that reduce developmental or operational risk.

E. If there are human spaceflight program elements, infrastructure, or organizations that are no longer contributing to progress along the pathway, the human spaceflight program should divest itself of them as soon as possible.

Recommendations for Implementing a Sustainable Program

The committee was not charged to recommend and has not recommended any particular pathway or set of destination targets. The recommended pathways approach combines a strategic framework with practical guidance that is designed to stabilize human space exploration and to encourage political and programmatic coherence over time.

If the United States is to have a human space-exploration program, it must be worthy of the considerable cost to the nation and great risk of life. The committee has found no single practical rationale that is uniquely compelling to justify such investment and risk. Rather, human space exploration must be undertaken for inspirational and aspirational reasons that appeal to a broad array of U.S. citizens and policy-makers and that identify and align the United States with technical achievement and sophistication while demonstrating its capability to lead or work within an international coalition for peaceful purposes. Given the expense of any human spaceflight program and the substantial risk to the crews involved, it is the committee's view that the only pathways that fit those criteria are ones that ultimately place humans on other worlds.

Although the committee's recommendation to adopt a pathways approach is made without prejudice as to which particular pathway might be followed, it was clear to the committee from its independent analysis of several pathways that a return to extended surface operations on the Moon would make substantial contributions to a strategy ultimately aimed at landing people on Mars and would probably provide a broad array of opportunities for international and commercial cooperation. No matter which pathway is selected, the successful implementation of any plan developed in concert with a pathways approach and decision rules will rest on several other conditions. In addition to its highest-priority recommendation of the pathways approach and decision rules, the committee offers the following priority-ordered recommendations as being the ones that are most critical to the development and implementation of a sustainable human space-exploration program.

NASA should

1. Commit to design, maintain, and pursue the extension of human presence beyond low Earth orbit (LEO). This step should include
   a. Committing NASA's human spaceflight asset base, both physical and human, to this effort.
   b. Redirecting human spaceflight resources as needed to include improving program-management efficiency (including establishing and managing to appropriate levels of risk), eliminating obsolete facilities, and consolidating remaining infrastructure where possible.

2. Maintain long-term focus on Mars as the horizon goal for human space exploration, addressing the enduring questions for human spaceflight: How far from Earth can humans go? What can humans do and achieve when we get there?

3. Establish and implement the pathways approach so as to maximize the overall scientific, cultural, economic, political, and inspirational benefits of individual milestones and to conduct meaningful work at each step along the pathway without sacrificing progress toward long-term goals.

4. Vigorously pursue opportunities for international and commercial collaboration in order to leverage financial resources and capabilities of other nations and commercial entities. International collaboration would be open to the inclusion of China and potentially other emerging space powers in addition to traditional international partners. Specifically, future collaborations in major new endeavors should seek to incorporate
   a. A level of overall cost-sharing that is appropriate to the true partnerships that will be necessary to pursue pathways beyond LEO.
   b. Shared decision-making with partners, including a detailed analysis, in concert

with international partners, of the implications for human exploration of continuing the International Space Station beyond 2024.

5. Engage in planning that includes mission requirements and a systems architecture that target funded high-priority technology development, most critically
   a. Entry, descent, and landing for Mars.
   b. Advanced in-space propulsion and power.
   c. Radiation safety.

In this report the committee has provided guidance on how a pathways approach might be successfully pursued and the likely costs of the pathways if things go well. However, the committee also concludes that if the resulting plan is not appropriately financed, it will not succeed. Nor can it succeed without a sustained commitment on the part of those who govern the nation—a commitment that does not change direction with succeeding electoral cycles. Those branches of government—executive and legislative—responsible for NASA's funding and guidance are therefore critical enablers of the nation's investment and achievements in human spaceflight, commissioning and financing plans and then ensuring that the leadership, personnel, governance, and resources are in place at NASA and in other federally funded laboratories and facilities to advance it.

Note

1 Although there is no strictly defined distinction between human spaceflight and human space exploration, the committee takes the latter to mean spaceflight beyond low Earth orbit, in which the goal is to have humans venture into the cosmos to discover new things.

THE COMMITTEE ON HUMAN SPACEFLIGHT of the Aeronautics and Space Engineering Board, Space Studies Board, Division on Engineering and Physical Sciences, of the National Research Council, was charged with assessing the goals, core capabilities, and direction of human spaceflight as directed by the National Aeronautics and Space Administration (NASA) Authorization Act of 2010.

Amitai Etzioni

 **NO**

Final Frontier vs. Fruitful Frontier: The Case for Increasing Ocean Exploration

Possible solutions to the world's energy, food, environmental, and other problems are far more likely to be found in nearby oceans than in distant space.

Every year, the federal budget process begins with a White House-issued budget request, which lays out spending priorities for federal programs. From this moment forward, President Obama and his successors should use this opportunity to correct a longstanding misalignment of federal research priorities: excessive spending on space exploration and neglect of ocean studies. The nation should begin transforming the National Oceanic and Atmospheric Administration (NOAA) into a greatly reconstructed, independent, and effective federal agency. In the present fiscal climate of zero-sum budgeting, the additional funding necessary for this agency should be taken from the National Aeronautics and Space Administration (NASA).

The basic reason is that deep space—NASA's favorite turf—is a distant, hostile, and barren place, the study of which yields few major discoveries and an abundance of overhyped claims. By contrast, the oceans are nearby, and their study is a potential source of discoveries that could prove helpful for addressing a wide range of national concerns from climate change to disease; for reducing energy, mineral, and potable water shortages; for strengthening industry, security, and defenses against natural disasters such as hurricanes and tsunamis; for increasing our knowledge about geological history; and much more. Nevertheless, the funding allocated for NASA in the Consolidated and Further Continuing Appropriations Act for FY 2013 was 3.5 times higher than that allocated for NOAA. Whatever can be said on behalf of a trip to Mars or recent aspirations to revisit the Moon, the same holds many times over for exploring the oceans; some illustrative examples follow. (I stand by my record: In *The Moondoggle*, published in 1964, I predicted that there was less to be gained in deep space than in near space—the sphere in which communication, navigations, weather, and reconnaissance satellites orbit—and argued for unmanned exploration vehicles and for investment on our planet instead of the Moon.)

Climate

There is wide consensus in the international scientific community that the Earth is warming; that the net effects of this warming are highly negative; and that the main cause of this warming is human actions, among which carbon dioxide emissions play a key role. Hence, curbing these CO_2 emissions or mitigating their effects is a major way to avert climate change.

Space exploration advocates are quick to claim that space might solve such problems on Earth. In some ways, they are correct; NASA does make helpful contributions to climate science by way of its monitoring programs, which measure the atmospheric concentrations and emissions of greenhouse gases and a variety of other key variables on the Earth and in the atmosphere. However, there seem to be no viable solutions to climate change that involve space.

By contrast, it is already clear that the oceans offer a plethora of viable solutions to the Earth's most pressing troubles. For example, scientists have already demonstrated that the oceans serve as a "carbon sink." The oceans have absorbed almost one-third of anthropogenic CO_2 emitted since the advent of the industrial revolution and have the potential to continue absorbing a large share of the CO_2 released into the atmosphere. Researchers are exploring a variety of chemical, biological, and physical geoengineering projects to increase the ocean's capacity to absorb carbon. Additional federal funds should be allotted to determine the feasibility and safety of these projects and then to develop and implement any that are found acceptable.

Iron fertilization or "seeding" of the oceans is perhaps the most well-known of these projects. Just as CO_2 is used by plants during photosynthesis, CO_2 dissolved in the oceans is absorbed and similarly used by autotrophic algae and other phytoplankton. The process "traps" the carbon in the phytoplankton; when the organism dies, it sinks to the sea floor, sequestering the carbon in the biogenic "ooze" that covers large swaths of the seafloor. However, many areas of the ocean high in the nutrients and sunlight necessary for phytoplankton to thrive lack a mineral vital to the phytoplankton's survival: iron. Adding iron to the ocean has been shown to trigger phytoplankton blooms, and thus iron fertilization might increase the CO_2 that phytoplankton will absorb. Studies note that the location and species of phytoplankton are poorly understood variables that affect the efficiency with which iron fertilization leads to the sequestration of CO_2. In other words, the efficiency of iron fertilization could be improved with additional research. Proponents of exploring this option estimate that it could enable us to sequester CO_2 at a cost of between \$2 and \$30/ton—far less than the cost of scrubbing CO_2 directly from the air or from power plant smokestacks—\$1,000/ton and \$50-100/ton, respectively, according to one Stanford study.

Despite these promising findings, there are a number of challenges that prevent us from using the oceans as a major means of combating climate change. First, ocean "sinks" have already absorbed an enormous amount of CO_2. It is not known how much more the oceans can actually absorb, because ocean warming seems to be altering the absorptive capacity of the oceans in unpredictable ways. It is further largely unknown how the oceans interact with the nitrogen cycle and other relevant processes.

Second, the impact of CO_2 sequestration on marine ecosystems remains underexplored. The Joint Ocean Commission Initiative, which noted in a 2013 report that absorption of CO_2 is "acidifying" the oceans, recommended that "the administration and Congress should take actions to measure and assess the emerging threat of ocean acidification, better understand the complex dynamics causing and exacerbating it, work to determine its impact, and develop mechanisms to address the problem." The Department of Energy specifically calls for greater "understanding of ocean biogeochemistry" and of the likely impact of carbon injection on ocean acidification. Since the mid-18th century, the acidity of the surface of the ocean, measured by the water's concentration of hydrogen ions, has increased by 30% on average, with negative consequences for mollusks, other calcifying

organisms, and the ecosystems they support, according to the Blue Ribbon Panel on Ocean Acidification. Different ecosystems have also been found to exhibit different levels of pH variance, with certain areas such as the California coastline experiencing higher levels of pH variability than elsewhere. The cost worldwide of mollusk-production losses alone could reach \$100 billion if acidification is not countered, says Monica Contestabile, an environmental economist and editor of *Nature Climate Change*. Much remains to be learned about whether and how carbon sequestration methods like iron fertilization could contribute to ocean acidification; it is, however, clearly a crucial subject of study given the dangers of climate change.

Food

Ocean products, particularly fish, are a major source of food for major parts of the world. People now eat four times as much fish, on average, as they did in 1950. The world's catch of wild fish reached an all-time high of 86.4 million tons in 1996; although it has since declined, the world's wild marine catch remained 78.9 million tons in 2011. Fish and mollusks provide an "important source of protein for a billion of the poorest people on Earth, and about three billion people get 15 percent or more of their annual protein from the sea," says Matthew Huelsenbeck, a marine scientist affiliated with the ocean conservation organization Oceana. Fish can be of enormous value to malnourished people because of its high levels of micronutrients such as Vitamin A, Iron, Zinc, Calcium, and healthy fats.

However, many scientists have raised concerns about the ability of wild fish stocks to survive such exploitation. The Food and Agriculture Organization of the United Nations estimated that 28% of fish stocks were overexploited worldwide and a further 3% were depleted in 2008. Other sources estimate that 30% of global fisheries are overexploited or worse. There have been at least four severe documented fishery collapses—in which an entire region's population of a fish species is overfished to the point of being incapable of replenishing itself, leading to the species' virtual disappearance from the area—worldwide since 1960, a report from the International Risk Governance Council found. Moreover, many present methods of fishing cause severe environmental damage; for example, the *Economist* reported that bottom trawling causes up to 15,400 square miles of "dead zone" daily through hypoxia caused by stirring up phosphorus and other sediments.

There are several potential approaches to dealing with overfishing. One is aquaculture. Marine fish cultivated through aquaculture is reported to cost less than other animal proteins and does not consume limited freshwater sources. Furthermore, aquaculture has been a stable source of food from 1970 to 2006; that is, it consistently expanded and was very rarely subject to unexpected shocks. From 1992 to 2006 alone, aquaculture expanded from 21.2 to 66.8 million tons of product.

Although aquaculture is rapidly expanding—more than 60% from 2000 to 2008—and represented more than 40% of global fisheries production in 2006, a number of challenges require attention if aquaculture is to significantly improve worldwide supplies of food. First, scientists have yet to understand the impact of climate change on aquaculture and fishing. Ocean acidification is likely to damage entire ecosystems, and rising temperatures cause marine organisms to migrate away from their original territory or die off entirely. It is important to study the ways that these processes will likely play out and how their effects might be mitigated. Second, there are concerns that aquaculture may harm wild stocks of fish or the ecosystems in which they are raised through overcrowding, excess waste, or disease. This is particularly true where aquaculture is devoted to growing species alien to the region in which they are produced. Third, there are few industry standard operating practices (SOPs) for aquaculture; additional research is needed for developing these SOPs, including types and sources of feed for species cultivated through aquaculture. Finally, in order to produce a stable source of food, researchers must better understand how biodiversity plays a role in preventing the sudden collapse of fisheries and develop best practices for fishing, aquaculture, and reducing bycatch.

On the issue of food, NASA is atypically mum. It does not claim it will feed the world with whatever it finds or plans to grow on Mars, Jupiter, or any other place light years away. The oceans are likely to be of great help.

Energy

NASA and its supporters have long held that its work can help address the Earth's energy crises. One NASA project calls for developing low-energy nuclear reactors (LENRs) that use weak nuclear force to create energy, but even NASA admits that "we're still many years away" from large-scale commercial production. Another project envisioned orbiting space-based solar power (SBSP) that would transfer energy wirelessly to Earth. The idea was proposed in the 1960s by then-NASA scientist Peter Glaser and has since been revisited by NASA; from 1995 to 2000, NASA actively investigated the viability of SBSP. Today, the project is no longer actively funded by NASA, and SBSP remains commercially unviable due to the high cost of launching and maintaining satellites and the challenges of wirelessly transmitting energy to Earth.

Marine sources of renewable energy, by contrast, rely on technology that is generally advanced; these technologies deserve additional research to make them fully commercially viable. One possible ocean renewable energy source is wave energy conversion, which uses the up-and-down motion of waves to generate electrical energy. Potentially-useable global wave power is estimated to be two terawatts, the equivalent of about 200 large power stations or about 10% of the entire world's predicted energy demand for 2020 according to the *World Ocean Review*. In the United States alone, wave energy is estimated to be capable of supplying fully one-third of the country's energy needs.

A modern wave energy conversion device was made in the 1970s and was known as the Salter's Duck; it produced electricity at a whopping cost of almost $1/kWh. Since then, wave energy conversion has become vastly more commercially viable. A report from the Department of Energy in 2009 listed nine different designs in pre-commercial development or already installed as pilot projects around the world. As of 2013, as many as 180 companies are reported to be developing wave or tidal energy technologies; one device, the Anaconda, produces electricity at a cost of $0.24/kWh. The United States Department of Energy and the National Renewable Energy Laboratory jointly maintain a website that tracks the average cost/kWh of various energy sources; on average, ocean energy overall must cost about $0.23/kWh to be profitable. Some projects have been more successful; the prototype LIMPET wave energy conversion technology currently operating on the coast of Scotland produces wave energy at the price of $0.07/kWh. For comparison, the average consumer in the United States paid $0.12/kWh in 2011. Additional research could further reduce the costs.

Other options in earlier stages of development include using turbines to capture the energy of ocean currents. The technology is similar to that used by wind energy; water moving through a stationary turbine turns the blades, generating electricity. However, because water is so much denser than air, "for the same surface area, water moving 12 miles per hour exerts the same amount of force as a constant 110 mph wind," says the Bureau of Ocean Energy Management (BOEM), a division of the Department of the Interior. (Another estimate from a separate BOEM report holds that a 3.5 mph current "has the kinetic energy of winds in excess of [100 mph].") BOEM

Should the United States Continue Its Human Spaceflight Program? by Easton

further estimates that total worldwide power potential from currents is five terawatts—about a quarter of predicted global energy demand for 2020—and that "capturing just 1/1,000th of the available energy from the Gulf Stream . . . would supply Florida with 35% of its electrical needs."

Although these technologies are promising, additional research is needed not only for further development but also to adapt them to regional differences. For instance, ocean wave conversion technology is suitable only in locations in which the waves are of the same sort for which existing technologies were developed and in locations where the waves also generate enough energy to make the endeavor profitable. One study shows that thermohaline circulation—ocean circulation driven by variations in temperature and salinity—varies from area to area, and climate change is likely to alter thermohaline circulation in the future in ways that could affect the use of energy generators that rely on ocean currents. Additional research would help scientists understand how to adapt energy technologies for use in specific environments and how to avoid the potential environmental consequences of their use.

Renewable energy resources are the ocean's particularly attractive energy product; they contribute much less than coal or natural gas to anthropogenic greenhouse gas emissions. However, it is worth noting that the oceans do hold vast reserves of untapped hydrocarbon fuels. Deep-sea drilling technologies remain immature; although it is possible to use oil rigs in waters of 8,000 to 9,000 feet, greater depths require the use of specially-designed drilling ships that still face significant challenges. Deep-water drilling that takes place in depths of more than 500 feet is the next big frontier for oil and natural-gas production, projected to expand offshore oil production by 18% by 2020. One should expect the development of new technologies that would enable drilling petroleum and natural gas at even greater depths than presently possible and under layers of salt and other barriers.

In addition to developing these technologies, entire other lines of research are needed to either mitigate the side effects of large-scale usage of these technologies or to guarantee that these effects are small. Although it has recently become possible to drill beneath Arctic ice, the technologies are largely untested. Environmentalists fear that ocean turbines could harm fish or marine mammals, and it is feared that wave conversion technologies would disturb ocean floor sediments, impede migration of ocean animals, prevent waves from clearing debris, or harm animals. Demand has pushed countries to develop technologies to drill for oil beneath ice or in the deep sea without much regard for the safety or environmental concerns associated with oil spills. At present, there is no developed method for cleaning up oil spills in the Arctic, a serious problem that requires additional research if Arctic drilling is to commence on a larger scale.

More Ocean Potential

When large quantities of public funds are invested in a particular research and development project, particularly when the payoff is far from assured, it is common for those responsible for the project to draw attention to the additional benefits—"spinoffs"—generated by the project as a means of adding to its allure. This is particularly true if the project can be shown to improve human health. Thus, NASA has claimed that its space exploration "benefit[ted] pharmaceutical drug development" and assisted in developing a new type of sensor "that provides real-time image recognition capabilities," that it developed an optics technology in the 1970s that now is used to screen children for vision problems, and that a type of software developed for vibration analysis on the Space Shuttle is now used to "diagnose medical issues." Similarly, opportunities to identify the "components of the organisms that facilitate increased virulence in space" could in theory—NASA claims—be used on Earth to "pinpoint targets for antimicrobial therapeutics."

Ocean research, as modest as it is, has already yielded several medical "spinoffs." The discovery of one species of Japanese black sponge, which produces a substance that successfully blocks division of tumorous cells, led researchers to develop a late-stage breast cancer drug. An expedition near the Bahamas led to the discovery of a bacterium that produces substances that are in the process of being synthesized as antibiotics and anticancer compounds. In addition to the aforementioned cancer fighting compounds, chemicals that combat neuropathic pain, treat asthma and inflammation, and reduce skin irritation have been isolated from marine organisms. One Arctic Sea organism alone produced three antibiotics. Although none of the three ultimately proved pharmaceutically significant, current concerns that strains of bacteria are developing resistance to the "antibiotics of last resort" are a strong reason to increase funding for bioprospecting. Additionally, the blood cells of horseshoe crabs contain a chemical—which is found nowhere else in nature and so far has yet to be synthesized—that can detect bacterial contamination in pharmaceuticals and on the surfaces of surgical implants. Some research indicates that between

10 and 30 percent of horseshoe crabs that have been bled die, and that those that survive are less likely to mate. It would serve for research to indicate the ways these creatures can be better protected. Up to two-thirds of all marine life remains unidentified, with 226,000 eukaryotic species already identified and more than 2,000 species discovered every year, according to Ward Appeltans, a marine biologist at the Intergovernmental Oceanographic Commission of UNESCO.

Contrast these discoveries of new species in the oceans with the frequent claims that space exploration will lead to the discovery of extraterrestrial life. For example, in 2010 NASA announced that it had made discoveries on Mars "that [would] impact the search for evidence of extraterrestrial life" but ultimately admitted that they had "no definitive detection of Martian organics." The discovery that prompted the initial press release—that NASA had discovered a *possible* arsenic pathway in metabolism and that thus life was *theoretically* possible under conditions different than those on Earth—was then thoroughly rebutted by a panel of NASA-selected experts. The comparison with ocean science is especially stark when one considers that oceanographers have *already* discovered real organisms that rely on chemosynthesis—the process of making glucose from water and carbon dioxide by using the energy stored in chemical bonds of inorganic compounds—living near deep sea vents at the bottom of the oceans.

The same is true of the search for mineral resources. NASA talks about the potential for asteroid mining, but it will be far easier to find and recover minerals suspended in ocean waters or beneath the ocean floor. Indeed, resources beneath the ocean floor are already being commercially exploited, whereas there is not a near-term likelihood of commercial asteroid mining.

Another major justification cited by advocates for the pricey missions to Mars and beyond is that "we don't know" enough about the other planets and the universe in which we live. However, the same can be said of the deep oceans. Actually, we know much more about the Moon and even about Mars than we know about the oceans. Maps of the Moon are already strikingly accurate, and even amateur hobbyists have crafted highly detailed pictures of the Moon—minus the "dark side"—as one set of documents from University College London's archives seems to demonstrate. By 1967, maps and globes depicting the complete lunar surface were produced. By contrast, about 90% of the world's oceans had not yet been mapped as of 2005. Furthermore, for years scientists have been fascinated by noises originating at the bottom of the ocean, known creatively as "the Bloop" and "Julia," among others. And the world's largest known "waterfall" can be found

entirely underwater between Greenland and Iceland, where cold, dense Arctic water from the Greenland Sea drops more than 11,500 feet before reaching the seafloor of the Denmark Strait. Much remains poorly understood about these phenomena, their relevance to the surrounding ecosystem, and the ways in which climate change will affect their continued existence.

In short, there is much that humans have yet to understand about the depths of the oceans, further research into which could yield important insights about Earth's geological history and the evolution of humans and society. Addressing these questions surpasses the importance of another Mars rover or a space observatory designed to answer highly specific questions of importance mainly to a few dedicated astrophysicists, planetary scientists, and select colleagues.

Leave the People at Home

NASA has long favored human exploration, despite the fact that robots have become much more technologically advanced and that their (one-way) travel poses much lower costs and next to no risks compared to human missions. Still, the promotion of human missions continues; in December 2013, NASA announced that it would grow basil, turnips, and Arabidopsis on the Moon to "show that crop plants that ultimately will feed astronauts and moon colonists and all, are also able to grow on the moon." However, Martin Rees, a professor of cosmology and astrophysics at Cambridge University and a former president of the Royal Society, calls human spaceflight a "waste of money," pointing out that "the practical case [for human spaceflight] gets weaker and weaker with every advance in robotics and miniaturisation." Another observer notes that "it is in fact a universal principle of space science—a 'prime directive,' as it were—that anything a human being does up there could be done by unmanned machinery for one-thousandth the cost." The cost of sending humans to Mars is estimated at more than $150 billion. The preference for human missions persists nonetheless, primarily because NASA believes that human spaceflight is more impressive and will garner more public support and taxpayer dollars, despite the fact that most of NASA's scientific yield to date, Rees shows, has come from the Hubble Space Telescope, the Chandra X-Ray Observatory, the Kepler space observatory, space rovers, and other missions. NASA relentlessly hypes the bravery of the astronauts and the pioneering aspirations of all humanity despite a lack of evidence that these missions engender any more than a brief high for some.

Ocean exploration faces similar temptations. There have been some calls for "aquanauts," who would explore the ocean much as astronauts explore space, and for the prioritization of human exploration missions. However, relying largely on robots and remote-controlled submersibles seems much more economical, nearly as effective at investigating the oceans' biodiversity, chemistry, and seafloor topography, and endlessly safer than human agents. In short, it is no more reasonable to send aquanauts to explore the seafloor than it is to send astronauts to explore the surface of Mars.

Several space enthusiasts are seriously talking about creating human colonies on the Moon or, eventually, on Mars. In the 1970s, for example, NASA's Ames Research Center spent tax dollars to design several models of space colonies meant to hold 10,000 people each. Other advocates have suggested that it might be possible to "terra-form" the surface of Mars or other planets to resemble that of Earth by altering the atmospheric conditions, warming the planet, and activating a water cycle. Other space advocates envision using space elevators to ferry large numbers of people and supplies into space in the event of a catastrophic asteroid hitting the Earth. Ocean enthusiasts dream of underwater cities to deal with overpopulation and "natural or man-made disasters that render land-based human life impossible." The Seasteading Institute, Crescent Hydropolis Resorts, and the League of New Worlds have developed pilot projects to explore the prospect of housing people and scientists under the surface of the ocean. However, these projects are prohibitively expensive and "you can never sever [the surface-water connection] completely," says Dennis Chamberland, director of one of the groups. NOAA also invested funding in a habitat called Aquarius built in 1986 by the Navy, although it has since abandoned this project.

If anyone wants to use their private funds for such outlier projects, they surely should be free to proceed. However, for public funds, priorities must be set. Much greater emphasis must be placed on preventing global calamities rather than on developing improbable means of housing and saving a few hundred or thousand people by sending them far into space or deep beneath the waves.

Reimagining NOAA

These select illustrative examples should suffice to demonstrate the great promise of intensified ocean research, a heretofore unrealized promise. However, it is far from enough to inject additional funding, which can be taken from NASA if the total federal R&D budget cannot be increased, into ocean science. There must also be an agency with a mandate to envision and lead federal efforts to bolster ocean research and exploration the way that President Kennedy and NASA once led space research and "captured" the Moon.

For those who are interested in elaborate reports on the deficiencies of existing federal agencies' attempts to coordinate this research, the Joint Ocean Commission Initiative (JOCI)—the foremost ocean policy group in the United States and the product of the Pew Oceans Commission and the United States Commission on Ocean Policy—provides excellent overviews. These studies and others reflect the tug-of-war that exists among various interest groups and social values. Environmentalists and those concerned about global climate change, the destruction of ocean ecosystems, declines in biodiversity, overfishing, and oil spills clash with commercial groups and states more interested in extracting natural resources from the oceans, in harvesting fish, and utilizing the oceans for tourism. (One observer noted that only 1% of the 139.5 million square miles of the ocean is conserved through formal protections, whereas billons use the oceans "as a 'supermarket and a sewer.'") And although these reports illuminate some of the challenges that must be surmounted if the government is to institute a broad, well-funded set of ocean research goals, none of these groups have added significant funds to ocean research, nor have they taken steps to provide NASA-like agency to take the lead in federally-supported ocean science.

NOAA is the obvious candidate, but it has been hampered by a lack of central authority and by the existence of many disparate programs, each of which has its own small group of congressional supporters with parochial interests. The result is that NOAA has many supporters of its distinct little segments but too few supporters of its broad mission. Furthermore, Congress micromanages NOAA's budget, leaving too little flexibility for the agency to coordinate activities and act on its own priorities.

It is hard to imagine the difficulty of pulling these pieces together—let alone consolidating the bewildering number of projects—under the best of circumstances. Several administrators of NOAA have made significant strides in this regard and should be recognized for their work. However, Congress has saddled the agency with more than 100 ocean-related laws that require the agency to promote what are often narrow and competing interests. Moreover, NOAA is buried in the Department of Commerce, which itself is considered to be one of the weaker cabinet agencies. For this reason, some have suggested that it would be prudent to move NOAA into the Department of the Interior—which already includes the United States Geological Service, the Bureau of Ocean

Energy Management, the National Park Service, the U.S. Fish and Wildlife Service, and the Bureau of Safety and Environmental Enforcement—to give NOAA more of a backbone.

Moreover, NOAA is not the only federal agency that deals with the oceans. There are presently ocean-relevant programs in more than 20 federal agencies—including NASA. For instance, the ocean exploration program that investigates deep ocean currents by using satellite technology to measure minute differences in elevation on the surface of the ocean is currently controlled by NASA, and much basic ocean science research has historically been supported by the Navy, which lost much of its interest in the subject since the end of the Cold War. (The Navy does continue to fund some ocean research, but at levels much lower than earlier.) Many of these programs should be consolidated into a Department of Ocean Research and Exploration that would have the authority to do what NOAA has been prevented from doing: namely, direct a well-planned and coordinated ocean research program. Although the National Ocean Council's interagency coordinating structure is a step in the right direction, it would be much more effective to consolidate authority for managing ocean science research under a new independent agency or a reimagined and strengthened NOAA.

Setting priorities for research and exploration is always needed, but this is especially true in the present age of tight budgets. It is clear that oceans are a little-studied but very promising area for much enhanced exploration. By contrast, NASA's projects, especially those dedicated to further exploring deep space and to manned missions and stellar colonies, can readily be cut. More than moving a few billion dollars from the faraway planets to the nearby oceans is called for, however. The United States needs an agency that can spearhead a major drive to explore the oceans—an agency that has yet to be envisioned and created.

Amitai Etzioni is University Professor and professor of International Affairs and director of the Institute for Communitarian Policy Studies at George Washington University.

EXPLORING THE ISSUE

Should the United States Continue Its Human Spaceflight Program?

Critical Thinking and Reflection

1. Exploring space is a great idea—but what's in it for us?
2. In a space program dominated by robotic spacecraft and landers, what role remains for human beings?
3. How will the U.S. government respond if China puts an astronaut on the Moon?

Is There Common Ground?

Those who argue over the merits of manned space exploration tend to agree that space is worth exploring. They disagree on whether it is necessary to send people into space when robots are already very capable and likely to be much more capable in a few years.

1. Just how capable are robots today? (There is a great deal of material on this question.)
2. Look up "telepresence" (see Tom Simonite, "The New, More Awkward You," *Technology Review*, January/February 2011; http://www.technologyreview .com/computing/26941/?a=f). Does this technology offer a compromise on the question of using either robots or humans in space?
3. Would telepresence also benefit ocean exploration?

Additional Resources

Augustine Commission, *Seeking a Human Spaceflight Program Worthy of a Great Nation* (October 2009) (http://www.nasa.gov/pdf/396093main_HSF_Cmte _FinalReport.pdf).

Robert D. Ballard, "Why We Must Explore the Sea," *Smithsonian* (October 2014).

Mark Schrope, "Journey to the Bottom of the Sea," *Scientific American* (April 2014).

Robert Zubrin, "How Much Is an Astronaut's Life Worth?" *Reason* (February 2012).

Internet References . . .

Ocean Exploration Trust

http://www.oceanexplorationtrust.org/

Ocean Explorer

http://oceanexplorer.noaa.gov/backmatter /whatisexploration.html

Space.com

http://www.space.com/11364-human-space -exploration-future-50-years-spaceflight.html

The Coalition to Save Manned Space Exploration

http://www.savemannedspace.com/

Unit 5

UNIT

The Computer Revolution

*F*ans of computers have long been sure that the electronic wonders offer untold benefits to society. When the first personal computers appeared in the early 1970s, they immediately brought unheard-of capabilities to their users. Ever since, those capabilities have been increasing. Today children command more sheer computing power that major corporations did in the 1950s and 1960s. Computer users are in direct contact with their fellow users around the world. Information is instantly available and infinitely malleable.

Some observers wonder about the purported untold benefits of computers. Specifically, will such benefits be outweighed by threats to children (by free access to pornography and by online predators), civil order (by free access to sites that advocate racism and violence), traditional institutions (will books, for example, become an endangered species?), or to human pride (computers have already outplayed human champions at chess, checkers, and go)? If computers can outthink humans at games, how long will it be before they are as intelligent and even as conscious as we are? What happens to our jobs and careers then? Do we have to worry about cyber-war? And must all software be produced as proprietary product?

Selected, Edited, and with Issue Framing Material by:
Thomas A. Easton, *Thomas College*

ISSUE

Will Robots Take Your Job?

YES: Kevin Drum, from "Welcome, Robot Overlords. Please Don't Fire Us?" *Mother Jones* (2013)

NO: Peter Gorle and Andrew Clive, from "Positive Impact of Industrial Robots on Employment," Metra Martech (2011)

Learning Outcomes

After reading this issue, you will be able to:

- Explain what kinds of jobs are now and may soon be suitable for robots.
- Discuss the impact of robotics on their future job prospects.
- Apply their understanding of how robots will affect future jobs in a discussion of career choices.
- Discuss how, if robots indeed do cause widespread unemployment, the world's economies will have to change.

ISSUE SUMMARY

YES: Kevin Drum argues that we are about to make very rapid progress in artificial intelligence, and by about 2040, robots will be replacing people in a great many jobs. On the way to that "robot paradise," corporate managers and investors will expand their share of national wealth, at the expense of labor's share, even more than they have in recent years. That trend, however, depends on an ample supply of consumers—workers with enough money to buy the products the machines are making. It is thus already time to start rethinking how the nation ensures that its citizens have enough money to be consumers and keep the economy going.

NO: Peter Gorle and Andrew Clive argue that robots are not a threat to human employment. Historically, increases in the use of automation almost always increase both productivity and employment. Over the next few years, the use of robotics will generate 700,000–1,000,000 new jobs.

The idea that technology threatens jobs is not new. In the early 1800s, the "Luddites" were textile workers who destroyed new weaving machinery that could be operated by unskilled labor. The movement faded away with the end of the Napoleonic Wars, but its name has continued to be applied to those who oppose industrialization, automation, computerization, and even any new technology. See, for example, Steven E. Jones, *Against Technology: From the Luddites to Neo-Luddism* (CRC Press, 2006).

Not surprisingly, modern computer technology arouses many job-related fears, for computers seem to be growing ever more capable. When IBM's "Watson" won a dramatic victory in the game of *Jeopardy*, many wondered if we were finally seeing true artificial intelligence. Kirk L. Kroeker, "Weighing Watson's Impact," *Communications of the ACM* (July 2011), notes that despite many dismissive comments, Watson is an excellent demonstration of the power of machine learning. Future applications of the technology will soon play important roles in medicine (extracting information from vast numbers of medical books and journals), law, education, and the financial industry. Many of these applications do not require that a robot look and act like a human being, but researchers are working on that, too; see Alex Wright, "Robots Like Us," *Communications of the ACM* (May 2012); and Dennis Normile, "In Our Own Image," *Science* (October 10, 2014).

"Robocars"—cars that drive themselves, with no human hand at the wheel—have already been demonstrated and their capabilities are improving rapidly; see Sebastian Thrun, "Toward Robotic Cars," *Communications of the ACM* (April 2010), and Alex Wright, "Automotive Autonomy," *Communications of the ACM* (July 2011). Before they can be broadly used, there must be changes in legislation (can you be guilty of OUI if the car drives itself?) and insurance, among other things; see "The Future of the Self-Driving Automobile," *Trends E-Magazine* (December 2010), and John Markoff, "Collision in the Making Between Self-Driving Cars and How the World Works," *New York Times* (January 23, 2012). Given such changes, we can expect to see job losses among taxi drivers and truckers, among others.

Robots may also cost other people their jobs. Jason Borenstein, "Robots and the Changing Workforce," *AI & Society* (2011), notes that robotic workers are going to become ever more common, and though new job opportunities are bound to arise from this, many jobs will disappear and the human workforce will change in many ways—including necessary education and worker income. Judith Aquino, "Nine Jobs that Humans May Lose to Robots," *Business Insider* (March 22, 2011), says the endangered list includes drivers, but also pharmacists, lawyers and paralegals, astronauts, store clerks, soldiers, babysitters, rescuers, and sportswriters and other reporters. John Sepulvado asks "Could a Computer Write This Story?" (CNN, May 11, 2012) (http://edition.cnn.com/2012/05/11/tech/innovation/computer-assisted-writing/index.html). By 2014, robowriters from the company, Narrative Science (http://www.narrativescience.com/), were already being deployed; see Francie Diep, "Associated Press Will Use Robots to Write Articles," *Popular Science* (July 1, 2014) (http://www.popsci.com/article/technology/associated-press-will-use-robots-write-articles). Farhad Manjoo asks (and answers) "Will Robots Steal Your Job? If You're Highly Educated, You Should Still Be Afraid," *Slate* (September 26, 2011) (http://www.slate.com/articles/technology/robot_invasion/2011/09/will_robots_steal_your_job.html). "Robots to Take 500,000 Human Jobs . . . for Now," *The Fiscal Times* (December 29, 2011), notes that every industry, from agriculture to the military, will be affected. Martin Ford, "Google's Cloud Robotics Strategy—and How It Could Soon Threaten Jobs," *Huffington Post* (January 3, 2012), says that "nearly any type of work that is on some level routine in nature—regardless of the skill level or educational requirements—is likely to someday be impacted by [robotic] technologies. The only real question is how soon it will happen." This foreboding

thought is echoed by Dan Lyons, "Who Needs Humans?" *Newsweek* (July 25, 2011). David J. Lynch is more optimistic in "It's a Man vs. Machine Recovery," *Bloomberg Businessweek* (January 5, 2012), he notes that businesses are buying machines more than hiring people, but "there's nothing wrong with the labor market that resurgent demand wouldn't fix." There may also be a need to consider the ethics involved, for as more robots enter the workplace, they will bring with them changed expectations (robots are tireless, and they don't need health insurance, retirement plans, vacations, and even pay; will employers expect the same of humans?); this may even mean restricting the use of robots; see Jason Borenstein, "Computing Ethics: Work Life in the Robotic Age," *Communications of the ACM* (July 2010).

Not everyone agrees on the degree of the threat. In "Will Work for Machines" (August 2014), *Scientific American*'s editors note that it is actually hard to tell whether there is a threat at all, for there is a serious shortage of data. David Bourne, "My Boss the Robot," *Scientific American* (May 2013), sees a future in which humans and robots collaborate to get jobs done more rapidly and efficiently than either could do alone. See also John Bohannon, "Meet Your New Co-Worker," *Science* (October 10, 2014). David H. Autor, "Polanyi's Paradox and the Shape of Employment Growth," report prepared for the Federal Reserve Bank of Kansas City symposium on "Re-Evaluating Labor Market Dynamics" (August 21–13, 2014) (http://www.kansascityfed.org/publicat/sympos/2014/093014.pdf), concludes that most "commentators overstate the extent of machine substitution for human labor and ignore the strong complementarities." Neil Irwin, "Why the Robots Might Not Take Our Jobs After All: They Lack Common Sense," *New York Times* (August 22, 2014), thinks robots aren't going to replace humans any time soon, except in very limited ways. See also John Tamny, "Why Robots Will Be the Biggest Job Creators in World History," *Forbes* (March 1, 2015 @ 9 AM) (http://www.forbes.com/sites/johntamny/2015/03/01/why-robots-will-be-the-biggest-job-creators-in-history/).

How bad might it get? Stuart Elliott, in "Anticipating a Luddite Revival," *Issues in Science and Technology* (Spring 2014), compares the capabilities of computers as reflected in the literature with job skills as defined in the Department of Labor's O*NET system. He finds that computers are already close to being able to meet skills requirements of 75 percent of jobs. "Safe" jobs that demand more skills are in education, health care, science, engineering, and law, but even those may be matched within a few decades. "In principle," he says, "there is no problem with imagining a transformation in the labor market that substitutes technology for workers for 80 percent of current jobs and then expands in the remaining 20 percent to absorb the entire labor force. [But} We do not know how successful the nation can be in trying to prepare everyone in the labor force for jobs that require these higher skill levels. It is hard to imagine, for example, that most of the labor force will move into jobs in health care, education, science, engineering, and law. . . . At some point it will be too difficult for large numbers of displaced workers to move into jobs requiring capabilities that are difficult for most of them to carry out even if they have the time and resources for retraining. When that time comes, the nation will be forced to reconsider the role that paid employment plays in distributing economic goods and services and in providing a meaningful focus for many people's daily lives." Marcus Wohlsen, in "When Robots Take All the Work, What'll Be Left for Us to Do?" *Wired* (August 8, 2014) (http://www.wired.com/2014/08/when-robots-take-all-the-work-whatll-be-left-for-us-to-do/), says that "The scariest possibility of all is that [the loss of jobs means] that only then do we figure out what really makes us human is work." William H. Davidow and Michael S. Malone, "What Happens to Society When Robots Replace Workers?"

Harvard Business Review (December 10, 2014) (https://hbr.org/2014/12/what-happens-to-society-when-robots-replace-workers), reach a similar conclusion: "Ultimately, we need a new, individualized, *cultural*, approach to the meaning of work and the purpose of life."

In the YES selection, Kevin Drum argues that we are about to make very rapid progress in artificial intelligence, and by about 2040, robots will be replacing people in a great many jobs. On the way to that "robot paradise," corporate managers and investors will expand their share of national wealth, at the expense of labor's share, even more than they have in recent years. That trend, however, depends on an ample supply of consumers—workers with enough money to buy the products the machines are making. It is thus already time to start rethinking how the nation ensures that its citizens have enough money to be consumers and keep the economy going. In the NO selection, Peter Gorle and Andrew Clive argue that robots are not a threat to human employment. Historically, increases in the use of automation almost always increase both productivity and employment. Over the next few years, the use of robotics will generate 700,000 to 1,000,000 new jobs.

YES ↵

Kevin Drum

Welcome, Robot Overlords. Please Don't Fire Us?

This is a story about the future. Not the unhappy future, the one where climate change turns the planet into a cinder or we all die in a global nuclear war. This is the *happy* version. It's the one where computers keep getting smarter and smarter, and clever engineers keep building better and better robots. By 2040, computers the size of a softball are as smart as human beings. Smarter, in fact. Plus they're *computers*: They never get tired, they're never ill-tempered, they never make mistakes, and they have instant access to all of human knowledge.

The result is paradise. Global warming is a problem of the past because computers have figured out how to generate limitless amounts of green energy and intelligent robots have tirelessly built the infrastructure to deliver it to our homes. No one needs to work anymore. Robots can do everything humans can do, and they do it uncomplainingly, 24 hours a day. Some things remain scarce—beachfront property in Malibu, original Rembrandts—but thanks to super-efficient use of natural resources and massive recycling, scarcity of ordinary consumer goods is a thing of the past. Our days are spent however we please, perhaps in study, perhaps playing video games. It's up to us.

Maybe you think I'm pulling your leg here. Or being archly ironic. After all, this does have a bit of a rose-colored tint to it, doesn't it? Like something from *The Jetsons* or the cover of *Wired*. That would hardly be a surprising reaction. Computer scientists have been predicting the imminent rise of machine intelligence since at least 1956, when the Dartmouth Summer Research Project on Artificial Intelligence gave the field its name, and there are only so many times you can cry wolf. Today, a full seven decades after the birth of the computer, all we have are iPhones, Microsoft Word, and in-dash navigation. You could be excused for thinking that computers that truly match the human brain are a ridiculous pipe dream.

But they're not. It's true that we've made far slower progress toward real artificial intelligence than we once thought, but that's for a very simple and very human

reason: Early computer scientists grossly underestimated the power of the human brain and the difficulty of emulating one. It turns out that this is a very, very hard problem, sort of like filling up Lake Michigan one drop at a time. In fact, not just *sort of* like. It's *exactly* like filling up Lake Michigan one drop at a time. If you want to understand the future of computing, it's essential to understand this.

What do we do over the next few decades as robots become steadily more capable and steadily begin taking away all our jobs?

Suppose it's 1940 and Lake Michigan has (somehow) been emptied. Your job is to fill it up using the following rule: To start off, you can add one fluid ounce of water to the lake bed. Eighteen months later, you can add two. In another 18 months, you can add four ounces. And so on. Obviously this is going to take a while.

By 1950, you have added around a gallon of water. But you keep soldiering on. By 1960, you have a bit more than 150 gallons. By 1970, you have 16,000 gallons, about as much as an average suburban swimming pool.

At this point it's been 30 years, and even though 16,000 gallons is a fair amount of water, it's nothing compared to the size of Lake Michigan. To the naked eye you've made no progress at all.

So let's skip all the way ahead to 2000. Still nothing. You have—maybe—a slight sheen on the lake floor. How about 2010? You have a few inches of water here and there. This is ridiculous. It's now been *70 years* and you still don't have enough water to float a goldfish. Surely this task is futile?

But wait. Just as you're about to give up, things suddenly change. By 2020, you have about 40 feet of water. And by 2025 you're done. After 70 years you had nothing. Fifteen years later, the job was finished.

If you have any kind of background in computers, you've already figured out that I didn't pick these numbers out of a hat. I started in 1940 because that's about when the first programmable computer was invented. I chose a doubling time of 18 months because of a cornerstone of computer history called Moore's Law, which famously estimates that computing power doubles approximately every 18 months. And I chose Lake Michigan because its size, in fluid ounces, is roughly the same as the computing power of the human brain measured in calculations per second.

In other words, just as it took us until 2025 to fill up Lake Michigan, the simple exponential curve of Moore's Law suggests it's going to take us until 2025 to build a computer with the processing power of the human brain. And it's going to happen the same way: For the first 70 years, it will seem as if nothing is happening, even though we're doubling our progress every 18 months. Then, in the final 15 years, seemingly out of nowhere, we'll finish the job.

True artificial intelligence really is around the corner, and it really will make life easier. But first we face vast economic upheaval.

And that's exactly where we are. We've moved from computers with a trillionth of the power of a human brain to computers with a billionth of the power. Then a millionth. And now a thousandth. Along the way, computers progressed from ballistics to accounting to word processing to speech recognition, and none of that really seemed like progress toward artificial intelligence. That's because even a thousandth of the power of a human brain is—let's be honest—a bit of a joke. Sure, it's a billion times more than the first computer had, but it's still not much more than the computing power of a hamster.

This is why, even with the IT industry barreling forward relentlessly, it has never seemed like we were making any real progress on the AI front. But there's another reason as well: Every time computers break some new barrier, we decide—or maybe just finally get it through our thick skulls—that we set the bar too low. At one point, for example, we thought that playing chess at a high level would be a mark of human-level intelligence. Then, in 1997, IBM's Deep Blue supercomputer beat world champion Garry Kasparov, and suddenly we decided that playing grandmaster-level chess didn't imply high intelligence after all.

So maybe translating human languages would be a fair test? Google Translate does a passable job of that these days. Recognizing human voices and responding appropriately? Siri mostly does that, and better systems are on the near horizon. Understanding the world well enough to win a round of *Jeopardy!* against human competition? A few years ago IBM's Watson supercomputer beat the two best human *Jeopardy!* champions of all time. Driving a car? Google has already logged more than 300,000 miles in its driverless cars, and in another decade they may be commercially available.

The truth is that all this represents more progress toward true AI than most of us realize. We've just been limited by the fact that computers still aren't quite muscular enough to finish the job. That's changing rapidly, though. Computing power is measured in calculations per second—a.k.a. floating-point operations per second, or "flops"—and the best estimates of the human brain suggest that our own processing power is about equivalent to 10 petaflops. ("Peta" comes after giga and tera.) That's a lot of flops, but last year an IBM Blue Gene/Q supercomputer at Lawrence Livermore National Laboratory was clocked at 16.3 petaflops.

Of course, raw speed isn't everything. Livermore's Blue Gene/Q fills a room, requires eight megawatts of power to run, and costs about $250 million. What's more, it achieves its speed not with a single superfast processor, but with 1.6 million ordinary processor cores running simultaneously. While that kind of massive parallel processing is ideally suited for nuclear-weapons testing, we don't know yet if it will be effective for producing AI.

But plenty of people are trying to figure it out. Earlier this year, the European Commission chose two big research endeavors to receive a half billion euros each, and one of them was the Human Brain Project led by Henry Markram, a neuroscientist at the Swiss Federal Institute of Technology in Lausanne. He uses another IBM supercomputer in a project aimed at modeling the entire human brain. Markram figures he can do this by 2020.

The Luddites weren't wrong. They were just 200 years too early.

That might be optimistic. At the same time, it also might turn out that we don't need to model a human brain in the first place. After all, when the Wright brothers built the first airplane, they didn't model it after a bird with flapping wings. Just as there's more than one way to fly, there's probably more than one way to think, too.

Google's driverless car, for example, doesn't navigate the road the way humans do. It uses four radars, a 64-beam laser range finder, a camera, GPS, and extremely detailed high-res maps. What's more, Google engineers drive along test routes to record data before they let the self-driving cars loose.

Is this disappointing? In a way, yes: Google *has* to do all this to make up for the fact that the car can't do what any human can do while also singing along to the radio, chugging a venti, and making a mental note to pick up the laundry. But that's a cramped view. Even when processing power and software get better, there's no reason to think that a driverless car should replicate the way humans drive. They will have access to far more information than we do, and unlike us they'll have the power to make use of it in real time. And they'll never get distracted when the phone rings.

True artificial intelligence will very likely be here within a couple of decades. By about 2040 our robot paradise awaits.

In other words, you should still be impressed. When we think of human cognition, we usually think about things like composing music or writing a novel. But a big part of the human brain is dedicated to more prosaic functions, like taking in a chaotic visual field and recognizing the thousands of separate objects it contains. We do that so automatically we hardly even think of it as intelligence. But it is, and the fact that Google's car can do it at all is a real breakthrough.

The exact pace of future progress remains uncertain. For example, some physicists think that Moore's Law may break down in the near future and constrain the growth of computing power. We also probably have to break lots of barriers in our knowledge of neuroscience before we can write the software that does all the things a human brain can do. We have to figure out how to make petaflop computers smaller and cheaper. And it's possible that the 10-petaflop estimate of human computing power is too low in the first place.

Nonetheless, in Lake Michigan terms, we finally have a few inches of water in the lake bed, and we can see it rising. All those milestones along the way—playing chess, translating web pages, winning at *Jeopardy!*, driving a car—aren't just stunts. They're precisely the kinds of things you'd expect as we struggle along with platforms that aren't quite powerful enough—yet. True artificial intelligence will very likely be here within a couple of decades. Making it small, cheap, and ubiquitous might take a decade more.

In other words, by about 2040 our robot paradise awaits.

AND NOW FOR THE BAIT and switch. I promised you this would be a happy story, and in the long run it is.

But first we have to get there. And at this point our tale takes a darker turn. What do we do over the next few decades as robots become steadily more capable and steadily begin taking away all our jobs? This is the kind of thing that futurologists write about frequently, but when I started looking for answers from mainstream economists, it turned out there wasn't much to choose from. The economics community just hasn't spent much time over the past couple of decades focusing on the effect that machine intelligence is likely to have on the labor market. Now is a particularly appropriate time to think about this question, because it was two centuries ago this year that 64 men were brought to trial in York, England. Their crime? They were skilled weavers who fought back against the rising tide of power looms they feared would put them out of work. The Luddites spent two years burning mills and destroying factory machinery, and the British government was not amused. Of the 64 men charged in 1813, 25 were transported to Australia and 17 were led to the gallows.

Since then, Luddite has become a derisive term for anyone afraid of new technology. After all, the weavers turned out to be wrong. Power looms put them out of work, but in the long run automation made the entire workforce more productive. Everyone still had jobs—just different ones. Some ran the new power looms, others found work no one could have imagined just a few decades before, in steel mills, automobile factories, and railroad lines. In the end, this produced wealth for everyone, because, after all, someone still had to make, run, and maintain the machines.

But that was then. During the Industrial Revolution, machines were limited to performing physical tasks. The Digital Revolution is different because computers can perform cognitive tasks too, and that means machines will eventually be able to run themselves. When that happens, they won't just put individuals out of work temporarily. Entire classes of workers will be out of work permanently.

In other words, the Luddites weren't wrong. They were just 200 years too early.

This isn't something that will happen overnight. It will happen slowly, as machines grow increasingly capable. We've already seen it in factories, where robots do work that used to be done by semiskilled assembly line workers. In a decade, driverless cars will start to put taxi hacks and truck drivers out of a job. And while it's easy to believe that some jobs can never be done by machines—do the elderly really want to be tended by robots?—that may not be true. Nearly 50 years ago, when MIT computer scientist Joseph Weizenbaum created a therapy simulation program named Eliza, he was astonished to discover just how addictive it was. Even though Eliza was almost laughably crude, it was endlessly patient and seemed interested in your problems. People *liked* talking to Eliza.

Robots will take over more and more jobs. As this happens, capital will become ever more powerful and labor will become ever more worthless.

And that was 50 years ago, using only a keyboard and an old Teletype terminal. Add a billion times more processing power and you start to get something much closer to real social interaction. Robotic pets are growing so popular that Sherry Turkle, an MIT professor who studies the way we interact with technology, is uneasy about it: "The idea of some kind of artificial companionship," she says, "is already becoming the new normal."

It's not hard to see why. Unlike humans, an intelligent machine does whatever you want it to do, for as long as you want it to. You want to gossip? It'll gossip. You want to complain for hours on end about how your children never call? No problem. And as the technology of robotics advances—the Pentagon has developed a fully functional robotic arm that can be controlled by a human mind—they'll be able to perform ordinary human physical tasks too. They'll clean the floor, do your nails, diagnose your ailments, and cook your food.

Increasingly, then, robots will take over more and more jobs. And guess who will own all these robots? People with money, of course. As this happens, capital will become ever more powerful and labor will become ever more worthless. Those without money—most of us—will live on whatever crumbs the owners of capital allow us.

This is a grim prediction. But it's not nearly as far-fetched as it sounds. Economist Paul Krugman recently remarked that our long-standing belief in skills and education as the keys to financial success may well be outdated. In a blog post titled "Rise of the Robots," he reviewed some recent economic data and predicted that we're entering an era where the prime cause of income inequality will be something else entirely: capital vs. labor.

Until a decade ago, the share of total national income going to workers was pretty stable at around 70 percent, while the share going to capital—mainly corporate profits and returns on financial investments—made up the other 30 percent. More recently, though, those shares have started to change. Slowly but steadily, labor's share of total national income has gone down, while the share going to capital owners has gone up. The most obvious effect of this is the skyrocketing wealth of the top 1 percent, due mostly to huge increases in capital gains and investment income.

In the economics literature, the increase in the share of income going to capital owners is known as capital-biased technological change. Let's take a layman's look at what that means.

The question we want to answer is simple: If CBTC is already happening—not a lot, but just a little bit—what trends would we expect to see? What are the signs of a computer-driven economy? First and most obviously, if automation were displacing labor, we'd expect to see a steady decline in the share of the population that's employed.

Second, we'd expect to see fewer job openings than in the past. Third, as more people compete for fewer jobs, we'd expect to see middle-class incomes flatten in a race to the bottom. Fourth, with consumption stagnant, we'd expect to see corporations stockpile more cash and, fearing weaker sales, invest less in new products and new factories. Fifth, as a result of all this, we'd expect to see labor's share of national income decline and capital's share rise.

These trends are the five horsemen of the robotic apocalypse, and guess what? We're already seeing them, and not just because of the crash of 2008. They started showing up in the statistics more than a decade ago. For a while, though, they were masked by the dot-com and housing bubbles, so when the financial crisis hit, years' worth of decline was compressed into 24 months. The trend lines dropped off the cliff.

How alarmed should we be by this? In one sense, a bit of circumspection is in order. The modern economy is complex, and most of these trends have multiple causes. The decline in the share of workers who are employed, for example, is partly caused by the aging of the population. What's more, the financial crisis has magnified many of these trends. Labor's share of income will probably recover a bit once the economy finally turns up.

Doctors should probably be worried as well. Remember Watson, the *Jeopardy!*-playing computer? In another decade, there's a good chance that Watson will be able to do this without any human help at all.

But in another sense, we should be *very* alarmed. It's one thing to suggest that robots are going to cause mass unemployment starting in 2030 or so. We'd have some time to come to grips with that. But the evidence suggests that—slowly, haltingly—it's happening already, and we're simply not prepared for it.

How exactly will this play out? Economist David Autor has suggested that the first jobs to go will be middle-skill jobs. Despite impressive advances, robots still don't have the dexterity to perform many common kinds of manual labor that are simple for humans—digging ditches, changing bedpans. Nor are they any good at jobs that require a lot of cognitive skill—teaching classes, writing magazine articles. But in the middle you have jobs that are both fairly routine and require no manual dexterity. So that may be where the hollowing out starts: with desk jobs in places like accounting or customer support.

That hasn't yet happened in earnest because AI is still in its infancy. But it's not hard to see which direction the wind is blowing. The US Postal Service, for example, used to employ humans to sort letters, but for some time now, that's been done largely by machines that can recognize human handwriting. Netflix does a better job picking movies you might like than a bored video-store clerk. Facial recognition software is improving rapidly, and *that's* a job so human there's an entire module in the human brain, the fusiform gyrus, solely dedicated to this task.

In fact, there's even a digital sports writer. It's true that a human being wrote this story—ask my mother if you're not sure—but in a decade or two I might be out of a job too. Doctors should probably be worried as well. Remember Watson, the *Jeopardy!*-playing computer? It's now being fed millions of pages of medical information so that it can help physicians do a better job of diagnosing diseases. In another decade, there's a good chance that Watson will be able to do this without any human help at all.

This is, admittedly, pretty speculative. Still, even if it's hard to find concrete examples of computers doing human work today, it's going to get easier before long.

Take driverless cars. My newspaper is delivered every day by a human being. But because humans are fallible, sometimes I don't get a paper, or I get the wrong one. This would be a terrific task for a driverless car in its early stages of development. There are no passengers to worry about. The route is fixed. Delivery is mostly done in the early morning, when traffic is light. And the car's abundance of mapping and GPS data would ensure that it always knows which house is which.

The next step might be passenger vehicles on fixed routes, like airport shuttles. Then long-haul trucks. Then buses and taxis. There are 2.5 million workers who drive trucks, buses, and taxis for a living, and there's a good chance that, one by one, all of them will be displaced by driverless vehicles within the next decade or two. What will they do when that happens? Machines will be putting everyone else with modest skill levels out of work too. There will be no place to go but the unemployment line.

WHAT CAN WE DO about this? First and foremost, we should be carefully watching those five economic trends linked to capital-biased technological change to see if they rebound when the economy picks up. If, instead, they continue their long, downward slide, it means we've already entered a new era.

Next, we'll need to let go of some familiar convictions. Left-leaning observers may continue to think that stagnating incomes can be improved with better education and equality of opportunity. Conservatives will continue to insist that people without jobs are lazy bums who shouldn't be coddled. They'll both be wrong.

Corporate executives should worry too. For a while, everything will seem great for them: Falling labor costs will produce heftier profits and bigger bonuses. But then it will all come crashing down. After all, robots might be able to *produce* goods and services, but they can't consume them. And eventually computers will become pretty good CEOs as well.

Solutions to this will remain elusive as long as we resist facing the real change in the way our economy works. When we finally do, we'll probably have only a few options open to us. The simplest, because it's relatively familiar, is to tax capital at high rates and use the money to support displaced workers. In other words, as The *Economist*'s Ryan Avent puts it, "redistribution, and a lot of it."

There's not much question that this could work, but would we be happy in a society that offers real work to a dwindling few and bread and circuses for the rest? Most likely, owners of capital would strongly resist higher taxes, as they always have, while workers would be unhappy with their enforced idleness. Still, the ancient Romans managed to get used to it—with slave labor playing the role of robots—and we might have to, as well.

Alternatively, economist Noah Smith suggests that we might have to fundamentally change the way we think about how we share economic growth. Right now, he points out, everyone is born with an endowment of labor by virtue of having a body and a brain that can be traded for income. But what to do when that endowment is worth a fraction of what it is today? Smith's suggestion: "Why not also an endowment of capital? What if, when each citizen turns 18, the government bought him or her a diversified portfolio of equity?"

In simple terms, if owners of capital are capturing an increasing fraction of national income, then that capital needs to be shared more widely if we want to maintain a middle-class society. Somehow—and I'm afraid a bit of vagueness is inevitable here—an increasing share of corporate equity will need to be divvied up among the entire population as workers are slowly but surely stripped of their human capital. Perhaps everyone will be guaranteed ownership of a few robots, or some share of robot production of goods and services.

But whatever the answer—and it might turn out to be something we can't even imagine right now—it's time to start thinking about our automated future in earnest. The history of mass economic displacement isn't encouraging—fascists in the '20s, Nazis in the '30s—and recent high levels of unemployment in Greece and Italy have already produced rioting in the streets and larger followings for right-wing populist parties. And that's after only a few years of misery.

So far, though, the topic has gotten surprisingly little attention among economists. At MIT, Autor has written about the elimination of middle-class jobs thanks to encroaching technology, and his colleagues, Erik Brynjolfsson and Andrew McAfee of MIT's Center for

Digital Business, got a lot of attention a couple of years ago for their e-book *Race Against the Machine*, probably the best short introduction to the subject of automation and jobs. (Though a little too optimistic about the future of humans, I think.) The fact that Paul Krugman is starting to think about this deeply is also good news.

But it's not enough. When the robot revolution finally starts to happen, it's going to happen fast, and it's going to turn our world upside down. It's easy to joke about our future robot overlords—R2-D2 or the Terminator?—but the challenge that machine intelligence presents really isn't science fiction anymore. Like Lake Michigan with an inch of water in it, it's happening around us right now even if it's hard to see. A robotic paradise of leisure and contemplation eventually awaits us, but we have a long and dimly lit tunnel to navigate before we get there.

KEVIN DRUM is a political blogger for *Mother Jones* magazine. He was a blogosphere pioneer when, after a stint in marketing, he went online as Calpundit in 2003. Prior to joining *Mother Jones*, he blogged at the *Washington Monthly's Political Animal*.

Peter Gorle and Andrew Clive

 **NO**

Positive Impact of Industrial Robots on Employment

Introduction

Study Aim

The study analyses the impact of the use of robots in the industrialized production of goods on employment. The study covers years 2000 to 2016.

Project Scope

The sectors considered are:

1. The large automotive players as well as the component suppliers.
2. Electronics and its interface with specialist plastics [solar cells, photovoltaics etc or other advanced materials], particularly clean rooms [but not the very specialised microchip manufacturing application].
3. Food and beverage, [health, cleanliness and safety*]
4. Plastics [and Rubber] Industry as such, not only in combination with Electronics, Chemicals and Pharmaceuticals, . . .

Other than the automotive sector, the brief specified that SMEs (Small and Medium Enterprises) up to 250 employees were specified as the target where possible. By agreement, this has been given less emphasis in the project as there is little available information on the use of robots specifically by smaller companies.

Industrial Robots Are the Target

Global markets are covered by the economic background data. The study then focused on six key countries. Brazil, China, Germany, Japan, Republic of Korea and USA.

Method

The project is based largely on analyses of economic data on the six selected countries.This has been combined with the data on Robot use provided by IFR [International Federation of Robotics].

Conclusions were drawn by the Metra Martech team based on economic and industry knowledge. There are considerable gaps in the information available and the main quantifications show orders of magnitude rather than precise numbers. These conclusions have been tested on IFR members in the countries. The testing process involved a two stage set of questions which were responded to by eighteen of these experts. The first question set established the validity of the main assumptions made by Metra Martech; the second was a more detailed set of questions, sent by IFR to selected experts. . . .

The Economic Factors: And Their Effects on the Use of Robotics

Displacement and Re-Employment

Where automation displaces people in manufacturing it almost always increases output. In some cases it allows such an increase in production and related decrease in unit price that it creates a whole new market and generates the need for downstream jobs to get the product to the consumer. It releases employees for other, often new jobs outside manufacturing. Historically, this has always been the case.

An alternative view is that this displacement in the future will be more difficult to place, as service robotics may take over many of the new job opportunities in human tasks such as in banking, fast food chains, and retailing petrol forecourts.

What is likely is that the growth of the production marketing, selling and maintaining of service robots will create the next wave of employment.

The USA has provided a good example, where the total number of people in employment has grown, driven by increase in population, increased participation by women and increased immigrant labour. The long downward trend in manufacturing as a proportion of total employment has been caused by failure to remain competitive in manufacturing as the industrialising countries have grown capacity. . . .

What is driving this trend to fewer employees in manufacturing is that manufacturers have steadily improved manufacturing productivity, largely by increasing the size of production units, automating tasks and sourcing components globally.

. . . [D]oubling use of robots in the past ten years in USA has not affected the trend. By contrast, Germany, which has proportionately many more robots, also doubled the number of robots and has achieved slightly higher growth with almost no reduction in manufacturing employment.

Pressure to increase productivity in the developed countries, has been precipitated by greatly increased competition from overseas manufacturers, and passing of high labour content production to the low labour cost areas.

Pressure to use robotics in the developing countries has been that, despite availability of low cost labour, consistency and accuracy required to compete with or meet the requirements of the developed markets, can sometimes only be achieved by robotics.

Five other economic factors have to be considered:

* Globalisation
* Increasing speed of technology development
* Age and skills profiles
* Wage levels
* Health and safety legislation levels

Globalisation of the Market

There has been very rapid growth of the very large developing markets of China and India.

These are low labour cost countries and while labour costs can be expected to level up around the world, these two countries are likely to be relatively low cost areas for at least 20 years. The markets are so large that they encourage the development of locally grown research and technology. This means the phase when China, for example, largely produced goods to western specifications is passing.

Two defences that the developed countries have to maintain their wealth creating production capacity [without putting up trade barriers] are:

1. To put more money into research and development. The success of the Frauenhofer Institutes in Germany, and the new 150bn Yen FIRST projects [Funding program for world leading Innovative R&D on Science and Technology] in Japan are examples of this.

2. To reduce dependence on high cost labour by introducing automation when it offers an economic alternative.

Increasing Speed of Technology Development

This is about the pace of technological development, and the opportunity which this provides for those who can introduce the new technologies. It results in the shortening of product life cycles. Shorter cycles call for more flexible robotics. The product sectors which are the target for this report are not all affected to the same degree by shortening life cycles. Length of production run is an allied factor. Increasing customisation of products, and the flexibility needed by smaller companies are likely to be met by the next generation of robots.

Age and Skills Profiles

The ageing populations in, for example China, Japan and Germany are often cited as an added reason for adoption of robotics. USA is also affected but to a lesser degree.

A very significant ageing is forecast, but if we consider the workforce, within the timescale of the survey, only Japan is significantly affected, with a projected 5% loss of people of employable age. The German situation will become critical in the following years, but is projected to be less than 2% loss in workforce because of ageing, between now and 2016. Our discussions with robotics experts identify specific problems with ageing workforce in the aerospace sector in USA, but this is outside the scope of the present study.

The existence of skills gaps is reported to be a problem, but this is more a question of education and training regimes than the effect of population ageing.

Several factors are involved in addition to age, the change in population as a whole, the change in people of [currently] employable age, the overall number of people employed and the success of skills training in the country. . . .

Skills Gaps

Even with increasing levels of technology training around the world, reports on the subject show that skills gaps are occurring. The recession has accelerated this. The idea of a jobless recovery [see extract below] favours investment in productivity rather than people. There is another factor connected to this which is the much greater computer and electronic interface skills of the up and coming generation. They also have higher expectations about the type of work they would like to do.

The problem is more of skills mismatch than overall skills availability. This is a structural training problem rather than a consequence of the ageing population.

- jobs are changing
- educational attainment is lagging. . . .

Wage Costs and Availability of Low Cost Labour

One of the arguments against robots, contested by the suppliers, is that they are less flexible in operation and demand more up-front investment than the employment of low cost [often immigrant in the developed countries] labour.

The high labour cost sectors are more likely to use robots.

The differences between the countries are large too, although the interpretation of comparative data is often difficult. . . .

Low Cost Labour

China, and to some extent Brazil, have had access to low cost indigenous labour.

Japan and to a lesser extent Korea have restricted incoming workers.

USA and parts of Europe have until recently allowed this inflow, and both areas have used fewer robots proportionately as a partial result of this, with the exception of Germany. The table shows very large differences in immigration. . . .

Health, Safety [H&S] and Environment

The increasing attention to these factors adds impetus to the employment of robotics in hazardous environments, or those involving great monotony. In the developed countries, H&S is a steadily advancing area; in the developing countries, progress is very sporadic.

According to the International Labor Organization (ILO), 270 million workers fall victim to occupational injuries and illnesses, leading to 2.3 million deaths annually, showing that the problem is significant.

There is pressure from consumer groups to force manufacturers in developing countries to look after their workers to a standard approaching that achieved by the developed world manufacturers, but progress is slow.

However, no specific new initiatives have been identified in the study so far, which would cause a *step change* in the current trend to gradual improvement of health and safety practices in the six countries being studied. . . .

Summary
Overall Rise in Employment

Overall paid employment has risen in most countries. In the six considered here, only Japan has seen a decline.

This is driven by increasing participation of women, and increases in population, including immigration in some cases. It is also caused by the increasing demand for services, and the creation of completely new products and markets, often related to the application of electronics to communication.

The statistics mainly point to reduction in employment in manufacturing in the developed countries, but this is often a small reduction. It coincides with an increase in output and an increase in robotics use except in the case of Japan.

The extra number that have gained employment in the years 2000 to 2008 is far greater than the small numbers losing their jobs in manufacturing.

The new jobs have been in:

1. distribution and services, some of the distribution jobs are the result of manufacturers outsourcing their distribution. In the past these jobs would have been classified as part of manufacturing.
2. and also in new manufacturing applications, particularly using technology advances to create new consumer products [mobile phones, computers, games etc].

In the industrialising countries, as could be expected, there has been a sharp rise in employment in manufacturing, as well as increase in output.

Productivity increases are not just caused by automation and robotics, but it is one of three main factors, along with increased size of manufacturing plants and the globalisation of sourcing. *Note: while the IFR numbers provide a clear basis from which to work, it has not always been possible to separate robotics from automation in our analyses.*

Individual countries differ greatly, the importance of manufacturing is only 11% of employment in USA . . . but 24% in Germany and as high as 27% in more recently industrialising countries such as the Republic of Korea.

The level of robotics use has almost always doubled, in all of the six countries [except Japan] in the eight years covered by the study. The proportion of the workforce that is unemployed has hardly changed in this period. . . .

Employment *Directly* Due to the Use of Robotics [World]

The robot industry itself generates on the order of 150,000 jobs worldwide, to which can be added the support staff and operators, another 150,000 people.

There are three other types of application where robotics create or preserve jobs. These are jobs which can only be done by robots.

I Where the product cannot be made to satisfactory precision, consistency and cost, without robotics.

II Where the conditions under which the current work is done are unsatisfactory [may be illegal in the developed countries], but where a robot will operate.

III Where [particularly] a developed country manufacturing unit with high labour costs is threatened by a unit in a low labour cost area.

Employment *Indirectly* Due to the Use of Robotics

A much larger source of employment, at least partly due to robotics, is the newly created downstream activity necessary to support manufacturing which can only be done by robots. We have been conservative in what we have chosen to include here. Some of the people we have spoken to, for example, would have liked us to have included large parts of the automotive sector sales and distribution employment. Our conclusion was that much of this infrastructure was in place before robots were widely used, and so not resulting from the use of robots.

The best example is the communication and leisure equipment business, from distribution to retailing. In the USA, this part of retailing is of the order of 1 million. In world terms this accounts for 3 to 5 million of jobs which would not exist if automation and robotics had not been developed to allow production of millions of electronic products, from phones to Playstations. . . .

Note that China now produces more cars than USA, but the number of robots used in vehicle manufacture in China is estimated at 28,000 compared with 77,000 in USA.

Robot density in a sector only provides a partial view of employment which is dependent on robotics. For example, use of robotics in the automotive sector does not cover all parts of the industry. However, large parts of the motor vehicle assembly sector would be lost to a country if it did not employ robotics. Probably not the components side, this is often highly automated but less likely to depend on robotics.

In the electronics sector some components could not be made without robotics, or could not be made at a cost which would sell, which would cause job losses not just in manufacture but downstream as well.

Potential for New Job Creation in the Years up to 2016

There are five main areas where new jobs may be created in the next five years by the use of robotics.

I. Continued development of new products based on the development of electronics and communication technology. One of the new areas identified, for example, is the manufacture of service robots. Another is the development and mass adoption of renewable energy technologies.

II. Expansion of existing economies and industries, notably automotive.

III. Greater use of robotics in the SME [small and medium enterprises] sectors, particularly in the developed countries, to protect or win back manufacture from the low cost countries, or to win back production which had been seen as hazardous, but which had been taken up by the developing countries.

IV. Greater use of robotics in the food sector [where current use is low] as processed meals develop, to meet more stringent hygiene conditions.

V. Expansion of the robotics sector itself, to cope with the growth in demand. We have assumed a 15% growth which adds 45,000 people.

Overall Effect

Direct employment due to robotics:

2 to 3 million jobs created in world manufacturing.

Considering the world population of industrial robots at just over 1 million, **that is 2 to 3 jobs per robot in use.**

Indirect employment downstream of this more than doubles this number.

For the future, 700,000 to 1 million new jobs to be created by robots in the next five years.

PETER GORLE is the managing director of Metra Martech, a firm specializing in industrial and economic analysis for governments and international organizations.

ANDREW CLIVE is a senior consultant with Metra Martech, a firm specializing in industrial and economic analysis for governments and international organizations.

EXPLORING THE ISSUE

Will Robots Take Your Job?

Critical Thinking and Reflection

1. What are "industrial" robots?
2. What kinds of jobs now held by humans may robots be able to do in the near future?
3. Why do robots threaten more than just industrial jobs?
4. In what ways might robots create jobs?
5. If robots take all the jobs, what will people do?

Is There Common Ground?

Computer technology (including robotics) is a rapidly growing field. Indeed, in the past whenever someone would say "Computers can't do X!" someone else would add "Yet!" They'd be right, too, for computers can now do a great many things their predecessors could not. Surely this applies to robotics as well, and robots have been expanding their presence in the workplace for decades. They will continue to do so, and Kevin Drum and Peter Gorle and Andrew Clive may well agree that there is a fine line between robots taking jobs and—in a faltering economy—robots keeping companies alive without hiring more humans. It is also worth stressing that the two selections reprinted here differ in their timelines. Kevin Drum says job loss will be severe before the middle of the twenty-first century. Peter Gorle and Andrew Clive say many (up to 1 million) jobs will be created in the next five years. If they had tried to project further into the future, perhaps they would have agreed with Kevin Drum.

1. Why have employers welcomed robots in the workplace?

2. What jobs seem to you to be out of reach for robots (so far!)?
3. Kevin Drum suggests that it is time to rethink our economy to achieve a more equitable distribution of national wealth. Where would you begin?

Additional Resources

Jason Borenstein, "Robots and the Changing Workforce," *AI & Society* (2011).

Erik Brynjolfsson and Andrew McAfee, *Race against the Machine* (Digital Frontier Press, 2011) (http://raceagainstthemachine.com/).

Kirk L. Kroeker, "Weighing Watson's Impact," *Communications of the ACM* (July 2011).

Aaron Smith and Janna Anderson, *AI, Robotics, and the Future of Jobs* (PEW Internet Research Project, August 2014) (http://www.pewinternet.org/2014/08/06/future-of-jobs/).

Alex Wright, "Automotive Autonomy," *Communications of the ACM* (July 2011).

Internet References . . .

MIT Computer Science and Artificial Intelligence Laboratory

http://www.csail.mit.edu/

Carnegie Mellon Robotics Institute

https://www.ri.cmu.edu/

Why Robots Will Be the Biggest Job Creators in World History

http://www.forbes.com/sites/johntamny/2015/03/01/why-robots-will-be-the-biggest-job-creators-in-history/

Selected, Edited, and with Issue Framing Material by:
Thomas A. Easton, *Thomas College*

ISSUE

Can Technology Protect Americans from International Cybercriminals?

YES: Randy Vanderhoof, from "Testimony Before the House Committee on Science, Space, and Technology, Subcommittees on Oversight and Research and Technology, hearing on 'Can Technology Protect Americans from International Cybercriminals?'" U.S. House of Representatives (2014)

NO: Charles H. Romine, from "Testimony Before the House Committee on Science, Space, and Technology, Subcommittees on Oversight and Research and Technology, hearing on 'Can Technology Protect Americans from International Cybercriminals?'" U.S. House of Representatives (2014)

Learning Outcomes
After reading this issue, you will be able to: • Describe the potential consequences of theft of credit card data.   • Explain what measures might be taken to prevent hacker attacks on the computer systems of major retailers.   • Discuss why, even with the best technology, cybercrime is unlikely to be stopped entirely.

ISSUE SUMMARY

YES: Randy Vanderhoof argues that as the United States' payment system shifts from credit cards with magnetic stripes (whose data, stored on merchant computer systems, are a prime target for hackers) to smart cards with embedded microchips (which do not make data available to hackers), the rate of credit card fraud will decline rapidly, as it already has in other countries.

NO: Charles H. Romine, Director of the National Institute of Standards and Technology's (NIST) Information Technology Laboratory, argues that technology is not enough to solve the cybercrime problem. The NIST works on smart card systems, but also develops guidelines, standards, and best practices essential to making the technology work. Fighting cybercriminals requires not just technology, but also policy, legal, and economic efforts.

Physicist Gregory Benford says he wrote the very first computer virus, way back in the late 1960s. It was not designed to do harm, just to test the idea of a program that could spread from computer to computer, but it was a virus. As computers became more sophisticated, so did viruses and other "malware." By the 1990s, there was much alarm about hackers (see Bruce Sterling, *The Hacker Crackdown: Law and Disorder on the Electronic Frontier,* Bantam, 1992; http://www.gutenberg.org/ebooks/101). With the advent of the Internet a little later, malware starred in credit card fraud, identity theft, and more. As the problem got worse, it gave rise to antivirus software and the computer security industry. Today cybercrime costs the United states a bit less than one percent of its Gross Domestic Product (GDP)(see "Net Losses: Estimating the Global Cost of Cybercrime: Economic Impact of Cybercrime II," Center for Strategic and International Studies, June 2014; http://www.mcafee.com/us/resources /reports/rp-economic-impact-cybercrime2.pdf).

Come the twenty-first century, and while computer security and fraud remain of concern, people have begun to worry about cyberwar. In June 2010, the Stuxnet worm attacked Iranian nuclear facilities. It used stolen digital certificates to take control over software and interfere with the normal function of nuclear power plants, electrical distribution systems, and oil pipelines. Early reports said the Stuxnet worm was so complex that it must have taken large teams of programmers, millions of dollars in funding, and many months of work to produce it. Iran insisted it had to be an Israeli-American cyber-attack, and on June 1, 2012, David E. Sanger reported in "Obama Order Sped up Wave of Cyberattacks against Iran," *New York Times*, that interviews with European, U.S., and Israeli officials have revealed that in 2006, President George W. Bush initiated the development of the Stuxnet worm under the code-name Olympic Games. Samuel Greengard, "The New Face of War," *Communications of the ACM* (December 2010), considers this a sign of the way wars will be fought in the future. "The risk of cyber-warfare is growing, and many . . . warn that political leaders aren't entirely tuned into the severity of the threat." It must be taken seriously, for it is only a matter of time before cyberwar is real. Richard A. Clarke and Richard K. Knake, *Cyber War: The Next Threat to National Security and What to Do about It* (HarperCollins, 2010), stress that because society is now totally dependent on telecommunications networks, it is also vulnerable to widespread, long-lasting damage. James P. Farwell and Rafal Rohozinski, "Stuxnet and the Future of Cyber War," *Survival* (February/March 2011), note that cyberwar "offers great potential for striking at enemies with less risk than using traditional means." They also note that many cyberwar techniques are rooted in cybercrime (viruses, worms, bot-nets, identity theft, hacking, fraud, and more).

The methods of defending against cyberwar and cyberterrorism are also rooted in the fight against cybercrime. Few people today do not have antivirus and/or anti-malware software on their computers. The U.S. government has long sought extensions to digital telephony and the Internet of traditional wiretapping laws that permitted law-enforcement agencies to listen in on the conversations of criminal suspects (see Declan McCullagh, "FBI: We Need Wiretap-Ready Web Sites—Now," *CNET News*, May 4, 2012; http://news.cnet.com/8301-1009_3-57428067-83 /fbi-we-need-wiretap-ready-web-sites-now/). After September 11, 2001, the War on Terrorism began and every tool that promised to help identify terrorists before or catch them after they committed their dreadful acts was seen as desirable. However, when the Department of Defense's Defense Advanced Research Projects Agency (DARPA) proposed a massive computer system capable of sifting through purchases, tax data, court records, Google searches, emails, and other information from government and commercial databases to seek suspicious patterns of behavior, many people objected that this amounted to a massive assault on privacy and was surely in violation of the Fourth Amendment to the U.S. Constitution (which established the right of private citizens to be secure against unreasonable searches and seizures; "unreasonable" has come to mean "without a search warrant" for physical searches of homes and offices and "without a court order" for interceptions of mail and wiretappings of phone conversations). This Total or Terrorism Information Awareness (TIA) program soon died although many of its components continued under other names; see Shane Harris, "TIA Lives On," *National Journal* (February 25, 2006). See also Hina Shamsi and Alex Abdo, "Privacy and Surveillance Post-9/11," *Human Rights* (Winter 2011).

Is cybercrime more like cyberwar? Matthew Goldstein, Nicole Perlroth, and David E. Sanger, report in "Hackers' Attack Cracked 10 Financial Firms in Major Assault," *New York Times* (October 4, 2014), that the hackers responsible for breaching JPMorgan Chase and nine other major financial firms, affecting more than 80 million homes and businesses, "are thought to be operating from Russia and appear to have at least loose connections with officials of the Russian government." There is now serious concern that a hacker attack could cause a major financial crisis. And with the involvement of foreign governments, it could easily be an act of war. John Stone is sure that "Cyber War Will Take Place!" *Journal of Strategic Studies* (February 2013); if commercial attacks are acts of war, the war may already be under way. At the end of 2014, Sony Pictures was hacked, embarrassing documents were released, and threats were issued to keep the movie "The Interview" (about the assassination of North Korea's leader) from being released; the U.S. government accused North Korea of the hacking and called it an act of cyberwar; see for example "Sony Hack: North Korea Threatens US as Row Deepens" (http://www.bbc.com/news /world-asia-30573040).

General Keith Alexander, head of the Defense Department's U.S. Cyber Command (http://www.defense.gov/home /features/2010/0410_cybersec/), is preparing as if cyberwar is a real threat. Peter Sommer and Ian Brown, "Reducing Systemic Cybersecurity Risk" OECD (Organization for Economic Co-operation and Development)/IFP (International Futures Programme) Project on "Future Global Shocks," 2011), conclude "that very few single cyber-related events have the capacity to cause a global shock. Governments nevertheless need to make detailed preparations to withstand and recover from a wide range of unwanted cyber events, both accidental and deliberate. There are significant and growing risks of localized misery and loss as a result of compromise of computer and telecommunications services." Simson L. Garfinkel, "The Cybersecurity Risk," *Communications of the ACM* (June 2012), argues that the reason why we have not already built more secure computer systems is that "it is more cost-effective to create systems without redundancy or resiliency." Gary McGraw, "Cyber War Is Inevitable (Unless We Build Security In)," *Journal of Strategic Studies* (February 2013), argues that this needs to change.

What is the best way to defend against cybercriminals and their more extreme cousins, the cyberwarriors? R. Scott Kemp, "Cyberweapons: Bold Steps in a Digital Darkness?" *Bulletin of the Atomic Scientists* (June 7, 2012) (http://www.thebulletin.org/web-edition/op-eds/cyberweapons -bold-steps-digital-darkness), argues that "We are at a key turning point . . . in which a nation must decide what role cyberweapons will play in its national defense. . . . for the United States and other highly developed nations whose societies are critically and deeply reliant on computers, the safe approach is to direct cyber research at purely defensive applications." According to Richard Stone, "A Call to Cyber Arms," *Science* (March 1, 2013), the U.S. and other governments are putting a great deal of effort not only into devising ways to defend against cyber-espionage and cyber-attacks against industrial,

defense, and commercial infrastructure, but also into ways to go on the offensive.

Most discussions of the topic focus on the role of technology in defending against cyber-attacks, and indeed on March 4, 2014, the United States House of Representatives' Committee on Science, Subcommittees on Oversight and Research and Technology held a hearing on "Can Technology Protect Americans from International Cybercriminals?" The YES selection is drawn from the testimony before this hearing of Randy Vanderhoof, executive director of the Smart Card Alliance. He argues that as the United States' payment system shifts from credit cards with magnetic stripes (whose data, stored on merchant computer systems, are a prime target for hackers) to smart cards with embedded microchips (which do not make data available to hackers), the rate of credit card fraud will decline rapidly, as it already has in other countries. His focus is very much on commerce, and given the JPMorgan Chase attack, perhaps that is appropriate. The NO selection is drawn from the testimony of Charles H. Romine, director of the Information Technology Laboratory of the National Institute of Standards and Technology. He argues that technology alone is not enough to solve the cybercrime problem. The NIST works on smart card systems, but also develops guidelines, standards, and best practices essential to making the technology work. Fighting cybercriminals requires not just technology, but also policy, legal, and economic efforts.

YES ⬎

Randy Vanderhoof

Testimony Before the House Committee on Science, Space, and Technology, Subcommittees on Oversight and Research and Technology, hearing on "Can Technology Protect Americans from International Cybercriminals?"

On behalf of the Smart Card Alliance and its members, I thank you for the opportunity to testify today. We applaud the Subcommittees' leadership and foresight in examining important issues in the payments industry, especially on increasing instances of international cybercriminals committing payment data breaches and the role of EMV (Europay, Mastercard, and Visa) chip payment technology to help secure the U.S. payments infrastructure.

The Smart Card Alliance is a non-profit organization established in 2001 that provides education about smart card chip technology and applications and operates a collaborative, open forum among leaders in various industries including payments, mobile, transportation, government, healthcare, and access security. The Alliance's members from the payment ecosystem include payment brands, card issuers, payment processors, merchants and technology providers.

Shortly after the four major payments brands, American Express, Discover, MasterCard and Visa, announced incentives to introduce secure EMV chip cards for the U.S. market and aligned timelines for fraud liability shift dates in 2015 and 2017, the Smart Card Alliance organized a new payments-only industry association, the EMV Migration Forum. The Forum was formed specifically to address issues that require broad cooperation and coordination across many constituents in the payments space to ensure the successful adoption of EMV-enabled cards, devices, and terminals across the U.S. market, and to ensure that migration in the U.S. market is efficient, timely and effective. The Forum has more than 150 member companies, including global payments brands, financial institutions, merchants, processors, acquirers, regional debit networks, industry associations and industry suppliers.

The Smart Card Alliance and the EMV Migration Forum have been the leading advocates for accelerating the adoption of secure payments technology to address the growing fraud problem in the United States and to ensure citizens traveling outside of the U.S. will have a safe and convenient payments experience.

The focus of my testimony will be on the state of payment card technology and the payments acceptance ecosystem, including differences between the magnetic stripe cards used in the U.S. and EMV chip cards used in more than 80 countries, the status of U.S. migration to EMV chip cards, and the benefits for the U.S. moving to EMV chip cards to increase security, reduce counterfeit card fraud, and reduce the likelihood of future data breaches by devaluing the payments data that is present in the retail and financial systems.

Increasing Instances of Cybercrime in the U.S. Highlight Need for EMV Chip Cards

Cybercrime targeting government and commercial enterprises is a growing problem in the U.S. In 2013, data breaches became more damaging, with one in three people who received a data breach notification letter becoming an identity fraud victim, up from one in four in 2012.

While cybercrime is a known threat across many industries, criminals are increasingly targeting retail store chains with sophisticated attacks in order to extract credit card data from millions of transactions. Attacks against

U.S. House of Representatives, 2014.

retailers are particularly damaging because of their effects on large numbers of consumers, banks and merchants at the same time. The results of a single attack, which we saw most recently with retailer Target, can be millions of dollars' worth of credit card fraud and the need to close and reissue tens of millions of payment card accounts to prevent further fraud. There are also other unquantified costs of payment data breaches, including the time and money to investigate and clean up after the breach, lost business and damaged reputations for the merchants and banks involved.

The opportunity for huge financial gains with little chance of criminal prosecution from these stolen card accounts also provides the incentive for hackers to penetrate deeper into compromised networks to extract additional personal information beyond payments data, including email addresses and phone numbers, putting consumers' privacy at further risk.

Increasing instances of attacks against retailers are due in part to the fact that U.S. magnetic stripe payment card information is highly valuable data for hackers, who can sell it on the black market to criminals for large profits. For example, the black market price for several million card accounts stolen from the Target breach was between $26.60 and $44.80 each prior to Dec. 19, 2013.

Criminals are willing to pay such high prices for U.S. magnetic stripe card data because of the ease with which that data can be used to create counterfeit payment cards for fraud. It's very simple to write stolen magnetic stripe payment card information to a different magnetic stripe payment card. This is why the U.S. is the only region where counterfeit card fraud continues to grow. The U.S. accounted for 47.3% of global fraud losses in 2012, despite only accounting for 23.5% of the total transactions, and U.S. issuer losses due to counterfeiting account for 26.5% of global fraud losses.

The financial industry has very strict data security standards, called the Payment Card Industry Data Security Standard (PCI DSS), in place to protect payments data and other sensitive personal information captured and stored by retail systems and processors. These standards and best practices are effective deterrents against a lot of criminal activity, but not enough for increasingly sophisticated criminals and attacks. Additional security measures are needed and are already used globally including EMV chip cards, advanced encryption technologies and tokenization.

EMV chip cards in particular can reduce the threat of financial cybercrime by removing the economic incentive for criminals. Replacing magnetic stripe payment data with secure EMV chip payment data devalues U.S.

payment data in the eyes of criminals because, if stolen, EMV chip payment data cannot be used to create counterfeit payment cards.

The positive news is that the U.S. payments system is undertaking a migration to EMV chip card technology, and this will present significant barriers for criminals engaging in payment card counterfeiting. Although the U.S. payments system is complex, the industry has recognized the need to move as quickly as possible to EMV chip card payments. I am encouraged by the movement and progress from all industry stakeholders towards implementation of the technology.

Next, I will explain EMV chip card technology and why it is secure, how it can help to address mounting U.S. payment data security problems, and what the current status of U.S. EMV migration is.

Introduction to EMV Chip Payment Technology

EMV chip payment cards are based on widely used and highly secure smart card technology, also referred to as "smart chip" technology. Smart cards—which can look like a card but can also take on different forms—have embedded integrated circuit chips, powerful minicomputers that can be programmed for different applications. Through the chip, the smart card can store and access data and applications securely, and exchange data securely with readers and other systems. Smart cards are ideal for many applications, especially payments, because they provide high levels of security and privacy protection, are easily carried, and do not require their own power source to operate effectively.

Smart cards are currently used to secure many applications worldwide, including:

- Identity applications including employee ID badges for physical access to buildings and secure computer and network access; citizen ID documents; electronic passports; driver's licenses; and online authentication devices. Today, smart card technology is used by all U.S. federal employees and contractors with Personal Identity Verification (PIV) credentials to secure access to government systems and buildings; in U.S. citizens' passports to secure identity information; and in federal programs like the TSA First Responder Authentication Credential (FRAC), the TSA Transportation Worker Identification Credential (TWIC) and the Department of Defense Common Access Card (CAC)

- Healthcare applications including citizen health ID cards; health provider ID cards; portable medical records cards. Smart card technology is now being recommended in legislation to create a pilot for a proposed Medicare Common Access Card (H.R. 3024)
- Mobile applications including billions of mobile phone subscriber identity modules (SIMs) in use today, plus in NFC-enabled phones to secure mobile wallets
- And lastly, with global payment standard EMV chip cards, now used in more than 80 countries worldwide with 1.6 billion payments cards issued to date, and the focus of this testimony

EMV: A Global Perspective

It was growing counterfeit card fraud that originally led the global payments industry to move to smart chip technology for bank cards and to develop the global EMV standard for bank cards based on chip card technology. The EMV specification, first available in 1996 and managed by EMVCo, defines the global interoperable standard for smart chip-based bank cards.

Financial institutions in Europe, Latin America, Asia/Pacific and Canada are issuing EMV chip cards for credit and debit payment or migrating to EMV issuance. According to EMVCo, approximately 1.6 billion EMV cards have been issued globally and 24 million point of sale (POS) terminals accept EMV cards as of Q4 2012. This represents 44.7% of the total payment cards in circulation and 76.4% of the POS terminals installed globally.

There have been a number of historical factors behind the adoption of EMV chip technology in these other countries. The most important factors have been high fraud rates and the cost and reliability of the communications infrastructure. In markets in Western Europe, Australia, Latin America, and Canada the rate of credit card fraud had been much worse than what the U.S. market has historically experienced. These higher fraud rates, plus the lack of low cost, reliable communications at the retail level, led countries to adopt EMV chip technology to enable greater security at the card and offline payments processing at the terminal level. Each of these markets are smaller than the U.S. market, with fewer financial institutions and merchants to convert to chip technology, so the business case to make the investment in EMV has been very strong. Countries that have implemented EMV chip technology have seen their counterfeit fraud decline by as much as 67%.

The U.S. is one of the last countries to move to EMV chip technology, but has now started its migration.

Between July 2011 and June 2012, American Express, Discover, MasterCard and Visa announced plans for moving the U.S. to an EMV-based payments infrastructure. The plans included a series of incentives and policy changes aligning around a target date of October 2015 for card issuers and merchants to complete their implementation of EMV chip cards, terminals and processing systems. ATM operators and retail petroleum outlets were given until 2016 and 2017, respectively, to complete their EMV migrations.

It is important to note that the target dates are not mandates, as U.S. payment brands do not have the ability to set requirements. What they can, and did, was mandate payments processors who connect through their global networks to support EMV chip data in transactions by April 1, 2013. This is the only mandate for U.S. EMV chip implementation.

The payment brands have offered card-issuing financial institutions and merchants an incentive to move to EMV chip technology in the form of a counterfeit fraud liability shift. After the target EMV chip migration dates, the payment brands will shift the responsibility for any fraud resulting from a payment transaction to the party using the least secure technology. This may be either the issuer of the card or the merchant accepting the payment card.

As an example, if a merchant can accept EMV chip cards and the cardholder presents a magnetic stripe card and there is fraud, the issuer would bear the liability for fraud. Conversely, if a cardholder presents an EMV chip card for payment and the merchant only accepts magnetic stripe cards, the merchant would be liable for any fraud. If both parties have deployed EMV and fraud results from that transaction, the current rules for fraud liability are applied.

This fraud liability shift ensures that those who have made the investment in EMV chip technology will not bear responsibility or cost from fraud from another stakeholder who has not made their system more secure. The goal of the liability shift is to encourage both issuers and merchants to move to EMV technology at the same time so that fraud is removed from the system, not shifted from one party to another.

Status of U.S. EMV Migration

The U.S. payments industry is approximately two years into the planned four-year migration to adopt EMV chip technology. Industry stakeholders have been meeting regularly at Smart Card Alliance conferences and EMV Migration Forum meetings and within other industry organizations to address issues that require coordination and cooperation among multiple payments industry participants to ensure a timely and cost effective industry-wide migration to chip technology in the U.S.

The migration to chip cards in the U.S. is complex, expensive and difficult to coordinate. The U.S. market is the largest individual market to convert to chip cards. With over 12,000 financial institutions that issue cards, an estimated 1.2 billion cards in the market, over 10 million POS devices in retail stores, and another 100,000 ATMs installed, the United States payments market is larger than all of Europe's payments markets combined. To date, an estimated 10 to 15 million chip cards have been issued to U.S. consumers, mostly to those who travel frequently outside of the U.S. and who benefit from having the same chip cards that are used in those countries' retail outlets and ATMs. This progress represents less than 2% of the total number of cards in the market. Retailers have replaced approximately 1 million of the more than 10 million POS terminals in stores, but nearly all of these are still operating only as magnetic stripe accepting devices until the software is tested and certified by the acquirers and the stores are ready to begin accepting chip cards.

Implementing EMV chip technology for U.S. debit is also very complex. Complexities result from having 19 debit networks for PIN debit card transactions and the need for compliance with the 2011 Federal Reserve Rule-making, "Regulation II, Debit Card Interchange Fees and Routing," interpretation of the Durbin Amendment under the Dodd Frank Act. The rulemaking requires that there be at least two unrelated debit card networks supported on each card issued and that merchants have the option to decide which network to route those transactions to each time a debit card is used.

Accommodating these debit routing rules through agreements among all of the debit networks and the global brands, as well as determining the impact of recent court decisions challenging the Federal Reserve rules, have created uncertainty among issuers and merchants about how to implement EMV chip technology for debit transactions. Today the industry is working on ways to comply with the current rules and still be able to accommodate potential changes that may result from further decisions by the courts, and progress has been made.

How EMV Chip Cards Prevent Counterfeit Card Fraud

Chip technology in conjunction with the global EMV payments application standard has proven to be the most effective tool to prevent counterfeit card fraud and

maintain the requirements for global interoperability of payment cards for issuers, merchants and consumers. The counterfeit fraud protection comes from two aspects of this technology:

1. The secure storage of the cardholder data inside the chip rather than on a magnetic stripe
2. The dynamic payment transaction data generated by the chip when it is presented to the payment reader for processing the card in a physical retail setting.

The chip itself is a powerful microcomputer with active defenses that prevent tampering with the application and the information it stores inside its memory. Even if chip data were to be copied, it could not be used to create a usable copy onto another chip card because each chip is programmed with a secret key known only to the issuer. The less secure magnetic stripe has no defenses to prevent a criminal from reading the stripe and reprogramming that same card data onto another magnetic stripe, creating an undetectable copy of the original card.

Chip-enabled terminals in retail stores are programmed to pass dynamic security information to the chip before the chip will pass the uniquely generated cryptographic electronic signature to the terminal to complete a payment transaction. This feature is the first line of defense against the use of counterfeit cards that is possible today with magnetic stripe cards.

The chip generates a one time, unique security code, called a cryptogram, for each chip payment transaction that is passed through the chip terminal and through the retailer's POS system and payments processing network. The security cryptogram is verified by the issuer processor to determine that the card used to start the transaction is authentic and that the transaction data was unique to that card. Therefore, a counterfeit copy of that card or a second transaction with the same unique card data would be detected by the issuer and the message normally sent back to the retailer to complete the transaction would deny the transaction.

In addition, EMV chip transactions do not include other data needed for magnetic stripe transactions. This means that any stolen data cannot be used to create a fraudulent transaction in an EMV chip or magnetic stripe environment.

The dynamic data generated by EMV chip cards and the omission of data used in magnetic stripe transactions greatly devalue any payment data that is present in the retailer's or third party processor systems since the chip data cannot be made into counterfeit cards to commit fraud. For example, if EMV chip data had been present in the retailers' systems that were recently victimized by a POS malware attack that extracted card transaction data, the impact of the data breach would have been significantly lessened for the merchant, the card issuers and the consumers through greatly reduced risk of counterfeiting and the resulting card fraud.

The EMV standard also supports additional security mechanisms including the manner with which consumers verify their identities, called Cardholder Verification Methods (CVMs). The EMV standard supports signature, PIN and/or no CVM. Chip-based payment cards that use signature as a CVM have all of the security benefits that the chip and the EMV transaction data provide for protection from counterfeiting and resulting fraud. Chip-based payment cards that use PINs as a CVM provide an added layer of security that prevents the physical card from being used if it is lost or stolen. In the U.S., card issuers will decide which CVMs they want to support based on customer profiles and card management considerations. Merchants can decide which CVMs available on each card they will accept in their retail outlets. As a result, it is likely we will see EMV chip cards issued with a mix of signature, PIN and no CVMs in the U.S.

The issuance of chip cards in the U.S. does not mean the elimination of the magnetic stripe altogether. Financial institutions will continue to issue chip cards with a magnetic stripe on the back for the foreseeable future in order to enable consumers to continue to use these cards at merchant locations that haven't yet upgraded to chip, or in some countries who have not yet adopted the EMV chip standard.

These magnetic stripes that will remain on the backs of bank-issued EMV chip cards do not pose a fraud threat to card issuers or consumers when chip-enabled merchant terminals are widely deployed. When issued on a chip card, a magnetic stripe has different information stored, so when swiped at an EMV chip-accepting terminal, it signals to the terminal that the card was issued with a chip. The terminal will then force the card to be used as a more secure chip card rather than as a less secure magnetic stripe card at that device.

Another scenario is where that chip card's magnetic stripe is copied and a card is created with that card's data written to another magnetic stripe on an unauthorized second card. When that counterfeit card is swiped at a merchant terminal that can process a chip transaction, the terminal would also direct the customer to use the chip. Because the chip doesn't exist on this counterfeit card, the transaction will be declined. If the counterfeit card is used at a terminal that does not support a chip, the card would be accepted unless the issuer flags the transaction based on certain usage analytics or if the cardholder reported the card lost or stolen.

After the fraud liability shift date, if the copied card made with the magnetic stripe data of a chip card is used at a terminal that does not support a chip, and the card is accepted even though it is a copy, the merchant would be responsible for that fraud because it did not have the more secure EMV chip handling capability that would have detected the card was a counterfeit. This is the reason for the liability shift discussed earlier; it's important for both the issuance and acceptance infrastructures to move to chip at the same time to provide the most protection from counterfeit card fraud.

In a third scenario where chip payment card data is intercepted and used to make an online purchase, there are additional security measures that online merchants use, including the three or four digit card security code printed on the card (and which is not available from either the magnetic stripe or the chip), the cardholder's billing address information, or both. Online purchases where the EMV chip is not used in the payment transaction, called Card-Not-Present (CNP) transactions, are not protected by the issuance of EMV chip cards. However, there are other ways to manage CNP fraud risk that are being used today and new technologies that are being developed to address this problem.

To summarize, the security features that EMV chip cards provide to the market in conjunction with the chip reading terminals and advanced payments processing upgrades to support dynamic data are a powerful set of tools to take counterfeit fraud out of the payments system. These security features reduce the likelihood of, or the resulting damage from, any future data breaches against retailers, processors and financial institutions.

Conclusion

In summary, the U.S. reliance on magnetic stripe payment cards has made the country a target for fraud. Evidence to support this are: the increasing attacks on U.S. retailers, of which the FBI found at least 22 instances in the past year, and the fact that the U.S. is the only region where counterfeit card fraud rises consistently. Hackers are motivated by the big profits that they can make from selling U.S. magnetic stripe payment data on the black market to criminals to make and use counterfeit magnetic stripe cards.

Joining more than 80 countries and implementing EMV chip technology will greatly devalue U.S. payment card data in the eyes of criminals because it cannot be used to create counterfeit chip or magnetic stripe cards. Other countries that implemented EMV chip payments saw fraud decrease by as much as 67%.

While the move to EMV chip payments in the U.S. is a complex and expensive undertaking, it is a critical one that will benefit our entire payments system. I am encouraged by the payments industry's recognition that we need to move EMV chip technology. I am even more encouraged by the fact that many of the largest financial institutions are now issuing EMV chip cards and big retail chains are moving quickly to put in place the chip-enabled terminals and working with their acquirer processors to enable those devices to begin accepting chip transactions by the October 2015 targeted completion dates.

Randy Vanderhoof is the executive director of the Smart Card Alliance, a nonprofit organization that promotes smart card chip technology to address the growing fraud problem.

Charles H. Romine  **NO**

Testimony Before the House Committee on Science, Space, and Technology, Subcommittees on Oversight and Research and Technology, hearing on "Can Technology Protect Americans from International Cybercriminals?"

Background

Cybertheft can occur at a scale unlike physical crimes. It can have multiple victims and a much larger impact than would be possible in conventional criminal activity. As we know, one breach can affect thousands—if not millions—of citizens. Cybertheft also can be perpetrated at the speed of electronic transactions. This makes interception difficult and places a strong reliance on preventive security controls. They also can occur without the physical presence of the criminal. This is possible because we work and live in an increasingly interconnected digital world. This introduces jurisdiction, legal and policy complexities as well as difficulty in attribution to the criminals themselves.

In response to the title of the hearing: "Can Technology Protect Americans from International Cybercriminals?"—my response would be: technology alone cannot solve these problems. However, we do believe that effective use of technology can make it more difficult for criminals to perpetrate these crimes, can make it easier for organizations to recover from serious incidents, and can, in some cases, prevent such incidents from occurring.

For example, technology can make it difficult to clone payment cards with stolen credentials or use the information to make online purchases. Smart cards using chip-and-pin technologies can make theft of the information stored on the card more difficult; however, often the attacks and exploits are not on the cards themselves, but are instead against the supporting payment infrastructure. We believe it takes a holistic approach that includes technology, training and awareness, policy, legal, economic and international efforts, to bring cybertheft, one of many different cyberthreats we face, under control.

With that background, today I would like to discuss some of the Department of Commerce National Institute of Standards and Technology's (NIST) activities that accelerate the development and deployment of security technologies and assist the US Government and other stakeholders and partners in protecting their information and communications infrastructure against cyberthreats, including cybertheft.

The Role of NIST in Cybersecurity

NIST's overall mission is to promote U.S. innovation and industrial competitiveness by advancing measurement science, standards, and technology in ways that enhance economic security and improve our quality of life. Our work in addressing technical challenges related to national priorities has ranged from projects related to the Smart Grid and electronic health records to atomic clocks, advanced nanomaterials, and computer chips.

In the area of cybersecurity, we have worked with federal agencies, industry, and academia since 1972, starting with the development of the Data Encryption Standard, when the potential commercial benefit of this technology became clear. Our role, to research, develop and deploy information security standards and technology to protect information systems against threats to the confidentiality, integrity and availability of information and services, was strengthened through the Computer Security Act of 1987 and reaffirmed through the Federal Information Security Management Act of 2002 (FISMA).

NIST accomplishes its mission in cybersecurity through collaborative partnerships with our customers and stakeholders in industry, government, academia, standards bodies, consortia and international partners.

Our broader work in the areas of information security, trusted networks, and software quality is applicable to a wide variety of users, from small and medium enterprises to large private and public organizations, including federal government agencies and companies involved with critical infrastructure.

We employ collaborative partnerships with our customers and stakeholders to take advantage of their technical and operational insights and to leverage the resources of a global community. These collaborative efforts, and our private sector collaborations in particular, are constantly being expanded by new initiatives, including in recent years through the National Initiative for Cybersecurity Education (NICE), the National Strategy for Trusted Identities in Cyberspace (NSTIC), the National Cybersecurity Center of Excellence (NCCoE), and in implementation of Executive Order 13636, "Improving Critical Infrastructure Cybersecurity."

NIST Cybersecurity Research, Standards and Guidelines

The E-Government Act recognized the importance of information security to the economic and national security interests of the United States. The Federal Information Security Management Act of 2002 (FISMA), Title III of the E-Government Act, included duties and responsibilities for NIST to develop standards and guidelines for Federal information systems.

The NIST Special Publications and Interagency Reports provide those management, operational, and technical security guidelines for Federal agencies and cover a broad range of topics such as Basic Input/Output System (BIOS) management and measurement, key management and derivation, media sanitization, electronic authentication, security automation, Bluetooth and wireless protocols, incident handling and intrusion detection, malware, cloud computing, public key infrastructure, risk assessments, supply chain risk management, authentication, access control, security automation and continuous monitoring.

Beyond these documents—which are peer-reviewed throughout industry, government, and academia—NIST conducts workshops, awareness briefings, and outreach to ensure comprehension of standards and guidelines, to share ongoing and planned activities, and to aid in scoping guidelines in a collaborative, open, and transparent manner.

In addition, NIST maintains the National Vulnerability Database (NVD), a repository of standards-based vulnerability management reference data. The NVD makes available information on vulnerabilities, impact measurements, detection techniques, and remediation assistance. It provides reference data that enable government, industry and international security automation capabilities. The NVD also plays a role in the efforts of the Payment Card Industry (PCI) to identify and mitigate vulnerabilities. The PCI uses the NVD vulnerability metrics to discern the IT vulnerability in point-of-sale devices and determine what risks are unacceptable for that industry.

NIST researchers develop and standardize cryptographic mechanisms that are used throughout the world to protect information at rest and in transit. These mechanisms provide security services, such as confidentiality, integrity, authentication, non-repudiation and digital signatures, to protect sensitive information. The NIST algorithms and associated cryptographic guidelines are developed in a transparent and inclusive process, leveraging cryptographic expertise around the world. The results are in standard, interoperable cryptographic mechanisms that can be used by all industries.

NIST has a complementary program, in coordination with the Government of Canada, to certify independent commercial calibration laboratories to test commercially available IT cryptographic modules, to ensure that they have implemented the NIST cryptographic standards and guidelines correctly. These testing laboratories exist around the globe and test hundreds of individual cryptographic modules yearly.

NIST Engagement with Industry

It is important to note that the impact of NIST's activities under FISMA extend beyond providing the means to protect Federal IT systems. They provide the cybersecurity foundations for the public trust that is essential to our realization of the national and global productivity and innovation potential of electronic business and its attendant economic benefits. Many organizations voluntarily follow NIST standards and guidelines, reflecting their wide acceptance throughout the world.

Beyond NIST's responsibilities under FISMA, under the provisions of the National Technology Transfer and Advancement Act (PL 104-113) and related OMB Circular A-119, NIST is tasked with the key role of encouraging and coordinating federal agency use of voluntary consensus standards and participation in the development of relevant standards, as well as promoting coordination between the public and private sectors in the development of standards and in conformity assessment activities. NIST works with other agencies, such as the

Department of State, to coordinate standards issues and priorities with the private sector through consensus standards organizations such as the American National Standards Institute (ANSI), the International Organization for Standardization (ISO), the Institute of Electrical and Electronic Engineers (IEEE), the Internet Engineering Task Force (IETF), and the International Telecommunications Union (ITU).

Partnership with industry to develop, maintain, and implement voluntary consensus standards related to cybersecurity best ensures the interoperability, security and resiliency of the global infrastructure needed to make us all more secure. It also allows this infrastructure to evolve in a way that embraces both security and innovation—allowing a market to flourish to create new types of secure products for the benefit of all Americans.

NIST works extensively in smart card standards, guidelines and best practices. NIST developed the standard for the US Government Personal Identity Verification (PIV) Card, and actively works with the ANSI and the ISO on global cybersecurity standards for use in smart cards, smart card cryptography and the standards for the international integrated circuit card. [ANSI 504; ISO 7816 and ISO 24727]

NIST also conducts cybersecurity research and development in forward looking technology areas, such as security for federal mobile environments and techniques for measuring and managing security. These efforts focus on improving the trustworthiness of IT components such as claimed identities, data, hardware, and software for networks and devices. Additional research areas include developing approaches to balancing safety, security, reliability in the nation's supply chain; enabling mobile device and application security; securing the nation's cyber-physical systems; enabling continuous security monitoring; providing advanced security measurements and testing; investigating security analytics and big data; developing standards, modeling, and measurements to achieve end-to-end security over heterogeneous, multi-domain networks; and investigating technologies for detection of anomalous behavior and quarantines.

In addition, further development of cybersecurity standards will be needed to improve the security and resiliency of critical U.S. information and communication infrastructure. The availability of cybersecurity standards and associated conformity assessment schemes is essential in these efforts, which NIST supports to help enhance the deployment of sound security solutions and builds trust among those creating and those using the solutions throughout the country.

Cybersecurity Framework

As you know, NIST has spent the last year working to convene the US Critical Infrastructure sectors to build a Cybersecurity Framework as part of Executive Order 13636. The Cybersecurity Framework, released last month, was created through collaboration between industry and government, and consists of standards, guidelines, and practices to promote the protection of critical infrastructure. The prioritized, flexible, repeatable, and cost-effective approach of the Framework helps owners and operators of critical infrastructure to manage cybersecurity-related risk. The Framework is already being implemented by industry, adopted by infrastructure sectors and is reducing cyber risks to our critical infrastructure, including the finance industry.

National Strategy for Trusted Identities in Cyberspace

NIST also houses the National Program Office established to lead implementation of the National Strategy for Trusted Identities in Cyberspace (NSTIC). NSTIC is an initiative that aims to address one of the most commonly exploited vectors of attack in cyberspace: the inadequacy of passwords for authentication.

The 2013 Data Breach Investigations Report (conducted by Verizon in concert with the U.S. Department of Homeland Security) noted that in 2012, 76% of network intrusions exploited weak or stolen credentials. In line with the results of this report, Target has revealed that the compromised credential of one of its business partners was the vector used to access its network.

NSTIC aims to address this issue by collaborating with the private sector to catalyze a marketplace of better identity and authentication solutions—an "Identity Ecosystem" that raises the level of trust associated with the identities of individuals, organizations, networks, services and devices online. NIST has funded a dozen pilots and supported work in the privately led Identity Ecosystem Steering Group (IDESG) to craft standards to improve authentication online.

National Cybersecurity Center of Excellence

In 2012, the National Cybersecurity Center of Excellence (NCCoE) was formed as a partnership between NIST, the State of Maryland, and Montgomery County to accelerate the adoption of security technologies that are based on standards and best practices. The center is a vehicle for NIST to work directly with businesses across various industry sectors on applied solutions to cybersecurity challenges. Today the NCCoE has programs working with the healthcare, financial services, and energy sectors in addition to addressing challenges that cut across sectors including: mobile device security, software asset management, cloud security, and identity management.

NIST and the NCCOE work extensively in standards and guidelines, as well as research and development in hardware roots of trust. Stronger security assurances can be possible by grounding security mechanisms in roots of trust. Roots of trust are highly reliable hardware, firmware, and software components that perform specific, critical security functions. Because roots of trust are inherently trusted, they must be secure by design. As such, many roots of trust are implemented in hardware so that malware cannot tamper with the functions they provide. Roots of trust provide a firm foundation from which to build security and trust.

In 2013, NIST and the NCCOE worked with government and industry partners on guidelines for hardware-rooted security features in mobile devices. These guidelines focus on device integrity, isolation, and protected storage features that are supported by roots of trust, and we continue our work to protect fundamental system firmware, commonly known as the BIOS. NIST continues working with key members of the computer industry on the use of roots of trust to improve the security of BIOS, computers and systems overall.

Additional Research Areas

NIST performs research and development in related technologies, such as the usability of systems including electronic health records, voting machines, biometrics and software interfaces. NIST is performing basic research on the mathematical foundations needed to determine the security of information systems. In the areas of digital forensics, NIST is enabling improvements in forensic analysis through the National Software Reference Library and computer forensics tool testing. Software assurance metrics, tools, and evaluations developed at NIST are being implemented by industry to help strengthen software against hackers. NIST responds to government and market requirements for biometric standards by collaborating with other federal agencies, academia, and industry partners to develop and implement biometrics evaluations, enable usability, and develop standards (fingerprint, face, iris, voice/speaker, and multimodal biometrics). NIST plays a central role in defining and advancing standards, and collaborating with customers and stakeholders to identify and reach consensus on cloud computing standards.

Conclusion

We at NIST recognize that we have an essential role to play in helping industry, consumers and government entities to counter cybertheft and cyberthreats. We look forward to continuing our work, along with our federal government partners, our private sector collaborators, and our international colleagues to establish and continually improve the comprehensive set of technical solutions, standards, guidelines, and best practices necessary to realize this vision. . . .

CHARLES H. ROMINE is director of the Information Technology Laboratory of the National Institute of Standards and Technology.

EXPLORING THE ISSUE

Can Technology Protect Americans from International Cybercriminals?

Critical Thinking and Reflection

1. Is there a difference between "cyberwar" and "cybercrime"?
2. Is all the worry about cybercrime just hype?
3. With conventional crime, it is possible to locate and arrest criminals. Why is it difficult to find cybercriminals?

Is There Common Ground?

Randy Vanderhoof and Charles H. Romine argue that technology must play a role in keeping intruders out of computer networks and limiting the damage they can do if they do get in. No one wants criminal hackers to be able to steal private information—usernames and passwords, in particular—so they can steal from bank accounts, use credit cards, steal identity, and even destroy financial institutions and the economy, disrupt electricity generation, shut down factories, shut down the Internet, or perhaps just mess with a city's traffic lights to cause traffic jams (among other things). Keeping them out is what cybersecurity is all about.

1. How do you protect your own computer? (passwords, firewalls, encryption, etc.)
2. Visit your campus IT department and ask how it protects the campus network from intruders.
3. Do you think similar measures would work against a cyber-war or cyber-terrorist attack?

4. Is knowing that you should NOT click links in mystery emails a technological defense? Or is it something else?
5. Many people use a single password for all the sites that demand one. Do you? How many passwords do you use? How strong are they?

Additional Resources

Richard A. Clarke and Richard K. Knake, *Cyber War: The Next Threat to National Security and What to Do about It* (HarperCollins, 2010).

Jonathan Clough, *Principles of Cybercrime* (Cambridge University Press, 2010).

R. Scott Kemp, "Cyberweapons: Bold Steps in a Digital Darkness?" *Bulletin of the Atomic Scientists* (June 7, 2012) (http://www.thebulletin.org/web-edition /op-eds/cyberweapons-bold-steps-digital-darkness).

P. W. Singer and Allan Friedman, *Cybersecurity and Cyberwar: What Everyone Needs to Know* (Oxford University Press, 2014).

Internet References . . .

EMV Connection

http://www.emv-connection.com/

Federal Bureau of Investigation, Cybercrime Page

http://www.fbi.gov/about-us/investigate/cyber

Net Losses: Estimating the Global Cost of Cybercrime: Economic Impact of Cybercrime II

http://www.mcafee.com/us/resources/reports /rp-economic-impact-cybercrime2.pdf

Smart Card Alliance

http://www.smartcardalliance.org/

United States Department of Defense, U.S. Cyber Command

http://www.defense.gov/home/features/2010 /0410_cybersec/

Selected, Edited, and with Issue Framing Material by:
Thomas A. Easton, *Thomas College*

ISSUE

Does the Public Have a Stake in How Drones Are Used?

YES: Amie Stepanovich, from testimony at U.S. Senate Judiciary hearing on The Future of Drones in America: Law Enforcement and Privacy Considerations, Judiciary Committee of the U.S. Senate (2013)

NO: U.S. Department of Homeland Security, Office of Inspector General, from "CBP's Use of Unmanned Aircraft Systems in the Nation's Border Security," United States Department of Homeland Security, Office of Inspector General (2012)

Learning Outcomes
After reading this issue, you will be able to: • Explain what unmanned aerial systems or drones are.   • Explain how they can be used to support the missions of various public agencies, including law enforcement.   • Explain how their use may impinge on citizens' right to privacy.   • Explain why domestic drone use is likely or unlikely to increase.

ISSUE SUMMARY

YES: Amie Stepanovich argues that the increased use of unmanned aerial systems (or "drones") to conduct surveillance in the United States must be accompanied by increased privacy protections. The current state of the law is insufficient to address the drone surveillance threat to the interests of the general public, who clearly have a stake (are stakeholders) in the issue.

NO: The U.S. Department of Homeland Security, Office of Inspector General, argues that planning is inadequate for the use of resources devoted to serving the purposes of the U.S. Customs and Border Protection (CBP) unmanned aircraft systems program, to provide reconnaissance, surveillance, targeting, and acquisition capabilities to serve the needs of stakeholders. The list of stakeholders does not include the general public, and privacy concerns are not mentioned.

Remote-controlled drones, more properly known as "unmanned aerial vehicles" or UAVs, first appeared on the modern battlefield over a decade ago. Today, according to Paul Scharre, "Why Unmanned," *Joint Force Quarterly* (2nd quarter 2011), there are thousands, and they include both UAVs and UGVs (unmanned ground vehicles, robotic bomb diffusers, and cargo carriers). They were initially used for reconnaissance, taking pictures of distant locations. Later they were armed and used for combat. Since they were not autonomous robots, there was never any risk that they would turn on their masters. Indeed, the risk to the masters is reduced because it is drones, not human soldiers, who go into harm's way.

As Scharre notes, the capabilities of the computers that control these machines are constantly improving and "more capable systems will be possible in the future." The result may be human-robot combat teams that are far more efficacious than humans alone. And as the cost of the necessary hardware and software continues to fall, the same technology will appear in the hands of adversaries, from nation states to terrorists. As a result, the military is motivated to continue developing better and better drones.

Yet it is not the military applications of drones that raise concerns in civilian circles. Many agencies find them appealing; see Nick Paumgarten, "Here's Looking at You," *New Yorker* (May 14, 2012). Law enforcement agencies find them appealing for tracking criminals, and the Obama administration has indicated that under very special circumstances armed drones could be used against terrorists (see Michael Isikoff, "Justice Department Memo Reveals Legal Case for Drone Strikes on Americans," NBC News, http://openchannel.nbcnews.com/_news/2013/02/04/16843014 -justice-department-memo-reveals-legal-case-for-drone-strikes -on-americans?lite). Emergency management folks want them for surveying the extent and severity of floods and fires and even for carrying supplies and cell phones to people in trouble. Amazon is reportedly planning to use them for package delivery (Alistair Blair, "Amazon Testing Delivery by Drone, CEO Bezos Says," *USA Today*, December 2, 2013). Researchers want to use them for environmental surveys. Environmental activists want to use them to look for offenses against environmental laws. And the Federal Aviation Administration is developing regulations to govern the use of drones in domestic airspace; see Paul Rosenzweig, et al., "Drones in U.S. Airspace: Principles for Governance," Heritage Foundation Backgrounder (September 20, 2012). Since there may be more than 10,000 drones in the air by 2020, such regulations will be essential. There is also a need to make their control signals hard to disrupt; see Kyle Wesson and Todd Humphreys, "Hacking Drones," *Scientific American* (November 2013).

Not surprisingly, many people see drones as both intrusive and threatening. Yet the numbers are perhaps less than overwhelming. A 2012 survey found that 44 percent support police use of drones; only 36 percent were opposed, while only a third were concerned about privacy; see Steve Watson, "Almost Half of All Americans Support Domestic Surveillance Drones," Infowars.com (September 28, 2012) (http://www.infowars.com/almost-half-of -all-americans-support-domestic-surveillance-drones/). Privacy advocates see their abilities to follow individuals, monitor political demonstrations, pick faces out of a crowd (the necessary software is under development), hover outside a window or over a backyard, and more—whether when operated by public agencies or by private interests (such as jealous spouses and private detectives)—as especially alarming. See "The Spies Above Your Backyard," *Scientific American* (April 2013). Tyler Wall and Torin Mona-

han, "Surveillance and Violence from Afar: The Politics of Drones and Liminal Security-Scapes," *Theoretical Criminology* (August 2011), find the use of drones dehumanizes people into targets for remote monitoring and destruction and removes reasons to refrain from action.

In "The Predator Comes Home: A Primer on Domestic Drones, Their Huge Business Opportunities, and Their Deep Political, Moral, and Legal Challenges," Brookings Institution, March 8, 2013 (http://www.brookings.edu /research/papers/2013/03/08-drones-singer), Peter W. Singer, director of the Center for 21st Century Security and Intelligence at the Brookings Institution, argues that the potential benefits of unmanned aerial systems (drones) are huge. And "While many are surprised by the existing use of robotics, the pace of change won't stop. We may have thousands now, but as one three-star U.S. Air Force general noted . . . very soon it will be 'tens of thousands' . . . of tomorrow's robots, with far different capabilities." Aerial robots will gain in intelligence and autonomy and the number of potential users will expand tremendously. The number of drones in the air may reach "tens of billions." There will therefore be a huge need for federal and state action to regulate the use of unmanned aerial systems, but much of the regulatory responsibility is likely to be borne by the courts.

The Association for Unmanned Vehicle Systems International (AUVSI), a manufacturers' organization, is lobbying intensely for laws that will permit drones to operate much more freely in U.S. airspace. In testimony before the Senate Judiciary Committee March 20, 2013, Michael Toscano, President and CEO of AUVSI, said that "The industry is at the forefront of a technology that will not only benefit society, but the U.S. economy as well. Earlier this month, my organization released a study, which found the unmanned aircraft industry is poised to help create 70,000 new jobs and $13.6 billion in economic impact in the first three years following the integration of unmanned aircraft into the national airspace." To the industry's dismay, a great many people find the prospect of drones being used within the United States an alarming prospect, perhaps because of their origins in war. Cities and states are passing laws against their use even as the industry lobbies Congress to promote their use. See Alec MacGillis, "Don't Fear the Reaper," *New Republic* (March 11, 2013). The Aviation Committee of the International Association of Chiefs of Police has formulated "Recommended Guidelines for the Use of Unmanned Aircraft" (http://www.theiacp.org/portals/0/pdfs/IACP_UAGuidelines.pdf) that include recognition of privacy and civil rights concerns and discourage the use of armed drones. The AUVSI has a Code of Conduct (http://www.auvsi.org/conduct) that calls for respect for individual privacy, rights, and concerns, but the code contains no penalties for those who ignore its requirements. Indeed its purpose seems to instill "confidence in our systems."

Will remotely controlled drones give way to autonomous robots? Will they be armed, and will they be tasked with deciding when and whom to kill? This has long been a theme in science fiction (see Fred Saberhagen's Berserker stories [e.g., http://www.amazon.com/Berserker-Saberhagens -Fred-Saberhagen-ebook/dp/B00A4Q4FLK/ref=sr_1_1?s= books&ie=UTF8&qid=1392907070&sr=1-1&keywords=- saberhagen+berserker] and David R. Bunch's Moderan stories [http://www.amazon.com/Moderan-David-R-Bunch/dp /B002TJT4LG]), but it is no longer just science fiction. In December 2012, the Department of Defense issued a Directive calling for "the development and use of autonomous and semi-autonomous functions in weapons systems, including manned and unmanned platforms" (http://www.dtic.mil/whs/directives/corres/pdf/300009p .pdf). Mark Gubrud, "US Killer Robot Policy: Full Speed Ahead," *Bulletin of the Atomic Scientists* (September 20, 2013), the new "policy in effect overrides longstanding resistance within the military . . . and signals to developers and vendors that the Pentagon is serious about autonomous weapons." Resistance to the policy has been developing rapidly (see Charli Carpenter, "Beware the Killer Robots," *Foreign Affairs,* July 3, 2013, and Richard Stone, "Scientists Campaign Against Killer Robots,"

Science, December 2013). In May 2014, the 117 state parties to the Convention on Certain Conventional Weapons (CCW; it currently bans or regulates the use of land mines, blinding lasers, and other weapons) will meet in Geneva, Switzerland, to discuss banning killer robots; see Mia Gandenberger, "CCW Adopts Mandate to Discuss Killer Robots," Reaching Critical Will (November 15, 2013) (http://www.reachingcriticalwill.org/news/latest- news/8583-ccw-adopts-mandate-to-discuss-killer-robots).

So far, the drones are not true robots; that is, they do not make their own decisions. Nevertheless, some people still find them worrisome. In the YES selection, Amie Stepanovich argues that the increased use of unmanned aerial systems (or "drones") to conduct surveillance in the United States must be accompanied by increased privacy protections. The current state of the law is insufficient to address the drone surveillance threat to the interests of the general public, who clearly have a stake (are stakeholders) in the issue. In the NO selection, the U.S. Department of Homeland Security, Office of Inspector General (OIG), argues that inadequate resources are devoted to serving the purposes of the U.S. Customs and Border Protection (CBP) unmanned aircraft systems program, to provide reconnaissance, surveillance, targeting, and acquisition capabilities to serve the needs of stakeholders. The OIG does not say "public be damned," but the list of stakeholders does not include the general public, and privacy concerns are not mentioned.

YES

Amie Stepanovich

"The Future of Drones in America: Law Enforcement and Privacy Considerations"

EPIC is a non-partisan research organization, established in 1994, to focus public attention on emerging privacy and civil liberties issues. We work with a distinguished panel of advisors in the fields of law, technology, and public policy. We have a particular interest in the protection of individual privacy rights against government surveillance. In the last several years, EPIC has taken a particular interest in the unique privacy problems associated with aerial drones.

The Federal Aviation Administration ("FAA") has been directed to fully integrate drones into the National Airspace by 2015. In 2012 EPIC petitioned the FAA, as it considers new regulations to permit the widespread deployment of drones, to also develop new privacy safeguards. The FAA heeded our warning, and is now considering privacy policies for drone operators. However, more must be done to protect the privacy of individuals in the United States.

We appreciate the Committee's interest in domestic drone use and its substantial impact on the privacy of individuals in the United States. In my statement today, I will describe the unique threats to privacy posed by drone surveillance, the problems with current legal safeguards, and the need for Congress to act.

I. Aerial Drones Pose a Unique Threat to Privacy

A drone is an aerial vehicle designed to fly without a human pilot on board. Drones can either be remotely controlled or autonomous. Drones can be weaponized and deployed for military purposes. Drones can also be equipped with sophisticated surveillance technology that makes it possible to spy on individuals on the ground. In a report on drones published by EPIC in 2005, we observed, "the use of [drones] gives the federal government a new capability to monitor citizens clandestinely, while the effectiveness of the . . . surveillance planes in border patrol operations has not been proved." Today, drones greatly increase the capacity for law enforcement to collect personal information on individuals.

We recognize that there are many positive applications for drones within the United States. With little to no risk to individual privacy, drones may be used to combat forest fires, conduct search and rescue operations, survey emergency situations, and monitor hurricanes and other weather phenomena. In Dallas, a drone used by a hobbyist photographer was able to pinpoint an instance of gross environmental abuse at a nearby factory. In Alabama, drones were recently used to assist in monitoring a hostage situation involving a young boy abducted off of the school bus.

However, when drones are used to obtain evidence in a criminal proceeding, intrude upon a reasonable expectation of privacy, or gather personal data about identifiable individuals, rules are necessary to ensure that fundamental standards for fairness, privacy, and accountability are preserved.

The technology in use today is far more sophisticated than most people understand. Cameras used to outfit drones are among the highest definition cameras available. The Argus camera, featured on the PBS Nova documentary on drones, has a resolution of 1.8 gigapixels and is capable of observing objects as small as six inches in detail from a height of 17,000 feet. On some drones, sensors can track up to 65 different targets across a distance of 65 square miles. Drones may also carry infrared cameras, heat sensors, GPS, sensors that detect movement, and automated license plate readers.

Recent records received by EPIC under the Freedom of Information Act demonstrate that the Bureau of Customs and Border Protection procured drones outfitted with technology for electronic signals interception and human identification. Following receipt of these documents, EPIC and a broad coalition of privacy and civil liberties organizations petitioned the CBP to suspend the domestic drone program, pending the establishment of privacy safeguards.

From U.S. Senate, March 20, 2013.

Much of this surveillance technology could, in theory, be deployed on manned vehicles. However, drones present a unique threat to privacy. Drones are designed to maintain a constant, persistent eye on the public to a degree that former methods of surveillance were unable to achieve. Drones are cheaper to buy, maintain, and operate than helicopters, or other forms of aerial surveillance. Drone manufacturers have recently announced new designs that would allow drones to operate for more than 48 consecutive hours, and other technology could extend the flight time of future drones into spans of weeks and months. Also, "by virtue of their design, size, and how high they can fly, [drones] can operate undetected in urban and rural environments."

Drones are currently being developed that will carry facial recognition technology, able to remotely identify individuals in parks, schools, and at political gatherings. The ability to link facial recognition capabilities on drones operated by the Department of Homeland Security ("DHS") to the Federal Bureau of Investigation's Next Generation Identification database or DHS' IDENT database, two of the largest collections of biometric data in the world, further exacerbates the privacy risks.

Law enforcement offices across the country have expressed interest in the purchase and use of drone technology to assist with law enforcement operations. Records released in 2012 by the Federal Aviation Administration show that over 220 public entities have already received approval to operate drones over the United States, including Police departments from Texas, Kansas, Washington, and other states. The Florida Police Chiefs Association expressed a desire to use drones to conduct general crowd surveillance at public events. News reports demonstrate that other police departments are not only interested in invasive surveillance equipment, but have also voiced interest in outfitting drones with non-lethal weapons.

II. Current Privacy Safeguards Are Inadequate

The Supreme Court has not yet considered the limits of drone surveillance under the Fourth Amendment, though the Court held twenty years ago that law enforcement may conduct manned aerial surveillance operations from as low as 400 feet without a warrant. In addition, no federal statute currently provides adequate safeguards to protect privacy against increased drone use in the United States. Accordingly, there are substantial legal and constitutional issues involved in the deployment of aerial drones by law enforcement and state and federal agencies that need to be

addressed. Technologist and security expert Bruce Schneier observed earlier this year at an event hosted by EPIC on Drones and Domestic Surveillance, "today's expensive and rare is tomorrow's commonplace." As drone technology becomes cheaper and more common, the threat to privacy will become more substantial. High-rise buildings, security fences, or even the walls of a building are not barriers to increasingly common drone technology.

The Supreme Court is aware of the growing risks to privacy resulting from new surveillance technology but has yet to address the specific problems associated with drone surveillance. In *United States v. Jones*, a case that addressed whether the police could use a GPS device to track the movement of a criminal suspect without a warrant, the Court found that the installation and deployment of the device was an unlawful search and seizure. Justice Sotomayor in a concurrence pointed to broader problems associated with new forms of persistent surveillance. And Justice Alito, in a separate concurrence joined by three other Justices, wrote, "in circumstances involving dramatic technological change, the best solution to privacy concerns may be legislative."

Regarding the invasive use of drones by commercial operators, current law does not anticipate the use of mobile devices that can hover outside a bedroom window or follow a person down a street. Legal standards should be established to protect people from a violation of reasonable expectations of privacy, including surveillance in public spaces. In considering legislation to address law enforcement use of drones, it would be appropriate also to establish privacy standards for the commercial use of drones.

III. Congress Should Establish Safeguards Related to the Use of Drones

As the Chairman has indicated, the privacy and security concerns arising from the use of drones needs to be addressed. In order to mitigate the risk of increased use of drones in our domestic skies, Congress must pass targeted legislation, based on principles of transparency and accountability.

State and local governments have considered a wide array of laws and regulations to prevent abuses associated with drone technology. A current survey demonstrates that over 30 states have proposed legislation to protect against unregulated drone surveillance of individuals. Most of these bills mandate a warrant requirement for the collection of information by drones operated by law enforcement officials.

Other bills require reporting requirements for drone operators. A bill in Georgia restricts law enforcement use of drones strictly to felony investigations, and a bill circulating in Oregon would require state approval for all drones, including federal drones, that would fly over the state's airspace.

Even as states consider these various measures, it would be appropriate for Congress to establish privacy standards for the operation of drones in the United States. First, Congress should require all drone operators, both public and commercial, to submit, prior to receipt of a drone license, a detailed report on the drones' intended use. This report should describe, the specific geographic area where the drone will be deployed, the mission that the drone is expected to fulfill, and the surveillance equipment with which the drone will be outfitted. Each of these reports should be made publicly available at a publicly accessible web site. A private right of action and, in certain instances, federal prosecution authority should be included to ensure that drone operators comply with the terms of these statements.

In order to prevent abuses associated with the use of this technology, a strict warrant requirement needs to be implemented for all drone surveillance conduct by law enforcement. A warrant requirement would establish a presumption that evidence obtained by means of an aerial search should require judicial approval. Statutory exceptions could be created for exigency in order to address drone use in emergency situations or when necessary to protect human life. In addition, mandatory public reporting requirements, similar to those required by the Wiretap Act, would increase the transparency and accountability of law enforcement drone operations.

Ongoing surveillance of individuals by aerial drones operating in domestic airspace should be prohibited. The invasiveness of drone technology represents a privacy risk to individuals as they pursue their daily activities. A drone, with the capability of staying aloft for hours or days at a time, could monitor a person's entire life as they go from home to work to school to the store and back. Even if law enforcement is not able to immediately discern exactly what a person says or does or buys at a particular location, simply tracking an individual's public movements in a systematic fashion for extended periods of time can create a vivid description of their private life. Broad, unregulated drone surveillance would have a chilling effect on the speech and expression rights of individuals in the United States. Drones should not be used as robotic patrol officers for law enforcement.

Finally, drone surveillance technology may allow the collection of information and images that would otherwise be inaccessible to prying eyes, such as activities within the home. Congress should prohibit drone operators from conducting surveillance of individuals that infringes on property rights. A federal "Peeping Tom" statute, recognizing the enhanced capabilities of aerial drones, would provide baseline privacy protection for individuals within the home. Additional provisions should prevent against any use of drones to collect information that would not otherwise be retrievable without a physical trespass.

Additional drone legislation should include:

- Use Limitations—Prohibitions on general surveillance that limit law enforcement drone surveillance to specific, enumerated circumstances, such as in the case of criminal surveillance subject to a warrant, a geographically-confined emergency, or for reasonable non-law enforcement use where privacy will not be substantially affected;
- Data Retention Limitations—Restrictions on retaining or sharing surveillance data collected by drones, with emphasis on personally identifiable information;
- Transparency and Public Accountability—A requirement for all federal agencies that choose to operate drones to promulgate privacy regulations, subject to the notice and comment provisions of the Administrative Procedure Act. In addition, the law should provide for third party audits and oversight for law enforcement drone operations.

These three principles would further help protect the privacy interests of individuals against both government and commercial drone operators.

IV. Conclusion

The increased use of drones to conduct surveillance in the United States must be accompanied by increased privacy protections. The current state of the law is insufficient to address the drone surveillance threat. EPIC supports legislation aimed at strengthening safeguards related to the use of drones as surveillance tools and allowing for redress for drone operators who fail to comply with the mandated standards of protection. We also support compliance with the Administrative Procedure Act for the deployment of drone technology and limitations for federal agencies and other organizations that initially obtain a drone for one purpose and then wish to expand that purpose.

AMIE STEPANOVICH is the director of the Domestic Surveillance Project at the Electronic Privacy Information Center (EPIC).

**Department of Homeland Security
Office of Inspector General**

 **NO**

CBP's Use of Unmanned Aircraft Systems in the Nation's Border Security

Executive Summary

We conducted a review of U.S. Customs and Border Protection (CBP) actions to establish its unmanned aircraft systems program. The purpose of the program is to provide reconnaissance, surveillance, targeting, and acquisition capabilities across all CBP areas of responsibility. Our objective was to determine whether CBP has established an adequate operation plan to define, prioritize, and execute its unmanned aircraft mission.

CBP had not adequately planned resources needed to support its current unmanned aircraft inventory. Although CBP developed plans to use the unmanned aircraft's capabilities in its Office of Air and Marine mission, its Concept of Operations planning document did not adequately address processes (1) to ensure that required operational equipment, such as ground control stations and ground support equipment, is provided for each launch and recovery site; (2) for stakeholders to submit unmanned aircraft mission requests; (3) to determine how mission requests are prioritized; and (4) to obtain reimbursement for missions flown on stakeholders' behalf. This approach places CBP at risk of having invested substantial resources in a program that underutilizes resources and limits its ability to achieve Office of Air and Marine mission goals.

CBP needs to improve planning of its unmanned aircraft system program to address its level of operation, program funding, and resource requirements, along with stakeholder needs. We made four recommendations that will aid CBP in maximizing the use of unmanned aircraft. CBP management concurred with all four recommendations.

Background

The mission of the Office of Air and Marine (OAM) is to protect the American people and the Nation's critical infrastructure through the coordinated use of integrated air and marine forces. Air and marine forces are used to detect, interdict, and prevent acts of terrorism and the unlawful movement of people, illegal drugs, and other contraband toward or across U.S. borders. The unmanned aircraft system (UAS) provides command, control, communication, intelligence, surveillance, and reconnaissance capability to complement crewed aircraft and watercraft, and ground interdiction agents. A UAS is composed of a long-endurance, medium-altitude remotely piloted aircraft, ground control station, ground data terminal, data and voice communications, and other ground support equipment required to operate and maintain the system. UASs provide reconnaissance, surveillance, targeting, and acquisition (RSTA) capabilities across all CBP areas of responsibility.

CBP began UAS operations in fiscal year (FY) 2004 with a pilot study conducted by the Office of Border Patrol to determine the feasibility of using UASs in the southwest border region. The pilot study proved the UAS was successful in providing RSTA and actionable intelligence to Border Patrol ground agents. In addition, the study concluded that UASs provided unique law enforcement capabilities, such as the ability to carry a variety of sensors and payloads and to remain airborne for extended periods without the limitations imposed by requiring onboard pilots. CBP has since expanded UAS operations to the Caribbean, gulf, and northern border regions.

CBP reported that, subsequent to the FY 2004 pilot, Congress appropriated approximately $240.6 million to establish a UAS program within CBP. CBP also reported that it has expended $152.3 million to purchase nine aircraft and related equipment. CBP had seven operational aircraft during our review. CBP received two additional aircraft in late 2011. CBP was awaiting delivery of a tenth aircraft purchased with FY 2011 funds. Each aircraft system costs approximately $18 million. In June 2011, CBP had 23 pilots who were capable of launching and recovering unmanned aircraft. UAS missions are launched and

From United States Department of Homeland Security, Office of Inspector General, 2012.

recovered from National Air Security Operation Centers (NASOCs) in Sierra Vista, Arizona; Corpus Christi, Texas; Cocoa Beach, Florida; and Grand Forks, North Dakota. An unmanned aircraft mission crew generally consists of a Command Duty Officer, Pilot-in-Command, Sensor Operator, and one or more contract technicians. . . .

Results of Review

CBP Needs to Improve Planning of Its UAS Program to Maximize Operations

CBP had not adequately planned for resources needed to support the current unmanned aircraft inventory. Although CBP developed plans to utilize the unmanned aircraft's capabilities in its OAM mission, its Concept of Operations planning document did not adequately address processes (1) to ensure that required operational equipment, such as ground control stations and ground support equipment, is available for each launch and recovery site; (2) for stakeholders to submit unmanned aircraft mission requests; (3) to determine how mission requests are prioritized; and (4) to obtain reimbursement for missions flown on stakeholders' behalf. This approach places CBP at risk of having invested substantial resources in a program that underutilizes resources and limits its ability to achieve OAM mission goals.

Resource Planning

CBP has not ensured that adequate resources are available to effectively operate its unmanned aircraft. CBP's Strategic Plan requires the agency to develop and implement a planning framework to incorporate investment, resource, and program management processes to ensure that CBP can acquire and effectively manage its resources. The plan requires CBP to accomplish its high-priority missions and objectives in a way that maximizes return on investment. CBP procured unmanned aircraft before implementing adequate plans to do the following:

- Achieve the desired level of operation;
- Acquire sufficient funding to provide necessary operations, maintenance, and equipment; and
- Coordinate and support stakeholder needs.

UAS Level of Operation

CBP has not achieved its scheduled nor desired levels of flight hours of its unmanned aircraft. The Office of Inspector General (OIG) estimates that, based on the contract performance specifications, seven UASs should support 10,662 flight hours per year to meet the mission availability threshold (minimum capability) and 13,328 flight hours to meet the mission availability objective (desired capability). However, resource shortfalls of qualified staff and equipment coupled with restrictions imposed by the Federal Aviation Administration, weather, host airfields, and others have resulted in CBP scheduling just 7,336 flight hours for its seven unmanned aircraft and limited actual flight hours to 3,909 hours. This usage represents 37 percent of the unmanned aircraft's mission availability threshold and 29 percent of its mission availability objective. Despite the current underutilization of unmanned aircraft, CBP received two additional aircraft in late 2011 and was awaiting delivery of a tenth aircraft in 2012. . . .

Funding of Operations and Maintenance

CBP reported that, since the UAS program's inception, Congress has appropriated a total of $12.6 million for operations and maintenance. The operations and maintenance funding category includes training, satellite links, facility rental, and contractor support. CBP also reported that from FY 2006 through FY 2011, it expended $55.3 million for operations and maintenance, but has not made a specific operations and maintenance budget request for the UAS program. This has resulted in a budget shortfall. According to CBP, it was required to transfer approximately $25 million from other programs in FY 2010 to address operations and maintenance funding shortfalls. As a result of CBP's insufficient funding approach, future UAS missions may have to be curtailed.

Funding of Equipment

CBP has not adequately planned to fund unmanned aircraft-related equipment. The procurement funding category includes aircraft and related equipment, such as ground control stations, ground support equipment, cameras, and navigation systems. This approach has resulted in insufficient equipment to perform UAS missions. For example:

- Corpus Christi NASOC received a maritime version of the Predator aircraft, which was placed in service in February 2011, but Corpus Christi did not receive a compatible ground control station. As a result, the Corpus Christi NASOC was not initially able to use the system's SeaVue maritime radar capability. However, Cocoa Beach NASOC transferred its backup ground control station to Corpus Christi to facilitate mission operations. A compatible ground control station is expected to be delivered in May 2012. This transfer was required because Corpus Christi was not designed for launch and recovery operations.

- On at least three occasions, NASOC Grand Forks could not conduct flight operations because maintenance could not be performed due to lack of ground support equipment. One aircraft was down for 4 days in January 2011 due to lack of wing-jacks and 3 days in February due to lack of go-jacks and fuselage stands. Another aircraft was down for 2 days in February 2011 due to lack of go-jacks and fuselage stands. Ground support equipment must be transferred from one NASOC to another because each NASOC does not have its own equipment.
- CBP does not have an adequate number of ground control stations to ensure safe operations. CBP's *MQ-9 Supplement to the Aviation Operations Handbook* requires a permanent ground control station and a mobile ground control station for the safe operation of unmanned aircraft. The handbook requires NASOC directors to submit written requests for relief from any provision of the handbook to the Executive Director of Test, Training, Safety, and Standards. At the time of our fieldwork, three of four NASOCs were operating without the required mobile backup ground control stations. However, only one of four NASOCs was granted a waiver to operate without this equipment.

Stakeholder Needs

CBP's planning has not adequately addressed coordination and support of stakeholders. Although CBP identified stakeholders and has flown missions on their behalf, it has not implemented a formal process for stakeholders to submit mission requests and has not implemented a formal procedure to determine how mission requests are prioritized. It also does not have agreements with exterior stakeholders for reimbursement of mission costs.

An OAM manager and stakeholders we interviewed said that CBP had flown missions to support the following stakeholders:

- Department of Homeland Security (DHS) agencies, including Office of Border Patrol, United States Secret Service, Federal Emergency Management Agency (FEMA), and Immigration and Customs Enforcement (ICE);
- Bureau of Land Management;
- Federal Bureau of Investigation;
- Department of Defense;
- Texas Rangers;
- United States Forest Service; and

- National Oceanic and Atmospheric Administration (NOAA).

Also, OAM management and stakeholders we interviewed discussed the following examples of missions performed by the UAS program:

- Provided NOAA with videos of dams, bridges, levees, and riverbeds where flooding occurred or was threatened;
- Provided FEMA with video/radar images of flooding;
- Provided surveillance over a suspected smuggler's tunnel, which yielded information that, according to an ICE representative, would have required many cars and agents to obtain;
- Provided radar mapping, or overlying radar images taken a few days apart, to show changes in location of flooding, allowing the National Guard to deploy high-water vehicles and sandbags to where they were most needed;
- At the request of the State Department, participated in discussions with another country on the use of unmanned aircraft;
- Participated in joint efforts with the U.S. Army to leverage capabilities of unmanned aircraft and test new technology; and
- Participated in efforts to establish a quarterly forum to share lessons learned with the Air Force and other government agencies.

Stakeholders we interviewed from NOAA, ICE, FEMA, and the Army National Guard were generally satisfied with support provided by the UAS program. However, they were unaware of a formal process to request UAS support and of how CBP prioritizes missions. CBP included a process to satisfy requests for UAS support in its *Concept of Operations for CBP's Predator B Unmanned Aircraft System, FY 2010 Report to Congress,* but this process was not implemented. Instead, tasking decisions are usually made by the Director of Air Operations at the NASOC with responsibility for the area of the stakeholder surveillance requirement. Missions are requested by various means, including from headquarters, Border Patrol agents, local law enforcement agencies, and other Federal agencies. We interviewed four stakeholders, three of whom recommended a standardized process to request UAS missions. A standardized process would provide transparency and ensure that requests are processed in a timely, predictable manner. This process would allow stakeholders to better plan their operations to meet mission needs.

The Robert T. Stafford Disaster Relief and Emergency Assistance Act, as amended, provides a system by which a

Presidential disaster declaration of an emergency triggers financial assistance through FEMA. CBP seeks reimbursement for services provided to FEMA under this Act since Federal agencies may be reimbursed for expenditures from the Act's appropriations. However, CBP does not have agreements to obtain reimbursement for missions flown on behalf of other stakeholders. When appropriate and authorized by law, obtaining reimbursement for such missions would provide additional funding needed for staff, operations and maintenance, and essential equipment.

Recommendations

We recommend that the Assistant Commissioner, Office of Air and Marine:

Recommendation #1:

Analyze requirements and develop plans to achieve the UAS mission availability objective and acquire funding to provide necessary operations, maintenance, and equipment.

Recommendation #2:

Develop and implement procedures to coordinate and support stakeholders' mission requests.

Recommendation #3:

Establish interagency agreements with external stakeholders for reimbursement of expenses incurred fulfilling mission requests where authorized by law.

Recommendation #4:

Postpone additional UAS purchases until recommendation #1 has been implemented.

. . . the actual funding is subject to changing Department and Agency criteria.

U.S. Department of Homeland Security, Office of Inspector General, serves as an independent and objective inspection, audit, and investigative body to provide independent oversight and promote excellence, integrity, and accountability within DHS programs and operations.

EXPLORING THE ISSUE

Does the Public Have a Stake in How Drones Are Used?

Critical Thinking and Reflection

1. What concerns over the use of drone technology will be most affected as the technology becomes cheaper and more available?
2. What is a stakeholder? What does the term mean in this context?
3. Why do many people not trust government agencies to be responsible in their use of surveillance technologies?
4. Is protecting national security more important than protecting individual liberties?

Is There Common Ground?

Most law enforcement and emergency management agencies seem to be aware that the public has a strong interest in their use of technologies that may impinge on privacy and civil liberties. They therefore go to some lengths to assure the public that they will be responsible in their use of such technologies. As noted in the Introduction to this issue, the Aviation Committee of the International Association of Chiefs of Police has formulated "Recommended Guidelines for the Use of Unmanned Aircraft" that include recognition of privacy and civil rights concerns and discourage the use of armed drones. Yet even though the public agrees that these technologies have useful roles to play, it remains concerned.

1. Has government ever abused its surveillance powers? (Recent news has extensively covered surveillance of phone and Internet messages by the National Security Agency or NSA.)
2. "Quis custodiet ipsos custodies" is an old Latin saying. What does it mean, and what is its relevance to this issue?

Create Central

www.mhhe.com/createcentral

Additional Resources

Ben Alusten, "The Terminator Scenario," *Popular Science* (January 2011).

Mark Gubrud, "US Killer Robot Policy: Full Speed Ahead," *Bulletin of the Atomic Scientists* (September 20, 2013).

Peter W. Singer, "The Predator Comes Home: A Primer on Domestic Drones, Their Huge Business Opportunities, and Their Deep Political, Moral, and Legal Challenges," Brookings Institution (March 8, 2013) (http://www.brookings.edu/research/papers/2013/03/08-drones-singer).

"Review of the 2012 US Policy on Autonomy in Weapons Systems," Human Rights Watch (April 15, 2013) (http://www.hrw.org/news/2013/04/15/review-2012-us-policy-autonomy-weapons-systems).

Internet References . . .

Living under Drones

http://www.livingunderdrones.org/

Rise of the Drones

http://www.pbs.org/wgbh/nova/military/rise-of-the-drones.html

Shadowview Foundation

http://www.shadowview.org/?gclid=CLeIqdX_2rwCFS7xOgoduWQATw

Unit 6

UNIT

Ethics

*S*ociety's standards of right and wrong have been hammered out over millennia of trial, error, and (sometimes violent) debate. Accordingly, when science and technology offer society new choices to make and new things to do, debates are renewed over whether or not these choices and actions are ethically acceptable. Today there is vigorous debate over such topics as the use of animals in research; cloning of both stem cells and whole organisms; and enhancing the human form with genetic engineering, electronic accessories, and even mechanical aids.

Selected, Edited, and with Issue Framing Material by:
Thomas A. Easton, *Thomas College*

ISSUE

Is "Animal Rights" Just Another Excuse for Terrorism?

YES: John J. Miller, from "In the Name of the Animals: America Faces a New Kind of Terrorism," *National Review* (July 3, 2006)

NO: Steven Best, from "Dispatches from a Police State: Animal Rights in the Crosshairs of State Repression," *International Journal of Inclusive Democracy* (January 2007)

Learning Outcomes
After studying this issue, students will be able to:
• Explain why animals are used in research.
• Explain why alternatives to the use of animals in research are sought.
• Describe the difference between "animal welfare" and "animal rights."
• Explain why society chooses to restrain extreme protests.

ISSUE SUMMARY

YES: Journalist John Miller argues that animal rights extremists have adopted terrorist tactics in their effort to stop the use of animals in scientific research. Because of the benefits of such research, if the terrorists win, everyone loses.

NO: Professor Steven Best argues that the new Animal Enterprise Protection Act is excessively broad and vague, imposes disproportionate penalties, endangers free speech, and detracts from prosecution of real terrorism. The animal liberation movement, on the other hand, is both a necessary effort to emancipate animals from human exploitation, and part of a larger resistance movement opposed to exploitation and hierarchies of any and all kinds.

Modern biologists and physicians know a great deal about how the human body works. Some of that knowledge has been gained by studying human cadavers and tissue samples acquired during surgery and through "experiments of nature." Some knowledge of human biology has also been gained from experiments on humans, such as when patients agree to let their surgeons and doctors try experimental treatments.

The key word here is *agree*. Today it is widely accepted that people have the right to consent or not to consent to whatever is done to them in the name of research or treatment. In fact, society has determined that research done on humans without their free and informed consent is a form of scientific misconduct. However, this standard does not apply to animals, experimentation on which has produced the most knowledge of the human body.

Although animals have been used in research for at least the last 2000 years, during most of that time, physicians who thought they had a workable treatment for some illness commonly tried it on their patients before they had any idea whether or not it worked or was even safe. Many patients, of course, died during these untested treatments. In the mid-nineteenth century, the French physiologist Claude Bernard argued that it was sensible to try such treatments first on animals to avoid some human suffering and death. No one then questioned whether or not human lives were more valuable than animal lives. In the twentieth century, Elizabeth Baldwin, in "The Case for Animal Research in Psychology," *Journal of Social Issues* (vol. 49, no. 1, 1993), argued that animals are of immense value in medical, veterinary, and psychological research, and they do not have the same moral rights as humans. Our obligation, she maintains, is to treat them humanely.

Today geneticists generally study fruit flies, roundworms, and zebra fish. Physiologists study mammals, mostly mice and rats but also rabbits, cats, dogs, pigs, sheep, goats, monkeys, and chimpanzees. Experimental animals are often kept in confined quarters, cut open, infected with disease organisms, fed unhealthy diets, and injected with assorted chemicals. Sometimes the animals suffer. Sometimes the animals die. And sometimes they are healed, albeit often of disease or injuries induced by the researchers in the first place.

Not surprisingly, some observers have reacted with extreme sympathy and have called for better treatment of animals used in research. This "animal welfare" movement has, in turn, spawned the more extreme "animal rights" movement, which asserts that animals—especially mammals—have rights as important and as deserving of regard as those of humans. Thus, to kill an animal, whether for research, food, or fur, is the moral equivalent of murder. See Steven M. Wise and Jane Golmoodall, *Rattling the Cage: Toward Legal Rights for Animals* (Perseus, 2000), and Roger Scruton and Andrew Tayler, "Do Animals Have Rights?" *The Ecologist* (March 2001).

As the idea that people must give informed consent to what is done to them in the name of research gained currency, along with the related idea that whatever is done should aim to benefit them, some people have tried to extend these ideas to animals. They say that just as scientists cannot do whatever they wish to humans, they cannot do whatever they wish to animals. Harriet Rivo, "Toward a More Peaceable Kingdom," *Technology Review* (April 1992) says that the animal rights movement "challenges the ideology of science itself . . . forcing experimenters to recognize that they are not necessarily carrying out an independent exercise in the pursuit of truth—that their enterprise, in its intellectual as well as its social and financial dimensions, is circumscribed and defined by the culture of which it is an integral part."

Among books that are pertinent to this issue are F. Barbara Orlans, *In the Name of Science: Issues in Responsible Animal Experimentation* (Oxford University Press, 1993); Rod Strand and Patti Strand, *The Hijacking of the Humane Movement* (Doral, 1993); Deborah Blum, *The Monkey Wars* (Oxford University Press, 1994); Tom Regan, *Empty Cages: Facing the Challenge of Animal Rights* (Rowman and Littlefield, 2005); and Paul Waldau, *Animal Rights: What Everyone Needs to Know* (Oxford University Press, 2011). Adrian R. Morrison provides a guide to responsible animal use in "Ethical Principles Guiding the Use of Animals in Research," *American Biology Teacher* (February 2003). Barry Yeoman, "Can We Trust Research Done with Lab Mice?" *Discover* (July 2003), notes that the conditions in which animals are kept can make a huge difference in their behavior and in their responses to experimental treatments.

The same research that leads to treatments for human illness also enhances the treatment tools of veterinarians. Thus Damon Linker, in "Rights for Rodents," *Commentary* (April 2001), can say, "Can anyone really doubt that, were the misanthropic agenda of the animal-rights movement actually to succeed, the result would be an increase in man's inhumanity, to man and animal alike? In the end, fostering our age-old 'prejudice' in favor of human dignity may be the best thing we can do for animals, not to mention for ourselves." An editorial in *Lancet*, "Animal Research Is a Source of Human Compassion, Not Shame" (September 4, 2004), insists that the use of animals in biomedical research is both an essentially humanistic endeavor and necessary. University of Pittsburgh assistant professor of anesthesiology and radiology Stuart Derbyshire writes in "Vivisection: Put Human Welfare First," *Spiked-Online* (June 1, 2004), that the use of animals in research is justified by the search for knowledge, not just the search for medical treatments, and reflects a moral choice to put humans first. Josie Appleton, "Speciesism: A Beastly Concept: Why It Is Morally Right to Use Animals to Our Ends," *Spiked-Online* (February 23, 2006), contends that the development of human civilization has been marked by increasing separation from animals. Humans come first, and it is entirely moral to use animals for own ends. Torturing animals is wrong, but mostly because it reflects badly upon the torturer. Wesley J. Smith, *A Rat Is a Pig Is a Dog Is a Boy: The Human Cost of the Animal Rights Movement* (Encounter, 2010), defends the stance that human interests must come before those of animals; granting rights to animals is an attack on human dignity.

Animal-rights extremists defend the opposing view vigorously, even going so far as to firebomb researchers' homes and cars; see Greg Miller, "Scientists Targeted in California Firebombings," *Science* (August 8, 2008). John Hadley, "Animal Rights Extremism and the Terrorism Question," *Journal of Social Philosophy* (Fall 2009), questions whether such extremist actions really fall under the "terrorism" label, but most people seems to have no trouble using the label. P. Michael Conn and James V. Parker of the Oregon National Primate Research Center describe in *The Animal Research War* (Palgrave Macmillan, 2008) how animals are used and protected in research and the benefits of their use, while also detailing the movement of terrorist tactics from the United Kingdom to the United States. In their view, "It is extremely important that an informed public know what is really going on and how it impacts on the future of health care and medical advances."

Yet the idea that animals have rights too continues to gain ground. Steven M. Wise finds in *Drawing the Line: Science and the Case for Animal Rights* (Perseus, 2002) that there is a spectrum of mental capacities for different species, which supports the argument for rights. Niall Shanks, in "Animal Rights in the Light of Animal Cognition," *Social Alternatives* (Summer 2003), considers the moral/philosophical justifications for animal rights and stresses the question of consciousness. Jim Motavalli, in "Rights from Wrongs," *E Magazine* (March/April 2003), describes with approval the movement toward giving animals legal rights (though not necessarily human rights). Jeffrey Stinson, "Activists Pursue Basic Legal Rights for Great Apes," *USA Today* (July 15, 2008), describes current efforts to grant such rights to the great apes. Paul Starobin, "Animal Rights on the March," *National Journal* (May 22, 2010), notes that the animal rights movement is shifting toward legislative efforts to meet their goals. In India, the use of live animals in most research has been banned;

see Linah Baliga, "Govt Bans Use of Live Animals for Education, Research," *Times of India* (April 17, 2012).

The animal welfare movement has led to important reforms in the treatment of animals, to the development of several alternatives to using animals in research, and to a considerable reduction in the number of animals used in research. See, for example, Robert A. Coleman, "Human Tissue in the Evaluation of Safety and Efficacy of New Medicines: A Viable Alternative to Animal Models?" *ISRN Pharmaceutics* (special section) (2011); Alan Dove, "The Search for Animal Alternatives," *Drug Discovery & Development* (May 2010); and Manfred Liebsch, et al., "Alternatives to Animal Testing: Current Status and Future Perspectives," *Archives of Toxicology* (August 2011). There is also a scientific Journal, ALTEX: Alternatives to Animal Experimentation (http://altweb.jhsph.edu/altex/index.html). However, it has also led to hysterical objections to in-class animal dissections, terrorist attacks on laboratories, the destruction of research records, and the theft of research materials (including animals).

The Animal Enterprise Protection Act (AEPA) was designed to prevent attacks on laboratories and researchers, and since its passage, such attacks indeed have diminished. Yet critics do object that it may have a chilling effect on legitimate protest; see Michael Hill, "United States v. Fullmer and the Animal Enterprise Terrorism Act: 'True Threats' to Advocacy," *Case Western Reserve Law Review* (Spring 2011), and Dara Lovitz, *Muzzling a Movement: The Effects of Anti-Terrorism Law, Money, and Politics on Animal Activism* (Lantern Books, 2010). One lawsuit was dismissed in March 2013 for failure to show that such "chilling" actually existed; see Rose Bouboushian, "Terror Fears of Animal Rights Group Tossed," *Courthouse News* (March 21, 2013).

In the YES selection, Journalist John J. Miller argues that animal rights extremists have adopted terrorist tactics in their effort to stop the use of animals in scientific research. Because of the benefits of such research, if the terrorists win, everyone loses. In the NO selection, Professor Steven Best argues that new laws against animal rights "terrorism" represent the efforts of animal exploitation industries that seek immunity from criticism. The new Animal Enterprise Protection Act is excessively broad and vague, imposes disproportionate penalties, endangers free speech, and detracts from prosecution of real terrorism. The animal liberation movement, on the other hand, is both a necessary effort to emancipate animals from human exploitation and part of a larger resistance movement opposed to exploitation and hierarchies of any and all kinds.

YES ↩

John J. Miller

In the Name of the Animals: America Faces a New Kind of Terrorism

Six days after the World Trade Center was destroyed, the New York Stock Exchange rang its opening bell and traders sang "God Bless America" from the floor: They wanted to send a loud-and-clear message to the world that al-Qaeda could not shut down the U.S. economy. Even though the Dow suffered its biggest one-day point-loss in history, the mere fact that buying and selling could resume so quickly marked an inspiring day for capitalism and against terrorism.

On September 7, 2005, however, terrorists struck again, and the NYSE still hasn't recovered. This time, they didn't target a couple of skyscrapers near the exchange, but rather a company called Life Sciences Research (LSR). It had recently qualified for a NYSE listing and its senior management had gathered on Wall Street to celebrate the occasion. Just a few minutes before the first trades were set to occur, NYSE president Catherine Kinney informed her guests that their listing would be postponed. It was immediately obvious to everyone from LSR what had happened: "A handful of animal extremists had succeeded where Osama bin Laden had failed," Mark Bibi, the company's general counsel, would say in congressional testimony the next month.

LSR is better known by the name of its operating subsidiary, Huntingdon Life Sciences (HLS), which is in the business of testing products on animals to assess their safety and comply with government regulations. Most people probably don't like to think about what goes on in these labs—vivisections of monkeys, for instance—but they also appreciate the importance of research whose ultimate goal is the protection and enhancement of human health. About 95 percent of all lab animals are rats and mice, but for animal-rights extremists who believe that "a rat is a pig is a dog is a boy" (as Ingrid Newkirk of People for the Ethical Treatment of Animals once said), the whole endeavor is deeply immoral. And some of them have decided that because the traditional practices of honest persuasion and civil disobedience haven't changed many hearts or minds, they must now adopt a different strategy—something they euphemistically call "direct action." These are efforts to intimidate and harass animal researchers and everyone who comes into contact with them. In recent years, hardcore activists have embraced property destruction and physical assaults. "This is the number-one domestic terrorist threat in America," says Sen. James Inhofe, an Oklahoma Republican. Keeping LSR off the Big Board probably represents their greatest achievement yet.

Red in Tooth and Claw

The animal-rights movement may be wrongheaded, but there's no denying that most of its members are motivated by genuine compassion for animals and a sincere commitment to preventing cruelty. There's also no denying that violence in their name has become a significant problem. Just as the pro-life movement is haunted by the murderers of abortion doctors, the environmental and animal-rights movements are cursed by their own packs of fierce radicals. A year ago, the FBI said that 35 of its offices were conducting more than 150 investigations into "animal rights/ecoterrorist activities." The number of illegal incidents involving these activities has risen sharply, from 220 in the 1980s and 1990s to 363 in just the last five years, according to a recent report by the Foundation for Biomedical Research, an association of businesses and universities that conduct animal research. (By contrast, abortion-clinic violence appears to be subsiding.)

"Other groups don't come close in terms of the financial damage they've done," says John Lewis, an FBI agent who until recently coordinated federal efforts against domestic terrorism. Not even militants in the mold of Timothy McVeigh, the man behind the Oklahoma City bombing in 1995? "We have an acute interest in all of these groups, but when the rubber meets the road, the eco- and animal-rights terrorists lately have been way out in front." Lewis estimates that they've caused around $100 million in damage, mostly property destruction affecting businesses, much of it from arson. This fall, eleven defendants will face trial in Oregon for causing an estimated $20 million in damage in five states.

Although animal-rights terrorism is fundamentally barbaric, its execution has assumed increasingly sophisticated forms. The campaign against Huntingdon Life Sciences began in the United Kingdom seven years ago with the formation of a group called Stop Huntingdon Animal Cruelty, or SHAC. Soon after, SHAC recruited members in the United States to focus on an HLS facility in New Jersey, using methods that were deployed to great effect in the U.K. A federal trial earlier this year—perhaps the most important trial ever held involving animal-rights extremism—put the group's methods on full display.

Many of SHAC's efforts targeted HLS directly. An electronic attack in 2002, for instance, caused the HLS server to overload. But other confrontations involved HLS employees away from work: cars vandalized in driveways, rocks tossed through the windows of homes, and graffiti messages such as "PUPPY KILLER" spray-painted on houses. Descriptions of these incidents were dutifully posted on SHAC's own website, often with an unnerving sense of glee. After a tire-slashing visit to the home of one HLS employee, for example, the SHACtivists seemed pleased that "his wife is reportedly on the brink of a nervous breakdown and divorce." These messages were meant to generate publicity, build a sense of momentum, and serve as models for activists spread across the country. In Britain, one top HLS employee was attacked by a group of hooded men wielding ax handles. "It's only a matter of time before it happens in the United States," warns Frankie Trull, head of the Foundation for Biomedical Research. "Everything they do over there eventually comes over here."

Intimidating employees in their private lives places pressure on HLS itself. But SHAC's harassment didn't stop with HLS employees. They also engaged in "tertiary targeting"—i.e., taking aim at companies with ties to HLS, plus their workers. Dozens of firms decided that doing business with HLS simply wasn't worth it. Deloitte & Touche, which had audited the HLS books, ended its relationship. Lawn gardeners quit. Even a security company that provided services to HLS succumbed to the abuse.

SHAC's methods certainly can be menacing, as transcripts from the trial make clear. One of SHAC's main targets was Marsh, a company that sold insurance to HLS. There was a smoke-bomb attack at an office in Seattle, forcing the evacuation of a high-rise building. In San Antonio, SHAC members glued the locks to a Marsh office and plastered the windows and doors of the building with pictures of a mutilated dog. Once they even stormed inside, screaming threats: "You have the blood of death on your hands! . . . We know where you live! You cannot sleep at night! We will find you!"

And they made good on these threats. Marsh employees were repeatedly harassed at home. There were late-night phone calls: "Are you scared? Do you think the puppies should be scared?" Other calls were more menacing: "We know where you live. You shouldn't sleep at night. You shouldn't rest until the puppies rest." Marion Harlos, who was managing director for Marsh in San Antonio, said that people went through her mail, ordered magazine subscriptions in her name, and rang her doorbell and dashed off in a kind of never-ending Devil's Night. Sometimes protesters would gather in front of her house, banging drums and hollering into megaphones. "They proceeded to parade the neighborhood, shout my name, that of my children," she said. "I was petrified. I was petrified for my children." The kids were kept indoors: "We did not know what was going to take place. Would someone be in the front yard? Would someone be in the back yard? Would someone come up and talk to them? Would someone try and take them?" To make a bad situation even worse, a neighbor threatened to sue Harlos, claiming that the ongoing presence of protesters was hurting property values. Harlos eventually moved.

Sally Dillenback, a Marsh employee in Dallas, had a similarly harrowing experience. A SHAC website published private information, some of it probably obtained by going through her trash: her home address, her car's license-plate number, and even her auto-insurance policy number. Most unsettling, however, was the information about her children: their names, the names of their schools and teachers, and descriptions of their after-school activities. "I felt that my family might be threatened with that kind of information being posted," she testified. The activists certainly didn't leave her alone; they plastered pictures on the side of her house, her mailbox, and her sidewalk. A SHAC website described the strategy: "Let the stickers serve to remind Marsh employees and their neighbors that their homes are paid for in the blood, the blood of innocent animals." On other occasions, animal-rights radicals held protests outside her home with drums and bullhorns. They followed her to church. The scariest moment may have been when Dillenback read an e-mail: "It asked how I would feel if they cut open my son . . . and filled him with poison the way that they, Huntingdon, [were] doing to animals." Her husband bought a semi-automatic shotgun, even though Mrs. Dillenback doesn't like guns: "He was wanting to protect the family."

Pundits in Black Ski Masks

Marsh employees were by no means the only tertiary victims of abuse. Two bombs went off at a California office of Chiron, a biotech company. Nobody was hurt, but the second explosion was delayed—a tactic sometimes used by terrorists to kill first responders. Workers at GlaxoSmithKline, a pharmaceutical company, also had their windows smashed and mail stolen. In one case, SHAC posted information about the spouse of a GSK employee who was undergoing treatment for alcoholism. Another employee was summoned to the Baltimore morgue to identify a dead relative—but when she arrived, she learned the call was a hoax.

Sometimes, the connections between SHAC targets and HLS were so tenuous as to be almost nonexistent. Elaine Perna, a housewife who is married to an executive who retired from the Bank of New York—another company with ties to HLS—confronted SHAC when protesters appeared on her porch. "When I opened the door, they were yelling at me through the bullhorn. One spat at my face through the screen and yelled obscenities at me, about me, about my husband." A defense lawyer's attempt to minimize the incident—"All Ms. Gazzola did was she screamed through the bullhorn, didn't she?"—irritated Perna: "They were yelling at me through a bullhorn, they were calling me effing this and my husband effing that and spitting in my face through a screen. Now, if you think that 'that's all,' you know, you can call it 'that's all.' But to me, it wasn't 'that's all.'" The mayhem didn't stop until the police arrived.

On March 2, a jury convicted six members of SHAC (at press time, sentencing had not yet occurred). This is an important victory, but animal-rights extremism isn't going away—groups such as Hugs for Puppies and Win Animal Rights are now on the scene, continuing their perverse crusade. They certainly don't lack for true believers. In Senate testimony last fall, Jerry Vlasak of the North American Animal Liberation Press Office announced that violence against HLS was "extensional self-defense" in behalf of "non-human animals." Recently, a mysterious full-page advertisement appeared in the *New York Times* and the *Wall Street Journal*. It featured the image of a man in a black ski mask, alongside the words "I Control Wall Street" and a short account of the NYSE fiasco. "Nobody knows who paid for it," says Trull. One theory proposes that a group of institutional investors are responsible; another claims that it's a backhanded attempt by animal-rights activists to raise anxieties even further. HLS still isn't listed.

Several members of Congress have tried to address this species of domestic terrorism by proposing legislation that would toughen the Animal Enterprise Protection Act, a law that was passed before the advent of "tertiary targeting." At the recent trial, prosecutors secured convictions against SHAC only because they were able to rely on anti-stalking laws. "They had to scour the federal code, looking for violations," says Brent McIntosh, a deputy assistant attorney general at the Department of Justice. "This is an enormous, surreptitious, and interstate conspiracy. We need to strengthen laws against it." Bills to do so have been introduced in both the House and the Senate, but a crowded legislative calendar probably means they won't be debated until a new Congress convenes next year.

The stakes are high. "Five years from now, we don't want to count up another $100 million in losses," says the FBI's Lewis. That's true, although the real costs of animal-rights terrorism aren't really quantifiable: They come in the form of medical discoveries that are delayed or never made, products that aren't approved, and careers that aren't started. Whatever the real price tag, one thing is certain: Each time an animal-rights terrorist wins, people lose.

JOHN J. MILLER is *National Review's* national political reporter. His latest book is *A Gift of Freedom: How the John M. Olin Foundation Changed America* (Encounter Books, 2005).

Steven Best

 **NO**

Dispatches from a Police State: Animal Rights in the Crosshairs of State Repression

Welcome to the post-constitutional America, where defense of animal rights and the earth is a terrorist crime.

In the wake of 9/11, and in the midst [of] the neo-liberal attack on social democracies, efforts to grab dwindling resources, and crush dissent of any kind, the US has entered a neo-McCarthyist period rooted in witch-hunts and political persecution. The terms and players have changed, but the situation is much the same as the 1950s: the terrorist threat has replaced the communist threat, Attorney General Alfred [sic] Gonzalez dons the garb of Sen. Joseph McCarthy, and the Congressional Meetings on Eco-Terrorism stand in for the House Un-American Activities Committee. The Red Scare of communism has morphed into the *Green Scare* of ecoterrorism, where the bad guy today is not a commie but an animal, environmental, or peace activist. In a nightmare replay of the 1950s, activists of all kinds today are surveilled, hassled, threatened, jailed, and stripped of their rights. As before, the state conjures up dangerous enemies in our midst and instills fear in the public, so that people willingly forfeit liberties for an alleged security that demands secrecy, non-accountability, and centralized power. . . .

The bogus "war on terror" has served as a highly-effective propaganda and bullying device to ram through Congress and the courts a pro-corporate, anti-environmental, authoritarian agenda. Using vague, catch-all phrases such as "enemy combatants" and "domestic terrorists," the Bush administration has rounded up and tortured thousands of non-citizens (detaining them indefinitely in military tribunals without right to a fair trial) and surveilled, harassed, and imprisoned citizens who dare to challenge the government or corporate system it protects and represents.

"The Animal Enterprise Protection Act"

While dissent in general has become ever-more criminalized in the dark days of the Bush Reich, animal rights activists especially have been caught in the crosshairs of state repression, targeted by "anti-terrorist" legislation that subverts First Amendment rights to protect the blood money of corporate exploiters. This is because the animal rights/liberation movement is not only one of the most

dramatic forms of resistance alive today (such as [is] evident in the dramatic raids, rescues, sabotage, and arson attacks of the Animal Liberation Front, a global movement), but also is an economic threat to postindustrial capital which is heavily rooted in science and research, and therefore dependent upon (it believes) animal experimentation.

In 1992, a decade before the passage of the USA PATRIOT Act, animal exploitation groups such as the National Association for Biomedical Research successfully lobbied Congress to pass a federal law called the Animal Enterprise Protection Act (AEPA). This legislation created the new crime of "animal enterprise terrorism," and laid out hefty sentences and fines for any infringement. The law applies to anyone who "intentionally damages or causes the loss of any property" of an "animal enterprise" (research facilities, pet stores, breeders, zoos, rodeos, circuses, furriers, animal shelters, and the like), or who causes an *economic loss* of any kind. The AEPA defines an "animal rights or ecological terrorist organization" as "two or more persons organized for the purpose of supporting any politically motivated activity intended to obstruct or deter any person from participating in any activity involving animals or an activity involving natural resources." The act criminalizes actions that obstruct "any lawful activity involving the use of natural resources with an economic value."

Like the category of "domestic terrorism" that is a keystone in the USA PATRIOT Act attack on civil liberties, the frightening thing about the AEPA is its strategic vagueness that subsumes any and every form of protest and demonstration against exploitative industries to a criminal act, specifically, to a *terrorist* act. Thus, the actions of two or more people can be labeled terrorist if they leaflet a circus, protest an experimental lab, block a road to protect a forest, do a tree-sit, or block the doors of a fur store. Since, under the purview of the AEPA, any action that interferes with the profits and operations of animal and environmental industries, even boycotts and whistle-blowing could be criminalized and denounced as terrorism. On the sweeping interpretations of such legislation, Martin Luther King, Mahatma Gandhi, and Cesar Chavez would today be vilified and imprisoned as terrorists, since the intent of their principled boycott campaigns was precisely to cause "economic damage" to unethical businesses. And since the AETA, like the legal system in general, classifies animals as "property," their "theft" (read: *liberation*) is unequivocally defined as a terrorist offense.

There already are laws against sabotage and property destruction, so isn't the AEPA just a redundant piece of legislation? No—not once [one] understands its hidden agenda which strikes at the heart of the Bill of Rights. The real purpose of the AEPA is to protect animal and earth exploitation industries from protest and criticism, not property destruction and "terrorism." The AEPA redefines vandalism as ecoterrorism, petty lawbreakers as societal menaces, protestors and demonstrators as domestic terrorists, and threats to their blood money as threats to national security. Powerful economic and lobbying forces, they seek immunity from criticism, to intimidate anyone contemplating protest against them, and to dispatch their opponents to prison.

Free Speech on Trial: The SHAC 7

Hovering over activists' heads like the sword of Damocles for over a decade, the AEPA dropped in March, 2006, with the persecution and conviction of seven members of a direct action group dedicated to closing down the world's largest animal-testing company, Huntingdon Life Sciences (HLS). Exercising their First Amendment rights, activists from the Stop Huntingdon Animal Cruelty (SHAC) campaign ran a completely legal and highly effective campaign against HLS, driving them to the brink of bankruptcy. Since 1999, SHAC activists in the UK and US have waged an aggressive direct action campaign against HLS, notorious for extreme animal abuse (torturing and killing 500 animals a day) and manipulated research data. SHAC roared onto the historical stage by combining a shrewd knowledge of the law, no nonsense direct action tactics, and a singular focus on one corporation that represents the evils of the entire vivisection industry. From email and phone blockades to raucous home demonstrations, SHACtivists have attacked HLS and pressured over 100 companies to abandon financial ties to the vivisection firm. By 2001, the SHAC movement drove down HLS stock values from $15/share to less than $1/share. Smelling profit emanating from animal bloodshed, investment banking firm Stephens Inc. stepped in to save HLS from bankruptcy. But, as happened to so many companies before them, eventually Stephens too could not withstand the intense political heat and so fled the SHAC kitchen. Today, as HLS struggles for solvency, SHAC predicts its imminent demise.

Growing increasingly powerful through high-pressure tactics that take the fight to HLS and their supporters rather than to corrupt legislatures, the SHAC movement poses a clear and present danger to animal exploitation industries and the state that serves them. Staggered and driven into the ropes, it was certain that SHAC's opponents would fight back. Throwing futile jabs here and there, the vivisection industry and the state recently teamed up to mount a major counterattack.

Alarmed indeed by the new form of animal rights militancy, HLS and the biomedical research lobby commanded special sessions with Congress to ban SHAC campaigns. On May 26, 2004, a police dragnet rounded up seven prominent animal rights activists in New Jersey, New York, Washington, and California. Hordes of agents from the FBI, Secret Service, and other law agencies stormed into the activists' homes at the crack of dawn, guns drawn and helicopters hovering above. Handcuffing those struggling for a better world, the state claimed another victory in its phony "war against terror." Using the AEPA, HLS successfully prosecuted the "SHAC 7," who currently are serving prison sentences up to six years.

After the SHAC 7 conviction, David Martosko, the noxious research director of the Center for Consumer Freedom and a fierce opponent of animal rights, joyously declared: "This is just the starting gun." Indeed, corporations and legislators continue to press for even stronger laws against animal rights and environmental activism, as the Bush administration encloses the nation within a vast web of surveillance and a militarized garrison.

In September 2006, the US senate unanimously passed a new version of the AEPA (S3990), significantly renamed the "Animal Enterprise *Terrorism* Act" (AETA). To prevent critical discussion, the Senate fast-tracked the bill without hearings or debate, and just before adjourning for the election recess. In November 2006, the House approved the bill (HR 4239), and President Bush obligingly signed it into law. Beyond the portentous change in name, the new and improved version extends the range of legal prosecution of activists, updates the law to cover Internet campaigns, and enforces stiffer penalties for "terrorist" actions. Created to stop the effectiveness of the SHAC-style tactics that biomedical companies had habitually complained about to Congress, the AETA makes it a criminal offense to interfere not only with so-called "animal enterprises" directly, but also with third-party organizations such as insurance companies, law firms, and investment houses that do business with them.

Thus, the Senate version of the bill expands the law to include "any property of a person or entity having a connection to, relationship with, or transactions with an animal enterprise." The chain of relations, like the application of the law, extends possibly to the point of infinity. As journalist Will Potter notes, "The clause broadens the scope of legislation that is already overly broad." This problem is compounded further with additional vague concepts such as criminalize actions that create "reasonable fear" in the targets of protest, making actions like peaceful home demonstrations likely candidates for "ecoterrorism."

As the Equal Justice Alliance aptly summarizes the main problems with the AETA:

- "It is excessively broad and vague.
- It imposes disproportionately harsh penalties.
- It effectively brands animal advocates as 'terrorists' and denies them equal protection.

- It effectively brands civil disobedience as 'terrorism' and imposes severe penalties.
- It has a chilling effect on all forms of protest by endangering free speech and assembly.
- It interferes with investigation of animal enterprises that violate federal laws.
- It detracts from prosecution of real terrorism against the American people."

ACLU Betrayal

A sole voice of dissent in Congress, Representative Dennis Kucinich (D-Ohio) stated that the bill compromises civil rights and threatens to "chill" free speech. Virtually alone in examining the issue from the perspective of the victims rather than victimizers, Kucinich said: "Just as we need to protect people's right to conduct their work without fear of assault, so too this Congress has yet to address some fundamental ethical principles with respect to animals. How should animals be treated humanely? This is a debate that hasn't come here."

One of the most unfortunate aspects of the passing of this bill was the failure of the American Civil Liberties Union to challenge it. The ACLU did indeed write a letter to Congress about the passing of the AETA, to caution against conflating illegal and legal protest, but the organization failed to challenge the real terrorism perpetuated by animal and earth exploitation industries, and ultimately consented to their worldview and validity.

In an October 30, 2006, letter to Chairman of the House Judiciary Committee F. James Sensenbrenner and Ranking Member John Conyers, the ACLU writes that it "does not oppose this bill, but believes that these minor changes are necessary to make the bill less likely to chill or threaten freedom of speech." Beyond proposed semantic clarifications, the ACLU mainly warns against broadening the law to include legal activities such as boycotts: "Legitimate expressive activity may result in economic damage. . . . Care must therefore be taken in penalizing economic damage to avoid infringing upon legitimate activity."

Thus, unlike dozens of animal protection groups who adamantly reject the AETA *en toto,* the ACLU "does not oppose the bill." In agreement with corporate interests, the ACLU assures the government it "does not condone violence or threats." It thereby dodges the complex question of the legitimacy of sabotage against exploitative industries. The ACLU uncritically accepts (1) the corporate–state definition of "violence" as intentional harm to *property,* (2) the legal definition of animals as "property," and (3) the use of the T-word to demonize animal liberationists rather than animal exploiters. Ultimately, the ACLU sides with the government against activists involved in illegal forms of liberation or sabotage, a problematic alliance in times of global ecocide. The ACLU thereby defends *the property rights* of industries to torture and slaughter billions of animals over the *moral rights* of animals to bodily integrity and a life free from exploitation and gratuitous violence.

The ACLU failed to ask the tough questions journalist Will Potter raised during his May 23, 2006 testimony before the House Committee holding a hearing on the AETA, and to follow Potter in identifying key inconsistencies in bill. Does the ACLU really think that their proposed modifications would be adequate to guarantee that the AETA doesn't trample on legal rights to protest? Are they completely ignorant and indifferent to the fact that the AEPA was just used to send the SHAC 7 to jail for the crime of protesting fraudulent research and heinous killing? And just where was the ACLU during the SHAC 7 trial, one of the most significant First Amendment cases in recent history? Why does the ACLU only recognize violations of the Constitution against human rights advocates? Do they think that animal rights activists are not citizens? Do they not recognize that tyrannical measures used against animal advocates today will be used against all citizens tomorrow? How can the world's premier civil rights institution [be] blatantly speciesist and bigoted toward animals? *Why will they come to the defense of the Ku Klux Klan but not the SHAC 7?* The ACLU's silence in the face of persecution of animal rights activists unfortunately is typical of most civil rights organizations that are too bigoted and myopic to grasp the implications of state repression of animal rights activists for human rights activists and all forms of dissent.

Animal Liberation as a New Social Movement

Corporate exploiters and Congress have taken the US down a perilous slippery slope, where it becomes difficult to distinguish between illegal and legal forms of dissent, between civil disobedience and terrorism, between PETA and Al Qaeda, and between liberating chickens from a factory farm and flying passenger planes into skyscrapers. The state protects the corporate exploiters who pull their purse strings and stuff their pockets with favors and cash.

The right to free speech ends as soon as you begin to exercise it. As the politics of nature—the struggle for liberation of animals and the earth—is the most dynamic fight today, one that poses a serious threat to corporate interests, animal and earth liberationists are under ferocious attack. The growing effectiveness of direct action anti-vivisection struggles will inevitably bring a reactionary and retaliatory response by the corporate–state complex to crack down on democratic political freedoms to protest, as well as new Draconian laws that represent a concerted effort by power brokers to crush the movement for animal liberation.

In the "home of the brave, land of the free," activists are followed by federal agents; their phone conversations and computer activity [are] monitored, their homes are raided, they are forced to testify before grand juries and pressured to "name names," they are targets of federal round ups, they are jailed for exercising constitutionally protected rights and liberties. Saboteurs receive stiffer prison sentences than rapists, bank robbers, and murderers.

There has never been freedom of speech or action in the US, but in the post-9/11 climate, where the USA PATRIOT Act is the law of the land, not the Constitution and Bill of Rights, activists are demonized as terrorists—not just the Animal Liberation Front (ALF), Earth Liberation Front (ELF), and SHAC, but also completely legal and peaceful groups like Food Not Bombs and vegan outreach organizations.

The massive police resources of the US state are being used far more to thwart domestic dissent than to improve homeland insecurity. While Big Brother is obsessed with the email, conversations, and meetings of people who know a thing or two about the duties of citizenship, the airlines, railways, subways, city centers, and nuclear power plants remain completely vulnerable to an attack, which, according to the elites, is imminent.

The contemporary animal liberation movement is an *extension of the new social movements,* and as such issues "post-materialist" demands that are not about higher wages but the end to hierarchy and violence, and a new relation with the natural world.

Second, it is a *postindustrial movement,* operating within a global postindustrial society where the primary aspects of the economy no longer center on processing of physical materials as much as information, knowledge, science, and research. Transnational corporations such as Monsanto, pharmaceutical industries such as GlaxoSmithKline, AstraZeneca, Novartis, and Pfizer, and drug testing corporations such as Huntingdon Life Sciences show the importance of science and research for the postindustrial economy, and thus the relevance of the animal liberation movement.

This movement also is an *anti-globalization* movement in that the corporations it attacks often are transnational and global in scope, part of what I call the Global Vivisection Complex (GVC). The GVC is comprised of pharmaceutical industries, biotechnology industries, medical research industries, universities, and testing laboratories, all using animal experimentation to test and market their drugs. As animals are the gas and oil for these corporate science machines, the animal liberation movement has disrupted corporate supply chains, thwarted laboratory procedures, liberated captive slaves, and attacked the legitimacy of biomedical research as an effective scientific paradigm.

Fourth, the animal liberation movement is an *abolitionist movement,* seeking empty cages not bigger cages, demanding rights not "humane treatment" of the slaves, opposing the greatest institution of domination and slavery ever created—the empire of human supremacy over millions of species and billions of animal slaves.

To an important degree, the historical and socioeconomic context for the emergence of the animal advocacy movement (in all its diverse tendencies and aspects) is the industrialization of animal exploitation and killing. This is dramatically evident with the growth of slaughterhouses at the turn of the 20th century, the emergence

and globalization of factory farming after World War II, and the subsequent growth of research capital and animal experimentation. To this, one would have to add expanding human population numbers, the social construction of carnivorous appetites, and the rise of fast food industries which demand the exploitation and massacre of ever-growing numbers of animals, now in the tens of billions on a global scale. Along with other horrors and modes of animal exploitation, the industrialization, mechanization, and globalization of animal exploitation called into being an increasingly broad, growing, and powerful animal liberation movement.

Animal liberation builds on the great abolitionist struggle of past centuries and is the abolitionist movement of our day. Animal liberationists are waging war against the oldest and last form of slavery to be formally abolished—the exploitation of nonhuman animals. Just as the modern economy of Europe, the British colonies in America, and the United States after the Revolutionary War were once entirely dependent on the trafficking in human slaves, so now the current global economy would crash if all animal slaves were freed from every lab, cage and other mode of exploitation. Animal liberation is in fact the anti-slavery movement of the present age and its moral and economic ramifications are as world-shaking, possible more so, than the abolition of the human slavery movement (which of course itself still exists in some sectors of the world in the form of sweatshops, child sex slavery, forced female prostitution, and the like).

The animal liberation movement is a profound threat to the corporate–state complex and hierarchical society in two ways.

First, it is a serious economic threat, as the planetary capitalist system thrives off animal exploitation with the meat/dairy and biomedical research industries. In the UK, for instance, where the animal rights movement has been particularly effective, drug-makers are the third most important contributor to the economy after power generation and oil industries. The animal rights movement has emerged as a powerful anti-capitalist and anti-(corporate) globalization force in its ability to monkeywrench the planetary vivisection machine and challenge transnational corporations such as HLS, GlaxoSmithKline, and Novartis.

Second, the animal rights movement is a potent ideological and psychological threat. The fight for animal liberation demands radical transformations in the habits, practices, values, and mindset of all human beings as it also entails a fundamental restructuring of social institutions and economic systems predicated on exploitative practices. The philosophy of animal liberation assaults the identities and worldviews that portray humans as conquering Lords and Masters of nature, and it requires entirely new ways of relating to animals and the earth. Animal liberation is a direct attack on the power human beings—whether in premodern or modern, non-Western or Western societies—have claimed over animals, since at least the dawn of agricultural society ten thousand years ago.

Total Liberation

As the dynamics that brought about global warming, rainforest destruction, species extinction, and poisoning of communities are not reducible to any single factor or cause—be it agricultural society, the rise of states, anthropocentrism, speciesism, patriarchy, racism, colonialism, industrialism, technocracy, or capitalism—all radical groups and orientations that can effectively challenge the ideologies and institutions implicated in domination and ecological destruction have a relevant role to play in the global social-environmental struggle. While standpoints such as deep ecology, social ecology, ecofeminism, animal liberation, Black liberation, and the Earth Liberation Front are all important, none can accomplish systemic social transformation by itself. Working together, however, through a diversity of critiques and tactics that mobilize different communities, a flank of militant groups and positions can drive a battering ram into the structures of power and domination and open the door to a new future.

Although there is diversity in unity, there must also be unity in diversity. Solidarity can emerge in recognition of the fact that all forms of oppression are directly or indirectly related to the values, institutions, and *system* of global capitalism and related hierarchical structures. To be unified and effective, however, anti-capitalist and anti-imperialist alliances require mutual sharing, respectful learning, and psychological growth, such that, for instance, black liberationists, ecofeminists, and animal liberationists can help one another overcome racism, sexism, and speciesism.

The larger context for current dynamics in the animal liberation movement involves the emergence of the neoliberal project (as a response to the opening of the markets that was made necessary by the continuous expansion of transnational corporations in the post-war period) which was crucial in the elites' effort to destroy socialism and social democracy of any kind, to privatize all social structures, to gain total control of all resource markets and dwindling resources, and to snuff out all resistance. The animal rights/liberation movement has come under such intense fire because it has emerged as a threat to operations and profits of postindustrial capital (heavily rooted in research and therefore animal experimentation) and as a significant form of resistance. The transnational elite want the fire crushed before its example of resistance becomes a conflagration.

Conversely, the animal liberation movement is most effective not only as a single-issue focus to emancipate animals from human exploitation, but to join a larger resistance movement opposed to exploitation and hierarchies of any and all kinds. Clearly, SHAC and the ALF alone are not going to bring down transnational capitalism, pressuring

HLS and raiding fur farms and laboratories will not themselves ignite revolutionary change, and are more rear-guard, defensive actions. The project to emancipate animals, in other words, is integrally related to the struggle to emancipate humans and the battle for a viable natural world. To the extent that the animal liberation movement grasps the big picture that links animal and human oppression struggles as one, and seeks to uncover the roots of hierarchy including that of humans over nature, they can be viewed as a profound new liberation movement that has a crucial place in the planetary struggles against injustice, oppression, exploitation, war, violence, capitalist neo-liberalism, and the destruction of the natural world and biodiversity.

Yet, given the profound relation between the human domination of animals and the crisis—social, ethical, and environmental—in the human world and its relation to the natural world, the animal liberation movement is in a unique position to articulate the importance of new relations between human and human, human and animal, and human and nature.

New social movements and Greens have failed to realize their radical potential. They have abandoned their original demands for radical social change and become integrated into capitalist structures that have eliminated "existing socialist countries" as well as social democracies within the present neoliberal globalization which has become dominant. A new revolutionary force must therefore emerge, one that will build on the achievements of classical democratic, libertarian socialist, and anarchist traditions; incorporate radical green, feminist, and indigenous struggles; synthesize animal, Earth, and human liberation standpoints; and build a global social-ecological revolution capable of abolishing transnational capitalism so that just and ecological societies can be constructed in its place.

Notes

For Feinstein's pathetic capitulation to the Green Scare and her sordid alliance with neo-McCarthyite Senator James "Global Warming Is a Myth" Inhofe (R-Okla.), see her press release. . . .

The text of the "Animal Enterprise Protection Act of 1992" is available online.

In states such as Oregon and California, related legislation has already passed which declares it a felony terrorist offense to enter any animal facility with a camera or video recorder "with the intent to defame the facility or facility's owner." See Steven Best, "It's War: The Escalating Battle Between Activists and the Corporate-State Complex," in *Terrorists or Freedom Fighters? Reflections on the Liberation of Animals* (Lantern Books, 2004), pp. 300–339 (eds. Steven Best and Anthony J. Nocella II).

For a more detailed analysis of the SHAC struggle in the context of political economy, see Steven Best and Richard Kahn, "Trial By Fire: The SHAC 7, Globalization, and the Future of Democracy," *Animal Liberation Philosophy and Policy Journal,* Volume II, Issue 2, 2004 . . .

On the SHAC 7 trial, see Steven Best and Richard Kahn, "Trial By Fire: The SHAC7, Globalization, and the Future of Democracy."

For the text of S3880, the final bill that passed in both houses, see . . .

Will Potter, "Analysis of Animal Enterprise Terrorism Act."

"Why Oppose AETA."

. . . Kucinich also challenged the AETA as being redundant and created a "specific classification" to repress legitimate dissent.

The ACLU letter to Congress is available at . . .

For a list of animal advocacy groups opposed to the AETA, see . . .

For Potter's testimony before the House Committee on the Judiciary Subcommittee on Crime, Terrorism, and Homeland Security see . . .

STEVEN BEST is an associate professor of philosophy at the University of Texas, El Paso. His most recent book (coauthored with Anthony J. Nocella) is *Igniting a Revolution: Voices in Defense of the Earth* (AK Press, 2006). According to his website (www.drstevebest.org/), "He has come under fire for his uncompromising advocacy of 'total liberation' (humans, animals, and the earth) and has been banned from the UK for the power of his thoughts."

EXPLORING THE ISSUE

Is "Animal Rights" Just Another Excuse for Terrorism?

Critical Thinking and Reflection

1. What is the difference between the "animal rights" and the "animal welfare" movements?
2. Why must drugs be tested for safety and efficacy?
3. Should extreme forms of protest be restrained for the good of society?
4. Do all animals (including cockroaches, for instance) have rights? If not, where do we draw the line?

Is There Common Ground?

Both the animal welfare and animal rights movements are rooted in awareness of past abuses of animals. Unfortunately, animal abuse is not just in the past. It shows up far too often in the daily news.

1. Check your local paper (or favorite news site) for stories on animal abuse. They may involve puppy mills, farms, dog tracks, dog or cock fighting, and more. Discuss what is being done about these cases, and by whom (animal welfare or animal rights groups).
2. Do some animals seem more deserving of "rights" than others? Does intelligence matter? Or, how closely are they related to us? (There have been proposals to grant great apes legal rights very similar to human rights; in Spain, in 2008, such rights were actually granted; see www .time.com/time/world/article/0,8599,1824206,00.html.)
3. How is animal welfare protected in your state? (See www.animallaw.com/.)

Create Central

www.mhhe.com/createcentral

Additional Resources

P. Michael Conn and James V. Parker, *The Animal Research War* (Palgrave Macmillan, 2008).

John Hadley, "Animal Rights Extremism and the Terrorism Question," *Journal of Social Philosophy* (Fall 2009).

Manfred Liebsch, et al., "Alternatives to Animal Testing: Current Status and Future Perspectives," *Archives of Toxicology* (August 2011).

Tom Regan, *Empty Cages: Facing the Challenge of Animal Rights* (Rowman and Littlefield, 2005).

Internet References . . .

Center for Alternatives to Animal Testing

The Johns Hopkins Center for Alternatives to Animal Testing (CAAT) promotes humane science by supporting the creation, development, validation, and use of alternatives to animals in research, product safety testing, and education.

http://caat.jhsph.edu/

Americans for Medical Progress

Americans for Medical Progress (AMP) nurtures public understanding of and support for the humane, necessary and valuable use of animals in medicine.

www.amprogress.org/animal-research

Selected, Edited, and with Issue Framing Material by:
Thomas A. Easton, *Thomas College*

ISSUE

Should We Reject the "Transhumanist" Goal of the Genetically, Electronically, and Mechanically Enhanced Human Being?

YES: M. J. McNamee and S. D. Edwards, from "Transhumanism, Medical Technology, and Slippery Slopes," *Journal of Medical Ethics* (September 2006)

NO: Maxwell J. Mehlman, from "Biomedical Enhancements: Entering a New Era," *Issues in Science and Technology* (Spring 2009)

Learning Outcomes

After studying this issue, students will be able to:

- Explain what transhumanism is.
- Explain why ethicists worry about "slippery slopes."
- Discuss why some people find the idea of enhancing the human body and mind objectionable.
- Discuss whether government should subsidize technologies that hold the potential to exacerbate differences among people.

ISSUE SUMMARY

YES: M. J. McNamee and S. D. Edwards argue that the difficulty of showing that the human body *should* (rather than *can*) be enhanced in ways espoused by the transhumanists amounts to an objection to transhumanism.

NO: Maxwell J. Mehlman argues that the era of routine biomedical enhancements is coming. Since the technology cannot be banned, it must be regulated and even subsidized to ensure that it does not create an unfair society.

In the early 1970s, scientists first discovered that it was technically possible to move genes—biological material that determines a living organism's physical makeup—from one organism to another and thus (in principle) to give bacteria, plants, and animals new features and to correct genetic defects of the sort that cause many diseases, such as cystic fibrosis. Most researchers in molecular genetics were excited by the potentialities that suddenly seemed within their grasp. However, a few researchers—as well as many people outside the field—were disturbed by the idea. Among other things, they feared that we were on the verge of an era when people would be so modified that they were no longer human. Some critics were also suspicious of the researchers' motives. Andrew Kimbrell, *The Human Body Shop: The Engineering and Marketing of Life* (HarperSanFrancisco, 1993), thought the development of genetic engineering was so marked by scandal, ambition, and moral blindness that society should be deeply suspicious of its purported benefits.

Since then the idea that human beings will one day be enhanced has grown. The idea now encompasses genetic changes to cure or prevent disease and modify height, muscle strength, and cognitive capabilities, the use of chemicals to improve performance in sports, and even the incorporation in the human body of electronic and robotic elements to add senses and enhance memory, thinking abilities, strength, and a great deal more. In fact, the idea has become a movement known as transhumanism that "promotes an interdisciplinary approach to understanding and evaluating the opportunities for enhancing the human condition and the human organism opened up by the advancement of technology" (see the Humanity+ site at http://humanityplus.org/). The goal is to eliminate aging, disease, and suffering. The transhumanist vision extends to "post-humanism," when what human beings become will make present-day humans look like chimpanzees by comparison. It even includes the possibility of uploading human minds into computers! See George Dvorsky, "Better Living Through

Transhumanism," *Journal of Evolution & Technology* (September 2008).

Some people find this vision frightening. Francis Fukuyama, "Transhumanism," *Foreign Policy* (September/October 2004), has called transhumanism "the world's most dangerous idea." Critics find changing human form and capability objectionable because they believe the result is in some sense unnatural. They believe that making some people more capable will exacerbate social distinctions and put those who can afford the changes in the position of old-fashioned aristocracies. Life will be even more unfair than it is today. Tom Koch, "Enhancing Who? Enhancing What? Ethics, Bioethics, and Transhumanism," *Journal of Medicine & Philosophy* (December 2010), finds transhumanism "a new riff on the old eugenics tune," and the result must be destructive.

Michael Bess, "Icarus 2.0: A Historian's Perspective on Human Biological Enhancement," *Technology and Culture* (January 2008), finds transhumanism in essence dehumanizing: "The technologies of enhancement threaten human dignity precisely because they tempt us to think of a person as an entity that can be 'improved.' To take this step is to break down human personhood into a series of quantifiable traits—resistance to disease, intelligence, and so forth—that are subject to augmentation or alteration. The danger in doing this lies in reducing individuals to the status of products, artifacts to be modified and reshaped according to our own preferences, like any other commodity. In this act, inevitably, we risk losing touch with the quality of intrinsic value that all humans share equally, no matter what their traits may be. In this sense, the well-intentioned effort to enhance a person can result in treating them as a mere *thing*."

Josh Fischman, "A Better Life with Bionics," *National Geographic* (January 2010), describes current work in developing prostheses controlled by nerve signals from nerves that have been surgically rerouted to communicate more effectively with the artificial limb's circuitry, a clear example of "improvement" of the human being. He also discusses electronic cochlear implants and artificial retinas. An accompanying editorial comment says that "Bionics is technology at its most ingenious and humane." Among the most recent developments in this line is an electronic implant that can give the paralyzed robotic arms; see Ian Sample, "Brain Implant Allows Paralysed Woman to Control a Robot with Her Thoughts," *The Guardian* (May 16, 2012) (www.guardian.co.uk/science/2012/may/16/brain-implant-paralysed-woman-robot-thoughts).

Among those who favor transhumanism, few come through more strongly than James Hughes, executive director of the Institute for Ethics and Emerging Technologies (http://ieet.org/). He has argued vigorously that enhancement technologies such as genetic engineering offer "such good that the risks are dwarfed" and finds "faith in the potential unlimited improvability of human nature and expansion of human powers far more satisfying than a resignation to our current limits." See his

"Embracing Change with All Four Arms: A Post-Humanist Defense of Genetic Engineering," *Eubios Journal of Asian and International Bioethics* (June 1996). Nicholas Agar, "Whereto Transhumanism? The Literature Reaches Critical Mass," *Hastings Center Report* (May–June 2007), finds that "transhumanism is a movement brimming with fresh ideas. Transhumanists succeed in making the intuitive appeal of posthumanity obvious even if they don't yet have the arguments to compel everybody else to accept their vision." Julian Savalescu and Nick Bostrom (a prominent founder of the transhumanism movement) provide a very positive overview in *Human Enhancement* (Oxford University Press, 2009). Susan Schneider, "Future Minds: Transhumanism, Cognitive Enhancement and the Nature of Persons," in Vardit Ravitsky, Autumn Fiester, and Arthur L. Caplan, eds., *The Penn Center Guide to Bioethics* (Springer, 2009), considers the question of whether people who have undergone extreme modifications are still the people they were before. Is personhood affected? Is the soul? "There are," she writes, "some serious issues which require working out." James Wilson, "Transhumanism and Moral Equality," *Bioethics* (October, 2007), finds that objections to transhumanism on the grounds that enhanced humans will be considered morally superior to unenhanced humans are groundless, for "once we understand the basis for human equality, it is clear that anyone who now has sufficient capacities to count as a person from the moral point of view will continue to count as one even if others are fundamentally enhanced; and it is [a mistake] to think that a creature which had even far greater capacities than an unenhanced human being should count as more than an equal from the moral point of view." David Gelles, "Immortality 2.0," *The Futurist* (January–February 2009), concludes that "skepticism of transhumanism is, arguably, natural. At the deepest level, living forever interferes with everything we understand about the world. . . . But such concerns may not matter any more." The change is already under way, and we may be underestimating how far it will go. See also Jonathan Weiner, *Long for This World: The Strange Science of Immortality* (Ecco, 2010). However, A. Rajczi, "One Danger of Biomedical Enhancements," *Bioethics* (July 2008), cautions that "By spending too much time, energy, and resources on enhancements, we could set back our pursuit of our deepest goals such as living happily and leading ethical lives." Philippe Verdoux, "Transhumanism, Progress and the Future," *Journal of Evolution & Technology* (July 2009), finds pursuing the transhumanist dream the safest route into the future. Philip Hefner, "The Animal that Aspires to be an Angel: The Challenge of Transhumanism," *Dialog: A Journal of Theology* (Summer 2009), finds that transhumanism "represents a fundamental challenge to our understanding of human nature, and in particular [with] what God has created us to become." Joanna Zylinska, "Playing God, Playing Adam: The Politics and Ethics of Enhancement," *Journal of Bioethical Inquiry* (June 2010), takes a different view of humanity's deepest goals and nature, for humanity coevolves with technology.

Maxwell J. Mehlman examines the future implications in *Transhumanist Dreams and Dystopian Nightmares: The Promise and Peril of Genetic Engineering* (Johns Hopkins University Press, 2012).

One way in which the change is already upon us appears in the realm of sports. Steven Kotler, "Juicing 3.0," *Popular Science* (August 2008), notes that the use by athletes of many enhancement techniques—reaction time stimulants, hormones that affect muscle, gene replacement, and even mechanical replacements for missing limbs—are going to become commonplace in the next few years. It may be necessary to accept enhancements as a legitimate part of athletics and other realms of endeavor. See Ivo Van Hilvoorde and Laurens Landeweerd, "Enhancing Disabilities: Transhumanism under the Veil of Inclusion?" *Disability & Rehabilitation* (December 2010), and Brendan Burkett, Mike McNamee, and Wolfgand Potthast, "Shifting Boundaries in Sports Technology and Disability:

Equal Rights or Unfair Advantage in the Case of Oscar Pistorius?" *Disability & Society* (August 2011).

In the YES selection, M. J. McNamee and S. D. Edwards discuss the idea that even to start on the transhumanist agenda is to set humanity on a "slippery slope" leading to disaster. They argue that of the several types of slippery slope, the one most threatening to transhumanism is the "arbitrary" slippery slope, meaning that the progression from the first change to the last is not based on any sense of the moral good, but only on subjective preference. They argue that this poses a challenge to transhumanists, to show that the changes they embrace *should* be embraced rather than just *can* be embraced. In the NO selection, Professor of Bioethics Maxwell J. Mehlman argues that the era of routine biomedical enhancements is coming. Since the technology cannot be banned, it must be regulated and even subsidized to ensure that it does not create an unfair society.

YES

**M. J. McNamee and
S. D. Edwards**

Transhumanism, Medical Technology, and Slippery Slopes

No less a figure than Francis Fukuyama recently labelled transhumanism as "the world's most dangerous idea." Such an eye-catching condemnation almost certainly denotes an issue worthy of serious consideration, especially given the centrality of biomedical technology to its aims. In this article, we consider transhumanism as an ideology that seeks to evangelise its human-enhancing aims. Given that transhumanism covers a broad range of ideas, we distinguish moderate conceptions from strong ones and find the strong conceptions more problematic than the moderate ones. We also offer a critique of Boström's position published in this journal. We discuss various forms of slippery slope arguments that may be used for and against transhumanism and highlight one particular criticism, moral arbitrariness, which undermines both forms of transhumanism.

What Is Transhumanism?

At the beginning of the 21st century, we find ourselves in strange times; facts and fantasy find their way together in ethics, medicine and philosophy journals and websites. Key sites of contestation include the very idea of human nature, the place of embodiment within medical ethics and, more specifically, the systematic reflections on the place of medical and other technologies in conceptions of the good life. A reflection of this situation is captured by Dyens who writes,

> What we are witnessing today is the very convergence of environments, systems, bodies, and ontology toward and into the intelligent matter. We can no longer speak of the human condition or even of the posthuman condition. We must now refer to the intelligent condition.

We wish to evaluate the contents of such dialogue and to discuss, if not the death of human nature, then at least its dislocation and derogation in the thinkers who label themselves transhumanists.

One difficulty for critics of transhumanism is that a wide range of views fall under its label. Not merely are there idiosyncrasies of individual academics, but there does not seem to exist an absolutely agreed on defini-

tion of transhumanism. One can find not only substantial differences between key authors and the disparate disciplinary nuances of their exhortations, but also subtle variations of its chief representatives in the offerings of people. It is to be expected that any ideology transforms over time and not least of all in response to internal and external criticism. Yet, the transhumanism critic faces a further problem of identifying a robust target that stays still sufficiently long to locate it properly in these web-driven days without constructing a "straw man" to knock over with the slightest philosophical breeze. For the purposes of targeting a sufficiently substantial target, we identify the writings of one of its clearest and intellectually robust proponents, the Oxford philosopher and cofounder of the World Transhumanist Association, Nick Boström, who has written recently in these pages of transhumanism's desire to make good the "half-baked" project that is human nature.

Before specifically evaluating Boström's position, it is best first to offer a global definition for transhumanism and then to locate it among the range of views that fall under the heading. One of the most celebrated advocates of transhumanism is Max More, whose website reads "no more gods, nor more faith, no more timid holding back. The future belongs to posthumanity." We will have a clearer idea then of the kinds of position transhumanism stands in direct opposition to. Specifically, More asserts,

> "Transhumanism" is a blanket term given to the school of thought that refuses to accept traditional human limitations such as death, disease and other biological frailties. Transhumans are typically interested in a variety of futurist topics, including space migration, mind uploading and cryonic suspension. Transhumans are also extremely interested in more immediate subjects such as bio- and nano-technology, computers and neurology. Transhumans deplore the standard paradigms that attempt to render our world comfortable at the sake of human fulfilment.

Strong transhumanism advocates see themselves engaged in a project, the purpose of which is to overcome the limits of human nature. Whether this is the foundational claim, or merely the central claim, is not clear. These limitations—one may describe them simply

---

as features of human nature, as the idea of labelling them as limitations is itself to take up a negative stance towards them—concern appearance, human sensory capacities, intelligence, lifespan and vulnerability to harm. According to the extreme transhumanism programme, technology can be used to vastly enhance a person's intelligence; to tailor their appearance to what they desire; to lengthen their lifespan, perhaps to immortality; and to reduce vastly their vulnerability to harm. This can be done by exploitation of various kinds of technology, including genetic engineering, cybernetics, computation and nanotechnology. Whether technology will continue to progress sufficiently, and sufficiently predictably, is of course quite another matter.

Advocates of transhumanism argue that recruitment or deployment of these various types of technology can produce people who are intelligent and immortal, but who are not members of the species *Homo sapiens*. Their species type will be ambiguous—for example, if they are cyborgs (part human, part machine)—or, if they are wholly machines, they will lack any common genetic features with human beings. A legion of labels covers this possibility; we find in Dyen's recently translated book a variety of cultural bodies, perhaps the most extreme being cyberpunks:

> . . . a profound misalignment between existence and its manifestation. This misalignment produces bodies so transformed, so dissociated, and so asynchronized, that their only outcome is gross mutation. Cyberpunk bodies are horrible, strange and mysterious (think of *Alien, Robocop, Terminator*, etc.), for they have no real attachment to any biological structure.

Perhaps a reasonable claim is encapsulated in the idea that such entities will be posthuman. The extent to which posthuman might be synonymous with transhumanism is not clear. Extreme transhumanists strongly support such developments.

At the other end of transhumanism is a much less radical project, which is simply the project to use technology to enhance human characteristics—for example, beauty, lifespan and resistance to disease. In this less extreme project, there is no necessary aspiration to shed human nature or human genetic constitution, just to augment it with technology where possible and where desired by the person.

Who Is for Transhumanism?

At present it seems to be a movement based mostly in North America, although there are some adherents from the UK. Among its most intellectually sophisticated proponents is Nick Boström. Perhaps the most outspoken supporters of transhumanism are people who see it simply as an issue of free choice. It may simply be the case

that moderate transhumanists are libertarians at the core. In that case, transhumanism merely supplies an overt technological dimension to libertarianism. If certain technological developments are possible, which they as competent choosers desire, then they should not be prevented from acquiring the technologically driven enhancements they desire. One obvious line of criticism here may be in relation to the inequality that necessarily arises with respect to scarce goods and services distributed by market mechanisms. We will elaborate this point in the Transhumanism and slippery slopes section.

So, one group of people for the transhumanism project sees it simply as a way of improving their own life by their own standards of what counts as an improvement. For example, they may choose to purchase an intervention, which will make them more intelligent or even extend their life by 200 years. (Of course it is not self-evident that everyone would regard this as an improvement.) A less vociferous group sees the transhumanism project as not so much bound to the expansion of autonomy (notwithstanding our criticism that will necessarily be effected only in the sphere of economic consumer choice) as one that has the potential to improve the quality of life for humans in general. For this group, the relationship between transhumanism and the general good is what makes transhumanism worthy of support. For the other group, the worth of transhumanism is in its connection with their own conception of what is good for them, with the extension of their personal life choices.

What Can Be Said in Its Favour?

Of the many points for transhumanism, we note three. Firstly, transhumanism seems to facilitate two aims that have commanded much support. The use of technology to improve humans is something we pretty much take for granted. Much good has been achieved with low-level technology in the promotion of public health. The construction of sewage systems, clean water supplies, etc, is all work to facilitate this aim and is surely good work, work which aims at, and in this case achieves, a good. Moreover, a large portion of the modern biomedical enterprise is another example of a project that aims at generating this good too.

Secondly, proponents of transhumanism say it presents an opportunity to plan the future development of human beings, the species *Homo sapiens*. Instead of this being left to the evolutionary process and its exploitation of random mutations, transhumanism presents a hitherto unavailable option: tailoring the development of human beings to an ideal blueprint. Precisely whose ideal gets blueprinted is a point that we deal with later.

Thirdly, in the spirit of work in ethics that makes use of a technical idea of personhood, the view that moral status is independent of membership of a particular species (or indeed any biological species), transhumanism presents a way in which moral status can be shown to be bound to intellectual capacity rather than to human embodiment as such or human vulnerability in the capacity of embodiment.

What Can Be Said Against It?

Critics point to consequences of transhumanism, which they find unpalatable. One possible consequence feared by some commentators is that, in effect, transhumanism will lead to the existence of two distinct types of being, the human and the posthuman. The human may be incapable of breeding with the posthuman and will be seen as having a much lower moral standing. Given that, as Buchanan *et al.* note, much moral progress, in the West at least, is founded on the category of the human in terms of rights claims, if we no longer have a common humanity, what rights, if any, ought to be enjoyed by transhumans? This can be viewed either as a criticism (we poor humans are no longer at the top of the evolutionary tree) or simply as a critical concern that invites further argumentation. We shall return to this idea in the final section, by way of identifying a deeper problem with the open-endedness of transhumanism that builds on this recognition.

In the same vein, critics may argue that transhumanism will increase inequalities between the rich and the poor. The rich can afford to make use of transhumanism, but the poor will not be able to. Indeed, we may come to think of such people as deficient, failing to achieve a new heightened level of normal functioning. In the opposing direction, critical observers may say that transhumanism is, in reality, an irrelevance, as very few will be able to use the technological developments even if they ever manifest themselves. A further possibility is that transhumanism could lead to the extinction of humans and posthumans, for things are just as likely to turn out for the worse as for the better (e.g., those for precautionary principle).

One of the deeper philosophical objections comes from a very traditional source. Like all such utopian visions, transhumanism rests on some conception of good. So just as humanism is founded on the idea that humans are the measure of all things and that their fulfilment is to be found in the powers of reason extolled and extended in culture and education, so too transhumanism has a vision of the good, albeit one loosely shared. For one group of transhumanists, the good is the expansion of personal choice. Given that autonomy is so widely valued, why not remove the barriers to enhanced autonomy by various technological interventions? Theological critics especially, but not exclusively, object to what they see as the imperialising of autonomy. Elshtain lists the three c's: choice, consent and control. These, she asserts, are the dominant motifs of modern American culture. And there is, of course, an army of communitarians ready to provide support in general moral and political matters to this line of criticism. One extension of this line of transhumanism thinking is to align the valorisation of autonomy with economic rationality, for we may as well be motivated by

economic concerns as by moral ones where the market is concerned. As noted earlier, only a small minority may be able to access this technology (despite Boström's naive disclaimer for democratic transhumanism), so the technology necessary for transhumanist transformations is unlikely to be prioritised in the context of artificially scarce public health resources. One other population attracted to transhumanism will be the elite sports world, fuelled by the media commercialisation complex—where mere mortals will get no more than a glimpse of the transhuman in competitive physical contexts. There may be something of a double-binding character to this consumerism. The poor, at once removed from the possibility of such augmentation, pay (per view) for the pleasure of their envy.

If we argue against the idea that the good cannot be equated with what people choose simpliciter, it does not follow that we need to reject the requisite medical technology outright. Against the more moderate transhumanists, who see transhumanism as an opportunity to enhance the general quality of life for humans, it is nevertheless true that their position presupposes some conception of the good. What kind of traits is best engineered into humans: disease resistance or parabolic hearing? And unsurprisingly, transhumanists disagree about precisely what "objective goods" to select for installation into humans or posthumans.

Some radical critics of transhumanism see it as a threat to morality itself. This is because they see morality as necessarily connected to the kind of vulnerability that accompanies human nature. Think of the idea of human rights and the power this has had in voicing concern about the plight of especially vulnerable human beings. As noted earlier a transhumanist may be thought to be beyond humanity and as neither enjoying its rights nor its obligations. Why would a transhuman be moved by appeals to human solidarity? Once the prospect of posthumanism emerges, the whole of morality is thus threatened because the existence of human nature itself is under threat.

One further objection voiced by Habermas is that interfering with the process of human conception, and by implication human constitution, deprives humans of the "naturalness which so far has been a part of the taken-for-granted background of our self-understanding as a species" and "Getting used to having human life biotechnologically at the disposal of our contingent preferences cannot help but change our normative self-understanding."

On this account, our self-understanding would include, for example, our essential vulnerability to disease, ageing and death. Suppose the strong transhumanism project is realised. We are no longer thus vulnerable: immortality is a real prospect. Nevertheless, conceptual caution must be exercised here—even transhumanists will be susceptible in the manner that Hobbes noted. Even the strongest are vulnerable in their sleep. But the kind of vulnerability transhumanism seeks to overcome is of the internal kind (not Hobbes's external threats). We are reminded of Woody Allen's famous remark that he wanted to become immortal, not by doing great deeds but simply by not dying. This will result in a radical change in our self-understanding, which has inescapably normative elements to it that need to be challenged. Most radically, this change in self-understanding may take the form of a change in what we view as a good life. Hitherto a human life, this would have been assumed to be finite. Transhumanists suggest that even now this may change with appropriate technology and the "right" motivation.

Do the changes in self-understanding presented by transhumanists (and genetic manipulation) necessarily have to represent a change for the worse? As discussed earlier, it may be that the technology that generates the possibility of transhumanism can be used for the good of humans—for example, to promote immunity to disease or to increase quality of life. Is there really an intrinsic connection between acquisition of the capacity to bring about transhumanism and moral decline? Perhaps Habermas's point is that moral decline is simply more likely to occur once radical enhancement technologies are adopted as a practice that is not intrinsically evil or morally objectionable. But how can this be known in advance? This raises the spectre of slippery slope arguments.

But before we discuss such slopes, let us note that the kind of approach (whether characterised as closed-minded or sceptical) Boström seems to dislike is one he calls speculative. He dismisses as speculative the idea that offspring may think themselves lesser beings, commodifications of their parents' egoistic desires (or some such). None the less, having pointed out the lack of epistemological standing of such speculation, he invites us to his own apparently more congenial position:

> We might speculate, instead, that germ-line enhancements will lead to more love and parental dedication. Some mothers and fathers might find it easier to love a child who, thanks to enhancements, is bright, beautiful, healthy, and happy. The practice of germ-line enhancement might lead to better treatment of people with disabilities, because a general demystification of the genetic contributions to human traits could make it clearer that people with disabilities are not to blame for their disabilities and a decreased incidence of some disabilities could lead to more assistance being available for the remaining affected people to enable them to live full, unrestricted lives through various technological and social supports. Speculating about possible psychological or cultural effects of germ-line engineering can therefore cut both ways. Good consequences no less than bad ones are possible. In the absence of sound arguments for the view that the negative consequences would predominate, such speculations provide no reason against moving forward with the technology. Ruminations over hypothetical side effects may serve to make us aware of things that could go wrong so

that we can be on the lookout for untoward developments. By being aware of the perils in advance, we will be in a better position to take preventive countermeasures.

Following Boström's speculation then, what grounds for hope exist? Beyond speculation, what kinds of arguments does Boström offer? Well, most people may think that the burden of proof should fall to the transhumanists. Not so, according to Boström. Assuming the likely enormous benefits, he turns the tables on this intuition—not by argument but by skilful rhetorical speculation. We quote for accuracy of representation (emphasis added):

> Only after a fair comparison of the risks with the likely positive consequences can any conclusion based on a cost-benefit analysis be reached. In the case of germ-line enhancements, the potential gains are enormous. Only rarely, however, are the potential gains discussed, perhaps because they are too obvious to be of much theoretical interest. By contrast, uncovering subtle and non-trivial ways in which manipulating our genome could undermine deep values is philosophically a lot more challenging. But if we think about it, we recognize that the promise of genetic enhancements is anything but insignificant. Being free from severe genetic diseases would be good, as would having a mind that can learn more quickly, or having a more robust immune system. Healthier, wittier, happier people may be able to reach new levels culturally. To achieve a significant enhancement of human capacities would be to embark on the transhuman journey of exploration of some of the modes of being that are not accessible to us as we are currently constituted, possibly to discover and to instantiate important new values. On an even more basic level, genetic engineering holds great potential for alleviating unnecessary human suffering. Every day that the introduction of effective human genetic enhancement is delayed is a day of lost individual and cultural potential, and a day of torment for many unfortunate sufferers of diseases that could have been prevented. Seen in this light, *proponents of a ban or a moratorium on human genetic modification must take on a heavy burden of proof* in order to have the balance of reason tilt in their favor.

Now one way in which such a balance of reason may be had is in the idea of a slippery slope argument. We now turn to that.

Transhumanism and Slippery Slopes

A proper assessment of transhumanism requires consideration of the objection that acceptance of the main claims of transhumanism will place us on a slippery slope. Yet, paradoxically, both proponents and detractors of transhumanism may exploit slippery slope arguments in support of their position. It is necessary therefore to set out the various arguments that fall under this title so that we can better characterise arguments for and against transhumanism. We shall therefore examine three such attempts but argue that the arbitrary slippery slope may undermine all versions of transhumanists, although not every enhancement proposed by them.

Schauer offers the following essentialist analysis of slippery slope arguments. A "pure" slippery slope is one where a "particular act, seemingly innocuous when taken in isolation, may yet lead to a future host of similar but increasingly pernicious events." Abortion and euthanasia are classic candidates for slippery slope arguments in public discussion and policy making. Against this, however, there is no reason to suppose that the future events (acts or policies) down the slope need to display similarities—indeed we may propose that they will lead to a whole range of different, although equally unwished for, consequences. The vast array of enhancements proposed by transhumanists would not be captured under this conception of a slippery slope because of their heterogeneity. Moreover, as Sternglantz notes, Schauer undermines his case when arguing that greater linguistic precision undermines the slippery slope and that indirect consequences often bolster slippery slope arguments. It is as if the slippery slopes would cease in a world with greater linguistic precision or when applied only to direct consequences. These views do not find support in the later literature. Schauer does, however, identify three non-slippery slope arguments where the advocate's aim is (a) to show that the bottom of a proposed slope has been arrived at; (b) to show that a principle is excessively broad; (c) to highlight how granting authority to X will make it more likely that an undesirable outcome will be achieved. Clearly (a) cannot properly be called a slippery slope argument in itself, while (b) and (c) often have some role in slippery slope arguments.

The excessive breadth principle can be subsumed under Bernard Williams's distinction between slippery slope arguments with (a) horrible results and (b) arbitrary results. According to Williams, the nature of the bottom of the slope allows us to determine which category a particular argument falls under. Clearly, the most common form is the slippery slope to a horrible result argument. Walton goes further in distinguishing three types: (a) thin end of the wedge or precedent arguments; (b) Sorites arguments; and (c) domino-effect arguments. Importantly, these arguments may be used both by antagonists and also by advocates of transhumanism. We shall consider the advocates of transhumanism first.

In the thin end of the wedge slippery slopes, allowing P will set a precedent that will allow further precedents (Pn) taken to an unspecified problematic terminus. Is it necessary that the end point has to be bad? Of course this is the typical linguistic meaning of the phrase "slippery slopes." Nevertheless, we may turn the tables here and argue that [the] slopes may be viewed positively too.

Perhaps a new phrase will be required to capture ineluctable slides (ascents?) to such end points. This would be somewhat analogous to the ideas of vicious and virtuous cycles. So transhumanists could argue that, once the artificial generation of life through technologies of in vitro fertilisation was thought permissible, the slope was foreseeable, and transhumanists are doing no more than extending that life-creating and fashioning impulse.

In Sorites arguments, the inability to draw clear distinctions has the effect that allowing P will not allow us to consistently deny Pn. This slope follows the form of the Sorites paradox, where taking a grain of sand from a heap does not prevent our recognising or describing the heap as such, even though it is not identical with its former state. At the heart of the problem with such arguments is the idea of conceptual vagueness. Yet the logical distinctions used by philosophers are often inapplicable in the real world. Transhumanists may well seize on this vagueness and apply a Sorites argument as follows: as therapeutic interventions are currently morally permissible, and there is no clear distinction between treatment and enhancement, enhancement interventions are morally permissible too. They may ask whether we can really distinguish categorically between the added functionality of certain prosthetic devices and sonar senses.

In domino-effect arguments, the domino conception of the slippery slope, we have what others often refer to as a causal slippery slope. Once P is allowed, a causal chain will be effected allowing Pn and so on to follow, which will precipitate increasingly bad consequences.

In what ways can slippery slope arguments be used against transhumanism? What is wrong with transhumanism? Or, better, is there a point at which we can say transhumanism is objectionable? One particular strategy adopted by proponents of transhumanism falls clearly under the aspect of the thin end of the wedge conception of the slippery slope. Although some aspects of their ideology seem aimed at unqualified goods, there seems to be no limit to the aspirations of transhumanism as they cite the powers of other animals and substances as potential modifications for the transhumanist. Although we can admire the sonic capacities of the bat, the elastic strength of lizards' tongues and the endurability of Kevlar in contrast with traditional construction materials used in the body, their transplantation into humans is, to coin Kass's celebrated label, "repugnant."

Although not all transhumanists would support such extreme enhancements (if that is indeed what they are), less radical advocates use justifications that are based on therapeutic lines up front with the more Promethean aims less explicitly advertised. We can find many examples of this manoeuvre. Take, for example, the Cognitive Enhancement Research Institute in California. Prominently displayed on its website front page . . . we read, "Do you know somebody with Alzheimer's disease? Click to see the latest research breakthrough." The mode is simple: treatment by front entrance, enhancement by the back door. Borgmann, in his discussion of the uses of technology in modern society, observed precisely this argumentative strategy more than 20 years ago:

> The main goal of these programs seems to be the domination of nature. But we must be more precise. The desire to dominate does not just spring from a lust of power, from sheer human imperialism. It is from the start connected with the aim of liberating humanity from disease, hunger, and toil and enriching life with learning, art and athletics.

Who would want to deny the powers of viral diseases that can be genetically treated? Would we want to draw the line at the transplantation of non-human capacities (sonar path finding)? Or at in vivo fibre optic communications backbone or anti-degeneration powers? (These would have to be non-human by hypothesis). Or should we consider the scope of technological enhancements that one chief transhumanist, Natasha Vita More, propounds:

> A transhuman is an evolutionary stage from being exclusively biological to becoming post-biological. Post-biological means a continuous shedding of our biology and merging with machines. (. . .) The body, as we transform ourselves over time, will take on different types of appearances and designs and materials. (. . .)
>
> For hiking a mountain, I'd like extended leg strength, stamina, a skin-sheath to protect me from damaging environmental aspects, self-moisturizing, cool-down capability, extended hearing and augmented vision (Network of sonar sensors depicts data through solid mass and map images onto visual field. Overlay window shifts spectrum frequencies. Visual scratch pad relays mental ideas to visual recognition bots. Global Satellite interface at micro-zoom range).
>
> For a party, I'd like an eclectic look—a glistening bronze skin with emerald green highlights, enhanced height to tower above other people, a sophisticated internal sound system so that I could alter the music to suit my own taste, memory enhance device, emotional-select for feel-good people so I wouldn't get dragged into anyone's inappropriate conversations. And parabolic hearing so that I could listen in on conversations across the room if the one I was currently in started winding down.

Notwithstanding the difficulty of bringing together transhumanism under one movement, the sheer variety of proposals merely contained within Vita More's catalogue means that we cannot determinately point to a precise station at which we can say, "Here, this is the end we said things would naturally progress to." But does this pose a problem? Well, it certainly makes it difficult to specify exactly a "horrible result" that is supposed to be at the bottom of the slope. Equally, it is extremely difficult to say that if we allow precedent X, it will allow practices

Y or Z to follow as it is not clear how these practices Y or Z are (if at all) connected with the precedent X. So it is not clear that a form of precedent-setting slippery slope can be strictly used in every case against transhumanism, although it may be applicable in some.

Nevertheless, we contend, in contrast with Boström that the burden of proof would fall to the transhumanist. Consider in this light, a Sorites-type slope. The transhumanist would have to show how the relationship between the therapeutic practices and the enhancements are indeed transitive. We know night from day without being able to specify exactly when this occurs. So simply because we cannot determine a precise distinction between, say, genetic treatments G1, G2 and G3, and transhumanism enhancements T1, T2 and so on, it does not follow that there are no important moral distinctions between G1 and T20. According to Williams, this kind of indeterminacy arises because of the conceptual vagueness of certain terms. Yet, the indeterminacy of so open a predicate "heap" is not equally true of "therapy" or "enhancement." The latitude they permit is nowhere near so wide.

Instead of objecting to Pn on the grounds that Pn is morally objectionable (i.e., to depict a horrible result), we may instead, after Williams, object that the slide from P to Pn is simply morally arbitrary, when it ought not to be. Here, we may say, without specifying a horrible result, that it would be difficult to know what, in principle, can ever be objected to. And this is, quite literally, what is troublesome. It seems to us that this criticism applies to all categories of transhumanism, although not necessarily to all enhancements proposed by them. Clearly, the somewhat loose identity of the movement—and the variations between strong and moderate versions—makes it difficult to sustain this argument unequivocally. Still the transhumanist may be justified in asking, "What is wrong with arbitrariness?" Let us consider one brief example. In aspects of our lives, as a widely shared intuition, we may think that in the absence of good reasons, we ought not to discriminate among people arbitrarily. Healthcare may be considered to be precisely one such case. Given the ever-increasing demand for public healthcare services and products, it may be argued that access to them typically ought to be governed by publicly disputable criteria such as clinical need or potential benefit, as opposed to individual choices of an arbitrary or subjective nature. And nothing in transhumanism seems to allow for such objective dispute, let alone prioritisation. Of course, transhumanists such as More find no such disquietude. His phrase "No more timidity" is a typical token of transhumanist slogans. We applaud advances in therapeutic medical technologies such as those from new genetically based organ regeneration to more familiar prosthetic devices. Here the ends of the interventions are clearly medically defined and the means regulated closely. This is what prevents transhumanists from adopting a Sorites-type slippery slope. But in the absence of a telos, of clearly and substantively specified ends (beyond the mere banner of enhancement), we suggest that the public, medical professionals and bioethicists alike ought to resist the potentially open-ended transformations of human nature. For if all transformations are in principle enhancements, then surely none are. The very application of the word may become redundant. Thus it seems that one strong argument against transhumanism generally—the arbitrary slippery slope—presents a challenge to transhumanism, to show that all of what are described as transhumanist enhancements are imbued with positive normative force and are not merely technological extensions of libertarianism, whose conception of the good is merely an extension of individual choice and consumption.

Limits of Transhumanist Arguments for Medical Technology and Practice

Already, we have seen the misuse of a host of therapeutically designed drugs used by non-therapeutic populations for enhancements. Consider the non-therapeutic use of human growth hormone in non-clinical populations. Such is the present perception of height as a positional good in society that Cuttler *et al.* report that the proportion of doctors who recommended human growth hormone treatment of short non-growth hormone deficient children ranged from 1% to 74%. This is despite its contrary indication in professional literature, such as that of the Pediatric Endocrine Society, and considerable doubt about its efficacy. Moreover, evidence supports the view that recreational body builders will use the technology, given the evidence of their use or misuse of steroids and other biotechnological products. Finally, in the sphere of elite sport, which so valorises embodied capacities that may be found elsewhere in greater degree, precision and sophistication in

the animal kingdom or in the computer laboratory, biomedical enhancers may latch onto the genetically determined capacities and adopt or adapt them for their own commercially driven ends.

The arguments and examples presented here do no more than to warn us of the enhancement ideologies, such as transhumanism, which seek to predicate their futuristic agendas on the bedrock of medical technological progress aimed at therapeutic ends and are secondarily extended to loosely defined enhancement ends. In discussion and in bioethical literatures, the future of genetic engineering is often challenged by slippery slope arguments that lead policy and practice to a horrible result. Instead of pointing to the undesirability of the ends to which transhumanism leads, we have pointed out the failure to specify their telos beyond the slogans of "overcoming timidity" or Boström's exhortation that the passive acceptance of ageing is an example of "reckless and dangerous barriers to urgently needed action in the biomedical sphere."

We propose that greater care be taken to distinguish the slippery slope arguments that are used in the emotionally loaded exhortations of transhumanism to come to a more judicious perspective on the technologically driven agenda for biomedical enhancement. Perhaps we would do better to consider those other all-too-human frailties such as violent aggression, wanton self-harming and so on, before we turn too readily to the richer imaginations of biomedical technologists.

M. J. McNamee is a reader in philosophy at the Centre for Philosophy, Humanities and Law in Healthcare, School of Health Science, University of Wales, Swansea, UK.

S. D. Edwards is a researcher at the Centre for Philosophy, Humanities and Law in Healthcare, School of Health Science, University of Wales, Swansea, UK.

Maxwell J. Mehlman

 **NO**

Biomedical Enhancements: Entering a New Era

Recently, the Food and Drug Administration (FDA) approved a drug to lengthen and darken eyelashes. Botox and other wrinkle-reducing injections have joined facelifts, tummy tucks, and vaginal reconstruction to combat the effects of aging. To gain a competitive edge, athletes use everything from steroids and blood transfusions to recombinant-DNA–manufactured hormones, Lasik surgery, and artificial atmospheres. Students supplement caffeine-containing energy drinks with Ritalin and the new alertness drug modafinil. The military spends millions of dollars every year on biological research to increase the warfighting abilities of our soldiers. Parents perform genetic tests on their children to determine whether they have a genetic predisposition to excel at explosive or endurance sports. All of these are examples of biomedical enhancements: interventions that use medical and biological technology to improve performance, appearance, or capability in addition to what is necessary to achieve, sustain, or restore health.

The use of biomedical enhancements, of course, is not new. Amphetamines were doled out to troops during World War II. Athletes at the turn of the 20th century ingested narcotics. The cognitive benefits of caffeine have been known for at least a millennium. Ancient Greek athletes swallowed herbal infusions before competitions. The Egyptians brewed a drink containing a relative of Viagra at least 1,000 years before Christ. But modern drug development and improvements in surgical technique are yielding biomedical enhancements that achieve safer, larger, and more targeted enhancement effects than their predecessors, and more extraordinary technologies are expected to emerge from ongoing discoveries in human genetics. (In addition, there are biomechanical enhancements that involve the use of computer implants and nanotechnology, which are beyond the scope of this article.)

What is also new is that biomedical enhancements have become controversial. Some commentators want to outlaw them altogether. Others are concerned about their use by athletes and children. Still others fret that only the well-off will be able to afford them, thereby exacerbating social inequality.

Banning enhancements, however, is misguided. Still, it is important to try to ensure that they are as safe and effective as possible, that vulnerable populations such as children are not forced into using them, and that they are not available only to the well-off. This will require effective government and private action.

A Misguided View

Despite the long history of enhancement use, there recently has emerged a view that it is wrong. The first manifestation of this hostility resulted from the use of performance enhancements in sports in the 1950s, especially steroids and amphetamines. European nations began adopting anti-doping laws in the mid-1960s, and the Olympic Games began testing athletes in 1968. In 1980, Congress amended the Federal Food, Drug, and Cosmetic Act (FFDCA) to make it a felony to distribute anabolic steroids for nonmedical purposes. Two years later, Congress made steroids a Schedule III controlled substance and substituted human growth hormone in the steroid provision of the FFDCA. Between 2003 and 2005, Congress held hearings lambasting professional sports for not imposing adequate testing regimens. Drug testing has also been instituted in high-school and collegiate sports.

The antipathy toward biomedical enhancements extends well beyond sports, however. Officially, at least, the National Institutes of Health (NIH) will not fund research to develop genetic technologies for human enhancement purposes, although it has funded studies in animals that the researchers tout as a step toward developing human enhancements. It is a federal crime to use steroids to increase strength even if the user is not an athlete. Human growth hormone is in a unique regulatory category in that it is a felony to prescribe it for any purpose other than a specific use approved by the FDA. (For example, the FDA has not approved it for anti-aging purposes.) There is an ongoing controversy about whether musicians, especially string players, should be allowed to use beta blockers to steady their hands. And who hasn't heard of objections to the use of mood-altering drugs to make "normal" people happier? There's even a campaign against caffeine.

If the critics had their way, the government would ban the use of biomedical enhancements. It might seem that this would merely entail extending the War on Drugs to a larger number of drugs. But remember that enhancements include not just drugs, but cosmetic surgery and information technologies, such as genetic testing to identify nondisease traits. So a War on Enhancements would have to extend to a broader range of technologies, and because many are delivered within the patient-physician relationship, the government would have to intrude into that relationship in significant new ways. Moreover, the FDA is likely to have approved many enhancement drugs for legitimate medical purposes, with enhancement use taking place on an "off-label" basis. So there would have to be some way for the enhancement police to identify people for whom the drugs had been legally prescribed to treat illness, but who were misusing them for enhancement purposes.

This leads to a far more profound difficulty. The War on Drugs targets only manufacture, distribution, and possession. There is virtually no effort to punish people merely for using an illegal substance. But a successful ban on biomedical enhancement would have to prevent people from obtaining benefits from enhancements that persisted after they no longer possessed the enhancements themselves, such as the muscles built with the aid of steroids or the cognitive improvement that lasts for several weeks after normal people stop taking a certain medicine that treats memory loss in Alzheimer's patients. In short, a ban on enhancements would have to aim at use as well as possession and sale.

To imagine what this would be like, think about the campaign against doping in elite sports, where athletes must notify anti-doping officials of their whereabouts at all times and are subject to unannounced, intrusive, and often indecent drug tests at any hour of the day or night. Even in the improbable event that regular citizens were willing to endure such an unprecedented loss of privacy, the economic cost of maintaining such a regime, given how widespread the use of highly effective biomedical enhancements might be, would be prohibitive.

A ban on biomedical enhancements would be not only unworkable but unjustifiable. Consider the objections to enhancement in sports. Why are enhancements against the rules? Is it because they are unsafe? Not all of them are: Anti-doping rules in sports go after many substances that pose no significant health risks, such as caffeine and Sudafed. (A Romanian gymnast forfeited her Olympic gold medal after she accidentally took a couple of Sudafed to treat a cold.) Even in the case of vilified products such as steroids, safety concerns stem largely from the fact that athletes are forced to use the drugs covertly, without medical supervision. Do enhancements give athletes an "unfair" advantage? They do so only if the enhancements are hard to obtain, so that only a few competitors obtain the edge. But the opposite seems to be true: Enhancements are everywhere. Besides, athletes are also tested for substances that have no known performance-enhancing effects, such as marijuana. Are the rewards from enhancements "unearned"? Not necessarily. Athletes still need to train hard. Indeed, the benefit from steroids comes chiefly from allowing athletes to train harder without injuring themselves. In any event, success in sports comes from

factors that athletes have done nothing to deserve, such as natural talent and the good luck to have been born to encouraging parents or to avoid getting hurt. Would the use of enhancements confound recordkeeping? This doesn't seem to have stopped the adoption of new equipment that improves performance, such as carbon-fiber vaulting poles, metal skis, and oversized tennis racquets. If one athlete used enhancements, would every athlete have to, so that the benefit would be nullified? No, there would still be the benefit of improved performance across the board—bigger lifts, faster times, higher jumps. In any case, the same thing happens whenever an advance takes place that improves performance.

The final objection to athletic enhancement, in the words of the international Olympic movement, is that it is against the "spirit of sport." It is hard to know what this means. It certainly can't mean that enhancements destroy an earlier idyll in which sports were enhancement-free; as we saw before, this never was the case. Nor can it stand for the proposition that a physical competition played with the aid of enhancements necessarily is not a "sport." There are many sporting events in which the organizers do not bother to test participants, from certain types of "strong-man" and powerlifting meets to your neighborhood pickup basketball game. There are several interesting historical explanations for why athletic enhancement has gained such a bad rap, but ultimately, the objection about "the spirit of sport" boils down to the fact that some people simply don't like the idea of athletes using enhancements. Well, not exactly. You see, many biomedical enhancements are perfectly permissible, including dietary supplements, sports psychology, carbohydrate loading, electrolyte-containing beverages, and sleeping at altitude (or in artificial environments that simulate it). Despite the labor of innumerable philosophers of sport, no one has ever come up with a rational explanation for why these things are legal and others aren't. In the end, they are just arbitrary distinctions.

But that's perfectly okay. Lots of rules in sports are arbitrary, like how many players are on a team or how far the boundary lines stretch. If you don't like being all alone in the outfield, don't play baseball. If you are bothered by midnight drug tests, don't become an Olympian.

The problem comes when the opponents of enhancement use in sports try to impose their arbitrary dislikes on the wider world. We already have observed how intrusive and expensive this would be. Beyond that, there are strong constitutional objections to using the power of the law to enforce arbitrary rules. But most important, a ban on the use of enhancements outside of sports would sacrifice an enormous amount of societal benefit. Wouldn't we want automobile drivers to use alertness drugs if doing so could prevent accidents? Shouldn't surgeons be allowed to use beta blockers to steady their hands? Why not let medical researchers take cognitive enhancers if it would lead to faster cures, or let workers take them to be more productive? Why stop soldiers from achieving greater combat effectiveness, rescue workers from lifting heavier objects, and men and women from leading better sex lives? Competent adults who want to use enhancements should be permitted to. In some instances, such as in combat or when performing dangerous jobs, they should even be required to.

Protecting the Vulnerable

Rejecting the idea of banning enhancements doesn't mean that their use should be unregulated. The government has several crucial roles to play in helping to ensure that the benefits from enhancement use outweigh the costs.

In the first place, the government needs to protect people who are incapable of making rational decisions about whether to use enhancements. In the language of biomedical ethics, these are populations that are "vulnerable," and a number of them are well recognized. One such group, of course, is people with severe mental disabilities. The law requires surrogates to make decisions for these individuals based on what is in their best interests.

Another vulnerable population is children. There can be little disagreement that kids should not be allowed to decide on their own to consume powerful, potentially dangerous enhancement substances. Not only do they lack decisionmaking capacity, but they may be much more susceptible than adults to harm. This is clearly the case with steroids, which can interfere with bone growth in children and adolescents.

The more difficult question is whether parents should be free to give enhancements to their children. Parents face powerful social pressures to help their children excel. Some parents may be willing to improve their children's academic or athletic performance even at a substantial risk of injury to the child. There are many stories of parents who allow their adolescent daughters to have cosmetic surgery, including breast augmentation. In general, the law gives parents considerable discretion in determining how to raise their children. The basic legal constraint on parental discretion is the prohibition in state law against abuse or neglect, and this generally is interpreted to defer to parental decisionmaking so long as the child does not suffer serious net harm. There are no reported instances in which parents have been sanctioned for giving their children biomedical enhancements, and the authorities might conclude that the benefits conferred by the use of an enhancement outweighed even a fairly significant risk of injury.

Beyond the actions of parents, there remains the question of whether some biomedical enhancements are so benign that children should be allowed to purchase them themselves. At present, for instance, there is no law in the United States against children purchasing coffee, caffeinated soft drinks, and even high-caffeine–containing energy drinks. (Laws prohibiting children from buying energy drinks have been enacted in some other countries.)

At the same time, it may be a mistake to lump youngsters together with older adolescents into one category of children. Older adolescents, although still under the legal age of majority, have greater cognitive and judgmental capacities than younger children. The law recognizes this by allowing certain adolescents, deemed "mature" or "emancipated" minors, to make legally binding decisions, such as decisions to receive medical treatment. Older adolescents similarly may deserve some degree of latitude in making decisions about using biomedical enhancements.

Children may be vulnerable to pressure to use enhancements not only from their parents, but from their educators. Under programs such as No Child Left Behind, public school teachers and administrators are rewarded and punished based on student performance on standardized tests. Private schools compete with one another in terms of where their graduates are accepted for further education. There is also intense competition in school athletics, especially at the collegiate level. Students in these environments may be bull-dozed into using enhancements to increase their academic and athletic abilities. Numerous anecdotes, for example, tell of parents who are informed by teachers that their children need medication to "help them focus"; the medication class in question typically is the cognition-enhancing amphetamines, and many of these children do not have diagnoses that would warrant the use of these drugs.

Beyond students, athletes in general are vulnerable to pressure from coaches, sponsors, family, and teammates to use hazardous enhancements. For example, at the 2005 congressional hearings on steroid use in baseball, a father testified that his son committed suicide after using steroids, when in fact he killed himself after his family caught him using steroids, which the boy had turned to in an effort to meet his family's athletic aspirations.

Another group that could be vulnerable to coercion is workers. Employers might condition employment or promotion on the use of enhancements that increased productivity. For example, an employer might require its nighttime work force to take the alertness drug modafinil, which is now approved for use by sleep-deprived swing-shift workers. Current labor law does not clearly forbid this so long as the drug is relatively safe. From an era in which employees are tested to make sure they aren't taking drugs, we might see a new approach in which employers test them to make sure they are.

Members of the military may also be forced to use enhancements. The military now conducts the largest known biomedical enhancement research project. Under battlefield conditions, superiors may order the use of enhancements, leaving soldiers no lawful option to refuse. A notorious example is the use of amphetamines by combat pilots. Technically, the pilots are required to give their consent to the use of the pep pills, but if they refuse, they are barred from flying the missions.

The ability of government regulation to protect vulnerable groups varies depending on the group. It is important that educators not be allowed to give students dangerous enhancements without parental permission and that parents not be pressured into making unreasonable decisions by fearful, overzealous, or inadequate educators. The law can mandate the former, but not easily prevent the latter. Coaches and trainers who cause injury to athletes by giving them dangerous enhancements or by unduly encouraging their use should be subject to criminal and civil liability. The same goes for employers. But the realities of military life make it extremely difficult to protect soldiers from the orders of their superiors.

Moreover, individuals may feel pressure to use enhancements not only from outside sources, but from within. Students may be driven to do well in order to satisfy parents, gain admittance to more prestigious schools, or establish better careers. Athletes take all sorts of risks to increase their chances of winning. Workers may be desperate to save their jobs or bring in a bigger paycheck, especially in economically uncertain times. Soldiers better able to complete their missions are likely to live longer.

Surprisingly, while acknowledging the need to protect people from outside pressures, bioethicists generally maintain that we do not need to protect them from harmful decisions motivated by internal pressures. This position stems, it seems, from the recognition that, with the exception of decisions that are purely random, everything we decide to do is dictated at least in part by internal pressures, and in many cases, these pressures can be so strong that the decisions may no longer appear to be voluntary. Take, for example, seriously ill cancer patients contemplating whether or not to undergo harsh chemotherapy regimens. Bioethicists worry that, if we focused on the pressures and lack of options created by the patients' dire condition, we might not let the patients receive the treatment, or, in the guise of protecting the patients from harm, might create procedural hurdles that would rob them of their decisionmaking autonomy. Similarly, these bioethicists might object to restricting the ability of workers, say, to use biomedical enhancements merely because their choices are highly constrained by their fear of losing their jobs. But even if we accept this argument, that doesn't mean that we must be indifferent to the dangers posed by overwhelming internal pressure. As we will see, the government still must take steps to minimize the harm that could result.

Individuals may be vulnerable to harm not only from using enhancements, but from participating in experiments to see if an enhancement is safe and effective. Research subjects are protected by a fairly elaborate set of rules, collectively known as the "Common Rule," that are designed to ensure that the risks of the research are outweighed by the potential benefits and that the subjects have given their informed consent to their participation. But there are many weaknesses in this regulatory scheme. For one thing, these rules apply only to experiments conducted by government-funded institutions or that are submitted to the FDA in support of licensing applications, and therefore they do not cover a great deal of research performed by private industry. Moreover, the rules were written with medically oriented research in mind, and it is not clear how they should be interpreted and applied to enhancement research. For example, the rules permit children to be enrolled as experimental subjects in trials that present "more than minimal risk" if, among other things, the research offers the possibility of "direct benefit" to the subject, but the rules do not say whether an enhancement benefit can count as a direct benefit. Specific research protections extend to other vulnerable populations besides children, such as prisoners and pregnant women, but do not explicitly cover students, workers, or athletes. In reports of a project several colleagues and I recently completed for the NIH, we suggest a number of changes to current regulations that would provide better protection for these populations.

Ensuring Safety and Effectiveness

Beginning with the enactment of the Pure Food and Drug Act in 1906, we have turned to the government to protect us from unsafe, ineffective, and fraudulent biomedical products and services. Regardless of how much freedom individuals should have to decide whether or not to use biomedical enhancements, they cannot make good decisions without accurate information about how well enhancements work. In regard to enhancements in the form of drugs and medical devices, the FDA has the legal responsibility to make sure that this information exists.

The FDA's ability to discharge this responsibility, however, is limited. In the first place, the FDA has tended to rely on information from highly stylized clinical trials that do not reflect the conditions under which enhancements would be used by the general public. Moreover, the deficiencies of clinical trials are becoming more apparent as we learn about pharmacogenetics—the degree to which individual responses to medical interventions vary depending on the individual's genes. The FDA is beginning to revise its rules to require manufacturers to take pharmacogenetics into consideration in studying safety and efficacy, but it will be many years, if ever, before robust pharmacogenetic information is publicly available. The solution is to rely more on data from actual use. Recently the agency has become more adamant about monitoring real-world experience after products reach the market, but this information comes from self-reports by physicians and manufacturers who have little incentive to cooperate. The agency needs to be able to conduct its own surveillance of actual use, with the costs borne by the manufacturers.

Many biomedical enhancements fall outside the scope of FDA authority. They include dietary supplements, many of which are used for enhancement purposes rather than to promote health. You only have to turn on late-night TV to be bombarded with claims for substances to make you stronger or more virile. Occasionally the Federal Trade Commission cracks down on hucksters, but it needs far greater resources to do an effective job. The FDA needs to exert greater authority to regulate dietary supplements, including those used for enhancement.

The FDA also lacks jurisdiction over the "practice of medicine." Consequently, it has no oversight over cosmetic surgery, except when the surgeon employs a new medical device. This limitation also complicates the agency's efforts to exert authority over reproductive and genetic practices. This would include the genetic modification of embryos to improve their traits, which promises to be one of the most effective enhancement techniques. Because organized medicine fiercely protects this limit on the FDA, consumers will have to continue to rely on physicians and other health care professionals to provide them with the information they need to make decisions about these types of enhancements. Medical experts need to stay on top of advances in enhancement technology.

Even with regard to drugs and devices that are clearly within the FDA's jurisdiction, its regulatory oversight only goes so far. Once the agency approves a product for a particular use, physicians are free to use it for any other purpose, subject only to liability for malpractice and, in the case of controlled substances, a requirement that the use must comprise legitimate medical practice. Only a handful of products, such as Botox, have received FDA approval for enhancement use; as noted earlier, enhancements predominantly are unapproved, off-label uses of products approved for health-related purposes. Modafinil, for example, one of the most popular drugs for enhancing cognitive performance, is approved only for the treatment of narcolepsy and sleepiness associated with obstructive sleep apnea/hypopnea syndrome and shift-work sleep disorder. Erythropoietin, which athletes use to improve performance, is approved to treat anemias. The FDA needs to be able to require manufacturers of products such as these to pay for the agency to collect and disseminate data on off-label experience. The agency also has to continue to limit the ability of manufacturers to promote drugs for off-label uses, in order to give them an incentive to obtain FDA approval for enhancement labeling.

An enhancement technology that will increase in use is testing to identify genes that are associated with non-disease characteristics. People can use this information to make lifestyle choices, such as playing sports at which they have the genes to excel, or in reproduction, such as deciding which of a number of embryos fertilized in vitro will be implanted in the uterus. An area of special concern is genetic tests that consumers can use at home without the involvement of physicians or genetic counselors to help them interpret the results. Regulatory authority over genetic testing is widely believed to be inadequate, in part because it is split among the FDA and several other federal agencies, and there are growing calls for revamping this regulatory scheme that need to be heeded.

Any attempt to regulate biomedical enhancement will be undercut by people who obtain enhancements abroad. The best hope for protecting these "enhancement tourists" against unsafe or ineffective products and services lies in international cooperation, but this is costly and subject to varying degrees of compliance.

To make intelligent decisions about enhancement use, consumers need information not only about safety and effectiveness, but about whether they are worth the money. Should they pay for Botox injections, for example, or try to get rid of facial wrinkles with cheaper creams and lotions? When the FDA approved Botox for cosmetic use, it ignored this question of cost-effectiveness because it has no statutory authority to consider it. In the case of medical care, consumers may get some help in making efficient spending decisions from their health insurers, who have an incentive to avoid paying for unnecessarily costly products or services. But insurance does not cover enhancements. The new administration is proposing to create a federal commission to conduct health care cost-effectiveness analyses, among other things, and it is important that such a body pay attention to enhancements as well as other biomedical interventions.

Subsidizing Enhancement

In these times of economic distress, when we already question whether the nation can afford to increase spending on health care, infrastructure, and other basic necessities, it may seem foolish to consider whether the government has an obligation to make biomedical enhancements available to all. Yet if enhancements enable people to enjoy a significantly better life, this may not be so outlandish, and if universal access avoids a degree of inequality so great that it undermines our democratic way of life, it may be inescapable.

There is no need for everyone to have access to all available enhancements. Some may add little to an individual's abilities. Others may be so hazardous that they offer little net benefit to the user. But imagine that a pill is discovered that substantially improves a person's cognitive facility, not just their memory but abilities such as executive function—the highest form of problem-solving capacity—or creativity. Now imagine if this pill were available only to those who already were well-off and could afford to purchase it with personal funds. If such a pill were sufficiently effective, so that those who took it had a lock on the best schools, careers, and mates, wealth-based access could drive an insurmountable wedge between the haves and have-nots, a gap so wide and deep that we could no longer pretend that there is equality of opportunity in our society. At that point, it is doubtful that a liberal democratic state could survive.

So it may be necessary for the government to regard such a success-determining enhancement as a basic necessity, and, after driving the cost down to the lowest amount possible, subsidize access for those unable to

Should We Reject the "Transhumanist" Goal of the Genetically Electronically and Mechanically Enhanced Human Being? by Easton

299

purchase it themselves. Even if this merely maintained preexisting differences in cognitive ability, it would be justified in order to prevent further erosion of equality of opportunity.

The need for effective regulation of biomedical enhancement is only going to increase as we enter an era of increasingly sophisticated technologies. Existing schemes, such as the rules governing human subjects research, must be reviewed to determine whether additions or changes are needed to accommodate this class of interventions. Government agencies and private organizations need to be aware of both the promise and the peril of enhancements and devote an appropriate amount of resources in order to regulate, rather than stop, their use.

Maxwell J. Mehlman is the Arthur E. Petersilge Professor of Law, director of the Law-Medicine Center, and professor of bioethics at Case Western Reserve University. His latest books are *The Price of Perfection: The Individual and Society in the Era of Biomedical Enhancement* (Johns Hopkins University Press, 2009) and *Transhumanist Dreams and Dystopian Nightmares: The Promise and Peril of Genetic Engineering* (Johns Hopkins University Press, 2012).

EXPLORING THE ISSUE

Should We Reject the "Transhumanist" Goal of the Genetically, Electronically, and Mechanically Enhanced Human Being?

Critical Thinking and Reflection

1. What is transhumanism?
2. What is a "slippery slope" argument?
3. What bodily or mental enhancements would you find desirable? Why?
4. Should government subsidize biomedical enhancements for those who cannot afford them? Why or why not?

Is There Common Ground?

"Common ground" is difficult to find here, for many of those who object to enhancing the human mind and body seem to draw rather arbitrary lines to distinguish between enhancements they find acceptable and those they do not.

1. Is the line between internal and external enhancements, or between new and old? Consider eyeglasses versus lens implants (done when cataracts must be removed), hearing aids versus cochlear implants, crutches and canes versus artificial hips and knees.
2. Do computers give us fundamentally new abilities for communication and memory expansion? Do we accept these abilities? Will it make a difference when we can implant our computers inside our heads?
3. What other technological enhancements of the human body and mind do most of us accept readily?
4. Does the list of acceptable enhancements expand as time goes on and technology progresses?

Create Central

www.mhhe.com/createcentral

Additional Resources

Josh Fischman, "A Better Life with Bionics," *National Geographic* (January 2010).

Andrew Kimbrell, *The Human Body Shop: The Engineering and Marketing of Life* (HarperSanFrancisco, 1993).

Julian Savalescu and Nick Bostrom, *Human Enhancement* (Oxford University Press, 2009).

Internet Reference . . .

Humanity+

Humanity+ is the leading transhumanist association, dedicating to promoting understanding, interest, and participation in the field of human enhancement.

http://humanityplus.org/